PUBLIC
PERSONNEL
ADMINISTRATION

Public Personnel Administration

Seventh Edition

O. GLENN STAHL

Harper & Row, Publishers
New York, Hagerstown, San Francisco, London

Sponsoring Editor: Dale Tharp
Project Editor: David Nickol
Designer: T. R. Funderburk
Production Supervisor: Will C. Jomarrón
Compositor: Maryland Linotype Composition Co., Inc.
Printer and Binder: The Maple Press Company

Public Personnel Administration, Seventh Edition

Library of Congress Cataloging in Publication Data

Stahl, Oscar Glenn, Date-
    Public personnel administration.

    First-4th ed. by W. E. Mosher, J. D. Kingsley, and
O. G. Stahl.
    Bibliography: p.
    Includes index.
    1. United States—Officials and employees. 2. Civil service—United States. 3. Per-
sonnel management—United States. I. Mosher, William Eugene, 1877–1945. Public
personnel administration. II. Title.
JK765.S68   1976   353.001   76-5809
ISBN 0-06-046387-2

Contents

v

Foreword

THIS EDITION CONTINUES the major revisions already incorporated in the sixth edition but elaborates on or modifies the material at various points so as to keep abreast of the latest developments and thinking in the administration of the personnel affairs of public enterprise. The major purpose remains the same: to bring together in one place the principal doctrine and ideas gleaned from both experience and research in the field.

Although this edition includes definition and classification of data and concepts for the sake of facilitating understanding, the prime emphasis is still to rationalize, to explain, to question, and to challenge. The concentration is on principle and reasoning, not on specific or time-oriented information. The book is concerned primarily with the continuing importance of subjects, with their significance and impact. Though giving due attention to current practice and problems, it is not merely a handbook or teaching aid—but the author hopes it will continue to be useful in university courses, in in-service training, and as a means for advancing among practitioners an appreciation of the many considerations that govern public personnel policy in all parts of the world.

Even more than in the previous edition it is necessary to relate the personnel function to its environment and to point up the essential public policy character of everything that has to do with government. This in no way diminishes, however, the intrinsic fundamentals that were stressed in the foreword to the sixth edition: the merit concept, the importance of work-centered motivation and of high prestige for the public service, the high standards of performance and conduct that must be maintained, and a balanced approach to the role of employee organization and to employee rights and obligations. If anything, the experience of the 1970s makes these fundamentals all the more relevant and all the more necessary. They are very much a part of the concept of an enlightened, vigorous, and responsive public service, not merely a fair, impartial, and nondoctrinaire public service.

The major subject-matter additions to this seventh edition concern equal employment opportunity for women and minorities and employee organization and collective representation. Not being a functional area in itself, the equal opportunity treatment is not presented as a separate chapter but is woven into the several chapters on staffing, as it was to a more limited extent in previous editions. The rapidly growing significance of unionism and collective negotiations in the public sector, however, has required elevating that subject to the status of a major part of the book, and the earlier single chapter has been expanded into three chapters.

The information and perspectives presented are the product of the experience and thinking of many persons in both the Western world and in countries struggling to reach higher levels of economic and political development. These practitioners are too numerous to permit acknowledgment individually. However, I am especially grateful to W. Donald Heisel and Nicholas J. Oganovic for helpful suggestions during the planning stages of this edition.

I have again relied heavily on the U.S. Civil Service Commission Library for published materials. It is still the single best source. Also, I am again appreciative of the careful manuscript reading by my wife, Marie Jane, whose thoughts always help in reducing error and improving readability. Whatever shortcomings remain in the volume are nevertheless my own responsibility.

O. Glenn Stahl

THE UTILITY OF GOVERNMENT

If government did not exist to maintain discipline and rationality in the affairs of men, we would have to create it to give vent to their aspirations. Its gamesmanship appeals to the sporting instinct; its lofty purposes evoke our compulsion for idealism; its power caters to the ambitious; its control of wealth attracts the venal; and its fallibility serves the inclination of every citizen who, imagining the emotion of ruling without its commitments, can indulge his boundless will to criticize. What other institution can provide such a combination?

OGS

PART I

The Modern Public Service

Constitute government how you please, infinitely the greater part of it must depend upon the exercise of the powers which are left at large to the prudence and uprightness of ministers of state.

Edmund Burke, "Thoughts on the Cause of the Present Discontents," *The Works of Edmund Burke, 1770,* London, Bell Publishers, 1902, vol. I, p. 332.

CHAPTER 1

The Services
of Civilization

THE BUSINESS OF the modern state is carried on for the most part by its administrative agencies. In any nation—old or young, small or large, developed or developing—this end-product of public policy known as public administration can be fully understood only in the context of the political system of that country and of politics internationally. Hence, a primary source for inspiration as well as information in arriving at this understanding is what has been happening on the world political scene.

POLITICS AND ADMINISTRATION to p. 8

The major political phenomena of the latter half of the twentieth century constitute an intricate and complex subject, but they are susceptible, at the risk of oversimplification, to relatively brief summary and analysis.

EXPANSION OF FUNCTIONS *The first and most obvious condition has been the tremendous expansion of government functions and responsibilities everywhere.* This most readily apparent of all political realities is explained by the revolutions in transportation and communication and in food production, by the companion developments of industrialization and urbanization, by the extraordinary degree of specialization of man's work and the resulting interdependency among groups and individuals, and by the increasing reach of all levels of formal education. Such conditions, in turn, create or intensify the array of public policy issues that occupy modern governments.

Herded as he is in great numbers in huge metropolitan regions, critically dependent on rapid transportation and communication, utilizing a myriad of

3

mechanical contrivances to meet basic human needs, and trying to live with a semblance of order and hope, modern man finds a growing public bureaucracy inevitable. As people come to rely more on technology to maintain life and happiness, the more technical and extensive public administration becomes. Economists estimate that in the United States at least a quarter of the gross national product is attributable to the activities of the "not-for-profit sector," comprised of government and nonprofit institutions. This part of our society accounts for almost two-fifths of all employment. It is also clear that for a number of decades the not-for-profit sector has been growing relatively more rapidly than the profit sector both in size of the labor force directly employed and of the national income produced.[1]

A few moments of thoughtful reflection will easily bring out why this condition is so striking in the United States: the vastly enlarged functions of state and local government in public education and community services (which have been the fastest growing), the great expansion of grants-in-aid by the federal government, the development of this nation as a world power with military, economic, and technical establishments girdling the globe, and the host of new challenges brought on by an affluent, urban society requiring a public response to energy needs, poverty, unemployment, water and air pollution, racial and sex discrimination, rapid transit and highway needs, housing requirements, new health hazards, burgeoning air traffic, a staggering volume of mail, the challenges of outer space, and so on and on. To one degree or another, similar growth pains confound almost every other nation of the world.

In short, new problems, new interrelationships, new perspectives have compelled new collective regulation, new controls, new initiatives. Government is a more conscious, a more ever-present feature of life everywhere than it has ever been before. There is simply more to do collectively, and there is consequently more government.

INCREASE IN INDEPENDENT STATES   *A second phenomenon is the substantial increase in the number of independent national states, as contrasted with the recent past.*[2] Largely the product of the break-up of several of the old colonial empires—British, French, Dutch, Spanish, Belgian, and Portuguese—this development has taken place predominantly in Africa and Asia. One problem induced by it has been the overwhelming contrast in size and importance between some of the tiny new states and the older, larger, more highly developed nations. Another has been the increased demand for leadership and overhead organization, adding significantly to the economic and political investment necessary to maintain a viable social order.

---

[1] See the relevant discussion in Eli Ginzberg, Dale L. Hiestand, and Beatrice G. Reubens, *The Pluralistic Economy*, New York, McGraw-Hill, 1965, pp. 193–195. Later indicators suggest that the trend has continued.

[2] Counting entities such as individual tribes, city-states, and the like might lead to a larger number at various points in history; but comparing the current number with the nineteenth and first half of the twentieth centuries clearly shows a marked increase, in fact about a doubling.

★ INTERNATIONAL ADMINISTRATION   *Third: there has been since World War II a corresponding expansion of governmental activity in the international realm.* Not only has there been, by treaty, a substantial delegation of decision-making to supranational agencies (from regional to worldwide), but a far wider scope and magnitude of functions have been undertaken by such international bodies. Aviation, health, technical assistance, economic investment, and a wide range of other fields are directed or regulated around the globe by international organizations[3]—which, while respecting the sovereignty of individual governments, exert a significant influence in specific fields tantamount to that of superstates. All governments, facing new and weighty issues in international trade and transportation, in monetary systems, in attendance at many hundreds of international conferences each year, in their realization of vital interdependency, find that almost all of their domestic departments are in some manner involved in foreign affairs or the international realm.

★ INTERDEPENDENCY   *A fourth political development is even more phenomenal: in the remarkably short span since World War II, the nations of the world have reached practically a universal awareness of the necessity for economic development in all countries,* including the need to stem the tide of population growth so that increases in productivity provide more than a treadmill effect. Efforts, with both goods and services, on the part of the wealthier states and of international agencies, to support and extend agriculture, water conservation, education, power production, transportation, industrialization, and family planning in the less fortunate areas of the world, are unprecedented in history. These efforts have included scholarships in the industrialized countries to train students and officials from less developed lands and support for universities and institutes within the latter nations to develop technology and a corps of informed civil servants.

Whether we attribute this development to a sense of mutual national dependency or to collective altruism, we have through it a brand new activity on the historical scene, involving many nations, both giving and receiving, greatly complicating the web of interdependent relations, and adding further to the machinery of government. The latter occurs not only among the major powers with huge organizations devoting full time to technical, educational, and economic assistance but also among the weaker nations that find it necessary to establish special units to coordinate requests and channel receipts of funds, goods, or personnel under various grants, loans, and projects.

★ DEPENDENCE ON CONSENT   *Fifth: regardless of the form of government—democratic, monarchic, totalitarian, or variants of these—there appears to be an increasing dependence worldwide on the consent of the governed.* Even dictators and the few remaining monarchs who really hold the reins of power keep their ears to the ground, carefully charting their courses so as not to

---

[3] Not only the U.N. Secretariat, but the various specialized bodies like the International Civil Aviation Organization, the World Health Organization, the World Bank, and many others.

move too far away from what public sentiment will tolerate. Certainly a pretense of reliance on the desires and demands of the people is an advance over earlier centuries when the "divine right" of kings rationalized absolutism. What a renewed sensitivity to the commonweal and concern for accountability to the public means for the brand of public servant in our bureaucracies, for his education and for his attitudes, is worthy of a major essay in itself.

CHANGES IN LEADERSHIP   *A sixth characteristic of the times, and perhaps related to the point just made, is the continuing, if not actually an increasing, instability (or should we say, frequency of change) in government leadership.* The political parties, the military juntas, the charismatic leaders, the cliques, the clans do not seem to last as long as before. None is invincible, as a review of current events will clearly show. Although sometimes overthrown by force or assassination, most political leaders or groups move out of office peacefully—more often than not the result of losing favor among the populace of their country. Rather than reflecting any basic disarray or trauma, this may simply be the natural product of expansion of democratic consciousness everywhere, but *it places great stress on the durability and quality of an administrative machine to assure uninterrupted social order and cannot escape being reflected in the processes and postures of governmental administration.*

BLENDING POLITICS AND ADMINISTRATION   In the light of these evolving conditions and *as a seventh factor in our list, it should not be surprising that the most youthful part of government—public administration—should lose some of its once touted sharp distinction from politics.* The evolution has been a curious one. The comparatively simple life in the early civilizations of the Orient, Egypt, the Greek city-states, Persia, the Roman Empire, and the Moghul Empire in India required only small and simple bureaucracies.[4] Administering justice, collecting revenue, and waging war were their principal components. Gradually, with the development of national states in Europe, bureaucracies became more formidable, but almost at the same time, as monarchs lost ground, control passed from their hands to those of legislatures. In the process bureaucracy became identified in the popular mind with oppression, an association lingering to this day. And the transfer of control to the legislative body brought with it abuses, most notably the tendency of parliaments to look with apprehension upon the kind of efficient administration fostered by their royal forebears and to regard the offices at their dis-

---

[4] No one has expressed it better than Woodrow Wilson, recognizing the contrast that had emerged by the late nineteenth century:

> The functions of government were simple, because life itself was simple. . . . There was no complex system of public revenues and public debts to puzzle financiers; there were, consequently, no financiers to be puzzled. No one who possessed power was long at a loss how to use it. The great and only question was: Who shall possess it? Populations were of manageable numbers; property was of simple sorts. There were plenty of farms, but no stocks and bonds: more cattle than vested interests. [From "The Study of Administration," *Political Science Quarterly*, June 1887, reprinted December 1941, p. 483.]

posal as private possessions or political currency. Thus, the first effect of the new dominance of legislative bodies was demoralization of the civil service. It is not surprising that political scientists at the turn of the twentieth century tried to mark off the realm of administration as one that must be clearly disassociated from political policy-making.

Recognition and acceptance of the blurring of lines between the deciding function and the doing are now hardly disputed, although in some countries, practice still seems to be based on the earlier conception of administration as a thing apart. While differences may be clearly evidenced at the extremes— such as a legislature wrestling with the scope and location of a long-range road-building program as contrasted with the operation of a piece of grading equipment preparing a surface for pavement—it is not so easy to say where administration begins when we refer to the work of an engineer whose designs prescribe exactly where bridges are to be placed, how many there must be, and what minimum safety standards must be provided; or a purchasing officer who decides how much material will be ordered, from what source, at what price, how far in advance, and delivered by what means. Such determinations by units of administration or by individual officials may actually have more impact on the economic welfare of hundreds of citizens or on the amounts of expenditure than would legislative policy decisions in many another field of activity. Who is to say that any costly, impact-laden decisions are not policy?

Without demeaning the importance, the necessity, or the consequences of the legislative and leadership processes of government, we cannot escape the fact that the great addition of this century to policy-making has been the constantly increasing role of the bureaucracy as a source not only of facts and experience but of ideas and solutions to public problems.[5] Indeed,

---

[5] The noted authorities on public administration, the Dimocks, assert flatly: ". . . in the modern world, bureaucracy is the chief policy maker in government" (Marshall E. Dimock and Gladys O. Dimock, *Public Administration*, 4th ed., New York, Holt, Rinehart and Winston, 1969, p. 3).

Herbert J. Storing is especially effective in his findings, expressed as follows:

> It is notorious that party politicians tend to learn moderation and responsibility when in office; but it is perhaps less generally recognized that one of their main teachers is the civil service. . . . Not only do civil servants exercise discretion in interpreting and applying the commands of their political superiors; they participate intimately in the formulation of those commands. They make proposals of their own and fight for them; they comment on the proposals of their political superiors— and may fight against them. They make a vital contribution to the process of deciding what is to be done. Government would come to a standstill if our "closet statesmen" in the civil service suddenly started doing only what they were told.
>
> . . . The cautious prudence and orderliness which tend to characterize the civil service are precisely that part of practical wisdom in which the party politician is likely to be deficient.
>
> [The position of career servants] enables them to mitigate the partisanship of party politics, and it gives them some protection from the powerful temptation, to which the party politician is always subject, to serve the people's inclinations rather than their interests.
>
> . . . In our mobile democracy, the civil service is one of the few institutions we have for bringing the accumulated wisdom of the past to bear upon political decisions.
>
> . . . The civil service is, then, in possession of certain institutional qualities which

in some fields, even the initiative frequently comes from the administrative agencies of government. In the case of the foregoing illustration concerning road construction the very content of the program—its scope, its emphasis, its duration—is likely to have originated in the bowels of the bureaucracy. A responsible bureaucrat of today is almost inescapably a policy-planner.

ADMINISTRATIVE PROFESSIONALISM   It is only a logical extension, then, to make *the eighth and final point in this list: to acknowledge the continually increasing technical character of modern public administration,* to recognize that as the governing of men covers more subjects, deals with more issues, faces greater complexity, and encounters growing technology, the administrative side of government takes on more and more the form of a collection of highly specialized, even professionalized, activities. Far from an army of clerks, government offices of today usually represent a galaxy of practically all of a nation's occupational pursuits and of many with no counterparts outside government. What is to be done cannot be so sharply drawn by legislators or prime ministers or governors or presidents that it can be effectuated by any intelligent, well-meaning person. Larger and larger measures of discretion have had to be left to technical judgment. Yet, many governments continue to be organized around the outmoded concept of administration as routine, repetitive operations in spite of the specialists and the powers that have inevitably accrued to their executive agencies.

PROBLEMS OF ADMINISTRATION

That there should be, as a consequence of the foregoing developments, accelerated attention to the critical problems of public administration every-

---

give it a title to share with elected officials in rule. It has a distinctive competence in the art of government and a unique knowledge of the problems of government, without which stable and intelligent government under modern conditions would be literally impossible. It has, moreover, a distinctive view of the common good which can guide and supplement the view likely to be taken by elected party politicians. On the foundation of its procedures, its rules, its institutional memory and foresight, its skepticism of political panaceas, and its protection from the whims of popularity, the civil service stands for the continuity and wholeness of American government.

Yet, Storing would not credit the career service with designing or pressing forward some of the major reconstructions of political direction in American history—such as binding the nation together following the Civil War or changing the basic role of government during the Roosevelt New Deal. In reference to the influence of the career official in such circumstances, he observes:

Even at his best he is not a political captain but a faithful, wise, and influential counsellor and servant. . . . It is not unfair to say of the bureaucracy (and perhaps of political parties too) that it contributes least to government in the most important cases, provided it is remembered that a government requires a capacity for everyday competence, prudence, and public-spiritedness, as well as a capacity for greatness. ["Political Parties and the Bureaucracy," in Robert A. Goldwin, ed., *Political Parties, U.S.A.,* Chicago, Rand McNally, 1964, pp. 152–157.]

where is hardly surprising. It seems inescapable that deciding what to do, however troublesome and complex, is not ordinarily as difficult as determining how to do it and, what is more, as actually getting it done. This is the raw stuff of administration—the "how," the effectuation—on top of its often being called upon to suggest the "what" at the outset.

A mere recitation of the critical problems of governmental bureaucracy indicates the marked degree to which they emerge from the eight phenomena just outlined. Apart from special issues peculiar to particular places and occasions, the problems of public administration may be summarized as follows:

1. *Planning*—applying to both the content of administrative programs and the means for financial sustenance. It is a never-ending process, commanding more and more technical methodology. It is a function easy to neglect, tempting to starve, even often overlooked. It requires analysis of every conceivable condition or contingency that might arise and generation of alternative plans to cope with each.

2. *Establishing a viable and fruitful relationship with sovereign sources*—mainly, working out the ethics and practice of communication between bureaucrat and legislator. A sensitive area, calling for great care and forbearance by public managers and legislative representatives, this relationship is all the more important as administration becomes more technical and professionalized. A heavy obligation rests on both to learn from each other and to establish relationships of trust. The legislator must not look upon every administrative move as an act of skulduggery, and the administrator cannot afford to view time spent with politicians as an encroachment on his schedule.

3. *Maintaining expertise*—an elementary necessity. Other branches of government, not possessing specialized knowledge or technique, must rely on the bureaucracy for expertise. Hence the bureaucracy must maintain an administrative and personnel environment that attracts and challenges, as well as nurtures, a high-quality staff. Expertise, always a scarce and fragile commodity, is fostered not only by solicitous care and feeding but, even more importantly, by reasonable organization of work and assignment of responsibility to make apt and full utilization of men's skills, by building motivation in the work to be performed, and by engaging the involvement and commitment of personnel to the specific program objectives of the organization employing them.

4. *Maintaining efficiency*—an older problem than expertise and always a vexing one. It is all the more critical in those nations that have not been noted for highly productive economies. The same elements of organization and personnel policy that serve expertise apply here. Although many governments are more efficient in serving public purposes than their constituencies usually give them credit for, public administration must never relax its effort to achieve or its prescription of and conformance to higher and higher standards.

5. *Maintaining responsiveness and accountability*—an ever-present obligation of administrators at all levels, as agents of public purpose, to serve, to conform with the collective will, to avoid taking unwarranted power into their own hands, and to make certain that public objectives are not scuttled by insolence, intolerance, or inaction. The very size and technical character of modern bureaucracy make this matter of accountability all the more vital. The imperious official who sees no need even to listen to the views of citizens' representatives, much less pay some attention to them, who takes all importunings by politicians as efforts to corrupt, who cannot imagine a genuine public interest in what he does, who feels no sense of duty to undertake or to urge change in practice where injustice or shortcomings are evident, does not fit the pattern for the modern public administration scene.

Little transitional thinking is necessary to perceive the relationship of the public personnel function to practically all of these critical problems and, in turn, to the major political phenomena of our times. Certainly expertise and efficiency are directly involved. Through training and career-advancement procedures a personnel system can also have a profound impact on attitudes of responsiveness and cultivation of proper relationships between public employees and public representatives. Administrative planning will founder without the support of personnel policies that induce high motivation. Personnel administration, with all its concerns as to productivity, benefits, and obligations, is also the focal point for issues relating to the nation's education system, the openness of the public service, its insurance against insularity, and its identification with national goals—and therefore is the vortex for measuring up to many of today's political realities.

In essence, the maintenance of quality performance—the merit concept—is the thread common to the imperatives of modern administration. It is a key to solution of so many problems, to facing up to the demands of the political phenomena of our times. For more than a century a most troublesome dilemma of democratic government has been finding how to reconcile a skilled, professionalized public service with responsiveness of government to public control. Indeed, what has seemed to be a contradiction—continuity *and* accountability—has itself provided the core of accommodation. It has come to be the very continuity and expertness of the bureaucracy that have ensured its ultimate responsibility to *all* the people rather than to a particular group or political party. It is thus a concern with quality and merit that constitutes the central theme of this book.

ADMINISTRATION—PUBLIC AND PRIVATE

Some of the historical roots of bureaucracy as we know it in the United States—the effort to make it the partisan currency of political leaders, its corruption at the turn of the century, and eventually its sheer size—have led to a gross underappreciation of the significance, the necessity, and certainly the fascinating and challenging character of most public enterprise. In the midst of "conspicuous consumption" of enormous quantities of worldly goods and services we neglect the essential services of government. Crowded schools, underpaid teachers, inadequate police forces, filthy streets, dilapidated park buildings, polluted streams and air, jammed airports, antiquated mail-processing systems, frustrating traffic congestion, poor distribution of medical care—all contrast sharply with lavishly equipped automobiles and television sets, luxury hotels, fancy packaging, rapid changes in clothing fashions, screaming advertising, and air-conditioning without exception in night clubs and bowling alleys but rarely in public schools or libraries. The American society is truly one of relative poverty in public services versus ever-increasing opulence in private goods.[6] Wants for many consumer goods are "contrived wants," stimulated by the ceaseless din of elaborate competitive advertising. Needs that cannot be fulfilled in the marketplace, that is, most public needs, are seldom so well recognized.

Nevertheless, as each decade passes by, America gives renewed attention and prestige to its public services, as it deals more boldly and energetically with its massive problems of concentrated populations, education, poverty, energy, pollution, and all that goes with them. Increasingly, men of responsibility and vision in both business and the not-for-profit sphere recognize the need for a "public philosophy" to offset our disposition toward purely private values.[7]

[6] No more brilliant statement of this condition has been made than that by John Kenneth Galbraith in *The Affluent Society*, Cambridge, Mass., Riverside Press, 1958. Also, for a rational approach to governmental expenditure and planning, see David D. Lloyd, *Spend and Survive*, Indianapolis, Bobbs-Merrill, 1960.

A Canadian official puts the issue clearly, with reference to municipal government:

> The issue rests on the allocation of our economic energies between the production of private goods and the provision of public services. . . . It is not the emotion-charged issue of private enterprise embattled against public incursions; it is not this at all. It is rather the issue of how we divide our energies between two broad classes of output—those whose distribution and individual levels of output can be effectively handled through a competitive market process, and those whose output and distribution cannot be determined by any known kind of market mechanism and must therefore be decided as matters of public policy. [Dr. Stewart Bates, then President, Central Mortgage and Housing Corporation of Canada, in an address at the International Municipal Assembly, U.S. Conference of Mayors, May 1960; published in *Public Management*, September 1960, p. 202.]

An opposite point of view is presented by Peter F. Drucker in *The Age of Discontinuity*, New York, Harper & Row, 1969, in which he urges "reprivitization" of much of what is already operated by government, on the grounds that it is already too big and clumsy and that its role should be simply to "govern" (whatever that is!). His case is not convincing to most people knowledgeable about politics and the public service.

[7] One study showed that many leaders hold views quite different from popular stereotypes about our society: Charles A. Nelson, *Developing Responsible Public Leaders*, A Report of Interviews and Correspondence with 52 Leading Americans, Dobbs Ferry, N.Y., Oceana Publications, 1963.

A distinguished political scientist has stated: "It is in the public service that the

It is appropriate therefore to draw attention not only to the organizational and personnel tendencies that are common to all enterprises but especially to those features of the public arena that distinguish it from private activity. The more important of these differentiating features are these:

1. *The services performed by the state are more urgent than those performed by private institutions.* The degree of urgency is, of course, relative to the times. Under conditions of a sparsely populated rural society inspection of canned food, regulation of air traffic, and disposal of sewage are hardly urgent, but they become eminently so in an urban society.

2. *The services performed by the state are generally of a monopolistic or semimonopolistic character.* Exceptions to this are the giant privately owned entities known as public utilities that are monopolies providing power, transportation, and communication facilities, but these are subject to such intensive governmental control that they are more like extensions of the state than of private enterprise. Indeed, in most countries of the world they comprise parts of the public service either as regular government departments or as public corporations.

3. *The conduct of public services is governed by relatively precise legal provisions,* so that it is impossible or at least extremely difficult for government administrators to expand or curtail activities or to change procedures without public attention or ratification.

4. *The supply of services by the state is not governed by market price.* The aim is to supply such services to all who need them and to treat all consumers equally. This objective especially compels the civil servant to maintain a role of strict impartiality, based on the principle of equality of individual citizens vis-à-vis their government. But this imperative has been mistaken to mean that the public worker must also be neutral, with no views or commitments relating to the mission of his department. There is a clear difference between being neutral and being impartial. If the requirement is construed to mean that all civil servants should be political eunuchs, devoid of the drive and motivation essential to dynamic administration, then the concept of impartiality is being seriously misapplied. Modern governments should demand that their hirelings have not only the technical but the emotional qualifications necessary for wholehearted effort. Commitment to a cause or to a program is usually as important as knowledge of its content and may spell the difference between a routine application of the rules and a wholesale dedication to achieving basic objectives.

---

future of mankind on this globe will be determined most directly. To the public servants will fall the responsibility of human survival; of social order; . . . of providing the services of civilization" (Stephen K. Bailey, "The Excitement of the Public Service," *Civil Service Journal,* July–September 1963, p. 9). The title of this chapter is borrowed from the Bailey statement.

5. *The business of the state, particularly in a democracy, is conducted very much in the public eye.* Even though the bulk of the permanent bureaucracy works in relative obscurity and takes no part in public advocacy on issues that divide political parties and are displayed in the news media, key civil servants are often in the limelight and all public workers at one time or another find their activities subjected to popular scrutiny in a way rarely if ever found in private enterprise.[8] As a consequence, matters such as selection, incentives, and ethical standards for government employees are more stringent and more difficult. It is not easy to reconcile the desirability of having enthusiastic workers with the need for continuity and for avoiding their taking sides publicly on issues that divide the nation (lest their privilege of continuity be challengeable and therefore jeopardized).

One perplexing aspect of the public-versus-private-administration issue is the propriety of use by government of private, especially profit-making, organizations to carry out specific parts of public functions. In the U.S. federal government especially, utilization of this device has developed imperceptibly into an almost concealed galaxy of activities by private corporations, universities, consulting and research enterprises, and some outfits set up exclusively for the purpose of taking contracts with the government, all of which in size of funds and employment collectively rival the government itself. The contracting technique has long been necessary for the acquisition of goods and services normally available in the marketplace, but the newer development largely in military, foreign aid, welfare, and research activities has been in the design of plans and policies that, while subject to approval by the duly constituted agencies of government, are so sophisticated and extensive that it stretches the average citizen's credulity to assume that these far-flung operations can be adequately supervised.

Without denying the advantages of pluralism and of the involvement of a variety of initiatives, the central issue is one of control and accountability. The question is whether the standards set for regular public functions should not apply to these organizations to which parts of public functions are sublet, whether the audits imposed on the bureaucracy should not be as tight for the contractors, whether the salaries and working conditions of employees of such

---

[8] It was well put long ago by Paul H. Appleby:

> Government administration differs from all other administrative work to a degree not even faintly realized outside, by virtue of its public nature, the way it is subject to public scrutiny and outcry. An administrator coming into government is struck at once, and continually thereafter, by the press and public interest in every detail of his life, personality, and conduct. This interest often runs to details of administrative action that in private business would never be of concern other than inside the organization. Each employee hired, each one demoted, transferred, or discharged, every efficiency rating, every assignment of responsibility, each change in administrative structure, each conversation, each letter, has to be thought about in terms of possible public agitation, investigation, or judgment. [*Big Democracy*, New York, Knopf, 1945, p. 7.]

enterprises should not parallel those in the civil service. When the funds supporting operations carried on by private contractors come from the same revenues as those supporting regular government bureaus, the question of the propriety of more liberal allowances for travel and purchasing or more generous salaries and benefits than those provided in such bureaus naturally arises. The subject deserves extensive inquiry and study, but it has been suggested that one good rule of thumb would be to outlaw any contracting-out of government functions where the work is performed on government premises, where it is for long periods (such as more than a year), where it makes use of government tools and equipment, where it involves work directly on an agency mission, where it parallels work already performed by civil servants, or where it requires immediate and direct government supervision of daily operations.

THE SIGNIFICANCE OF SIZE

Whether or not some facets of the state's functions are concealed by devolutions through contracting to private organizations, government at all levels is of immense proportions and will probably continue to grow. The great army of public servants in the United States (not counting almost three million uniformed men and women in the military services) had passed well beyond the fourteen and one-half million mark by 1975, accounting for over one-sixth of the total gainfully employed persons in the country. They are distributed among major jurisdictions as shown in the table below.

TOTAL PUBLIC EMPLOYMENT

Federal	*2,840,000*
Public Education (state & local)	*6,202,000*
State (non-education)	*1,798,000*
Local (non-education—city, county, & other)	*3,794,000*
Grand Total	*14,634,000*

NOTE: These rounded figures are derived from 1974 data as reported in Bureau of the Census, *Public Employment in 1974*, Washington, D.C., May 1975, reporting information for October 1974; and from U.S. Civil Service Commission data for December 1974. They include both full-time and part-time employees. If the numbers were adjusted to "full-time equivalent" (allowing for accumulation of fractions of time served by part-time workers), the gross figure would be about one and three quarter-millions less. The difference occurs mostly in public education.

The range and variety of government jobs are as comprehensive as a dictionary of all human occupations. In the federal service alone there are thousands of different classes of positions in 1500 distinct occupations, ranging from the most specialized scientific and medical research posts to all the skilled crafts, as well as the more widely known administrative, professional, postal, and clerical categories. In the upper reaches of the service nearly all incumbents have had a college education, with a majority holding graduate degrees. State jobs, although of more limited scope, run the gamut from the unskilled to the most highly technical. And one would go far before he discovered a business enterprise employing as great a variety of skills as are found in a modern city government.[9]

Size of the public payroll is always a matter of continuing concern to thoughtful persons and an obsession with some. Curiously, nothing like this attention is devoted to the millions indirectly employed by government through contracts or supplying goods and services largely utilized by government. It is especially anomalous to find the lack of scrutiny and control exercised by the taxpayer over the numbers, pay, and performance of these so-called private workers as compared with the fish-bowl existence of direct civil servants. When one takes into account the delivery of close to one hundred billion pieces of mail a year, the payment of tens of millions of checks to social security retirees, veterans, and vendors, the guidance of thousands of aircraft per day into safe airlanes, the policing of the purity of foods and drugs, the operation of school systems from kindergarten though graduate school for many millions of students, the processing of over one hundred million tax returns each year, the ferreting out of smugglers, counterfeiters, dope peddlers, and kidnappers, the exploration of what goes on everywhere from outer space to inside a human cancer cell, the special services demanded by the people for businessmen, farmers, veterans, young people, old people, poor people, and the armed forces, it is little wonder that a giant bureaucracy is necessary.

THE PERSONNEL FUNCTION

No amount of railing against bureaucratic bigness will minimize the need for larger and larger public services in an ever-expanding and more complicated world society. And no schemes for devolution, by contract or otherwise, to private initiative and competition will eliminate the problems of size or the need for some kind of ultimate accountability. Those troubled with big government are merely troubled with big countries, burgeoning metropolitan areas, and severe problems. Size and complexity are inescapable. Energies should not be dissipated in fruitless escapes from reality. It is more productive to try to build into our public services the conditions and the incentives that will make for the kind of competent, dedicated, rewarded, and responsive public employees who have long characterized the best of government. There are no substitutes for that.

[9] A most illuminating, popular description of bureaucracy is found in John D. Weaver, *The Great Experiment, An Intimate View of the Everyday Workings of the Federal Government,* Boston, Little, Brown, 1965. Contains real-life vignettes of the fascinating work going on; a good antidote for persistent beraters of public servants and their accomplishments.

IMPORTANCE

This is the task of public personnel administration, managing the human resources of man's largest and most difficult undertaking—government. Many nations need especially to look at the formalities of their personnel systems. Gearing them to the needs of modern government calls for structures and policies quite different from those that fit the circumstances of the nineteenth century. There is no more constructive field to which the nations of the world could repair than to reappraise and reshape their public personnel administration to serve late-twentieth-century democracy.

DEFINITION

Personnel administration is *the totality of concern with the human resources of organization.*[10] It is one of the organization's major linkages with its environment. It applies in microcosm the values, the ethics, the philosophy of that environment, and it in turn influences the environment. To whatever extent this is true in any organization, it is all the more true in the public service—simply because of its size and its relationship to the whole people.

Personnel administration is something of a state of mind. It is an attitude compounded of understanding both the forces which shape manpower needs, supply, and problems and, at the same time, the importance of human will and personality. It is a kind of continual educational process for employer and employee alike. It is management's conscience as well as its privilege; it is employees' obligation as well as their rights. It is enlightenment in the fusing of organizational goals with individual needs. The important human need to achieve, to be creative, to perform satisfying work, is consistent with the essence of organization, the need to get work accomplished in an orderly,

---

[10] Although from time to time I use the phrase "human resources," I do not find it practical as an adjective, such as in "human resources management" or "human resources planning." For titles and subject headings there is nothing wrong with the older terms *personnel administration* or *personnel management*. In fact, overuse of the word *resources* reminds me of something reforming economists taught us long ago—that labor should not be viewed as a *commodity*. Nevertheless, for the convenience of conveying meaning and for the sake of variety in expression, I do not disdain the use of "human resources" entirely. As an alternative to the word *personnel*, it at least helps avoid the tiresomeness of repetition.

Even more frequently I employ the word *manpower*. I am aware that various individuals object to the use of the term because they feel it excludes women. However, the alternative, especially in conjunction with functions like "planning," is to use cumbersome phraseology like "human resources planning." Furthermore, I do not accept the contention that all words with *man* in them, such as *chairman* or *manpower* are not generic and do not embrace both sexes. The first meaning of "man" in all standard dictionaries is "human being," not "male." Wherever I use the words *man*, *manpower*, *he*, or *him* in this book, I refer to human beings of both sexes, except where the connotation is obviously limited to the male sex.

Incidentally, the term *personnel* in its modern context was first used by the U.S. Civil Service Commission in its report of 1909 and by the Secretary of Commerce and Labor in 1910. It was later borrowed by private businesses and other institutions and has persisted to this day.

effective manner. This is why one of the emphases of this book is on *work-centered* motivation.

THE STATE OF THE ART

Periodically we are led to believe that the personnel function is in dire straits, that it has failed to live up to the highest expectations. As in so many other aspects of life, of course, the quality and results of personnel management vary widely at different times, in different sectors of society, and in different individual institutions. But over the decades of experience and study of this author, there is no question that almost all of the objectives of wise, compassionate, and constructive personnel administration are being more adequately met today than they ever were in the past. This is probably true to some degree in all nations and societies, but it is especially true in the United States. Workers enjoy more latitude, receive higher real income, are protected by more benefits, and contribute more to productivity than at any other time in history.

The dismal interpreters of doom and despair usually lack some perspective on history. Whether or not the personnel function is given its due recognition in the halls of academia, corporate board rooms, or government departments, what it has been concerned with has profoundly changed even in the past few decades. This is not to say that there is little room for improvement, either in the techniques of personnel administration or in the articulation and conceptualization of its objectives and roles. Nevertheless, we can enter a thorough study of this field with confidence not only that it deserves our scrutiny but that formidable progress has been made in its pursuit.[11]

[11] A practical and factual perspective on the status of the working population in America is cogently presented in the following column by a noted journalist, when ushering in a new year:

> As we move into 1975, national morale is shaky.
>
> Across the front pages march the grim phalanxes of inflation, recession, scarcity, crime and corruption with heavy tread.
>
> They have sent out stabs of fear that good times are forever gone and our system is crumbling under the forces of disintegration.
>
> On newsstands, national magazines challenge passersby with apocalyptic covers: one depicts a well-to-do family sitting down to a Christmas dinner of empty plates; another trumpets "The End of Affluence: The Last Christmas in America"; a third cover announces that we are "Coming Around to Socialism."
>
> Erudite pundits blithely tell us that the edifice America has built is junk, and now will come tumbling down about us.
>
> Great difficulties loom before us in 1975, no one can doubt that. But before writing off the future or jumping into a briar patch of quack nostrums, a little stock taking is in order.
>
> Remember the 1950s? That decade opened on a surge of Korean War inflation, followed with three back-to-back recessions.
>
> Hanging over the chronically depressed economy were two spectres that promised untold trouble. Remember? One was automation, which threatened to bring mass unemployment by wiping out millions of traditional jobs; the other was the after-effect of the postwar baby boom.
>
> What would happen, went the refrain, when 70 million kids poured into the school system and then the job market? The mathematical extrapolations were

ghastly. At the levels of growth and capacity, which were then current, the incoming hordes would be locked out, first without classrooms and teachers, then without jobs, houses, hospitals, highways.

To ward off a catastrophe that would bring on a breakdown of society, we would have to spend more, train more and construct more in two decades than in all the previous years of our national life combined. Stagnant America lacked the will and the vision, the critics said; it couldn't be done.

Well, we did it. What we accomplished just yesterday is worth reviewing. For if we grasp what we have done, then we shall gain a sense of what we can do. This may help us meet the challenge of reviving the economy and developing new energy sources.

Part of the story is chronicled in the book, "The Real America," by Ben Wattenberg, an author with a nose for doomsday cant and an uncanny gift for making the cold statistics come to life. Other facts have been gathered by my staff.

Here's the story, all carefully documented:

• Since 1950, we have made it possible for—hold your hats—74 million people to be enrolled in schools today. That's one third of the nation! Nine million are in college, more than double the 1960 figure. From our poorest homes, earning from $3,000 to $5,000 a year, 21 per cent enter college. Of our college population, 60 per cent are the children of parents who did not attend college. Thus, while we went about our ordinary business, we produced the greatest miracle of upward mobility in human history.

• Since 1950, employment has expanded fast enough to absorb almost all those postwar babies. Manual labor and menial jobs declined. But the ditch digger re-emerged at a bulldozer operator and the maid as a bank teller.

• Since 1950, America has constructed from scratch a suburbia that houses 35 million people. In a twinkling, as it were, we erected the physical equivalent of a new nation, containing more houses, furniture, bathtubs, vehicles, stores, theaters, libraries, communications equipment, paved roads and public services than the efforts of centuries have accumulated in such advanced nations as France, Great Britain or Italy. Aesthetes may deride these look-alike homes on their quarter acres, but they represent the best material living conditions ever created for working people anywhere.

• Since 1950, the median income of the American family has doubled. With inflation taken into account, average family income, measured in constant 1972 dollars, has risen from $4,500 to more than $11,000. Distress over inflation and fear of recession cause us to forget this gain. But there it is, the greatest and broadest increase in well-being ever recorded.

• Since 1950, working conditions have improved dramatically. Shameful conditions still exist in some industries, and they must be relentlessly exposed. But for most people, gains have been impressive. Work begins later and retirement comes earlier, cutting 10 to 15 years off the working life. In 1949, 61 per cent of our workers got paid vacations of two weeks; by 1972, 87 per cent got paid vacations of four weeks or more.

• What of the poor? Since 1959, poverty has been cut in half; the percentage of families below the poverty line has dropped from 22 to 11 per cent. Substandard housing fell from 16 to 7 per cent. In the past dozen years, 14 million Americans crossed over the poverty line.

We who have wrought these advances in our time have not suddenly atrophied and fallen sterile, ready for the ideological embalmers. Whatever innovations the new era calls for, we'll be equal to them. [Jack Anderson, "U.S. Will Overcome Challenges Again," *The Washington Post*, January 2, 1975.]

CHAPTER 2

The Personnel Function in Society

INVOLVED AS IT IS with the human side of management and in view of the large portion of almost everyone's life spent in a work situation, the personnel function is in a central role in the processes and problems of civilization. As we have noted, it supplies a major linkage of an organization with its environment, and this is especially true when the organization is a public agency serving all citizens. Personnel administration is greatly influenced by what transpires in society as a whole, it must be responsive to those impacts, and in turn it may exercise a profound effect on the operations of society.

Without doubt the most pervasive influence on public personnel management in modern times has been the expansion of government everywhere, affecting principally the scope and magnitude of public employment and contributing therefore to its complexity and dynamism. But other factors in modern life also exert their impact. Some of the more important of these are examined in this chapter.

A common thread running through most of the interactions elaborated here is the tendency to accept government employment as an enormous balance wheel and a model in the economy. To some extent this is unavoidable, but the effects of this tendency on the effectiveness of the public service—a condition essential to a viable civilization—is seldom evaluated. The point should be borne in mind especially as we examine the first few of the major influences on and consequences of public personnel policy.

THE MANPOWER ENVIRONMENT [1]

We are much more conscious nowadays of manpower as an economic and social resource. Within the precepts of a free society we abhor manipulation, but we recognize the necessity of trying to find all available means to motivate and channel people into occupational pursuits which society requires and which will make the best and fullest use of their skills and potential. Social scientists observe that we have the human resources to maintain and even improve high living standards providing we support more education, recognize the shift to higher skill requirements, and make proper use of young people, older persons, women, and minority groups.

But we are also told that without adequate support and guidance the labor market and public education cannot be relied upon to produce the numbers and types of professional, technical, and skilled manpower that the economy now requires for growth.[2] In the affairs of nations it is especially notable that appropriation of funds to get a new program under way is not enough, for money without trained men is pretty sterile. Even a highly developed country like the United States has had to learn that specific technical skills were not automatically available in the market for the asking. The implication of these hard facts is bound up in one word: *planning.* The term, in spite of much misunderstanding, does not simply mean *conjectural forecasting* and certainly not *regimenting.* It does mean carefully analyzing alternative probabilities, being prepared with alternative plans to meet whatever condition arises, bolstering those educational institutions and programs that have the potential for relieving shortages, and deliberately trying to find all reasonable means to guide people into productive use of their talents. To a considerable extent we are already engaging in these very processes, but concepts have not caught up with haphazard practice.

Government has reacted with impressive speed and bounty in subsidizing the fields of natural and physical science, but it has done far less well in other areas and it continues to neglect analysis of and preparation for its own manpower needs. As a result, it is not as imposing a competitor in the labor market as its sheer size might warrant. Some of the procedures that are called for are discussed in a later chapter.

Other aspects of the manpower picture also imply effects on the public personnel front. One has been the greater mobility of many segments of the labor force, a subject which will be dealt with in the discussion on the impact of technology. Another is the desire of a larger proportion of the work force, particularly those with some college education, for "meaningful work" and less emphasis on monetary reward. Although this subject is dealt with at some length in the chapter on the will to work, suffice it to say at this point that the public service, because of its broader and more impact-

[1] See footnote 10 in Chapter 1.
[2] See the foreword, especially pp. 4 and 5, in Eli Ginzberg, *Manpower Agenda for America*, New York, McGraw-Hill, 1968.

laden functions, should have a tremendous head start over industry in providing attractive work challenges. The advantage of serving society's deepest needs over repackaging detergents or redesigning automobile interiors can be lost, however, if government fails to create the participative and stimulating work environment essential to capitalize on the intrinsic fascination of its duties.

A further environmental consideration arises from efforts to extend to government services the pattern of union-management relations that has developed in recent decades in private industry. This pattern evolved out of conflicts implicit in an exploitative absentee ownership characterizing early capitalist enterprise and from the countervailing power sought by militant labor organizations. The history and circumstances of the public service, to say nothing of the ultimately political character of all activity in the name of government, have been quite different. The implications of this parallelism approach now advocated for union-management issues in government employment will be explored in the chapters on employee organization and representation.

SOLVING SOCIAL PROBLEMS

An effect of the manpower market worthy of separate analysis is the persistent tendency to view government employment as a sort of gigantic eleemosynary institution, to hold that public jobs must be dispensed primarily on the basis of need or reward, for example, to the political party faithful, to various localities on the basis of population, to those in need of employment, or to groups to which the public owes an obligation. In this milieu the view of the government as an overwhelmingly important employer, entitled to acquire the ablest personnel it can attract and hold, tends to get lost.

This welfare concept was most clearly evidenced historically in legal provisions such as prohibitions against holding two jobs at once (even where the hours of work and duties are compatible), restrictions on the number of members of one family who may work in government, residence requirements in states and localities and the apportionment rule in federal headquarters, keeping the salaries and benefits in the higher career jobs comparatively modest, preferential treatment for veterans and their families, and excessive limitations on the removal process—most of which practices exist in practically every jurisdiction in the United States. Only on the logic that public jobs constitute a form of pay-off could such laws be rationally defended.

EQUAL OPPORTUNITY

One of the most significant developments of the 1960s and 1970s has been the renewed[3] emphasis on equal opportunity for all—regardless of race, sex,

---

[3] The term *renewed* is used because the objective of equal opportunity was always intrinsic in the idea of merit, but broader problems in society as a whole forced re-

or ethnic origin—to jobs in both the public and private sectors of the economy. The main reinforcement to personnel management has been to build more support for sound methods of attraction and selection among candidates for employment. It has also had a substantial effect on job analysis and design, on recruit orientation and other in-service training, on motivational understanding, and on research.

Insofar as these society-wide efforts have contributed to greater awareness of personnel policy and to modes of maintaining a rational relationship between work needs and the talents of workers, it has enhanced the concepts and the techniques of the personnel function. Where these efforts have, on the other hand, degenerated into new forms of discrimination or "quotaism," misguided devices to seek artificial "representativeness" by ethnic groups or others on a numbers-ratio basis, then society's pressure for equal opportunity has been prostituted. In such instances it has become not only a disservice to objective professionalism in the personnel process but has contributed to a deterioration of public services and employee behavior, has set back attainment of the sound aims of true equal opportunity, and has handicapped improvement of the conditions, the self-esteem, and the ultimate welfare of population groups that have heretofore been discriminated against.

As the noted black psychologist Kenneth Clark has observed:

> I cannot express vehemently enough my abhorrence of sentimentalistic, seemingly compassionate programs of employment of Negroes which employ them on Jim Crow double standards or special standards for the Negro which are lower than those for whites.
>
> This is a perpetuation of racism—it is interpreted by the Negro as condescension, and it will be exploited by them. Those who have been neglected and deprived must understand that they are being taken seriously as human beings. They must not be regarded as peculiar human beings who cannot meet the demands more privileged human beings can meet. . . . I suspect that the significant breakdown in the efficiency of American public education came not primarily from flagrant racial bigotry and the deliberate desire to create casualties but from the good intentions, namely, the sloppy sentimentalistic good intentions of educators to reduce standards of low-income and minority group youngsters. . . .[4]

Not only does the sheer number and variety of groups requiring attention create self-defeating pressures, but the effort to extend suitable preferences in employment to each causes conflicts and confusion almost to the point of being absurd. Currently there are so many groups targeted for "special

---

examination of the methods for ensuring such opportunity. See the author's pamphlet, *A Fair Look at Fair Employment*, Chicago, International Personnel Management Association, 1971.

[4] Kenneth B. Clark, "Efficiency as a Prod to Social Action," *Monthly Labor Review*, August 1969, pp. 55–56.

emphasis" in job placement—minorities, the disadvantaged, women, youth, older workers, the handicapped, veterans, etc.—that such groups compete with each other, and the efforts in their behalf are self-defeating. Not only does no one appraise whether such efforts really serve a useful purpose, but certainly no one appraises the impact on the public service.[5]

[5] Concern for the problem is well expressed in this editorial by Robert Perrin, vice president for University Relations at Michigan State University.

The federal government has almost succeeded in doing the impossible: It is turning the white, Anglo-Saxon Protestant male into a minority.

With its latest law requiring employers to take "affirmative action" to hire Vietnam-era veterans, the government has now brought one more major minority group under its protective umbrella, leaving the WASPish non-veteran and perhaps a few obscure subcultures still outside the privileged fold.

Affirmative action, for those unacquainted with governmental euphemisms, has become Washington's all-purpose answer to discrimination, past and present. It is aimed not merely at insuring equal opportunity; it calls for, in the words of one directive, "positive action . . . to overcome the effects of systematic institutional forms of exclusion and discrimination." Simply having non-discrimination policy is insufficient because "a benign neutrality in employment practices will tend to perpetuate the *status quo ante* indefinitely."

Therefore, the program requires employers to make "additional efforts to recruit, employ and promote qualified members of groups formerly excluded, even if that exclusion cannot be traced to particular discriminatory actions on the part of the employer," but the cutting edge is the establishment of hiring "goals" and timetables for women and minorities to create a properly balanced work force.

Determining the availability of these "excluded" persons—in the numbers necessary and with requisite qualifications—is far from an exact science. Goal setting usually is predicated on a group's proportionate representation in the local labor force or, in the case of faculty, on the number of Ph.D.s graduated nationally in specified disciplines. As a measuring device to determine how many women or minorities might be available, each leaves much to be desired.

The affirmative action concept was initiated by President Johnson in 1965 when he issued Executive Order 11246 to require employers who are also federal contractors (which includes most major employers and educational institutions) to hire regardless of race, color, religion or national origin. Two years later, the order was amended to include sex. Minorities were defined as blacks, Spanish-surnamed, American Indians and Orientals (now "Asian-Americans"). Failure to comply could mean a loss of federal funds.

Successive orders and laws emanating from Congress and the Executive Branch since have enfolded one more group after another. In January 1973, for example, the Federal Register contained guidelines from the Department of Labor requiring employers to include in their affirmative action efforts members of various religious and ethnic groups "primarily but not exclusively of Eastern, Middle and Southern European ancestry, such as Jews, Catholics, Italians, Greeks, and Slavic groups." Fortunately, the guidelines did not apply the proportional representation yardstick or ask for numerical goals for each category.

Congress also has passed Title IX of the Higher Education Act which prohibits discrimination on the basis of sex "under any educational program or activity receiving federal financial assistance," effectively blanketing in virtually all of organized education.

. . .

. . . the popularity of stamping "affirmative action" on every governmental ukase continues unabated. Last summer, the Labor Department published rules based on the Vocational Rehabilitation Act requiring employers receiving federal funds to establish affirmative action plans for the physically and mentally handi-

The danger is not merely the direct damage to the quality of administrative performance; the danger is equally the bad image of the public service created—one that public jobs are by nature rewards, or worse still, welfare dispensations existing for the purpose of providing incomes to the needy or the deserving. The moral fabric of a society is surely in less danger by resort to the "negative income tax," a guaranteed income, or any other such device

---

capped. Again, it was not merely non-discrimination in hiring that was required, but active recruiting and other positive measures.

Most recently, in December, Congress passed, over the President's veto, the Veterans Assistance Act. And there it was in the fine print: Employers must "take affirmative action to employ and advance in employment qualified service-connected disabled veterans and veterans of the Vietnam era." The conference report accompanying the bill noted that the affirmative action requirement "does not necessarily mean, however, that specific numerical goals and timetables will be made applicable to contractors and subcontractors *at this time*" (emphasis added).

. . .

. . . the fear remains that imposition of the layer upon layer of affirmative action plans either will be impossible to live with or will turn the process into a charade. Already, employers are so caught up with the gathering of statistics and the interminable governmental paperwork that they are losing sight of the principal objective of equality of opportunity. One also hears the cynical jokes about scoring multiple affirmative action points by hiring a black woman who has converted to Judaism or a handicapped veteran with a Spanish-surname.

Here, then, is the real danger of the federal government's blanket approach to the problems of "excluded" groups. The over-use of affirmative action is devaluing the currency of equal opportunity commitments. As employers attempt to draw up, and then carry out and defend, plan after plan dealing with the recruiting, hiring and upgrading of such diverse categories as minorities, women, ethnic and religious groups, the handicapped and now veterans, the necessary moral commitment will become lost or impotent in a bureaucratic maze.

As a result, the effectiveness of endeavors to meet the very real employment problems of these groups can only diminish. The people covered by the plans will continue under the illusion that they have some special assistance until, inevitably, expectations collapse. The collapse will be especially hard as rising unemployment shrinks the job market.

Up to a point, affirmative action has had its beneficial effects. It has forced employers to review the means by which they recruit, hire, promote and establish job qualifications, with the result that many artificial barriers and attitudes affecting women and minorities have been removed. Certainly, the quaint academic hiring procedures long indulged in by higher education have undergone a welcome modernization, and the colleges and universities are the stronger for it. If nothing else, the requirement that job vacancies be posted has opened up many new opportunities for those long disenfranchised in the employment market.

But it also can be argued that there are enough laws now on the books, such as the Civil Rights Act of 1964, the Equal Employment Opportunity Act, the Equal Pay Act, the prohibition against hiring discrimination because of age (not yet requiring goals), and Title IX which, together with enforcement arms, assure a strong legal foundation for equal opportunity and compliance.

So before affirmative action is carried to the ultimate absurdity with, say, a hiring plan required for WASPs and "all others," it is time to refocus on the real problems and their solutions. These will not come from statistics or a preoccupation with competing goals and plans, but from a moral as well as a legal compunction to act. [Robert Perrin, "Making Everybody into a Minority," *The Washington Post*, February 10, 1975.]

than it is by a corrosion in the public mind of the prestige of government employment.[6]

NEED FOR IMPROVED ADMINISTRATION OF MERIT

One must nevertheless acknowledge that the public service in its employment policy must be above reproach in assuring fair treatment to all citizens. Unfortunately, the motivation for some of the special "drives" to favor certain groups has grown out of frustration at thoughtless and indefensible discriminatory practices that have crept into the abracadabra of some so-called merit systems or were injected by careless or unprincipled managers and selecting officials. Any merit system worthy of the name must live up fully to the merit objective, making especially certain that artificial barriers and requirements are not created that have little or nothing to do with gauging the prospects of candidates' performance and making certain that genuine efforts are made to probe all sectors of society as sources of candidates.

We must also not overlook the importance of questioning traditional organization of work into jobs. Too often this has been the product of precedent or habit, with little thought given to logic or optimum utilization of men's skills. There is certainly no violence done to the philosophy enunciated here if jobs are redesigned so as to shred out routine duties from technical work, thus reducing the need for higher skilled workers and creating opportunities for lesser skilled applicants all at the same time. When there is an oversupply of low skills in the labor market and an undersupply of high skills, this procedure of job redesign makes common sense. It may mean that where there had been two positions with mixed duties, both calling for considerable education or experience which was really only essential for the more difficult duties, two new jobs may be created, one in which the higher duties are concentrated and the other with the lesser functions, the latter thereby requiring only minimal preparation. But this is a far cry from deliberate downgrading of standards and requirements without alteration of actual duties, a practice which can only lead to disastrous consequences for performance of public functions.

---

[6] A scholar in India, where there is a "reservation" of posts in the states for backward classes or castes, cites these flaws in the Indian experience:

> In the first place, the system of reservation undermines efficiency and morale of the civil service by inducting candidates of sub-standard quality into administration. Secondly, it makes backwardness a privilege, with the consequence that more and more communities keep up an agitation for their inclusion in the list with a view to reaping the special advantages. Thirdly, the communities included in the Backward Classes are themselves on various levels of backwardness, some being relatively more advanced than others. The lion's share of the special benefits accrues to the less backward among the Backward Classes, which is really contrary to the intentions underlying the system of reservation. And, worst of all, it perpetuates caste and class distinctions, which have been the bane of our society. [S. R. Maheshwari, *Indian Administration*, New Delhi, Orient Longmans, 1968, p. 257.]

Assuming a first-rate merit operation—free of outmoded standards or ill-advised testing processes—there is no place in the public service for special preferences or use of public jobs to serve welfare purposes. The standard of merit, and merit alone, is the only one yet discovered that can assure a quality service and at the same time avoid ridiculous competition to exploit the public payroll and to curry favor with one problem group or another in order to serve interests other than getting the government's work done effectively.[7]

CREATING JOBS

Although related to the foregoing discussion, programs to use the public service as a corrective in times of serious unemployment in the general economy deserve separate attention. Such steps were first taken in the Great Depression of the 1930s and have been repeated, in different forms, on several occasions since then. The theory is that if the general welfare is threatened by a high rate of unemployment in the private sector, then it is up to government to do something about it. One of the most popular methods and one with the quickest impact is to create more jobs in the public sector to help take up the slack. Most recently this has taken the form of federal grants to state and local units of government to develop programs of public usefulness in which large numbers of the unemployed can be readily hired.[8]

Few can quarrel with the notion that urgent and larger concerns of public policy must sometimes override the more limited objectives of manpower management in the regular public service. Some of the more recent programs, however, have sought to achieve this objective plus assuring that persons so hired under emergency unemployment relief also have more than temporary opportunities within the continuing state or municipal civil services. So long as such aims are attained without damage to the quality of the service or to the opportunities of persons already in the service or of those otherwise not in the emergency relief group, the process is relatively unassailable. Usually, sensible procedures can be devised to accomplish multiple purposes. One method is to keep the special unemployment programs separate from the regular service (as they were in the 1930s) until the new workers can be assimilated one by one into regular jobs on a merit basis.

On the other hand, when the zeal to ensure enduring employment overcomes fairness to others and flouts the effectiveness of the public service, it is no longer in the best interests of the public as a whole. Like some other welfare-oriented efforts, it eventually prostitutes the service and weakens its capacity to manage some of the very government activities that are in the interest especially of all sectors of the weak and underprivileged.

[7] See also the discussion of veteran preference in Chapter 9.

[8] A basic work on the subject is Harold L. Sheppard, Bennett Harrison, and William J. Spring, eds., *The Political Economy of Public Service Employment*, Lexington, Mass., D. C. Heath, 1972.

THE IMPACT OF TECHNOLOGY

We have already explored the extent to which the state in an urban society has acquired an unprecedented array of technical functions. We have observed the expanding range of occupations embraced. But the influence of a technological age runs still deeper.

Using an ever-increasing proportion of higher skills means acquisition of more highly educated people. Not only do persons with advanced education tend to have shorter careers (by going into full-time work later in life), but they are also more mobile. Professionals especially think of their identification with a field of work rather than with a particular employer. They are more likely to look upon employment in the civil service as an interlude rather than an exclusive career. Even those whose principal roots remain in the governmental field find themselves moving from jurisdiction to jurisdiction or accepting excursions into university teaching and research or into service abroad in education or technical assistance in developing countries.

Government agencies still imbued with the ideal of attracting competent people in their youth and holding them for lifelong careers in the same environment will have to revise their approach. Personnel systems must make accommodation to the "in-and-out" type of career. Policies which accept and encourage entry at all levels and departures for long periods with no loss of privileges are the order of the day. Actually this situation has been a blessing in disguise, for it helps to keep a bureaucracy in touch with the society it is supposed to serve in a way in which corps of civil servants insulated for life from other pursuits can rarely achieve. But personnel administrators must be prepared with new flexibilities in recruitment, in pay, in tenure, and in retirement provisions.[9]

Another effect of the growing technology is on in-service training. In fact, it has been the single strongest influence in training's coming of age. Relaxation of restraints on prolonged absences for full-time training, payment of tuition and expenses, a proliferation of in-plant courses to keep staffs current with rapid changes in technique—all have become commonplace and almost invariably received at least their initial impetus from the compelling needs of engineers, medical men, scientists, and technicians working in government laboratories, experiment stations, plants, and offices. It was not too long ago when such massive investment in training by government as employer would have been looked upon as an adverse reflection on recruitment and selection practices or on management or both. Unfortunately a few jurisdictions still see it that way.

[9] The subject was given intensive attention, as it affected professionals in less developed countries, at a U.N. seminar held in Tashkent, USSR, in October 1969. See *Report of the United Nations Interregional Seminar on the Employment, Development and Role of Scientists and Technical Personnel in the Public Service of Developing Countries*, 3 vols., United Nations, New York, 1970.

Along with other effects the heyday of technology has also brought with it a headiness on the part of many professionals, particularly scientists, who have come to think of themselves as such a special breed that they require separatism and privileges not available to the common herd or even to other professionals. Some, having been pampered beyond their powers to absorb without undue ego-inflation, have spent more time seeking further aggrandizement of their status than in doing their jobs. Revisions in important policy elements have indeed been called for, but wholly separate personnel systems for scientists are not ordinarily justified.

In fact, the age of technology imposes obligations as well as prestige upon the scientist in government. Because he is in the public service he has a special responsibility to be more than a scientist, to rise above his specialization. He owes a loyalty to public programs, to public objectives, and to his organization. His is not the independent choice to conduct research on what pleases him alone. He is a member of a team established to achieve certain goals, and his performance may properly be judged on his contribution to those goals.

INTERGOVERNMENTAL RELATIONS

The fathers of the American federal system would have difficulty recognizing their handiwork today. Through a century of legislative extensions and judicial interpretations, responding to nationwide needs, the national government is clearly preeminent. No small part of this nationalizing trend has been the product of the superior taxing power of the federal government and its massive grant-in-aid endowment of state and local governments. The independent status of state and local administrative machines has been substantially altered over the years. Criteria for performance, controls over expenditure, and personnel standards have had a profound effect on the nature and caliber of administration in these jurisdictions.

GRANTS AND MERIT

Since 1940, including subsequent extensions, all states receiving federal grants for welfare, employment security, public health, vocational rehabilitation, and civil defense have had to insure that at least these branches of their civil services operate under a merit system of employment, in this case supervised by the federal government. With minor exceptions the application of this mandatory stimulus to administrative improvement has met with unalloyed praise from all quarters. Even more important, it laid the groundwork for establishment of modern personnel policies on a statewide basis in those states that had not adopted such plans on their own volition. The significance for the quality of state administration can hardly be overstated.

INTERGOVERNMENTAL PERSONNEL PROGRAM

The interdependence of public jurisdictions in personnel matters has evolved rapidly since the 1940s. The International Personnel Management

Association and other professional groups in their own specialized areas have exerted a profound and positive influence on the general level of personnel management all over the country. State and local employees may participate in training programs run by federal agencies, some conducted especially for them, some available on a tuition basis.

Federal legislation now provides help to state, municipal, and county governments by subsidizing personnal management improvement and training programs with grants of funds, by establishing merit system standards, by encouraging and supporting operation of statewide personnel systems, by technical assistance in personnel methodology, by cooperative entry examining, by special fellowships for state and local civil servants, by interstate compacts in recruitment and training, and by fostering mobility of key workers among jurisdictions.[10] In turn, a number of states now authorize internal mobility of civil servants and assignment to the federal service. Also, local residence requirements are rapidly disappearing.

FEDERAL CONTROLS

The concept of "revenue sharing" developed in the 1970s was founded on the idea of allowing greater latitude administratively among state and local governments without denying them the benefits of federal money. However, except for the intergovernmental personnel program just referred to, other legislation has tended to regulate in considerable detail the manner in which states, counties, and cities hire, pay, and develop their employees. Such measures do not provide constructive assistance, technical or financial, but impose on these public jurisdictions controls that seek to parallel the expanding federal regulation of private industrial personnel management.

Examples of such restrictions are seen, most prominently, in enforcement of equal employment opportunity, establishment of public jobs to relieve unemployment, requirements for occupational health and safety, and extension of minimum wage and overtime pay provisions heretofore limited to the private sector. In addition, further constrictions may be in the offing, such as those setting standards for retirement systems and pending bills that would require all jurisdictions to bargain with employee unions on most conditions of employment, possibly replacing many parts of state or local laws governing personnel systems.[11] Without challenging the superficially

---

[10] This unique program, administered by the U.S. Civil Service Commission, was established under the *Intergovernmental Personnel Act of 1970*, signed January 5, 1971. So far, it has not been generously supported with funds to meet anything like the overall needs of state and local governments.

[11] The principal federal laws that have already imposed detailed controls are: (1) the *Occupational Safety and Health Act of 1970* (signed December 29, 1970, effective April 29, 1971), which requires the states to maintain comprehensive safety and health programs for all public employees; (2) the *Equal Employment Opportunity Act Amendments of 1972* (signed and effective March 24, 1972), which extend equal opportunity standards designed for private business to government employees; they have caused confusion of the directives and jurisdiction of the Civil Service Commission (over merit provisions) with those of the Equal Employment Opportunity Commission; (3) the *Comprehensive Employment and Training Act of 1973* (signed December 28, 1973,

worthwhile objectives of most of such federal intervention, a basic question arises as to whether it does not upset some fundamentals of the federal system, particularly the high degree of decentralization that has been the system's bulwark, the desirability of having local citizens and taxpayers control their own local governments, and the great flexibility and room for experimentation that has always characterized the system.

In spite of such developments in the way of absolute standards and controls, the more constructive features in federal personnel policy affecting state and local governments—as exemplified in the Intergovernmental Personnel Act—still offer much promise. Whatever the degree of decentralization and latitude remaining, the potential for a higher quality of personnel practice in American public services is good.

POLITICS AND THE PATRONAGE

The administration of government personnel systems on the basis of merit has gained great currency but has by no means overrun the field. Large segments of the American public service, as will be seen in the next chapter, are still plagued with a philosophy of "to the victor belongs the spoils" or "we need the jobs to ensure responsibility." Advantage to entrenched interests and indifference on the part of the public have contrived to maintain job patronage in large sectors of nearly a third of the state capitals, in many smaller cities, in almost all rural government, and in a few units of the federal

---

effective July 1, 1974), which calls for manpower plans embracing public workers and the creation of public jobs in high unemployment areas, entailing minute controls on kinds of jobs established and on hiring practices; and (4) the *Fair Labor Standards Amendments of 1974* (signed April 8, 1974, with provisions effective on varying dates, May 1, 1974, to January 1, 1975), which apply minimum wage, overtime pay, and age discrimination prohibition provisions to state and local governments, the provisions on overtime being especially onerous and costly by attempting to fit types of employment normally involving much "standby time" (e.g., fire protection, police, etc.) into the traditional overtime mold. At this writing, the Act's application to state and local governments has been suspended by the Chief Justice, pending constitutional review by the full Supreme Court of the United States.

During the same period, the only legislation involving a retreat in federal controls is a provision (effective January 1, 1975) in the *Federal Election Campaign Act Amendments of 1974* that reduces earlier prohibitions on political activities of state and local employees by no longer prohibiting them from leadership, fund-raising, and electioneering in political campaigns but continuing to deny their being candidates themselves, their coercing contributions from other public employees, and their using official authority to affect the result of an election.

The most serious threat to state and local government independence is posed by bills (still pending at this writing) that would require collective bargaining with unions on varying ranges of personnel policy and working conditions, leading to collective agreements that might reduce the power of the local citizenry to regulate personnel policy through law. Also, although not a threat to most public retirement systems, a study is now under way by congressional committees to determine whether federal regulation of vesting, of fiduciary standards, or of other features of public retirement plans is desirable. A report is due by December 31, 1976, called for by the *Employee Retirement Income Security Act of 1974*, which is aimed at counteracting the inadequacy of private pension schemes.

service. Although unique in its form, government job patronage is not radically different in impact from nepotism in private corporations and cliquism in educational institutions, but because it is in the public service its deleterious effects are more serious.

A test of party membership or service in order to hold government jobs is hardly compatible with the ideals of competency and impartiality held up for modern public service. Where the infection exists it thrives not only at the point of entrance but in every aspect of personnel movement, utilization, and reward. A career supervisor who gained his post on merit can have no discipline over politically appointed subordinates.

Related is the behavior of some legislators who misuse their power over appropriations or substantive legislation to bully their way into executive matters beyond their rightful jurisdiction. In an effort to please a constituent or satisfy his own whims, a legislator may try to influence an appointment or promotion or interfere with a proposed separation. It is to the credit of most of them, however, that they stay above such petty activities. Some assist a constituent only to the extent of getting the facts on a personnel transaction, recognizing that matters such as selection, discipline, removal, and advancement are the more proper and feasible domain of administration.

On a more general front, legislative bodies often try to make a showing to their electors of careful, economizing scrutiny over the employment and pay practices of government departments and at the same time preoccupy themselves with currying the favor of that special body of voters, public employees, by assiduous protection of their interests. Standing committees of the Congress and of state legislatures view the civil service as their special domain, but frequently find it awkward to maintain a posture of watchdog and protector at the same time. In any event, public personnel administration is necessarily responsive to this interest insofar as it can legitimately be.

CAREER CONTINUITY AND POLITICAL LEADERSHIP

We have already called attention to the unavoidable intermixture of policy-making and administration. The power of career bureaucrats over policy may rest less on their esoteric knowledge than on their advantageous position to initiate new programs.[12] Nevertheless, politically elected or appointed executives must give leadership to and make use of the bureaucracy. This is part of the machinery of responsiveness and accountability. It is to be sharply distinguished from patronage practices, the use of the public payroll up and down the line as a reward for political service. But it creates another strong tug on the arm of the personnel function.

[12] See the interesting discussion by Herbert A. Simon in "The Changing Theory and Changing Practice of Public Administration," Chapter 4 in *Contemporary Political Science: Toward Empirical Theory*, Ithiel de Sola Pool, ed., New York, McGraw-Hill, 1967.

Note again the points made previously in Chapter 1 on "Blending Politics and Administration."

Personnel management must indoctrinate career personnel with an attitude of responsiveness to political leadership without sacrifice of professional integrity. Independent-mindedness must be in delicate balance with loyalty to superior officers. The career man should not mistake obsequiousness for responsibility, or rashness for individuality and freedom.

The ideal permanent civil servant gives his full measure of service and devotion whatever he may think of his political superior, but he also has the courage to state his case emphatically when he thinks his boss is wrong or when the chief's proposals violate law or principle. When these are matters of _judgment,_ that is, where there is a range of choices, then he must ultimately abide by and give effect to decisions made, or else he must accept political vulnerability for his defiance. Only when he is so certain of his case that he is convinced that most reasonable men are bound to see it his way can he dare risk insubordination. Otherwise, to avoid compromising either his conscience or his superiors, his only recourse is to resign.[13]

A particularly trying period occurs when new political leadership takes over the bureaucracy following an election. The transition is sometimes painful to career man and new official alike. But it need not be. One of the strengths of a good personnel system in government is the degree to which it fosters smooth transitions to new political leadership, breeds mutual respect and understanding, and promotes clear definition of the respective roles of career and political officers.

The personnel system in the public service must contrive conditions, requirements, and safeguards that produce this balance in forces and attitudes. Some flexibility in selection of key assistants and constructive placement and mobility of top career men is just as essential to this objective as are continuity and competence in the rank and file of the service.

It is interesting that in the federal government during some administrations the career service was the largest single source from which presidential appointments to assistant secretaryships were made. In addition, many other selections were made from among persons who had long government experience in a noncareer capacity. The fiction that career men were lacking in the ability and imagination to adapt to changes in party or philosophy gave way to recognition that they were fully as successful in top policy positions as those with more political but less administrative experience.[14] Similar findings apply to the many career people appointed to lesser political posts.

Following the events of the early 1970s commonly referred to as the "Watergate" scandal, further support for the several ideas expressed here came from a distinguished panel of experts in public administration which had been commissioned by the National Academy of Public Administration. In

---

[13] See the further discussion in Chapter 16, "Public Service Ethics in a Democracy."
[14] This conclusion is based on the study by Dean E. Mann, with Jameson W. Doig, _The Assistant Secretaries: Problems and Processes of Appointment_, Washington, D.C., The Brookings Institution, 1965.

connection with various issues involving politically appointive posts in the federal service, this panel not only recommended a limitation on the proliferation of such positions but also advanced the novel proposals that new appointees be "encouraged or even required" to attend educational sessions dealing with their public responsibilities and their relations with career personnel and that they commit themselves to serve at least two years in their assignments.[15] Certainly these conditions would not be too much to ask of the political side in the needed accommodation between career and noncareer officials. As a matter of fact, orientation programs for political appointees were finally started in the federal service in 1975.

✗ THE DECLINE OF MANAGERIAL LICENSE ✗

During the early stages of the movement to recognize the importance of administration, it was common to hear the contemporary managerial philosophers proclaim that executives should not be expected to assume responsibility for a segment of work unless they had control over all the policies and conditions affecting the outcome, that their authority to determine inputs must be commensurate with their responsibility for results. We have long since learned, especially with the advent of more behavioral research, that this plausible-sounding dictum was vastly overstated.

Of necessity, there are are all kinds of constraints that the modern manager must live with. He faces increasing demands for *shared* decision-making—citizen or client insistence, pressures of employee unionization, deeper penetration by the press, in short all the elements of the need to survive in a "negotiating society." The days of the independent autocrat are gone. Even the subtle requirements for technical growth and adaptation, to maintain competence, are a constraint of their own. The realities of human motivation, the built-in resistances of employees and colleagues, the need to win support from all quarters—all these constitute another category of limitation on executive prerogative.

An observant researcher in the human aspects of organization experience once pointed out: "The realities of modern organizational life place the manager at any level of the organization in a position where he cannot control many things which affect the results for which he is responsible. It is foolish indeed to emphasize the logical idea that his authority must equal his responsibility. . . ."[16] The power to control rests not on authority but on selection of the means of influence most appropriate to the circumstances. To paraphrase further, one might say that it is easy to be an autocrat. The real

---

[15] *Watergate: Its Implications for Responsible Government*, A Report Prepared by a Panel of the National Academy of Public Administration at the Request of the Senate Select Committee on Presidential Campaign Activities, March 1974, pp. 106–107.

[16] Douglas McGregor, *The Human Side of Enterprise*, New York, McGraw-Hill, 1960, pp. 158–159.

challenge is how to achieve within bounds that are inescapable. The old single-minded preoccupation with fortifying executive power is outmoded and misguided. It is not only undesirable; it is realistically impossible.

THE INSTRUMENTS OF DEMOCRACY

Of all places where managerial license cannot and should not exist, it is in the public service. Strangely, we have always acknowledged the virtues of a government of checks and balances, but somehow we overlooked this in the pressure over the first half of the twentieth century to augment and sustain executive power.

Even the presidency has felt the stinging reaction to the excesses and abuses of power in a democracy. After the departure from office in disgrace of both a Vice President and a President within one year, it will be a long time before the American people will tolerate any more earmarks of an "imperial" presidency.

The trauma of events at the apex of government in the 1970s has its lessons for managers up and down the line in public administration. For this reason it is well to examine at this point an organizational thesis that until comparatively recently had become almost a fetish.

LINE AND STAFF

The thesis referred to is the conventional, simplistic distinction made between "line and staff." According to this theory, the functions for which the organization was created—carrying the mail, putting out fires, running a mental institution—are the "line" functions, and those existing *as the result* of creating the organization—personnel management, financial control, supply services—are "staff."

It follows from this construct that the line functions are paramount and that the staff must *serve* the line. Staff is therefore advisory and should not control, while line is the "doing" side of the operation and should not be inhibited but only helped by the staff activity. Hence, the only test for the propriety and adequacy of the personnel function, as one of the staff duties, would be its degree of support and service to the original functions of the organization. It is commonplace to hear the assertion that personnel administration is not an end in itself.

Up to a point this makes sense. Certainly in the broadest context management of government personnel exists in order to further the ends of government. Indeed, a *work-centered* approach to manpower motivation would support this thought. Except to meet extraordinary economic emergencies or under the most crass forms of the spoils system, government work is not created just to make jobs for people. Government does not exist in the first instance in order to hire, pay, discipline, and motivate its administrative workers.

The trouble comes in carrying this idea too far, in applying it at all levels in public organizations, and in ignoring the realities of the public interest. The fact is that once a government agency exists, the matter of *how* it does its job is often as important as *what* it does. The staff activities, including the personnel function, usually have the most to do with this *how* factor. How people are hired and how they are paid may be so critical at a given point in time that they may even override in importance any subdivision of the line function. They may, indeed, be a sound constraint on the line manager.[17]

THE PLACE OF THE PERSONNEL FUNCTION

The public's rightful interest in government personnel policy and operations is very real. Whether motivated by a concern for efficiency and economy or by a desire to facilitate proper entrance into the service, the public has a legitimate concern with how personnel work—from hiring to firing—is carried on in the bureaucracy.

When we talk about staff "service" to a line activity, we must bear in mind the scope of the two functions we are relating. *Governmentwide* personnel policy—in a city, a state, or the federal service—is very likely more important and vital than many *single segments* of the line function. The effectiveness of employee pay policy across the board certainly outstrips the matter of efficiency in issuing dog licenses. It is even more important to assure human competency throughout the service than to predict the weather with accuracy.

Not that such objectives are necessarily in conflict; usually they are not. But neither is it wise to insist that *by definition* a staff duty is subservient to a line duty. Many a personnel principle must be maintained even if it interferes at the moment with the desires of a particular line official or of an outside interest group concerned with his success, precisely because the personnel goal is presumably serving a larger and longer-range end of good government than is the immediate success of the activity supervised by that official.

The wise executive does not worry about artificial distinctions between line and staff. He may not even use the terms. He thinks about what is important. He may use personnel administration, just like budget administration, as one means of assuring a certain standard of uniformity and quality in getting the line functions performed—the *how* factor. He knows that the public has a right to be concerned about the employment and treatment of government personnel. And it is usually a much larger public than that concerned, for example, with the issuance of grazing permits, the regulation of labeling on canned oysters, or the construction of rural electric lines. The man-

[17] This general thesis is elaborated in the author's articles in *Public Administration Review*: "The Network of Authority," Winter 1958, and "More on the Network of Authority," Winter 1960. Douglas McGregor later advanced much the same reasoning, debunking line-staff fetishes in chapter 11, *op cit*. He observed: "Every member of lower and middle line management is subject to influences from staff groups which are psychologically indistinguishable from the authority exercised by his line superiors" (p. 146).

agement of fourteen million persons who constitute the federal, state, and local civilian bureaucracy in America is a most significant government function. It has indeed become an end in itself, ranking close in importance to almost any of the major operations of the public service—because it is woven through all of these and determines in large measure their effectiveness.

SPECIAL INTEREST GROUPS

As in the case of other governmental activities, the public personnel function has its special interest groups. Unfortunately, they are not so influential as to present a united front of substantial power in support of sound administration. Examples of such groups are found in the National Civil Service League, a citizens' organization that has historically fostered extension of the merit system, and professional associations like the American Society for Public Administration, the International City Management Association, and the International Personnel Management Association, which help establish norms for technically sound personnel operations.

Employee unions and war veteran organizations only rarely concentrate their energies to support sound administration, their chief orientation being toward gaining improved conditions for their membership, with or without regard to the public interest. Occasionally, in a crisis, their voices can be counted on to defend the merit system, but few of the great advances in public personnel administration can be ascribed to their initiative.

This is not to condemn organizations established primarily to foster the welfare of government employees; much is to be said in their defense in a later chapter. Rather it is simply to say that *there is ordinarily no special interest group in any jurisdiction doing battle in the legislative halls continuously to bring about better, more imaginative, more creative personnel management.*

Sporadically and temporarily, a League of Women Voters, a local civil service league, or some other group in an individual state or municipality will campaign or lobby for a new merit-system law, but it usually relaxes when the law is passed. Other than in such instances, it would seem that a new law or policy is strongly advocated by interest groups only if it promises to save money (as with taxpayers' leagues) or ensure benefits for some public employees or applicants (as with unions, veteran organizations, or groups representing the concerns of women or minorities).

Few influential voices speak out for the long-range interests of the public in general—namely, high-quality performance and management in government services. Typically, the government personnel official has no substantial outside clientele, no powerful interest group among the general citizenry actively pressing for such measures as improved recruitment, more adequate research, or broader training and educational programs. Initiation of such measures almost invariably must come from within the bureaucracy.

PUBLIC PERCEPTIONS OF GOVERNMENT SERVICE

No analysis of environmental influences is complete without some discussion of the susceptibility of the civil service to mercurial public attitudes toward it. The ups and downs of the prestige of public employment are attributable at least as much to external factors as they are to internal behavior.

In the United States, as well as some other countries, overreaction to whatever gets journalistic attention seems to be a predictable cultural habit. Trying times of disillusionment and corruption, instead of leading to a strengthening of institutions, often result in further handicaps to their operation in the public interest.

An example is the periodic paranoia demanding "openness" in all administrative determinations. While democratic responsiveness requires considerable attention to methods for citizen participation, open hearings, and free inquiry by the news media, like all good things such procedures can be pressed to the point of absurdity. When performed without regard to the need for careful technical analysis and reflection, with too much insistence on current and continuous disclosure and on decision-making before citizen observers, the consequences of this preoccupation generally involve discouragement to a professional approach to administration, a stifling of initiative and innovation, and, in the long run, a subversion of the benefits of a more rational openness in managing the public weal.[18]

Another result of well-meaning but overzealous citizen pressures has been a drastic resort to the courts. The judiciary was not designed for administration; yet, more and more of the details of management—particularly those relating to personnel—seem to be challenged and ruled on in lawsuits. To some extent these judgments have exerted reasonable and proper prods or restraints on executive agencies, but on as many occasions the courts have stepped well beyond basic interpretation of the law and have encroached seriously on the latitude of administration to exercise discretion and to give common sense an adequate role. The result too often has been not only a further stifling of administrative creativity but, even worse, a careful hedging-about of all action with excessively detailed written procedures that reduce management to computerlike decision-making, laborious redundant work processes, and hamstrung productivity.

These latter-day evidences of a proclivity to clamp down on the bureaucrats are simply more sophisticated versions of longstanding desires of Americans to control and contain their governors. Although the extreme frontier attitudes of negativism about anything governmental have expired along with witchcraft and the pony express, the persistence of distrust and

---

[18] See the excellent critique on "The Costs of Openness" by Harlan Cleveland in an address before the American Society for Public Administration in April 1974 at Syracuse University. Major excerpts from the speech appeared in *The Washington Post*, January 11, 1975.

overweaning constraint is curious in this day when so much, of necessity, has been entrusted to public agencies and when their functions have become more imperative than ever.

Traditionally, Americans looked upon government as incidental to the main business of life. Many top-quality young people failed even to consider the desirability of entering upon a public service career. Some happened into it by accident only to become intrigued by its challenges and to remain. Educational institutions and vocational counselors have been slow to interest their students in employment with public agencies. But somehow governmental jurisdictions have managed to attract a reasonable share of the country's best talent.

The importance of the work itself again comes to the fore. Repeatedly, studies have shown that reasons given by civil servants for remaining in public employment are heavily weighted with satisfaction in performing interesting, sometimes exciting, tasks. From this we may take the cue that at least for the professions and management occupations, where the need is greatest anyway, we would do well to interest qualified citizens in the great issues facing our society, pointing out that the ambitious, mentally alert individual can most readily get involved with these fascinating challenges by working for the government.[19]

Over the years thoughtful leaders in business, education, and politics have spoken up to give the public service its due. The National Civil Service League, the Rockefeller Foundation, and other public-spirited organizations annually recognize outstanding civil servants with significant awards. Professional associations and other groups likewise often honor public employees for achievements in the service of society.

Distinguished panels like the Sixth American Assembly and the Second Hoover Commission stressed some time ago the need to root out the folklore of deprecation about the civil service and to enhance the prestige of public employment as the best insurance for attracting high-quality manpower.[20] Much of the misinformation and misconception about the public service has been gradually corrected, but pockets of mythology persist. It is a fact of life to which the public personnel function must ever be alert so as to decry the

[19] The most comprehensive survey of prestige factors was Franklin P. Kilpatrick, Milton C. Cummings, Jr., and M. Kent Jennings, *The Image of the Federal Service*, Washington, D. C., The Brookings Institution, 1964.

[20] Sixth American Assembly, *The Federal Government Service: Its Character, Prestige, and Problems*, New York, Columbia University Graduate School of Business, 1954; Commission on Organization of the Executive Branch of the Government, *Personnel and Civil Service*, Washington, D.C., 1955, and *Task Force Report on Personnel and Civil Service*, Washington, D.C., 1955.

An interesting insight into honorable careers is the book describing the lives of eight Rockefeller Award winners: Delia and Ferdinand Kuhn, eds., *Adventure in Public Service*, New York, Vanguard Press, 1963. Attention is called also to the excellent volume by John D. Weaver, *The Great Experiment, An Intimate View of the Everyday Workings of the Federal Government*, Boston, Little, Brown, 1965.

blanket assaults, to make certain that real flaws in the service are eliminated, and to feel free to advertise its qualities and achievements without inhibition.

*   *   *

THE RANGE OF INFLUENCES upon personnel administration is obviously broad and penetrating. Its impact on society is, in turn, equally impressive. This environment makes all the more clear that the rock upon which the bureaucracy can most safely rest is the merit system, the subject to which we now turn.

CHAPTER 3

Development of the Merit System

THE MOST DISTINCTIVE characteristic of today's public service in the United States as contrasted with that of the nineteenth century is the merit system. No other development has been as responsible for stimulating professionalization and competence in government employment. Along with the reorganization of functions, budget planning, and fiscal controls, the merit system has shaped the nature and the quality of American bureaucracy at the very time when it was assuming a more prominent role in American life.

The practice of using public jobs as rewards for political party service was found to be entirely inconsistent with two imperatives: the popular pressure for equality of opportunity to work in government and the increasingly technical and critical character of government functions. After muddling through strained periods of part spoils system and part merit for many years, the nation happily has reached a point where merit is clearly dominant. Yet, there are still provinces of patronage surviving, primarily in state and local jurisdictions, and there are still apologists for the practice.

The thesis sometimes advanced that a reasonable amount of patronage is necessary to nourish the particular kind of party machinery existent in this country is based on the false premise that motivation for party work can come only through winning jobs. As a matter of fact, this kind of reward in the past may account for the caliber of workers too often found in party hierarchies. A change in the incentive system can also improve the quality and motivation of party workers. The improvement that has gradually taken place in recent decades may be due in large part to the fact that most party workers must of necessity look to other satisfactions, rather than to jobs, as their reward.

The following analysis is most convincing:

> American political parties have, after all, been getting along without patronage to various extents for some time now, and they have survived. Even many large metropolitan cities, whose patronage needs the scholars emphasize, have managed without it. The political party has its causes and justification deep in the American political process and not in the dispensation of political privileges. Patronage is necessary to a certain type of party operation, but others can be maintained without it. The old machines and local party organizations relied on patronage, but they were rooted in social and economic conditions that are disappearing. As they disappear, so will the parties and patronages they fostered.
>
> Ultimately, the decline of patronage will, among a number of causes, speed the parties to further centralization, to the heightening of their ideological content, to a greater reliance on group participation in politics, to greater nationalization of the candidate image and party campaigning, and to the establishment of some modicum of party discipline.
>
> There is something almost quaint in these days of big parties, big government, and advertising agency politics about a political institution that conjures up images of Boss Tweed, torchlight parades, and ward heelers. As the great day of patronage recedes into history, one is tempted to say that the advancing merit systems will not kill patronage before it withers and dies of its own infirmity and old age.[1]

Before summarizing the history of the patronage and the evolution of its antidote, we should examine more closely what is meant by a merit system.

DEFINITION OF MERIT SYSTEM

Initially the concept of merit system applied solely to the manner of entrance into the service. Indeed, the term appears not to have been used at all in the early years of civil service reform. Erroneously the phrase *civil service* still lingers with a connotation of appointment by examination simply because the subject of reform came to be confused with its nature. But the more accurate designation is merit system. Civil service, after all, merely distinguishes civilian pursuits in government from military. A civil service can literally be manned under either a patronage or a merit system.

Nowadays, the term *merit system* is commonly used not only to convey a form of selection for entrance to the service but also to embrace other aspects of the personnel system—advancement on merit, pay related to the nature of the job and to quality of performance, and desirable working

[1] Frank R. Sorauf, "The Silent Revolution in Patronage," *Public Administration Review*, Winter 1960, p. 34.

conditions. In its broadest sense a merit system in modern government means *a personnel system in which comparative merit ar achievement governs each individual's selection and progress in the service and in which the conditions and rewards of performance contribute to the competency and continuity of the service.*

The entrance and usually the promotion features of a merit system are ordinarily founded on a plan of open, competitive examinations (not necessarily written tests) by which candidates are appraised as to their *relative* fitness for duty in a position, an occupation, or a service.[2] The U.S. Civil Service Commission, in a publication designed for acquainting new political leadership with the career service, has declared that "open competition" consists of the following principal elements:

1. Adequate publicity. Job openings and requirements must be made public so that interested citizens have a reasonable opportunity to know about them.
2. Opportunity to apply. Citizens who are interested must have a chance to make their interest known and to receive consideration.
3. Realistic standards. Qualification standards must be reasonably related to the job to be filled and must be applied impartially to all who make their interest known.
4. Absence of discrimination. The standards used must contain factors which related only to ability and fitness for employment.
5. Ranking on the basis of ability. The very essence of competition implies a ranking of candidates on the basis of a relative evaluation of their ability and fitness, and a selection process which gives effect to this ranking.
6. Knowledge of results. The public must be able to find out how the process works, and anyone who believes that the process has not been applied properly in his own case must have a chance for administrative review.[3]

Such are the formal ingredients of that aspect of a merit system relating to entrance into government positions. But these should be accepted as only the bare outline. Much depends, for example, on the content of standards "reasonably related" to job requirements. These must be high enough to assure competence but not so high as to be unrealistic in terms of available personnel. They may concentrate on the knowledge and skills needed but should not neglect the candidates' genuine interest in the work and the objectives of the organization. Contrary to the doctrine sometimes advanced, requiring that candidates evidence a real sympathy and even zeal for the program is wholly compatible with, in fact sometimes essential to, attainment of true merit. Motivation and drive can be especially vital to new, uncharted activities. Likewise, only the facade of a merit system is main-

---

[2] The nature and uses of such examinations are discussed fully in a later chapter.
[3] U.S. Civil Service Commission, *The Federal Career Service—At Your Service*, Washington, D.C., 1973, section on "Selecting the Career Worker."

tained when jurisdictions fail to seek out energetically the participation of the very best candidates, who are not likely to be among those eagerly seeking employment. But more about these considerations in subsequent chapters.

HISTORY OF THE MERIT SYSTEM

To appreciate the crusade against the spoils system and the eventual development of positive management aims in personnel administration requires a brief review of this facet of American political history.[4]

Colonial America grew up under a spoils system. Public office had been treated by the British aristocracy as the special preserve of a privileged class, which led colonial legislatures first to try to restrict the appointing power of royal governors and, after the Revolution, to frame measures to prevent reappearance of this monopoly. This accounted for the overreliance on popular election of administrative officers in the new states and in 1820 for the tenure limitations in the youthful federal service that provided for automatic separation of many appointees every four years. It was this very rotation that became the foundation of a new favoritism.

In spite of chaos in the states and cities and then the four-years law, it is generally conceded that the first presidents maintained substantial standards of competence in the federal service, although political orthodoxy was by no means omitted as an element of fitness for office. But the full flower of rotation in office and rationalization of the patronage did not bloom until the administration of Andrew Jackson. In effect, the attitudes and traditions springing from an individualistic, pioneer society found their most complete expression in Jacksonian democracy. In the context of the times it seemed entirely laudable to counter the equation of fitness with wealth and aristocracy that had evolved during the forty years from Washington through Jefferson[5] with a more democratizing practice consistent with the equalitarian conditions of the frontier. Paradoxically, though, the eventual entrenchment of the political spoils system itself became a menace to the continuance of democratic government.

It was the progressive degradation and degeneration of public life under the spoils method that finally called forth a movement in the 1860s which

[4] The most thorough and authoritative historical studies are Leonard D. White, *The Federalists, The Jeffersonians, The Jacksonians,* and *The Republican Era,* New York, Macmillan, 1948, 1951, 1954, 1958; and Paul P. Van Riper, *History of the United States Civil Service,* New York, Harper & Row, 1958—the best single volume history.

An excellent brief history of early civil service reform is provided in U.S. Civil Service Commission, *Biography of an Ideal,* Washington, D.C., 1974. A basic early work is Carl R. Fish, *The Civil Service and the Patronage,* Cambridge, Mass., Harvard University Press, 1904. An especially insightful treatment is found in Herbert Kaufman's "The Growth of the Federal Personnel System," appearing in Sixth American Assembly, *The Federal Government Service,* 2nd. ed. of papers prepared for the Assembly, Wallace S. Sayre, ed., Englewood Cliffs, N.J., Prentice-Hall, 1965.

[5] See the interesting data amassed by Sidney H. Aronson, *Status and Kinship in the Higher Civil Service,* Cambridge, Mass., Harvard University Press, 1964.

demanded reform of the civil service in the name of governmental efficiency and public morals. The disastrous turnover, in which experience was systematically scrapped; the exaltation of inexperience and incompetence; the stagnation in administrative policies; the favoritism and partiality in the ordinary conduct of public business; and the taboo that grew up about public service as a career—combined to make reform imperative.

Carried on by a small group of high-minded, public-spirited men, the movement focused initially on three limited goals: (1) minimal examinations for certain clerical jobs in Washington, D.C., (2) limitation on removals from office for partisan reasons, and (3) prohibition against the longstanding custom of levying assessments on officeholders for party purposes. But even these aims were not achieved until need for a more drastic reform was perceived.

Four subsequent developments were the most important in finally leading to that reform through the historic Civil Service Act of 1883: (1) the courage and dogged persistence in advancing reform by idealists such as George William Curtis; (2) the organization by 1877 of the New York Civil Service Reform Association, followed by other state groups, culminating in the National Civil Service Reform League;[6] (3) the report on the British civil service prepared by Dorman B. Eaton, appointed by President Hayes; and (4) the assassination of President Garfield at the hands of a disappointed office seeker. This last sorry happening, indirectly chargeable to the patronage practice, so crystallized sentiment for reform that temporizing and compromise were no longer feasible.

The original Civil Service Act, based on the English model, created a bipartisan commission responsible to the chief executive and provided for filling government positions by open competitive examination, but initially it applied to only a limited portion of the headquarters service (known as the departmental service) in Washington. Fortunately it authorized the President to extend coverage by executive order, and such extension took place gradually over the years until by the mid-twentieth century the Act's provisions applied to nearly all sectors of the federal establishment over which it was feasible to apply a wholesale formal system and which were not otherwise covered by statutory personnel provisions.[7]

Meanwhile, contemporary stirrings of reform were taking place at the state level, with New York leading off by adopting a statute in the same year as the federal law, 1883, followed by Massachusetts (1884), Wisconsin and Illinois (1905), Colorado (1907), New Jersey (1908), Ohio (1912), California and Connecticut (1913), Maryland (1920), and most of the others after 1935. The larger cities during the same period began undertaking

---

[6] Now the National Civil Service League.

[7] No effort is made here to catalogue the details of all these extensions, but reference may be made to a convenient summary: National Civil Service League, *The Presidency and the Civil Service*, Washington, D.C., 1967. It covers the administrations of Theodore Roosevelt through Lyndon Johnson.

personnel system reform, but counties and other rural jurisdictions made little headway.

EVOLUTION OF THE PERSONNEL FUNCTION

While the notable feature of the period from 1883 to the 1930s was the negative aim of limiting the spoils system by establishing competitive entrance requirements for public jobs and by placing bipartisan control agencies in a strategic position to check any cheating on this objective, the period since then has been characterized by an expansion of the scope and concepts of public personnel administration. The need for government to be not only qualified but expert, motivated, stable, and, above all, responsive to democratic control has necessitated a more positive and comprehensive approach to the management of its human resources.

Indicative of the numerous milestones since the 1930s that have marked the path of progress into an era of aggressive and positive management of personnel affairs in government are the following steps:

1. The report *Better Government Personnel* by the Commission of Inquiry on Public Service Personnel (1935), which stressed the need for a career service that would attract the best minds of the nation.
2. The establishment by the President in 1931 of the Council of Personnel Administration (later the Federal Personnel Council, and now the Interagency Advisory Group), made up of federal personnel directors who became an important force in improvement of personnel administration.
3. The development in the 1930s and 1940s of comprehensive, modern programs of personnel management in such agencies at the Department of Agriculture, the Tennessee Valley Authority, and the Social Security Board, the latter entity becoming absorbed eventually into the Department of Health, Education, and Welfare.
4. The report *Personnel Administration in the Federal Service* by the President's Committee on Administrative Management in 1937, which suggested various antidotes to the then negative and restrictive activities of the federal Civil Service Commission.
5. A series of executive orders elaborating on the personnel responsibilities of federal agencies and the Commission, beginning with Franklin Roosevelt's order of 1938 establishing personnel divisions in each department.
6. The gradual excursions of some states and major cities into fields of in-service training, grievance systems, and modern job-classification and pay systems.
7. The recommendations of the two Hoover Commissions and the Sixth American Assembly to which reference has already been made and which in large measure have been implemented.
8. The state merit systems required by the federal Social Security Act in 1940 and subsequent intergovernmental cooperation all along the per-

sonnel front, especially as reflected by the Intergovernmental Personnel Act of 1970.

9. Passage and implementation of the Government Employees Training Act of 1958 in the federal service.
10. The increased role of employee unions in determining personnel policy and the development of a formalized and more sophisticated union-management consultation and bargaining procedure in the federal government and in many cities and states.
11. The establishment in 1966 of an Executive Assignment System in the federal government, recognizing the special placement, training, and incentive policies needed for the upper reaches of the career service.
12. The increasing reliance on behavioral science research to foster genuine zeal on the part of the work force in the program aims of public enterprises.
13. Extension in 1972 of equal employment opportunity standards to government employees, requiring careful reappraisal of selection methods.

The changes in emphasis have been clear: a competent civil service could not come just from initial employment on a competitive basis and "equal pay for equal work." The big job of personnel management was emerging as that of securing the ablest people for the public service and of maintaining a well-trained, satisfied, productive work force. Paralleling developments in private industry, this meant enlargement of the personnel function to embrace much more than recruiting, testing, and pay standardization. It has meant making the public service attractive as a career for the cream of the graduates from the nation's schools and colleges. It has meant expanded in-service training for orientation, for skill improvement, for increasing employee potential for advancement, for creating a sense of "belonging" and a sense of unity and common purpose in an organization—all factors that are vital to high productivity.

The new role of personnel administration, further, has meant inclusion of internal placement policies and methods to insure promotion and transfer opportunities, so that the filling of positions is not wholly a matter of looking to formal examination registers. It has meant stimulation of recreation programs; provisions for personal counseling; establishment of services and conveniences for employees that made life in the organization more satisfying—loan funds, employee libraries, car sharing, improved eating and sanitary facilities, and the like. It has meant the inauguration of positive incentives—special salary increases for superior work, cash awards, honor awards. It has meant supervision of relations with employee organizations, with full recognition of employees' rights to organize and negotiate collectively on matters affecting their work status and conditions.

These developments have not, of course, been uniformly applied or uniformly successful. Too large a number of jurisdictions still hold back from an enlightened personnel policy. But general acceptance of at least the broad features of the merit concept in public employment has been validated again and again.[8] Perhaps we are finally giving meaning to the phrase coined so long ago: "the best shall serve the state."

SCOPE OF MERIT SYSTEMS

FEDERAL   In the federal civil service, as already noted, the break with the patronage system has been rather complete, in spite of periodic abuses of merit requirements that crop up from time to time. The point is that legally the principles of merit cover all but small segments of the service, and most deviations that get public attention are violations of law and regulation, not the result of inadequate coverage.

Except for a few categories of jobs like those of attorneys and certain overseas posts, employment and advancement in the federal executive agencies and departments are genuinely controlled by *what* a person knows and how he performs rather than *who* he knows. Even in the excepted categories mentioned various degrees of the merit process come into play. There are hardly any career jobs filled solely on the basis of party service or personal favoritism. This takes into account that special merit systems, to one degree or another independent of the general system administered by the Civil Service Commission, cover many thousands of jobs in agencies such as the Postal Service, the Department of Medicine and Surgery of the Veterans Administration, the Tennessee Valley Authority, the Federal Bureau of Investigation, the Panama Canal, the Energy Research and Development Administration, the Nuclear Regulatory Commission, the Public Health Service commissioned corps, and the Foreign Service. The largest category of "exempt" jobs is certainly not open to political influence, namely, those filled by foreign nationals at American defense bases or other missions overseas.

The following table clearly demonstrates the steady progress of the merit idea in the federal government over the years.

---

[8] As evidenced by the number of states adopting statewide merit systems in the 1960s and 1970s and by an opinion poll showing 70 percent of the people from all over the country and all walks of life favoring merit for public jobs up to the highest policy-making level. American Institute of Public Opinion, *The Washington Post*, August 6, 1966.

A first-rate summary of progress in the development of the public personnel function in the United States appears in U.S. Civil Service Commission, *Biography of an Ideal*, Washington, D.C., 1974. It includes two informative sections that bring the history of achievement up to date: "The Past Fifteen Years, 1958–1973," and "State and Local Personnel Administration."

An authoritative guide for state and local governments in establishing a statutory base for a merit system, with discussion of alternative features, is *Guidelines for Drafting a Public Personnel Administration Law*, Chicago, International Personnel Management Association, 1973.

FEDERAL EMPLOYEES SUBJECT TO MERIT PERSONNEL POLICIES

Year	Number of Employees in Civil Service	Number Under General Merit System	Number Under Special Merit Systems	Percentage Under Merit
1884	131,200	13,800	—	10.5
1900	208,000	94,900	—	45.6
1930	580,500	462,100	—	79.6
1950	1,934,000	1,641,900	—	84.9
1970	3,000,000	2,565,000	110,000	89.1
1975	2,840,000	1,741,000	817,000	90.1

NOTE: The recent reduction in proportion under the general merit system, subject to the jurisdiction of the Civil Service Commission, is accounted for entirely by the quasi-industrial status accorded the U.S. Postal Service under the Postal Reorganization Act, which went into effect in 1971.

Total employees in the left-hand column include those in the General Accounting Office and Government Printing Office, which are in the legislative branch rather than the executice branch of the government but are subject to the general merit system. Likewise the "special merit systems" column includes the Library of Congress, also in the legislative branch. Other special systems (all provided by law) included in that column are: Energy Research and Development Administration, Nuclear Regulatory Commission, commissioned corps of the Public Health Service, Federal Bureau of Investigation, Foreign Service, Panama Canal, Postal Service, Tennessee Valley Authority, and the medical and nursing employees in the Veterans Administration.

Major groups not under formal merit systems (though various degrees of merit are followed in employment for most of them) are: foreign nationals working in American defense bases and embassies abroad (accounting for well over half the exemptions), American teachers in schools for military dependents abroad, consultants in all departments, student aides, attorneys in all departments, and county committeemen of the Department of Agriculture.

The data are based on information supplied by the U.S. Civil Service Commission. Some figures are estimates, and all are rounded to the nearest hundred or thousand. The percentages under merit for 1930 and 1950 would have been larger if the necessary statistics had been available; some of the special systems were in existence in those years.

STATES   As for state personnel administration based on merit, the most powerful initial impetus was the federal intervention provided by the Social Security Act, effective in 1940.[9] Because of this requirement that federal funds for welfare, employment security, health, and other grant programs must be administered by state agencies operating under merit systems, *every state has*

[9] The best overview of this federally directed program, including recommendations for improvement, is found in these documents: *Progress in Intergovernmental Personnel Relations*, Report of the Advisory Committee on Merit System Standards, Washington, D.C., Department of Health, Education, and Welfare, 1968; and *More Effective Public Service*, The First Report to the President and the Congress by the Advisory Council on Intergovernmental Personnel Policy, January 1973, and The Supplementary Report, July 1974, Washington, D.C. The latter advisory council was authorized by the Intergovernmental Personnel Act but has not been continued beyond its initial assignment.

at least a major portion of its civil service subject to modern personnel practices.

In addition, as previously mentioned, many states on their own have adopted and implemented statewide merit systems. By 1975, the number in this category was thirty-four. Several of these, however, are inadequately supported with funds or otherwise are poorly administered. A few additional states have some elements of a personnel system beyond that required by the federal grant-in-aid laws, with features such as statewide position-classification or training programs or extension of competitive merit processes to departments other than the grant-receiving units but still short of statewide. The remainder ensure merit only in the grant programs.

Diversity and complexity are hallmarks of state personnel administration. In addition to the variations occasioned by parts of all state services coming under federal standards, special systems often exist for groups such as state police and state universities. Often these are provided for separately by law. Consequently, it is common to find several different personnel systems at the state level.

The next stage of advancement for the states, and indirectly all subunits of states, came from the financial and technical assistance provided by intergovernmental personnel legislation.[10] At the same time, it should be understood that the mere presence of a merit system law is no guarantee of sound personnel management, a lesson bitterly experienced in several of the states. Adequate funds and affirmative concern by chief executives are absolute requisites to success. A number of states fall short in both categories.

On the other hand, most states carry on a very creditable operation, and some have distinguished themselves by innovative steps that are in the vanguard of the field. One such forward move has been the establishment in a number of states of a single personnel director with broad executive powers to conduct the personnel program, subject to check by a bipartisan body with respect to basic policy and employee appeals.

CITIES   At least as progressive as the states, indeed more so in many cases, are the major cities. Every large municipality has a merit system, and almost all of those in the one-hundred-thousand-population class or above have at least the bulk of their public services run under such a plan. Even in smaller cities, especially those with the city-manager form of government or where there are statewide merit requirements, the practice is gaining rapidly—a development that has steadily moved ahead since the 1930s. In a major policy statement on municipal government the National League of Cities has been

---

[10] The Intergovernmental Personnel Act of 1970. See the discussion on Intergovernmental Relations in Chapter 2. A study that helped make the case for the 1970 Act was W. Brooke Graves, *Federalism and Public Employment*, Washington, D.C., Federal Professional Association, 1965. Principal credit for development of the legislation goes to the U.S. Civil Service Commission and the staff of the Senate Committee on Government Operations.

emphatic in its advocacy of merit principles to govern personnel management in American cities.[11]

COUNTIES   In that blighted area of American politics, the county, the story is different. Except in a few urban or suburban counties and those in states such as California, New York, and New Jersey that require merit systems in their counties, this earmark of modern management is rarely to be found. Rural counties are almost invariably devoid of modern personnel policies and methods. However, the rural county government is clearly declining in importance as a political unit. In total government employment the nearly three thousand such counties represent collectively only a small fraction of the American public service.[12]

JURISDICTION OF MERIT PROCEDURES

Under the typical civil service law, the central personnel agency is given jurisdiction over specified groups of positions; according to some civil service parlance, these positions are in the "classified service." The term *classified* in this sense has nothing to do with the grouping of positions into classes upon the basis of duties. In the federal service and others the term *classified* has been dropped. Positions subject to the merit system are in the "competitive service" or the "career service."

NONCAREER CATEGORIES   The following are usually not subject to merit system control: elective officials, those appointed to special boards and commissions, heads of departments, and occasionally experts who may be permanent or temporary employees working under special contract. These are said to be in the "unclassified," "excepted," or "noncareer" service.

DEGREES OF COMPETITION   The merit system and competition are not necessarily synonymous terms. The typical law also vests in the personnel agency or the chief executive the authority to determine which positions under merit jurisdiction will be filled by open competition, which filled by "non-

[11] *National Municipal Policy*, Adopted at the Forty-ninth Congress of Cities, 1972. The statement in section 4.200 is obviously drawn from the declaration of policy in the opening provision of the Intergovernmental Personnel Act of 1970.

Data on the merit system in cities reflect its wide applicability, in direct correlation with city size. By 1974 allegedly over 95 percent of municipal employees were covered by merit systems, although there is no way to evaluate how many of these systems exist in name only. Two facts are clear, however: the proportion covered by merit is largest in the big cities (those with populations of 250,000 and up); and, whatever the precise count, anything close to a 90-percent figure constitutes an impressive record for acceptance of the merit principle. See Andrew W. Boesel, "Local Personnel Management," *The Municipal Year Book, 1974*, Washington, D.C., International City Management Association, pp. 92–93.

[12] The best overall summary of developments in state and local government appears in *Biography of an Ideal, op. cit.*

competitive" examination,[13] and which exempted from any requirements whatsoever. This process simply involves determining the method of selection most desirable in connection with each category of position.

It may be stated categorically at this point that the spirit, if not the letter, of the merit system demands open competition wherever feasible. If the best are to serve the state, they can ordinarily be discovered from a number of applicants only through such competition. A noncompetitive examination procedure may result in qualified appointees, but there is usually no reason to believe that it results in the *best*-qualified. This is a distinction that needs to be kept constantly in mind. It is not necessarily implied that competition can be only by means of the traditional ranking of candidates by numerical rating. They may also be grouped into broad categories of quality, recognizing that for many jobs examination methods do not lend themselves to fine distinctions.

Furthermore, there are positions which it is not feasible to fill through competitive methods and where "the conditions of good administration" warrant the use of other means. In general, they fall into two groups: (1) certain positions of a highly technical nature, the qualifications for which are such that only a few persons can meet them; (2) certain positions which are so undesirable for one or another reason that very few applicants can be discovered by any recruiting methods. It is obviously futile to attempt to fill a position by open competition if extremely few candidates compete. The freedom of choice given the appointing officer enables him, in such instances, to select whom he will from the applicants, and he might as well have followed such a procedure in the first place.

Unfortunately, however, many positions which do not fall in either of these groups have been placed in a noncompetitive class in the various jurisdictions.[14] All too frequently, under pressure from appointing officers or others or because of an inadequate examining staff, positions are included in this class which could be filled without difficulty by competitive methods. When this is the case, the variation is being employed to weaken rather than to strengthen the merit system.

EXEMPT CATEGORIES   In the exempt class are found those positions which may be filled without examination of any kind. Usually, these fall into four groups: (1) laborers, (2) positions of a "confidential" or "policy-determining" character, (3) part-time or temporary positions, (4) positions which have not been filled satisfactorily by examination methods. Varying reasons

[13] The noncompetitive examination is synonymous with the "pass" examination (as employed under the federal law of 1871). The incumbents of noncompetitive positions are selected by the appointing officer, subject only to their meeting certain standards, which may include passing a test. There is no relative ranking of eligibles on the basis of examination results.

[14] In general, the proportion of noncompetitive positions should be small, although in case of emergency this method of selection offers the advantage of speed.

are behind the exemption of each of these groups. That of laborers is widely defended because of the nature of the employment and on the specious ground that labor jobs are too unimportant for the attention of the personnel agency. Employees whose work is of a confidential nature, like private secretaries or personal assistants to top officials, are commonly exempted to give the appointing officer a free hand in the choice of those upon whom he depends most directly. Part-time or temporary positions are often exempted for two reasons: in the first place, the length of employment and its character may not warrant the effort and expense of selection by examination; in the second place, it has often been difficult to secure qualified workers who would accept temporary employment. Finally, there may be a few positions with duties or requirements of so peculiar a character that selection by examination does not yield the best results.

The exemption of specific positions from the ordinary processes of merit selection offers one of the most serious and widely exploited possibilities of abuse to be found anywhere in the system. This is the place, more than at any other, where the personnel agency becomes a focal point for partisan political pressures. We are not speaking here of the legitimate exemption of positions of the confidential or policy-determining variety mentioned previously. Such jobs, carrying with them responsibility for espousal and public advocacy of the very policies and views of the party leadership in power that are involved in partisan debate, are essential to accountable political control. Their availability therefore to that party leadership does no violence to the merit principle. It is when political selection is applied to jobs which by no stretch of the imagination have these characteristics that the damage is done, for such a practice is nothing less than outright, old-fashioned patronage.[15]

The merit ideal was most recently reaffirmed in the fact that during the disastrous Watergate period, in which scores of persons were involved, not one career civil servant was even *accused* of wrongdoing. In its reaction to this sorry episode in American political history, the panel of the National Academy of Public Administration spoke firmly of the need to ensure "strict enforcement of the laws and regulations forbidding political considerations in career personnel actions."[16]

*   *   *

IN SPITE OF islands of anachronism that remain to be conquered, the merit idea clearly has such a foothold in the American governmental scene that it

---

[15] With respect to the U.S. Civil Service Commission's authority to exempt certain positions from competition, a former official close to the process has observed: "Although fault may be found with individual decisions, the over-all statistics tend to support a record of almost continuous expansion of the competitive service. Any ground that has been surrendered has been yielded grudgingly against superior fire power" (Donald R. Harvey, *The Civil Service Commission*, New York, Praeger, 1970, p. 50).

[16] *Watergate: Its Implications for Responsible Government*, Washington, D.C., March 1974, p. 112.

is difficult to foresee any serious setbacks that could cause retrogression. Efforts on the part of some public employee organizations to substitute union contracts for personnel laws have not, as yet, widely interfered with merit processes. Certainly it has been demonstrated that job patronage is by no means necessary to the maintenance of political party responsibility. The merit method has no substitutes in providing the conditions of competence and continuity that are essential to operation of the complex administrative machine of modern government. Undoubtedly the principles and practices of good management could never have been extended to the sphere of public administration had not civil service reform created a stable body of qualified public employees.[17] As it has developed into an affirmative style of modern personnel management bent upon seeking out, motivating, rewarding, and making effective use of talent for the general welfare, the merit system has provided a far more effective answer to the need for popular control of far-flung big government than the rewarding of party workers with jobs ever did or could.[18]

[17] Directed against the now widespread practice of making distinctions among people on the basis of ability and merit, one occasionally hears attacks, inspired by a perverted egalitarianism, on what is cynically called the "meritocracy." Of course, the recognition and reward of merit (if that be what meritocracy means!) is a characteristic of much deeper significance in our society than its prevalence in the public service. Undoubtedly the most effective answer to this attack is contained in John W. Gardner's classic, *Excellence; Can We Be Equal and Excellent Too?* New York, Harper & Row, 1961. A careful reading of this short but powerful essay is strongly recommended.

The defense of merit recognition is also well capsuled in the following:

> The principle of equality, both in the religious tradition and in the secular doctrine, does not imply that all men have equal capacities or that they are entitled to equal rewards. These interpretations of the meaning of equality are put forward by opponents and not by its friends. What we derive from the religious tradition is the sentiment that, without reference to his capacities, each person is of infinite worth, no matter of what race or nationality, of what class or social condition. [I. B. Berkson, *Ethics, Politics, and Education*, Eugene, University of Oregon Books, 1968, p. 210.]

Indeed, one might ask if equality thus correctly defined could ever survive in a society that fails to identify, use, and honor meritorious ability and achievement.

[18] As this book was going to press, last-minute note was taken of a significant document of December 23, 1975, published by the U. S. House Committee on Post Office and Civil Service and prepared by a former Executive Director of the U. S. Civil Service Commission, Bernard Rosen. Entitled *The Merit System and the United States Civil Service*, this monograph presents a candid and cogent analysis of recent strains on the federal bureaucracy and the capacity of the merit system to withstand them, as well as trenchant proposals for further strengthening of merit processes and organization. It is one of the best "inside views" of what is right and wrong with government personnel administration that has appeared in the past several decades.

PART II

Structure of a Personnel System

The ideally perfect constitution of a public office is that in which the interest of the functionary is entirely coincident with his duty. No mere system will make it so, but still less can it be made without a system, aptly devised for the purpose.

John Stuart Mill, *Representative Government,*
London, Parker, Son & Bourne, 1861, vol. II, p. 194.

CHAPTER 4

Career
Systems

THE TERM *career* is an old one. It has been widely used to denote the progression of an individual in a field of work throughout the employable years of his life. A career in business or in a profession is a commonly understood concept. Sometimes it means devotion to a specialty; sometimes it means a series of employments which are only loosely related to each other. In either case, it usually implies some degree of success. *Career* is a pleasant term. It is something that everyone who expects to work for a living would like to have.

For many years public services have sought to embrace within their personnel systems the concept of careers. Consciousness of its importance in the United States was accelerated at the time of the report of the Commission of Inquiry on Public Service Personnel in 1935. This body fostered, particularly for the federal civil service, the idea that a merit system for selection was not enough. It urged the creation of conditions that would provide true careers for those who entered the service, with careful selection of young persons at the various levels of graduation from educational institutions and with real opportunities for satisfying advancement to retain them in the service for a lifetime. This philosophy has continued to influence the planning of public personnel systems since that time. Paralleling the efforts of private industry and the military services, emphasis has been placed on the "holding power" of the employer. Early recruitment, generous retirement systems, competitive pay, and other factors have evidenced this endeavor.

COMPARTMENTALIZATION   In most government jurisdictions, the typical career has been within the confines of a single department or bureau. The larger the jurisdiction, the more common this appears to be. In the U.S. government this compartmentalization of careers is further demonstrated by the separate career systems that exist alongside the general civil service: four different military systems, the Postal Service, the Coast Guard, the Foreign Service, the commissioned corps of the Public Health Service, the Coast and Geodetic Survey, medical services in the Veterans Administration, and the separate merit systems for agencies such as the Federal Bureau of Investigation, the Nuclear Regulatory Commission, the Tennessee Valley Authority, and the Energy Research and Development Administration. The different pay system, collective bargaining arrangements, and other special features of the gigantic Postal Service, representing nearly one-fourth of federal civilian workers, clearly make it a separate career service.

Even within the general civil service there are many lifetime careers entirely inside such specialized bureaus as the Forest Service, the Social Security Administration, the Bureau of Standards, and the Internal Revenue Service. Careers in state and large municipal services are likewise commonly limited to individual units—a department of health, a water department, a highway or street department, and the like. Nevertheless, particularly among the occupations that cut across agencies in a jurisdiction, there are many persons who move from department to department and bureau to bureau as they climb up the career ladder.

Of growing importance in the development of career system patterns is the recognition of the public service as a place for parts of careers as well as for some lifetime careers. The movement of persons, particularly those in professional, research, and managerial fields, among industrial, educational, and public places of employment is a distinctive American phenomenon that will increase as time goes on. Instead of blighting career opportunities in any one place, this trend enlarges the scope of such opportunities. More important, it augurs well for the mutual enrichment of and understanding between public and private sectors of our society.

MOBILITY NEEDS   At the same time, there is now greater encouragement for movement among the three levels of public employment—federal, state, and local.[1] A good example of a career pattern that has regularly involved movement from one jurisdiction to another is that of city manager, for which the whole advancement tradition has been one of progression from smaller municipalities to larger and more important ones. More recently, state after state has been dropping residence requirements for employment and authorizing movement of personnel internally within the state and to the federal

[1] See the discussion on intergovernmental relations in Chapter 2. Assignment among jurisdictions, particularly of federal civil servants, is facilitated under provisions of the Intergovernmental Personnel Act. The number of employee exchanges between the federal government and the states and localities, including educational institutions, has reached into the thousands.

government without loss of benefits. Thus, the monolithic career, identified with one institution or government, will surely be less emphasized in the future than in the past.

ALTERNATIVE PATTERNS   The foregoing introductory comments alone are sufficient to suggest that there are considerations relating to career systems besides the more obvious functional aspects concerning selection methods, promotion devices, and insulation from political party manipulation. Modern public personnel administration must concern itself with the patterns through which careers operate. Should they be monolithic, providing lifetime service in one organization in one place? Should they involve all units in a particular state, municipality, or other government entity? Should the public service be viewed as a wholly distinct place for careers in contrast to private employment, education, or the professions? Can careers best operate within the scope of a position-classification scheme or will they flower only under plans like those used in our military services?

Obviously, there are no single right answers to these questions applicable to all situations. Conditions imposed by the breadth and limitations of given occupations, size of organizations, personal interests of individuals, methods of compensation, status and prestige, tenure, and various other factors all combine to influence what career system patterns should be like and what they can be like in given instances. With full recognition of the diversity of conditions under which application can be made, this chapter is devoted to an analysis of some of the kinds and problems of career systems found in most public organizations.

CATEGORIES OF CAREER SYSTEMS

Depending on the point of view, career systems may be classified roughly according to their scope, their limitations on entrance, or their orientation for reward and rank. The first two methods of classification may be disposed of comparatively briefly. The matter of orientation of the system will require more extended treatment. These approaches to different kinds of career systems are not mutually exclusive; any one career system may be subject to classification by each approach separately.[2]

---

[2] For a discussion of career systems, see Everett Reimer, "Modern Personnel Management and the Federal Government Service," in Sixth American Assembly, *The Federal Government Service: Its Character, Prestige, and Problems*, New York, Columbia University Graduate School of Business, 1954.

See also Frederick C. Mosher, *Democracy and the Public Service*, New York, Oxford University Press, 1968; and O. Glenn Stahl, "Of Jobs and Men," *Public Administration Review*, July/August 1969, pp. 379–384, first published in the *Indian Journal of Public Administration*, April–June 1968. The latter article is a detailed critique of the practical application of many closed, functional rank-in-corps systems.

PROGRAM CAREERS AND ORGANIZATION CAREERS

As already indicated, a career system may be built on the idea that men and women are going to stay in a certain program—insurance regulation, highway construction, employment service, scientific research—or they may be geared to permit or encourage movement among various programs throughout a large, diversified department or among various agencies in a government jurisdiction. The scope of a career system may even be designed to permit and encourage movement among jurisdictions themselves.

Various conditions of employment affect the degree to which movement of employees is permitted or encouraged. A common system of job identification and pay is a most important factor. Ability to transfer from one unit to another through open competition or noncompetitively (that is, without having to take a competitive examination again) may be another one. When movement between departments or governments is involved, the transferability of retirement rights and eligibility becomes significant. The presence or absence of such conditions can extend or limit the likelihood of an employee's choosing his next point of advancement outside his existing organization.

EFFECT OF SPECIALIZATION   Of course, modern technology and the proliferation of occupational specialties make it unlikely that the majority of people will find their careers in more than one or a few agencies in any government jurisdiction. The most common limitation on how far or how widely a person can move is the scope of his own occupation. A chemist is not likely to find a place in a finance office; a tax specialist could hardly expect to work in a laboratory. Except in top commands, even the military services have had to modify drastically their longstanding view of the role of the career officer as a generalist who could be expected to carry out almost any assignment. The age of specialization has circumscribed the orbits within which any officer can be expected to serve competently, in accordance with his own education, training, and experience. Certainly the schemes of rotation are vastly different from what they were a half century ago.

Nevertheless, there are many occupations which do exist throughout an entire government service or at least in more than one agency. Examples of the more obvious variety are stenographer and secretary, general clerk, accountant, personnel officer, and attorney, to name but a few. As stressed elsewhere, many career systems could be improved by establishing conditions which encourage the movement of personnel, even those in highly specialized occupations, across bureau and department lines. Also, the possibility of logical progression from one occupation to another—such as personnel officer to general executive, or secretary to administrative assistant—is often overlooked by the artificial fences that are built into some personnel systems.

INTERORGANIZATIONAL MOVEMENT   The immense value of cooperative endeavor or exchange of specialists between federal and state or local governments has been amply illustrated in the fields of agriculture and public health. There is probably more contact and movement among government levels in these two professional areas than in any others, because liberal legislation of longstanding permitted a variety of patterns: service in state posts by federal health officers; hybrid positions (partly federal, partly local) such as those of county agricultural agents; and some movement back and forth, as in agricultural extension work.

Stumbling blocks that still stand in the way of careers having intergovernmental scope are (1) limitations—some of them imposed by practice rather than law—on lateral entry above junior levels into a service, (2) absence of reciprocal exchange of retirement benefit eligibility, and (3) disparity in salary scales. The retirement problem is partially solved by (1) the extension of national old-age insurance coverage as a floor under all public retirement plans that avail themselves of the connection (but not all have done so) and (2) the liberal provisions of the Intergovernmental Personnel Act (IPA), permitting service outside a jurisdiction to count toward pension eligibility.[3] It should be noted that even the salary problem is not all one-sided; that is, the federal government is by no means uniformly the most generous employer. Some of the larger states, like New York, California, and Michigan, and large cities, like Detroit and Los Angeles, have as high or higher pay scales than does the national civil service.

CLOSED AND OPEN CAREERS

CLOSED SYSTEMS   Through the device of low maximum age limits for entrance and the filling of upper-level positions almost entirely from within, some career services have what is referred to as a *closed* system. There are numerous instances of it in the various nations of the world, especially in association with a rank-in-corps system as described later. But the scheme is also well known in the United States although not generally characteristic of its civilian public services.

The officer corps of the military services, except in time of great expansion, are almost invariably replenished by the commissioning of new junior officers, with practically no intake at middle or senior levels. The Foreign Service and the Public Health Service commissioned corps provide further examples of what is, to all intents and purposes, a closed system. Under all such systems the concept is that substantial opportunity for advancement can

---

[3] Although the social security "floor" is still applicable in the federal service only to temporary employees, the provisions of the IPA eliminate many retirement inhibitions on mobility of career people by allowing credit for nonfederal service toward the retirement of federal workers and by paying retirement premiums into state system when state and local employees are assigned to the federal government. Also, see t' discussion in Chapter 23.

be assured only if the hierarchy is refueled by personnel from the base, preserving the upper ranks for those already in the service. Unfortunately, there is a tendency to use the generic phrase *career system* to designate such plans exclusively, as if to say that only by such an arrangement can careers be truly achieved. There has come to be in recent years, however, some relaxation of the bars to lateral entry in a number of these schemes, so that they are not as inbred as many of the closed systems in other countries.

Along with the above features, a closed system usually includes provision for "selection out." The theory is that officers reaching a certain intermediate or moderately high rank must either meet certain standards to merit further promotion or be retired prematurely from the service. Such separation customarily takes place after the officer has been "passed over" for promotion two or three times. The theory tends not to be applied in as many instances as conditions might seem to warrant, but it should be noted that where it is used it has a curious effect. The officer is not separated because of ineffectiveness at his existing level but because he does not seem promotable. When coupled with the almost automatic promotion aspect of a rank-in-corps system, this, of course, helps avoid the embarrassment of too many "chiefs" in the higher ranks. But it also leads to a sad waste of manpower which is perfectly competent at one level but unable to rise above it. The solution would seem to lie in more limited and selective promotions commensurate with the actual number of higher posts, rather than assuming that total separation from the service is less ignominious than not being promoted.

OPEN SYSTEMS   The *open* type of career system, as the term implies, permits entrance at any or all grade levels (by rank or position). Entrance is, of course, governed by whatever qualification requirements and competition a jurisdiction prescribes for each category. Those already in the service always have a natural advantage (intimate knowledge of the program, performance already known to selecting officials, ready access to the selection process, etc.), so that it would be erroneous to claim that outsiders have equal access to all job openings or that insiders lack adequate assurance of advancement opportunity. But the important feature is that infusion of new blood at middle and upper levels is not precluded, and in fact it does occur under more than emergency conditions.

Specific bureaus and professions may, by their very specialized nature, operate as if they are closed even under an avowed open system. Many an instance could be cited in any or all jurisdictions of the United States. Nevertheless, the type of open system typical of most American practice is much to be preferred over the closed, self-contained personnel schemes found so many civil services in Europe, in South America, and in the countries reflecting a British or Napoleonic colonial legacy such as India and some the African nations. Since open systems of the indigenous American o are clearly more flexible, they make greater allowance for entry personalities and ideas at levels where they are likely to count and, in actual practice, permit almost as much opportunity for advancement of permanent staff. With the new emphasis on more highly mobile careers, with the compelling need for modern bureaucracy to be in touch with the people, the old-fashioned closed systems of nineteenth-century origin are indeed anachronisms.

JOB-ORIENTED CAREERS AND RANK-IN-CORPS

The third major classification of career systems is by their orientation as to rank and status. In the one type, the focus of the plan is on the assignment —the job to be performed—and the fitting of an individual into the job. Careers of individuals derive from a succession of such assignments, more or less unplanned. Such careers may cut across departments, programs, even occupations—so long as the careerist, under specified and varied modes of competition, meets the demands of each post assumed. Hence the designation rank-in-job, or the job-oriented system.

In the other type, usually in conjunction with a more or less closed entry policy, the focus is on the person. Assignment, training, utilization, rank, and recognition are viewed in terms of the individual and the corps to which he "belongs" rather than in terms of a hierarchy of positions. Rank has more to do with length of service, relationship to others in the same group, and general aptitudes demonstrated than to level of job occupied or to performance on a particular job. Thus, the designation rank-in-corps.[4]

The theoretical differences between the two concepts can be so drawn as to make them seem utterly incompatible. Actually, the application of each approach in many places in the United States and abroad has been so modified with features of the other that conceptual compromise does seem to be possible if not always practicable.[5] But the perennial debate over the relative merits of the two calls for an evaluation here on both theoretical and practical grounds.

RANK-IN-JOB   Obviously the job-oriented concept is the newer of the two basic ideas. Originating in the United States and Canada, it is the most commonly applied plan in the large industries as well as the public services of these two highly productive societies. Largely through the gradual impact of American technical assistance abroad, plus a bit of international osmosis, a number of other countries, notably the Philippines, Thailand, Iran, a few nations in Latin America and the Middle East, the Soviet Union, and to a certain extent Japan, have likewise put the rank-in-job idea into operation.

[4] The more commonly used term has heretofore been *rank-in-man*, but it does not seem to be as descriptive of the actual features of the arrangement as rank-in-corps, because the plan is so heavily weighted with the idea of "membership" in a clearly defined and closely knit group with common backgrounds and ideals.

[5] How the two systems may be reconciled is well stated by Harold H. Leich, "Rank in Man or Job? Both!" *Public Administration Review*, Spring 1960, pp. 92–99.

Otherwise, partly as the extension of European colonial influences, we would have to say that rank-in-corps is still the prevailing philosophy in most large civil services around the world.

The job-oriented concept, with its attendant methodology of orderly classification of positions on the basis of duties and responsibilities (either required or assumed), is especially compatible with the rationalization of organization. It is the logical corollary of systematic subdivision of responsibilities and the specialization of labor. The position, as a segment of an organization plan, is in effect a part of administrative planning. Ideally, for the sake of efficiency, its composition and relationships must be known and specified before work can start. Rank-in-job fits in nicely with managerial efforts to clarify lines of responsibility, to avoid conflict and overlapping in administrative operations, to establish clear-cut modes of procedure, and to facilitate coordination among all the parts of a far-flung administrative machine. The very knowledge of actual duties being performed under all assignments contributes to these ends.[6]

Perhaps the most significant single aspect of the job-oriented approach is the manner in which it affects the compensation of workers. As will be developed more fully in subsequent chapters, pay under this system is synchronized with classes of positions in an effort to give meaning to the old slogan "equal pay for equal work." It was the quest for an objective criterion to determine pay that gave the job concept its impetus in the public service.

Nevertheless, this tying of pay to jobs or job levels did not go so far as to ignore other proper governors of compensation. Thus, most compensation schedules geared to position-classification plans provide room for pay adjustment and advancement on the basis of performance and length of service as well as job demands. Furthermore, wisely administered classification plans permit considerable flexibility in interpretation of what the job is. Managers are given wide latitude in establishing and changing the content of positions. Where the nature of the work is susceptible to such effects and an incumbent's particular talents leave an imprint on the very duties and impact of a position, it can be created or changed around the individual. Finally, pay on the basis of work categories and levels has been conducive to bargaining with employee unions on prevailing pay and its proper application to the service, because comparison with industrial wages or with other jobs in a given area could be made in objective terms of duties performed in defined categories of jobs, the product of position classification.

---

[6] A comprehensive and persuasive defense of the job concept and its contribution to effective performance appears in Albert P. Ingraham and Carl F. Lutz, "Managing Positions—the Key to Effective Organization, Compensation, and Productivity," *Human Resource Management*, Summer 1974, pp. 12–21. Also, for an able analysis of the 'tfalls of overreliance on rank-in-corps, see Chapter 2, "Jobs and Rank," by Carl F. 'z and James P. Morgan, in *Police Personnel Administration*, O. Glenn Stahl and ard A. Staufenberger, eds., Washington, D.C., Police Foundation, 1974.

RANK-IN-CORPS   It is no wonder that those rank-in-corps systems that still exist in the United States have borrowed heavily from rank-in-job. To facilitate the matching of men's skills with job needs, many corps systems have modified their assignment and pay practices and thus accommodated to the world of specialization. This has meant altering a man's rank on the basis of the assignment instead of his relative position in the corps.

Yet it is clear than rank-in-corps has continued to possess enough allure to survive here and around the world. It has the special appeal of ensuring an esprit de corps where such a loyalty to group consciousness is especially valuable, as in military services. It is almost invariably associated with personnel conditions where a high degree of mobility is expected of incumbents. Membership in a group, instead of status in a job, is contributory to an acceptance of mobility, although mobility has also been induced under position-oriented systems by the simple expedient of making it a prerequisite for promotion. By not having pay so inexorably geared to the job, a rank-in-corps plan has great pay flexibility when a person's abilities are needed on a certain assignment: the threat of a downgrading does not have to be overcome, or the enticement of a higher grade does not have to be indulged.

Perhaps the most attractive feature of rank-in-corps in that it puts tenure at a level above the position held and in the service as a whole. If a unit is reorganized or eliminated or certain posts abolished, the officers under such a system who happen to be in the positions adversely affected are not out of jobs, as is often the case under the position-oriented plan. Since their status and rank inhere in the total service instead of a transitory assignment, they are simply readied for another assignment. If net reductions in staff are necessary, broader considerations than the last post held are taken into account. A similar effect can be achieved under the job concept only through laborious, complex procedures designed to trace and maintain tenure rights through a combination of seniority or other factors among those in a common occupation and area.

RELATIVE ADVANTAGES   It is perhaps easy to exaggerate the advantages of one system and therefore the flaws of the other, but careful examination of experience with both plans suggests that neither is inherently so bad as its opponents make out. For example, certain doubtful practices, especially in military forces, have long been associated with the rank-in-corps concept— pay and advancement strictly on the basis of longevity and seniority, assignment without regard to the wishes or interests of the individual assigned, and undemocratic social stratification. The inherent characteristics of the rank idea, however, by no means require these appurtenances. In fact, the only inherent feature of the concept is that status (pay, prestige, rights, etc.) resides in the individual regardless of the nature of his assignment.

On the other hand, systems of position classification are often criticized on the grounds that they create too many fine occupational distinctions and too many levels of pay, require labored and very detailed job descriptions, demand a special jargon of mystic phrases, and interfere with variation in pay on the basis of individual performance. Again, the objections are being leveled at tangential applications of an idea rather than at the idea itself. The core of the position concept bears repeating: it is simply that status depends upon the work performed rather than upon the previous service of the individual. Further, it requires a system of putting positions into classes on the basis of their duties and responsibilities. Even a system of position classification does not require that *pay* be governed strictly by assignment. Thus, the proposal that top-level career executives be permitted to transfer from job to job without loss in pay status, regardless of the classification of their positions, can be made compatible within a framework in which integration of position classification with pay is the accepted order for the bulk of the service.

FOREIGN RANK SYSTEMS   On the international level it is easier to come down hard in favor of the rank-in-job system, for the simple reason that in so many countries the civil services have failed to adapt to at least some of the utilities of that system. The classic model was the British system, with its former elite Administrative Class, but even more aggravated forms of rank-in-corps ideas prevail elsewhere. These usually take the form of a series of highly independent cadres or "services," usually one for each major professional or technical field, topped off with a not-very-clearly-defined "generalist" category usually termed *administrative*.

The weaknesses of these systems lie primarily not in the manner by which pay is determined but in the extraordinary degree to which assignments are straitjacketed, so that only membership in a given group can gain a certain post even if someone in another group is obviously better qualified. By predetermining that specified posts "belong" to a particular corps (and without any duties analysis of such posts, for the most part), future matching of skills to jobs is unusually confined. By setting apart an earmarked battery of positions as the private and closed preserve of a chosen (and usually a self-governing) group, the members of which acquire their special prerogative by winning entrance at a very youthful age on the basis of an academic examination whose validity has rarely been tested, these civil services handicap their internal flexibility, create invidious strains among occupational groups, divert attention away from the work and into group protectiveness, and help ensure insulation from the needs and interests of the people and sometimes even of elected political leadership.

The situation is further aggravated by the tendency to skim off all the top career posts as the exclusive property of just one corps, the administrative class or service. High-quality professionals are thereby precluded from access to the most powerful and senior career assignments, simply because these are defined out of their orbits and into one of "administration." Thus, medical doctors quite capable of holding and eager to serve in the upper career positions of health ministries are barred because they did not enter the service as "members" of an administrative corps. Engineers in road building or hydroelectric construction, agriculturists in soil conservation or grain production and storage, resent domination by men, often their juniors, who are rotated in over them with no program knowledge or commitment.[7]

At least as serious is that in many of these rank-in-corps systems the isolated groups become inbred and more concerned about the welfare of the group than of the job to be done. In fact, one would go far to find a system better calculated to ignore the imperative of work-centered motivation. The ingrown character of such cadres is a major barrier to administrative reform in many a nation.[8]

Still other shortcomings have been noted in the rank-in-corps approach. An attitude tends to be built up among members of a corps that promotion is practically a right, as evidenced by resistance to competition from the outside and by promotions becoming so far out of correlation with duties assigned that there are either too few persons of adequate rank to assign to principal posts or too many persons promoted to the highest ranks. The result in the latter case is that many of them must be used on assignments well beneath their skills, a practice wasteful of manpower, demoralizing, and conductive to misconceptions about the value to the service of duties being performed. Likewise, under this system in its most aggravated forms, planning for future recruitment becomes quite unrealistic, because so little of it relates to a careful analysis of the actual numbers of assignments needed, categorized by skill requirements. Finally, imbalances in specialization frequently occur, because work needs are contorted to fit into the confines of some predetermined generalist or specialist categories that are not responsive to new occupational technology.

A growing awareness of these flaws in hard-and-fast classes, services, or cadres was dramatically demonstrated by the findings of the Fulton Committee in the United Kingdom in 1968 and the interest they generated in civil service circles around the world.[9] The British civil service had been under mounting attack as becoming out of tune with the times. Illustrative of the criticism of the long-fabled Administrative Class is this statement about its mid-nineteenth-century origins in contrast with modern governmental realities:

---

[7] The issue is discussed at length in Stahl, *op. cit.*

[8] Speaking of some of the parallel systems in the United States, Frederick C. Mosher observes: "Rank, once acquired, is a more important determinant of prestige and sometimes of influence than are position, current responsibilities, and performance" (*op. cit.*, p. 145).

[9] *The Civil Service*, vol. I, Report of the Committee, 1966–1968, Lord Fulton, Chairman, presented to Parliament by the Prime Minister and the Chancellor of the Exchequer by Command of Her Majesty, June 1968, London, Her Majesty's Stationery Office. Other volumes put out by this committee consist of testimony and evidence supplied to and gathered by it in pursuance of its mission.

The image of the administrative civil service eventually created by these reforms [resulting from the Northcote-Trevelyan Report of 1854] was that of intelligent, highly educated, incorrupt and distant officials, administering an essentially regulatory system of government, in which the emphasis was on fair and equal treatment for all persons under the law, rather than on positive ideas to promote social and economic change.[10]

The Fulton Committee expressed strong impatience with the failure of the British civil service to consider the demands of jobs and to provide a rational means of assignment of men to posts on the basis of skills needed. They found the system of "classes" (variously called "services," "corps," or otherwise under other similar systems) to be too crude an instrument for matching men to jobs, calling attention to two erroneous assumptions: "that any job can be categorised as appropriate to one or other of the classes; and that it will then be most appropriately filled by selection from the members of that class, . . ."[11] Instead of concentrating on tasks appropriate to particular *classes*, the civil service, according to the committee, should place the main weight "upon an analysis of the results required from each individual *job*, their relative importance to the work of the Service as a whole, and the consequent search for the man with the right qualities and qualifications to produce those results."[12]

Similar conclusions were arrived at by study commissions in two countries, Pakistan and India, whose systems had been modeled after the British one (as it had operated in the nineteenth century), and Pakistan has already abolished its system in line with its study.[13] Meanwhile the civil service of Spain was reorganized with the aim of combining certain features of the corps system with position classification.[14] Several smaller nations are moving in the same direction. A U.N. workshop among Asiatic countries in 1968 likewise concluded that job criteria should play a greater role in the structuring of personnel systems and particularly in the processes for selection and placement, to ensure better capitalization on expertise and specialization.[15]

[10] The Fabian Society, *The Administrators; The Reform of the Civil Service*, Fabian Tract 355, London, June 1964, p. 3.

[11] *The Civil Service, op. cit.*, p. 68.

[12] *Ibid.*, p. 69. Even before World War II a keen American observer found the British civil service unprepared for postwar technological needs, unrepresentative of major sectors of society, and structured to foster elitism: J. Donald Kingsley, *Representative Bureaucracy; An Interpretation of the British Civil Service*, Yellow Springs, Ohio, Antioch Press, 1944.

[13] Pakistan began dramatic changes in late 1973, consistent with the *Report of the Pay and Services Commission*, 1962 (not released until 1969). Action in India has been less impressive, not yet giving effect to the rather moderate recommendations in the *Report on Personnel Administration*, Administrative Reforms Commission, 1969.

See also the discussion in Chapter 27 relating to developing countries in general.

[14] *International Review of Administrative Sciences*, 1964, Summaries, pp. i and ii. The principal criticism of the corps system was that it fostered "compartmentalization and resistance to change."

[15] U.N. Economic Commission for Asia and the Far East, *Workshop on National Personnel Systems*, Bangkok, 1968.

How far nations in the midst of civil service reform will go in modifying their long-entrenched systems remains to be seen. The exigencies of specialization and technology are exerting a strong influence to alter or eliminate the compartmentalization of civil servants into arbitrary cadres determined at entrance and to permit freer movement to posts based on individual qualifications rather than on membership in a corps. In this process the American practice of position classification has been held up as a facilitating device.[16] Certainly it promotes an understanding of what job demands are and a matching of the skills of individuals with those demands. It provides no predetermined avenues of promotion, no career insurance, but it charts the various occupational ladders and, by defining duties and qualifications needed, makes it possible for any and all to move upward and outward depending on the knowledge and skills they have acquired en route as well as in their youth.

It is for this reason, as well as its relation to pay standardization, that a full chapter is devoted in this book to position classification. This does not mean that position classification, especially in any specific form, should be taken in doctrinaire fashion as the source of all good personnel administration. Rather it must be examined for its essential contributions, its most fruitful uses, the limits of its application, and those features in which technique needs to be improved.

THE HIGHER CIVIL SERVICE

Because the unusual demands on the upper reaches of a civil service call for special incentives, optimum mobility, and extraordinary training, the personnel system required for such levels should not be confused with the more general career system established for a total service. Consequently a brief discussion here is in order.

As governments have become bigger and more heterogeneous, attention has been drawn increasingly to the qualities that should be expected of senior civil servants. Whatever their field of concentration, they must especially possess the capacity, be exposed to the range of experiences, and develop the insight and vision necessary to a breadth of view and mature judgment. Traditionally these qualities had been sought through the creation and nurturing of the kinds of administrative cadres discussed in the foregoing section on rank-in-corps versus rank-in-job. Indeed, students of public administration in the United States, having become enamored with successful

---

[16] One area where the variegated U.S. federal systems could stand their own reform is in connection with the American Foreign Service. With every national agency now having responsibilities in the international arena, the separatism and exclusiveness of the Foreign Service are no longer called for. A flexible and increasingly mobile general civil service can easily supply the framework for all overseas assignments and thereby enhance the perspectives and decrease the provinciality of both domestic and overseas civil servants and avoid inbreeding. See pp. 303–304 in Stahl, "Reveries and Perspectives upon Transition," *Public Administration Review*, May/June 1970.

institutions such as the British Administrative Class, had long urged establishment of such a corps in this country.

Gradually, however, it became clear that creation of an elite group—destined from college graduation onward to provide the talent for senior posts—was not in the best democratic tradition and did not necessarily achieve the objective of top men combining expertise, breadth, and responsiveness. Hence, later proposals for the federal civil service took the form of a plan for certain special policies to apply to the three highest grades, both administrative and specialized, namely: recognition of persons at these levels as constituting a more or less mobile group of executives and specialists who would be given special training opportunities, would have greater incentive for mobility, would retain their grades (or ranks) regardless of assignment, would enjoy special emoluments and recognition, and would be retained on the payroll even when a current assignment was eliminated.

HOOVER COMMISSION PLAN

This in essence was the proposal of the Sixth American Assembly in 1954 and the second Hoover Commission in 1955, the latter terming its idea a plan for a "senior civil service."[17] Modifying the position-classification principle and seeking to overcome the tendency for the government's best career talent to be confined to individual departments or programs, the senior civil service was conceived both as a more suitable personnel system for executive levels and as a means of providing a dependable and flexible supply of top-level career people that would (1) give political department heads more latitude in assigning and utilizing higher civil servants and (2) preserve a strong career tradition for this group, thus more tightly insulating the career service from the temptation of political tampering. The tenure of a career man exposed to direct relationships with political leaders would not be dependent upon his retention in any particular position, while political executives would not be deprived of the knowledge, skill, and continuity of a career group and could move members freely even though they were obliged to fill career posts only with senior civil servants.

The important distinction between this proposal for recognition of a horizontal band of high-level talent and the vertical cadres discussed earlier is that membership in the senior civil service was to be acquired by promotion from any sector or specialization within the civil service, regardless of mode of entry or designation, and could even be partially fed by competitive entry from outside. This "upper crust" of the service was to include scientists, doctors, engineers, accountants, economists, lawyers, budget planners, personnel specialists, and many others, as well as a variety of generalist types.

---

[17] Sixth American Assembly, *op. cit.*; and Commission on Organization of the Executive Branch of the Government, *Personnel and Civil Service*, Washington, D.C., February 1955, recommendation no. 6, and *Task Force Report on Personnel and Civil Service*, Washington, February 1955, chapter 3.

It differed markedly therefore from functional cadres in other countries and even from American institutions such as the Foreign Service and the Public Health Service officer corps, in that there was to be no elite group that by virtue of a particular brand of education and initial mode of entry (or even mid-career selection) had exclusive access to the topmost grades or posts. In other words, it could not have been classified as a closed career system, nor was it exactly a rank-in-corps scheme. It dispensed with some of the restrictions of the position-classification process, but jobs were still to be classified according to duties, and incumbents of the three upper grades could retain as their personal rank any grade once achieved regardless of subsequent assignments. Also, tenure was to be in the service as a whole rather than a job, so that individuals would have some active status even if their positions were abolished as the result of program change.

EXECUTIVE ASSIGNMENT SYSTEM

Although legislation was never passed to establish the senior civil service, some of its objectives have been approximated in the Executive Assignment System established by executive order in 1966, especially when we take into account also the broadly conceived training program now offered by the Federal Executive Institute in Charlottesville, Virginia, the increased stress on mobility, and much improved salaries at upper career levels. The Executive Assignment System, the product of several years of planning by the U.S. Civil Service Commission, applies to the great majority of positions in the three grades known as General Schedule (or GS) 16, 17, and 18.[18] Separating out those jobs that are clearly noncareer by nature of their relationship to political leadership, the system is characterized mainly by a centralized perpetual inventory of the detailed backgrounds of all persons in the civil service in these three grades plus the one below (GS-15), an inventory which must be consulted by appointing officials whenever a position in the top three grades is to be filled. The inventory embraces practically all occupations and agencies of government. Under specified conditions a department may extend its search for talent outside the service. When this is done, special boards and panels, in collaboration with the Commission, are established to insure reliance on merit procedures and to pinpoint selection to the requirements of the job. Individual agency training programs, capped by the very advanced explorations at the Federal Executive Institute into world issues and problems of leadership, help groom middle-management people for the higher responsibilities.[19]

Although the Executive Assignment System represents a move in the

---

[18] Executive Order 11315, November 7, 1966. Since the provisions of the order merely make the essential amendments in the Civil Service Rules, a complete description of the system must be obtained from other explanatory documents available from the Civil Service Commission.

[19] See the further discussion of top leadership training, including the Federal Executive Institute, in Chapter 13, "Staff Development and Training."

right direction, much remains to be done to achieve all that may be hoped for in the nation's upper civil service. On the credit side, in addition to the exemplary training programs, is the fact that for the first time there is centralized knowledge of the total reservoir of talent reposing throughout the service. Thus, the base for executive search is substantially broadened, better use can be made of talent wherever it may be located, civil servants have more hope of opportunities for personal development and challenging assignments, instances where an individual's skills are misplaced or underutilized are reduced, and increased mobility is generated.

CONTINUING NEED

Nevertheless, the system does not go far enough. The federal service is still plagued with too many subsystems of recruitment and classification policy applying to individual groups or specializations.[20] This inhibits a true federal-wide program. Invulnerability to separation or demotion when jobs disappear, contemplated by the senior civil service proposal, has not been achieved. There is little or no central planning for meeting executive needs. Distinctions between career and political-leadership posts are too fixed and artificial. Most of all, too much obeisance is still paid to the independent selection authority of individual department heads. Until the last-named precept is more boldly challenged, fruitful mobility and full utilization of executive talent in the federal civil service will continue to be a goal instead of a reality. Abandonment of the position concept will not eliminate the barrier to the desired mobility within broad functional fields. The barrier will bend only to the superior power of central direction and control over the manpower resources for key career assignments.[21]

To deal with some of these deficiencies, proposals have been made in recent years by the U.S. Civil Service Commission for executive personnel systems that would carve out special policies for application to the upper levels of the civil service. The most significant common features of these plans would: clarify career and noncareer roles at senior ranks, establish more penetrating reviews of qualifications by specialist boards, permit more flexible pay and assignment authority to foster effective utilization, promote responsiveness to political leadership without politicization of careerists, and give them greater protection from any other misuse or abuse.[22] So far such

[20] For example, the special laws for designated numbers of scientific positions (so-called PL 313 type), the postal system, the medical-care positions in the Veterans Administration, the commissioned corps of the Public Health Service, the Foreign Service, etc.

[21] Changes in statutes and some reinterpretation of the Constitution may be called for, but a great deal could be accomplished by more forthright assertion of authority already vested in the presidency and the Civil Service Commission. For example, the Commission does not fully use its referral and approval authority to *insist* on consideration by an agency of outside candidates.

[22] All such plans would require legislation. The panel of the National Academy of Public Administration endorsed the basic features of such a plan in its report, *Watergate: Its Implications for Responsible Government*, Washington, D.C., March 1974, pp. 112–113.

Interesting comparisons may be made with an earlier survey, David T. Stanley, *The*

plans have not been designed to cover top jobs in all major segments of the service; they stop short of guaranteeing assignments when programs change; they do not deal with irrational limitations on executive pay; and they fail to take the bold step of central control over assignments—all of which are essential to an imaginative system to achieve the highest motivation and most profitable utilization of top talent for the federal government.

In spite of only partial accomplishments, still inadequate proposals, and continuing unfulfilled needs, the advances of recent years have been productive. They clearly demonstrate, in contrast to yesteryear, the increasing prestige of the senior levels of the service. Sophisticated training and development activities and somewhat greater mobility are already the accepted order of the day. In changes yet to come, the proper balance between the position-oriented and corps-oriented patterns will no doubt come closer to reality. When the major elements of a system giving special attention to the upper civil service are once established, the U.S. government will be on the road to meeting the nation's needs for a respected, expert, and responsive body of higher executive and professional manpower.

 THE CALIFORNIA MODEL

Meanwhile, the state of California has operated successfully a "Career Executive Assignment" (CEA) system under which special selection, pay, and tenure provisions apply to approximately five hundred key posts that are in close contact with elected or other political officials. Open to regular civil service employees from all occupations, these designated career managerial jobs have been gradually filled, as they became vacant, through a rigorous examination and selection process. The salaries of incumbents are in five basic levels, determined by comparison with key positions that are relatively stable in nature. Differential maximum rates for any one level and salary bonuses are used to reward unusual contributions or outstanding performance. Finally, and most distinctive, incumbents may be removed from such assignments without recrimination and without jeopardy to their return to their former civil service positions.

Created to provide greater flexibility in key assignments and managerial incentives, while preserving career tenure, the CEA system has apparently worked quite well and has weathered several transitions in state political administrations. Only a handful of individuals are transferred out of the system each year. Hence, mobility within the system and acceptance of top-side career expertise has permitted accommodation to even substantial shifts in political philosophy but avoided partisan manipulation or other misuse of the higher civil service.[23]

Higher Civil Service; An Evaluation of Federal Personnel Practices, Washington, D.C., The Brookings Institution, 1964.

[23] For a first-decade appraisal of the plan, see: John Birkenstock, Ronald Kurtz, and Steven Phillips, "Career Executive Assignments—Report on a California Innovation," *Public Personnel Management*, May–June 1975, pp. 151–155.

CHAPTER 5

Classification of Positions

THE FOUNDATION OF a job-oriented career system is a position-classification plan. Such a plan is a prerequisite for any system that regards the nature and content of each position as central to good organization and to motivation based on the work to be performed.

Position classification is the organizing of jobs in an enterprise into groups or classes on the basis of their duties, responsibilities, and qualification requirements. The subject is work performed or to be performed, the process is analysis and evaluation, and the result is classification or arranging of work units into classes.

Duties classification represents one of the most far-reaching developments in the public personnel field since the inauguration of merit system laws. It carries in its train influences that affect every branch of employment policy and most aspects of general administration.[1]

---

[1] An excellent treatment of the subject in pamphlet form is U.S. Civil Service Commission, *Classification Principles and Policies*, Personnel Management Series No. 16, Washington, D.C., June 1963.

The older but still standard work on the subject is the report by a committee of the Civil Service Assembly (later the Public Personnel Association and now the International Personnel Management Association), headed by Ismar Baruch, *Position Classification in the Public Service*, Chicago, 1941, reprinted 1965. A revised edition is now in process, under the leadership of Harold Suskin.

Another first-rate treatment is that by Carl F. Lutz and James P. Morgan, appearing as Chapter 2, "Jobs and Rank," in *Police Personnel Administration*, O. Glenn Stahl and Richard A. Staufenberger, eds., Washington, D.C., Police Foundation, 1974.

ITS CLARIFYING ROLE

One of the products of such job standardization is the systematic use of titles that reflect actual duties. Neither a financial nor a personnel agency can properly perform its functions unless titles and their definitions are realistic. This need is apparent not only in connection with pay but also in matters of selection, placement, promotion, transfer, and training. It should be noted, of course, that a corps or rank system can also produce standardized titles but not necessarily on the basis of duties.

The interest of both the government and the workers dictates a rational grouping of positions on the basis of functions and responsibilities. This fact underlies the rapid expansion of the concept, the general objective of which is efficient management as well as equitable treatment of employees by accurate definition, orderly arrangement, and fair evaluation of positions.

It is well at this point to emphasize that a duties classification plan is not the same thing as a pay plan. Duties classification may be a vital element upon which a compensation structure is based and administered. But compensation, as explained in a succeeding chapter, must also be governed by other factors, such as quality of performance and length of service, to say nothing of basic economic and social considerations; furthermore, classification serves many uses other than governing pay. The fact that the two are distinct is best illustrated by the fact that compensation can be changed without affecting the classification plan, and classes of positions can be rearranged on a pay schedule without changing the schedule.

DEVELOPMENT OF THE CONCEPT

The roots of the cry "equal pay for equal work" lie deep in American history, with origins as far back as the early half of the nineteenth century, when federal employees sought reform of their chaotic pay situation. But this was not the only motivation for establishment of position classification throughout the public service, leading eventually to the technique's being applied in almost all major cities and states as well as in the federal government.

Among the numerous other factors which contributed to the origin and development of this important innovation, several stand out prominently. The first of these was the adoption of the merit system itself. If positions were to be filled upon the basis of merit, it became necessary to know what constituted the duties of various groups of positions and what qualifications were required. Logically, then, the merit system demanded some form of occupational classification.

The merit factor was linked at the end of the first decade of the century with a general demand for increased governmental efficiency. Reform was in the air, and across the land where there was a renewed interest in public service problems. The classification idea fitted admirably into these wider objectives. It not only was a means to more expert selection and management of personnel but contributed directly to the accomplishment of the broader aims of efficiency and economy. Thus, if the organization set-up was to be rationalized, if lines of authority in the administrative hierarchy were to be clarified, if more direct control was to be exercised over the flow of work, it became necessary first of all to study the duties of the various positions involved and to discover the lines of authority and the relationships existing among them. Moreover, the new principles of centralized financial control also demanded classification if their full possibilities were to be realized. Uniform accounting required a uniform job terminology in place of a hodge-podge of nondescript and conflicting titles.

Thus, each of the broader movements—for merit and for efficiency—contributed to the development of the other, and jurisdiction after jurisdiction felt their impact. At the same time, they were accompanied by the renewal of an old demand on the part of public employees, the demand for equal pay for equal work. Disregard of this principle was the cardinal social vice at which position classification soon came to be directed.

Parallel with the pressure for equal pay for equal work in the public domain, especially during and after World War I, management in many large industries was taking up job analysis with increasing enthusiasm. The stimulus here came largely from the desire to systematize and improve factory operations down to the point of specific tasks and steps in an individual worker's job. Job analysis went hand in hand with time and motion study. Although at first looked upon suspiciously by employee unions as a device to get around collective bargaining, job evaluation has gradually come to be widely accepted as offering the most solid ground for common understanding of the jobs for which rates were being set and for job-to-job comparison. It is often less palatable, however, to craft-type occupational unions than it is to industrial-type unions, since the former fear occasions under which occupational comparisons would place their particular craft at a disadvantage.

Job analysis in industry, therefore, was first used to increase efficiency and production; secondarily and later, its use for standardization and equalization of pay became evident. Thus, job analysis led to job evaluation and classification. In government the chronology was generally just the reverse. The first emphasis was on pay, with incidental recognition that defining job classes facilitated recruitment and examination. Later other uses of job evaluation and classification—as a vital technique and source of data in organization and procedures improvement, in training, etc.—were stressed in the public service.

The history of the movement in the U.S. government includes, for the most part, abortive efforts to introduce classification until the Congressional Joint Commission on Reclassification of Salaries reported in 1920 on the deplorable lack of uniformity in titles and pay in the departmental (headquarters) service. Compromise between the recommendations of this commission and those of the Bureau of Efficiency culminated in the Classification

Act of 1923, one of the great milestones in public personnel legislation. Creating a central Personnel Classification Board to enforce its provision in the departmental service, this law clearly established the principles of grouping positions into classes on the basis of their duties and responsibilities and of "equal compensation for equal work, irrespective of sex."

Significant extensions and improvements in the Act and, of course, substantial revisions in the pay scales prescribed have taken place since 1923. Notable structural changes have included (1) application of classification to white-collar occupations in the field, (2) vesting of ultimate control authority in the Civil Service Commission, and (3) replacement of the old law by a completely new Classification Act of 1949.[2] This latter Act for the first time made a clear distinction between establishment of job evaluation standards (a task assigned to the Civil Service Commission) and classification of individual positions (a function left to the departments and agencies, subject to the Commission's postaudit and power to correct misclassifications). Pay and classification features of the Classification Act do not apply to the Postal Service, which is governed by separate legislation, or to blue-collar jobs paid prevailing rates set under the federal wage system.

In most state and local jurisdictions the evaluation and classification of positions is performed by the central personnel authority, with individual departments making recommendations.

DEFINITIONS AND USES OF CLASSIFICATION

It is not surprising that conditions in America in general and the nature of our approach to personnel problems in particular should have strongly influenced the character of the duties classification plans developed in this country. The emphasis upon *expertise*, upon the selection of prior-trained technicians and workers with special skills, determined the general character of the classification system. The relatively precise type of occupational classification is more characteristic of the United States than of any other country.

Positions, of course, may be classified upon a number of bases—according to geographical location, organization unit, and so forth—depending upon the use that is to be made of the classification. But the purpose of a duties classification is to aid in the handling of personnel matters such as salary administration and the recruitment process, entrance qualifications, and the nature of the testing program. The classification, therefore, must be based on those characteristics which render positions similar or dissimilar from the standpoint of these purposes of personnel management.

Basic to a duties classification plan are the concepts of *position* and *class*. A position, which may be either occupied or vacant, must be differentiated from the incumbent of the position. It is characterized by certain duties and responsibilities, which call for the time and attention of some one individual.

---

[2] *U.S. Stat.* 954, October 28, 1949. Codified in 5 U.S. Code 5101–5115.

Of course, an incumbent's capacities or lack of them may be the reason why an occupied position contains the duties it does, but the personal characteristics of the individual are extraneous except as the duties performed reflect them.

If positions are the raw materials of classification, the class is the operating unit. As defined by a technical committee, a class is a

> group of positions sufficiently alike in respect to their duties and responsibilities to justify common treatment in selection, compensation, and other employment processes, and sufficiently different from positions of other classes to justify different treatment in one or more of these respects. While defined as a group of positions, a class may sometimes consist of but one position where no others of the same kind exist in the service being classified.[3]

To each such class or category there is assigned a distinguishing title.

To summarize, the principal uses and advantages of position classification may be listed as follows:

1. Facilitating other personnel objectives:
   a. It provides a rational criterion for control of pay levels by making it possible to equate whole classes of positions with common salary ranges.
   b. It reduces a variety of occupations and positions to manageable proportions so that recruitment, qualification requirements, examination, and selection can be made for whole classes of positions or more at a time.
   c. It defines in objective terms the content of jobs (or what is expected) against which the performance of incumbents (how well it is done) can be measured.
   d. It furnishes job information upon which the content of orientation and other in-service training can be based.
   e. Although it does not of itself guarantee a good promotion and placement policy, it supplies a systematic picture of opportunities and position relationships, which is essential to an orderly promotion and placement procedure.
   f. It provides a foundation for common understanding between supervisor and employee as to the job and pay, which facilitates employee-management relations and helps promote work-centered motivation.

---

[3] Preliminary Report of Section A on the "Development, Adoption and Administration of Classification and Compensation Plans," *Proceedings of the 20th Annual Meeting of the Civil Service Assembly*, Buffalo, 1927, p. 113. This definition is still standard, although in 1951 California broadened the meaning to embrace several levels of work with different pay ranges (facilitating movement of personnel among similar jobs without competitive promotion examinations) and in 1955 the federal government began use of varying pay steps for the same grades in recruitment for hard-to-fill occupations.

2. General aids to an organization:
   a. By use of standard class titles, it establishes uniform job terminology.
   b. It clarifies, by requiring definition and description of duties, the placing of responsibility in each position.
   c. It provides an orderly basis for translating needs for positions into fiscal terms, thus facilitating budgetary procedures.
   d. It provides information on job content that aids in the analysis of organization problems and procedures by bringing out points of duplication, inconsistency, and the like in the work process.
3. Particular values in the public service (the foregoing points apply to all organizations, public or private, whereas two others have special significance in government):
   a. It assures the citizen and taxpayer that there is some logical relationship between expenditures for personal services and the services rendered.
   b. It offers as good a protection as has been found against political or personal preferment in determination of public salaries.

Both of these last points assume that the pay plan is definitely governed by a system of position classification.

STEPS IN EVALUATION AND CLASSIFICATION

In general, the processes employed in the development and application of a classification plan include four basic steps: (1) analyzing and recording the duties and other distinctive characteristics of the positions to be classified (job analysis and description); (2) grouping the positions into classes upon the bases of their similarities; (3) writing such standards or specifications for each class of positions as will indicate its character, define its boundaries, and serve as a guide in allocating individual positions to the class and in recruitment and examinations; and (4) allocating individual positions to the classes thus described. Three of these have to do largely with the setting up of the plan; the fourth, with the initial step in its administration. They all reflect processes that are repeated continuously in the day-to-day administration of position classification and therefore warrant some description here.

Certain preliminary considerations are important. Since the classification plan will be useful only to the extent that it is understood and accepted by management and employees and is kept on a current basis, it is important that all parties have a real share in its development, execution, and revision. This calls for careful explanation to department and division heads of the objectives and processes of classification, for meetings with employees of each unit for the same purpose, for bringing in representatives of employee unions in the planning stages, and for opportunities for all to contribute suggestions and criticisms at various stages. In various jurisdictions representative workers' committees have aided in the process. Furthermore, the technicians who conduct the study need to acquaint themselves with all the organizational and functional information about the governmental entity to be classified that may be derived from sources such as budgets, charts, annual reports, payrolls, laws, and ordinances.

JOB DESCRIPTION AND ANALYSIS

The development and operation of a classification system, the determination of lines of promotion, and the application of the principle of equal pay for equal work all depend upon the adequacy of the information with respect to individual positions. This information needs to be of three basic sorts: (1) information concerning the duties of the position—the tasks ordinarily assigned to the incumbent; (2) information concerning the responsibilities of the position—the degree of supervision under which the work of the position is performed, the extent to which the exercise of independent judgment is required, and the like; and (3) information concerning the knowledge and skill necessary for adequate performance of the duties of the position.

SOURCES OF INFORMATION   In seeking this information it is not enough to study the work of the various positions in isolation. No adequate picture of authority or responsibility can be secured without an analysis of the work of the particular organizational units in which the positions under review are located, or without comprehension of the relationship of the individual position to other positions and to the whole hierarchy of authority.

This necessary information may be secured by various means and from a number of sources. In the first place, certain basic facts regarding the general organizational set-up, the broad lines of authority, and similar matters may be gathered from preliminary study as suggested previously, which will at best offer only leads and signposts. The really fundamental data can be secured only by interviewing organization heads, administrators, and supervisors, and by studying the individual positions themselves.

The latter procedure, which is most basic to the classification process, may take several forms. The first and most usual one, at least in initial surveys, is to study the position through the employee himself—that is, to ask each employee to fill out a questionnaire or duties sheet describing his duties and responsibilities. Because of the complexity of the classification task and in view of considerations of expense and expediency, the questionnaire method of obtaining basic data has been widely followed.

QUESTIONNAIRES   Questionnaires have evolved from open-end types, leaving wide discretion to the writer, to more specialized types, each for a specific occupation and listing concrete items or questions to be checked or answered. Thus, a draftsman might fill out a different form from that of a file clerk, a janitor a different form from that of a mine inspector. Although they are admirably suited to later follow-up checks in almost all cases, the usefulness of such specialized questionnaires in initial surveys is largely confined to occupations which are found in almost any organization, such as typists and stenographers, or to relatively homogeneous or unifunctional organizations, such as a police department or a fire department, where there is no great variety of occupations. Otherwise specialized questionnaires require too much preliminary analysis of the positions to be covered if they are to be relevant and are to go to the right employees. Hence, it is common to find specialized questionnaires used for part of a survey and more general forms for the rest of it. Whatever their form, job analysis questionnaires must attempt to elicit information on the nature of the work, the knowledge required to do it, its complexity, how it is carried out, what supervision is exercised by others over it, and what responsibility for the work of others is inherent in the position.

The usual approach in use of a questionnaire is to have each completed form reviewed by the supervisor of the employee who prepared it and, in turn, by the division or bureau chief. This serves the purpose of correcting misstatements or overstatements and providing supplementary information that the incumbent of the job may not have explained. However, even with this check some experts argue that the questionnaire yields results of dubious value if what is intended is an unbiased, true picture of a position. They point out not only that different employees will use different terms to express the same thing, but that some will be taciturn, some prolix, some self-deprecatory, and some inclined to exaggerate. Hence it has been urged that basic descriptions be prepared only by skilled job analysts following desk audits and interviews with employees and supervisors, with differences in interpretation or understanding worked out in three-cornered discussion. This, in turn, is questioned on the ground that it is too time-consuming and expensive. Furthermore, the questionnaire method probably provides the best opportunity for each employee and supervisor to participate in the process of job analysis and to recognize that he has had an active part.

ALTERNATIVES   As in many administrative problems, what is apparently a dilemma can usually be met by a combination of two alternative procedures. The questionnaire can be used for the basic data. Following preliminary review of this material, classification technicians can then round out the picture by spot-check interviews, particularly where more than one job of a kind is found. This is not a perfect solution for one-of-a-kind positions, but at least those with the most inadequate questionnaire responses could be singled out for subsequent desk audit. In the case of multiple jobs of a kind— such as stenographers in a pool, card-punch operators, claims examiners, probationary police officers, file clerks in a central file room—a device that has been found useful is to invite the employees whose questionnaires have been reviewed to select one or two of their number to represent them in the interview with the job analyst. This procedure, supplemented by discussion with the supervisor, has the advantages of securing the necessary first-hand information, getting the benefits of numerous interviews out of one, and giving employees as full an opportunity to participate as is consistent with an economical survey.

PARTICIPATION   One principle which deserves stress in the development of a classification plan, as in many other phases of personnel management, is that the formulation should be a cooperative effort, with wide participation by the people most affected—the supervisory officers and the employees. Apart from an actual change of salary rates there is nothing that comes closer home to both groups than the classification of their positions. Stimulating their interest and enlisting their cooperation in the first stage—the job description and analysis—is therefore very important.

Although these procedures and precepts are expressed in terms of an initial survey, it should be understood that they apply in the same fashion to periodic reanalyses of jobs—which are the main concern of those many jurisdictions in which position classification has long been in operation.

GROUPING POSITIONS INTO CLASSES

When the job analyses and descriptions have been completed and the classifying agency is thus equipped with a blueprint of each position, the stage is set for the actual arrangement of positions into classes. Any classification is the systematic arrangement of items into groups upon the basis of common or distinguishing factors, to the end that the mind may more readily grasp what would otherwise be an anarchy of detail. As applied to position classification, the aim is to arrange the variety of individual positions into groups of various sorts upon the basis of similarities and dissimilarities—to distribute positions into classes and classes into such occupational groups as are necessary for purposes of easy use and reference.

CONTENT OF A CLASS   A *class*, as previously defined, is a group of positions sufficiently alike in respect to their duties and responsibilities to justify common treatment in the various employment processes. Thus, all positions the duties of which are "under general direction, to stand watch at a public bathing-beach of a state park to prevent drowning and other accidents" may be in the lifeguard class in a state classification plan. Individual job descriptions are tentatively distributed according to those of like occupation (accountants, typists, engineers, and the like) and then broken down into levels or zones of difficulty, namely, classes. The information on the questionnaires, supplemented by interviews, provides the basis upon which the tentative groupings can be made. Such a distribution will usually result in the establishment of several hundred or more classes.

MAKING DISTINCTIONS   The process of classification is one that requires discrimination and judgment. It is a far cry from any mechanical procedure. Persons unfamiliar with the problems involved would be surprised at both the variety of government positions and the difficulty of determining likenesses and differences among them. Many borderline cases invariably appear. The question will arise, for example, whether a telephone operator who spends one-third of her time on routine typing should be classed as an operator or as a typist, or whether a special typist-operator class should be formed. Generally speaking, the effort should be made to have as limited a number of classes as is consistent with the purposes for which the classification is designed.

Although borderline cases of this sort are not in any sense unusual, they can ordinarily be classified without serious difficulty. Greater difficulties are usually involved in discovering and evaluating the factors that distinguish a position from or render it similar to others in the same occupational field. Most activities are represented in the public service in various degrees of difficulty and responsibility, and at this point the discrimination and judgment of the classifier are taxed to the utmost. What factors, for example, cause a position to be classed as assistant biologist rather than as biologist of higher class? As a basis for these determinations, careful analyses must be made of the kind and degree of supervision exercised from above and over others, of other responsibilities, such as the need for independent judgment, and of the relative difficulty and importance of the work.

CONTROLLING FACTORS   These so-called allocation factors or classification factors are the stock in trade of the job evaluator's technique. In attempting to relate a position to other positions or to a previously established class of positions, he must consider matters such as knowledge and skills required to perform the work, decisions that must be made, variety and scope of the work, intricacy, status of the work when presented to the employee, latitude in determining tasks and priorities, originality required, control by others, consequences of actions taken, responsibility for planning, responsibility for the work of others, and often various other elements or subelements. The permutations and combinations that are possible and that add to the complexity of the classifier's task, demanding the utmost in analytical logic, are almost infinite.

POINT-RATING   The usual approach to this process in the public service is to rely heavily on abstractions and subjective judgment. In industry, where factory and office jobs have been peculiarly susceptible to quantitative measurement, personnel men have been more enamored of the mechanical, mathematical type of techniques. Numerical weights are often assigned, for example, to given degrees of each particular job element, all of which may be added up, averaged, or what not, to arrive at an overall "weight" for the job. The class itself then would be largely defined in terms of a range of figures. When total job weights fall in that range, they are in that class.

The foregoing description may be an oversimplification of many well-thought-out "point-rating" devices that are particularly useful in evaluating manual or routinized work. But great care must be exercised in accepting quantitative schemes as precise measuring tools merely because they use mathematical terms that sound very scientific. More often than not, the basic evaluation must still rest on certain judgments of intangibles, certain arbitrary estimations of value and difficulty. The evaluation of positions is not an exact science. It is an orderly application of system and logic to what is otherwise chaos and confusion. It need not be made to appear precise in order to be defended.[4]

The processes involved in deciding on final classifications must be checked at every point by further excursions into offices and other work places to secure additional information on borderline cases and to gain first-hand observations of the work at employees' benches or desks. What such steps, along with the preceding ones, initially achieve is a tentative set of job classes. Under continuing administration of the plan, almost identical steps are followed to determine where new or changed jobs fit into established classes.

PREPARATION OF CLASS STANDARDS

After tentative classes are established, the task of writing the class standards or specifications is taken up. This calls for the capacity to generalize from a considerable number of details. The objectives are to define a class in such a way as to distinguish it clearly from every other class and to provide a clear and sufficient guide for the allocation of positions to classes. The specification also standardizes titling and includes a statement of minimum and desirable qualifications necessary to perform the work.

Such a class specification is tentatively arrived at by analysis and then synthesis of the positions which appear to be similar enough to be classed together. This tedious process requires great skill and objectivity to seek out the significant "allocation factors" and to so combine them that they form a logical progression of classes. Often it leads to revision of the original rough grouping of classes.

There is considerable discussion among the technicians about the proper uses and form of the class specification. The traditional thinking has been that it should be an all-purpose tool: a guide to psychometricians in the

---

[4] Illustrative of the evolution that is inevitable even in major, well-established job evaluation systems is the basic reappraisal of structure and processes that occurred in the U.S. federal system in the 1970s. The Job Evaluation Policy Act of 1970 (approved March 17, 1970), after affirming congressional support for "a coordinated job evaluation and ranking system for all civilian positions, to the greatest extent practicable," called upon the Civil Service Commission to study and report within two years on plans to implement this objective, including proposals on methods of job alignment.

Although an elaborate set of recommendations emanated from a special task force set up by the Commission, no changes in coverage or basic structure embracing all the satellite personnel systems in the government have been put into effect. However, some interesting and innovative methods for evaluation and relative ranking have evolved and are in the process of development within the federal service. The framework for these approaches is referred to as a "factor/point rating method." It seeks to exploit the attractions of quantitative devices but to minimize their artificiality and overdependence on them. See the explanation in Harold Suskin, "Testing a New Approach to Job Evaluation," *Civil Service Journal*, July–September 1974, pp. 24–31.

preparation of tests; an official source of information for the legislative body, the employees in the jurisdiction, and the general public; a basic outline for in-service training activities; and a measuring rod for the use of classifiers who have to evaluate positions in order to determine if they fall within the class. However, some classification analysts have suggested that the specification should be recognized as primarily their tool, that the other uses are more illusory than real, and that a standard that provides more precision should therefore be employed. Thus, some have urged the use of charts which present each factor in a class on a scale, facilitating the analytical process of the classifier when he is checking a specific job against the class definition. Actually this approach is not very different from that in common use in private industry.

GIVING EFFECT TO THE CLASSIFICATION PLAN

The next steps are those of installation and administration: (1) adoption of the plan, (2) determination of the agency to administer the plan, (3) promulgation of the class standards, (4) initial allocation of positions to classes, (5) adoption of formal rules for the administration of the classification, and (6) provision for and hearing of appeals on allocations.

Several of these aspects require scant comment. The classification plan may be adopted preferably by administrative action provided there is a commitment by the legislative body to set pay rates or to authorize the setting of rates in accordance with the plan. The central personnel authority is the logical agency of general administration. It is already charged with the functions of recruitment, examination, and the like, and usually with that of recommending or setting pay rates, matters most directly affected by classification. In the great majority of jurisdictions in the United States in which a duties classification has been adopted, the personnel agency is in fact charged with its administration.

The concentration of the U.S. Civil Service Commission's authority on setting standards and on postauditing classifications points the way to a development that must ultimately take place in all large-scale jurisdictions, namely, that the operating departments should carry out position classification and other personnel operations following standards and procedures set down by the central personnel agency, with these guides established in consultation with line executives. In such circumstances the problems of maintaining uniformity and bringing about standardization will abate without destroying operating speed and flexibility. Final postaudit authority, however, must be lodged in a single agency, which may also serve as an appeals body to which an employee may turn in case of dissatisfaction with the classification of his position.

One point worth stressing in the otherwise routine step of promulgating the class standards (originally or when later revised) is the necessity for issuing a tentative set for criticism by both top management and employees. As indicated earlier, it is important for the whole development to be a cooperative affair, since its future effectiveness depends critically on its being understood and accepted in the organization. This is one of the points in the process where participation can be encouraged. The give and take in full-fledged hearings and discussion on criticisms of the proposed specifications will serve as much as anything to impress all parties with the complexity of the problem, with the desirability of compromise at proper points, and with the continuing need for strict objectivity and impartiality in application of the plan. Such discussion can best take place *before* determination of the allocation of individual positions to each class, thereby focusing attention in the first instance on the general guide rather than on where John Doe's position falls.

Sound administration also requires the provision of facilities for hearing appeals and grievances concerning allocations or other aspects of classification, whether the complaints come from departments or from individual employees. Few personnel matters more seriously affect the individual worker than his classification. It is imperative, therefore, that he be given an opportunity to be heard if he feels that his work has been improperly evaluated. This not only is a means of enhancing employee cooperation but may also serve to bring to light mistakes in classification which might otherwise long remain unnoticed. Most jurisdictions make some provision for appeals on classification.

Finally, even where the classification plan has been adopted through legislative action, there will still remain the necessity for detailed rules of administration to supplement the provisions of the law. These should be adopted at the outset by the agency charged with administration and given proper publicity so that all persons affected may be acquainted with them.

CONTINUOUS ADMINISTRATION

So far we have been referring principally to the various steps and techniques involved in the development and installation of position classification in government offices where no plan had existed. Much of what has been said about technique applies with equal force to what is done on a continuous basis after that, and certainly continuity is of equal importance to the quality of the plan itself. Some of the most serious classification problems, from the standpoint of administration, have to do with keeping the classifications up to date and abreast of changes in the service.

Administration is a continuous process, and constant effort is required to keep even the best classification plan serviceable. Because of changes in personnel, in governmental functions, and in the structure of the public service, no sooner is a classification plan adopted than its revision and adaptation must be undertaken. We know well that the public service itself is not static, nor are the personalities of those who are appointed to operate and direct it. A road engineer who was once asked how soon repair crews should be set to work on new highways replied, "The day they are open to the public." So it is with a duties classification. As soon as it is installed, revision is called for.

COOPERATIVE ENDEAVOR

Although the various aspects of administration cannot be treated in detail within the scope of a single chapter, a few of them warrant some comment. At the outset it should be emphasized that successful administration depends upon close cooperation between the operating departments and the personnel agency. The maintenance of a current record of changes in the character of positions, occurring through the creation of new positions, the reassignment of duties within an organization unit, or the assumption of increased responsibility by an incumbent, depends in the first instance upon the operating authorities' awareness of the changes and their promptness in reporting them to the classification agency.

It is therefore essential that the rules for administration specify that no substantial change in the duties or responsibilities of existing positions be made or new positions created without notification to the classifying authority, whether within or outside the operating department. Logically, supervisors occupy the best observation posts for perceiving changes in the duties performed by their subordinates and for initiating moves looking toward the reclassification of one or more positions.

KEEPING UP TO DATE

In spite of the most conscientious efforts to maintain currency through these means, unreported changes are almost certain to occur. Because of this, periodic audits or resurveys are essential to keep the classifications in tune with the facts of the situation. Indeed, the accepted policies of some jurisdictions call for a continuous reclassification survey. Only under such a procedure can the interrelationship of all jobs in a given organizational unit be studied all at once, with the least duplication of effort and with the maximum yield of job information. This survey procedure is fortunately possible in combination with various others.

For example, there is a widespread practice of checking on the classification every time the incumbent of a position changes. This is, in effect, a check to see whether the duties about to be assigned are actually the same as those which influenced the current allocation. If not, the position is redescribed and reevaluated to see if it still falls in the same class. This is an opportune time to effect corrections without jeopardy to employees already carrying out the duties.

Then, of course, every *new* position must be studied and classified. Operating heads must think through the position thoroughly in order that its duties and responsibilities may be clearly enough developed for evaluation purposes before assignment of an incumbent can take place.

Whatever the method, the necessity to keep up with the dynamics of an organization is the point on which many classification plans go awry. The budgetary approach to "positions," for example, often leads to using for recruitment and pay purposes a position authorized many years earlier for quite a different purpose than currently contemplated—making perhaps the title, the class, and the qualifications required inappropriate to the current need. This happens because executives overlook the evolution that takes place in job duties and fail to reread an initial description of the job before saying, as they scan a list of titles, "We should fill this position right away."

Once a classification plan is adopted, it is pointless to do anything less than provide for continuous, painstaking maintenance on a current basis, else once different positions that have actually become similar to each other remain in different classes, and some former cognates that have become quite different continue in the same class. Such a program often seems expensive. But to stint too much on this out-of-pocket cost may create still higher hidden costs growing out of lowered morale, poor production, delayed operating programs, excessive pay for simple work, and low pay for responsible work (resulting in poorly qualified executives and professionals)— all normal concomitants of inadequate, hasty, or out-of-date classification.

Most job analysis occurs in this day-to-day continuous application of classification to new or changed positions. Many position classifiers in the public service have had no experience in developing or installing a classification system. They have only worked on keeping what exists in line with a previously established plan. Nevertheless, the techniques of position analysis and comparison, the use of "allocation factors," the reasoning and judgment and weighting involved in the initial evaluation are necessarily applicable to new positions, resurveys, and reappraisals. As already suggested, everything that has been said regarding technique under "Grouping Positions into Classes" applies to the long-range, continuing task. There are some special problems, however, of particular concern to the classifier who is keeping job allocations up to date, such as evaluating positions that have duties of varying classes ("mixed positions") and positions that vary in importance with different seasons or periods ("cyclic positions"), maintaining continuous understanding of classification objectives and methods on the part of employees and supervisors, and protecting the integrity of the classification plan.

EFFECT OF INCUMBENCY

One of the considerations likely to affect the currency of classifications, particularly in professional and managerial occupations, is the impact of the incumbent's capacities on the job. Some work is highly susceptible to change as the result of the special talents or interests of the incumbent. Organization should never be so rigid as not to capitalize on the innovative or unusual proclivities of its key employees. While a machine operator may not be able, even subtly, to change the character or level of his job, the design engineer, the attorney, or the organization and methods analyst might readily do so. Reliance on his judgment and/or the scope of his assignments may grow as the result of his skill, insight, and capacity. Or the job may narrow down because of his personal limitations. Progressive jurisdictions recognize these changes, even though they may take place gradually, by an eventual reclassification of the position at a more appropriate level— up or down. It will be readily understood that personal flaws of the incumbent may not be the basis for many *reductions* in job level, because reassignment to a *different* job (even when lower) is usually the happier solution in such cases. But job growth due to the positive abilities of an employee is frequent enough to demand regular attention in the classification process. This also imposes the obligation on the part of administrators to take the responsibility of acknowledging the superior work of those whose jobs stand out for such recognition.

AN OPEN PROCESS

Another consideration in good classification administration is the need to avoid making the evaluation process a mysterious bit of priestcraft, fathomable only to an initiated few. Program supervisors have as much stake in proper internal alignment of jobs as they do in getting the most favorable classifications possible for their employees. They are likely to feel a sense of responsibility in this regard when they are themselves involved in the evaluation procedure. Position classifiers who try to keep their techniques a secret usually do not have successful relationships throughout their organizations. Operating supervisors clearly need some training and advice in the principles and methods of sound position classification in order to participate in job appraisal, but whether trained or not some of the most effective systems are those in which they do so participate. Especially in the evaluation of professional positions, panels of program officials who themselves have knowledge in the occupations involved and knowledge of the classification standards to be applied have frequently maintained better job alignment through their pooled judgment than would have been possible by job analysts working on their own. The developing role of the job classifier nowadays is to serve as an equal partner, rather than an exclusive authority, with operating supervisors who have been motivated to share the responsibility for keeping positions properly classified.[5]

INTEGRITY

It also goes without saying that job evaluation will bring on more evils than it cures if it is allowed to become the cat's-paw of political or personal preferment. Legislators or others who bring pressure to favor a friend in the service with an unwarranted reclassification and administrators who succumb

[5] See O. Glenn Stahl, "The 'System' Takes the Rap," *Civil Service Journal*, October–December 1961.

to such pressure not only breed cynicism and disrespect for the whole process but soon come to find that they can maintain no valid system at all when they are unable to defend their actions. The only classification plan that works is one administered with the utmost integrity.

POST AUDIT

In a decentralized job evaluation system, questions insistently arise on postaudit regarding misclassifications that have occurred, especially the issue of how far to go in making a correction that would result in reducing the grade of an incumbent. It is usually management's fault if a job has been placed in too high a level in the occupational structure in which it belongs. The solution to this in the U.S. federal service has been to allow retention of a salary achieved (though not the grade) so long as the same employee remains in the post. Some experts would go further and allow the grade itself to stand throughout current incumbency.[6] Better alternatives include altering the duties to justify the grade or, even more desirable, transferring the incumbent to another job that warrants the grade already attained. In any event, all agree that when a misclassified job is vacated, it should be filled at its correct level.

EVOLVING PLANS

Discussion of continuous administration should not be concluded without recognition of one other important point—the need to keep the plan itself current. The class specifications themselves are not necessarily timeless standards. They are susceptible to change because of technological changes, changes in occupations themselves (in knowledge required, scope of subject, professionalization, machines used, or the like), and changes in the nature and scope of public functions, to say nothing of change simply because of a better understanding or keener evaluation of the field of work. Thus, the plan—the body of class definitions—itself evolves. The importance of this point is too frequently overlooked. Some plans have persisted for several decades with few or no changes. Everything that has been said regarding the initial development of the plan, including participation of line management and employee groups, applies with equal force to keeping it fresh and realistic.

JOB DESIGN

As previously stated, one major purpose of job analysis in private industry has been to increase production. With some notable exceptions, public jurisdictions have been slow to make this application of the process. Although

---

[6] Gilbert A. Schulkind, "Monitoring Position Classification—Practical Problems & Possible Solutions," *Public Personnel Management*, January–February 1975, pp. 32–37.

some of the earlier users of the time-and-motion studies first employed in this connection carried job design and refinement too far, thereby gaining the opposition of organized labor, public personnel administration could profit from this experience and make more sophisticated use of techniques to plan more consciously and standardize more methodically the elements of various positions. The output of many clerical and mechanical jobs in the public domain as well as the private, such as office machine operators, typists and stenographers, supply clerks, and file clerks, are already being measured and having norms of performance set for them. Certain aspects of the work of investigators and inspectors would lend themselves to such measurement and standardization; even supervisory positions can sometimes be analyzed in terms of objective criteria such as variety of functions supervised, volume of goods or expenditures under their control, and similar quantitative indexes. The cooperation of workers themselves is a fruitful source of energy to tap when undertaking such analysis and rationalization of job content.

An important application of job design comes in the adaptation of jobs to the labor market. One of the most common areas of managerial neglect is in the establishment or reinstatement of positions without careful appraisal of whether a particular combination of duties is practical, efficient, or conducive to finding an incumbent with the right balance of qualifications to perform satisfactorily in the post. Job analysis and classification provide the raw material to make that appraisal by presenting what each principal duty requires in the way of skills or knowledge and by showing the relative difficulty and level of different functions.

As technology progresses, shortages of personnel with specialized experience or training will continue to plague employers. Yet such shortages could be considerably abated by concentration of those duties that absolutely require higher skills into as few positions as possible, so that more routine functions could be, in turn, concentrated in jobs demanding less of candidates and incidentally less of the payroll in wage levels. Unless the organization of work because of sequence, geographical dispersion, or otherwise makes such a practice unavoidable, the analytical approach would reduce instances in which any one position has a wide span of duties ranging from complex to menial.

The advantage of conscious and careful job design is evident not only in a labor market of short supply. As already noted in an earlier chapter, job restructuring makes it possible to employ persons who were for one reason or another deprived of adequate schooling or good experience and to develop them in an organization, with training and skillful supervision, to assume responsibilities they could never have qualified for at the outset. In other words, sound job design also takes advantage of an oversupply of low skills or even so-called unemployables in the market. Some studies have shown that persons with little formal training or experience perform better at routine tasks than those who are overqualified. Yet many organizations continue to ask engineers and technicians and school teachers to spend large segments of their time on repetitive or menial tasks that could be as well or better performed by lesser-qualified and lower-salaried personnel.[7]

*   *   *

THE IDEA AND practice of position classification has given solid enough support to the job-oriented type of career system that it has earned an established place in the imperatives of modern management. It has influenced markedly all aspects of personnel administration and many facets of general management. It is still not a precise instrument, and perhaps it need not be as long as it is not mistaken for such, but it is not likely to be replaced as the foundation for personnel administration pertaining to at least the great bulk of the modern public service.

[7] The best up-to-date case for the manifold benefits of job analysis appears in Albert P. Ingraham and Carl F. Lutz, "Managing Positions—the Key to Effective Organization, Compensation, and Productivity," *Human Resource Management*, Summer 1974, pp. 12–21.

NOTE relating to Chapter 6, *Compensation*: Because of an important report issued in December 1975, after the present volume was set in page proof and when there was no space available in Chapter 6, the following statement should be read in connection with that chapter:

A special panel of high government officials, headed by the Vice President, has recommended major changes in federal systems of pay and benefits. Reaffirming the principle of comparability with nonfederal employment as the governing criterion for total compensation, this body proposed these principal revisions in the process of establishing such comparability: (1) that fringe benefits as well as pay be included when gauging total compensation; (2) that rates and benefits in nonprofit organizations and state and local government be included along with those in strictly private enterprise; (3) that clerical and technical occupations be compensated on a locality-rate basis (like blue-collar jobs), while professional and managerial occupations continue on a nationwide scale; (4) that employee performance have greater influence on within-grade pay increases in the professional-managerial group; and (5) that various technical improvements be made to reduce the frequency of surveys, strengthen statistical processes, rid the blue-collar wage system of inequities, set more defensible premium pay, increase schedules for top executives, and provide more recruitment incentives. Most of the recommendations would require legislation and are likely to meet with resistance among employee unions and in the Congress. *Report to the President of the President's Panel on Federal Compensation*, December 1975, Washington, D. C.

CHAPTER 6

Compensation

IN NO PHASE of personnel administration is the possibility for misunderstanding and conflict greater than in that of compensation. This generalization applies equally to private and to public employment. In the latter case the citizens are the employers and, as taxpayers, have come to insist on an economy plank in every platform, in every campaign, irrespective of party. The administrator finds himself, therefore, confronted with conflicting pressures, one from the public servants desirous of a liberal wage policy and one from the taxpayers eager to have expenses reduced.

Of course, the problem is not even that simple. Taxpayers want economy, but they also want public services. Economy of program, the reduction of activities to their bare essentials, is one thing; an attempt to secure a wide variety of public services cheaply is something else. Taxpayers *should* want the kind of pay policy and levels that will secure and retain an able staff, public employees who can give good service. To harmonize the interests of all groups and to retain their confidence and support is a challenge to the constructive ability of both legislator and administrator.

Payment for personal services constitutes the largest single item in the operating budgets of state and local governments, and it is outweighed among federal expenditures only by defense costs, debt retirement, and social benefits. Thus the interest of the taxpayer is both direct and controlling. Likewise the concern of the civil servant is very real. Both interests converge at the point of the consequences of a compensation policy. An overly generous plan is costly and unnecessary; a niggardly or inequitable plan produces low morale and decreased efficiency.

The subject of compensation may be discussed under two general headings: (1) the development of general pay policy and levels, and (2) the construction and administration of pay schedules.[1] The first is primarily a matter for legislative determination, making use of executive analysis and recommendations; the second is primarily a matter for executive action. Unfortunately, the tradition in the United States is for the legislative body to act with little or no executive participation in the first area and to encroach deeply into the second. With the exception of small jurisdictions, executive agencies ought to establish pay scales, once basic policy and limits have been set by the legislature. Actually this is the practice in most nations of the world.

The consequences of legislative involvement in the details of pay scales and policy have been: wide disparity in salaries, inequitable pay relationships, and sluggish response to the inexorable pressures of the salary market. Fortunately, the federal government and a number of states and municipalities have moved in the direction of executive prescription of pay scales in accordance with broad principles or amounts of money established by legislative bodies. A delicate and technical subject such as pay can be determined effectively, within the boundaries of general public policy and procedure, only through the expertise available in the executive branch.[2]

GENERAL PAY POLICY AND LEVELS

For many years public pay scales in this country were characteristically low in comparison with the rest of the economy. This can still be said of many

[1] The most complete modern treatise on the subject is Kenneth O. Warner and J. J. Donovan, eds., *Practical Guidelines to Public Pay Administration*, Chicago, International Personnel Management Association, vol. I, 1963; vol. II, 1965.

[2] The federal service now provides a model in administratively determined pay scales through the system used for its major white-collar pay systems. (Pay schedules for trade and other blue-collar jobs had long been set administratively.) The first step was the milestone enactment, the *Salary Reform Act of 1962*, which first put into law the principle of keeping career salary levels comparable with those in private enterprise.

Following abortive attempts by Congress to keep up with the pace of change in the economy (although several upward adjustments were enacted), it finally passed the *Federal Pay Comparability Act of 1970*, which reincorporated the principles of the 1962 law but, more importantly, empowered the President to establish the rates for the General Schedule, the Foreign Service, and the special medical and nursing schedules in the Veterans Administration. (The Postal Service, under the *Postal Reorganization Act of 1970*, was excluded, following original coverage in the 1962 act, but it also is required to maintain comparability with the private sector even in establishing salaries and other benefits by collective agreement with postal unions.) The President acts on recommendations made jointly by the Chairman of the Civil Service Commission and the Director of the Office of Management and Budget, who are required to consult a Federal Employees Pay Council, composed of five representatives of employee unions, and an Advisory Council on Federal Pay, composed of three pay and labor experts appointed by the President. Under the 1962 Act, final pay schedules had still been dependent on congressional enactment.

The main problem under the 1970 Act has arisen from efforts of the President to limit or defer pay increases in times of economic stress, which have led Congress on several occasions to override executive action by special legislation. So far, however, the principle of administrative determination has held fast. (Also, see note, p. 92.)

smaller jurisdictions. In almost all, it is standard to find pay lagging behind at the executive and professional levels while measuring up well or exceeding prevailing pay at lower, more routine levels. Public scales tend to be more compressed, top to bottom, than those in private employment. And public rates increase less rapidly than private during time of advancing living costs but hold steadier during times when costs retreat.

What, then, should be the controlling considerations in setting public service compensation? Obviously many factors must be taken into account—the nation's wealth and national income, productivity of workers, labor supply, social and ethical values, tradition and custom, and the like. Most of these are of an economic nature, a fact which suggests discussion of that area first.

ECONOMIC CONSIDERATIONS

One of the most complex problems in theoretical economics is that of determining the share of labor in the value of goods produced. It is not possible within the scope of this chapter to inquire into this problem or to examine the various economic theories of value and wages. However, it must be recognized that there is a vital relationship, first, between the total amount spent for wages and the total productivity, and second, between the amount spent for wages and the proportions of the total income going to the other factors in production. As society is economically organized at present, there is thus a practical limitation upon the height to which the general level of *all* compensation can go—a limitation determined first by the total productivity of industry, and second by the irreducible requirements of the various other elements affecting production. A wage set with due regard to these considerations is regarded as an "economic" wage, and private establishments paying "uneconomic" wages are likely to be forced out of business.

SPECIAL CIRCUMSTANCES OF GOVERNMENT   In the case of public enterprises, the situation is somewhat different. In most of the services which it supplies the government possesses a monopoly. It is not subject to the rigorous process of competition, nor is it under the same pressure to accept the marginal productivity or commodity theory of labor as is private industry. The theoretical limit to what the government can spend in salaries and wages is determined only by the state of the taxpayer's pocketbook and by the extent to which it is important for the government to compete in the labor market.

Although the government in theory could disregard some of the economic factors involved in wage determination, there are considerations which make it necessary for public services to fix pay with some regard to the "economic" levels set is private industry. Regardless of the theory of wages or of labor accepted, the government competes with private employers in the labor market. Thus, assuming other things to be equal, if the general level of pay in public employment is substantially lower than that in private industry, the government will find it difficult or impossible to recruit qualified persons into the service. On the other hand, if the public scale is substantially higher, the result may be to drain the more efficient workers from industry, thus reducing its productivity. This is entirely aside from the questions of ethics or expediency involved. From the latter standpoint, it is exceedingly doubtful whether sufficient support could be secured for a program which, in effect, meant unfair competition with private industry. In short, the prevailing or market rate must be considered as a major factor in the determination of government pay policy.

Moreover, it is largely through some consideration of prevailing rates that the government can give weight to the major economic factors involved in salary determination. To carry on public services, pay cannot be made to depend directly upon market demand for those services. Under such circumstances, the primary economic guide is supplied by the prevailing conditions in the labor market, which reflect the interplay of many economic forces.

PREVAILING RATE PROBLEMS   The competitive market rate is not, however, a perfect guide in establishing pay levels in the public service. Still leaving ethical or social considerations out of account, there are three major difficulties encountered in basing a public wage policy primarily upon prevailing rates: (1) the practical difficulty of determining what the market rate is for any particular class of positions, (2) the fact that large groups of public servants have no comparable counterpart in private industry, and (3) geographic variations.

The term *market* or *prevailing* refers to an abstraction. There is no such thing as a *single* prevailing rate. Salaries for identical jobs vary from locality to locality, from concern to concern within the same industry and the same locality, and from individual to individual within the same concern. There are, then, many going rates, ranging from niggardly to liberal. The problem of pay policy is not solved merely by discovering the rates paid for various types of work in private employment. It is still necessary to make a choice, and that choice should be influenced by reference to concerns which are known to maintain good employment policies and with which the government may be expected to compete.

This fact, however, does not invalidate the collection of wage data from private employers according to standard job specifications or the use of such data as a factor in determining the general wage levels in the public service. Although it is apparent that the competitive market rates supply only a variable standard, some criterion is better than none. This has been recognized in many of the more progressive public jurisdictions, where surveys of wages paid in private employment have been made and used as guides in determining public salary structures.

The second difficulty with the application of the competitive market rate to public employment arises from the fact that vast numbers of public employees are engaged in occupations without parallel in private employment, such as police officers, fire fighters, crop, meat, and dairy inspectors, and dozens of other classes. In such cases, the pay must be fixed with regard to the going rates for work of comparable complexity and skill and the rates for other public jobs that are comparable to some in private enterprise. This requires cross-occupational job analysis and evaluation.

The U.S. Government, in setting rates for trades and other blue-collar employees, recognizes that only rough justice is possible even in the skilled trades for which prevailing rates have been a traditional guide in collective bargaining. After setting a floor and a ceiling on rates for a locality and discounting discriminatory rates for irrelevant factors such as sex, race, and religion, it in effect makes exceptions to market rates by the use of job evaluation, that is, seeing to it that each class of jobs bears a reasonable pay relationship to others in terms of complexity, responsibility, and skill. The same approach governs white-collar pay setting, except that the schedules are nationwide.

The third problem grows out of the wide disparity in pay conditions in a country as large as the United States. It is one thing for a municipality to survey prevailing compensation for selected classes of employment in its own locality. It is quite another for the federal civil service to determine which jobs should be paid on local rates and which should go on a nationwide scale, and whether in the latter case, to follow nationwide averages or to allow for special rates at least in high cost areas.

Another aspect of this variation in conditions among localities is the question of where to draw boundaries of areas in which different rates are provided. This is a problem not only for the federal government but for large states with quite disparate competitive situations as between rural and metropolitan areas. How far into the suburbs or surrounding counties should the city rates apply? Obviously the answer to such a question is fraught with all kinds of political overtones and pressures. The most workable solution is to pattern the pay area after the employment and commuting habits of the population. Fortunately, the U.S. Bureau of the Census publishes periodic reports with such data on major metropolitan areas.

SOCIAL AND ETHICAL CONSIDERATIONS

Although from an economic standpoint government is somewhat freer in setting its pay policy than are most private establishments, from social and ethical standpoints it is less free to do as it wishes. The state, charged with providing for the common welfare and with establishing and maintaining desirable social conditions, is under a special obligation to its servants that many private employers are not. Moreover, the bargaining power of public employees is limited, because of (1) the absence of effective organization among many civil servants, (2) limitations upon the right to strike and to engage in political activities, and (3) the specialized character of much government work, which makes it difficult for the civil servant to leave the service for private employment. Thus, there is a special obligation upon the state to treat its employees fairly. The weak bargaining position in which many public servants find themselves produces a situation conducive to arbitrary treatment and discrimination. The chief restraint against unfairness must be self-imposed, on the ground that the government should be a "model employer." Unfortunately, such self-restraint has been noticeably absent in many public jurisdictions.

LIVING WAGE   There is a crying need for the recognition and acceptance of general social principles as a basis for pay policy. One of the most frequently advocated principles is the living wage. Most contemporary references to a minimum wage are, in reality, references to a minimum living wage. The arguments for the living wage are not primarily economic but ethical. They are based upon the contention that every citizen of a civilized community should be assured the means to a reasonable scale of living according to the standard prevailing in the community.

To determine the minimum living wage requires first a decision on the general living standard to be provided, and second the study of cost-of-living budgets as a basis for determining the amount necessary to maintain that standard. Both of these are intimately related to the question of whether the minimum is to provide a living wage for a single man, a single woman, a married worker, an average family, or some other unit. Obviously, what might be a living wage for a person with no dependents would not provide a living for a family of five.

One solution to this problem is the family allowance system, under which a minimum living wage is set for a single person and increments are added for dependents. This has some advantages over a theoretical family standard, and most of the major European governments have at one time or another paid family allowances to their civil servants. Moreover, commissioned officers in the U.S. military forces have traditionally been remunerated under such a system. Even without special allowances and taking into account the lack of precision in any so-called standard of living, reasonable approximations can be made. The safe procedure for a jurisdiction genuinely desiring to put a defensible floor under its pay structure is to study all available data from such sources as the U.S. Bureau of Labor Statistics and to assume that its rock-bottom wage will support a small family (say, one of four).

PAY CEILINGS   Related to these considerations is the matter of pay ceilings. Although private industry seems to experience very little social pressure against excessively high salaries, the public service almost everywhere, and especially in the United States, has traditionally been the object of the most insistent pressure, sometimes to the extent of imposing unreasonable limitations on top-level compensation. In fact, legislative bodies and political heads have a better record in establishing socially justifiable minimum pay than they do maximum. Often in their anxiety to get political credit for generosity to the more numerous rank and file, they give short shrift to the upper grades of the service.

Executives (both career and noncareer) and other higher-bracket employees must maintain a standard of living that enables them to associate with their counterparts in private pursuits with dignity and self-respect. This is just as important an application of social and ethical considerations as is an adequate minimum wage. The compression or narrow range of some public pay schedules is shocking in view of the normal popular rejection of such leveling, socialistic practices. It would seem that the mistaken and unfortunate mythology portraying public servants as tax-eating parasites, overpaid and underworked, is visited mostly upon executive and professional ranks, the very levels where the most devoted and industrious employees are usually found.

It is gratifying, however, to observe in recent years a marked improvement in public salaries throughout the nation. Although many smaller jurisdictions have a long way to go to catch up, most American governments have adopted an unprecedented series of upward pay adjustments all along the line. Minimum rates have generally kept up with living standards; long underpaid groups like school teachers and police have been brought into more reasonable relationship with other sectors of employment, both public and private; and civil servants with the greatest responsibilities have in many locations been placed at salary levels that are quite respectable for an affluent society and enable them to hold their heads high in professional and managerial circles. As usual, however, this favorable report is not consistently applicable among all jurisdictions, and the future stresses of keeping up with an inflationary economy are always to be faced.[3]

One might surmise from the foregoing discussion that monetary compensation is the be-all and end-all of modern management. There is no intention here to ignore the many other factors influencing the attractiveness and holding power of public employment which are discussed elsewhere in this book. But when pay for services rendered is demonstrated to be unfair in relation to others or unworthy of a wealthy nation, then it is most likely to be the controlling factor in acquiring and motivating the best talent to work for government. There is no dispute here with the psychological theories

[3] Although it had substantially caught up with the private sector in the late 1960s, pay at the highest career levels in the federal government has lagged again in recent years, so that executives and professionals in the top several grades of the General Schedule and their counterparts in the other career pay systems are frozen at a point thousands of dollars below what comparability with private executive pay justifies. This is largely due to unrealistic ceilings imposed in the laws on the subject, in which members of Congress find it difficult to tolerate their own compensation being below the second highest level in the noncareer pay brackets, which in turn restrict the top salaries under the career schedules. Even the Comptroller General of the United States has described the situation as "untenable" (*Critical Need for a Better System for Adjusting Top Executive, Legislative, and Judicial Salaries*, Report to the Congress, February 25, 1975). (Also, see note, p. 92.)

that when pay is fair and adequate, other motivational influences—such as the nature and organization of work, quality of supervision, and challenge of assignments—may then operate with far greater effect.

In brief, it may be said that the private enterprise that cannot pay defensible compensation is uneconomical and socially destructive, whereas the state which does not do it is imposing a kind of serfdom on its workers. No employer can, over the long pull, successfully neglect social considerations in determining its basic pay structure; for the state, they must be ultimately controlling.

OTHER CONSIDERATIONS

Beyond economic competition and social policy, still other factors enter into determining general pay levels. The more significant of these, as conditions of employment, are hours of work, provisions for vacation and sick leave, relative security of tenure, and retirement benefits—all of which may be translated into indirect compensation elements. But other parts of this book will demonstrate how difficult it is to quantify these factors in an accurate enough way to permit comparison between governmental units or between any one government and private employment. While *some* public services may be said to provide more advantageous perquisites in *some* of these areas, it is impossible to arrive at any generalized conclusions on the overall status of public employment in this respect.

CONSTRUCTION AND ADMINISTRATION OF PAY SCHEDULES

General pay policy governs the overall responsiveness of compensation to economic and social determinants and the ability of an employer to maintain a quality work force. The translation of this policy into salary or wage schedules and the application of such schedules to specific cases create much of the structure of a personnel system.

It is this second function which must be and ordinarily is carried on by the executive branch of a government. The specific agency to do this is the personnel agency, which normally operates or oversees the operation of the position-classification plan. The intimate relationships between classification and compensation, the importance of compensation to recruitment and incentive, the many problems of equity involved—all combine to make it imperative that the personnel organization have the leadership role. This is not to disparage collaboration with the budget and fiscal planning activity, but the latter's role is more important in winning executive and legislative support for a far-sighted basic policy.

SALARY AND WAGE SURVEYS

A prerequisite to construction of a rational pay schedule is thoroughgoing knowledge of what is going on in the general labor market. Smaller jurisdictions may have to rely for this information on published reports or the action of nearby communities. Major jurisdictions are more likely to have to conduct independent surveys of their own to supplement such sources.

The standard practice in gathering pay data consists of the following steps: (1) selecting a representative set of position classes that typify major segments of the civil service involved and are likely to be found in reasonable numbers in the outside market, (2) writing brief descriptions of these classes that will help identify comparable classes in private or other public employment, (3) soliciting by questionnaire or personal visit the existing pay rates, pay schedules, work hours, bonus or extra pay provisions, and other relevant information for each of these classes from all or a representative sample of employers that hire substantial numbers of people in these categories, and (4) compiling these data in a systematic way to determine the spread of rates found for each class and the most suitable statistical method that reflects the central or "prevailing" tendency of these rates.

We have already taken note of some of the problems inherent in ascertaining prevailing rates. The foregoing steps go far to minimize these problems, but one that deserves special mention here is the selection of employers from whom rate data are solicited. Except in relatively narrow local surveys, it is impractical to include every employer who hires one or more persons in the class under study. Decisions often must be made to exclude the very smallest employers in order to reduce the survey load. This also has the advantage of concentrating on those employers who have the most impact on going rates. In addition, some employers exclude themselves by refusing to supply the necessary information, and there is ordinarily no law requiring them to do so. The only bait that can be used is the promise of making the overall results of the survey available to them for application to their own situations.

Employee unions frequently seek to confine data-gathering to employers who set pay under union contracts. This may offer no problem in many cases, but, where large portions of the workers in a given class are not paid under contracts, the public service cannot ignore noncontract rates as part of the true market situation. Government jurisdictions can, however, decline to average in the rates of notoriously low-paying employers who appear to deviate markedly from the level around which all other employers tend to cluster.

Comprehensive surveys are conducted annually by the Bureau of Labor Statistics covering various trades and clerical occupations in metropolitan areas and a substantial number of professional and managerial occupations on a nationwide basis, following the procedure outlined previously. It is this survey that is used by the federal government to set salary schedules for practically all groups of white-collar positions, since the classes used are common to both the civil service and private industry.[4] Trades and labor jobs (blue collar) are surveyed separately and locally by the government to derive rates for application to such jobs in each area of the country in which federal establishments are located.[5] State and local governments often draw upon these sources but also, where they deem it useful, conduct independent surveys of their own.

One point is especially clear: it would be next to impossible to carry on anything like the sophisticated survey process set forth if it were not for the existence of position classification. Valid comparisons between public and private employment are feasible only through job analysis and description, and, as we shall see in the next section, the finding of prevailing pay data for selected job classes can be extended to all other classes only by use of this well-established procedure.

CONSTRUCTION OF SCHEDULES

Separate pay scales for each separate occupation would require prevailing pay information on each occupation. We have already seen that gathering any such quantity of data would be wholly impracticable. Surveys can be made ordinarily only for selected classes of jobs that typify both the public service and the employers being surveyed.

Hence, most jurisdictions aggregate classes of comparable level from different, but often related, occupations into common grades, so that the same pay range can be used for a whole gamut of position classes instead of just one. This keeps the number of specific pay ranges down to a manageable order, but most significant to our present subject, it makes it possible to extend to a broad spectrum of jobs the pay findings fitting a few that are representative of that level. Obviously, then, we are back to reliance on the elementary principles of position evaluation and classification.

The preceding chapter describes how classes are created and how individual jobs are allocated from time to time to such classes. Construction of a pay schedule requires a similar process in bringing together classes themselves, as distinguished from individual jobs, into rank order. Thus, the number of grades required by combinations of the various levels of classes in many occupations will be the number of grades required for the total salary or wage schedule. Stopping short of separate schedules for each occupation, some states and cities establish several schedules, one for each group of occupations that have certain common denominators, such as for clerical, professional, or police. The federal service has a separate schedule for the Postal Service, one for trades and labor jobs in each major locality, and one for each of several special personnel systems, like the Foreign Service, but

---

[4] The procedure, authorized initially by the *Salary Reform Act of 1962* and reaffirmed in the *Federal Pay Comparability Act of 1970*, involves a careful matching of representative job levels between the private sector and the federal government. It is probably the most exacting and thorough process of gauging private pay and gearing public pay to it that exists anywhere.

[5] Under the Coordinated Federal Wage System.

the extremely broad variety of occupations embraced by the Classification Act is housed in a single schedule of eighteen grades.[6] All of these are adjusted from time to time so that they may be maintained as comparable to prevailing pay as practicable.

In effect, then, in a schedule of general application, some occupations may use some of the grades, but not all, while others may employ all or other grades in the schedule. Naturally, they may overlap, so that any one grade may embrace classes from many occupations, some of which concentrate in the lower reaches of the schedule and others in the middle or higher ones. For example, the more routine occupations would be found in the lower grades, and, overlapping the upper levels of these, there would start the lower rungs of technical or professional occupations, which in turn would likely extend to the very top grade.

In relating classes to pay scales, there is also the question of the number of levels into which a given occupation can be divided. If the classification has been pressed to the point of recognizing in separate classes all possible distinguishable zones or gradations of difficulty and responsibility, that many separate pay ranges will have to be established. If the object in the classification is to keep the number of levels at a minimum consistent with the natural pattern of major distinctions in the particular occupation, then considerably fewer grades for pay purposes will probably be required. The tendency in recent years is in the direction of the latter approach.

This is one of the points at which the relationships between classification and pay are almost inextricable, even though quite separate in substance. Some technicians will still argue for numerous distinctions in level in an occupation simply because the distinctions can be rationalized on job evaluation grounds; that is, differences can, by great refinement in reasoning, be made. It seems more feasible, however, to require no more distinctions than are absolutely necessary for the recognition of genuine differences in skill, ability, or knowledge required and of the usual hierarchical structure of positions in the occupation. This not only simplifies the subsequent process of determining which classes individual positions fall into by reducing the number of break-off points or borderlines; it also simplifies the establishment of pay ranges by permitting more "room" or flexibility in pay between classes. Hence, the nature of the classification plan vitally affects the way in which the compensation structure can be set up.

SALARY OR WAGE RANGES

The several rates of pay that constitute one grade or level are usually referred to as a salary or wage range.[7] Normally such a pay range consists of a

---

[6] The General Schedule, from which the designations GS-1, GS-2, etc., are derived.

[7] The term *salary* is commonly used for compensation expressed in monthly or annual figures and paid to white-collar employees; the term *wage* is commonly used for compensation expressed in hourly rates and paid to blue-collar (trades, crafts, and manual) workers.

minimum rate, one or more intermediate rates, and a maximum rate. The minimum is usually the starting rate for a new employee in a particular level, although there are exceptions to this that will be considered later in this section. The rate used for comparison with prevailing pay should ordinarily be that intermediate rate which is the midpoint or average at which employees in the grade are currently being paid, since the outside rates with which comparison is made represent such modes or means of the ranges existing in the surveyed enterprises.

BREADTH   Maximum rates are customarily the highest amounts that may be paid to employees whose jobs fall in the range. As a general rule, good practice has dictated that a maximum rate should be about 25 to 30 percent above the minimum of each grade. In this way the scope of the range can reflect the relative importance of the grade, thus permitting larger pay increments in the higher levels. It is an accepted truism that a salary increase within range which might seem significant to a duplicating machine operator would seem insulting to a senior executive.

UTILITY   The spread between minimum and maximum rates is founded on the theory that factors other than the job level should have an influence on compensation of individuals. Among other purposes, rates within a range are normally used to recognize an employee's increased value and usefulness while he remains on the same job. Unfortunately, in most pay systems this had led to the asumption that progress is automatic and relatively unvarying among different employees, because in most cases everyone receives increases within range at the same pace, based obviously on pure seniority. In some instances a minimal standard of performance is required to earn an increase, and a few jurisdictions permit more rapid advancement in rates for superior performance. But more often than not governments fail to exploit the incentive potential of the pay range.

A good case can be made that a certain amount of salary progress should be forthcoming for everyone good enough to keep on the job. One could say that the employer's responsibility toward the worker increases as the latter's length of service increases. Furthermore, the reservations about and lack of objectivity of many schemes of performance evaluation, as pointed out in a later chapter, are understandable. But one cannot escape the conclusion that some plan to ensure that increases do not go to substandard performers and to recognize meritorious achievement with accelerated increases is the preferred approach. Certainly the widespread custom of automatic increases without relation to performance has little to commend it from the standpoint of good administration.

OVERLAPPING   Two other aspects of the size and use of pay ranges deserve attention. One is the matter of overlapping of ranges between grades. If the ranges are to be of adequate breadth then it is almost inevitable that the upper ends of at least some ranges will have to overlap the lower ends of those above. This should occasion no problem in the promotion of employees from grade to grade, because an arbitrary advance in an amount equivalent to one or two within-range rates can automatically apply in any case where the individual is already at a rate as high or higher than the entry rate of the new grade.

SPECIAL RATES   The other subject has to do with the use of special rate ranges for classes of positions that are in short supply and therefore hard to fill. No matter how faithfully a pay structure is kept up to date and responsive to the prevailing market rates on a general basis, there will always be some occupations for which going rates are far out of line with the overall market, thus making it extraordinarily difficult for a rule-bound employer like a government agency to attract qualified candidates. In an age of rapid changes in technology such instances multiply. Blending the pay of very hard-to-fill jobs into the standard salary schedule when other employers are offering much higher rates is hardly a satisfactory practice.

Consequently, in spite of the violence done to strict job evaluation and equal-pay-for-equal-work principles, the only solution is to authorize temporary deviation from the standard rate ranges for those specific occupations where unusually heavy competition can be demonstrated. It is preferable that this be accomplished by setting a special rate range for each specific class and that the power to do this be vested in the personnel authority. The jobs affected remain in their proper grades and revert to the regular rate range whenever market conditions change sufficiently to warrant it or whenever the regular schedule, by virtue of subsequent change upward, catches up with the special temporary rates. This is the policy in meeting unusual demands followed by the federal civil service, and it has worked well.

ALLOWANCES AND DIFFERENTIALS

PAYMENT IN KIND   Many public employees, especially those working in hospitals and other institutions, work under conditions that make it necessary for them to accept part of their pay in kind—meals, lodging, and laundry, for example. When such is the case, standard values need to be computed for the services provided so that deductions can be made from their cash compensation. The value of such maintenance must take into account not only the outright cost to the government but the reasonable value of the items to the employee during the particular period and in the particular locality when and where he is employed. In this manner salary standardization is maintained and equitable treatment to all is assured, since everything of monetary value received is in effect calculated as part of pay.

EXTRA EXPENSE   In other instances, employees work under conditions where they must go to extraordinary expense for transportation, housing, or meals. This is also true when any employee travels on official business or moves his family to accept a new post at the behest of his employer. Under such circumstances it is reasonable to provide standard allowances that approximate the extra costs to the employee rather than reimburse for itemized expenditures.

GEOGRAPHIC DIFFERENTIALS   Provision of a variety of pay differentials is an essential part of any comprehensive compensation structure. One of these is geographic differentials to allow for differences in living conditions or costs in different areas of a state or of the country.[8] Although still used in a few instances in the federal service, cost of living is a more or less discredited basis for a pay differential, because adjustment of rate ranges to meet high pay competition can better serve the basic purpose of attracting or keeping a much needed staff. However, differentials to induce people to take assignments where housing, educational facilities for children, or environmental conditions are poor are often justifiable. Such is the justification for many differentials now paid to persons working at foreign posts or in isolated territories where living circumstances or health hazards create hardships for the average family. In these cases the extra pay is not for higher costs; indeed, no amount of money could buy a correction of the conditions. Rather it is simply an inducement to offset the ordeal.

HAZARD   An especially troublesome issue occurs in connection with efforts to compensate in the form of special differentials for work in highly hazardous surroundings or with dangerous materials, such as duties around a nuclear reactor, under risky atmospheric conditions, near explosives or highly contagious viruses, in submarine or airplane testing, and the like. Some argue that hazard should be taken into account as an important contributing factor in evaluating the position. Others feel that degree of hazard is not as measurable as the duties of a job and that therefore recognition of hazard must be based on some arbitrary monetary measure of its importance in the recruitment and retention of employees on the work in question.

There is a question regarding the desirability of trying to meet the hazard problem by extra pay. Many officials contend that hazard should be controlled by safety engineering and training, by careful selection of employees where special skills are required to avoid harm, and by careful adjustment of working time or conditions, and that more adequate injury compensation and family benefits in case of death should be looked upon

[8] "Differentials" as used here refer to special increments, usually percentage adjustments, added on to standard pay rates throughout the range, and usually to all levels within a scale. This is not the same thing as "locality rates," wherein the basic schedules are devised initially in comparison with prevailing rates for comparable work in the particular locality or commuting area. The latter method already applies to trades and labor occupations in the federal service. Experts have suggested that, instead of nationwide rates (even with occasional special differentials), the system of locality rates ought to be used for postal and various clerical and office occupations for which pay standards vary widely across the country. The idea makes sense. (See note, p. 92.)

as economic protection for the individual and his family. This view, however, does not take into account the uncontrollable hazard—as in test pilot assignments—where extra pay is simply designed to induce a person to accept and stay on a job which requires him to risk his neck. Although extra pay for hazardous employments should be avoided as much as possible, the prevailing practice in private industry for comparable jobs should probably be a controlling consideration. There is little doubt that the long-range goal for public employers facing this issue should be to reduce and control the occupational hazards themselves.

SPECIAL PAY   Although not exactly belonging under the heading "differentials," several other aspects of pay may for convenience be mentioned here. These are overtime, night, and holiday pay. Most jurisdictions have found it necessary to provide overtime pay, usually approximating one and one-half times the basic pay, for at least the lower-level jobs. Also, many activities carry on around the clock, such as hospitals, public buildings operation, certain military installations, and to some extent even mass clerical operations where space or machinery limitations require more than one shift. The complexities in administering these special pay provisions are enormous but are probably justified by the added ease of recruiting and retaining personnel for duty outside a normal work week.[9]

Whatever the purpose of the allowance, differential, or special pay feature may be, the best procedure is for the legislative body to authorize the personnel agency to set the actual rates in accordance with clearly stated objectives and criteria, following consultation with all interested parties.

ADMINISTRATION OF PAY POLICIES

Much has already been said about administrative measures essential to creating and operating a sound compensation structure and the organs and information necessary to this objective. But a few addional comments are warranted to round out the full story.

INSTALLATION   One has to do with the initial installation of a general pay plan. A common issue arises from the very likely prospect that current salaries for some positions will be above or below the range authorized for the class under the new system. It is easy enough to provide that those underpaid be

---

[9] Extension of the *Fair Labor Standards Amendments of 1974* to government jurisdictions may cause considerable dislocation and expense in municipalities and other governments particularly because of overtime pay provisions. "Time and a half for overtime," a hallowed condition in most industrial employment and already common in most public service jobs, does not fit very well into the kinds of employment peculiar to government, such as fire-fighting, police duty, etc., which of necessity entail much "standby" or no-work time. Counting such time the same as full duty is an unjustifiable distortion and unduly expensive to taxpayers. Challenged on constitutional grounds by the National League of Cities, the law is temporarily suspended by court order, but the specter of this unwarranted intrusion on local self-government still hangs over all municipalities.

raised to the proper level, but those overpaid pose a dilemma. Since living standards derive from income already enjoyed, reductions can cause hardship and resentment. On the other hand, to maintain out-of-line salaries impairs the uniformity of schedules and violates equal pay for equal work. The most satisfactory solution has been to allow current employees paid in excess of their class range to keep their existing rate during incumbency of the job but without opportunity for salary advancement until the scale catches up. The off-standard rate would not attach to the position but to the person, and every effort should be made under this policy to find a placement of each employee so frozen that will warrant his existing pay.

REVISIONS   As in the case of classification plans, compensation systems are about as good as their maintenance. This means that from the beginning the overall policy should include an automatic periodic action by executive agencies to initiate a reappraisal of the pay structure. Ideally this should be an annual review. The availability of prevailing pay data from official and private sources leaves little excuse for neglect even if an independent survey cannot be undertaken.

In this connection it should be noted that over a period of time various experiments have been conducted by states and cities to find some foolproof scheme to permit salary schedules to adjust automatically with changes in cost-of-living or price indexes. Unfortunately these sliding-scale plans have suffered from overreliance on one factor to control pay. They have several drawbacks: original base rates come to be viewed as sacrosanct, making the correction of any inherent inequities the more difficult; prevailing pay is not given sufficient independent attention even though this is the one economic criterion that encompasses the interaction of almost all economic forces; price indexes indicate only changes in prices and do not measure the kind and amount of goods and services that families buy or their total family expenditure; and dependence on living-cost changes ignores changes in labor's share of economic gain that may have been secured by increased productivity, organized union bargaining, or other effects. A good example of this latter point is found in public school teaching: if teachers had been caught with a cost-of-living clause that was accepted years ago, their salaries would not have increased anywhere near the amount that has been reached by the change in their relative position vis-à-vis other kinds of employment.

*   *   *

THE IMPORTANT LESSON to be learned is that flexibility and adaptability are the cardinal virtues of a modern, serviceable compensation system. Continuous adjustment should be taken for granted. The customary reaction to crisis and the desire to "settle the matter once and for all" is most illadvised. Of primary importance, therefore, is the need to charge the personnel agency with responsibility for regular reviews and surveys to keep public employee pay abreast of all the considerations that are involved in this difficult but vital aspect of personnel administration.

PART III

Staffing

When you make an appointment be careful to allot it to the man adapted
to it and not one lacking for needful capacity. . . . Not every duty can be
assigned to every man. . . . Give the work, therefore, to one who is expert in
it and thus avoid annoyance.

Kai-Ka'us-ibn-Iskandar, *Qabus Nama* (Letters of a
Persian Chieftain in A.D. 1082), trans. in
Reuben Levy, *A Mirror for Princes,* New York,
Dutton, 1951, pp. 225–226.

There is nothing I am so anxious about as good nominations, conscious that
the merit as well as the reputation of an administration depends as much
on that as on its measures.

Thomas Jefferson, *Writings*, memorial ed.,
April 8, 1801, vol. IX, p. 248.

An increasing number of bright and able people must become involved in
the development of public policy. Ours is a difficult and exhilarating form of
government—not for the faint of heart, not for the tidy-minded, and in
these days of complexity not for the stupid. We need men and women who
can bring to government the highest order of intellect, social motivations
sturdy enough to pursue good purposes despite setbacks, and a resilience of
spirit equal to the frustrations of public life.

John W. Gardner, *No Easy Victories,*
New York, Harper & Row, 1968, p. 6.

CHAPTER 7

Manpower Planning and Attraction

THE ORIGINAL INTEREST of civil service reformers centered in the selection process. The merit system was designed to assure selection of the best who applied but not to influence the sources of application. The task was conceived to be a negative one, keeping out the unfit rather than encouraging the best to present their credentials. It was naively assumed that if political favoritism could be excluded, men of ability would somehow find their way into the public service. The assumption long ago proved to be erroneous, yet only slowly did the negative emphasis give way to positive methods to induce highly qualified persons to present themselves for consideration.[1]

As the labor market became tighter and tighter and the scarcity of talent in many specialized fields more and more evident, this problem of recruitment took on still a further dimension—namely, the need for planning. But for a long time, just as governments have acted as if the supply of manpower is infinitely elastic, so have they tended to overlook the desirability of systematic planning to acquire it. Thus, the two conditions preceding formal selection that are most critical for the ultimate product— (1) manpower analysis and planning,[2] and (2) affirmative policies of re-

---

[1] See the discussion by James W. Fesler, *The 50 States and Their Local Governments*, New York, Knopf, 1967, especially on p. 379, where he observes that the best people have to be sought out and cannot be expected to turn up as applicants, because at least in many professions "being an applicant and being a supplicant are scarcely distinguishable." On p. 391 he stresses the need for political executives to be so interested in attaining their program goals that they become committed to search for the caliber of people who can best help them attain those goals.

[2] Again, we do not apologize for using the generic term *manpower*. See footnote 10 in Chapter 1.

cruitment and attraction to the service—have been among the more neglected aspects of the public personnel function.

ANALYSIS AND PLANNING

No organization can afford to replenish its supply of raw materials, equipment, or other goods on a haphazard basis, without systematic means for projecting ahead the types and quantities needed. It knows that it takes time to produce and transport these physical items, and that they are not always available at the snap of a finger. But few organizations take the same care with the replenishment of their manpower. Large industries have begun to take this process seriously, and a number of governmental jurisdictions are at least working at it in selected segments of their work forces, as in the case of management internships and certain professional categories, but overall schemes of analysis and projection of manpower needs are still more honored in lip service than in practice.[3]

The major feature of modern society that makes such neglect foolhardy is change. The expansion of automation, unceasing mutations in technology, revisions in occupational technique and content, continuous extension and elaboration of educational offerings, to say nothing of the normal vicissitudes of public policy and programs, together make for unending shifts in emphasis and demand on the supply of manpower. Planning would be comparatively simple if it were not for the inexorable operation of such phenomena.

Government, above all, as it has assumed an ever more important role in society, must be mindful of both its own inescapable needs for personnel of all stripes and its impact on the total labor market. Leading manpower economists have directed special attention to public employment in these strong terms: "Clearly, the nation cannot afford either mediocrity or severe shortages in the public service. Government must have access to substantial proportions of its talented, highly educated and trained, and creative men and women."[4]

REQUISITES FOR ASSESSMENT

Manpower analysis is less a settled discipline than it is a philosophy and technique in the process of development. It is perhaps, like the classical

---

[3] In a survey in late 1972 of 354 private and public employers, it was found that 22 percent of local governments, 43 percent of private corporations and state governments, and nearly 90 percent of federal agencies were carrying out modern manpower planning, but only two-thirds of these programs covered all positions in the respective organizations (District of Columbia Government Personnel Office, *Manpower Planning: The State of the Art*, Washington, D.C., April 1973, pp. i and ii).

[4] The National Manpower Council, *Government and Manpower*, New York, Columbia University Press, 1964, p. 4.

The demand for professional and technical workers is expected to increase by about 45 percent during the 1970s, twice the rate for all workers (U.S. Department of Labor, *News Release*, January 7, 1970).

definition of the ballet, "a science on top of which an art is precariously balanced." But there are some principles and conditions that have emerged from limited experience that deserve enunciation. Even the most sophisticated methodology is but an empty exercise without foundation on sound principle. The principles in this case relate to various environmental factors and to the importance and use of data.[5]

BASIC CONSIDERATIONS   Certain background considerations, while elementary and perhaps obvious to some, deserve first mention:

1. Manpower assessment for government services cannot be considered in a vacuum. The current and future needs of the private sector in the economy should not be ignored, especially for occupations in short supply.
2. A fine degree of precision cannot be expected, especially in initial forecasts of manpower needs, but knowing at least the order of magnitude among various occupations helps in planning educational and training programs, recruiting campaigns, and selection processes.
3. The growth of certain occupations and the number of their practitioners may be limited by scarcity of equipment, space, or technology (for example, sophisticated laboratory equipment, electronic devices, nuclear reactors, or the like).
4. Numbers to be projected may have to be increased for each occupation by an estimated percentage to allow for workers who must be away from the job for advanced training and to allow for less than top productivity of partially trained workers.
5. Careful job reengineering or redesign may be desirable in some activities if necessary functions are to be fitted to the trained manpower available. The demand for scarce technical or professional personnel can be reduced by greater use of more quickly trained subordinate workers who can perform segments of major tasks or processes. At the same time, this process increases opportunities for use of lower-skilled manpower that may be in excess supply.
6. In all personnel planning it is desirable to take into account the training and development possibilities on the job, the adaptations feasible following initial employment.
7. It is important, especially in developing economies, to give high status to mechanics, craftsmen, and technicians—people who can fix things, who are not afraid to work with their hands. Unfortunately, acquiring education or training in many places has been equated with white-collar

[5] The author draws heavily in the planning section of this chapter from his paper "Analyzing Manpower Requirements for the Public Service," prepared for the conference sponsored by the U.N. Economic Commission for Africa, in Addis Ababa, Ethiopia, May 1964, in which the public personnel agencies and institutes of public administration of most African nations were represented.

employment and disdain for manual skills. Yet it is usually this very middle-level manpower that is in serious short supply.

Manpower estimation and projection methods are of little value unless considerations like the foregoing are governing. Environmental factors, the motivational climate, and the occupational prestige values of a people are more basic than the mere devices to gauge the kind and number of posts to be filled. It is better that manpower assessment not be undertaken at all than to neglect principles of the kind just enumerated.

ADEQUATE DATA   Furthermore, analyses and predictions can be no better than the data on which they are based. Reliable information must be available from the general economy as well as from the public service itself. For example, there must be census data at hand on the distribution of the population by broad occupation, the numbers and varieties of graduates from different levels in the education system, and, if possible, unemployment statistics, mobility habits, and the rate of growth or decline of major occupational categories. From within the service itself there must be accurate information on the size and location of all government facilities, the occupational distribution, numbers of persons employed and separated (by category) each year, kinds and amounts of in-service training under way or planned, and, to be sure, developments in the way of new, expanding, or contracting government activities anticipated by public planning or budgeting agencies.

Manpower needs and availability are also affected by other factors, such as birth rates, health and longevity, labor organization, vocational guidance, and military conscription. Knowledge about all such conditions will enrich and make more realistic and useful any analysis of personnel needs and of how they may be met.

Such analyses are more dependent on data about the past in proportion as a nation's public services become more and more stabilized; they are more dependent on predictions about the future to the degree that its public agencies are in transition or are rapidly expanding and changing. Therefore, more reliance can be placed on past turnover as the clearest predictor of manpower needs in a stable employment situation than is the case in a newly developing civil service. Nevertheless, there are precedents that mirror the future in almost every situation. Every government has some experience with the volume of services and kinds of public servants needed in the past, even under previous regimes. A cardinal precept, therefore, is that manpower assessment is inevitably and in great measure characterized by analysis of immediate past history.

Another sine qua non is some form of classification of posts. With or without the most modern techniques of job evaluation, there must be some method of categorizing positions by occupational nature and skill requirements. A common job language is a prerequisite of data collection.

Finally, there are several essentials in the *use* of data for manpower assessment:

1. Periodic analyses and forecasts must be kept up to date. If both annual and longer-range (such as five-year) projections are made, the product of each year's analysis must extend and hence revise the previous long forecast. Thus the process continues indefinitely, refining each projection into the future on the basis of the current year's analysis of fresh information.
2. The results of an analysis and forecast must be used. Nothing affects the quality of a product quite as adversely as an awareness by all parties that it has little or no practical application.
3. Manpower analysis must have the full support of the heads of government. Unless the chief executive and legislative body back the assessment process, it will suffer from lack of resources, lack of data, and lack of utility.

ESTIMATING, COLLECTING, AND RECORDING PROCESSES

In an assessment of government manpower some systematic thinking must be given to the scope of public functions, which may run the gamut from postal services to the generation of atomic energy. For example, a public jurisdiction must look at the current status and prospects for continuance or expansion of activities such as its weather service, air traffic control, social security, agricultural research, and public roads construction. No effort will be made here to explore such questions in depth. For purposes of this chapter, it is sufficient to proceed directly from scope of functions to broad methods of reducing them to quantitative and qualitative factors.

Some functions lend themselves readily to quantitative analysis of these kinds:

1. *Workload:* It is often necessary to estimate the amount of work that may be involved and then to make some judgment as to how many people must be employed to keep up with it. This may be true of delivering mail, auditing tax returns, handling customs, maintaining repair of roads, and the like. The degree of mechanization of the work to be achieved will, of course, affect the manpower requirements.
2. *Standard of performance:* In some instances, the standard of performance desired may be the determining factor. This is especially true where there are no physical workload units to accumulate. Examples might be standards set for teacher-pupil ratios, numbers of public health service officers for each unit of population, number of police officers per unit of population, and so on.
3. *Comparison:* In other cases, we may look at the experience and practice of other jurisdictions to note the staff size and structure of various activities, perhaps for such functions as a national banking system, water

conservation, census, and narcotics control, as well as for the overhead functions of maintaining government structure itself, that is, the budget office, the personnel office, the audit office, and the like.

With respect to qualitative requirements, one must decide on what kinds of skills are needed in the public service for each function and at what levels those skills must be possessed. Here it is helpful, as briefly suggested earlier, to have the following:

1. *Skills classification*—an orderly means of identifying and describing work in such a way that it can be assigned some standard nomenclature or classification and that the kinds of education, training, and experience needed to perform it can be established.
2. *Resource information*—adjusting qualitative requirements to the resources available. This is of particular importance in developing nations. The effect may work two ways in a country without adequate middle-level manpower. On the one hand, it may be necessary to use college-trained lawyers, economists, and engineers at clerical and mechanical levels until nonprofessional manpower is developed for such work. On the other hand, it may be equally necessary to use nonprofessionally trained teachers, accountants, and social workers until adequate numbers of professionally trained people in these fields are available. The responsible leaders of government must decide on the level of staff skills desired for each function.

It would follow, of course, that if estimated requirements, either quantitative or qualitative, were initially based on either objective (such as workload) or subjective considerations (such as standard of performance or professional skill level desired), careful attention should thereafter be given to trends and changes in such bases (in particular, such changes as population growth, economic development, government workload, new skills produced by the educational system, and feasibility of higher standards of performance).

Concurrent with or following estimation of general requirements for some period in the future, it is necessary to collect and record information regarding the current and projected work force in each sector of public employment. This constitutes a base upon which personnel officials may project needs by occupation. From such a tabulation it is possible to see the size and occupational distribution of the staff, the numbers needed for normal replacement, and the projections of need by occupation into the future.

The occupational data from various departments may be accumulated by simply adding up the individual reports. But this is possible only when all of the figures are reported under a standard system of occupational definitions. Normally, these occupational facts should be reported annually.

Likewise, annual estimates of loses and expansion would be called for. As to the matter of recording loses, it is important to distinguish between (1) those who leave an occupation entirely (that is, by resignation, death, retirement, or movement to a different occupation) and (2) those who merely leave a particular office or job but remain within the occupational category.

Projections, in turn, may be translated from overall public service requirements into occupational needs by

—accumulating estimates of program growth or contraction for each governmental organization;
—relating this to the current occupational distribution in each such unit;
—translating program needs into occupational categories;
—adding numbers needed to replace current employees, applying past turnover experience; and
—indicating a final projection for each occupation for one or more periods ahead.

A further refinement may consist of estimating what proportion of projected needs can or should be filled by trainee or entry-level personnel in the occupation and what proportion requires direct appointment of journeyman-level or fully operating professional personnel.

Hence, basic data collection forms supplied to each reporting unit can provide, at one and the same time, a means for reporting data, for tabulation and accumulation of data, and for projection of needs by occupation.

DETERMINING PROBABLE SOURCES OF MANPOWER

Having pulled together the analyses and estimates from individual offices of the government, the personnel staff next considers sources for supplying the need. How many people are being trained in the occupation, either in general educational institutions or in specialized institutes established in the service? How many more can be attracted to enter into training? How many can be attracted or moved from other occupations or from other employers in the region or country?

These and other questions require a program of reporting by various organizations somewhat parallel to reporting on the work force. Thus, each governmental entity, such as a department of agriculture or of public works, may be asked to list those educational institutions or other sources at home or elsewhere from which it expects to draw candidates for employment, including how many are available from each such source per year. If there are any duplications among these sources, as submitted by individual departments, these must be weeded out by the personnel staff. Such source data can be reported on parallel forms with information arranged by occupation, so that these lists can be laid alongside the work-force estimates and conclusions drawn about what should be done to help assure that supply will match demand for each category.

CONCLUDING STEPS

Following collection of information and analyses by individual parts of the government on both work-force and supply data, individual tally sheets for each separate occupation make it possible to consolidate all of the information regarding a particular occupation that exists in more than one government establishment and to see at a glance the picture regarding the current situation, future needs, and the degree to which existing sources offer a possibility of supplying those needs. The net deficit of needs that are not being planned for indicates the degree to which special preparations are required, such as additional or accelerated training, reengineering of jobs to accommodate to skills available, or stepped-up recruitment.

No great purpose is served by reporting and tabulating work-force and supply information unless some decisions are made and action taken based on the data. For example, should more money be put into vocational schools? Should recruitment begin for a particular occupation, and in what places? Where there appears to be no early hope of finding an adequate supply of a particular skill, should job analysts try to dissect the work and organize it into two or more subskills, each of which might be trained for in a shorter time than the overall skill? Should special government training programs be inaugurated? Such are the issues that are pointed up by a sound program of manpower analysis.

There are two concluding observations that appear overriding: (1) Since much depends on estimates, it is clear that the best of plans will only provide an approximation; but this is much better than not knowing even the approximation. (2) Manpower planning must be attuned to the specific situation. No master design can fit all conditions. Hence, each operation must be especially tailored to fit conditions of a particular jurisdiction. Some of the variables that will influence methods of analysis and estimating are the scope and extent of development of various government functions; the extent of public education; the nature and development of the public personnel system (methods of hiring, pay, tenure, mobility, retirement, discipline, and training); the adequacy of census data; and the existence and refinement of manpower information for the economy as a whole.

It is better that there be an awareness of these considerations than for any employer to copy too quickly the practices already in operation in another location.[6]

---

[6] For a number of years until 1970 the U.S. Civil Service Commission produced governmentwide employment projections for four-year spans in most nontrade occupations in the federal service, reported in a brief but interesting annual document, *Federal Workforce Outlook*. Unfortunately it was of such little interest to operating managers that it was discontinued. So far, what passes for manpower planning in government agencies is compartmentalized by department or program with scant attention to overall government needs and trends.

RECRUITMENT AND ATTRACTION POLICIES

Following assessment of personnel needs and estimation of probable capacity of the economy to fill those needs, a government personnel agency must discover specific sources of good candidates, both outside and inside the service, and systematically cultivate those sources. Of course, there is much more to the total selection process, but the step of active recruitment and attraction of potential employees is fundamental to the attainment of a genuine merit system.

THE FIELD OF RECRUITMENT

Superficially, all persons possessing specified qualifications are prospective recruits for the public service. But, in actuality, various circumstances contrive to place limitations on the area open to government recruitment. Attention has already been given, at some length, to two most powerful conditions: (1) the attitudes prevailing in the general population toward public employment, or, in other words, the prestige such work has in the popular mind; and (2) the salaries and emoluments offered by governments. Although there has been notable relief on both scores in recent years, both have historically in the United States tended to blight the efforts of public jurisdictions to secure the quality and quantity of manpower to which they should have been entitled. The only offsetting forces have been: (1) the sheer attraction of much government work, based on its glamour, challenge, or fascination (but such pulling power has been confined to limited areas of activity); and (2) periodic conditions of unemployment in the general economy.

In addition, the character of the education system and various self-imposed restrictions, such as citizenship, residence, age limits, sex, and veteran preference, have likewise taken their toll on the recruitment field. Each of these deserves some analysis.

EDUCATION   The state as employer is always influenced by the state as educator, and the character of the education system to a considerable extent determines that of the civil service. For a long time the emphasis in American educational institutions on acquisition of specialized techniques to the neglect of conceptual understanding, a natural concomitant of minute division of labor, had led civil services to minimize educational achievement as an index to capacity and to build much of the selection process around fitting individuals already trained into more or less rigidly specified pigeonholes. Acknowledging that this era has pretty much passed, we may still perceive some of its unfortunate effects, especially on the public mind.

Almost all jurisdictions with a personnel program worthy of the name have emphasized two features: (1) recruitment of young people educated in a variety of disciplines to enter training internships, with a view to their ultimately being used in a variety of managerial or program posts; and

(2) in-service training to enlarge the perspectives of specialists who necessarily got their start in the organization in relatively narrow fields of work. As we observed in the chapter on career systems, many governments of the world had approached this subject differently: keeping each technical field as it developed in a separate compartment, and providing another and coordinating compartment for those specializing in "administration"—a function usually undefined. By and large, the American practice of accepting specialists of all stripes and giving them growth experiences and training within the government, permitting any and all to reach whatever top rungs they demonstrate fitness for, has worked best and contributed to a better motivated, more cohesive work force.

In spite of earlier disdain of public administrators for education per se, except the most technical kinds, the mutual cooperation that has evolved between public jurisdictions and universities in the past few decades has been little short of miraculous. Planned and purposeful visits of government recruiters to college campuses are now the rule rather than the exception, even though some college placement officers have yet to update their own perceptions of what government employment is all about. In this closer liaison much has been studied and learned about college graduates and their success on the job, including the finding that personal characteristics and capacity are more important to later success than is the prestige or alleged quality of the institution attended.[7] Likewise it has been found time and again that the best students are more attracted by the nature and challenge of the work than they are by "fringe" benefits, a lesson still not appreciated by many employers.

AFFIRMATIVE ACTION   Beginning in the 1960s public agencies in the United States have been mindful of the need to extend their campus recruiting efforts to include all schools and all races. It had been common for institutions which had predominately black or other minority students to be overlooked in the scouring of the country for candidates. Although the response is not always encouraging, the only sensible policy that can be followed in a free, open society is to bring the same, perhaps even more, resources to bear upon recruitment campaigns in these colleges as anywhere else, in order to make certain that talent of whatever race or color is earnestly sought for government service careers. Reluctance of graduates of neglected institutions to give credibility to the genuineness of such efforts should not discourage continued emphasis on them, for time and sincere attempts to make good placements will surely offset understandable suspicions. The only way any minority group can be gradually brought into more meaningful participation in a society that has discriminated against it is to make sure that its members are given every

---

[7] For example, consult the findings of the U.S. Civil Service Commission in its nationwide network of university recruiting experiences and its test research. Also, note Alexander W. Astin, "Undergraduate Achievement and Institutional Excellence," summarized in *Science*, August 16, 1968, pp. 661–667.

avenue, every bit of information, and every opportunity to enable them to compete on personal merit and fitness alone.

CREDENTIALISM   Before we leave the subject of education as an influence on the field of recruitment, a word must be said about the tendency to rely too heavily on college degrees or other school credentials as *automatic* indicators of quality. As some thoughtful persons have contended, we have become an overcredentialed society. Each occupational group, from barbers to medical doctors, has organized itself in such a way as to make its "club" hard to enter, to attain a kind of exclusiveness. Invariably this becomes expressed in the form of some licensing, certification, or educational qualification that originally had a meritorious objective in seeking to eliminate charlatanism and fakery but, more often than not, was designed long before validation techniques on the relevancy of specific requirements to performance were well developed. Indeed, most of them have been established by arm-chair cerebration of eager leaders in the occupation rather than objective job analysis and study of job success.

Naturally, with the onset and expansion of the merit system in public employment, such arbitrary standards were seized upon by personnel agencies as convenient eliminators that would simplify the processing of mass applications. The most notorious offender was public education itself, by establishing for the teaching profession (usually embedded in state law) minimum requirements, in number of credit hours, for all manner of special courses in educational methods. Strangely, these standards seldom called for anything as stringent in the subject matter being taught. Thus, it has not been uncommon for persons with demonstrated experience and ability gained in teaching abroad or in private schools to be ineligible to teach in public ones. A majority of states still do not require language teachers to be able to speak the language they are to teach but exclude highly qualified speakers of the language if they have not had the requisite number of hours in education courses.[8] Nowhere is there a better illustration of the tenacious and myopic restrictions imposed by an organized profession (except possibly in the medical field) than those that have successfully been saddled on the public by the schools and departments of education in the various states.

Some relief in the arbitrariness of educational requirements has been

---

[8] The hazards of overreliance on positive and detailed education requirements are brilliantly exposed in an address "Changing the Pecking Odder," delivered by the then U.S. Commissioner of Education, Harold Howe II, before the College Entrance Examination Board, in Chicago, October 24, 1967. He expressed concern that "the route into an increasing number of occupations is a specific educational route and, for some professions, that route begins close to infancy and makes no provision for detours."

Albert H. Aronson described overemphasis on licensure and diplomas as "equating persons by status in a caste," ignoring individual abilities, and as categorizing "the anointed and the unanointed." It limits entrance to a field "from related ancillary work, developing artificial shortages and promoting a closed guild approach. . . ." From an address, "Capacity, Credentials and Careers," delivered at the Institute on New Careers in Warrenton, Virginia, March 4, 1968.

forthcoming in many jurisdictions for a wide range of occupations, but those in public education have been slowest to change. No public merit system should prescribe precise degrees or courses as absolute essentials for entry to any position or career without allowing for acceptance of the "equivalent" experience or training that may be offered by extraordinary candidates who can obviously perform the work successfully.

CITIZENSHIP   Briefer attention may be given to the other constraints on the recruitment field. One of these is citizenship. Practically all American jurisdictions have some requirement that candidates be U.S. citizens. Ordinarily this is not unreasonable, but occasionally exceptions are necessary. Some units of government, including the federal service, have the authority to waive this requirement, usually to fill highly specialized posts for which candidates are extremely rare. Also, a major exception is in the employment of thousands of foreign nationals at military bases and other U.S. establishments abroad.[9]

RESIDENCE   A more serious limitation arises out of the restriction of candidates for state or local government to residence in local areas of such jurisdictions. This is another hangover of the concept of public jobs as gift property, bound up with the idea that each community should "take care" of its own. Although the most routine jobs may just as well be filled by local residents, the place of residence of persons in technical or professional fields hardly contributes to an appraisal of their relative qualifications to do the work. It is to the credit of many public jurisdictions that residence restrictions are gradually being deemphasized. At least key positions have long been filled from broader than local labor markets. Also, the long-standing apportionment provisions of the federal civil service law, requiring distribution of appointments to the headquarters service in Washington, D.C., in proportion to state population, have been waived for so many categories of employment and candidates that they are no longer important constraints.

AGE   Age limits likewise are loosening up. Although minimum age requirements are still common, these have become sufficiently realistic for the most part that they certainly do not interfere with direct recruitment from school. At the other end of the scale, maximum age limits, the public service has usually had a more enlightened policy than much of private business. The federal government has no maximum limit in the competitive civil service, and it has a mandatory retirement age higher than most other employers. The growing proportion of the population in the middle- and upper-age brackets and positive efforts in government welfare programs to

---

[9] The situation in state and local civil services is somewhat different than in the federal government. Courts have begun to question the constitutionality of rejection of noncitizens by states, as a violation of the Fourteenth Amendment on "equal protection of the laws."

overcome foolish and unreasonable restrictions on age have combined to change the antiquated ideas on this subject entertained by many employers.

Chronological age is no measure of competence or even of good health. About the only circumstances under which age restrictions may properly continue are: for the minimum, to protect against the exploitation of children; and for the maximum, to apply to jobs calling for extraordinary physical stamina or agility, such as electric lineman, mining engineer, or heavy-duty truck driver, and to trainee jobs in which the investment in training must be recouped by some prospect of continued employment for a number of years.

VETERAN PREFERENCE   Since the subject of preference in public employment for military veterans is dealt with at length in a later chapter,[10] suffice it to say here that, insofar as it exists, it is a constraint on the field of recruitment in view of the handicap placed on nonveterans. Preference does operate, however, to relax for veterans themselves some of the other constraints, such as educational, age, or physical requirements.

SEX   Finally, there has been the sex barrier to recruitment, its elimination the product of a lengthy struggle and one not yet concluded. Although there are few formal prohibitions against the employment of women, sex discrimination does continue in the latitude left to appointing officials who in some places may still specify "male only" when requesting lists of eligible candidates without having to prove that women would be unsuitable for the work. Other places, like the federal service, allow the official such leeway only in very limited cases, and then he must fully support the absolute necessity for it.

In brief, then, as far as the sources for recruitment are concerned, the personnel agency has a consistent, though twofold, task: (1) to eliminate or modify those restrictions of the recruitment field that are not contributory to an effective public service and (2) to enlist into competition as many promising candidates as possible so that real meaning is given to the objective of selecting the best.

METHODS OF RECRUITMENT AND ATTRACTION

Getting the most competent and promising people to make themselves available has not always been a major aim of public merit systems. As indicated earlier, the practice of posting unattractive civil service examination announcements in post offices and city halls reflected outmoded assumptions that qualified candidates were clamoring for jobs and that the main thrust of a personnel agency's task was to keep the crowd down to manageable proportions. This conception of the nature of the labor market has been

[10] Chapter 9.

recognized as mistaken for so long that few jurisdictions can now be accused of harboring such notions.

Typical of the more enterprising recruiting methods used by public agencies and destined to be further developed are these:

1. Intensive cultivation of newspaper, radio, and television outlets for news about public job opportunities, usually on a "public service" basis but often supplemented by imaginative paid advertising. College and trade journals are also useful media.
2. Maintenance and use of extensive mailing lists of schools, labor unions, vocational counseling offices, and particularly of organized occupational groups—professional, technical, or trade—including their membership lists, where appropriate. Depending on the occupation, the relevant organizations or their memberships are circularized with attractive and informative data about job and career opportunities.
3. Inviting individuals to specify their vocational interests for future reference. When positions open up, such expressions (coded and recorded on electronic equipment) yield automatic mailing lists for distribution, direct to potential applicants, of information about examination and hiring procedure.
4. Careful development of long-term institutional relationships with teachers, editors, influential professional men and women, and labor leaders.
5. Preparation and strategic distribution of well-illustrated pamphlets, each on a separate occupation or profession in the service and the career possibilities it offers.
6. For college-level positions, particularly at junior entrance level, a career directory like that produced by the U.S. Civil Service Commission. It indexes and illustrates opportunities by college major as well as by occupational field and emphasizes the kind of work programs in which the positions exist. This is a valuable tool to have available in liberal numbers in university placement offices.
7. Periodic visits, displays, and programs directed to college campuses to interest students in government work.
8. Maintaining dramatic and informative exhibits of government careers at conventions, state fairs, and similar assemblages where large numbers of persons are in attendance.
9. Holding "open house" periodically in those agencies which have functions that lend themselves to public display—whether it be the local waterworks or a space science laboratory.
10. Personal letters to college seniors or high school seniors in relevant institutions.
11. Use of tourist bureau materials—colorful, descriptive booklets and maps—especially for out-of-area prospects.
12. Exploitation of contest publicity to attract interest in public institutions and jobs.

It will be observed that many of these techniques are of an institutional character, that is, not designed to recruit for a specific need of the moment but to develop a general awareness and sympathetic understanding by a segment of the public regarding a government jurisdiction or some of its functions.

The significance of a systematically developed recruitment policy cannot be overemphasized. The very character of any organization will in the long run depend on the quality and character of the recruits who are brought in from time to time. Many methods have been devised and tried out which should be adapted to local conditions. Resourcefulness and ingenuity should constantly be brought into play. The employment market is ever changing, as are the demands of the public agency. Contacts with education institutions should be assiduously cultivated, not alone because their officers can serve as employment aides in securing leads, but also because they may be stimulated to organize or modify courses which will provide better preentry training for prospective public servants.

Furthermore, it is incumbent upon the personnel agency to test the success of its various recruitment policies by keeping a check on the results. Just as advertisers and advertising agencies check on the effectiveness of their publicity efforts, so should the personnel agency evaluate its publicity practices.

Finally, the status and prestige of the public service are immeasurably improved through advances in public employment policies. These advances must be maintained. There can be no resting on the oars. The employment market in a healthy economy is a highly competitive one. With its new and expanding functions the government as an employer can ill afford to content itself with anything less than the better, if not the best, ability available.

APPLICATION PROCEDURE

The goal of recruiting activities is the production of an adequate number of qualified applicants for employment. Recruitment ends with an application; the examining process begins with one. Application procedures constitute, therefore, the connecting links between recruitment and other aspects of the selection process. In addition, they make important contributions to individual placement, discussed at another point in this book. Their proper handling is, therefore, of strategic importance.

It goes without saying that the two most fundamental requisites of sound application procedure are (1) to facilitate determining whether the applicant is basically qualified to compete and (2) to ensure that unnecessary barriers to admission to competition are eliminated. The design of the application form and the processes through which it is put by personnel officers must take these objectives into account. Even as an information tool, the form not only must yield data for immediate selection purposes—identification, education, experience, etc.—but should ordinarily fit in as a part of permanent personnel records if the applicant is eventually employed, lending itself to ready supplementation in future years to cover added education, professional honors, and the like.

A word should be inserted here about the outmoded practice of calling for a separate application for each examination or occupation for which the applicant wishes to be considered, a traditional shortcoming of the American version of the merit system. A single application for any occupation or post that the candidate is qualified for has been tried successfully in many places and certainly makes sense. The applicant should not have to predetermine the positions for which he may qualify. Under this procedure the old method of separate application for each examination, with precise closing dates for each, is discarded.

The common procedure now consists of so-called open-continuous registers of eligible candidates built up and maintained by a constant supply of fresh applications from new candidates. Of course, where written tests are held periodically or where the recruitment is directed at temporary employment, such as summer jobs for students, cut-off dates must be established. In any event, except to bring applications up to date when long periods have elapsed, there is no reason (with all the modern recording and duplicating equipment available) for any jurisdiction not to accept a one-time application for a variety of posts under the same personnel system.

Another approach in this regard is to broaden the whole examination procedure, from recruitment and application to examination and placement. By this is meant the use of broad-coverage examinations under which many kinds of positions are filled at comparable levels and for which general intelligence tests and only general educational or experience qualifications are prescribed, such as the several broad-band examination procedures of the federal civil service, the best known of which is the Professional and Administrative Career Examination,[11] directed at but not confined to college graduates.

Applications must be thoroughly audited before the formal examination, whether written or not, in order to (1) check for completeness of data on application forms, (2) determine that the applicant has met the legal requirements for eligibility, and (3) determine that the applicant meets minimum entrance qualifications.

The most difficult step in the review, and the one requiring the greatest amount of technical knowledge, is unquestionably that in which the presence or absence of minimum training and experience qualifications is ascertained. It is difficult to define objectively the factors involved and to assess properly the many possible combinations of "equivalent" training and experience. Although the complex question of rating these factors will be discussed at a later point, the task of ascertaining the fact of eligibility in terms of qualifications may be touched upon here. It is by no means simple. Even when the fields of acceptable education and experience have been

---

[11] Formerly the Federal Service Entrance Examination.

defined in specific terms, unforeseen combinations will emerge. Decisions must be made as to the circumstances under which the applicant's education will affect the acceptability of certain experience, and vice versa. Types of experience unfamiliar to the reviewer may emerge and require a careful study of their relevance to the work applied for. Only well-trained examiners are competent to perform this phase of the review, assisted by various devices to help standardize the process as much as possible.

It should be added that applications may be rejected not only because an individual proves ineligible by failure to meet legal or qualification requirements but also for fraud or misrepresentation.

Finally, there should be a right of appeal. This is both a natural concomitant of a democratic, open service and a form of insurance to permit correction of inevitable mistakes and to serve as an incentive to the examining agency to keep its review processes as accurate as possible. No process or agency is so infallible that it would not profit from the challenges presented by appeals. Normally the person or body reviewing appeals of applicants should be someone or include someone other than those involved in the original decision of rejection.

*   *   *

A MERIT SYSTEM does not live up to its name unless it plans systematically to replenish its manpower, unless the field within which it may seek applicants is a broad and unfettered as possible, and unless it uses as modern and as aggressive recruitment methods as it can find or invent. If the manpower assessment and recruitment program does not reach out and attract the best minds and skills to apply for employment, then the rest of the staffing process consists merely of a sorting out among the mediocre and the ill qualified.

CHAPTER 8

Methods of Examination

THE CORNERSTONE OF public personnel systems is built upon competitive examinations, the answer to the twin demands of democracy and of good administration. Historically they were the means by which equality of opportunity was to be united with efficiency. From the beginning, the merit system has placed special emphasis upon formal selection procedures.

However, as evident from the preceding chapter, selection of persons for employment is as dependent on securing the interest and willingness of good candidates to apply as it is on separating the strong from the weak. What is said in the present chapter about selection methods must be taken as relative. The utility of sound and discriminating selection procedures is questionable, to say the least, if the raw material of selection—the candidates —includes few or no individuals worthy of appointment. Hence, overdependence on even the most modern type of formal selection tools and neglect of building an attractive organization, of assuring career opportunities, of maintaining satisfactory working conditions and compensation, and of pressing aggressive recruitment can be a most disappointing and disillusioning experience.

Nevertheless, the methods of examination can be very important. Other factors being equal, they can spell the difference between a top-notch service and a mediocre one. No merit system worthy of the name can afford to take less than a fully professional approach to examining applicants for employment. In today's government, with its world-shaking responsibilities and its vast range of occupations and skills, nothing less than the best examination system ought to be tolerated. This is especially true when we consider the need to select for potential leadership as well as for immediate jobs.

To avoid confusion, emphasis must also be placed on some matters of definition. In many places, particularly in schools and colleges, the terms *examination* and *test* (usually meaning written test) are commonly used synonymously. They are not necessarily synonymous in the public service. *Examination*, the broader term, usually embraces a number of steps—sometimes in combination, sometimes used alternatively—designed to facilitate comparative selection. Among these steps there may be any of a variety of *tests*, written, oral, or otherwise. Perhaps the meanings will be clearer as we explore the underlying assumptions of an examination process and the varying forms of examination.

FOUNDATION FOR THE EXAMINATION PROCESS

The purposes and techniques of examination for employment in the public service are not peculiar to modern times. Records of several ancient civilizations—the Chinese, Egyptian, Persian, Greek, Roman—show evidences of interest, ranging from identification of problems in examining to remarkably substantial efforts in dealing with them. But not before this century had the matter been reduced to a science.[1]

FACTORS IN EMPLOYMENT SELECTION

The starting points for modern examining processes are basically two: (1) a determination of the objective for selection, which may be a given position, occupation, program, or service-wide career; and (2) a setting of basic standards for selection, that is, what skills and knowledge are necessary to meet the preceding objective.

At one time the emphasis in public merit systems was on "practical testing" to fill a specific job. Nowadays much more attention is given to selection of persons who possess a capacity for growth and development. Not that all candidates can anticipate advancement to the top rungs, or even that all selection must be so focused on long-range placement; nevertheless, a great deal of government recruiting and selection must be fashioned to ensure at least an adequate intake of the highest-caliber people at all levels so that there will be no dearth of talent when movement upward or outward in the service takes place.

---

[1] For comprehensive textbooks on the theory and techniques of psychological measurement, see Lee J. Cronbach, *Essentials of Psychological Testing*, 3rd ed., New York, Harper & Row, 1970; and C. H. Lawshe and Michael J. Balma, *Principles of Personnel Testing*, 2nd ed., New York, McGraw-Hill, 1966. The standard work for government is J. J. Donovan, ed., *Recruitment and Selection in the Public Service*, Chicago, International Personnel Management Association, 1968.

The best up-to-date technical manual for the public service is also published by the latter organization: Grace H. Wright, ed., *Public Sector Employment Selection; A Manual for the Personnel Generalist*, 1974. It covers the standard processes on a how-to-do-it basis, as well as dealing thoroughly with current problems of validation of tests and legal issues.

The second starting point calls for the establishment of specific requirements for entry, whether for individual positions or a broad field of work. Such requirements are commonly referred to as "qualification standards" or "qualification requirements." When applied to a single position or occupation such standards are ideally derived from the process of job analysis discussed earlier. These standards must first of all be expressed in terms of the particular knowledge and skills required to perform the work involved.

Knowledge and skills are in turn translated into the specific or general education and/or experience requirements that are deemed to demonstrate the possession of such knowledge and skills. This is a weak link in many selection systems. Job analysis does not produce a qualification standard expressed in terms of a number of years of education, training, or experience. It can only shed light on how much or what kind of knowledge, capacity, or skill is needed. What may actually demonstrate the possession of these requisites is part of the examination process itself. There is a great temptation arbitrarily to translate skills needed into concrete education and experience requirements. Therefore, such requirements must frequently be kept at a bare minimum so as to give full play to the operation of more refined procedures, such as valid written tests, to distinguish among candidates as to how well they evidence possession of skills and information needed for the work.[2]

Other elementary factors that are taken into account in devising selection methods are:

1. *Public relations.* A selection or examining process must be plausible and acceptable to be successful. Even when it is technically sound, consideration must be given to whether the procedure superficially appears to be sound—that is, whether it has "face validity."
2. *The status of the employment market.* In times of labor shortage every employer, including the public service, is sometimes forced to accept lower standards and therefore less able recruits than might be desired. This affects the rigidity with which certain examination standards can be adhered to. It also calls for more strenuous recruitment efforts. On the other hand, when large numbers of people are unemployed, entrance standards can sometimes be tightened to avoid useless testing of unneeded numbers of applicants.
3. *Cost utility.* The "ideal" selection process for any given purpose is not always attainable if it is extremely costly. Few techniques are so thoroughly proved that an employer can afford to ignore their cost in relation to their specific purpose and their probability of producing exceptionally good results. During World War II the Office of Strategic Services spent many weeks examining each candidate for overseas intelligence work, but such an expensive process could hardly be justified in order to assure us of honest postal clerks, efficient firemen, or even competent highway engi-

---

[2] See the discussion of overreliance on arbitrary credentials in the section "The Field of Recruitment" in the preceding chapter.

neers. The point is that in using such devices we might not improve on the effectiveness of much simpler and cheaper processes sufficiently to warrant such an extraordinary outlay for these needs, which are less critical than spying behind enemy lines in time of war.

Any well-conceived examination—particularly a written, oral, or performance test—is an instrument for measuring or evaluating a sample of behavior as a basis for prediction of probable future behavior. Its essence is to extract a cross-section of a typical life situation in which the behavior of the candirates may be evaluated by observation or review. How this is achieved may perhaps be clearer as this discussion unfolds.

CRITERIA FOR THE EFFECTIVENESS
OF SELECTION METHODS

Three primary considerations enter into the effectiveness and the propriety of examination processes: objectivity, validity, and reliability.

OBJECTIVITY   One of the prime reasons for professionalizing all steps in the examining system is to ensure thoroughgoing *objectivity*. Only those devices which disregard extraneous factors such as race, religion, politics, sex, residence, and chronological age can be considered thoroughly objective. The objectivity sought is in terms of identifying those characteristics of mind and skill necessary to the given purpose, and only those necessary, whether the purpose be to fill a particular position or to begin a career.

VALIDITY   Examinations, especially in the form of written tests, should also have *validity*, that is, they should actually measure what they purport to measure. A perfectly valid test would rate prospective employees in exactly the same relationship to one another as they would stand after trial on the job. Perfect validity is practically impossible to achieve. Reasonable validity, however, is not only possible but indispensable.[3] Selection upon the basis of tests which have no known validity may be little different from selection upon the basis of the turn of a card. Yet some public personnel agencies in the United States are still using tests which have not been subjected to this criterion.

The process of determining the validity of a test involves statistical correlation between the test results and some criterion of efficiency on the job. Where the worker is engaged in production activities to which it is easy to adapt unit measurements, the question of the criterion presents no problem. Thus, the efficiency of a typist can be gauged by the speed and accuracy of the work accomplished, that of an assembler by the number of pieces assembled in a given time, and so forth. But the simplicity of the problem disappears when

[3] A useful reference is Edwin E. Ghiselli, *The Validity of Occupational Aptitude Tests*, New York, John Wiley, 1966. For a sound but brief treatment, see Vernon R. Taylor, *Test Validity in Public Personnel Selection*, Chicago, International Personnel Management Association, 1971.

attention is directed toward an adequate criterion of efficiency for police officers, let us say, or civil engineers or psychiatrists. In these cases and many others the researcher must rely upon appraisals by those closely acquainted with the work of the employees.

There are two procedures by which the validity of a test is determined, each supplementary to the other. In the first instance, the test may be administered to employees of known ability already on the job. If those employees who are known to be most efficient score highest on the test while the least efficient employees score lowest, the test has validity. The second procedure in checking on the validity of a test, and one that should be employed to supplement the foregoing, consists in follow-up studies of the performance of those employees who have been selected through it. No test can be said to be truly valid until both these procedures have been employed. Underfinancing has prevented enough endeavor along these lines in public personnel agencies.

One of the benefits of contemporary pressures for equal employment opportunity has been to awaken greater interest in validity studies. Managers and legislators, as well as personnel specialists, now appreciate the importance of investing resources to verify the appropriateness of selection measures.[4]

---

[4] Unfortunately, this healthy pressure for equal opportunity is occasionally marred by court decisions that demonstrate a shocking misunderstanding of the meaning of validity. For example, in a number of cases, examinations are declared biased against minority candidates on the mere grounds that more minority members fail the test than members of the majority white groups, when such a condition can be explained by a variety of causes. In one such case, when the U.S. Circuit Court of Appeals of the District of Columbia asserted in a split decision in 1975 that the district police department's extrance examination discriminated against blacks, Judge Spottswood Robinson III supported the decision on grounds that were irrelevant to the merits of the examination itself. Referring to the higher proportion of blacks who failed the test, he argued: "This phenomenon is the result of the long history of educational deprivation, primarily due to segregated schools, for blacks. Until arrival of the day when the effects of that deprivation have been completely dissipated, comparable performance on such tests can hardly be expected." The point might just as well have been made in defense of the test. It was not designed to take into account educational deprivation or any other factor that might have influenced the backgrounds of candidates. The purpose, among others, was to measure some skills in the use of the English language; the fact that some candidates had not acquired such skill in adequate amount, no matter what their color, was precisely what the test sought to ferret out. It is understandable that the one judge of the three-man panel who opposed the majority decision, Judge Roger Robb, retorted with the observation: "In short, issuing a badge and a gun to a semiliterate cannot transform him into a competent police officer. . . . In my judgment, the majority opinion is a step backward that will lead to debasing the quality of our police force" *Davis* v. *Washington et al.*, February 27, 1975.

In spite of these occasional decisions that illustrate fuzzy, illogical, and sometimes downright prejudiced thinking, most court opinions ruling in this area have focused on the relevance of the examination in question to the occupation for which it is designed. When they have done so, they have reinforced the plea that conscientious personnel officers have been making for years—to spend the time and money necessary to ensure that tests really measure what they purport to measure. This is the thrust of the oft-cited 1971 decision of the U.S. Supreme Court in *Griggs* v. *Duke Power Company*, which is further discussed in footnote 10 in this chapter.

The best discussion of court decisions on the general subject of testing is in Chapter 8, "Validation Concepts and Legal Issues," by Mary Tenopyr, in Wright, ed., *op. cit.*

RELIABILITY   Finally, by the *reliability* of a test is meant the consistency with which it serves as a measuring instrument. If a test is reliable, a person taking it at two different times should make substantially the same score each time. Under ideal conditions a test can never be any more than a sample of the ability being measured. Because of this fact the sample should be as representative as it is possible to make it. No test is of value in personnel work unless it has a high degree of reliability. This is usually determined by one of three methods: (1) by giving the test to the same group at two separate times and correlating the resultant series of test scores, (2) by giving two or more different (but equivalent) forms of the same test and correlating the resulting test scores, or (3) by giving the test only once but dividing the items and correlating scores on one-half of the items with scores on the other half.

LIMITATIONS OF SELECTION METHODS

THE CRITICS   From time to time skepticism is expressed about the use of technical measuring instruments, especially written tests, for purposes of college entrance or employment. Some attacks on testing have been useful in forcing psychologists to take greater care in the choice of test items and to warn school and personnel officials against use of tests for wrong purposes, while others have been more in the nature of wild broadsides displaying a complete lack of understanding of the process.[5] Also, the misuse of phrases such as "psychological testing" (which refers to almost any kind of mental test) when dealing with what is really only a very limited field properly known as "personality testing" (which all reputable test experts acknowledge is the most tenuous area of appraisal and which is questioned later in this chapter) has led to wholesale condemnation of ethical, scientific-oriented practices along with underdeveloped aspects and the depredations of charlatans. Some writers, having gained a little acquaintance with the most discredited devices and practices, proceed to censure the entire concept.

The most serious damage done by the extremists has been to divert attention away from legitimate and responsible criticism of testing. Frustration over the poor test showing of people deprived of good schooling should not be used to deprive such persons still further of learning of the need for

[5] Several books, such as the following, stirred up interest in the subject in the early 1960s: Martin L. Gross, *The Brain Watchers*, New York, Random House 1962; Banesh Hoffmann, *The Tyranny of Testing*, New York, Crowell-Collier, 1962; and Vance Packard, *The Pyramid Climbers*, New York, McGraw-Hill, 1962. The Gross book, while professing to deal with all testing, actually treats only personality assessment, which has long been challenged by competent measurement psychologists. Neither the Hoffmann nor the Packard volume cites any real supporting evidence for its charges. But, all three, as may be guessed from their titles, are colorfully written and thereby gained considerable notoriety.

Other critics had been William H. Whyte, Jr., in *The Organization Man*, New York, Harper & Row, 1956, and Jacques Barzun in *The House of Intellect*, New York, Harper & Row, 1959; but these writers were more directly questioning reliance on pure intelligence as a sole criterion of success, a doubt that would certainly be shared by many managers.

correction of their deficiencies. Test makers and test users may be blamed for not having come up with devices to gauge qualities such as creativity, imagination, and drive. They may be blamed for not having been as determined as they might have been in warning against or preventing misuse of or overreliance on tests for purposes for which they were never intended and could never fully serve. But there are sound and supportable means to measure a variety of mental abilities and aptitudes that serve many educational and vocational purposes.[6]

One problem is that too many people have had too blind a faith in tests. None of the tests or other selection devices described in this chapter is infallible. But putting them to uses which presume that they are is certainly fallible; acting as if a difference of a fraction of one percentage point on two test scores is actually a measurable difference is certainly fallible, to say nothing of being dishonest. Even validity as a statistical concept deals with groups, not individuals; a test that is valid generally (the results of which conform to job performance better than could be expected by chance alone) cannot be so precise in predicting the performance of any given individual.

IMPORTANCE OF BALANCE   The practice to be guarded against is relying too exclusively on a single device, particularly when it is a written test. The less-than-perfect character of individual techniques of measurement is no cause for despair or abandonment; skilled technicians can find combinations in which the strengths of one method offset the weaknesses of another. Such balance in examination devices also ensures that the various levels of adaptability of candidates to different modes of examination or testing are accommodated. One of the most important caveats in the selection process is to avoid reliance on a *single* examination technique.

Furthermore, no formal device should be viewed as a substitute for judgment but only as an aid to judgment. The reason for seeking objectivity, validity, and reliability in an examination is not to circumvent judgment but to analyze it, direct it, and reinforce it. That is another reason why a single technique alone should not comprise a full examination. A balance of techniques, each supplementing the other, plus allowing room for responsible judgment—if necessary by multiple groups of reviewers—would seem to provide the only safe procedure.

DEFINING THE OBJECTIVE   The worst sins in examining are not inherent in written tests or any other single instrument. They derive from *using the wrong selection instrument*, that is, using something that is inappropriate for

---

[6] Says John W. Gardner: "Whatever their faults, the tests have proven fairer and more reliable than any other method when they are used cautiously within the limits for which they were designed." And ". . . it must never be forgotten that the tests introduced an objectivity into the measurement of human abilities that never existed before." *Excellence: Can We Be Equal and Excellent Too?* New York, Harper & Row, 1961, pp. 49 and 48.

gauging abilities really needed in a given occupation or field of work. A test may be completely appropriate for measuring a particular kind of capacity but highly ineffective for measuring another. An even more common error is to presume that an identified capacity is needed for a given job when careful analysis and research demonstrate that the assumption is incorrect. When the wrong measuring instrument is used under such circumstances, too often the resulting criticism is directed against the instrument itself instead of against the bad judgment that led to misuse of the measure.

UTILITY OF TESTS   The fact is that carefully validated and standardized measurement goes far to reduce the elements of chance and caprice that would otherwise be present in the selection process. The person who can judge ability intuitively is nonexistent. The use of sound research techniques to find the best instruments pays off, even in those areas where there is the greatest scoffing at tests—such as in application to highly disadvantaged, educationally deprived persons. It has been demonstrated, for example, that candidates with little experience and low skill often have greater motivation and actually perform better at routine jobs than persons with more extensive job experience and higher intelligence.[7] The best tests to search out this kind of motivation and to lower the chances of the overqualified can then be employed in narrowing the field down to the most promising candidates for the work at hand. This is an illustration of how psychological measurement can be used to further sound selection even when it runs counter to previous habits of thinking.

In short, if there is anything wrong with the science of tests and measurements, it is the failure to press the inquiry further, to put resources into the process of finding the best combination of methods, and to recognize throughout that there is no single royal road to good selection, that human judgment must not be ruled out. The critics of testing have no substitute procedures to suggest that would do the sorting and winnowing that are unavoidable in all large employment situations. They would better serve the ends of justice if they made their attack on the failure to make the best use of existing instruments, on the niggardliness of public agencies in supporting test research, and on those who would deny management its responsibility to exercise judgment at those stages in the selection process where it is an essential ingredient.

FORMS OF EXAMINATION

The forms which objective examinations can take may be conveniently classified into five, but they are almost invariably used in various combinations. The one that is most common, because it is one of the elements in

---

[7] As discovered in a survey of the literature and federal civil service experience conducted by Ernest S. Primoff of the Bureau of Policies and Standards, U.S. Civil Service Commission, and reported in a paper "Motivation and Interest in Doing Work at Jobs at the Lowest Level," March 1968.

almost any employment examination, is the systematic evaluation of education and experience. It may be relied upon heavily for filling professional and managerial occupations but is almost always supplemented by one or both of two other forms: oral tests and standardized qualification inquiries. The remaining two forms are written tests, to which we have already given some attention, and performance tests.

SYSTEMATIC EVALUATION OF EDUCATION AND EXPERIENCE

In addition to serving as a standard upon which to judge admission to the full evaluation process itself (the examination), the evaluation of education and experience is also a kind of examination which can differentiate among candidates as to their degree of fitness for a position or occupation. Because the application blank alone, supplemented occasionally with other papers, is usually the vehicle for this evaluation, the candidates need not be brought together for the purpose. Hence, this process, which can be handled via the mails, is often referred to as an "unassembled" examination, whereas written and performance tests are "assembled" examinations.

The rating of training and previous work history is considered more difficult than rating assembled tests, because of such problems as (1) standardizing the evaluation process, (2) securing equal performance by the examiners, (3) providing in the rating guide for many permutations and combinations of education and experience, (4) recognizing variability and qualitative factors in experience, and (5) recognizing the relevance of experience not provided for in the rating standard. However, the processes can be sufficiently standardized and quantified so that different reviewers can come to reasonably close conclusions on the same case. Human error is usually reduced by the simple device of having two examiners independently rate each case.

In any event, the important task of evaluating education and experience cannot be left to rule of thumb. It is a major factor in most selection procedures. Hence, its objectivity and validity must not be overlooked.[8]

WRITTEN TESTS

Pencil-and-paper tests are used by most public personnel agencies in the United States, and their development constitutes one of the major contributions of government to personnel administration. They are commonly included in examinations for entrance-level positions and for others for which aptitudes, intelligence, or concrete knowledge are prime determinants. They do not, of course, suffer from the rating difficulties inherent in appraising training and experience, and they especially offer great help where no experience is required or present. In other words, a written test is easier to evaluate objectively, and the technical proficiency required of the reviewers is ordinarily much less. In its administration the written form is also simpler and cheaper

---

[8] The best explanation of what is involved in this kind of examination is found in the two chapters by Albert P. Maslow, "Evaluating Training and Experience" and "The Unassembled Examination" in Donovan, *op. cit.*

than the oral or performance types of tests, since it can be given to a large number of individuals at the same time.

FREE-ANSWER FORM   Written tests may be divided into two broad classes, variously called either subjective and objective, or free-answer and short-answer. Of the two, the subjective or free-answer is the older form. Practically everyone is familiar with it. It consists of questions which the applicant is free to answer as he thinks best.

This type of examination is much easier to set up than the objective type but is accompanied by serious disadvantages. Possibly the most weighty is the difficulty of evaluating the answers in any uniform or reliable manner. From the standpoint of the applicant, serious objections may also be raised. The essay or free-answer examination places a premium on literary ability, an attribute often unrelated to the duties of the position for which the test is given. Under such circumstances, test validity is impaired, and public relations will almost certainly suffer. The subjective test is, of course, of the highest value in the selection of employees for positions in which literary skill plays a part. Moreover, if properly employed in a modified form, it may be useful in rating candidates for positions in which the ability to select and organize facts or to analyze complex problems is relevant. In a few jurisdictions significant experiments have been undertaken in the production of modified free-answer tests for higher positions. By the careful phrasing of specific questions, employment of a large number of items, and development of rating keys, some of the usual disadvantages of this type of examination may be minimized and a partially objective type produced.

OBJECTIVE FORM   The impetus toward the adoption of the short-answer or objective type of examination was originally supplied by the extensive use of this form in general psychological tests. As the designation "short-answer" suggests, this type of examination is distinguished more by the form of the answer than by that of the question. The task of the competitor, from the mechanical standpoint, is reduced to a minimum; his answers are in a single mark or a word or underline. The short-answer form is widely used by public personnel agencies. One of the most popular forms of the short-answer test is the multiple-choice type, with its several variations, including the analogy and degree-of-truth tests.

The most popular varieties of short-answer tests are particularly well adapted to the testing of intelligence or specific knowledge, although the short-answer form may be extended in many ingenious directions. Their advantages lie in their objectivity, in the fact that both the tests and the results can be standardized, in the ease with which they may be administered, and in the fact that the duties of occupations can be more completely covered by an examination of this type than by the free-answer variety. Finally, the short-answer test is often preferred by candidates.

One more point deserves emphasis: written tests provide a unique opportunity to appraise a *sample* of a candidate's capacity or knowledge. Whatever their form, their utility must be judged in those terms. They can never by themselves be all-knowing determinants of a person's potential. Of all the forms of measurement, written tests have drawn the most fire of the critics. Nevertheless, they must continue to be major elements in winnowing down differences among candidates when the test results square with performance on the job.

PERFORMANCE TESTS

The assembled tests now employed in industry and the public service include a large number that are neither oral nor written. These are commonly referred to as performance tests, although any examination may actually be considered a matter of performance. Among the tests that may be classed in this group are actual demonstrations on the job (involving use of tools or equipment), various specialized tests of alertness and agility, and job-miniature tests involving the use of apparatus similar to that to be used on the job. All of these have one thing in common: they employ some kind of performance other than writing or speaking. For the most part they involve motor reactions. The most common examples of performance tests are those for stenographic and typing work and for skilled trades.

For want of a better place to treat it, we may classify under the performance heading a type of examination plan that links selection with training and trial on the job. It is finding favor especially among certain police and other agencies. Under this procedure final appointment is delayed until the new recruit has successfully passed a rigorous academy training program and also a number of weeks under close observation in actual field performance. Where undertaken successfully such a plan represents a sophisticated blend of several forms of evaluating an individual's potential for continuing assignment on the staff.

ORAL TESTS

Providing an opportunity to appraise candidates on the basis of what they say orally is usually referred to as an oral test. Here we are not concerned with the employment interview, which has existed from time immemorial. Such an interview is little more than a highly subjective, last-stage "get-acquainted" discussion for a selecting officer to size up a candidate after the field has been narrowed to the final few. This comes after formal testing is completed.

As has been previously explained, any test worthy of the name implies a process founded on as much objectivity as can be extracted from a situation. Oral tests embrace a variety of carefully designed measures to get at each candidate's knowledge or behavior via his facility in speech. They range from systematic probing for what information, views, or skills a person possesses that he can state orally, to observation of his personality and general behavior as evidenced by his conversation with one or more examiners or with other candidates. In any case it is a carefully constructed and planned affair. As little is left to chance as possible.

Oral tests of individuals to ascertain knowledge or achievement are rare in the public service. This purpose is readily and much more economically served by written tests. Oral tests of this kind are largely confined to scholastic arenas.

Public jurisdictions have, however, used oral testing widely to measure attributes of behavior, such as poise, leadership, alertness, social awareness, speaking ability, and general responsiveness to social stimuli, that are not readily ascertained through other means. A basic assumption underlying the use of such a test is that a real-life situation is created in which the individual can react spontaneously and, in doing so, reveal temperament, oral skill, and character attributes of which he is perhaps unaware but which the observer can note and interpret.

Such a test is most successful in a group, that is, where several candidates are observed interacting. A specific set of test objectives is defined, and a detailed specification of points or factors to be observed and rated is set forth. The problem or subject put before the group is carefully presented, and always in the same manner to each group in the same test. In order to pool or balance judgments and thus reduce subjectivity, more than one observer is usually involved, and such observers must ordinarily be carefully trained and, if possible, become "professional" at the process.

Even under such circumstances the group oral test is fraught with perils. There can be a failure to discriminate between that performance which is relevant, material, and reliable and that which is not. Also, such a test provides opportunity for analysis of only a very small part of oral behavior, to say nothing of a person's total behavior. Sweeping conclusions can be far from the true mark. Hence, it is rational to conclude that such oral tests must never constitute the only element in an examination; also, they can serve their most useful purpose if not used to produce fine rating distinctions among candidates but simply to eliminate obviously marginal people who might pass other elements of the full examination or to discover exceptional people who have potential for special or advanced assignment upon employment.

STANDARDIZED QUALIFICATION INQUIRIES

Particularly for positions of substantial responsibility another ingredient may appear in the examination procedure. This is variously referred to as the reference inquiry, qualification check, or personal investigation. Candidates may meet all requirements in terms of education and experience qualifications, have an excellent written test record, and still be unsuitable for employment by reason of character, temperament, quality of performance, or similar factors which cannot be fully weighed in the formal testing program. Reliable information on questions of this kind can be secured only through careful inquiry by a trained staff.

Whether confined to mailing out a standard questionnaire to the candidate's former employers and acquaintances or involving a face-to-face or telephone inquiry by a trained investigator, such a procedure must entail a systematic means of acquiring and recording information in such a fashion that different recorders will note similar results on the same case and that such notations can be readily evaluated and, if practicable, quantified for examination rating purposes. This kind of check may be given a weight in the total examination, or it may be used simply to eliminate the clearly undesirable who manage to surmount the other hurdles in the examining process.

Investigations may, of course, be used for purposes supplementary to the examination itself rather than as an integral part of it, for example, to verify statements made on the application or simply to collect information regarding character and integrity. Occasionally, such an investigation may occur or continue after appointment and during the probationary period. The best practice dictates that a qualifications investigation be concluded before selection and appointment in order to avoid expensive and unnecessary orientation and turnover.

The personal investigation tends to be a rather costly process and is almost prohibitive as a form of rated examination except where comparatively few candidates are involved. Nevertheless, its value for technical and managerial posts in incalculable. In such instances the investigation is an essential step even if it follows the general examination and is used just as a final weeding-out measure before selection.

Special forms of examination used in promotion determinations are dealt with in the chapter on selection from within the service.[9]

THE OBJECTS OF MEASUREMENT

Now we come to a classification of tests as to purpose, that is, as to *what is measured*. Generally, one could say that all testing seeks to measure either capacity or achievement, but this is an oversimplification. Hence, a somewhat more refined breakdown is presented.

GENERAL ABILITIES

The most widely known and extensively employed psychological test of capacity is the general intelligence test. There is still some disagreement among psychologists regarding what exactly the various standardized tests of abstract intelligence measure. In general, however, those who have designed the tests mean by intelligence just what is popularly meant by it: smartness, alertness, the ability to adjust readily to new situations, and so forth.

Experts may disagree on whether general intelligence is a combination of just a few special capacities or aptitudes or of a great range of specific abilities, but a combination it certainly is. In any event, it is not necessary

[9] Chapter 10. See particularly the discussion on assessment centers.

to formulate a careful definition of intelligence in order to use intelligence tests. The pertinent question is: are they of any value in the selection process? If they are selective and the selections made upon the basis of the tests have some positive relationship to later adjustment to the job situation, they serve an important utilitarian purpose.

There is a considerable accumulation of evidence to show that a positive relationship exists between performance on intelligence tests and educational achievement, and numerous investigations have indicated a relationship between intelligence, as measured by general intelligence tests, and vocational success. The evidence suggests not only that certain determinate minima of intelligence are essential in many occupations, but also that an individual can be too intelligent for a particular job, causing unnecessary turnover. Thus, it seems probable that there are upper and lower limits within which the most likely candidates for many positions may be bracketed. Tests of general intelligence are even found frequently to give better results in predicting success in specialized positions than do specialized knowledge tests.

As a consequence of such findings, the general abilities or intelligence test is the most common instrument found in modern employment testing batteries. In content it usually consists of measurement of such capacities as verbal ability, abstract reasoning, quantitative (arithmetical) reasoning, and spatial visualization—obvious ingredients for success in many walks of life. So much research and standardaization has gone into intelligence test development that a number of widely known general instruments are available to any qualified employer who wishes to purchase the technique.

Eagerness of some critics to discredit intelligence tests have led them to seize upon certain court decisions as prohibiting such tests. As a matter of fact, no judicial determinations known to this writer have done anything of the kind. They have simply declared that a test must measure some factor important to actual performance of the work involved.[10]

Here we have a further illustration of the importance of using realistic measuring instruments. Because an intelligence test is not predictive of per-

[10] A widely cited case has been that of the U.S. Supreme Court in 1971, *Griggs* v. *Duke Power Company*, which held that an employer is prohibited under the Civil Rights Act from requiring a high school education or passing of an intelligence test when these standards are not related to successful performance of work for which the standards are prescribed. In this instance the Duke Power Company had set these requirements for movement from one kind of menial laboring work, mostly outside, to another order of manual duty in its "inside" departments. To all intents and purposes, the device seemed to be calculated to discriminate against black incumbents.

The point here is that the Court specifically authorized the use of professionally developed ability tests that served a demonstrably "reasonable measure of job performance." Nor did the Court interdict the use of tests of general mental abilities or mechanical comprehension that could be demonstrated as relevant in specific employment situations. It merely rejected the uncritical use of an intelligence quotient or other label having no relevance to the conditions for which the individual was being evaluated.

The best analysis of this decision appears in Albert H. Aronson, *The Duke Power Company Case*, Chicago, International Personnel Management Association, 1971.

formance for some kinds of work does not mean that it cannot be used for others where its use *is* predictive. Most of the recent legal and professional determinations relating to such testing simply reinforce the essential elements of useful and fair selection processes, for which there are no substitutes:

1. Careful analysis and verification of the real talents and abilities needed to perform successfully in an occupation, a job, or a career; and
2. Careful research to ascertain the best available selection instruments to measure the presence of such qualities in candidates for employment.

Reiteration of these elementary principles must not, however, conceal another truth. Concerning ourselves with "job relatedness" should not blind us to the continuing need to recruit for careers and not just for individual niches in the job structure. If we were to be confined to testing for qualities needed only in an entry job, what kind of human potential would we be recruiting for future promotion? It was the bane of the public service before the great strides of the 1930s that it selected personnel primarily for the short run. In our anxiety to ensure fairness we must always be concerned with what we are examining for—today's job or potentiality for a career. In many fields this is where "general ability" is important, and testing for long-range promise cannot be dismissed out of hand as unfair discrimination against minorities.

SPECIAL ABILITIES OR APTITUDES

Besides the basic elements found within so-called general abilities tests, some of the particular areas of capacity for which specialized intelligence or aptitude tests have been developed are mechanical, number facility, memory, word fluency, and finger dexterity. These have been isolated through the process of factor analysis—identifying the discrete characteristics and validity studies which help determine their varying degrees of importance in a variety of occupations and activities.

Since many specific aptitudes have now been isolated through the foregoing process and various combinations of these aptitudes are found to be related to success in different fields of work, differential test batteries have been constructed to provide, with a minimum amount of testing, an index of these different aptitudes. In other words, a battery of tests is designed which will identify and measure each of a number of specific human aptitudes. Scores on each of these tests are correlated with success in many different jobs, and optimum weighting (the relative effect on the total score) of each test for each job is determined. For some jobs, a certain minimum score on a particular aptitude test will be essential, but ability above that amount will not be correlated with success. In such cases, a minimum score on that test should be required, but that score should not be combined with other test results in ranking candidates. Thus, with a single test battery, candidates' potential can be ascertained and ranked for many different jobs. This not only provides an economical means of testing but also permits better placement of candidates.

Before leaving the subject of special abilities, we cannot overlook the fact that in this area there is probably more room for development than in any other aspect of employment examination. We have already taken the test makers to task for doing little about measuring qualities such as creativity, imagination, and drive. It is certainly regrettable that there appear to be no reliable devices to gauge the presence of these capacities. In many fields of work they are more important than intelligence itself, provided some minimum intelligence level has been attained. Most employers would rather have at least their key staff composed of people who are inventive, who can see alternatives, who have the energy and the insight to tackle problems with relish, than to have geniuses in the sense of those with raw intelligence. But it must be acknowledged that finding the criteria and standardizing the measures for such qualities is a delicate, frustrating, and almost insoluble task. The most that can be done at this point is to plead for more resources to be invested in the study of these elusive qualities in man, of the manner of their display, and of how they might be captured in an examining situation.

ACHIEVEMENT

Achievement tests, as distinguished from aptitude tests, have been widely employed; the older civil service examinations were of this type. They are useful in the selection of employees already possessed of particular job skills but are only incidentally indicative of the possibilities of future development. Tests of this character may be classified as education, trade, and demonstration or performance tests.

Whenever a test aims to discover the extent to which an individual has mastered specific subject matter, usually of an academic type, that is an *education test*. It may be a test of spelling ability as employed in most clerical examinations; of knowledge of sociology, economics, or government, as employed in a battery for junior social workers; or of surveying methods in an examination on drafting or engineering.

There are many standardized education scales available to the personnel administrator. In general, however, officials have preferred to devise their own education tests, because many of the standard scales have been standardized upon the basis of results with students and require considerable adaptation before they can be used with employable adults.

Trade tests are also education tests, but for purposes of discussion they may be differentiated. The trade test is designed to measure the degree to which a person possesses a given occupational knowledge. Thus, we may have trade tests not only for carpenters, toolmakers, and others in the skilled trades groups but also for clerical workers, accountants, architects, city planners, and many others.

Another variety of achievement test is the so-called *performance* (or practical or demonstration) *test.* This is the type of testing done when an applicant for a job as paver is asked to pave a section of street, or an architect to design a structure, or a diesinker to cut a die. Practical tests of this kind are universally employed in industry and have had wide usage in civil service.

For professional and managerial occupations the achievement test is becoming less popular, largely because it seldom reveals much about a candidate's ultimate potential. The general and special abilities tests have become more meaningful for this purpose. In other words, how far a person is likely to go is more a function of his basic capacity and how he utilizes it than of how much he knows about a specific field.

However, the achievement test is particularly useful for determining when a person with some experience but without requisite educational background—as, for example, in engineering or accounting—actually possesses the necessary technical knowledge and understanding to permit his entrance or transfer into a professional field. In other words, it may be used to measure whether he has the equivalent of the formal education commonly required for the profession, having acquired what he knows by a combination of unique work experience and personal study. This type of achievement testing is sometimes called an "education-equivalency" test.

HEALTH AND PHYSIQUE

Examinations by a medical staff to determine physical fitness for a job are by no means confined to those positions which require special strength or agility. To ensure reasonable continuity and avoid unnecessary charges on the retirement system, it is common to require basic health examinations of all appointees to the public service. Needless to say, these are customarily given only to those selected or about to be selected for actual employment, since they rule a candidate either "in or out" and need not be part of the original screening steps.

Many positions require special physical attainment—strength, endurance, agility, coordination, or other qualities. Examples are police officers, firemen, sanitation workers, and many kinds of laborers. In these instances the physical examination may include special features and be part of the basic examination process on which all candidates are rated. It is also common to find minimum and maximum height and weight qualifications for such jobs—many of which, however, are of doubtful validity.

There is considerable feeling that arbitrary physical standards such as those relating to height, weight, or specific physical skills, not being always related directly to job success, are given too much emphasis. Employers could rely on a general physical examination and postappointment training to assure good performance. So many other variables enter into the physical fitness of a candidate for a particular task that the efficacy of arbitrary standards is, at the least, questionable.

PERSONALITY AND EMOTION

The fact that many personal traits of a temperamental or emotional sort are closely related to vocational success has long been recognized. Their identification and measurement, however, have proved extremely difficult. Although a number of interesting experiments have been made in this field, such tests leave much to be desired in the way of reliability and standardization. This does not imply that personnel agencies with a competent staff and facilities would not do well to experiment with them. No aspect of the personnel program is more fertile for research. But they must be used with great caution and circumspection. Unfortunately, personality testing has been beset by overzealous efforts at shortcuts which have discredited the entire field.

Emotional stability is particularly critical for success in executive positions. As a result there has been widespread interest in efforts to gauge personal and emotional adaptability to the stresses of the job. The fact that failure is so often attributable to emotional maladjustment rather than lack of occupational skill has accentuated this interest. Numbers of industrial firms have employed psychiatrists or psychologists to conduct extensive analyses of individual employees, particularly when under consideration for advancement to critical key positions. But these are expensive and time-consuming procedures (they often take several days), a far cry from some of the simple paper-and-pencil tests that purport to measure personality.

Seldom are such comprehensive psychiatric tests practicable or even needed for original entrance. A few municipalities have been known to employ brief psychiatric interviews to test police candidates just before final appointment, on the theory that the public cannot risk entrusting weapons for purposes of law enforcement to individuals who are not thoroughly mature and stable. Wartime selection of intelligence officers entailed very complex and extensive procedures to assure the selection of persons who would perform effectively and withstand the strains and pressures of such assignments —and the processes were carried out with remarkable success. But these are radical measures for radical purposes.

As far as most short-time personality testing is concerned, relying primarily on written testing or picture interpretation, the validity yet achieved is far from what a public jurisdiction would require. As in the case of any experimental market, it would be well in this one for the employer to follow the injunction of *caveat emptor*—"let the buyer beware"—before accepting a personality test.

ADMINISTRATION OF EXAMINATIONS

Few public jurisdictions are so self-sufficient that they can afford to develop and maintain in alternate forms all the examinations that are required to serve the great variety of occupations that exist in modern government.

This is particularly true in the case of written test materials. Only the federal government and a few major states and cities rely totally on their own resources for this purpose.

TEST AVAILABILITY   For the great majority of jurisdictions the following practices demonstrate the widespread interdependence that exists in written test construction:

1. The International Personnel Management Association provides a regular test consulting service to all its member agencies, including an extensive test exchange and a number of original standard tests (as for police and fire personnel).
2. The Bureau of Intergovernmental Personnel Programs of the U.S. Civil Service Commission supplies technical assistance to the states on testing matters.
3. Joint examinations are held by different jurisdictions in common geographic areas, thus lightening the burden of test construction and permitting specialization by each government unit involved.
4. Program specialists in a government jurisdiction are frequently called upon to help set up tests in their respective occupational fields, thus spreading the effectiveness of a small staff of professional psychometricians.
5. More and more standard tests for intelligence and special aptitudes are being supplied by reputable commercial and professional organizations.

TECHNICAL PROBLEMS   Some of the technical problems in administering competitive examinations are substantial and are seldom appreciated by the general public.[11] For example, there is the matter of arriving at the relative weights to be given to different parts of the examination, such as training and experience, written test, and oral test. Even among the parts of a written test itself, each separate segment weights itself if it is not deliberately weighted by design. Ideally the relative importance to be attached, for example, to education or to the verbal facility part of a written test should be governed by that element's relative correlation with job success or with the particular aspect of success which it is expected to measure. Statistical techniques are available which permit expression and balancing of these values.

A frequently used approach is the "hurdles" concept. Under this procedure the candidate must pass each part of the total examination before he can take the next part. Thus, if a candidate passes the rating of education and experience, he is permitted to enter the written test; then if he passes that, he

[11] The best discussion of the problems is found in Donald R. Harvey, *The Civil Service Commission*, New York, Praeger, 1970. He observes:

the principle of filling jobs through civil service examinations has become so widely accepted today that many people endorse and espouse it without really comprehending the complexity of living up to it. Sponsors of the merit system have tended, if not to oversimplify, then to subordinate the problems of administration, so that it has been difficult to draw attention to them lest this action be interpreted as a challenge to the principle itself. [P. 50.]

may be given the oral test; and so on. Those who fail any hurdle are "out" at that point. This succession of hurdles is most effective if the most valid part of the examination is given first, that is, the part that correlates best with job success. Obviously, if the most valid test is not given first, there is greater risk that qualified people who might have done well on other parts of the examination may be eliminated too early and many who stand no ultimate chance be subjected to too many hurdles.

Another commonly misunderstood problem is that of the "passing" mark. Some merit system laws or regulations fix this point inexorably at 70 or some other figure, on the assumption that there is some magic to such a number on a scale of 100. Actually, the concept of any fixed figure is meaningless. The passing point is more properly a function of how many eligible candidates are needed and at how stringent a point it is desired to cut off eligibility. Besides, what amounts to 70 on one examination may have no relationship to 70 on another.

Most examiners get around this problem by giving attention first to the "raw score" and then deliberately setting the passing point. The raw score is most readily illustrated by the gross number of possible right answers on a written test (a test with 150 items has a potential raw score of 150). From an assessment of how many eligibles are needed, what previous experience with the test has indicated, and how many persons are taking the examination, the psychometrician decides on a passing point (variously called cutting point, critical score, etc.) that will yield enough high-quality eligibles to provide more than enough recruits for the number of jobs to be filled. This point, which on the 150-item test may be a raw score of, say, 90, then becomes 70 for legal passing purposes, and the raw scores between 90 and 150 are compressed on a scale of 70 to 100.

Obviously, then, 70 even on the same test may represent a different standard of achievement at different times. This is as it should be. There is no point to having either too many or too few people pass. When there are too many, those eligible but not selected are misled into false expectations; when there are too few, the needs of the service are not met.

DATA PROCESSING   Modern examination administration in large jurisdictions is a big business. In the federal civil service, for example, a great many examinations are processed annually by a nationwide network of boards of examiners and field offices for two to three million applicants. On a lesser scale, but still involving large numbers, are found the examining activities of the major cities and largest states. Clearly such operations can be carried on rapidly and effectively only with up-to-date machine methods. Automatic electronic data-processing equipment is employed at such points as the following in the examining process:

1. Notifying potential applicants of examination dates and procedure.
2. Indexing candidates' qualifications as to education and experience, permitting quick sorting and finding of those with special skills.

3. Maintaining subject files of written test items.
4. Scoring written tests.
5. Notifying candidates of rating results.
6. Certifying lists of eligibles.
7. Compiling data on characteristics of the examinees as to education, age, residence, etc., for use in research studies.
8. Maintaining continuous follow-up on candidates (or employees) for use in test validity studies.

Any such uses of machine processes require the reduction of all data to numerical codes, with the result that vast quantities of information can be stored on discs, tapes, or cards and subsequently called up, sorted, and tabulated for almost any purpose. Much of the drudgery of mass examining operations has thereby been eliminated, with the added dividend, in contrast with yesteryear, that information is far more extensive, far more readily available, and in far better condition for analysis and research—a sine qua non of effective examinations in the public service.

APPEALS   An important step in the examination process is the consideration of appeals on examination ratings. Unless candidates are given an opportunity to appeal these ratings, there is the possibility that favoritism will be charged. Moreover, there is always the possibility of a mistake, and there should be some machinery set up by which mistakes can be rectified. This fact has been recognized by progressive public personnel agencies in the United States. In a number of jurisdictions, the matter of appeals on examinations has been completely standardized.

*   *   *

THE IMPORTANCE OF test validity and reliability is so great that no more fitting plea can conclude this chapter than one for increased attention to and funds for test research. There is still too little scientific analysis and control in various phases of testing and selection. The major civil service testing agencies should be equipped with strong research staffs which will bring together the output and findings of psychological research laboratories and make independent checks on the results of their own testing programs. Even the staff of the U.S. Civil Service Commission is still inadequate. Unfortunately, such activities do not seem to be appreciated by the budgeteers and legislative appropriation committees. Yet there are few aspects of personnel administration where more is to be gained in the way of improving efficiency than in the measurement and prediction of the performance of candidates for jobs. Until more legislators and executives are appreciative of the values of personnel research in this and other phases of the field, public personnel administration will fall short of all that is expected of it.

CHAPTER 9

Selection: From Outside the Service

THE PROBLEM OF staffing a government agency is one of filling positions or occupational categories from any of several sources. When an appointing officer is considering the establishment of a new job or wishes to fill a vacancy, his attention should be turned to all practical sources of candidates, whether inside or outside the service. Thus, initial recruitment and selection are inextricably bound up with movement of employees already in the service from job to job. This chapter and the one following attempt to discuss the many ramifications of this whole subject. It is only for convenience and because the steps for securing candidates from outside the service necessarily vary from those for selection from within that we have divided the subject into two chapters. This chapter deals with those aspects of initial selection which follow the entrance examination process.

EMPLOYMENT LISTS AND THEIR USE

ESTABLISHING LISTS Following the application procedure and the rating of examinations, the next step in the employment process is to compile the list or register of eligible candidates. This is usually composed of the names of all those who possess the requisite qualifications and who have received the passing grade on the examinations. These are ranked in the order of their relative standing, from the highest to the lowest, except as such ranking is disturbed by the preferential ratings given war veterans. Since large numbers of veterans present themselves for appointment to government positions and preferential treatment is granted them in almost every jurisdiction, special attention is given to this subject later in this chapter.

Separate eligible lists are usually maintained for each class or broad field of positions for which examinations are given. They can be properly established, however, only upon the basis of a comprehensive duties classification. Otherwise they cannot be closely related to the occupations to be filled, and, furthermore, unnecessary duplications may result.

TIMELINESS   If employment lists or registers are to provide a fruitful source of good candidates, then they must be promptly set up and maintained. With the use of automation and other devices most public jurisdictions have managed to overcome what was once a common problem of taking too long to establish lists and too long to make appointments from them once they were established. Also, the trend toward keeping registers available and in use on a continuous basis—and therefore allowing new applicants who qualify to be placed on them from time to time—has mitigated some of the old questions, such as whether time limits should be put on lists before they are replaced by new ones. Under the modern procedure registers are, in effect, renewed almost daily with fresh candidates. But it is common practice eventually to drop any names that are consistently passed over (for good reason, presumably) for an extended period, say, one to three years. In this way, the list is a continuing and up-to-date source of qualified, and hopefully available, people.

STEPS IN USING LISTS   After eligible lists are in existence, three succeeding steps are necessary to bring new employees on duty: (1) requisition of names by the employing departments, (2) certification of the most qualified available by the personnel agency, and (3) appointment by the employing department. If the examination system worked perfectly, that is, if it ranked candidates in the precise order of their later performance on the job, such subsequent steps would be of no great consequence. But intangible factors such as initiative, personality, and appearance are not usually evaluated by the formal examination (at least not with any dependability), and yet they may spell the difference between success and failure in many lines of work. It is in the course of these subsequent steps that such factors may be taken into account.

REGULAR CERTIFICATION   Almost all merit systems permit the certification of three or more names to the appointing official in order for him to take into consideration any of the personal factors that are critical to job performance. Needless to say, this is also the point at which such officials may exercise (consciously or unconsciously) some of their pet notions or even prejudices about prospective workers. Fear of such undermining of the merit objective has led some well-intentioned practitioners to argue that only one candidate per job vacancy should be certified, in other words, that the appointing officer should have no choice. Such a stand overlooks two inexorable facts: first, that the examining process can never be so perfectly valid that it ensures the ranking of applicants in exact order of overall merit; and second, that responsible administrators should quite properly be given some latitude in making the final choice of individuals whose performance must contribute positively to the success of their operations. As long as the jurisdiction has genuine policies of nondiscrimination as to race, sex, religion, or other extraneous conditions, fully backed by its chief executive, and as long as these administrators have themselves been selected by an above-board process, there should be less risk in allowing this administrative discretion than in denying it.

CATEGORY RATING   As a matter of fact, the real issue is whether the "rule of three" is not too restrictive rather than too loose. The Tennessee Valley Authority many years ago pioneered—and with considerable success—the process of submitting flexible numbers of candidates to appointing officials, depending upon the number who appeared to be of approximately equal merit on paper and upon the general state of the register. The first Hoover Commission in 1949 had suggested grouping candidates for the federal service into broad categories instead of numerical ranks,[1] and the U.S. Civil Service Commission at one time followed up on this proposal by suggesting that such "category rating" be made applicable at least to professional and other higher-level jobs, with other flexible procedures to apply to lower ranks.[2] Undoubtedly the rock on which these meritorious ideas foundered was veteran preference, which had developed a vested interest in the rule of three, as will be seen later in this chapter.

CATEGORY CERTIFICATION   While still relying on numerical or percentage scores, there are several mechanistic ways (besides the rule of three or five or any other arbitrary number) of determining which candidates should be certified in the top eligible group. These devices are founded on full recognition that examination ratings are not absolutely precise measures and that all applicants within a certain *range* of examination ratings are approximately equal in qualifications potential for the type of positions being filled. Thus, if a number of candidates have the same rating, such a certification rule does not limit the personnel agency to certifying just three with a rating of, say, 99, while totally excluding those with 98 or 97 who are, for all intents and purposes, indistinguishable from those with 99.

At least two examples, which have already been adopted in a number of state merit systems, illustrate this more flexible certification procedure. One is known as the "rule of ranks." Under this process, all persons with examination ratings in the top *three numerical scores*, no matter what the total number of persons happens to be, are certified. In other words, all names in the top

---

[1] Commission on Organization of the Executive Branch of the Government, *Personnel Management: A Report to the Congress*, Washington, D.C., February 1949, pp. 18–19.

[2] U.S. Civil Service Commission, *66th Annual Report*, fiscal year ended June 30, 1949, which cites a letter to the Senate in which this recommendation was made.

three numerical ranks, not just three names from the *top* rank, are available for consideration by the appointing official. A more complex application of the same basic idea is sometimes referred to as the "rule of reliability." In this case, the number of applicants certified is based on the particular examination's statistical reliability. Thus, a "band-width," or number of numerical ranks, within which all candidates can be considered approximately equal in merit, is determined for each examination, based on the degree of the examination's reliability in predicting success on the job. That is, the more reliable the examination, the narrower the band-width and the fewer the number of applicants certified. Under this alternative, the number of ranks certified could well be more than three.

The net effect of such realistic certification procedures is not too different from broad category ratings themselves, in that all candidates with generally equal potential are considered in the same group. However, the *category certification* devices, as distinguished from *category rating*, simply provide more flexible use of numerical ratings instead of supplanting them with somewhat more subjective rating classes.

SELECTIVE CERTIFICATION   Quite a few years ago the U.S. Civil Service Commission pioneered in making registers flexible by setting up less specialized examinations and using "selective certification" to reduce the total number of lists which have to be kept up to date. The Commission or one of its boards of examiners passes on requests from appointing offices for panels of candidates with particular qualifications not possessed by all on the list; then only the top persons meeting such special needs are certified. This is now a common procedure in the use of college-level entrance examinations.[3] Such a process is almost mandatory in view of the great variety of positions now appearing in the classification plan of any fair-sized jurisdiction.

Selective certification is prostituted if it is used for any non-job-related purpose. Thus, if a few positions in a common category require the ability to speak Spanish, this procedure is most appropriate to single out those top candidates who have that extra job-related qualification. But if it is used to select Spanish-speaking competitors just to reach some predetermined "quota" where jobs skills do not call for such capacity, it adulterates the whole process.

BLOCK CERTIFICATION   In addition to "selective certification," which helps reconcile the need for examinations of broad coverage with the demand for more and more specialties in the service, another certification device of utility is that of "block" or "pool" certification. Particularly where the number of eligible candidates is less or little more than the number of vacancies or under other conditions where practically everyone on the list above a certain

---

[3] The most notable one being the Professional and Administrative Career Examination, under which a wide variety of federal managerial and social science entry positions are filled. Similar vehicles apply to middle- and upper-level positions.

rating can be assured of being offered a job, all interested users of the register are given the entire list to choose from and may select at random. The net result is no different than if the rule of three had been laboriously applied, except that it is more efficient and faster.

PROVISIONAL APPOINTMENTS   There are, of course, merit system loopholes which tempt the patronage seeker. One of these is "provisional appointments,"[4] which were intended to permit the government to fill positions even when eligible lists were not immediately available. Obviously, exploitation of this safety valve coupled with a policy of starving the personnel agency for funds with which to keep up its examination program can be rather effective in circumventing the merit system. Hence, it is common to provide time limits or other restrictions on provisional appointments, in order to allow time to develop an appropriate employment list and to ensure an enduring selection that fully comports with the merit principle.

TEMPORARY AND EMERGENCY APPOINTMENTS   Other types of exceptional appointments which all jurisdictions require are temporary and emergency appointments. One is for temporary positions and therefore of limited duration; the other is to permit hiring of employees to meet emergencies such as forest fires or natural disasters. In either case it is ordinarily impractical to have employment lists already available, except where temporary jobs are seasonal and repetitive. In spite of the dangers of abuse which these conditional appointment powers may create, such authority is essential to a flexible personnel system.

VETERAN PREFERENCE

Practically every nation has been faced at one time or another with the problem of what to do with its creditors, that is, with those who risked life and limb in its service. The solutions from time immemorial have fallen into two categories: the granting of a gratuity or pension, and the granting of a job. Often both have been used at the same time. In the case of the job, it has usually been the public service that has been opened to the veteran on a preferred basis.

Government policy-makers are thus confronted with a dilemma. On the one hand, good administration demands that the public service be restricted to the most fit, the best qualified for the work to be performed. On the other, humanitarian as well as political considerations have persuaded legislative bodies that the state itself should provide suitable occupations for this category of citizen that served in its defense. To this end, most jurisdictions have made veterans a privileged class so far as public employment is con-

---

[4] Called Temporary Appointments Pending Establishment of a Register, or "TAPER," in the U.S. civil service.

cerned. This policy has been threatened in recent years by the competing preference sometimes sought for ethnic or minority groups.

NATURE AND EXTENT OF PREFERENCE

The history of preference policy and laws in the United States is too complex to permit a simple recounting here. Suffice it to say that before World War II statutory provisions on the subject were confined to rather general statements of policy enjoining appointing officials to give disabled or other veterans (and eventually their wives) preference over others of equal qualifications. The details by which this was accomplished were established by executive authority and usually went beyond the strict requirement of the law. In any event, by World War I the policy was clearly established in the United States that government jobs were to be regarded as a gratuity so far as veterans were concerned and that the state as administrator was to bow to the state as almoner.

FORMS OF PREFERENCE   The customary device used both in the federal service and in the fifty states is tied in with merit system procedure. Thus, five additional points are usually given on examination ratings to veterans (and ordinarily to their wives or widows) and ten to disabled veterans, with a degree of ten percent disability qualifying for the latter. Another feature in the federal policy is that disabled veterans must be listed at the top of a register, regardless of earned rating, except for professional positions above entry level.

Curiously, it was the Veterans' Preference Act of 1944 which, in first embedding such preferences into statutory form, at the same time legislated a merit system rule that had theretofore been instituted only by executive action, namely, the rule of three in certification. Although many state and municipal personnel laws had the certification process set up in statute, the U.S. Civil Service Act had, up to 1944, left to the President and the Civil Service Commission determination of the *method* of ensuring selection of the best.

In addition to tying the Commission's hands in this manner (and preventing sensible procedures such as category rating), the Act of 1944 prevented the Commission from establishing any minimum education requirement for entry to examinations except for certain professional occupations which the Commission must determine cannot be performed by a person without such education. Although this latter provision has not proved to be a serious handicap and may partially account for the federal civil service being less credential-bound than many of the states, it is clear that in its enthusiasm to guarantee preference for veterans the Congress went well beyond basic preference policy and legislated personnel employment procedures to a degree of detail unparalleled anywhere else in the world.

The federal law extends preference to apply to the employee appeals process and to retention during reductions in staff but omits its application to promotions. In the states, on the other hand, only a few give play to preference in staff reductions or appeals, but a number do provide for preference in promotion examinations. Most state preference laws cover local subdivisions, so that provisions in cities within a state are usually similar. Some states and cities have limited preference to one-time use by the veteran or to a period within several years following his discharge from military service or following a war. Prior to the Korean and the Vietnam hostilities there was a noticeable move afoot in the states to moderate some of the more drastic preferences legislated immediately after World War II.

Interestingly, it was the very mechanics of merit examination, rating, and certification that led to the precise forms of preference in the employing process. In those portions of state and city services still untouched by the merit concept, preference becomes, to all intents and purposes, absolute. In the federal service, it was not until 1953 that veterans were required to earn a passing grade on an examination before receiving premium points. Until that time the extra points could bring a failing candidate up to passing.

PEACETIME VETERANS   It is also significant that even the 1944 Act was confined to veterans who served during wartime or national emergency. This policy lasted for twenty-two years when, through a little noticed provision in the Veterans' Readjustment Benefits Act of 1966, it was reversed by extending preference also to peacetime veterans, in other words, anyone who served in the military services as long as six months. How such a policy can be justified on the grounds of reward for sacrifice or risk-taking could be labeled a thoroughgoing mystery if it were not for the suspicion that it grew out of the desire of key Congressmen to curry favor with the leadership of veterans' organizations, which must continually find fuel to stoke the fires of membership.

IMPACT   Little wonder that most of the public services in the United States contain anywhere from substantial and disproportionate numbers of veterans in their employment to overwhelming majorities. Following major conflicts like World War II, when many millions of men under arms were demobilized, this caused little dislocation, because the great bulk of employables, particularly those starting out on a civilian career, were veterans and most of the competition was among themselves. However, this is hardly the case when not only the dischargees from lesser conflicts but anyone with more than token service in military uniform (including men who chose it voluntarily as a career and are retired at an early age) may enter civil services with a special advantage and often are able to retain their posts in preference to nonveterans with longer service in the civil departments of government. Nor can it be overlooked that by its very nature veterans preference discriminates heavily against women in public employment.

REHIRING   Before turning to a more extended discussion of the justification and rationality for preference, we should take note of a related matter that is often confused with preference. This is the right of conscripted veterans to be rehired by the employer with whom they were engaged when they were drafted for duty to their country. It goes without saying that whenever the nation has some degree of compulsory military service, those men already in the government's employ who are drafted should be accorded genuine assurance of a right to return to their civilian pursuits without loss of any equities that may have accrued to their former colleagues while they were away.

Because of its critical relationship to the concepts of merit and equal opportunity, to say nothing of justice and social desirability, veteran preference deserves rather full attention here as an issue of long-range public policy for civil administration.

JUSTIFICATION FOR PREFERENCE

POLITICAL APPEAL   Enthusiasm for veteran preference in public employment rises and wanes in almost direct correlation to the public consciousness of its indebtedness to the generation which risked, and sometimes suffered, the supreme sacrifice in defense of the country's interests. Invariably when men's minds are on the pursuits of peace, usually some years after the last involvement of the nation in hostilities, there are moves to modify or restrict veteran preference. But at the height of or immediately after engagement in international conflicts, such movements are completely swamped by the urge of legislators to outdo each other in devising rewards for the veteran.[5]

[5] Examples of studies or proposals at various times in recent history, most of them anomalously succeeded by laws to extend rather than limit preference, are:

A. John F. Miller, "Veteran Preference in the Public Service," in Commission of Inquiry on Public Service Personnel, *Problems of the American Public Service*, New York, 1935, which presents the best resumé up to its time.
B. International Personnel Management Association (then the Civil Service Assembly), *The Employment of Veterans in the Public Service in the United States: A Report to the Assembly by the Committee on Veteran Employment Policies*, Chicago, August 1944; and National Civil Service League (then the National Civil Service Reform League), *Report of the Committee on Veteran Preference*, New York, 1945; both of which committees urged that preference not apply in promotions and that appointment preference be limited to a period of five years after a war or after discharge of the veteran, whichever is later.
C. Frederick C. Mosher, "Is Veteran Preference the Answer?" *Personnel Administration*, January 1946, pp. 1–7, who concludes that preference is wanting whether viewed from the standpoint of offsetting sacrifices, compensation for valor, or reward for service, and accordingly urges readjusting the veteran to the status he could reasonably expect to have attained if he had not been drafted, including full credit for his military experience and assistance in obtaining training and placement.
D. Sixth American Assembly, *The Federal Government Service: Its Character, Prestige, and Problems*, New York, Columbia University Graduate School of Business, 1954, p. 183; and Commission on Organization of the Executive Branch of the Government, *Task Force Report on Personnel and Civil Service*, Washington, D.C., February 1955, pp. 114–115; both of which groups proposed the five-year limitation first put forward by the IPMA and NCSL committees ten years earlier.
E. President's Commission on Veterans' Pensions, *Veterans' Benefits in the United States: A Report to the President*, Washington, D.C., April 1956, p. 319, which

PROSPECTS FOR CHANGE   A period following America's involvement in Southeast Asia is not a happy one in which to expect reform, but independent-minded people will continue to challenge the current concepts of preference as long as they are fixed in the statute books. The "professional veteran," representing organizations of veterans, will of course continue to resist change. It is the declared policy of the American Legion, for example, that it will not tolerate any "weakening" of the Veterans' Preference Act of 1944, a threat from which many a congressman runs scared in an election year.

The principal proposal over the years has been to limit employment preference to a few years after discharge or following hostilities, whichever is later in a given situation. It emerges from so many sources and so persistently (as indicated in footnote 5) that the reasoning behind it merits some analysis. It represents clearly an effort to achieve a balance in the obligation of the state to meet the genuine problem of employment of veterans during a period of demobilization while maintaining a high-quality administrative machine in which all citizens, veteran and nonveteran alike, have an equal stake.

ALTERNATIVE RATIONALES   In essence there are two basic philosophies underlying veteran preference in public employment: (1) the idea of preference as a continuing reward for service to the country and (2) the concept of preference as a readjustment aid to help veterans adjust to civilian life. Both concepts are evident in current policy, although the reward theory is the more heavily relied on and the one usually articulated by the average citizen. Acceptance of one or the other of these fundamental approaches to a rationalization of the subject, however, leads to substantially different conclusions regarding the kind and degree of preference that are appropriate.

REWARD THEORY   Under the reward philosophy government jobs become a form of gift, to be equated with pensions, bonuses, free medical care, and the like. Therefore, it is perfectly logical for a veteran to enjoy the benefits of the reward at any time he chooses to avail himself of it. Furthermore, it is

---

also recommended entrance preference and special appeal rights for only "a limited period," continuing preference in hiring and retention to be confined to disabled veterans with at least a 30-percent disability.

F. Bernard L. Gladieux, "Veteran Preference: Twenty Years After," *Good Government*, Winter 1964, pp. 61–69, who seriously challenged, with considerable statistical evidence, whether preference was justifiable or even needed or useful. Mr. Gladieux was Chairman of the Board of the National Civil Service League.

G. Commission on California State Government Organization and Economy, *Management Manpower Requirements*, Sacramento, California, February 1965, which recommended that for the state service hiring preference be restricted to periods of national emergency and the succeeding five years, granted only once, and applied only to positions below the managerial and policy-setting levels.

H. One veterans' organization, the American Veterans' Committee (AVC), which came out for the following limitations at its 1972 convention: (1) limiting preference to initial appointment and (2) opposing absolute preference in state and local civil services. See *Congressional Record*, November 8, 1972, p. E9169.

only on this theory that various forms of preference after a veteran is in the service can be defended—for example, preference in promotions and transfers and in retention during staff reductions. In fact, if we accept the reward idea as the main reason for preference, there is really no substantive limit as to the forms and degree that preference might logically assume. We would make the reward as generous as possible. The only limitation would be the burden on the economy and the willingness and ingenuity of citizens and legislators to develop new forms of gratuity. A continuation of this philosophy could lead to a gradual increase in the number of persons entitled to preference and in the already high proportion of the public service made up of veterans.

A major flaw in this line of reasoning is that it ignores the sacrifices and hazards endured by nonmilitary groups in the population who are equally patriotic and actually may be more exposed to the dangers of modern warfare than are some military personnel. In an atomic age, how can we distinguish between the valor of the civilian aircraft spotter and that of the soldier who may or may not actually go to battle? Or between the civilian telephone operator who mans a post during an attack and the officers on a desk assignment in the Pentagon? This is not to disparage military service but only to point up the pitfalls of the reward approach in recognition of such service through public jobs.

READJUSTMENT THEORY   The readjustment concept starts from a substantially different premise. Rewards for military service and achievement would be provided in ways other than use of public office. It is reasoned, nevertheless, that because men are removed from their normal civilian pursuits during time of war, their employer (the government) is under special obligation to see to it that they are restored to a situation in civil life as nearly approximating where they otherwise would have been as practicable and to make this adjustment as swiftly and smoothly as possible. Hence, providing an advantage in reemployment of a veteran with this same employer—this time as a civilian—seems entirely logical. It is especially defensible when the advantage can be granted without compromise of the general proposition of merit in public service selection processes. By and large, the more common preference devices of added points on a passing grade have reasonably achieved this objective.

The readjustment concept has further implications, however. It would not support absolute preference, such as placing names at the top of a list. It would not offer a basis for continuing initial employment preference to a veteran after the first few years following his release from military service. Finally, it would not rationalize provision of preferential treatment of veterans after they are already in the service, such as in promotions, in reductions in staff, and in appeal processes.

Obviously it is the readjustment concept that is behind the various proposals for a time limit on preference in entrance to the public service. It is the only concept that can be defended without going blindly down the path of placing the government's responsibility to one sector of its citizenry ahead of its responsibility to all, of risking the reduction of its administrative agencies to a state of mediocrity. Eventually it is those veterans failing at other lines of endeavor who seek the sanctuary of the public service when special entrance privileges are available to them for life. Especially now that preference rights are extended in the federal service to peacetime veterans, the threat in the future is all the greater—and without even the excuse of doing a favor for those who actually saw combat or otherwise saw service during a period of hostilities.

It seems clear that until enough politicians muster the courage to resist the blandishments and threats of the professional veteran, little improvement in preference provisions will be forthcoming, although it is easier to get modification at state and local levels than at the national.[6] There is reason to believe that rank-and-file veterans are not actually carrying on a crusade for civil service preference. Several studies over the years have shown this, notably one conducted by the National Civil Service League which indicated little support by veterans for favoritism in lay-offs and even substantial questioning of the need for advantage in entrance examinations. Those who favored giving the most to veterans tended to be World War I men, active members of veterans' organizations, those with only elementary school education, and those with low incomes.[7]

In short, it is the readjustment theory of the state's responsibility to its military creditors that offers a reasonable basis for action on this thorny subject. Under this theory preference would be *a temporary privilege during a period immediately following international conflicts, would not extend to in-service favoritism, and would not apply at all to peacetime veterans.* Here, then, is another area for statesmanship in the never-ending quest for the upgrading of American public services.

AFFIRMATIVE ACTION FOR EQUAL OPPORTUNITY

In other chapters much has already been said about the importance and challenge of ensuring that all citizens have a fair and equal opportunity to employment in the public service.[8] Lest it be assumed that indefensible

---

[6] As evidenced by stirrings in various places, such as Pennsylvania and Minnesota. See Orville C. Peterson, "Too Much Veterans Preference," *Minnesota Municipalities,* March 1967. On the other hand, North Dakota in 1973 first extended to veterans top preference in state, county, and city jobs.

[7] "Veterans Aren't So Sure About Veterans' Preference," *Good Government,* July–August 1959.

[8] Note the discussion in Chapter 2 on "the Personnel Function in Society," in Chapter 7 on "Manpower Planning and Attraction," and in Chapter 8 on "Methods of Examination." Still more is covered in Chapter 10 on "Selection: From Inside the Service."

A useful tool for achievement is a U.S. Civil Service Commission pamphlet, *Equal Employment Opportunity in State and Local Governments—A Guide for Affirmative Action,* Washington, D.C., 1972. It suggests a variety of procedures to ensure equal opportunity for minority groups and women.

practices working to the disadvantage of women or minority groups are anathema only in the recruitment and examination stages of the employment process, attention should be drawn here to the special caveats that concern the final steps in appointment.

The concerns and rulings of the U.S. Commission on Civil Rights and the Equal Employment Opportunity Commission have understandably concentrated on the formal aspects of employment—the requirements for job entry, recruitment practices, and examination processes. This has also been the focus of attention of the courts when judicial procedures have been brought to bear on public employment. To be sure, these are important points at which to bring the proper pressure for conformance to the equal opportunity principle. So-called affirmative action programs have, for example, especially stressed the need to reach heretofore neglected strata of society to ensure that all are aware of their opportunities to work for government.

Nevertheless, well-run merit systems have acquitted themselves commendably in the employment of women and minority members of the American work force.[9] In the experience of this author, the most serious handicaps to equal opportunity have been the maljudgments made by individual administrators and selection officers in their insistence on certain entry requirements and in the final steps of selection from among certified eligible candidates. Although this is a more subtle area to deal with, it is a realistic one if we are to eradicate the last vestiges of prejudice and myopic thinking in public employment.[10]

---

[9] See the impressive record of various state and local jurisdictions and the federal service in O. Glenn Stahl, *A Fair Look at Fair Employment,* Chicago, International Personnel Management Association, 1971.

Note should be taken here of a book that insists that good personnel management, especially basing selection and placement on job analysis, is what best ensures affirmative action to bring about true equal opportunity: Clement J. Berwitz, *The Job Analysis Approach to Affirmative Action,* New York, Wiley, 1975.

[10] The legitimate objectives of equal opportunity and affirmative action to help ensure that opportunity are sometimes obscured by misguided efforts to acquire quick "representativeness" by all sectors of society in public agencies or other institutions. Almost invariably, overzealous and hastily devised processes lead to "reverse discrimination," that is, giving preference to persons of minority races, women, or others regardless of their standing compared with better-qualified individuals. This was allegedly the case when the University of Washington Law School established a dual admission system for minority and nonminority applicants for admission. When a white male, DeFunis, was denied admission, he sued on the grounds that he had been discriminated against on account of his race. After being admitted under state court order and continued in school under order by a single U.S. Supreme Court justice (William O. Douglas), his case finally came before the full Supreme Court, a bare majority of which declared the matter moot, since DeFunis by that time was already near graduation. Justice Douglas, nevertheless, in a noted dissent, argued that the Court should have ruled on the issue and contended as regards the plaintiff: "Whatever his race, he had a constitutional right to have his application considered on its individual merits in a racially neutral manner." In rejecting proportional representation, Justice Douglas also said:

> The State . . . may not proceed by racial classification to force strict population equivalencies for every group in every occupation, overriding individual preferences. The Equal Protection Clause commands the elimination of racial barriers, not

THE PROBATIONARY PERIOD

One more feature of the selection process at initial entry warrants special mention—the use of a probationary period following appointment during which the appointee must demonstrate his capacity to perform the work before his employment becomes final. Almost without exception, personnel laws or rules provide for such an extension of the formal examining stage, usually for periods of six months to a year and sometimes varying as among different groups of positions.

In effect , the probationary period is part of the examining and selection policy, adding trial on the job to the more artificial conditions of formal examination. It affords administrators and personnel officials an opportunity to gauge those intangible and personal qualities of a new employee that are not assayed by tests or other examining techniques. It is a check on the whole selection procedure and also provides a means for remedying awkward or inappropriate placements. The only substantive question that has been raised about the policy is that it may foster unrealistic assumptions of permanency once probation is successfully completed, whereas meeting work standards should be a *continuing* requirement in all jobs.

The major reservation about the impact of the trial period is its lack of use by supervisors who are too often inclined to let a relationship drift without using the occasion for a clear understanding of the tentative character of the contract with the new recruit, for positive development of the employee's understanding of the organization and his role in it, for clarification of all that is expected of him, for positive training, for correction of flaws in his work, for remedial placement where it might improve a situation, and for weeding out, when all else fails, those who do not measure up to the demands of the assignment. Conscientious use of the probationary period for the foregoing purposes can be a vital capstone to a well-rounded selection procedure.

To ensure effective capitalization on the idea, some jurisdictions have provided that a probationer will be automatically separated unless the supervisory official supports a positive certification that his work has been sufficiently satisfactory to warrant his continuance in the organization. This device is referred to as a "positive probationary period," as contrasted with the more standard situations in which the employee may achieve continuing status automatically unless the supervisor remembers to evaluate and report

---

their creation in order to satisfy our theory as to how society ought to be organized. [*DeFunis* v. *Odegaard*, 1974.]

These are significant statements, coming as they do from a justice noted for his liberal views.

In other instances around the country, either courts or administrative bodies concerned with civil rights enforcement have had to restrain public executives bent upon achieving representativeness overnight by fiat regardless of comparative qualifications.

For a comprehensive analysis of the various meanings of "representativeness," see David H. Rosenbloom, "Forms of Bureaucratic Representation in the Federal Service," *Midwest Review of Public Administration*, July 1974, pp. 159–177.

on his performance before the deadline. Forcing the supervisor or manager to give full consideration to an appraisal and to make a definite decision on the employee may also be achieved by requiring a report from him at some point prior to the end of the period. Either procedure is likely to avoid attainment of relative permanency by default.

* * *

STILL OTHER CONSIDERATIONS may be explored in a study of the initial selection process, but the foregoing subjects of employment lists, veteran preference, affirmative action, and probationary periods are the most important. We may proceed, then, to a review of the policies and practices relating to selection of personnel from the resources already within the organization or jurisdiction.

CHAPTER 10

Selection: From Inside the Service

As INDICATED AT the outset of the preceding chapter, the process of selection for staffing is primarily one of filling positions, regardless of the source of the candidates. The fact that staffing from within involves a source closer at hand and requires special methods of recruiting and selection is ample reason for separate treatment of that subject in this chapter. Even more important, however, is that filling positions from among persons already in the service implies movement of personnel by *promotion and transfer.*

In initial recruitment we are not fully concerned with the morale of the entire recruitment field, that is, the general public as a whole, except to ensure open access and to maintain good public relations. In selection from within, on the other hand, we must be very much concerned with the morale of the whole recruitment field, namely, the employee group which comprises the organization. Opportunity for advancement and the chance to make the best possible use of one's capacities form one of the wellsprings of human motivation. The proper determination of positions which can be filled by selection of the ablest employees for advancement, the development of employees to their maximum usefulness, and the proper balance between inside and outside recruitment lie at the very heart of good personnel administration.

PROMOTION ISSUES

Many public jurisdictions have made considerable progress toward the goals just enunciated. Others, however, still fall far short of a reasonably good system. Even among those that have achieved some success, as have the more progressive state and municipal governments and the federal service, there is considerable disagreement over form and method.

BASIC POLICY   There is still much vagueness about what is meant by a "promotion program." From the nature of the generalizations on the subject some personnel specialists and employee groups appear to assume that all employees are to be *guaranteed* promotions to new responsibilities from time to time; others jump to the conclusion that outside recruitment is undesirable except for the *lowest* rung in the civil service structure. Not enough people see a promotion program as part of a general staffing policy, a policy for filling positions with the ablest available talent, of which outside recruitment is another integral part at many levels in the structure.

Some highly inbred government organizations take satisfaction in a tightly knit promotion-from-within policy. Yet they are seldom among the best-run agencies. It may be that occasionally the one-time unskilled office boy who becomes bureau chief is a near genius at things administrative and achieves brilliant success, but more often than not he is, without extraordinary capacity and much formal training, dismally unfit for a top post. Many are the clerks in executive positions who are still operating them as clerical jobs. No— the intent of a sound promotion policy is not to rule out encroachments from the outside and to ensure inbreeding.

SENIORITY   Nor is it to emphasize years of experience. Too often the highly touted "twenty years of experience," before which all those within hearing are expected to bow down, is merely one year of experience multiplied twenty times. Staying power is not by itself a virtue unless it has been accompanied by progress and growth. And so we must especially give thought here to what is perhaps the most basic and compelling issue of all in promotion policy: the concern for objectivity and the contest between merit and seniority for the role of dominant criterion.

The classical complaint about flexible promotion systems is invariably that too many decisions under them are capricious, that "favorites" (whatever that may mean) are given preference too often, and that merit is an unattainable illusion; and indeed evidence can almost always be adduced to make at least some semblance of a case for existence of such behavior in any jurisdiction. But along with the risks of caprice and favoritism we must consider the infirmities of the alternative: relying on that most objective of criteria, seniority. If clumsy efforts at applying merit deserve disapprobation, then seniority, however well operated, deserves absolute condemnation. The question is: which produces the more serious and longer-range ill effects? The employee's wounds of being passed over (even unjustifiably) in favor of a younger or newer candidate may be severe, but they usually heal in time, and, what's more, he usually has another chance. In contrast, the dead hand of disincentive, the downright stagnation so often observed in seniority-ridden organizations leave shortcomings in the performance and spirit of an enterprise that are almost impossible to eradicate.[1]

ROLE OF JUDGMENT   However, we cannot face the issue merely in terms of the lesser of two evils. Every effort can be made to sharpen the modes of appraisal, to objectify the process of selection by pooling judgments and by avoiding overconcentration of selection authority, and otherwise to make merit as practical, objective, and real as possible. When all is said and done, this is what this chapter is all about. But, in the last analysis, there will always have to be a certain amount of hard-headed subjective judgment in promotion, just as in original appointment—especially when one is predicting what a person's "potential" appears to be.

And here is where administrators (to say nothing of others speaking for the public interest) need to make their stand. Even if performance evaluation systems are faulty and need constant repair, even if human beings make fallible judgments—to make judgments is the reason managers and supervisors exist. It is idle to assume that their reasoning counts for so little that their latitude must be hobbled by arbitrary seniority rules. If such judgments—however subjective they may have to be—count for naught, one might as well try running an organization on an anarchistic basis, with no supervisors at all.

Individual employees are in no position to see themselves in perspective in relation to other competitors for promotion. Yet it is ordinarily the disgruntlement of the few that dictates mechanical, seniority-laden promotion policies. Outstanding people rarely complain and rarely have cause to do so. In any event, we must keep reminding ourselves that *an organization, especially a public one, is not the private property of those who work there,* and it exists for purposes that override any ambitions of its employees to achieve higher rank or pay.

If our choice lies only between relying on managerial judgment and responding to pressure for a system that works automatically, then in the interest of productivity and the public welfare we must choose managerial judgment. The encrustations of seniority around the world constitute clearly the most serious of any conceivable deficiency, and experience suggests that they must be avoided almost at all costs. But hopefully, managerial judgment need not be devoid of rationality and fairness. The task is to make

---

[1] Felix A. Nigro has put it well:

> In appraising morale and worker satisfactions, a distinction should be made between 'resentments' caused by unfair treatment, and the sense of disappointment naturally experienced by the unsuccessful candidates. For the organization as a whole most employees will be more satisfied and the public better served, when recognition is on a merit basis, rather than on time-serving. [*Management-Employee Relations in the Public Service*, Chicago, International Personnel Management Association, 1969, p. 52.]

it as objective as is humanly feasible. We must avoid indefensible personal favoritism, certainly, but above all we must avoid the oversimplified versions of promotion that result in little more than the progressive advancement of mediocrity or the periodic elevation of durability.

UPGRADING MINORITIES AND WOMEN   An aspect of promotion policy receiving emphasis in recent years grows out of the affirmative action efforts to make certain that various ethnic groups and women, while having initial access to public jobs, do not lose out in the promotion process. Without doing violence to the merit principle, many jurisdictions have of necessity had to reexamine their traditional devices to adjudge employees for promotion to new or higher responsibilities. These efforts, both in the federal service and among state and local governments under pressure from federal legislation as well as federal grant programs, are generally along the following lines:

1. Expansion of in-service training opportunities, covering more areas of subject-matter and including basic skill training. At one time initial training in basic skills, such as typing, stenography, computer operation, manual crafts, and the like, was considered inappropriate for the public employer on the grounds that acquisition of such skills was the responsibility of the individual to obtain from general educational sources, especially from the public schools. The increased sensitivity to the deprivations of minority groups in the educational process, however, has resulted in a transformation of this attitude. It is now widely recognized that, to make it possible for many heretofore-discriminated-against people to advance in the service, their concentration in menial jobs can be broken only by equipping them with skills and knowledge that will enable them to compete with their more fortunate colleagues for more useful and rewarding positions.
2. Adjusting training techniques to accommodate to the special needs of educationally deprived persons. This often involves attention to language used in training manuals and presentations, especially when directed to groups not always as comfortable with everyday business English, such as Spanish-speaking persons or ghetto blacks. It also includes more imaginative use of visual aids.
3. Constant attention to methods of measurement in the process of selection for promotion. Just as in initial entry, the considerations of validity and reliability are vital to ensure against discrimination on any grounds irrelevant to the needs of the jobs being filled.[2]
4. Education of selection officers to ensure that in the final steps of selection for promotion no one is ruled out because of his or her sex, race, religion, or other condition unrelated to the work.

[2] See the discussion in Chapter 8.

No promotion policy is worth the paper it is written on, no matter how refined its techniques, if it allows the narrow and myopic prejudices of even a few misguided officials to prevent minority groups, women, or any other category of employees from access to advancement solely on the basis of their knowledge, skill, and personal attributes. The mythology of racial or sexual differences in capacity has long ago been thoroughly discredited.[3] All persons, whatever their origins, must in a democratic society have completely equal chances to contribute their talents to the work of that society. The vast array of public services in this country has already gone far to set the example and must continue to do so.

At the same time, we cannot afford to overlook that individual differences among people do exist and that promotion policy and practice must be directed at these genuine differences. Zeal to ensure fairness and opportunity to all must not be prostituted so that lesser competence is elevated over greater competence. The sooner all personnel policy can be divested of "special emphases" and focused on the qualities of individuals, regardless of any category to which they may belong, the better our public services will be.

OTHER POLICY INGREDIENTS   Before turning to an exploration of the scope of promotion opportunity, the area of competition, methods for selection, and the use of reassignment and transfer for employee development or readjustment, we should take note of several other ingredients of sound selection policy that are usually missing in organizations that do not justify the adjective "livewire." Some of these essentials are: (1) practical and understandable qualification standards for positions; (2) adequate records and machinery that provide a means for identifying the best candidates within the unit; (3) good measures of overall competence and potentiality; (4) comprehensive training programs to keep the staff alert to new developments and to prepare promising men and women for advancement and for supervision; (5) promotion and transfer across division lines within a bureau, department, or jurisdiction, ensuring as broad a field of selection and opportunity as possible; and (6) clear distinction between clerical jobs, requiring manipulative skills and aptitudes, and executive jobs, requiring superior training, imagination, and ability, so that the latter are not filled by default primarily from the ranks of the former but go to employees with the education, the breadth of view and experience, the capacity to deal in ideas as well as with "things," the gifts and character to lead, to innovate,—yes, and to make the rational judgments in promotion of others that are espoused here.

[3] For a lively and informative exposition of the breakdown of the myths and prejudices about women in executive jobs, see Edith M. Lynch, *The Executive Suite— Feminine Style*, New York, Amacom (American Management Association), 1973. For some methodology to help bring about upward mobility for women and minorities see U.S. Civil Service Commission, *Equal Employment Opportunity in State and Local Governments—A Guide for Affirmative Action*, Washington, D.C., 1972.

SCOPE OF PROMOTION OPPORTUNITY

Several conditions affect how much promotion opportunity an organization really has: (1) the kind of career system that exists;[4] (2) the initial recruitment and examining policy, that is, the degree to which people are selected on the basis of capacity for advancement; (3) the number of key posts that are reserved to political appointment; (4) the proportion of career-type appointments from the outside above junior levels; (5) the size and heterogeneity of the organization; and (6) the elements of dynamism, growth, or change in the organization's program of work. The impact of most of these factors on the chances for promotions within the ranks is fairly clear, but several points warrant some further explanation.

For a long time American jurisdictions were inclined to found much of their junior-level recruitment upon the basis of acquiring ready-made skills instead of looking for broader abilities. In the larger places this has drastically changed. The creation of internships and training grades has underscored the now common practice of recruiting expressly for advancement. Such an approach is most applicable to the professions and various managerial occupations. Clearly it makes promotion from within more practical from all points of view.

Likewise, in the early days of civil service reform, the exclusion of a great many higher-level positions from merit system coverage had the effect of cutting off promotion possibilities for competitively appointed employees at a considerably less than desirable plane. Both the expansion upward of merit systems and the increasing reliance on career groups as a source for political or policy-making appointees have combined to mitigate this impact. Finding the optimum point beyond which careerists should normally not aspire is not easy, but to maintain a democratically controlled and responsive bureaucracy maximum promotion-possibility must give way to leaving at least the very top posts open to the choice of political leadership.[5]

And the same may be said for operating an open service within the career ranks. It has been demonstrated many times that a closed career system is not necessary to assure reasonable frequency and volume of promotion. The advantage of filling higher positions from within is obvious, but it is also clear that much is to be gained by leaving the door ajar for some infusion of "new blood." There may be little profit in looking outside to fill the majority of jobs in lower-ranking occupations or in lines of work peculiar to government employment. But, particularly for technical and managerial-type assignments, living up to the ideal of finding the best available talent may require at least a check on what the outside market can offer. It is a

[4] In the several senses discussed in Chapter 4.

[5] Of course, selection of career people for such posts should by no means be precluded, but when it is done, they cannot expect their career status to attach to the exempt position. As indicated elsewhere, career ranks have sometimes been a principal source for presidential or other political appointments in the federal service.

healthy procedure to see every now and then how people in the organization "stack up" against other competition. An occasional selection from outside can provide far more of a boon to an agency's outlook and to its resistance to provincialism than it does discouragement to the aspirations of its employees. And, of course, sometimes "outside" means merely another agency in the same or related governmental jurisdiction, in which case we are still talking about promotion from within—all of which leads to our next topic, the "area" or the "field" within which promotion opportunity is conceived and practiced.

AREA OF SELECTION AND PROMOTION

The extent of the area from which promotional candidates are recruited is affected by a number of factors. The most obvious is the size of the particular service or the particular occupation. Other things being equal, the appointing officers and the personnel agency will have wider choice in a large service or in a heavily populated occupation. But just as important are those limiting factors to be found within the particular service itself. These include the qualifications set up to govern promotion, the restriction of candidates to certain grades or classes of the service or to certain departments or establishments, the methods of promotion employed, and the transfer policy.

At the outset, it should be clearly recognized that promotion placement is as dependent upon a sound duties classification as is original placement. Only when the positions within the organization have been grouped in logical relation to one another, when lines of promotion have been clearly indicated upon the basis of the duties of the various positions, can a promotion policy be administered intelligently. The presence of a classification scheme means order; it facilitates a bird's-eye view of all positions and their interrelationships.

ORGANIZATIONAL MYOPIA   One of the most serious limitations on the area of promotion, from the standpoint both of the quality of selections and its effect on the whole service, is the common restriction of competition for higher positions to those within the particular bureau or office in which these positions are located. Such confinement of the promotion area, particularly if transfers between offices are likewise inflexible, has these unfortunate consequences: (1) the narrower the breadth of competition, the more likely the ultimate choice will be less than the best; (2) such a policy results in great inequalities in promotion opportunities among various branches of the service; and (3) it prevents the development of a service-wide point of view and stultifies the kind of mobility that contributes to the making of top-notch executives.

There are, of course, a number of influences that explain the persistence of this practice. It is, first of all, in the line of least resistance. There is a natural unwillingness to disturb a team of workers in one unit by advancing someone from another unit into it or moving out one of the team to another unit. Further, workers in any one unit usually feel they have a kind of vested right in their branch of the organization. Also, it may sometimes be argued that the work of various units is so different that employees even of the same class are not readily transferrable among units.

The question is how weighty these considerations are in comparison with what is lost by keeping the field narrow, and also whether differences in work among units cannot be taken into account in the evaluation process. The ultimate criterion is the good of the whole service. Even allowing for suitable breaking-in periods for outsiders, more often than not vacancies in any one unit will probably be filled largely by people from the lower ranks in that unit. The lesson here is not to favor moving employees in from the other parts of the service without reason but to make certain that they are not precluded from such placement because of arbitrary, thoughtless, or habitual exclusion.

DATA ADEQUACY   One of the problems in making a service-wide promotion policy work is that of having the right information in the right place at the right time. Adequate records on the demands of positions plus useful data on the qualifications of all employees are indispensable. They are much more important than insistence on service-wide competitive testing, which may get too far away from appraisal of actual demonstrated performance in favor of results in the relatively artificial atmosphere of a written test. However useful the latter may be in initial entry, they are appropriate within the service only when the candidates under consideration are without the specific experience required in the job being filled, as, for example, when non-supervisory employees are being reviewed for a supervisory post. In such case, testing for the presence of qualities that could not have been demonstrated on the job makes sense. The materials that must be used in the majority of promotion decisions, however, undoubtedly will be the records of experience, training, performance, and predictions of potential that are continuously maintained.

EFFECT OF SIZE   Another factor is size, both of the total service and of the occupation in which promotion is being made. Wherever there are large numbers of people engaged in a field of work concentrated within one organizational entity, the scope of competition may be quite adequate to assure management a chance to find as good a pick as it could get anywhere and to provide employees a periodic opportunity to move upward. Under such circumstances there is little point in extending the competition to a service-wide scope. But, more often than not, people in related occupations and with similar skills are scattered among various branches of a governmental jurisdiction. Then the question becomes simply one of the practicality of size in determining the promotion area.

What may be practical for a municipality with a few thousand employees may not be feasible for even one federal department, several of which are beyond the hundred-thousand class. What may be service-wide in a moderate-sized state or a fairly large city may be bureau-wide, or department-wide, or locality-wide in the federal civil service. In line with a comprehensive policy applying to all branches of the national service, all agencies have systems and techniques designed to make promotion opportunity as much a reality as possible within a gigantic, sprawling bureaucracy. These include elaborate indexes to employee qualifications, schemes for publicizing vacancies, participation of employee organizations and managers in developing plans, and a variety of evaluation devices, including written tests only where directly supportable, for making selections. In view of the scattering of federal establishments across the land, there is still room, however, for more cooperation among the smaller units of various departments located in any one metropolitan area or region.

The separatist attitude so typical of government agencies at all levels, federal, state, and local, cannot be defended in the light of the criteria for sound promotion systems advocated here. Greater mobility is the byword of today and of the foreseeable future. To avoid artificial obstructions to the free and natural upward flow of talent, there can be no arbitrary restrictions on the promotion area except where it is obvious that to extend it further would serve no useful purpose in locating the ablest employees and placing them where both they and the jurisdiction would profit from the full utilization of their capacities.

METHODS FOR DISCOVERING AND USING TALENT

Wherever a central personnel authority exists, whether in a government or a large corporation, there is frequently debate over the operating manager's hand in promotions. His acquaintance with employee performance and promise and his responsibility for getting the work out are strong forces that compel vesting considerable freedom of choice in his judgment, a fact of life we have already stressed. On the other hand, if every supervisory official were left maximum freedom, we would not very likely have the service-wide approach that is at least as compelling for the larger good of the entire jurisdiction. The dilemma can never be perfectly resolved, but approximations can be reached when these officials participate in developing a system, are forced to think in terms beyond their own specific bailiwicks, and become acquainted with the problems and issues of good selection methods, their validity, and their risks. The logical role of the personnel agency is one of leadership, pointing out what needs to be determined, introducing knowledge of techniques and principles, establishing final policy, and supervising the continuing requirements that seem most advisable.

Furthermore, in a well-conceived career system, analyses of employee aptitude and potential should be conducted soon after employment and followed at reasonable intervals with deeper appraisals. Although adequate to the job for which he was originally selected, an employee may have potential for different types of work which he can perform even better. This is not often a fact known to any one supervisor. Although trial on many jobs may be an ideal method to gauge a person's prospects, it is not practical to sample more than a tiny fraction of the wide range of tasks usually available in a public agency, and many positions require special knowledge or skills that can only be developed through training or substantial experience.

In reality, there are much better opportunities for evaluating employee aptitudes and potential than there are for evaluating applicant qualifications for initial entry to the civil service. For one thing, the employee's interests can be probed more deeply than the applicant's because of the opportunity for closer observation and interviewing. Also, outside applicants in their effort to demonstrate their capacity for the particular work for which they are applying sometimes bias their statements to emphasize part of their repertoire of abilities, whereas after an employee is fully oriented to an organization and to its interest in him he is open to a wider variety of devices for discovery of more of his talents. Under a continuing inventory of employee worth, ample and more accurate information is available for use in deciding on promotions.

Among the measures used to determine promotability, the following would seem to be the most prominent: (1) comparison of previous education and experience, (2) comparison of performance within the organization, (3) trial on the job, (4) objective testing of skills and aptitudes, and (5) the one that repudiates all the other four—seniority. Having already devoted considerable space to the last one, we hardly need to say more here, other than to acknowledge this method's rigid objectivity and simultaneously to deplore its lack of validity.

MEASURING ACHIEVEMENT

The first two measures have this in common: they may be carried out coterminously with the use of some of the same devices—the maintenance of personal achievement records and of locator mechanisms that will help sift out qualified candidates wherever they may be in the organization. The nature and utility of such devices warrant some amplification.

PERSONAL ACHIEVEMENT RECORDS Comprehensive records are the basis of any successful program of promotion and transfer. These should cover examination records, performance reports, special abilities, education and training, experience, hobbies, interests—anything that may be of probative value from the placement standpoint. They should, moreover, be kept current. Information concerning the acquirement of a special skill or interest, completion of a training course, admittance to the bar, certification as a public accountant, and similar matters should be recorded promptly. It may easily be the deciding factor in the selection of a candidate for promotion.

Many departments request that employees inform the personnel office of all changes in their qualifications and interests which might conceivably have a bearing on promotion, lay-off, and similar matters. The whole burden of keeping records up to date should not be placed upon the employee, however. The maintenance of adequate records is a personnel function of basic importance and should therefore be the responsibility of the personnel office. Where a central file is maintained and a system of interorganization transfers and promotions has been set up, the task will naturally fall to the central personnel agency. In other instances it may be the responsibility of the department personnel offices. Periodic surveys of employee qualifications help ensure up-to-dateness.

INDEX TO QUALIFIED CANDIDATES   Even though records are up to date, they are of little use unless there is some easy method of finding all those that would be relevant in reviewing candidates for a particular vacancy. In large organizations this process can be facilitated by the application of tapes, punch-cards, or other electronic methods. Such instruments do not, of course, increase the reliability of the records, but they do enhance the certainty that when a vacancy occurs all persons in the organization possessing the necessary qualifications will be considered. In smaller organizations other devices may be employed. Many agencies have successfully used a cross-occupational card index system, which catalogues each employee under all the occupations, skills, and kinds of positions he seems to be qualified for. The catalogue is a supplementary record device which enhances the value of the personal information on file.

Whatever the device for finding all candidates who meet minimum qualification requirements for the job, this step is merely one of developing the recruitment field. The punch-card data or occupational index card is simply a means to pull the full records on each employee, and this information then constitutes the basis for the referral of the best candidates and for the final selection. Furthermore, such indexes do not always provide an adequate check on the *potentiality* of employees for work different from or higher than that which they have been performing. This lack is particularly observed in seeking adequate measures to predict leadership skill and aptitude when considering nonsupervisory employees for promotion to supervisory jobs. The central importance of good supervision to all that is held up as ideal in personnel management clearly makes better selection of supervisors a prime requisite in modern administration.

USING THE DATA   The use of personal achievement records and indexes to qualified candidates brings up another important point, namely, who shall use them and make the judgments? We have already stressed the individual manager's role in a final selection, but his step comes at the very end of the process. Much winnowing and culling must occur before that step.

By and large, these principles may be enunciated: the first sorting and narrowing of the volume of names that are pointed up by the mechanical contrivances may be made by the professionals in the process—the personnel officials; the next, and more serious, state of developing a final list to go to the appointing official should be the product of the judgment of a committee, panel, or other duly constituted group of responsible and knowledgeable persons in the organization who understand the requirements of the job being filled, the promotion standards being followed, and the qualifications of all the candidates. These may be different groups for different types of jobs. It is an expensive procedure but not nearly so expensive as placing too much reliance on the isolated judgments of isolated managers and opening the selection process to all kinds of complaints and resistance. There is not only safety but wisdom in numbers. Pooling judgments in the final winnowing stage can reduce markedly the doubts and suspicions about how people got on the final list.

Perhaps needless to add, a flexible promotion policy would permit some flexibility in the number of names to be certified. Normally the number should range anywhere from at least two to no more ordinarily than five. This should provide ample opportunity for the selecting officer to do the final interviewing and exercise those subjective but essential judgments that are vital to all responsible administration.

TRIAL ON THE JOB

The next measure is trial on the job, perhaps the ideal technique by which to judge the promotability of employees for higher responsibilities—but one with grave procedural faults. The device of temporary assignment to a higher post permits observation of the facility with which employees adapt to the new requirements and of their possession of those intangible qualities which are so critical but so difficult to gauge otherwise. But the possibility of wholesale use of the technique is obviously very limited. Where one-of-a-kind positions are being filled, especially when there is no lengthy advance period before they become vacant or where there are more than two or three good candidates for a given job, it is usually quite impractical to delay final selection by a series of "details" or "secondments" of all candidates in succession. And it is clearly impolitic to single out one candidate, give him the exclusive chance to demonstrate his wares, and thereby preclude others from the same chance.

There are some circumstances, however, under which trial on the job may be feasible. One is to make maximum use of subordinate staff to replace higher officials while the latter are on vacation. In this fashion, over a period of years, a record on the performance of at least several likely prospects could be built up. Of course, there would have to be some sort of competition arranged to determine who were given the opportunities to substitute for the boss. Another occasion occurs when the retirement of a supervisor is known long in advance, say a year or more ahead. Finally, where there are multiple jobs of a higher level that are more or less identical and where there is a fairly continuous series of promotions into these jobs, a planned program of trial assignments could be the regular order of the day.

EVALUATIONS OF POTENTIAL

WRITTEN TESTS   The nature and limitations of written tests have already been thoroughly explored. Their successful use in the promotion situation tends to be concentrated in those instances where candidates under consideration have had no opportunity to display their prowess in the job or line of work involved, such as in filling supervisory positions when only nonsupervisory candidates are available or in the case of jobs for which all the candidates are in *related* but not the *same* kind of work. In these circumstances the internal recruitment task is somewhat parallel to that in measuring the relative abilities of persons from outside the organization or jurisdiction.

Also, formal written test competition may be useful in a very large organization, such as a mass clerical or mechanical operation or a metropolitan police force, where a number of higher jobs may be filled at any one time and the number of eligible candidates within the organization is substantial. In such cases the techniques of comparing performance in the past may not be refined enough to permit the number of distinctions that will be necessary. In any event, it is unlikely that written tests can be profitably used for promotion without their being combined with evaluation of past performance, special achievements or recognition that the employee-candidates have experienced, and their particular interests and goals.

ASSESSMENT CENTERS   Perhaps the most promising evaluation method for filling managerial and supervisory posts is the assessment center or assessment laboratory, terminology that refers to a process, not a place. Following earlier experimentation largely in private enterprise, a number of public jurisdictions in North America and the United Kingdom have reported notable success with the method.[6]

Actually the process consists not of a single device but a battery of evaluative and practice methods, and it places considerable emphasis on multiple judgments in appraisal. Although there are wide variations (as there should be for different situations), the principal ingredients are: one to three days of concentrated evaluation of a group of eight to twelve candidates; job-simulation exercises, including management games, "in-basket" trials, simulated interviews, oral or written exercises, and fact-finding sampling; occasional written tests or intensive interviews; and pooled assessment of each candidate by teams of professional assessors and managers who spend full

[6] See the illuminating articles in *Public Personnel Management*, September–October 1974: William C. Byham and Carl Wettengel, "Assessment Centers for Supervisors and Managers," pp. 352–364; and Donald S. Macrae, "An Academic Laboratory Report," pp. 367–377. A lengthy bibliography appears in the Macrae article.

time observing and reviewing candidate performance. Participants usually receive feedback on their performance.

The particular array of exercises or tests is always designed to be carefully related to the needs of the positions being filled, whether they be middle-manager jobs, police captains or chiefs, internships, senior executive posts, or entry slots into executive development programs. The substantial dependence on job analysis, the participation of top management in setting job requirements, the large amount of information accumulated on each person being evaluated, the formal methods of recording that information, and the use of trained observers are reasons given for the outstanding validity and utility of the assessment center technique. The feature of relying on multiple judgments is shared by other panel-evaluation methods, of course, but it is undoubtedly a major contributor to the success of this process as well.

PSYCHIATRIC TESTS   In this connection mention should be made of the general neglect of psychiatric tests. Public agencies have been slow to avail themselves of the knowledge and instruments of psychologists and psychiatrists in predicting the emotional maturity and adjustability of employees. The processes are lengthy and expensive, making them almost prohibitive for initial entry processes, but they offer considerable hope in gauging the personal attributes within the service that are so vital to many positions, such as those at executive level.

OTHER CONSIDERATIONS

PUBLICITY   Several other aspects of the promotion problem should be considered before closing this section. One is the issue of publicity about vacancies. That there should be general publicity within the organization as to lines of possible advancement and as to the prerequisites necessary for higher positions cannot be gainsaid. This can usually be accomplished through the device of employee handbooks, bulletin board announcements, and occasional flyers reminding employees and supervisors of the preparation required for various kinds of work and outlining training opportunities available both on and off the job.

There is considerable dispute, however, over the wisdom and necessity of publicizing vacancies as they occur. Employee organizations and many personnel specialists urge the following arguments in support of posting and advertising vacancies within the organization. First of all, no record or mechanical selection system is infallible. There may always be qualified individuals who have been overlooked and who should have consideration. Moreover, employees are not going to believe the system is infallible, even if it is, and are likely to be suspicious of unpublicized promotions. Second, the knowledge that promotions are regularly being made is an incentive of real potency. Conversely, there is nothing so deadly as the impression that an organization is static. Publicizing of promotion opportunities thus serves to bring whatever movement of personnel exists to the attention of the staff. Finally, the task of weeding out the applications of unqualified persons is not, in most instances, so formidable as to be decisive. Furthermore, it presents an excellent opportunity for calling the attention of the more ambitious employees to their deficiencies and to the means of overcoming them. Rejection can thus be turned into a positive asset if properly handled.

On the other hand, the arguments usually advanced against publicizing vacancies as they occur are that (1) the record system is so well devised that all qualified persons are known to the personnel office, (2) general publicity produces such a mass of applications as to handicap seriously the selection process, (3) knowledge of vacancies to which they are not appointed merely makes for unrest and dissatisfaction among large numbers of employees, and (4) many able employees are not disposed to apply when the initiative is left entirely to them. As to this last point, professional pride, particularly among technical and higher-level workers, leads many to feel that their qualities should be known and appreciated by top management and that they should not be reduced to the humiliation of "selling their wares" in order for management to discover them. This is an understandable reaction of sensitive and competent people of high education and attainment. Even among the rank and file, it is far from true that ambition and aggressiveness in promoting one's progress are in direct correlation with one's ability and skill.

These are potent and reasonable objections. The work of the organization must go on, and the filling of vacancies must not be unduly held up. As in many other personnel policy issues, the problem is not a simple black-or-white alternative. Under some conditions, as where special vacancies exist that are not filled frequently, it may be desirable to supplement existing candidate-finding systems with publicity which will elicit voluntary applications from interested employees. However, where similar jobs in relatively large numbers are periodically vacant because of normal turnover, it seems idle to post vacancies on bulletin boards in any precise sense. Such announcements would invariably be out of date as soon as they went up. The possibility of employee application may be better encouraged by disseminating the general information that certain types of positions are filled from time to time and that the qualification requisites are thus and so.

SOME SPECIAL CAVEATS   The observations in this chapter on the subject of promotion indicate what a complex process it is and how futile is the expectation of finding some simple and automatically operating measure. Here are problems to test the capacity of the most skilled administrator and to provide ample scope for that cooperation between the departments and the personnel agency without which the personnel system is of little value. In the last analysis, promotion, like all placement, must be handled upon the basis of careful individual judgments, although the establishment of formal bases of selection, if not too rigidly prescribed, aids the administrator by narrowing his problem.[7]

An ideal promotion policy is not just a sugar plum for employees. It is, first of all, a plan to ensure management that it will have the benefit of the best talent in the organization for the toughest jobs and a reasonable explanation for the promotions it makes when its actions are questioned. This is at least half of the case. The other half is to ensure employees that promotions are made strictly on the basis of merit and that opportunities are broad and open so as to minimize the danger of dead ends or unfairness.

One final note of caution should be entered. Promotion policy is not something to be predicated on a high-powered sales technique. Employees should not be whipped into a continuous frenzy over promotion opportunity. No organization is so constructed that all can expect eventual promotion to the top few rungs of the ladder; in fact, there is room for only a small minority to climb beyond the middle levels. Besides, many employees are perfectly content to stay in their existing positions and, if let alone, will continue to work with a high order of efficiency. Any program that overemphasizes the necessity for "getting ahead" may only make many employees feel a sense of inadequacy and may eventually decrease their overall usefulness. Here, as in so many fields, moderation is the watchword.

MOBILITY, REASSIGNMENT, AND TRANSFER

As may already have been implied, not all selection from within the service involves movement upward. Mobility in its fullest meaning also refers to movement laterally and outward. The horizontal channels can be as important and motivating as the vertical ones. They may permit changes in duties at the same level or only changes in supervisors but, whatever their character, they are almost certain to produce a diversification of experiences. Transfers laterally—that is, without change in rank or pay—may be called for by organizational demands (expansion, contraction, shifting policies or methods, seasonal loads, etc.), or by need for development of the individual or for making better use of his skills. In either case, the process can be entered into without much formality, certainly without any competitive features.

IMPORTANCE OF MOVEMENT

Transfer can and should be used quite deliberately to extend an employee's horizons and broaden his exposure to the work of the enterprise. Nothing has better training value than the job; so, why not use it construc-

---

[7] Illustrative of the complexities and need for adaptations in promotion policy is the situation in American police departments. A useful discussion appears in Chapter 6, "Promotion," by Benjamin Shimberg and Robert J. di Grazia, in *Police Personnel Administration*, O. Glenn Stahl and Richard A. Staufenberger, eds., Washington, D.C., Police Foundation, 1974.

tively for training and development purposes?[8] It matters not whether a public jurisdiction has a job-oriented career system or a rank-in-corps plan; in either case, laterial mobility may be exploited to the fullest. And, as already contended in the case of promotions, such a policy helps break down the traditional separatist tendencies among government agencies. Creatures of legislatures, they are customarily treated as isolated units, resulting in much of the rivalry and inflexibility that perpetuate the sins and omissions of bureaucracy—conditions that an insistent and enlightened transfer policy can go far to prevent.

We observed earlier how intergovernmental mobility was being fostered by the Intergovernmental Personnel Act.[9] Internal mobility within a jurisdiction is at least as important in achieving effective staff utilization and development, and it is much easier to accomplish. It embraces, of course, not only lateral transfer but promotion and advancement as well. Systematic movement, especially of managerial and professional employees, to diversify their experiences and to make the most productive use of their talents is more and more being recognized as a cardinal feature of good personnel policy.

HANDICAPS TO MOBILITY

Unfortunately, many public jurisdictions do not provide the incentives to make such mobility practical and attractive. Especially in the case of state and federal governments, where *geographical* moves are often involved, movement of an employee and his family may be an expensive affair. If the employer does not absorb all or almost all such costs, a serious damper is placed on what is otherwise a facile way of developing staff and building capacity for greater responsibility.

Although the federal government covers most travel and moving expenses for moves in its own interest, it is far less generous than progressive private employers when it comes to helping employees dispose of homes in one location and acquire new ones in another, meeting all kinds of readjustment costs, covering extra education expenses for children, and carrying various other burdens incidental to transfers. In fact, it is now commonplace among multifacility industries to dispose of an employee's home in his old location and help him acquire one in the new area, with no financial loss to the employee (as otherwise often occurs, considering the vicissitudes of the real-estate market in various places at various times).[10] Such assumption of responsibility by the employer is still not looked upon in government as a proper charge for personnel development or, in other words, a legitimate cost of doing business.

[8] See the further discussion in Chapter 13 on using the job constructively for training.

[9] See the discussion on intergovernmental relations in Chapter 2.

[10] The practice has become of such proportions that the Equitable Life Assurance Society, one of the country's largest insurance companies, now provides a special service to many private firms by taking care of all these real-estate transactions for them. This enterprise, called the Equitable Relocation Service, charges its clients a percentage of the capital expenditures involved.

REMEDIAL PLACEMENTS

Bad placements resulting from the imperfections of the examining and selection processes and placements in which the incumbents are unhappy or maladjusted can also be corrected by a liberal practice of transfers. For both these and for developmental transfers, the personnel office or agency must maintain adequate records as a basis for rational reassignment and must keep its doors open to employees who seek a change in atmosphere.

One point is certain: if there is a conflict between the exigencies of a dynamic transfer policy and the privilege of managers to make final selections, then the latter power must give way—for the dangers of provincialism and inbreeding are more devastating than occasional denial of freedom of choice to an appointing official. In fact, one of the criteria for filling managerial posts should be insistence that the candidate be as free as humanly possible of the common habits of being protective of the manpower under one's own limited supervision or being resistant to the introduction of new blood from outside.

*   *   *

OUR EXPECTATIONS OF selection from within—the promotion and transfer policies and practices—are without question very high. We must avoid both extremes: the stagnation of no promotion or transfer opportunity and the dead hand of inbreeding. At the same time, we must assure the filling of positions with the best available persons and guarantee fairness to all within the organization. Clearly this is no small order.

PART IV

Motivation and Effectiveness

When an institution, organization or nation loses its capacity to evoke high individual performance, its great days are over.

Every institution . . . should be prepared to answer this question posed by society: "What is the institution doing to foster the development of the individuals within it?"

The good society is not one that ignores individual differences but one that deals with them wisely and humanely.

John W. Gardner, *Excellence: Can We Be Equal and Excellent Too?* New York, Harper & Row, 1961, pp. 96, 142, and 75 respectively.

CHAPTER 11

Liberating the Will to Work

THERE IS NO truth more evident from experience and research than this: *work* is the lifeblood of man's existence. It is as natural for man to work and to want to work as it is for him to rest. Members of the simplest societies have regularly engaged in productive pursuits, in the arts of handicrafts, even when food was in abundance and climate was such that clothing and shelter were all but unnecessary. Human beings are not by nature sloths—whether their existence depends on their expenditure of energy or not.

This driving force, so pervasive in history and so common among all races and climes, seems to be composed both of an inner need to achieve and a response to external challenge. From the findings of Toynbee to the lessons of space exploration we have caught glimpses of the influence of challenge. From the wisdom of ancient philosophers to the researches of modern psychologists we have learned of the satisfaction and fulfillment that comes from constructive effort. Men who have thought more than superficially about the subject know that work can be fun, and most of us have at one time or another had just such an exhilarating experience. That great sage about human affairs, John W. Gardner, has observed, "What could be more satisfying than to be engaged in work in which every capacity or talent one may have is needed, every lesson one may have learned is used, every value one cares about is furthered?"[1]

If the true recreation is work, then certainly the activities of govern-

[1] From his address at the Thirteenth Annual Career Service Awards Banquet, National Civil Service League, Washington, D.C., April 21, 1967, as printed in the *Congressional Record*, vol. 113, no. 63, April 25, 1967.

ing, both at the political and the administrative levels, would share with few other pursuits the real excitement, team play, novelty, risk, and competition that are characteristic of genuine diversion. The only reservation is whether government is conceived of and organized to exploit this natural advantage of possessing more than the usual share of exciting, challenging functions, more than the common quota of conditions calling upon the fullest investment of men's talents, their lessons learned, their values cherished.

What has been said may seem more relevant to statesmen and to higher administrative posts than to the rank and file. But the point is that wise management can extend the effects far down into the organization when today's understanding of motivational influences is given rein. For the fact is that broad ethical drives combined with the stimulus of tackling society's major problems suggest a pattern of managerial behavior that can treat each employee as if he himself is a worthwhile human being bent upon doing his utmost to help get the job done. As managers become more like coaches concerned with the training and conditioning of their teams and with field strategy rather than with calling every play, as they behave more like teachers than rule enforcers, as they perform more as planners and less as plan executors, the prospects are good that the people beneath them will acquire, in varying degrees, some of the breadth, the strains, and the excitement that are too often found in management jobs alone.[2]

In short, the assumption that the average person dislikes work and will avoid it if he can has been shown to be wrong. And the companion assumption that most employees must be coerced, controlled, directed, and threatened with punishment before they will exert effort toward organization objectives is equally in error. Again and again, scientific research as well as common sense has demonstrated how much the opposite concepts are true.[3]

If we accept that man generally wants to work and derives great satisfaction from a productive concentration of his energies, then the management problem becomes one of reconciling his objectives with those of the organization. Achieving those objectives would be one of the employee's greatest rewards. If we accept that creative capacity is widely distributed in the population, as history certainly suggests, then the management problem becomes one of contriving organizational relationships that give as much vent to human self-expression and self-realization as possible. Here lies the avenue to optimum effectiveness and innovation.

Instead, much of government as well as industry has placed its emphasis

---

[2] Paraphrased from Saul W. Gellerman, *Management by Motivation*, New York, American Management Association, 1968, p. 271.

[3] The extensive literature and research in human behavior, motivation, morale, and leadership is only partially reflected in the bibliography for this chapter at the end of the book. Social science, since World War II especially, has contributed from all its disciplines and in a wide variety of projects the insights that are summarized in this chapter. The contrast between the concepts of man as work-shunning and man as work-needing is based particularly on the "Theory X" and "Theory Y" analysis by Douglas McGregor, *The Human Side of Enterprise*, New York, McGraw-Hill, 1960.

on off-the-job rather than on-the-job satisfactions. Management has assumed that it should draw the attention of the worker to "fringe" benefits—to time off from the job, to insurance plans, to bonuses, to retirement—and all the other perquisites that can be enjoyed anywhere except at the work place. As one author put it: "The work becomes a barrier which must be endured in order both to collect the reward and to have the opportunity to enjoy it."[4] Similarly, some of the mechanization and de-skilling of tasks, to conform to new technology, has deprived much work of its meaning. Fulfillment can rarely be achieved on an assembly line.

It is in view of the conclusions just expressed that a basic tenet throughout this volume has been the high value placed on *work-centered motivation*. This chapter highlights the story behind this thesis, providing a resumé of the concepts and research that shed light on human behavior and motivation and an analysis of some of the practices and forces that stultify or liberate man's natural will to work.

THE MEANING OF MOTIVATION

VARYING INFLUENCES

Motivation varies with environment and conditions of life. When the most basic human physical needs—food and water, sexual gratification, protection from bodily harm—are not being met, these become the most important areas in which incentives may operate. A man dying of thirst in the desert will do anything within his power for a drink; but under conditions where he knows his thirst can always be readily quenched, the drive for liquid fades into the background.

Similarly, in a poor society where standards of satisfaction of human physical wants are low, the means to purchase a higher scale of satisfaction, namely, income (through pay or in other forms), becomes paramount. As such satisfactions are more fully realized, other motivations loom larger. In an affluent society with a high minimum standard of "creature comfort," pay is rarely the number-one motivator. Research studies time and again have shown that in public service and industrial environments in the United States pay usually ranks second, third, or lower, on a scale of motivating factors. Ahead of it—the order depending on the specific activities and the particular conditions in a work place, occupation, or hierarchy— are factors such as credit and recognition, challenging work, a congenial work group, freedom to make decisions, security of tenure, fair and equal opportunity for advancement, and the quality of supervision.

RELEVANCE OF PERSONNEL POLICY

Motivation to perform and morale, its concomitant, do not refer to matters separate from the various aspects of personnel administration dis-

---

[4] Mason Haire, *Psychology in Management,* New York, McGraw-Hill, 1956, p. 154.

cussed in other chapters. Certainly, in those organizations in which there is no apparent rationality underlying compensation and reward, it would be pretty difficult to achieve high motivation or morale; where selections and promotions are made on some basis other than merit, respect for one's employer or his mission is not likely to be very high; and where performance is evaluated perfunctorily or unfairly, there is not very fertile soil for development of a genuine *esprit de corps.*

In a broad sense, therefore, the inculation of morale, of that spirit, that state of mind, which expresses itself in loyalty, enthusiasm, cooperation, pride in the service, and devotion to duty, is the end of the whole personnel system. Every aspect of the personnel program from recruitment to retirement may be handled so that it is either an incentive or a depressant to individual and group morale. In a very real sense, this whole work is devoted to a consideration of ways of building and maintaining this most valuable asset of any organization.

"Morale is the capacity of a group of people to pull together persistently and consistently in pursuit of a common purpose," according to one authority,[5] and in the words of another: "the possession of a feeling . . . of being accepted and belonging to a group of employees through adherence to common goals and confidence in the desirability of those goals."[6] The importance of such factors to the effectiveness or productivity of any enterprise can hardly be overestimated. Just as public administration is essential to the collective operations of an advanced society, so the elements of morale and work-centered motivation are vital to modern administration.

HIGH STANDARDS

Before examining some of the ingredients of motivation and morale in more detail, it is well that we take note of a very significant point: the concern with how employees work together, how they are influenced and led, and how they are given opportunity to perform should not be mistaken for sentimentality or softness. Some well-meaning people have misunderstood attention to these matters, equating it with a surrender to mediocrity and maudlin pandering to every employee's whim. The strength of sound human attitudes and relationships in an organization depends as much on high expectations and standards as anything else. There can be little motivation in the work without respect by all for the quality of the service or the product. Supervised as well as supervisor share this responsibility. We are not just speaking of what managers should *do for* employees. It is a two-way street.

Insistence on high standards of performance comports much more with job satisfaction than do laxity and indifference. The employee is de-

---

[5] Alexander Leighton, "Applied Science of Human Relations," *Personnel Administration,* July 1947, p. 4.

[6] Milton J. Blum and James C. Naylor, *Industrial Psychology: Its Theoretical and Social Foundations,* New York, Harper & Row 1968, p. 391.

prived of the fullest sense of achievement if he is never shown how much better his work could be. Correction, firmness, or discipline may engender a temporary feeling of resentment, but such action, constructively done without destroying the individual's self-respect, can also instill a realization that there is more to be achieved—which sooner or later appeals to the compelling human need for a sense of success, of approval, of recognition. Many a worker has done some of his best work while smarting under the sting of strong criticism. Pride in high standards and discipline is very much like that experienced by members of a crack athletic squad or a superior debating team.

BASIC EMOTIONAL NEEDS

If easy or slipshod work, if an empty kind of happiness or detached contentment are not the underlying wants of employees, then what are the wellsprings of their motivation and their adaptation to the environment? A synthesis of social science findings and concepts would suggest that for an organization to function most effectively its members must satisfy these fundamental needs: need for a feeling of security, for a sense of achievement, and for a sense of belonging. The broadest and most basic of all is the need for security; in its fullest interpretation it may incorporate the others.

SECURITY   By a sense of security psychologists do not mean economic security, although that may be part of the meaning. Certainly it is not just security of tenure in a job, although tenure based on considerations irrelevant to performance may prevent realization of the broader concept. What is meant is security in knowing what is going on, security in the feeling that one's work is wanted, that one's boss and colleagues are going to react in some predictable way to certain actions rather than by caprice, and that one has a reasonable opportunity to get self-expression into his work. It means that one must be given as much freedom to "create" as is consistent with coordination of effort among many human beings, to utilize his mind and his skill as fully as possible.

ACHIEVEMENT   Part of the meaning of security is found in the second area of satisfaction—that derived from achievement and recognition. This sense of success refers to the feeling that one is making progress, that there is general acceptance of one's work, that one is achieving what he set out to achieve, and that one is realizing the potentialities of his skill and his ability. Such emotional satisfaction is affected not only by what he accomplishes but also by how those with whom he works react to what he accomplishes. People work not for bread alone but for the satisfaction of social acceptance. We also know that standards set unreasonably high do not always make a success experience possible.

At this point we must reiterate the importance of the character and prestige of the work itself as a motivating factor. This is, of course, more valid in professional work and in the higher reaches of an organization than in menial jobs. Time and again surveys have shown that the major recruiting attraction and principal holding power for highly trained people is the work to be done.

Although this resource cannot be tapped as dependably perhaps in jobs involving repetitive manual tasks, there is still much there that can be accomplished. Some of the sense of achievement in a work force can be lost through failure to recognize the pleasure to be found in almost any kind of work. This fact, of course, has implications for the organization of tasks: where mechanistic, material, or layout considerations may dictate one pattern, this may not take job satisfaction for the worker into account. It is for this reason more than any other that we see a trend away from that routinization of tasks in industry which had narrowed jobs down to absurd specializations, as on assembly lines.

But most important, there is an advantage in this respect for government employment, because the public service more than industry is fortunate in having many routine jobs that entail interesting and sometimes fascinating duties. Also, there is always the satisfaction growing out of the importance of even simple work for the public welfare or safety. These considerations are too infrequently emphasized in both the recruitment and the supervision of public employees.

BELONGING   Finally, there is the matter of "belonging." An office, a plant, or a laboratory is as much a social unit as it is a productive enterprise. To work at his best an individual must feel that he has a personal place of value in the work group, that he belongs, that he counts, that he has worth as a human being, not just as an impersonal producer. Without this assurance of being "one of the gang," the worker feels unwanted, behaves like an outsider, and is in a most unlikely state of mind for high motivation.

To be sure, conditions of the work environment are rarely so perfect that the needs for security, achievement, and belonging are fully met. Circumstances vary in the degree to which they satisfy these needs, and there are infinite varieties of combinations. Also, individuals vary considerably in the degree to which their needs in these directions have to be satisfied in order to keep them working as useful members of a group. But it does not take much research to warrant the observation that the policies and attitudes of the organization, the behavior of the employee's colleagues and supervisors, and his own adaptability go far to determine whether these elementary emotional needs are sufficiently satisfied to make the employee an effective producer.

THE LANDMARK STUDY

The first major research study that drew attention dramatically to the problems of human behavior in the work place was that made in the Hawthorne plant of the Western Electric Company in Chicago, beginning in the late 1920s.[7] The conclusions that were significant were incidental to the original purposes of the study. The company had started out to explore the effect of good lighting on certain work groups. It discovered that when lighting was increased step by step over a period of time, production increased correspondingly. Fortunately, the investigators were thorough researchers and decided to check their findings by *reducing* the amount of light. To their astonishment, production continued to rise and did so until the lighting was no brighter than moonlight.

Psychologists and engineers from Harvard University and from the company staff were called in to probe more deeply. They found, after much painstaking effort, that the workers in the test groups had come to feel important—because they were being given all this attention! They had a feeling of not being "bossed." The researchers seemed more interested in the workers' welfare than in production—and as a result, production continued to go up. Where individuals had problems at home, they depended critically on a favorable social climate in their work situation to make up for it. In other words, the Hawthorne studies were revealing what the philosophers have been saying for centuries—that one's efforts are affected more by one's *attitudes* than they are by physical surroundings. The problem in management is to discover those attitudes and influence them as favorably as possible. The Hawthorne studies, carried on to some degree over a period of sixteen years and costing a million dollars, were milestones in the development of personnel administration. Stuart Chase has said: "If managers of factories the country over were intimately aware of what the research men at Hawthorne discovered, American industry would be *revolutionized*."[8]

CONTINUING BEHAVIORAL RESEARCH

During or not long after pursuit of the Hawthorne studies two names stood out as the most brilliant evidence of pioneering thinking and exposition in this emerging new approach to industrial management—Ordway Tead and Chester I. Barnard.[9] The ideas of these two men, cogently expressed, were amazingly consistent and prescient of the findings of somewhat later research. Tead expounded the thesis that the widest freedom for personal initiative and sharing in the results were the requisites for capitalizing on the normal desires of both workers and managers to produce high quality

[7] The study is described in full in F. J. Roethlisberger and William J. Dickson, *Management and the Worker*, Cambridge, Mass., Harvard University Press, 1939. A popular description appears in Stuart Chase, *Men at Work*, New York, Harcourt, Brace Jovanovich, 1945, chapter 2.

[8] Chase, *ibid.*, p. 9.

[9] Principal works: Ordway Tead, *The Art of Leadership*, New York, McGraw-Hill, 1935, and *The Art of Administration*, New York, McGraw-Hill, 1951; and Chester I. Barnard, *The Functions of the Executive*, Cambridge, Mass., Harvard Business School, 1938. Both men, in addition to being philosophers about their interests, occupied top leadership posts for extended periods in business and public service. The foregoing books will be considered classics for a long time to come.

at a high level. Barnard emphasized the greater role of nonmonetary incentives in motivation as compared with pay, along the same lines later supported by objective research. In many other respects the insights of these two intellectual giants were corroborated by scientific analyses of behavior, attitudes, and productivity in American industry. Only a superficial summation of the outstanding features of these later research efforts can be made here.

IN INDUSTRY   Since the 1930s the studies undertaken in U.S. business concerns have grown prodigiously both in numbers and in scope and variety. Many have been carried out by teams of university men of interdisciplinary make-up—representing cultural anthropology, economics, social psychology, sociology, and political science. Gradually, the enthusiasm and techniques for such inquiries spread to Canada, the United Kingdom, and the continent of Europe. Regrettably, not many of these scientific studies have been made in public jurisdictions, although the federal government contracted for some in its military operations and in some of its science-oriented activities.

The scope of the research has embraced almost every conceivable aspect of managerial and employee behavior and motivation.[10] Early projects included some based on experiments in child psychology, out of which came such conclusions as these: a democratic environment is far more productive than a laissez-faire type with practically no leadership, and is at least as productive as an authoritarian environment but with fewer strains in the way of conflicts and jealousy. Other inquiries have shown that supervisors who were "employee-centered," that is, genuinely interested in the concerns and aspirations of their staff, tended to head higher-producing units than did those who were more authoritarian and were continually hammering away at the need for production. Some have demonstrated that optimum contributions can be expected of workers when they are treated like mature adults and not like dependent children. A few have pointed out some differences between productivity and contentment with the work situation, showing that keeping employees happy was not always the way to enlist their maximum drive to do a good job. Based on experiments in a wide variety of industrial situations, the less authoritarian kind of supervision, under which employees are given as much leeway as possible in making decisions or de-

---

[10] An indication of the range of publications on the subject may be seen in the bibliography. The most notable concentration of researchers has been at the Institute for Social Research, University of Michigan, under the directorship of Dr. Rensis Likert. But the number of psychologists, sociologists, political scientists, and other professionals at various research institutes and universities who have conducted studies and published in the field is quite large. In addition, many others have interpreted and synthesized the findings of the research men, often adding theories of their own, and published them in textbooks and popular writings aimed primarily at the business world.

The volume of studies continues to mount, but the findings remain basically consistent with the summation of principles set forth in this chapter.

termining the course of their work, has generally been found by social scientists to be the most satisfactory.

SMALL GROUPS   Psychologists and sociologists have also joined forces to concentrate study on the behavior and relationships of small groups. Indeed, small group research has almost come to be a discipline unto itself. Whereas psychologists had previously studied the individual's responses to his environment, many now study the influence of the group on the individual or that of the individual on the group. Whereas sociologists had ordinarily focused on whole societies or institutions, many now record and analyze the behavior of small groups. Since all organizations consist of a number of comparatively homogeneous small groups at some level in the hierarchy, the products of this research can have wide application. Most of the group study, however, has been directed to the industrial setting.[11]

OTHER EMPHASES   Still other investigations have brought out the virtues of "management by objectives," which means emphasis on goals, with maximum reliance on employees to work out the methods for reaching them. Other approaches have been labeled as "cybernetics," or a "systems approach," which espouse the doctrine of comprehensiveness—that is, diagnosing and treating each situation in terms of every conceivable factor present, from the most general to the most specific environmental influences and effects. New conceptualizations of organization of tasks, delegations of authority, and teamwork have also added to the impressive results of wide-ranging inquiries.

RESEARCH INSTITUTIONS   Outstanding among the enterprises that have led the field in behavioral research is the Institute for Social Research at the University of Michigan, but notable contributions have also been made from the schools of business, the departments of psychology or sociology, or the schools or institutes of public administration at some of America's best-known and most innovative educational institutions—Harvard, Yale, Princeton, Stanford, Chicago, Massachusetts Institute of Technology, Minnesota, Syracuse, Ohio State, and Southern California, to name only the most prominent. Not only is the integration of several disciplines sufficiently developed to ensure continual growth of this embracing field of behavioral science, but the opportunities for new inquiries are unending in view of the ever-growing scope and variety of conditions and functions in modern organzation. Few studies are applicable precisely to environments other than the one in which the research is undertaken. Every enterprise and every set of circumstances require their own special analyses, and the changes in time and technology demand repetition of an inquiry to verify its continuing relevance to reality.

---

[11] The bibliography contains several references reporting on this field, along with the many others touching on the entire range of behavioral research.

The market for continued growth of behavioral science research, therefore, looks very good indeed.

THE KEY FINDING It may be presumptuous to attempt to generalize too much from all these scientific and philosophic efforts. Human problems are always the most difficult to isolate, to understand, to predict. We must guard against any appearance of advocating "canned" techniques or rules. But if there is a single most repeated finding that emerges from the research products already available, it would seem to be the one that says something like this: *reliance on the work itself to be its own reward and constructing it as much as possible on the concept that employees are by and large mature, self-willed, self-motivated people who want to achieve and to share in achievement—is the most reliable management and personnel philosophy to develop optimum effectiveness in reaching an organization's objectives.* The future, it would seem, may bring further elaboration or refinements but not likely a fundamental alteration in the thrust of this idea. The thesis is well put in this summation:

> most of us need . . . a dare, a challenge, a test to see what we amount to. This is much more likely to be provided by an organization which is constructed on the basis of a deep and abiding faith in the capacities of men and women than by one which is skeptical of such capacities and seeks to compensate for human weakness rather than capitalize on human strength.[12]

USING WHAT IS KNOWN

H. L. Mencken is credited with the statement: "There is always an easy solution to every human problem—neat, plausible, and wrong." If this bit of cynicism is taken to mean that we should be wary of pat formulas and panaceas to solve human behavior problems, it is very much worth bearing in mind. If, on the other hand, it is taken to disparage our having any guideposts at all in conducting human affairs, it is seriously overdrawn. There is equal wisdom and less danger of contradictory interpretation in this assertion by Alexander Leighton: "The striking thing about this new science of human relations is not the vast areas of what is unknown—which many are fond of emphasizing—but the degree to which *what is known is not used.*"[13]

All phases of organization and management should be designed to contribute to human motivation and capitalize on the will to work. Some of

---

[12] James C. Worthy, *Big Business and Free Men*, New York, Harper & Row, 1959, p. 118. An excellent summary of deductions from research appears in Edward E. Lawler III, "Worker Satisfaction, Job Design, and Job Performance," *Good Government*, Summer 1972, pp. 12–15.

[13] As stated to Eileen Ahern, "Preventive Psychiatry in Industry," *Management News*, January 28, 1949, p. 3.

these are implicit in the doctrine and experience enunciated throughout this volume as part of the personnel function. At this point, therefore, it seems appropriate to sketch a few activities and attitudes of management and employees that may contribute to work-centered motivation and are founded on faith in the virtues of personal dignity, human determination, and individual differences, but which are not discussed explicitly in other chapters.

ORGANIZATION OF TASKS

We have already noted in the introductory comments of this chapter the relevance of work content to job satisfaction. The more meaning the work has to the worker, the more likely it will serve his basic emotional needs; the more routinized, dull, or irrelevant tasks become, the less they can contribute to these ends. Consequently, job simplification (except to make use of and to develop low-skilled laborers) has been giving way to job enlargement.

The original scientific-management school of thought, devotees of Frederick Taylor and his preoccupation with job routinization, did contribute much to the engineering of mass production but in the process threatened to reduce the man on the assembly line to a stereotyped, mindless automaton. No movement has been so thoroughly discredited. The new science starts from the assumption that man wants and needs to tax his own capacity, and the objective evidence is abundant that acting on this assumption brings about far superior results. Thus, the modern trend is to make the tasks, even on assembly lines, as broad or varied or challenging as physically possible.[14]

Putting aside the industrial parallel and focusing more directly on public services, the concept of job enlargement would be expressed in measures such as (1) making people responsible for whole integrals of a function, instead of breaking it into fine specializations with separate employees or groups concentrating on each; (2) permitting workers to follow through on tasks or projects from start to finish, rather than perform just a single segment in the process; (3) introducing as much diversification as feasible into a unit's activities; (4) delegating the maximum authority for decision-making to each layer in the hierarchy; (5) training employees to grow beyond what-

---

[14] An example is reported by Robert N. Ford in *Motivation Through the Work Itself*, New York, The American Management Association, 1969, in which he describes the "job enrichment" program of the American Telephone and Telegraph Company and suggests how the approach may be applied elsewhere. In these significant studies the job environment and rewards were held constant while tasks were improved for experimental groups of workers by providing greater chance for achievement, recognition, responsibility, advancement, and psychological challenge and growth. These groups almost invariably exceeded uninvolved groups on a number of criteria—turnover, quality of customer service, productivity, lowered costs, lower absence rates, and source for managerial upgrading. As author Ford observed: "The surroundings of the task can produce dissatisfactions, but not long-run satisfaction" (p. 39). It takes the work itself to produce the latter.

ever tasks they have been performing; and (6) rotating employees from time to time among different assignments to give them the flavor and stimulus of new experiences and challenges. Whether we are talking about processing tax returns, directing traffic, reading meters, surveying rights-of-way, making medical examinations, conducting research, inspecting food, or adjudicating claims, many of the foregoing techniques can be exploited to build on the concepts derived from the research and ideas reported in this chapter.

At least two influences complicate efforts to achieve results along these lines in government establishments: one is the introduction of automation, especially electronic data-processing; the other is the tendency for legislative bodies to overprescribe procedure and to be intolerant of action or decision by anyone less than the "top man." The mitigating factor in the first instance is that more new and challenging occupations have been created to make use of machines, even though some manual work is reduced to a very menial level. In the other case, we may have to accept that, the need for bureaucratic responsiveness and responsibility being what it is, some actions will have to be reviewed at headquarters or by higher echelons regardless of the advantage of relying more fully on civil servants in field offices or other lower levels in the hierarchy. Citizens and their representatives will continue to demand such action. But few are the governmental enterprises where there is no room for further delegation of authority to make decisions. The more common reason for absence of delegation is the lack of trust in people, coupled with inadequate standards and training to make delegation practicable.

The kinds of administrative issues discussed here may appear to go well beyond what is customarily thought of as personnel administration. But where else in the organization should the stimulus for the proposed actions come from except the personnel office? Who else should have the knowledge, the insight, and the will to press for change other than the personnel specialist? The point is that job enlargement is dictated by findings and concerns about the motivation of people, and where this subject is not part of the interests and responsibility of those giving full time to personnel matters, there personnel management is indeed a very sterile function.

PARTICIPATIVE MANAGEMENT

Approaches to the direction of men's work which in some fashion make use of their participation in shaping policy and procedure have gained great currency in progressive management. This participative emphasis takes various forms.

INDUCING PARTICIPATION　Sometimes it is expressed formally through committees or boards, where employees make their views known on policy issues that affect their work or their welfare. Other evidences of the approach may be characterized as management by winning consent, as distinguished from management by command. Instead of the traditional issuance of orders, such management enlists employees' involvement in defining and reaching an objective, in doing it cooperatively, in exercising some choices in methods taken to reach goals, and in seeing and participating in the results.

Occasionally referred to as democratic management, the participative approach is clearly consistent with the concept of work-centered motivation.[15] It does not, of course, imply decision by majority or anything of the kind. It does mean frequent consultation by the supervisor with his staff, guiding them to arrive jointly at decisions, and providing the free environment in which they become accustomed to apply their own intelligences rather than to receive instructions on every detailed step or task. A teaching atmosphere thereby replaces a command atmosphere.

This doctrine should not be taken to mean that there are never any circumstances when positive, decisive action by a supervisor is called for. "Intelligent autocracy" may sometimes be necessary, and more productive, than "democracy." Whenever peace at any price becomes a goal instead of the long-range goals of the organization, the point of participative management is missed. Participative management is important because it usually contributes to both productivity and tranquility. If, for any reason (problem personalities, unusual stress, or other conditions), it does not contribute to productivity, then it must be reappraised. There are circumstances when strong, positive leadership is necessary to shake an organization out of a lethargy born of misguided tolerance of damaging behavior. Participation is not license; it presumes a wide sharing of responsibility, not a negation of it. Excessive permissiveness can be just as unfortunate as blind despotism.

ENCOURAGING SUGGESTIONS   Another form of the participative environment relates to work improvement efforts, whereby employees are encouraged to propose changes in work processes or organization. Special procedures set up for this purpose have generally been referred to as suggestion systems. Having passed through phases during which "suggestion boxes" were distributed throughout the establishment and later when management or employee committees were created to pass on the feasibility of suggestions, most of these systems have evolved to stress the processing of suggestions through regular supervisory channels so as to avoid either the appearance or the fact of "end runs." Emphasis on group rather than individual suggestions for work improvement has also developed, to reduce the accent on personal rivalry and competition at the expense of teamwork.[16]

---

[15] Like a political democracy an organization democracy reflects the conviction that people are capable of initiative and responsibility, of intelligent judgment and the ability to adapt to changing situations. Conversely, an authoritarian organization reflects an assumption of management that its subordinates are incapable of acting wisely without rigid supervision from above. [James C. Worthy, *op. cit.*, p. 56.]

[16] The Tennessee Valley Authority and industries that use the "Scanlon Plan" have had considerable success with management-union cooperative committees that process ideas for improvement, subject them to critical review, and, where appropriate, develop alternative proposals that are collectively arrived at.

Suggestion systems are of value only to the extent that they have the full endorsement of the supervisory line at all levels, induce the active participation of employees and their formal organizations, and, above all, produce good and useful suggestions. Also, when suggestions are impractical —and under even the most ideal conditions some will inevitably be—the reasons should be explained to the suggestor. When they are sound, needless to say some form of recognition should go to the employee, if only a word of commendation or publicity about his contribution; and, of course, the fullest recognition comes from the actual adoption and effective application of the suggestion.[17]

Suggestion systems are always in danger of being "oversold" by enthusiastic partisans. They constitute only one avenue for developing a participative climate in an enterprise and must be viewed in perspective with other aspects of the particular motivational environment. The making of suggestions has sometimes been so artificially stimulated that the suggestion process became more central in the employee's mind than the work itself. It should be a natural and continuing part of creativity and open-mindedness on the job, not a procedure apart and one diverting attention away from the job.

LEADERSHIP: ITS ELEMENTS AND IDENTIFICATION

What has been said about motivation and the will to work almost automatically defines the kind of leadership necessary in an effectively operated activity. But leadership is an elusive quality, and research that has been focused directly on the topic has demonstrated that a variety of personalities in a variety of situations can be successful leaders. No stereotype of character or style provides a formula for all places at all times. Nevertheless, it is clear that respect for and trust in others is invariably an ingredient of behavior that must be present.

So many have pontificated for so long on the substance of leadership that no attempt will be made here to embrace all aspects of the subject. It will suffice for our purposes to enumerate a few of the more prominent features of good leadership and describe how they may be discovered and developed.

QUALITIES NEEDED   Most students of leaders and of the impact of their actions conclude that there is need for high intelligence but, more significantly, for imagination, creativity, and innovative capacity on the part of leaders. Generally, the successful leader also has a strong drive for accomplishment, good facility with language (especially orally), and mature, stable emotional health as well as sound physical health. Such qualities, plus those implied by

---

[17] The pros and cons of dispensing cash awards for adopted suggestions, along with other forms of achievement recognition, are discussed in the succeeding chapter on performance evaluation and incentives.

the needs of their subordinates, would seem to complete the prescription. Obviously, this leaves room for many kinds of personality, many alternative forms of behavior, and display of many other abilities.

Executive skills, it has been observed, may be thought of in three major categories: technical, human, and conceptual.[18] The higher up the ranks a person moves, the more the first order of ability—subject-matter knowledge—becomes subordinated to the other two. The conceptual role (thinking, innovating) and the human role (motivating, inspiring) are more dominant at upper levels but especially so in the public service, where the top executive may be an influential figure. The higher placed the executive, the longer the intellectual and emotional shadow he casts over the organization. First-line supervisors and middle management tend to reflect upon their subordinates the attitudes and spirit they sense in top managers, that is, their own superiors. One would expect, then, that the attributes of good supervision and leadership would be the most sought-after capacities in filling managerial posts at all levels.

SELECTION FOR LEADERSHIP   In spite of this expectation, the fact is that the traditional criterion for elevating employees to higher responsibilities has been the degree of their technical knowledge or skill. Although such capacity should never be ignored, there is considerable room left for taking into account the human and conceptual abilities. Efforts to do just this have been experimented with in many enterprises during recent decades, but with varied results. The big problem is that of making executives out of specialists. Vocational and professional schools all too often turn out graduates quite unprepared for managerial responsibility, but few can climb very far in their chosen field without some administrative duties, that is, some direction and accountability for the work of others. The day of the scientist, engineer, medical officer, or accountant working in isolated splendor from his fellows has disappeared from this interdependent world. And this is all the more true in the public sector where teamwork and coordination are exposed to almost daily scrutiny.

The obligation imposed on public administration is therefore threefold: (1) to insist on the inclusion of more of the social sciences, humanities, and communication subjects in technical school curricula, (2) to look for and measure the possession of human and conceptual skills among existing employees, and (3) to train and retrain supervisors, managers, and non-supervisory workers in what is known about motivation, leadership, and all the other aspects of getting a collection of people to work together toward common goals. Preentry and postentry education along these lines is discussed in the chapter on training; also, much of what has been said in the chapters on examination and selection is applicable to the matter of iden-

---

[18] Robert L. Katz, "Skills of an Effective Administrator," *Harvard Business Review*, January–February 1955, pp. 33–42.

tifying and choosing men and women for leadership jobs. But a few special points are worth emphasis here.

Selection for leadership has not been wholly without reason or design in the past. Many officials have the knack of observing human and conceptual skills in others. In filling supervisory posts they steer away from persons who display anxieties when they are up against the obligation to make decisions; they watch out for individuals who always find it necessary to blame others for mistakes or inadequacies in which they shared; they avoid men and women who get easily upset or aroused; they are wary of people who seldom have a new idea of their own. In short, they have found that some of the worst mistakes in selecting supervisors can be avoided by a shrewd calculation of the potential of nonsupervisory candidates.

But this is not a very practical procedure when there are hundreds of candidates and scores of supervisory jobs to be filled. It is not a very reliable procedure when the judgment is being made repeatedly by only one official. In other words, more formal and objective devices are often essential if the task is to be performed with reasonable validity and dependability. Hence, there must be substantial reliance on tools such as aptitude tests, assessment centers, and, for key positions, even psychiatric examinations—at least to narrow the field of candidates. In all such measures, the pooling of judgment by several persons who observe the behavior of candidates or who are familiar with their records and progress is usually a sound and reliable element.

Such approaches, plus ample investment in in-service training, normally go far to minimize the ever-present problem of locating and utilizing leadership capacity.

CLOSING COMMUNICATION GAPS

This author is most skeptical of any effort to formalize good communication within an enterprise by some special "program," but it is desirable that we be conscious of the existence and the quality of this phenomenon, of the fact that communication exists in one form or another regardless of what is done about it, and of the value of being deliberate about making improvements where they appear to be needed.

Many writers have stressed the reality of "informal organization" and of the "grapevine" as a means of transfer of information and news among the staff. Too often this is the major channel of communication, because management does not open up the overt channels or because it fails to take employees into its confidence. As a result, the informal channels frequently convey misinformation rather than facts. Any group of people associated together to get work done is in essence a social organism that devises its own ways of keeping alive through exchange of intelligence as to "what is going on." The answer to poor communication lies not in suppression of these natural, informal channels (which is impossible anyway) but in keeping a two-way flow of information free of obstructions, so that the informal track does not have to be so heavily relied upon.

Research in communication within industrial organizations led to articulation of a few principles which may be summarized as follows:

1. Communication—oral and written—is the lifeblood of an enterprise. It is the means by which human beings work together.
2. Communication is a two-way process. Employees should know the goals of the organization, why management is proceeding the way it is, what changes are in the works. Management should know what employees are thinking and feeling, what ideas they have to get the job done.
3. Communication involves *receiving* and *understanding* as well as telling. Words, ideas, or proposals do not always mean the same thing to the receiver and the transmitter. A breakdown in understanding can occur because the communicator does not put himself in the other fellow's shoes. A supervisor may not proceed carefully in making his instruction, or an employee may not properly prepare a supervisor for a new idea that he springs.
4. Normally, the more freedom and encouragement given to self-expression and the more care taken to provide people with the reasons for action, the less communication difficulty there will be.
5. Good communication is an essential concomitant of delegation of authority and reliance on the good sense and good intentions of the staff. Along with participation, it is the "stuff" of the decision-making process.

It is hardly necessary to point out the consistency of the preceding generalizations with recognition of the dignity and importance of the individual and with nourishment of the basic desires of a work force for security, achievement, and identification. Concurrent with various methods for stimulating employee expression and getting at employee opinion is management's obligation to see that employees are so thoroughly informed about the current problems and aims of the organization that they truly become interested partners in the enterprise.

SOLVING PERSONAL PROBLEMS

Enlisting group participation may be the best way to set goals, work out strategies, and solve group problems, but not all stresses and strains of the work environment are wholesale in nature. Some are very much localized to the individual and quite personal. Instead of the usual group-wide applications of training, task restructuring, participative management, leadership determination, and communication improvement, we are concerned here with matters that involve an individual quite apart from his colleagues and sometimes entail consideration of his mental health.

Because of the finding that workers responded constructively to an interest in them as persons and that off-the-job circumstances often had an impact on their energy concentration, the Hawthorne researchers were the first to urge a continual program of confidential interviews with employees to permit them, when they wished, to give voice to their concerns or dissatisfactions and to encourage their personal involvement in arriving at solutions to problems.[19] With techniques of "nondirective" interviewing, usually referred to as "counseling" (something of a misnomer, if it is taken to mean positive advice) but bordering on the methodology of psychiatric interviewing, the objective is to draw out of an employee his innermost feelings about his work situation, his problems, or his anxieties, to help him analyze the reasons behind his condition, and to lead him to make adjustments in those instances where neither his supervisor nor the organization can do much about it.

Alcoholism, marital problems, maternity, persecution complexes, concerns about family budgets or debts, child care, housing, recreation needs, vocational aspirations—are all examples of subjects that may understandably so preoccupy an employee that they interfere either with his work product or his relationships with other people. Obviously they are not problems ordinarily susceptible of resolution by his supervisor, and many of them he does not feel like sharing with colleagues. Hence, many progressive enterprises provide professional counselors to engage in confidential listening and assistance to the troubled employee. Such a service is especially needed in organizations that employ sizable numbers of lower-paid, lesser-educated workers, who have neither the knowledge nor the funds to seek help in the community at large. Having developed rapidly in American industry and government during World War II, counseling is now a more or less settled service that is usually found in combination with other employee relations functions of a personnel office in modern government establishments.

But some employee problems are serious enough to require more substantial attention, either in terms of treatment or prevention. Instances of mental and emotional instability are as prevalent in the work place as much as in any other area of human activity. Some surveys have shown that the great majority of failures on the job are attributable to emotional disorders and not to technical inadequacies. Scrutiny of almost any collection of dismissal cases or other maladjustments will bear out that what is often termed *incompetence* is more likely induced by a mental health failure rather than an intellectual deficiency. When things are going smoothly, there may be little difference shown on the job between stable and unstable employees; but when the pressure is on and difficult situations develop, petty annoyances become major issues in the minds of some. In modern organizations, an expanding role is being found, therefore, for the fully trained clinical psychologist or psychiatrist, whose job it is to spot situations where trouble

[19] Roethlisberger and Dickson made this their concluding plea, as a long-range program to improve morale. *Op. cit.*, pp. 590–604.

might develop, to diagnose cases, and to suggest or provide for more extended treatment in instances that warrant it.[20]

The preventive approach, as in the society at large, makes sense. It is foolish to wait for mental breakdowns before making use of the services of psychiatrists. Special attention should be given to supervisors and executives, who probably have more than their fair share of the strains of organizational living. Professional assistance is useful at the point of selecting key officers, as well as in probing more deeply when the going gets rough. Group preventive therapy, in which "role playing"[21] and other techniques are used, can be helpful to the supervisory employee to understand his own drives and those of others, to face the unexpected, to handle subordinates' problems better, to delegate authority to act, and to reduce the load on himself. This process is sometimes referred to as "sensitivity training," but the latter term has also unfortunately been used to describe some bizarre and questionable practices.

The interesting and promising efforts to achieve a status of mental-health maintenance in modern organizations are still in a developmental stage. As more professional research and attention is devoted to the industrial health area, there should be more progress and tangible accomplishment to report.

ADJUSTMENT OF GRIEVANCES

Some of the problems that inevitably arise in any organization can be resolved through a formal system of adjustment of grievances, but even if they cannot, a procedure for such adjustment is an absolute essential to any self-respecting enterprise. Whether well founded or not, grievances undermine morale and effective performance. Let an individual harbor the notion that he is being abused on any ground whatsoever, and his attention to and interest in his work are bound to decline.

INEVITABILITY OF COMPLAINTS   No matter how well an undertaking is run, unsatisfactory conditions of one sort or another are endemic. Where any considerable group of human beings are intimately thrown together, disagreements and complaints are certain to develop. Human frailty being what it is, incompatibility, misunderstanding, unfriendly rivalry, jealousy, and numerous other shortcomings can make for the friction that destroys the will

---

[20] An example of a book devoted exclusively to industrial mental health problems is Harry Levinson, *Emotional Health in the World of Work*, New York, Harper & Row, 1964. The author is an official of the Menninger Foundation.

[21] Having employees play roles in mock discussions, interviews, or confrontations in which a hypothetical problem or conflict is postulated and each individual acts out how he would be expected to behave in the circumstances outlined. Those who take part are sometimes thrust into roles opposite from their real-life ones and thereby learn from the experience. For those who observe, the dramatization clarifies the issues and evokes critical analysis of what should or should not have been done by the actors to achieve a desired result.

to work of any staff. Improper placements, unfair pay relationships, faulty tools or equipment, thoughtless misassignments of tasks, delays in securing materials, drafts, glare, dirt, and what-not can make for dissatisfaction and often strident complaint. Conditions which arise from deliberate changes in work processes or personnel or from deterioration of physical properties may be discovered and remedied by an alert management, but many others will go undiscovered. The consequent discontent is not likely to be realized unless there is some machinery for bringing the causes into the open where they can be dealt with.

DEFINITIONS   This is the purpose of a system for learning about and acting on grievances and complaints. Where it is not established voluntarily, employee organizations are certain to demand its creation. In fact, one of the most elementary features of formal agreements between management and unions is provision for settlement of grievances. In these circumstances the term *grievance* may embrace concerns with interpretation of such labor contracts as well as individual complaints.[22]

In the industrial world little or no distinction is made between complaints on matters of the sort listed here and objections to or appeals against overt actions of management for disciplinary or other purposes. Even in government a common procedure may be used for resolution of all such employee complaints. The distinction between the two categories lies not so much in procedure for resolution as in the nature of the subject being considered.

Because they relate so intimately to disciplinary actions by management, formal appeals against such actions are discussed in the chapter on that subject. For convenience, however, and because of their relationship to so many other aspects of the positive motivational environment, grievances as defined here are presented in this chapter. It may be noted also that there is a connection between suggestion systems and grievance procedures, since remedies for grievances may take the form of constructive suggestions. In any event, in all such processes the important consideration is to keep the channels from rank and file open to higher officialdom.

ADJUSTMENT PROCESS   Complaining to immediate supervisors has decided limitations. Although grievances can often be adjusted by this means, and the wise executive makes a conscious effort to maintain sympathetic contacts with his subordinates, not all complaints of employees are susceptible to this treatment. Many grievances, for example, may be against the supervisory officer himself, in which case they would not likely be taken to him and would only rankle in the mind of the employee. Others may relate to issues clearly beyond the control of the supervisor. He may be able to remove the cause of some petty irritations, but further avenues, just as in the case of receiving suggestions for work improvement, must also be open.

[22] Other aspects of management-labor relations are discussed in Chapters 19–21.

The typical procedure does call for taking an issue up with the supervisor first, unless the complaint is against him personally, in which case it goes directly to the next level in the line. Most public agencies require a decision to be rendered at one or more points in the hierarchy but at some point permit the aggrieved employee to present his case before an impartial hearing officer or committee that may, if the employee so elects, conduct an oral hearing. The hearing officer, grievance committee, or panel usually has the duty of advising the head of the organization (or in extremely large entities, perhaps the deputy) on an equitable disposition of the matter. This process guarantees an independent review to the aggrieved person but preserves management's opportunity to take responsibility and make its own adjustments. There is a variety of methods for composition of such hearing committees, but commonly there is some provision for employee participation in selection of members. Sometimes this takes the form of union representation on the committee, sometimes employee election, or, most frequently, selection of one member by the aggrieved employee or his union, one by management, and the third (who serves as chairman) by agreement between the other two.

There is general acceptance of the policy in public jurisdictions which invites either suggestions or complaints from rank-and-file employees and encourages their participation in efforts to remedy conditions. The importance of grievance machinery lies not so much in its frequent use as in the fact of its availability, operating somewhat as a safety valve.

ATTITUDE SURVEYS

A final technique in this galaxy of practices—all of which have the common denominator of facilitating an open communication network—is known as the attitude survey. As distinguished from reliance on employee initiative in bringing problems to attention—as in the case of suggestions, personal problems, grievances, or the like—the attitude survey is a management initiated diagnostic tool to find out what employees are thinking about, what is motivating them, what is bothering them, what gives them satisfaction or fails to give them satisfaction on the job. As in the case of counseling, formal survey of employee attitudes by questionnaire and interview was first stimulated by the Hawthorne studies.

The technical aspects of an attitude survey are in the actual construction of questionnaires and the conduct of interviews. These must be so designed that the questions will elicit specific and accurate responses and will supply data that can be readily consolidated and interpreted. The process calls for professional knowledge and skill. Also, in organizations of more than a few thousand persons, there are questions of distribution and sampling, since covering everybody may be too costly and no more useful than a good cross-section of opinion. Among other considerations, the techniques of the public opinion poll are relevant to the analysis of employee attitudes.

A number of experts on the subject advocate an attitude survey as a periodic affair—not as a substitute for other programs, such as participative management or supervisory training—but as a supplemental check on how everything is going. More often than not, organizations that have used attitude surveys have failed to give sufficient continuity to the process by following through with succeeding surveys. Perhaps in many cases the findings are so surprising that a repeat performance is unconsciously shied away from. In other cases, however, follow-up surveys have been used with profit, often showing how conditions that had been corrected following the preceding survey had noticeably improved employee attitudes toward their jobs.

There are no theoretical limits to the subject-matter scope of a survey. Surveys may be on specific areas of question, such as physical working conditions, or on the whole range of the employment relationships, covering pay, supervision, advancement, health, safety, quality of workmanship and product, equipment, hours, vacations, and literally everything that might conceivably affect the employee's attitude toward his job and the organization. They may also seek to get employee reaction to substantive policy in day-to-day operations.

Needless to say, a survey is worth no more than the effort expended to do something about what it reveals. Practices or conditions that seem to be sound and well received deserve further strengthening or emphasis. Those that are sources of dissatisfaction should be corrected or abandoned. As a matter of fact, even before a survey begins, management and supervisors should be conditioned to accept the results as objectively as they can and to commit themselves to doing something about them. One of the surprising results of many attitude surveys is how significant for employee morale minor irritations become. In numerous instances the difficulty is not with pay or hours of work or even "the boss" but with petty annoyances or oversights that suggest that management is not concerned about human welfare in the organization.

Although a chapter could be written on this subject alone, space confines us to this introduction to a very practical tool for diagnosis of personnel ills. Where it is used continuously and seriously for evaluating the effectiveness of administrative practices, and where positive action is taken over a period of years to meet the needs shown, employee attitudes can be improved to the benefit of the organization, the public, and the employees themselves.

*　　　*　　　*

IN SPITE OF the burgeoning research in behavioral science, there is no established practice of providing for it in individual public jurisdictions. To be of maximum usefulness such studies must be tailor-made to serve the needs of each locale and must be of a continuous nature. The fact that government performance on the whole compares favorably with that of the most effective private enterprises is no cause for complacency. With the continuing development of technology, the growing complexity and scope of governmental activity, and the critical reliance on administrative agencies as the instruments for effecting public policy, there is more reason than ever for attention to the problems of motivation and morale and for substantial and unceasing investment in social science research in the public service.[23] To put the need in the broadest terms, it is an indispensable requirement in the forward march of democracy.

[23] See Chapter 26 on personnel research in general.

CHAPTER 12

Evaluation
and Incentives

No ORGANIZED ENTERPRISE can escape making judgments about the behavior and effectiveness of members of its staff. Assignment, advancement, reward, discipline, utilization, and motivation—all depend ultimately on such judgments, whether they are formalized and recorded or whether they are simply implicit in the decisions and actions of management. The literature dealing with the evaluation of performance continues to be of formidable proportions. Yet, despite this attention it remains an almost intractable problem and one that has produced frequent disillusionment.

The central difficulties seem to be twofold: (1) finding the ways to appraise and report performance that are meaningful and useful in their impact on the work to be done; and (2) finding the ways to carry on the process and apply its results in full recognition that the process itself is a prime factor affecting employee motivation and morale. The second one is the principal object of debate, inquiry, and soul-searching. Most managers (and employees, for that matter) would probably agree that evaluation should (a) maintain or improve performance, not retard it; (b) support supervisory responsibility for the ultimate effectiveness of the work performed; and (c) assure reasonable equity and dignity in human relationships. This is no small order.

No matter how well the inescapable determinations about individual or group performance are made and accepted, making use of these judgments is still another source of concern. Consequently, the subject will be reviewed in this chapter both in the light of what has already been said about motivation and in conjunction with the incentive power of special awards.

206

THE ADEQUACY OF PERFORMANCE REPORTING

In spite of the universal necessity of passing judgment on the performance of others in so many aspects of modern civilization—in political, economic, social, and administrative contexts—research on the subject has been relatively limited and, for the most part, confined to the fringe issues of formal measurement devices and to their objectivity and validity. The reasonableness of purposes served, the compatibility among these purposes, the question whether performance is all that should be weighed, the impact of the evaluation process on the performer—all these are problems that have received scant attention from social scientists. Just enough has been done to provide a research base for some of the instinctive misgivings that executives have voiced over the years. But answers to the persistent question of how unavoidable appraisals can escape readily apparent pitfalls are considerably less satisfactory than answers to many other problems of human relationships. About all a rational treatment of the subject can attempt is to draw upon what is known from experience and modest research and to season this knowledge with a generous quantum of intuition, insight, and speculation.

OBJECTIVES

In more specific terms than those mentioned in the introductory paragraphs of this chapter, any effort to evaluate and report on performance in a work enterprise should serve essentially these ends:

1. Clarification of what is expected—that is, to develop standards of satisfactory performance, setting forth what quality and quantity of work of a given type is acceptable and adequate for pursuing the functions of the organization.
2. Fortifying and improving employee performance—by identifying strong and weak points in individual achievement, recording these as objectively as possible, and providing constructive counsel to each worker.
3. Refinement and validation of personnel techniques—serving as a check on qualification requirements, examinations, placement techniques, training needs, or instances of maladjustment.
4. Establishment of an objective base for personnel actions—namely, in selection for placement and promotion, in awarding salary advancements within a given level, in making other awards, in determining the order of retention at times of staff reduction, and in otherwise recognizing superior or inferior service.

The traditional method for serving these purposes has been to require every supervisor and manager at fixed intervals (such as a year) to follow certain prescribed criteria, to render a judgment about how each subordinate measures up to these, to record these conclusions on a "rating" report of some kind, to discuss the results with the employee being appraised (a later development), and to submit the reports to his superior officer for review, after which they were to be deposited at some central point in the personnel office for future reference. Various ways of accomplishing these several steps, including the utility and shortcomings of each way, are outlined briefly later. At this point it seems useful to analyze some of the problems encountered in almost every effort to follow this general pattern —that is, to make and record formal evaluations or ratings at periodic intervals.

RELIANCE ON A SINGLE TOOL

The very breadth of the objectives just cited should have suggested otherwise, but in both industry and government the perennial error has been to attempt to achieve all ends with a single evaluation device. The typical annual performance rating, stretched and contorted to be usable for future promotion comparison, for diagnosing training needs, for salary advancement, and for order of lay-off, to serve as a stimulus to better performance, and, above all to represent an honest and valid appraisal, has naturally been found wanting. No known method of ordering judgments or recording them has been able to satisfy such diverse purposes all at the same time. Consequently, current thinking has been directed toward the use of special methods, each tailored to suit a particular purpose.[1] For example, in the matter of promotion it has been concluded by many that selection for unknown future vacancies—with their variety of special qualification requirements—cannot be geared to previously recorded appraisals of past performance. Thus, the solution has been to seek further evaluations aimed directly at promotability of employees, as distinct from past performance per se, or to rely on ad hoc appraisals at the time candidates are actually under consideration for a specific vacancy, rather than to store up ratings for future reference without knowing the precise use likely to be made of them.

GAUGING "POTENTIAL"

Related to the single-tool issue is the failure to look beyond past performance as a predictor for the future. So much attention has been focused on past performance that measures of a man's potential not demonstrated on his existing job has been underplayed. Too often aptitudes or skills actually possessed by a person but not brought into evidence in past positions are overlooked.

It is for this reason that aptitude tests are often useful in promotion selection supplementary to performance records. This is a sound procedure, provided the abilities tested are genuinely needed in the post being filled.

---

[1] One piece of evidence discrediting all-purpose ratings has been the research conducted in the General Electric Company as reported in Herbert H. Meyer, Emanuel Kay, and John R. P. French, Jr., "Split Roles in Performance Appraisal," *Harvard Business Review*, January–February 1965, pp. 123–129.

The best example is when selections must be made from among nonsupervisory employees to fill supervisory jobs. This simple fact that in personnel matters the past is not always prologue gives the lie to those who would base promotions to new jobs entirely on performance in quite different jobs or, worse still, on simple seniority.

Another means to get at employee potential has been to ask supervisors to appraise this factor separately from performance.[2] Such a process obviously must be quite subjective, since it rests entirely on a general sizing up of a person by a superior official who may or may not be good at this kind of exercise. A tangential issue is whether or not the employee should be entitled to know what his supervisor thinks of his future. Even though there is almost general accord on the practice of allowing employees to know the details of the appraisals of their past performance, management tends to shrink from revealing so intangible a prediction as that represented by appraisal of potential. Clearly it is fraught with all kinds of dangers of misjudgment or prejudicial behavior by supervisors, but these flaws can be minimized by making certain that action based on "potential" ratings is taken only when they are made by several different officers who have some acquaintance with the employee involved. Furthermore, they merely represent formalization of predictive judgments that are going to be made anyway at one point or another.

THE PROBLEM OF FIXED PERIODS

Requiring supervisors annually or at some other fixed period to render a written evaluation on each employee has been the bane of modern rating systems. Supervisors are reluctant to go over old ground with long-term employees especially, and they often recoil from the artificiality of a process which seems to say: "Today I consider how my employees are doing," as if all the rest of the time does not count. Many do not hesitate to deal forthrightly with their subordinates on their daily work products or behavior, giving counsel on what is wrong and what might improve the situation as each occasion requires, but shrink from an effort to sum this all up and confront each employee with a periodic accounting of his total performance. In fact, some feel that this forced confrontation is at best awkward, replete with possibilities of each party saying the wrong thing, and at worst disruptive of what may otherwise be a salutary relationship.

Consequently, various ways to circumvent the dilemma between the genuine need for some kind of reporting and the problem of fixed periods have been devised. One has been to eliminate frequent ratings for long-term employees and require an appraisal on them only once every five years, or whenever they change jobs, and then only to verify if there has been any marked change in conduct or production. Another is to gear performance

[2] A number of U.S. federal agencies, including the Foreign Service, have tried this approach, usually with moderate success.

reports to specific events instead of to the calendar, so that they are made only when new supervisors have taken over, when employees are new to the job, when reorganizations have taken place, when the job content or technology has been changed, or on similar occasions. Still another variant is to confine regular reporting only to exceptional performance, either unusually superior or unusually poor, so that no reports at all need be made on the great majority of workers in any given category. Under this last condition the appraisal and whatever motivational influence it might have are left to the day-to-day supervisor-employee relationship.[3]

OVERALL EVALUATIONS

Another implicit error in past practice has been to assume that we can analyze all of the faults and strengths of an employee, add them up in some fashion, and come to some neat overall conclusion—expressed by an adjective, a percentage or numerical value, a letter category, or some other device —that makes it possible to compare him as a whole with someone else. This is a most doubtful, if not actually a dangerous, procedure. Individuals on similar work may differ from each other in such a way that the strengths of one are in the very areas in which the other is weak. One employee may be good at meeting and dealing with people but not so good in expressing himself in writing; the other may be just the opposite, facile at paper-and-pencil articulation but shy and dull when it comes to face-to-face communication. If the job requires both skills in some measure, who is to say which employee is the better of the two? Together, with a deft organization of the work, they may make a pretty good team, even though individually they have shortcomings. Looking at the situation as a whole, no one can say that the total effect is not contributory to getting a good job done.

One solution to this problem of overall rating is to abandon the summation or conclusion but keep the analytical part of the report. Thus, a report might point up certain areas of activity or aptitude in which the individual excels and others in which he needs improvement, but refrain from facilely labeling the total man into some grand category derived from

---

[3] As long ago as the reports of the two Hoover Commissions on the federal civil service (1949 and 1955), there was a lack of support for regular periodic ratings. The first comimssion urged that "ability and service records" be used only for supervisor-employee conference, with a view to developing employee performance, and not to govern salary increases, lay-offs, or dismissals (Commission on Organization of the Executive Branch of the Government, *Personnel Management: A Report to the Congress*, Washington, D.C., February 1949, p. 33).

The second Hoover Commission followed this up with the recommendation that only exceptional performance—the kind demonstrating promotion potential, misplacement, or need for special recognition or dismissal—be reported. It advised that a rating system "should not be an end in itself" (Commission on Organization of the Executive Branch of the Government, *Personnel and Civil Service*, Washington, D.C., February 1955, pp. 62–65).

For the most comprehensive treatment of the evaluation process, touching on practically all the issues discussed in this chapter, see Felix M. Lopez, Jr., *Evaluating Employee Performance*, Chicago, International Personnel Management Association, 1968.

these elements, especially if the latter is used as a means for comparison with others. An employee is usually able to recognize and accept his shortcomings in very specific aspects of his work but finds invidious and ego-shattering any attempt to pin a descriptive label on his total worth. Without such summary ratings it is doubtful that there would be as many challenges to supervisory judgments in the form of appeals against appraisals. Employees are not so likely to object to the "profile" of their behavior but may well resent any oversimplified conclusions drawn from it. They may feel, and sometimes rightly so, that what they excel in offsets what they do poorly. In any event, an analytical profile of performance can be even more useful in future applications than the summary evaluation, since the latter with its usual "halo" effect may detract attention from the concrete performance elements that are really important.[4]

WHAT TO APPRAISE

It is the employee's performance, not himself, that should be the subject of analysis. In spite of the common sense of this statement as it appears to us now, the fact is that traditional rating systems focused the supervisor's attention primarily on personal traits and characteristics of people rather than on the actuality of what they did. Thus, emphasis was placed directly on items such as tact, initiative, integrity, ingenuity, dependability, and the like. The alternative, and the one more commonly stressed nowadays, is to require evaluation simply of actual and concrete achievements or behavior on the job, without trying to translate this into a picture of the employee's personality. This approach is, of course, consistent with the concept of management by objectives wherein evaluation is concentrated on results, not just on technique. The supervisor, who sees only a segment of the employee's life and behavior, is less likely to appreciate the person's generic traits than he is to gauge what emerges from the employee's mind or hands as a work product. Hence, the reporting system that is likely to evoke the most reliable findings is one that asks supervisors to cite and measure specific instances of performance in terms of what the job demands are.

There are, to be sure, some difficulties with trying to report actual performance and specific behavior. Most important, it requires that rating forms be geared to each general category of work, so that the reporting official can be prompted to take note of each significant element of performance. The same form could not be used for police officers, stenographers, teachers, and nurses. Each occupation calls for quite different kinds of tasks, and there are vastly different criteria for and ways of observing their accomplishment. Perhaps the only things common to all jobs are the basic human

---

[4] The foregoing analytical approach would be in less danger of running afoul of the trenchant criticism of performance appraisals made by Douglas McGregor, who challenged the notion that supervisors can justifiably "play God" when they judge the whole man ("An Uneasy Look at Performance Appraisal," *Harvard Business Review*, May–June 1957, pp. 89–94).

personality traits of the type referred to previously, which explains why early rating systems tended to concentrate on them. But the extra work called for in developing specialized appraisal forms for at least broad categories of occupations is completely justified on the grounds that evaluation must, if it is not to run afoul of many other pitfalls, focus on the realities of the employee's work, on the quality and quantity of his output, whether it is a service or a product. Specialized forms are the only means so far devised to facilitate this emphasis.

Another problem is that of assuring that the performance or on-the-job behavior reported is representative and not exceptional. It is very easy to recall the exceptional and to overlook the normal. About the only solution to this problem is to maintain a constant campaign alerting people to it through written instructions on the evaluation process and through training programs for supervisors. Usually the design of the report form itself will also help to remind the evaluators of the need to look at performance in total perspective.

OBJECTIVITY AND VALIDITY

The act of evaluating performance is one of relating the work of individuals, in respect to factors found significant in the work, against some standard or norm. The standard may be subjective (as in the case of the quality of a piece of administrative writing) or objective (as in the case of the number of audit vouchers accurately processed), but it must be there. The aim is to make the standard as objective and consistent as possible. Otherwise evaluations will be of low reliability, for the criterion of comparison will vary from one supervisor to another and with one supervisor as applied to different employees. This has been one of the most frustrating aspects of all efforts at improving performance appraisal, and it will continue to attract the interest of research men everywhere. The most that can be said here is to allude to the following discussion concerning employee participation in setting work standards. Under this approach, the norms may not be perfect, but at least those who are being measured against them will have had a hand in their establishment.

One of the incessant aims of appraisal systems has been to reduce to a minimum the element of personal bias that may enter into reporting. At one time experts sought to obviate bias by devising mechanical scoring systems, by which the evaluator's individual markings on specific points were aggregated by a process unknown to him. But this was hardly satisfactory when it produced results that mystified or disappointed both him and his subject, to say nothing of having the basic drawbacks of any overall summary ratings. About the only protection against bias that can be relied on is heavy investment in sound and comprehensive methods for supervisory selection and in thorough and continuous training of supervisors and prospective supervisors in the obligations and techniques of good supervision.

EMPLOYEE PARTICIPATION

Evaluation methods are worthless unless they have the full understanding, participation, and acceptance of the employees being appraised. In fact, the most progressive thinking on the subject concludes that supervisor and employee should *share* in the evaluation process, from start to finish.

A participative approach begins with the setting of work standards themselves, that is, the goals or norms by which success is to be judged—a subject to which some reference has already been made. Where numerous workers are engaged in comparable tasks, this can be accomplished by a group effort in which the supervisor is leader and convenor but in which a serious attempt is made to arrive at a group consensus on standards of quality and quantity that are in the interests of the organization as a whole but are also within the bounds of reasonableness so far as human realization is concerned. A similar process can be pursued with one-of-a-kind workers on an individual basis. Experience has demonstrated that standards of performance which employees have helped shape are the most durable, the most valid, and the most operable.

In addition, there must be participation in the evaluation itself. With due allowance for the reservations about periodicity already stated, the wise supervisor begins his appraisal, not merely ends it, by consultation with the person being evaluated. Citing the standards that have been the product of a joint effort, he solicits as much self-analysis as possible from an employee and tries to make his final report a reflection of concurrence between the two parties. In aggravated cases this may not always be an attainable goal, but it is usually worth the try.

Not to lose sight of some of the points made in foregoing paragraphs, it should be understood, of course, that the participative process is most successful when it is used at a point of need that is obvious to both supervisor and employee alike, not merely to meet some thoughtless requirement for annual review that, in some cases at least, may mean plowing old ground over and over again. Also, emphasis should always be on the constructive side, that is, on improvement, not just evaluation for evaluation's sake. And it should be noted that workers improve most when specific goals are set and when the behavior of the supervisor during an appraisal session is consistent with his usual style and behavior on the daily job.

IMPACT OF APRAISALS

As we stated at the outset of this chapter, one of the most important considerations in performance evaluation is the impact the process itself has on employee attitudes and performance. It took many years of experience before this factor was recognized and expressed, and only in the decade of the 1960s did research begin modestly to penetrate this facet of the subject. We have learned, for example, that sometimes the process of appraisal, particularly when it is a repetitive one with little relevance to the needs of the moment, inhibits good performance rather than insures it. This is especially true when there have been flaws in the employee's performance and these are brought to his attention in an inept fashion. Nor does it follow that a periodic reminder to an employee as to how good he is necessarily serves to maintain his level of accomplishment. It may even motivate him to slacken up a little because of overconfidence.

There is no question that, by and large, employees need to "know where they stand" in the eyes of their superiors. The error comes in applying average truths as if they are universal and invariable. For example, take the case of an employee whose weaknesses are tolerable though nonetheless real. He meets minimum standards, perhaps by extra effort or other offsetting characteristics, so that management is not prepared to do anything very drastic about his shortcomings. It decides that the deficiencies are more or less irreparable and that the organization would best live with them, make any necessary adjustments, and adapt the employee's positive talents in some direction that minimizes the effects of the weaknesses. In the face of this bit of reality, traditional rating philosophy would have that management, once a year or during some other interval, bring up to the employee what these weaknesses are. The chances are that these repeated reminders would only serve to develop him into a thoroughly unsatisfactory employee. The persistent laying-it-on-the-line theme would tear down his ego to the point where he loses all self-respect.

In short, periodic reminders are not likely to be very productive of the object of improving performance unless they introduce something new to the situation or unless the time has come to jolt an employee into a new pattern of behavior. As has been shown, they may even be counterproductive. Employee performance—to say nothing of the subtleties of the ongoing supervisor-employee relationship—is a delicate and sensitive issue. Wholesale handling of infinite varieties of situations without regard to human differences and the sundry emotional needs of employees is almost certain to precipitate anything from disappointment to disaster.

DISCLOSURE

An issue of some consequence to employees, and one often exploited by their union representatives, is the question of their having access to the results of the rating process. Of course, with the participative approach described earlier, the problem does not arise. But there was a time when ratings were considered so confidential that they were kept locked up in the office safe. Needless to say, such a procedure did not contemplate their use as instruments for positive improvement of performance. Even today final recordings are viewed by some managers as reports for the eyes of management only. It is highly doubtful whether a cooperative spirit can be sustained very long where employees are not allowed to see what the record says about their past performance.

A more complex problem arises when we refer to appraisals of "potential." We alluded to the issue in conjunction with the earlier discussion of that subject. The prevailing thought, in contrast with that regarding performance reports, is that the highly subjective predictions implicit in supervisory descriptions of potential are purely opinion, can therefore be used only in combination with other devices that shape an employee's future, and would dry up into meaningless drivel if they had to be revealed (and therefore, in a sense, "justified") to employees. If management makes adequate use of the techniques of multiple judgment, both in potential appraisal itself and in the promotion process, there should be ample assurance to the employee that an off-hand view of his prospects by some one individual will not be controlling in determining his future.

ADMINISTRATION

A few precepts regarding the operation of an evaluation system, however formalized or informal it happens to be, may be safely enunciated. For one thing, it is imperative that any formal procedure be simple, expeditious, and not unduly burdensome on supervisors. Processes and forms that demand hours of study and consultation on each case at specific points in time invariably break down. Even where formal recording is expected only for extraordinary performance, it is wise to keep the load on already busy supervisors at a minimum so as not to encourage ignoring the exceptional performance that should unquestionably be reported. Simplicity and brevity of any written tools supplied to the evaluator are therefore standard bywords.

Of equal merit is the need for continuous training of rating officials in the objectives and processes of evaluation that are used in the organization. Many difficulties can be reduced, if not eliminated, by adequate attention to a sophisticated program of enlightenment on this complex and controversial subject. Frank acknowledgment of its limitations and pitfalls and full participation of managers at all levels in development and critical audit of the system will go far to elicit the understanding and cooperation of the operating branches of the service. Training and participation are in many ways parts of the same concept. The one must be achieved largely through the other, and they may be pursued through planned conferences that serve both purposes.

Any system that leads to written reports should provide for some systematic review of lower-level determinations by higher echelons in the hierarchy. Where managers above the first rating level have some contact and acquaintance with an employee's work, they should be participants at some point in the evaluation. Likewise, this is the point where unevenness in the practices or judgments of various supervisors may be brought into closer harmony. It is only here that the overly permissive supervisor and the unusually rigid or austere one can have their deviations from the norm made clear to them and their attitudes and appraisal practices brought into more acceptable balance.

Most students of the subject in recent years have concluded that performance reports, if they are to facilitate good performance, should not be instruments of discipline. To the extent feasible the process should be nonpunitive. Wherever performance is so wanting that there is no alternative to a self-respecting manager but to dismiss or demote an employee, this should be done forthwith at the time when conditions call for it, not as the result of "discovering" the circumstances on the occasion of a performance review. The latter should be reserved for the explicit purpose of joint analysis between supervisor and subordinate as to where the work stands, a taking stock of how things are going and how each of them can contribute to more effective achievement. It need be no more threatening or punitive than inventorying materials and supplies; more difficult and requiring more care, yes, but not more offensive.

The matter of administration should not be closed without another reference to participation. To encourage sound and useful appraisal, management should be mindful that both in the design of the system and in its operation there should be ample opportunity built in for all interested parties—supervisors, managers, and employees—to participate in the total process. In those instances where formal ratings have some effect on personnel actions, provision should also be made for any employee rated adversely to appeal the judgment rendered to some impartial hearing officer or committee that would be empowered to advise top management on final disposition, just as if it were any other kind of grievance.

METHODS OF EVALUATION

It must be frankly acknowledged (if it is not already self-evident!) that many rating and reporting systems used in the past have provided rather crude and imperfect means for estimating and recording the facts and effects of individual work performance. Nevertheless, there are lessons to be learned from a brief review of the more prominent of these, including systems widely used in the public service. These lessons supplement the insights which may be derived from a more analytical treatment such as that just completed. No effort is made to touch upon every practice ever publicized, but at least the best-known ones deserve passing mention. The task for the future is to extend dramatically the research efforts in this field so that precepts and principles can be sustained or altered and the best of experience can be aggregated into doctrine and standard practice that will serve the high purposes all good public administrators seek.

Some of the methods or devices for evaluation are a matter of history but will be included here because of their dominance at one time. Others still employed are interwoven in the list. It should be noted that some good practices already mentioned, such as participation of employees in setting performance standards, mutual goal setting, gearing appraisals to occasions when needed, reduction of formal reports on long-term employees, and evaluation of results instead of traits—are overriding approaches that may be integrated with any of a number of specific evaluation devices or forms. They are all practices from which the rating devices themselves, as well as the organizations using them, are likely to profit. Here, then, are some of the principal recording and reporting methods:

1. *Production records:* Many kinds of work lend themselves to measurement of actual units of production. Typical would be typists, file clerks, voucher auditors, claims examiners, machine operators, and the like, although some modern office machines (such as duplicators) set their own pace which cannot be affected by the operator. The production counts in repetitive operations provide an unusually good opportunity to develop employee participation in setting the norms or standards by which each employee's production will be judged. Also, they have the advantage of being thoroughly objective. They can rarely, however, provide the only relevant measure needed in a given situation. Almost always there is a quality as well as a quantity factor that must be considered, and in many jobs the behavior of the employee in relation to fellow workers, clients, or others must also be taken into account.

2. *Man-to-man comparison:* Inaugurated by the Army in World War I, this device involved selection of key officers as representative of certain degrees of a particular factor being rated. It was an attempt to avoid the blanket type of appraisal and overemphasis on qualities that may or may not be important to execution of the duties. It sought to objectify judgments by describing that for each trait the reporting officer visualize the best, the poorest, and three intermediate steps in terms of individuals he knew, and then render an opinion about the officer being evaluated on that scale. Although an advance over previous systems used in the military services, it suffered from these deficiencies: it concentrated attention on traits instead of tasks; it specified qualities of too general a nature; and it overlooked that the yardsticks of other-officer behavior selected by individual raters were not necessarily comparable. Man-to-man comparison, with some of these flaws moderated, has been used from time to time in other settings.

3. *Rating schedules:* A wide variety of schemes has been in vogue over the years that consist of listed factors on which judgments are to be made and a scale of numerical or other degrees to apply to each factor. These range from assignment of numerically or alphabetically expressed values by the rater on each factor, which are in turn added up to produce an overall conclusion, to more elaborate devices in which scores of factors are included or in which the evaluator checks specific statements that seem to him descriptive of the person being appraised. Almost all of these have failed to serve their purpose, either because they opened the door to all kinds of inconsistencies among raters or because they were too complex and difficult to handle.

4. *Graphic rating scales:* In and effort to standardize the scales used on each factor appraised and to reduce inconsistencies, the so-called graphic

rating scale evolved, which consists essentially of (a) a list of traits or functions to be rated, arrived at by analysis of factors leading to success or failure on the job; and (b) various descriptive phrases denoting the several degrees to which strong or weak evidence of the factor's presence in an employee's performance is noted. As the rating form is set up, these descriptive phrases are placed along a horizontal line graphically representing the entire range of the quality under review. They then serve as a guide to the supervisor, who is instructed to place a check mark at a numerical point on the line where he feels the phrase most aptly describes the employee's behavior or performance in regard to that quality.

Variants of the graphic scale emerge from time to time, including some in which the descriptive phrases are sharpened and honed by clearance with hundreds of supervisors who choose which phrases best represent different numerical values along the horizontal scale. In another approach, known as the behaviorally anchored scale, the format is structured through an elaborate participative process in which performance factors and examples of high, medium, and low performance ("anchors") are identified by the employees to whom they will apply. Factors and anchors are not finally set until successive samples of incumbents have formulated and reviewed them; and ultimate ratings are usually made by two supervisors in each case in order to minimize bias.

The graphic scale has been less than wholly satisfactory, however, because it relies on translation of qualitative judgments into quantitative terms under circumstances in which the factors evaluated are too complex or general to permit genuine standardization. In essence, the appearance of precision, arrived at by what are actually arbitrary weights given to each item, is misleading. The stamp of scientific method is being placed on essentially subjective judgments. It should be acknowledged, however, that if there is no adding up of scores on each factor and therefore no summary rating, and if the factors used relate to actual job behavior rather than surmised personal traits, such a device can facilitate supervisor-employee analysis and discussion, and the gradations on individual items measured against a realistic norm may be more valid standing alone than when they are aggregated.

5. *Critical incident method:* This method of appraisal requires as a first step determining the major performance requirements of the job and hence would vary with different occupations. A form is then provided that permits the supervisor to record from time to time any actual critical incidents in an employee's work that illustrate either good or poor performance. The resulting work sheet becomes a realistic record of some concrete experiences that will serve as a profile of the employee's pattern of behavior, bringing out both effective and ineffective incidents. It can be useful in facilitating employee consultation, and it has the virtue of focusing on facts. However, it does run the risk of overemphasis on unusual behavior, because it leads the supervisor into looking for those incidents that typify the especially good or bad, to the possible neglect of performance that is average but even more typical of the individual's total behavior.

6. *Free-written or narrative reports:* A number of organizations have used simple narrative reports, either periodic or as the occasion requires, as the means to record evaluations. Sometimes these are structured by use of outlines or guides to assist the evaluator and to ensure completeness and care in making the appraisal. In other cases the device is "open end," allowing the supervisor to express himself as he sees fit on the aspects of performance he chooses to cover. Assuming that no summary ratings or conclusion about "the whole man" are attempted, narrative reports make possible maintenance of records on performance that might otherwise be lost or forgotten but without the flaws of more formal or scaled devices. Furthermore, they permit flat statements of fact, to which employees are not as likely to take exception as they are to moralizing categorizations of their performance. Free-written reports do not lend themselves to ready comparative treatment, but the doubts about such a use of evaluations are sufficient to make this shortcoming unimportant. They can be most effective in future placement and in developing mutual understanding between supervisor and subordinate.

7. *Coaching appraisal:* As the term implies, this style of evaluation has more to do with the evaluator's relationship with the person being appraised than with any forms or devices used. Under this concept a continual joint exploration with the employee as to how he is getting along is emphasized. The evaluation is purely for the purpose of fostering mutual understanding and improving performance. Insofar as it is a continuous process on the job, and not confined to specified periods, one might look upon the approach as an overall mode of supervision rather than a rating method.

8. *Variations as to who does the appraising:*

(a) *Multiple or group appraisal:* Evaluation of an individual by several other persons at the same time has been used in government agencies and business establishments primarily for application to upper-level supervisors and executives. It usually consists of appraisal of the manager's performance and potential by a panel of superiors acquainted with his work from different vantage points, including his line supervisor; review of the group's conclusions by the next higher level of management authority to relate them to overall organization effectiveness, possible reassignments, and the like; discussion by the superior with the subject individual, pointing out strengths and weaknesses and suggesting action growing out of the group appraisal and review; and guiding development of the person through further training, greater delegation of authority, rotational assignment, committee work, and comparable steps. Variations on the technique include, for example, the possibility of permitting the subject executive to choose one of the members of the panel which will make the group appraisal in his case. The process, having arisen from concern with executive development, illustrates the advantage of special-purpose evaluation over the omnibus methods that have encountered so many difficulties and raised so many doubts. It is an expensive process but undoubtedly worth the cost when dealing with key employees.

(b) *Self-appraisal:* Most experiments with self-rating by employees have shown that they are generally more severe in estimating their performance value and sizing up where they need to improve than are their supervisors. Whether there is a formal means for employee self-appraisal or not, certainly it is profitable for the supervisor to take the subject of the evaluation in on the process and to help him and lead him, if necessary, into an appraisal in which he recognizes his own faults and virtues. This is likely to make the process a mutually acceptable one and relieves the supervisor of making the judgment alone. The problem of performance evaluation and recording becomes a joint enterprise, as much the responsibility of the employee as it is of his chief. As in so many aspects of this subject, however, room must be left for determination of those instances where the technique may be useful and where it may not.

(c) *Appraisal of peers and superiors:* Sometimes referred to as mutual rating, this participative approach entails evaluation of each member of a work unit by all of his associates—by his colleagues and subordinates as well as his supervisors. The collective result, reflecting the interaction of the judgments of peers and subordinates in addition to superiors, may develop a very balanced and no doubt interesting profile of the individual employee's behavior on the job. Although this little-used method does not ensure objectivity, it helps preclude bias, and although it does not produce neat summaries about people that permit comparison with others, it introduces all the advantages of wide participation and it can serve very constructive guidance and counseling purposes. At least it deserves more research attention than it has so far received.

THE FUTURE

It is quite clear from analysis of the basic problems of evaluation and of the various methods tried over the years in both the public and private arenas that no one package of ideas emerges as the final answer to the never-ending quest for serving constructive purpose and comporting with human needs. We hazard the prediction, nevertheless, that future developments will stress supervisor-employee understanding through various participative processes; profile analyses instead of summary ratings; evaluation of facts of performance rather than traits or standardized elements; special methods for each separate purpose (such as promotion, training, retention, or special recognition); and evaluation as the occasion demands instead of for pre-established periods.

THE INCENTIVE VALUE OF AWARDS

When employees go beyond what the job requires, when their achievement is exceptional, when their performance is unquestionably outstanding, it is entirely consistent with the natural achievement motivation that they should expect some recognition of the fact. This recognition may take place, of course, in a considerable variety of ways. They may be looked up to favorably by their colleagues, they may have the satisfaction of seeing their handiwork or ideas put into tangible operation, or they may ultimately get promoted to new and higher responsibilities as a result. But such forms of recognition may not suit all cases or may not be feasible for reasons unrelated to the employee's performance. Consequently, there has grown up a substantial body of principle and practice that seeks to supply modes of recognition where they might not otherwise be present or to emphasize or add to other forms. Generally, these are referred to as "incentive awards."

FORMS OF AWARD

Awards may take the form of special citations or honors, monetary gifts, or elevation to some coveted membership or rank in a professional body of some kind. They may be given to individuals or to groups. They may be in response to a continuing level of accomplishment, to some specific one-time achievement, or to generation of an idea or suggestion that is valued highly by the organization.[5] Psychologists are generally agreed that positive incentives are preferable to those that are merely directed at blocking the doing of wrong, and awards certainly fit the definition of positive incentives. Negative or punishment incentives do not clarify the right way to do something, and it is impossible to foresee and contrive enough negative devices to block all the wrong paths. There is no question that awards for the most part are looked upon favorably, that they exert a positive influence on an employee's motivation, and that they can be valuable supplements to those motivations that are derived from the work and the job itself.

The problems come from determining the nature of the award, especially the relative merits of cash and honorary awards, and determining its recipient, particularly the question of group as compared with individual recognition. Of course, there can be emotions of resentment and disappointment stirred up by the granting of awards, but these are the natural risks of any process that makes distinctions among people and are not peculiar to an awards system.

The idea of cash awards is still widely accepted, although skepticism is voiced in some quarters that it may overemphasize individual gain at the expense of cooperation with the group, that it puts a premium on secrecy and isolation of the employee's efforts from the group effort, and that it raises the issue of equitably relating the award to the value of the suggestion or service rendered.[6] Thus, both the cash and the emphasis on the individual are challenged at one and the same time. There is certainly much to support the position that rewards for suggestions or for superior performance should

---

[5] Reference has already been made to this subject in connection with the discussion on suggestion systems in Chapter 11.

[6] A principal contender for this point of view has been the Tennessee Valley Authority. The question of cash awards was rejected in favor of publicity and other forms of recognition by vote of its joint union-management committee. TVA's notable success in employee relations makes its conclusions worthy of serious attention, although they also raise questions as to the overzealous desire of unions to play down individual differences.

come through the ordinary channels of increased official esteem, public recognition, and, of course, salary advancement and promotion. There is also merit to the argument that honors of various kinds are more respected than doling out money. Likewise, any policy must take into account the range of difference among workers as to their reaction to awards of any kind. What may be a true incentive in one time and place may have little or no effect in another. Expectation of award may spur one employee to extra effort and leave another employee quite indifferent.

EXTENT OF USE

In spite of all these qualms, the use of special awards in general and cash awards in particular seems to grow rather than contract.[7] It is possible that we have here an illustration of the need to have a well-stocked inventory of devices available when it comes to forms of recognition. With no derogation of the basic truths that emerge from the overriding importance of the job itself and the esteem of colleagues and superiors as prime motivators, it is evident that the more artificial stimulants such as cash awards are useful too, at least in a respectable proportion of cases.

It is also possible that some organizations have succumbed too readily to the thesis of equalitarianism and collective sameness—whether it stems from the tendency of business concerns to thwart rather than promote competition, of civil services to assure absolutely equal treatment, or of trade unions to ignore individual differences. John W. Gardner has described trade-union practices as containing "a veritable coral reef of accumulated defenses against extreme emphasis upon individual performance."[8] Has anyone thought whether unions represent exceptional employees as well as the average? In broader terms, Gardner makes this statement: "When an institution, organization or nation loses its capacity to evoke high individual performance, its great days are over."[9]

It is not necessary to make a case for cash awards or honorary awards or

---

[7] Many cities and close to half of the states make effective use of cash awards.

In the federal service, cash awards for employee suggestions adopted and for superior performance total many millions of dollars each year. In addition, special salary advancements within the General Schedule pay ranges are awarded for exceptional achievement. Approximately one of every ten employees is recognized in one of these ways each year. Over the two-decade life of the special incentive awards programs, the measurable benefits to the government have reached significantly into the billion-dollar range, and the awards have gone to employees in total numbers that far exceed the size of the federal work force at any one time.

It is therefore difficult to conclude that monetary awards serve little incentive purpose. Management and employees are not likely to maintain such support for a process having low incentive value.

[8] *Excellence: Can We Be Equal and Excellent Too?* New York, Harper & Row, 1961, p. 111.

[9] *Ibid.*, p. 96. At another point he observes: ". . . in an organization or society characterized by extreme equalitarianism the greatest threat lies in *external competition*, i.e., from aggressive organizations or societies which have not fettered their most talented and energetic people" (pp. 24–25).

any other kind of distinctive recognition as the final answer to all evaluation and incentive problems. It is only that they should not be too readily written off on grounds that they inhibit teamwork. They may or may not, but it is quite likely they are entirely consistent with the need to stimulate *individual* excellence if a technological society is not only going to maintain itself but improve.

NEEDS OF PROFESSIONALS

Before leaving the subject of awards, we must take note of the special role of incentives for that growing body of workers known as professionals. As has been mentioned before, engineers, scientists, doctors, social workers, and professional people in general may identify themselves more with their profession than with the organization in which they happen to be employed. A chemist thinks of himself as a chemist first, and a employee of a particular laboratory second. He is more concerned about the regard of colleagues in his profession than he is about the appraisal of executives in his current place of employment.

This is not to be deplored. Organizations merely need to recognize the fact and behave accordingly. Such professional pride can be the foundation for strong motivation and morale, and management can still build strong organizational identification even though it may be secondary. But it may be more practical to capitalize on recognition given by outside groups, through awards or otherwise, than to insist on employer-centered awards. An example is the use of outside professional groups to decide on the granting of awards.[10] Another is the employer's financing of participation of technical personnel in professional meetings and in the leadership of professional societies.

Finally, we must acknowledge that the most important single incentive for the public employee is the confidence that the American people accord to their government and the degree to which they give its personnel an honored place in American life. The rising prestige of public employment in this country is a hopeful sign that the caliber of public administration will continue to improve.

*   *   *

IN CONCLUDING THIS chapter, one more quotation from that very quotable thinker, Gardner, is most fitting: "The sorting out of individuals according to ability is very nearly the most delicate and difficult process our society has to face."[11] If that be true, it is indeed strange that so much of the research on appraisals and incentive has been on the fringes of the subject. How do different techniques and approaches help or hinder motivation and improvement of performance? What are the merits and risks of various forms of participation in evaluation? What systems of appraisal or award best serve what purposes? How and when is consultation with an employee about his

[10] See the discussion on "Public Perceptions of Government Service" in Chapter 2.
[11] *Ibid.*, p. 71.

work most effective? What methods of evaluation and recognition are most in keeping with human dignity, sound discipline, and a democratic environment? These and numerous other questions deserve at least a modest proportion of the unstinted resources poured annually into the investigation of the behavior of material phenomena. Incentives and evaluation will continue to be uncertain and troublesome if problems of human behavior continue to rank so low in mankind's research attention as compared, for example, with the fission or fusion of the atom.

CHAPTER 13

Staff Development and Training

TODAY, AN OBSERVANT person engaged anywhere in the world of work can see that training is widely accepted as a necessary function of managing a large enterprise. The development of the staff is the very essence of supervision, and it clearly assumes a role of great significance to the quality of service and long-range effectiveness. The relentless press of technology, the inexorable fact of change, the ceaseless clamor of social problems—all combine to make the adaptability and continuing preparation of the work force at least as important as its initial acquisition and its motivation.

These generalizations seem so patently true nowadays that it seems strange that attitudes which were quite different could have been sustained at any point in recent times. Yet, the concept of formalized training as a natural and continuing activity of the employer is one that has seen its main development, with rare exceptions, since the 1930s. By and large, its beginnings were in enlightened private industry and in the orientation programs for types of work in the public service that had no counterparts outside, such as police work, foreign diplomacy, and public education. In these latter cases, of course, the roots of in-service training systems can be traced to much earlier dates. But training and development as a general facet of the overall managerial process, regardless of the uniqueness or special demands of particular functions, is a relatively new phenomenon.

THE STATUS OF TRAINING

The resistance to investment in training in the public service that men of imagination encountered among politicians and some administrators as late as the 1930s and 1940s was founded primarily on the thesis that employees hired under a merit system must be presumed to be qualified, that they were already trained for their jobs, and that if this was not so it was evidence that initial selection of personnel was at fault. Fortunately this shortsighted view was not long-lasting. Gradually there was an awakening to the inescapable realities that explain the basis for the manifold staff development activities that are found today throughout the American public service and in the administrative and technical agencies of almost every country of the world.[1]

THE NEED

Some of these realities are perhaps obvious but nevertheless deserve setting forth here:

1. People are recruited not for specific niches alone but for broad categories of jobs, some of which are scattered throughout the organization, and therefore require orientation in the work of the particular agency or unit.
2. Public programs rarely remain static (being frequently revised by legislation), and the quickest way to adjust a going concern to such changes is through deliberate, orderly training of its employees.
3. Many occupations are entirely or almost entirely limited to the public service (police, fire-fighters, tax assessors, food inspectors, mail carriers, sanitary engineers, social workers, and many others), so that the specific skills required are seldom acquired in general educational institutions.
4. Occupational fields usually evolve. Neither medicine, nor engineering, nor accounting, nor even stenography remains quite the same. Training is the process through which specialists can keep abreast of their specialty as well as avoid the limitations of the narrow expert.
5. It is more efficient to improve the skills of existing employees to an optimum level than to rely on initial recruitment to provide a hypothetical supply of the highest skilled available.
6. Films, talks, interesting reading materials, seminars, planned staff conferences, or other training devices go much further in creating enthusiasm for the work than does learning by trial and error.
7. In order to achieve cohesiveness and coordination in an agency, it is important for employees to understand the aims and functions of the rest of the organization, not by chance or in fragments, but by an orderly study of policies and programs presented in a manner that builds mutual respect and confidence.
8. Training frequently accounts for the difference between organizations in qualities such as knowledge of employees about the activities and rules of

[1] Two authoritative works that depict the tremendous range and volume of training going on around the globe, especially in public services are Fred Tickner, *Training in Modern Society*, Graduate School of Public Affairs, State University of New York at Albany, 1966; and Department of Economic and Social Affairs, Public Administration Branch, *Handbook of Training in the Public Service*, New York, United Nations, 1966.

their total organization as well as their own jobs, courtesy and attitude toward the public, interest in the work, and skill and speed in performing a service. Whether they be in restaurant or grocery chains, airlines, or government bureaus, such differences are easy to detect and are often accounted for by variations in the scope and quality of each organization's training practices.

9. Training of some kind necessarily takes place in any work situation, if only by osmosis; the question is whether it will be systematic or haphazard, efficient or wasteful, effective or useless. Unless it is well conceived, planned, and carefully consummated it is unlikely to measure up to the more desirable of these conditions.

One might take the foregoing facts of life as a kind of charter for in-service training in government employment. But even with their wide acceptance, attitudes and circumstances of management can counteract their impact. One of the most common problems is to persuade managers and supervisors to risk losing staff members by training them for better things. Those who try to hold on to their best employees fail to contribute talent to other parts of the organization where it may be needed, inhibit career opportunities, and discourage people from working in the organization. Their resistance to releasing their most promising subordinates for training is unfair to the employees, to the organization as a whole, and eventually to themselves.[2]

THE MILESTONES

Being purposeful and systematic about educational processes in government establishments is so vital to their success that it is worth taking note of the milestones in public service training in the United States in recent decades:

1. The rapid development in the 1930s and 1940s of university schools and programs for preentry education in public administration.
2. The establishment in 1937 of a Bureau of Public Service Training in the

[2] The case is well stated in the following:

When a manager does a good development job, when his organization earns a reputation for quality results on time, the employees reporting to him have frequent promotional opportunities. Indeed, the manager who really works at development will *seek* better jobs for those employees who he feels are ready for greater responsibilities. He invents ways to display their talents to others and bring their accomplishments to the attention of higher-level managers. The more capable men go on to bigger and better things; those who are less able leave for more suitable jobs elsewhere.

Although this high turnover places an inevitable hiring and training burden on the manager or supervisor, it also brings many benefits. The organization is eternally fresh; it looks at questions from many angles; it never develops an ingrown inflexibility about problem solutions. And, because the prospect of upward mobility is attractive to capable employees, staffing presents no insuperable difficulties in the long run. [Marion S. Kellogg, *Closing the Performance Gap; Results-Centered Employee Development*, New York, American Management Association, 1967, p. 201.]

New York State Education Department to aid in the development and coordination of training programs for state and local employees.

3. The trail-blazing in-service training programs of the Tennessee Valley Authority, the Social Security Board, and a few other New Deal agencies in the 1930s.

4. The executive order of 1938, authorizing the Federal Civil Service Commission "in cooperation with operating departments and establishments, the Office of Education, and public and private institutions of learning, [to] establish practical training courses for employees in the departmental and field services of the classified civil service,"[3] and authorizing the appointment of a personnel director in each of the departments and certain administrative agencies.

5. The provision of federal funds, under the George-Deen Act, for subsidizing training programs for state and local officials to be carried on under auspices approved by the Vocational Education Division of the Office of Education.

6. The enormous impetus given to in-service training as the result of wartime governmental operations that called for maximum use of orientation and skill-improvement training to build efficient administrative organizations in a hurry.

7. The encouragement given to training programs by the reports of both the first and second Hoover Commissions (1949 and 1955).

8. The passage of the Government Employees Training Act in 1958, authorizing, among other things, broad use of outside institutions for federal training.

9. The executive order of 1967 which for the first time spelled out in no uncertain terms the responsibilities of the Civil Service Commission and federal departments in continuing education of federal employees.[4]

10. The expansion of programs especially designed for executives and upper-level supervisors, including the establishment of several training centers in the federal government and some of the states, and culminating in the opening of the Federal Executive Institute in Charlottesville, Virginia, in 1968, the answer to the long-sought administrative staff college paralleling such institutions in the military services and in other countries.

11. The growth of training in state and local jurisdictions, particularly the larger ones, to develop the orientation, improved skill, and supervisory capacity of public employees.

[3] Order Extending the Competitive Classified Service, No. 7916, June 24, 1938, sec. 8. Although superseded in 1947 by Executive Order 9830, in 1953 by Executive Order 10440, and in 1967 by Executive Order 11348, the earlier order is still a milestone in view of the "legitimacy" which it created for training.

[4] Executive Order 11348, April 20, 1967. This order was the outgrowth of a report by a presidential task force of distinguished citizens entitled *Investment for Tomorrow*, in which detailed recommendations were made for further strengthening of the training policies and programs of the federal service.

12. The enormous boost given to training for state and local employees by the Intergovernmental Personnel Act of 1970, under which various special courses are conducted specifically for this purpose by the U.S. Civil Service Commission and through which state and local participants in regular federal training programs number scores of thousands per year.
13. The development of university programs in large metropolitan centers providing out-of-hours courses in managerial and technical subjects of primary interest to federal, state, and local government employees.
14. The inauguration of the first institution developed especially for training state and local government managers, the National Training and Development Service.

These developments have been in addition to the earlier programs of preparation at the preentry level pointing to public service.

Before we delve more deeply into the in-service aspects of training, it is desirable that we review briefly the role and status of preentry education directed toward public employment, as it has been undertaken by American colleges and universities.

PREENTRY EDUCATION

University-level curricula aimed at preparation for the public service have gradually been extended over the years. Most typical and of longest vintage have been the offerings, usually leading to academic degrees, designed for the more specialized governmental callings such as forestry, public health, welfare, highway engineering, recreation, library science, city planning, agriculture, and, most common of all, elementary and secondary school teaching. A few institutions have shaped their courses to fit the requirements of the Foreign Service. A number have established schools of public administration or public affairs, which serve the double purpose of preparing young people for work in the general managerial fields and of supplementing technical and professional education with orientation to government service.

BREADTH OF FIELDS

The great bulk of recruits to public jobs, however, come from educational backgrounds much the same as those of entrants to the nonpublic sector. In the professional fields of medicine, law, economics, statistics, accounting, engineering, and the sciences, graduate school programs are generally concentrated on the substance of the field with little or no regard for the locus of the graduate's ultimate employment. Obviously, an increasing proportion of such graduates have been entering upon public service careers; and the brunt of acquainting them with public issues, with governmental machinery, and with the problems of administering the huge complexes serving the public interest has therefore fallen upon government agencies themselves.

The in-service training aspects of this obligation will be discussed later in this chapter.

Meanwhile, the growth and elaboration of bureaucratic forms and methods has brought into being a host of occupations that were unheard of at the turn of the twentieth century and were still sparse in size as late as the 1920s. They still have not, for the most part, reached the status of full-fledged professions in the traditional sense, but they are of a character calling for the intellect and the perspective of persons with an advanced education. Typical of these newer pursuits (which we have referred to as "managerial") are budget administration, personnel management and all its subspecialties, organization and methods analysis, computer programming and operation, property management, public purchasing, administrative research, public information development, and related activities.

Graduates in fields such as economics, political science, and public administration made heavy inroads into these occupations, but most public jurisdictions in the United States did not exert a special effort to attract college-level men and women to them until after World War II. Consequently, in too many places such jobs were filled by able but ill-prepared people from the clerical ranks. Since that time, so much emphasis has been placed on attracting persons with baccalaureate and graduate degrees in the social sciences and humanities that the era of concern about too many incumbents of narrow outlook has all but passed. The outstandingly successful Federal Service Entrance Examination, its successor, the Professional and Administrative Career Examination, and comparable instruments in many of the major states and cities typify the nationwide talent hunt for young people of imagination and administrative potential that has taken place. The kinds of persons sought have been those with the exposure to knowledge and the appreciation of values that would enable them to perform not only in the managerial-type work mentioned but also in those uncharted and unanticipated assignments modern government must perennially create.[5]

EUROPEAN APPROACHES

The United States did not go the way of the British and continental tradition or of their colonial offsprings in Asia and Africa, under which "administration" was viewed as a thing apart and therefore a field of work for which recruitment was to be made more or less exclusively from one or another brand of liberal arts education. The British, for example, since the mid-nineteenth century, had assumed that the best and to some extent the

[5] Under the 1968 amendments to the Higher Education Act, finally funded in 1975, the federal government makes grants to institutions of higher education for establishment and improvement of programs to prepare graduate and professional students for public service careers and for establishment of public service fellowships.

As an indication of the number of institutions that are concerned with public service education, there are over 70 member institutions in the National Association of Schools of Public Affairs and Administration.

only education that prepared men for high administrative responsibilities was training in the classics. Although there had come to be gradual modification in this dictum by the mid-twentieth century, a major overturn of the policy was not signaled until the Fulton Committee Report was made in 1968.[6] That body sought to move away from the elitism of an exclusively prepared corps of "generalists" (who lacked subject-matter skills) to man key positions in the career service toward a more open system, like that in the United States, where persons from any or all specializations could aspire to and be developed for the highest posts.

COUNTERACTING SPECIALIZATION

Meanwhile, the problem in the American civil services was the lack of breadth and vision associated with overspecialized educations. For a time it appeared as if no one was being prepared for the higher responsibilities. Even the schools of public administration tended at first to focus too much on the tool subjects of budgeting, personnel management, and methods analysis. But, with rare exceptions in civilian public employment (such as the Foreign Service), the mistake was not made here to preempt key administrative positions for a special breed of men. Instead, we turned to in-service training and to sending specialists to school as the means to develop our administrative talent. As a result, a better reconciliation between the compulsions of specialization and the need for breadth of understanding and an overall point of view seems to have been achieved. More and more nations that first followed the European closed model are turning to the American open system.

Another aspect of the impact of specialization on public services in the United States has been the problem of getting technological education to become less specialized. Since so many graduates of engineering, law, medical, and technical schools of one kind or another inevitably enter government employment, it would seem reasonable to expect these institutions to augment their curricula with more orientation to governmental affairs. The primary, if not the exclusive, emphasis in these schools still seems to be on private practice even in the face of decreasing proportions of their graduates moving in that direction. As a matter of fact, more course work in communication, the social sciences, administration, and literature would serve well the ambitious engineer, lawyer, doctor, or technician even in the private sphere, because delivery of professional services must increasingly be achieved through complex organizational frameworks. If their careers are to rise above mediocrity, experts such as these will not be able to escape administrative responsibility.

If the solution is to institute more five-year and six-year programs, as some engineering schools have already done, then it might develop for the public service more well-rounded specialists and relieve somewhat the load

---

[6] See the discussion on openness and rank-in-corps in Chapter 4, "Career System."

of new training and retraining that has had to be carried on within the service. Perhaps in those places where schools of public affairs or public administration exist, these units of a university could render one of their highest services by doing more in the way of supplementing the curricula of the technical and professional schools with some imaginative orientation in the subject areas suggested previously.

One of the best proofs of the need for emphasis on general administrative understanding and capacity on the part of technical men is the void that exists when experts in health, sanitation, agriculture, engineering, and even education try vainly to establish mechanisms for absorption and application of their skills in a young or developing country. They are all too often dismayed by the lack of infrastructure on which to build. They assume the existence of machinery or habits of behavior to which they had become accustomed in the United States. Usually the new environment affords too little knowledge, tradition, and administrative structure to provide the necessary underpinnings for making use of the advice the fledgling society is getting. And the American specialist is all too often ill equipped to diagnose the problem, create the climate, develop the understanding, or suggest the organizational machinery or devices necessary to make the technology they are proposing practicable on a continuing basis. Time and again men who know the problems of economic, political, and social development abroad have asserted that the difficulty is not the absence of or failures in transmitting technical information but the lack of administrative arrangements to get programs put into effect. Since technical assistance abroad is so commonly expected of senior specialists in this country, it behooves us as a nation to give more attention to the rounding-out of our technicians both at the point of preentry education and of in-service training.[7]

Universities, in addition to their general educational role, are also playing an increasingly important part in the in-service training of government employees, a subject which will be touched upon later in this chapter.

IN-SERVICE TRAINING POLICIES AND PURPOSES

In-service training is never fully accomplished; it is always in process. It is concerned with initiating new recruits. It focuses generalized knowledge on specific functions of government programs. It seeks to keep employees abreast of developments in their fields of activity, in government aims and strategy, and in national and worldwide conditions that affect their work. It helps to equip them for higher responsibilities or to diversify their skills. It is, like so many of the other personnel duties of the organization, a never-ending proceeding.

---

[7] See the discussion relating to technical assistance in Chapter 27, "Public Personnel Policy Around the World." The reader is also urged at some time in his study of this subject to savor the wisdom in the classic piece by Harold J. Laski, "The Limitations of the Expert," *Harper's Magazine*, December 1930, pp. 101–110.

Management and employees share responsibility for the learning experiences that are presumed to develop from training. Management must help set the goals and provide the opportunities; employees must provide the initiative and persistence to permit their development to take place. At its most elementary level, training takes place when a supervisor or a colleague advises, guides, or assists an individual in doing his work. In more formal terms, it consists of planned courses, conferences, reading, drills, practice sessions, tours, surveys, task forces, home assignments, or any of a number of other organized techniques to generate the learning experience. In all of this effort the supreme task of management is to infuse the whole organization with a common spirit, a universal understanding of the objectives of the enterprise and the relation of individual assignments to these objectives. Training is not only a part of management; in many ways it *is* management. It is not only a facet of each employee's experience; it *is* his experience.[8]

POLICY FOUNDATIONS

Responsibility for training and development of the staff, like any other element of the managerial process, can best be emphasized and communicated by a written understanding within the organization as to the meaning, aims, methods, and obligations of its pursuit. It should be developed with intensive participation of managers, supervisors, and representatives of employees. It should direct attention to how training is part of every supervisor's job and an obligation of every employee. It should establish machinery for continuous overseeing of the administration of training policies and programs. More specifically, it should include standard practice on such points as the various forms of training and of diversifying experience, kinds of training done on government time, how group training can be arranged for, responsibility the organization will take for after-hours training, use of outside educational facilities, training records and their use in promotion eligibility, selection of instructors, services of the training staff, materials and films available, evaluation procedures, costs that can and cannot be borne by the organization, and any statutory requirements or limitations that might apply.

Basic to staff development policy are some fundamental concepts that deserve some elaboration at this point:

1. *Learning is a lifelong process.* There is no period when a person stops getting an education. This is just as true of living within a work enterprise as it is anywhere else. It is wrong to assume that some people in an organization are trained and some are not; all learn from their environment, their colleagues, their supervisors, and their subordinates. All acquire some kind of exposure that may be called training. The question

---

[8] The title of this chapter includes the phrase "staff development" because the word *training* standing alone conveys to so many people an image of formal classes only.

is whether it is organized, deliberate, well thought out, purposeful, and skillfully executed.

2. *The job itself is a formidable instrument for training.* This includes but is not confined to letting a person grow *in* his job. It also refers to planned reassignment to different jobs—in other words, mobility or opportunities for new experiences on new jobs. Such a policy does not require periodic or wholesale reassignment at fixed intervals. It does call for seizing every opportunity to enliven and sharpen the interest of staff members by occasionally exposing each of them to a fresh set of responsibilities or at least an assignment which is partially new. Exchanges of assignment for substantial periods or other means of diversification can be useful in achieving this end. Some organizations achieve dynamism by frequent reorganizations, resulting in numerous shifts in assignment. Stagnation on the same job is just the opposite of the kind of growth implied by good in-service training.

3. *Another instrument of training is found in the very process of administration.* This refers principally to the degrees of delegation and reliance that are vested in workers. Such an approach is particularly applicable to professional and managerial personnel, but it also applies right down to the lowest clerical echelon. An individual learns as he bears responsibility, and he learns more when his superiors give him some feeling of confidence. It is through the process of reliance on people and the confidence that they learn from their own experience that they actually grow and develop. In short, supervisors should not be afraid to allow employees the opportunity to make a mistake.[9]

4. *There is a great advantage in introducing fresh, new, and even controversial ideas into an organization.* This may be done by calling in outside consultants occasionally to speak—including those whose views are known to differ from ideas prevailing inside. Some would even counsel keeping controversial figures on the staff for the deliberate purpose of providing a disturbing influence! Most important of all is the need to inject points of view which, while not necessarily conflicting, are at least enlarging. For example, in the community recreation department it might be wise to prod the staff over a period of months with such subjects as cultural anthropology, the role of government in modern society, manpower requirements for the coming decade, the importance of water resources, or the psychological bases for racial tensions. At least the staff might begin to see people, streams, and government controls from more than a parochial slant. Sometimes the most dramatic improvement on the job occurs when people get away from it and acquire a new perspective.

In effect, then, the training policy may more accurately be termed the *growth* policy of the enterprise, for the ramifications and significance of that

---

[9] Reference should again be made to the discussion on work-centered motivation in Chapter 11.

policy to development of the organization are at least as vital to success as any other aspect of human resources administration.[10]

DIAGNOSING TRAINING NEEDS

Like training itself, analysis of needs is a continuous process; it is not something that can be done once and for all. A number of conditions give signs of training needs: low production, slow service, low mobility of personnel, poor supervision, lack of coordination, client complaints, and the like. Although such situations may often be observed without any formal analysis, the need may be brought more sharply into focus and better coordinated with other solutions (rarely can such ailments be alleviated by one treatment alone) if some time is spent on a careful survey of the facts. These may take the form of questionnaires to supervisors and representative employees, suited to the occasion or on some periodic basis. Training needs may well be reported on in conjunction with job analysis, setting standards of performance, and evaluation of performance. Whatever the method used, administrators, with the professional aid of their training staff, must continually be on the alert to ascertain in what areas and in what forms training efforts should be undertaken for the good of the organization and its mission.

RESOURCES FOR TRAINING

In-House Activity   Determining what formalized training may best be contracted for with existing educational institutions or professional associations and what may more efficiently be performed within the jurisdiction itself is a policy issue that must be answered almost daily. Where courses of instruction are intended for employees in occupations scattered in several or all departments and not concentrated in one, the central personnel agency may well be the vehicle through which the training may be conducted. This would be in addition to its natural function of leadership, stimulation, advice, and evaluation of the training activity throughout the jurisdiction. In a large governmental entity like the federal service or one of the more populous states or cities, central training is a common phenomenon. It has built up to a major operation of the U.S. Civil Service Commission, for example.[11]

[10] The basic premises for training and its goals were set forth as follows by the Presidential Task Force on Career Advancement:

- Self-development requires employee initiative and persistence
- Learning arises from experiences which change the individual or the group
- The best learning occurs when supervisors develop work environment which encourages employees to seek it actively
- Training provides management-sponsored, goal-oriented learning experiences
- Work itself provides a variety of experiences which managers can use for training
- Training meets the organization's needs for change. [*Investment for Tomorrow,* Washington, D.C., 1967, p. 14.]

[11] Annual reports show that many thousands of federal employees annually attend programs conducted by that agency, extending from a few days to two months and covering a wide range of subject areas. Still greater numbers attend courses in federal operating agencies other than their own. Under the Government Employees Training Act of 1958, each agency sending employees pays tuition to the agency giving the training.

Because of its area of program specialization a single department of government may be in the best position to provide training in a certain field —for example, in health, fiscal affairs, urban development, or other fields where one agency is obviously dominant but where there is a "need to know" in various other branches of the jurisdiction that have some involvement with the subject. There is no reason why such a department should not be the locus for the specialized offerings of this type, no matter from what parts of the government the participants come. Likewise, specialists who could serve as instructors and are available from only one department might be borrowed by other agencies needing their services for training. Such mutual arrangements may well be prompted and coordinated by the central personnel agency.

To be sure, large agencies with big training needs of their own and adequate resources with which to meet them would be expected to operate the mine-run programs to serve their own employees. In the federal civil service this is where the overwhelming bulk of training is done. But in the much smaller jurisdictions this is less likely to be the case.

One of the major facilities for training used by states and cities is the federal government itself. For many years several federal agencies—for example, those concerned with health, agriculture, and housing—have been empowered to develop courses for and train employees in counterpart agencies of these subsidiary jurisdictions. More recently this authority has been extended so that any federal department in pursuance of its legitimate functions may admit state and local government employees to its training programs, and the U.S. Civil Service Commission in particular may not only do this but also design courses especially for state and local personnel.[12] In addition, many thousands are trained each year in states and cities through financing under the Intergovernmental Personnel Act, other federal legislation, and local resources.

OUTSIDE INSTITUTIONS   The one remaining source that any government in the country may draw upon for educational purposes is that available from already established institutions—universities, technical institutes, and training instrumentalities of professional associations. The criteria for calling upon such resources usually are the ready availability of course-work being offered by such institutions, the inability of the jurisdiction to develop an equivalent program for itself, the possibility of acquiring a better, professionally prepared program than it coud develop alone, and the likelihood of being able to purchase the training at lesser or no greater cost than it would expend if it were to develop and run it itself. Consequently, all but a few of at least the major governmental jurisdictions in the United States take advantage of

---

[12] Authorized by individual program legislation, then generally by the Intergovernmental Cooperation Act of 1968, and substantially extended by the Intergovernmental Personnel Act of 1970. By 1974 over 70,000 state and local employss per year were participating in federal training sessions.

this ready-made resource.[13] Certainly the propriety of public agencies turning to tax-supported institutions, such as state or municipal universities, requires no argument. But other educational enterprises have also equipped themselves to make in-residence courses and facilities available to governments, particularly for executive training. Even the federal service, with extensive resources of its own, finds it useful to send personnel to private and public institutions of learning.

Some of the schools that have achieved national prominence with programs of his kind are the Harvard Graduate School of Public Administration, Princeton's Woodrow Wilson School of Public and International Affairs, the Maxwell School of Citizenship and Public Affairs at Syracuse, the Institute of Public Administration at the University of Michigan, the Graduate School of Public Affairs of the State University of New York at Albany, and the School of Public Administration at the University of Southern California. In addition, courses offered by various graduate schools of business throughout the country are often used by government agencies that subsidize the advanced managerial training of their key people.

Professional associations of public administrators in various fields, headquartered principally in Chicago and Washington, D.C., provide continuous courses and institutes for training of specialists and executives primarily from states and cities. Examples are the International City Management Association, International Personnel Management Association, American Public Welfare Association, American Public Works Association, and Municipal Finance Officers' Association.[14] Programs by these and other societies are conducted at many points throughout the country.

In addition, the Brookings Institution in Washington, D.C., a privately endowed research enterprise focusing on public issues, has been noted for its seminal conferences for government executives and for acquainting business leaders with governmental operations. More recently, the National Training and Development Service, with financing by foundation sources and Intergovernmental Personnel Act funds, has been conducting a number of special seminars and workshops for state and local administrators, supplemented by a series of brief publications designed especially for their concerns.

On top of the official use of programs run by universities or professional associations, a number of institutions located in large metropolitan centers cater to the personal educational interests of government employees in their geographical areas by offering evening courses especially designed to meet their needs. For these programs the public employee pays his own way and

[13] The volume of reliance on general educational institutions may be discerned from examination of annual reports of the U.S. Civil Service Commission, from annual publications such as the *Book of the States*, put out by the Council of State Governments, and occasional special surveys like the one by that Council, *Fringe Benefits in State Government Employment*, Chicago, May 1968 (Table 12).

[14] The renowned 1313 East Sixtieth Street building adjacent to the University of Chicago campus still houses many such professional groups, although a number have moved or established additional offices elsewhere, notably in Washington, D.C.

attends the institution on his own time. Outstanding examples of universities engaged in this kind of activity are The American University, George Washington University, and the Graduate School of the Department of Agriculture[15] in Washington, D.C., the University of Southern California in Los Angeles, Denver University, Wayne State University in Detroit, Nova University in Florida, the University of the City of New York, and New York University. In Washington and other locations, a number of universities have established "off-campus" class centers in or adjacent to government quarters.

As for instructional staff, when formal training courses are developed and conducted by a government agency for its own employees, the planning, design, and general content of the program are the responsibilty of a specialized training staff, usually associated with the personnel office, as will be noted in the discussion on adminstration of training. But these staff members more often than not do not serve as the technical instructors in the courses. The latter must therefore be drawn from within the organization, from neighboring agencies or governments, or from universities. Hence, this is another way in which outside institutions may be called upon—as suppliers of teaching talent. Larger jurisdictions, however, are usually able to rely chiefly on the reservoir of skilled and informed personnel within their own borders for their instructional leadership.

THE ENDS OF TRAINING

Regardless of what classification of training activities as to purpose is contrived, there invariably seems to be some overlap among the different aims articulated. For our analysis, the following listing may suffice, even though it does not necessarily represent absolutely discrete end-objectives:

1. INDUCTION AND ORIENTATION   In addition to actual on-the-job instruction by supervisors, a variety of means are employed to introduce new employees to the organization, to their segment of its work, and to the conditions of employment that will affect them and their future. Formal schools or courses are set up in many places to serve these ends, such as the academy of the Federal Bureau of Investigation, the Foreign Service Institute, police and fire-fighting schools in major cities, and the like. Obviously this mode of orientation is practicable only when a number of new appointees are brought together at some one time.

An increasingly common technique of orientation is the so-called internship, under which a series of job assignments is combined with formal training sessions to acquaint the recruit with the scope and significance of the organization's activities and equip him for the first steps in an anticipated career. Of particular value in the managerial occupations, although

---

[15] The latter is a quasi-private institution, subsidized with space and a certain amount of leadership from the Department of Agriculture. Its courses are open to all who have the requisite preparation for specific subjects, including government employees from other departments (who are its principal customers) and citizens at large.

not unknown in scientific pursuits, internships have proliferated in many states, cities, and federal agencies. Many city managers and federal administrators are the products of such entry-training systems. The federal government has extended the idea to middle-management levels by selecting employees with a few years of experience for special broadening opportunities to orient them to government as a whole and thereby increase their ultimate usefulness. Still another variant is the summer or intermittent employment of college students, especially those headed for the professions, in a systematic series of assignments that can lead to full-time appointment upon graduation, with much of their orientation already out of the way. Also, those government establishments engaged in construction, maintenance, or industrial-type activities often provide apprenticeship programs in the skilled trades and crafts.

Supplementing all these methods of orientation has been the use of handbooks and other published or filmed materials. Such instruments are especially useful for getting across the functions of various elements of the organization, information about the personnel system, and rules about employee conduct and performance.

2. PERFORMANCE IMPROVEMENT   Sometimes referred to as "refresher" courses, the intention here is to keep employees up to date in their respective fields of activity. Such programs may emphasize new ways of getting the job done, new laws or regulations relative to the work, technological developments outside, and other aspects of change, whether they apply to tax assessment, sanitation, forestry, accounting, or foreign trade. Reliance on independent educational institutions has been especially profitable in this connection, since they are of necessity concerned with vanguard thinking and achievement in almost every line of endeavor. Fortifying and improving performance in already established professions has been a particularly challenging task because of the rapidity of change in technology, to say nothing of the persistent tendency of professionals to become smug about their expertise.[16] It falls to in-service training, making use of such outside resources as may be accessible, to supply most of the correctives for the limitations and myopias of the specialist.

3. BROADENING STAFF USEFULNESS   Not entirely separable from the performance-improvement objective is a still more complex aim of extending and expanding the horizons and utility of staff members, without particular regard to their fields of concentration. It may cover a wide variety of subjects and subsidiary purposes; it may mean broadening for the current job or

---

[16] "Professions are subject to the same deadening forces that afflict all other human institutions: an attachment to time-honored ways, reverence for established procedures, a preoccupation with one's own vested interests, and an excessively narrow definition of what is relevant and important" (John W. Gardner, *No Easy Victories*, New York, Harper & Row, 1968, p. 42).

preparation for another. It always contains at least a tinge of something added, something beyond that for which the employee had been initially prepared. Typical of these kinds of program objectives are:

—*Improvement of supervision:* Aimed at both present and prospective supervisors, supervisory training probably takes on a greater variety of forms than any other. It is commonplace in many public jurisdictions, and its subject matter ranges from work planning and process analysis to sharpening motivational understanding and skills. The main emphasis is usually on the leadership and human side of management for the simple reason that this area is the most likely to have been neglected in the earlier preparation of supervisors. Role playing and sensitivity training have been widely employed in this process.

—*Preparation for greater responsibility:* Aside from any further augmentation of the employee's education for higher responsibilities initiated by him and at his own expense, such as in evening courses or home study, the employer must also be interested in readying staff members all along the line for a larger role in the organization. It may embrace teaching to the unskilled much needed skills not readily available in the labor market, or it may involve exposure of higher-level employees to the stimulating influences of a graduate seminar on great issues of our time. It may entail indoctrination in more sophisticated use of computer technology, or it may incorporate course work in determining the cost-effectiveness of alternative policy decisions. Whatever its nature or its level, its aim is to develop a reservoir of talent in the organization upon which to draw as vacancies up the line occur. Or, even where promotability is not the direct or central purpose, the point is to diversify that talent so that it may be used more flexibly in an atmosphere of unrelenting change.

4. DEVELOPING TOP LEADERSHIP   Training of executives at the highest rungs of the hierarchy, although at one time an unheard-of exercise, has become fashionable if not commonplace. Whereas at one time it was most difficult to persuade officials at these levels to spend any considerable portion of their time on a planned learning experience, they now compete with each other for the opportunity. The assumption that their very arrival at high positions was ample evidence of their possession of all the requisite qualities needed for leadership and policy-making has all but disappeared. The gamut of methods employed to hold the interest and stretch the minds of highly competent, experienced men and women includes formal retreats of several weeks to several months at a university facility, planned rotation in key assignments, capitalizing on sophisticated group appraisals, and exposure to graduate programs in the liberal arts and humanities. There is almost universal acceptance that getting away from the pressures of the job and spending private and social hours in residence at an educational center provides opportunities for the administrator to reflect on himself and his

role, to acquire a different perspective on his current position and others with which it relates, to exchange experiences with executives who have comparable responsibilities and problems, and in general to develop fresh insights into the place of his job and his program in today's world.

No better method of achieving these ends has been found than that provided by the administrative staff college. Getting its start in Britain and Western Europe, this type of institution has spread to many countries. The idea was a long time aborning in the United States but finally saw the light of day in the form of the Federal Executive Institute established by the U.S. Civil Service Commission at Charlottesville in 1968. This facility accommodates sixty federal officials in the very top career grades for a seven-week residential period, scheduled four times a year, plus several three-week and one-week seminars. It offers an imaginative array of unique learning experiences that challenge even the jaded and self-satisfied mind. Executive seminar centers for employees of slightly lower rank offer two- or three-week programs at Oak Ridge, Tennessee, Berkeley, California, and King's Point, Long Island. All the programs seem to be eminently well received.

Highly relevant to top leadership training is, of course, wise use of the job itself. By this is meant the judicious use of reassignment and rotation to broaden the perspective of managers while they are on the way up the ladder of promotion. Recent research has verified the natural assumption that variegated experiences in a series of assignments not only extend an individual's qualifications and help demonstrate his potential but also help the organization avoid managerial stagnation and provide it with a pool of experienced persons ready to fill normal vacancies or to meet the needs of organizational expansion.[17] Some would argue that planned job rotation may well be the single most viable technique for managerial development.

Illustrative of planned use of jobs as training vehicles is the promising new program inaugurated in 1974 in the federal service for a small group of rising managers. Under this plan, following nationwide competition, twenty-five to thirty civil servants at GS-15 from various departments spend a full year away from their regular jobs, a period including seven weeks of formal seminar work at the Federal Executive Institute, a series of special sessions with key federal officials, and one or more developmental work assignments in established positions located in agencies other than their own. Although participation carries no built-in promise of reassignment or promotion, participants clearly have enhanced their opportunities for further growth and assignment.

STATE OF THE ART

There can be little doubt that training and development as an integral part of management is here to stay. The era of lack of receptivity is over. Each

[17] Gary G. Kaufman, "Managerial Mobility: A Cost-Benefit Analysis of Job Rotation," *The Bureaucrat*, January 1975, pp. 462–485.

year around one million members of the federal civilian work force take part in some facet of in-service developmental activity sponsored and paid for by the national government. Levels of training activity in many state and local governments are gradually reaching comparable proportions.

Today's training issues center not on legitimacy but on problems of planning, methodology, organization, administration, and evaluation—subjects that require some exposition in their own right.

IN-SERVICE TRAINING METHODS AND ADMINISTRATION

Some of the forms and modes of in-service training have been alluded to in the analysis of training policies, resources, and objectives. Also, it should be clear that the learning process takes place under such a variety of circumstances that it is most difficult to say where casual, chance training lets off and planned, purposeful training begins. For our purposes here we can only hit the high spots and leave detailed reports on educational methodology to the many publications already accessible in this field.[18]

METHODS

We have already noted that the most common training influences in any work enterprise are the daily guidance of the supervisor passed on orally to the employee and the total impact of the entire communication system within the organization. But these are highly unstructured channels by which intelligence is transmitted and not very susceptible of systematic analysis. Most formalized training, on the other hand, could be classified into three types: controlled assignments, reading, and group sessions.

CONTROLLED ASSIGNMENTS   As previously stated, one of the most effective methods for managerial training is planned use of job assignments. It likewise has proved its efficacy in the systematic rotation associated with internships. If we learn at all by doing, deliberate diversification of work experience is surely one of the more effective methods for development. It enables the individual to see and appreciate the work and problems of an organization from more than one of its internal vantage points. It may occur at any stage in career development.

Planned movement of field-station heads and other professional or middle-management personnel has long been a practice in a number of highly effective federal agencies, including the Forest Service, the Food and Drug Administration, the Public Health Service, the Internal Revenue Service, the Social Security Administration, and the Foreign Service, all of which are major entities within their respective departments. More recently, a number of state and local jurisdictions have profited from using the same technique.

---

[18] A good nontechnical review is found in Chapters 8 and 9 of the U.N. handbook on training, *op. cit.*

In addition, the conscious use of understudies, a means of grooming under close supervision persons expected to succeed to key posts, constitutes a kind of controlled assignment. To be successful the understudy technique requires the formalities of competition and selection on merit to take place before a person is chosen as an understudy, not after. It can be a most reasonable device provided it is not operated outside the normal constraints of promotion based on relative merit.

READING   Assigned reading may, of course, be supplementary to any other form of training. It is usually coupled with formal course work, but it also shows up in the form of correspondence courses and in the issuance system of the public agency involved. Thus, the readability and usability of all instructional and policy materials, handbooks, procedure manuals, or periodic bulletins become essential characteristics of any agency's effort to maintain a well-informed work force. Sometimes the general issuance system and correspondence courses are the only contacts with headquarters for the isolated field-station or itinerant employee. They are hardly a substitute for face-to-face discussion and interchange of ideas, but this makes all the more important a deliberate policy of seeing to it that they are well done. Another mode of reliance on the written word for educational ends is the systematic circulation of periodicals and new books relating to the agency's field of work to all employees who are in a position to gain from studying them. This, in turn, along with many other good reasons, dictates the absolute necessity for all but the very smallest organizations to have a specialized library of their own, and one which is prepared and inclined to keep the staff alert to all that is going on in the subject-matter areas relevant to the agency's mission.

GROUP SESSIONS   Group sessions may also take many subsidiary forms. Periodic staff meetings between supervisor and members of his team, while usually very informal, can be very fruitful devices for staff growth, to say nothing of keeping the supervisor on his toes. When they are conducted in a participative atmosphere, with a spirit of free exchange of ideas, they can serve a much higher purpose than one of just being a transmission belt for issuing orders. On a larger scale, occasional assemblies of all or large sectors of the employees of an organization in any one location, in which the head of the activity and his key colleagues take part, may also contribute markedly to an esprit de corps and to group identification with the organization's goals.

Of course, the most commonly recognized kind of group training session is the formal class or course patterned after the prototype in general educational institutions. However, the variations in instructional method that may be used with the assembled group are almost infinite. In the reference to a number of these here, it should be noted that each may be used in combination with any of the others; they are not, and indeed should not be thought of as, individually exclusive pedagogical methods.

The most traditional technique is, to be sure, the formal lecture, in which the expert of presumed superior knowledge, insight, or experience relates to the class what he thinks they ought to understand. It is frequently criticized as too nonparticipative but nevertheless continues to be employed widely because of its sheer convenience and the occasional attraction of a well-known speaker. In spite of its limitations, the lecture has some obvious advantages of directness and of capitalizing upon the wisdom of extraordinary minds that will always make it a feature of many training classes.

Sometimes coupled with lectures is the widely used discussion group, which may be just a question-and-answer session or, under skillful guidance, a real occasion of give-and-take among the participants and the leader. Case studies are often included as bases for such discussions. Another stage closer to full participation is represented by the seminar or conference, in which a structured agenda or series of questions may be followed but in which the meeting "belongs" to the group and the object is to emerge with either some group conclusions or a determination to pursue issues further, either as a group or as individuals.

A further and still more participative approach is the group-project technique, variously known as the task force, syndicate, or project method. This usually entails assignment of a small number (say, three to six) persons from the larger group to work jointly on a research or study project that presents a real challenge, requires much study and discussion among the members and possibly a certain amount of subdivision of labor, and results in a written or oral report on findings and conclusions to the plenary group. The syndicate method used in the British Administrative Staff College at Henley achieved international renown among all those concerned with educational processes among working adults. It takes time and careful planning. Unquestionably, the variants on this group-project device have established themselves as among the most sophisticated and effective learning techniques in adult education.

Also of British origin is the conference method employed by the Coverdale Organization of London. Used in British industry, in several civil service institutions, and on this continent in programs arranged for international and other organizations, this approach concentrates on managers' strengths, seeking to equip them to learn from their own experience, to observe the reactions of others more accurately, to measure their own progress, to make better use of the talents of others, and otherwise to increase their own practical skills in management.

There are, of course, a number of specific participative methods that could be spelled out, among them role-playing and the group-diagnostic processes known as sensitivity training.[19] These devices involve an acting out of real-life situations that make the technique particularly useful for dealing

---

[19] The best source of articles on this popular but controversial technique is found in Robert T. Golembiewski and Arthur Blumberg, eds., *Sensitivity Training and the Laboratory Approach: Readings About Concepts and Applications*, Itasca, Ill., F. E. Peacock Publishers, 1970.

with human behavioral subjects. As in all educational programs, there is also room in in-service training for full exploitation of demonstration techniques, for field observation trips, and for mechanical or electronic visual and oral presentations of various kinds—wherever the nature of the subjects, the state of the knowledge, and the type of participants lend themselves to the use of such training aids.

ADMINISTRATION OF TRAINING

ROLE OF MANAGEMENT   Although we have stressed that training is essentially the line supervisor's responsibility, the larger the organization the more it is necessary that somebody or some office give full-time professional attention to the overall business of in-house educational policies and practices. The training specialist is cast in the role of advisor and coordinator, but he must also be a stimulator, a provocateur, and an evaluator. He may occasionally function as an instructor in some aspects of orientation or supervisory training, but his usual responsibility is to take leadership in joint efforts with management to design a program, to secure appropriate instructors and conference leaders, and to see that formal courses are operated efficiently and effectively. He must be a master of educational philosophy and method, but, above all, must be broad-gauged and possessed both of a keen insight into human behavior and a full grasp of the mission of his agency. Among his duties will be conducting surveys and discovering training needs; conducting research in training methods; working with operators in planning the content and methodology of courses; maintaining ready access to qualified instructors both within and outside the activity; preparing training materials; arranging for services from outside institutions; preventing duplications or gaps in training; and directing the evaluation of training programs. Obviously, his is part of the overall personnel management responsibility.

INSTRUCTORS   One of the difficult but extremely vital steps in developing group-training programs is the selection and preparation of those who are expected to help instruct others. As we have seen, many will be drawn from within the organization, but the training officer must be thoroughly acquainted with the resources that may be called upon from the outside. Also, he must recognize that the average practitioner, whatever his specialty, seldom possesses an inborn flair for translating his knowledge to others, that is, for teaching. The training officer must be relentless but skillful in training the trainer. He must see that the instructor appreciates the relation of theory in his field to practice, that he does not get lost in details, that he knows how to speak before a group and to elicit discussion, and that he is flexible enough to employ modern learning aids and techniques that are relevant to his subject.

EVALUATION   Perhaps the most underdeveloped aspect of training is its evaluation. Some may despair of attempts at evaluation of any training effort because they seek precision and certainty. At best, we can only approximate the quality of training results, since training deals with intangibles and may be only one of several circumstances that can be held accountable for a given effect. But this does not mean abandonment of the effort. And there are at least quasi-scientific methods that help determine the extent to which a particular program is effective.[20]

No one can object to the use of whatever objective data or quantitative measures are available to appraise a training program, but opportunities for such are likely to be few and far between. It is usually necessary to rely on questionnaires given to the training participants themselves, on follow-up interviews and inquiries some period after completion of the course under review, on the collective observations of managers and supervisors or others in a position to gauge the situation at least subjectively, or on some combination of these approaches. More often than not, such inquiries do elicit a reasonable appraisal, providing some basis for recasting a program to serve more precisely the objectives it sought to achieve. Of most importance, of course, is any evidence of improved job performance, service, or effectiveness that may have been part of the aim—even if other influences may also have contributed to these results. Traffic fatality rates as an indicator of highway patrol effectiveness, fire incidence rates as a measure of fire-fighters' training, speed and accuracy criteria as marks of improvement among welfare case workers, claims examiners, or voucher auditors, are examples of how the end results in program performance may suggest whether a certain training effort had any impact or not.

An example of acute need to evaluate and continuously refocus training on changes in the community and the work environment is found in municipal police training. This is one of the reasons that police administration is so complex and illustrates why all law enforcement methodology, especially training, must be ever adaptive to surrounding circumstances.[21]

Evaluation of training may easily be confused by uncontrollable events, such as new statutes, new top executives, budget changes, newspaper campaigns, political controversy, and other extraneous factors. They will have to be discounted insofar as it is possible. At all events, it is desirable to keep evaluation focused on the purposes the training was intended to serve and to search for all the indicators that may exist as to whether those purposes are being reasonably achieved. In the final analysis, however, a certain amount of training will have to be taken on faith. No one can *prove* that an educated man is a better man, but we have an instinctive feeling that his existence has something to do with the quality of a civilization. So it is with in-service training. It is next to impossible to measure the pay-off in some of

[20] One of the few detailed accounts of evaluation method is William R. Tracey, *Evaluating Training and Developing Systems*, New York, American Management Association, 1968. At time of writing, the author was director of instruction at a U.S. Army school.

[21] A useful discussion appears in the chapter by Robert Wasserman and David Couper, especially pp. 126–138, in O. Glenn Stahl and Richard A. Staufenberger, eds., *Police Personnel Administration*, Washington, D.C., Police Foundation, 1974.

the efforts at broadening the horizons of executives, for example. We have to have faith that there is more risk of narrow and provincial judgment when they do not have such exposures than when they do.

*   *   *

IN CONCLUSION, WE must remind ourselves that a staff grows and develops not just by use of formal training alone but also by living with an environment, with an attitude of management, permeating all operations, that makes growth and development natural, attractive, and satisfying. It seems to be a fact of life that the very existence of complex bureaucratic structures fosters inertia, resistance to change, and acceptance of the status quo. As John M. Pfiffner was once heard to say, "organizations resist intellect." The perpetual task of staff development is to help intellectual influences blow their fresh winds through the stale airs of bureaucracy.

CHAPTER 14

Health, Safety, and Welfare

UNLIKE MATERIAL OBJECTS, government servants are not to be used today and scrapped tomorrow. The cultivation and development of human resources as a function of work enterprises is a theme prominent throughout many parts of this book, but particular attention is drawn here to those extra responsibilities of the public employer for employee welfare—those aspects of working conditions and worker concerns for which a special institutional accountability must be maintained. Keeping employees "fit," in the physical sense, is clearly a legitimate goal of management. Measures to contribute to the health and also to the social and economic well-being of the staff, as means to conserve human resources and to maximize human performance, deserve special comment at this point, over and beyond what may be inferred along these lines from other chapters.

HEALTH MAINTENANCE

That health is a national asset and therefore a national responsibility is widely accepted. Inherent in this recognition are the manifold activities of public health and welfare agencies in disease prevention or, more broadly stated, health conservation. Compulsory health insurance not only applies to the older sector of the population but gains adherents daily for wider application. Group health insurance and related protections abound in all employment, both industrial and governmental. Long ago the safety movement, stimulated by workmen's injury compensation laws in the states, helped legitimize the practice of having physicians and nurses engaged full time at

248

places of work. Employers also became aware that absenteeism due to sickness and possible subsequent employee turnover entailed costs of operation in excess of any cost of maintaining the health of the work force. Public agencies, in the meantime, had relied heavily on generous sick leave provisions as a form of health insurance.

Evolution of these various evidences of enlightenment suggests that the basic aims of a broad-gauged health and medical program on the part of the modern employer are these: (1) to procure and assist in proper placement of personnel who are physically fit to perform, (2) to train employees in personal hygiene and health care, (3) to reduce loss of work time, and (4) to generate peace of mind among members of the staff about their personal well-being. To achieve such aims requires an array of activities which may be conveniently summarized under two headings: (1) those preemployment or on-the-job health services such as physical examinations, treatment of accident injuries and minor illnesses, health education, and supervision of sanitary and other conditions affecting health; and (2) provision of comprehensive group insurance for general health care for employees and their families.

While health functions cannot ordinarily be performed directly by the personnel agency or office, that organization should guide and coordinate them. It certainly has a vital stake in employee health, not only because it is charged with the maintenance of an efficient staff but because health administration intimately affects other aspects of personnel management, such as setting minimum physical requirements for work, control of attendance, administration of leave policies, and disability retirement. In organizations of more than the smallest size, at least one full-time industrial physician would normally find his time profitably occupied. Public jurisdictions have the advantage of being able to call upon general public health agencies, industrial hygiene divisions, or a medical branch in a labor department to provide such professional services. It has not, however, been a field in which public personnel establishments have been in the vanguard to work out such arrangements, leaving much of the ground-breaking development in employee health matters to private business concerns.[1]

---

[1] The Occupational Safety and Health Act of 1970, while occasioned mainly by needs in private industry, also imposed nationwide requirements on public employers. It required all states to develop and maintain comprehensive health and safety programs for all public employees in their jurisdictions, coupled with assurance of federal assistance. The Department of Labor administers the program within the federal service as well as the nationwide program. Money grants are available for research and demonstration projects on health and safety standards and practices in the work place. Safe and healthful physical environs, adequacy of safety equipment, provision of certain health services, proper accident reporting, and intensive employee consultation procedures are cardinal features of the program.

For a good summary of the operation of the program in government, see Walter O. Jacobson, *Compliance with the Occupational Safety and Health Act*, Personnel Report No. 741, Chicago, International Personnel Management Association, 1974.

ON-THE-JOB HEALTH MEASURES

In the discussion of the selection process it was pointed out that physical examination is a common hurdle to be cleared by prospective entrants into public services. This requirement is essential not only to a rational hiring practice but also to operation of injury compensation and retirement systems.

EXAMINATIONS Physical examinations in no way preclude effective utilization of physically handicapped persons in government jobs, as promoted among all employers by the President's Committee on the Physically Handicapped. Indeed, it is through such examinations that the most effective placements can be made on the basis of candidates' true skills and capacities. Also, the preentry examination sifts out those who have a contagious disease or are physically incapable of handling the stresses of some work, and further, discovers defects that should be considered in wise placement. Moreover, it may bring to light insipient predisposition to certain ailments that can be periodically checked to avoid later illness. Naturally, records of results of preentry examinations should be filed with other health records for future reference.

The fact of good health at the time of entrance does not preclude the possibility of deterioration thereafter which may result in decreases in performance and danger to the health of fellow workers. Therefore, the logical extension of a thorough-going program is a periodic medical examination, but these are not nearly so common in government employment as the preentry check-ups. Good standard practice should especially include a complete review, every year or so, of the physical condition of key executives and other categories of civil servants who are exposed to unusual strains or hazards.

EMERGENCY TREATMENT Since accidents happen even where there is a well-managed safety program, progressive employers always establish facilities for the prompt and effective treatment of injuries. To meet the tests of speed and adequacy requires an emergency health room in every large establishment or building, staffed with at least one full-time nurse and either a full- or part-time physician. Actually, this aspect of a medical program has been given more support in public agencies than other health activities, but many health rooms are understaffed and the quality of service varies greatly from one organization to another.

If reduction in lost time on the job is to be successful, the medical department cannot be confined to treatment of injuries but must be prepared also to diagnose and treat minor illnesses on the job. Usually more time is lost through illness than through accident. Experience shows that the medical office can make a considerable contribution by concentrating on a few prevailing illnesses. The greatest offender is the common cold; next come other respiratory diseases and digestive troubles.

OTHER MEASURES   Much absenteeism can be prevented by proper sanitation, early diagnosis and treatment, and health education, all essential responsibilities of an employee health service. Likewise, if sick-leave use is to be reasonably controlled, visiting nurses and physicians may be necessary. But health service staffing is seldom adequate to permit visits to the homes of absent employees.

Often the most effective work of a medical division is accomplished through health education. This includes dissemination of information on ordinary matters of personal hygiene, such as sleep, cleanliness, and diet, and also instruction in home remedies for colds and other common ailments. Public health departments or hospitals in most jurisdictions are usually equipped to provide this kind of service and frequently cooperate in health educational activities when requested to do so by the personnel agency.

GROUP HEALTH INSURANCE

At this point we turn to the concern of the employer with the health of workers beyond the work place and likewise the health of their dependent families. One of the benefits of employment is the opportunity it usually provides to participate in prepayment family medical care and hospitalization plans at low group rates. Although some plans are maintained by workers on their own, it is now commonplace for public employers to sponsor the arrangement and to pay half or more of the insurance premiums required. The trend in private labor contracts is toward noncontributory plans in which the employer pays all the cost, whereas some public jurisdictions still require the employee to pay the full cost. In any event, some kind of group arrangement is all but universal in the public service.

The largest carriers of these plans are the nationally affiliated Blue Cross and Blue Shield hospitalization and medical-surgical programs. Depending on location, coverage is also provided by various comprehensive care group-practice clinics such as the Group Health Association in Washington, the Kaiser program on the West Coast, and the Health Insurance Plan of Greater New York. Private insurance group policies, which reimburse for specified expenditures for medical and hospital care, serve all or parts of the government plans. Coverage of health insurance for federal employees, first put into effect in 1960, embraces all these types of programs (the choice being up to the employee) and constitutes the largest single insurance scheme in the United States. Almost all civil servants in the national government have availed themselves of this protection, for which the government pays a substantial share of the cost and deducts the employee's share from his pay check.

One of the issues plaguing group-health insurance is the skyrocketing cost of hospital care and surgery, necessitating a constant increase in insurance rates, whether paid by employer, worker, or both. There is increasing concern that the universal method of paying for health care by the risk-sharing insurance device may have turned out to be a social guarantee that hospitals and doctors can charge what they wish and have their incomes assured. However, one of the reasons that running hospitals and clinics has become so expensive is that most of the paramedical occupations, such as nurses and medical technicians, have only in recent years achieved salary levels commensurate with the training required and in more balanced relation to other high-skill vocations. The true cost in the past has unfortunately been concealed behind niggardly pay policies for all but the physicians themselves.

ACCIDENT PREVENTION AND SAFETY

Accident prevention receives its impetus in industry from two primary sources: (1) from the desire to eliminate production losses due to accidents; and (2) from workmen's injury compensation laws in the states which make employers responsible for industrial accidents by requiring them to pay higher premiums when they have higher accident rates. Thus, private employers have a financial incentive for accident reduction, and generally it has been effective. Public service institutions, however, are ordinarily not required to make the cost of accidents a charge against their budgets. Hence, whereas business concerns have been forced to embark upon safety programs for their own protection, many government agencies have not been under any such compulsion.

SAFETY PROGRAMS

A well-constituted safety program deals with both accident prevention and amelioration and with fire prevention and protection. Its development and administration require some central authority that has the definite backing of the personnel executive. The program requires a continuous process of reporting on the number, character, severity, and cause of accidents. This, in turn, means reporting on prescribed forms, investigation by competent officers, and analysis in a central office.

Accidents are due either to working conditions, machine failures, and the like, or to personal or human factors such as carelessness or ignorance. In the case of the former a competent safety engineer may be able to improve the physical circumstances of the work so that many accidents are prevented. The class of accidents due to carelessness or inexperience calls for a different mode of treatment, namely, safety education. Techniques for safety education entail formal instruction, establishment of safety committees, exploitation of all means of communication, contests, and numerous other devices to keep the attention of employees. Whatever the program content, it can be successful only if someone is specifically charged with responsibility for this aspect of personnel administration.

The utility of safety programs in public jurisdictions has been demonstrated time and again. Dramatic reductions in accidents and in resultant injury-compensation payments have been made in quite a few municipalities, states, and federal agencies. But, with the best of prevention, there will probably always be a certain number of unpreventable accidents. The problem here is one of amelioration, decreasing the seriousness of the consequences of accidents. One of the means to achieve this is through quick treatment and prompt hospitalization where called for. Obviously, this can be best assured by provision of adequately staffed and well-located health and first-aid rooms, to which reference has already been made.

Neither must fire prevention and protection be slighted. Government buildings must be fireproof insofar as that condition is attainable, with adequate fire escapes and other exits to accommodate the maximum number of occupants of each building. Regular inspections are also desirable to eliminate situations conducive to fire, and, of course, fire drills and other educational devices should be fully exploited.

INJURY COMPENSATION

Regardless of the usual absence in the public service of tax incentives (such as occur in most states under private workmen's injury compensation laws), most governmental jurisdictions do have some provision for compensating employees when they must lose work time because they have the unfortunate experience of being injured or acquiring a disease under circumstances attributable to the job. Until recent years these benefits have not ordinarily been very generous. Even in the federal service it was not until 1974 that an injured employee could draw full pay for up to forty-five days following the event, plus enjoying a number of other benefits that have for years been characteristic of compensation under union contracts in private industry.[2]

PHYSICAL WORKING CONDITIONS

Although many county courthouses, a number of city halls, and even a few state and federal office buildings still typify the kind of office space reminiscent of the 1880s, the fact is that the great majority of public servants are now housed in relatively modern structures. The rapid growth of government itself has necessitated vast expansion and replacement of outworn buildings, quite apart from considerations of good personnel policy. The sheer volume of modern facilities has made the acceptable standard for good work space widely evident, even to the casual observer. All that is needed here is a brief allusion to the principal factors involved in good physical working conditions—ventilation, lighting, noise, space, seating, and sanitation.

VENTILATION   Ventilation may approximate perfection when atmospheric conditions regularly meet these criteria: (1) a normal proportion of oxygen is present, (2) temperature and humidity fall within the comfort zone, (3) the

[2] Federal Employees' Compensation Act Amendments, P.L. 93-416, September 7, 1974.

air is free from dust, odors, and abnormal concentrations of bacteria, and (4) there is continual circulation of air. Under ordinary urban conditions, and particularly with a large work force, adequate ventilation can usually be achieved only if a modern central air-conditioning system is employed. Attainment of this objective is more than merely desirable, not only because of its bearing on fatigue and efficiency but also because of its impact on health. Where public employees are still located in buildings without air-conditioning or other high-quality ventilation, there is almost invariably a noticeable loss in the expenditure of energy for productive work.

LIGHTING   Even though it may play a secondary role to psychological factors,[3] the question of proper lighting is nevertheless important from several standpoints. Eyestrain, for one thing, is known to be a contributing cause of fatigue. Moreover, poor lighting conditions, if long continued, may result in permanent impairment of sight, particularly for persons engaged in very close work. Aside from humanitarian considerations, such a result may lead to unnecessary injury compensation cases, to premature retirements, and to generally lowered efficiency—all of which baneful effects are costly. Whether natural or artificial light or both are employed, adequate standards should be maintained by means of systematic tests. The photometer is an inexpensive and indispensable aid in making light surveys. As for criteria, it is generally accepted that artificial lighting should approximate daylight as far as possible, that combinations of indirect and direct light are superior to either alone, that fluorescent bulbs are more versatile and economical than incandescent, and that the color of walls and ceilings is an important factor in securing agreeable and salutary effects.

NOISE   Just as one uses a photometer to test the adequacy of lighting, so also may the amount of noise be gauged with a sound-level meter by registration of electrical impulses. Despite the lack of dependable standards, observations made with use of a sound meter can lead to reduction if not elimination of conditions in the work place that give rise to disturbing noise. In offices noise can be reduced by provision of soft or resilient floor covering, by selection of typewriters and other necessary machines at least partly on the basis of their quietness, and by treating walls with effective sound-absorbents. Planning office layout can help by isolating noisy office equipment, by keeping typing operations separate from interview rooms, by erecting partitions at reasonable intervals, and by other such efforts. Overcrowding itself, of course, may also be a factor contributing to unnecessary noise.

SPACE AND EQUIPMENT   Although operators of office machines such as typewriters may not complain of noise distraction, some studies have shown that noise adds to fatigue without employees' realizing it. A common error in government offices, even in relatively modern buildings, is to force ad-

[3] See the discussion of the Hawthorne studies in Chapter 11.

ministrative and technical employees who are expected to do creative work to sit at desks adjacent or close together—often four, or as many as ten or a dozen, to a small room. Concentration on a problem or a report becomes almost impossible when one or more others in the room are engaged in necessary telephoning or conferences with their colleagues. The amount of production lost under such circumstances is well-nigh incalculable. Certainly it is far greater than any savings in space or in the cost of installing simple partitions. One solution is to provide small, quiet private or semiprivate offices for all employees who are called upon to do research, solve technical or management problems, conduct interviews, carry on extended telephone or personal conferences, develop policy proposals, or otherwise perform more than repetitive or manual tasks. The total space required need be little greater than is used in the open "bull pen" type of office space, and the cost of half-partitions or other movable partitions is easily offset by increased effectiveness and productivity of the staff.

Since a close connection has been demonstrated to exist between working posture and fatigue, the question of proper seating requires attention. Work must be so arranged that posture can be varied and that good posture is possible. Too little concern has been shown for the seating of most government employees, although use of adjustable typist chairs is a common exception to this neglect.

SANITATION   General cleanliness is an elemetary requirement for satisfactory work space. Cleaning of floors and windows and dusting of furniture are tasks best done outside of daily working hours by a special force. Aside from these more or less obvious elements of good sanitation practice, there must also be adequate and accessible drinking water, clean and uncrowded toilet facilities, and, where appropriate, suitable wash and locker rooms. It is usually desirable that the employee health office, not merely the building maintenance crew, have the dominant voice in supervision of sanitation and any other physical environmental conditions that may have an impact on the staff's welfare and performance.

The general impression created by surroundings on workers who spend the best part of their waking hours on the job can be a potent attitudinal factor. Other things being equal, the person who works seven or eight hours every day in clean, cheerful, and comfortable quarters is likely to have a very different outlook from one who is forced to exert himself in drab, dirty, or uncomfortable surroundings. Quite apart from any attendant losses in efficiency, anything less than desirable standards for the physical environment is indefensible on broader grounds.

WELFARE AND OTHER COOPERATIVE ACTIVITIES

Customarily, public employers maintain or permit a variety of services at or adjacent to the work place that facilitate employees' adjustment. Cafeterias and stores, savings and loan offices, cooperative purchasing, legal aid services, and sundry recreational activities are typical of what is available in many jurisdictions.

To avoid any flavor of paternalism of the type so odious in the old-fashioned "company towns" and to permit more democratic control, many such activities are carried on under the auspices of employee unions or welfare associations, with the governmental entity providing certain support through provision of space and initial capital investment. This is the manner in which many eating facilities, credit offices, athletic leagues, and recreational events are sponsored. This is not to say that welfare services of this type must be left entirely to employee-group initiative. There is a management obligation here to stimulate such activities, where possible, and to see to it that enterprises such as cafeterias and snack bars meet suitable standards as to sanitation and impact on health. It is to the advantage of the employer especially to see that attractive eating facilities are maintained that provide adequate and healthful diets at low cost.

Notable among employee-operated welfare organizations are several in the federal service. The largest is Government Services, Incorporated (commonly referred to as GSI), which operates most of the employee cafeterias and dining rooms in government buildings in Washington, D.C., and nearby areas, and runs several recreational facilities. An example of a smaller group is the Welfare Association of the Department of Agriculture, which engages in similar services.

GROUP LIFE INSURANCE

Group life insurance entails the usual financial protection against loss of life, based on term insurance (with no cash surrender value), at low rates made possible by the random spreading of the risks among members of a fairly selective group. Life insurance, on either a contributory or noncontributory basis, is much less common among public jurisdictions than is health insurance, although the federal government's life insurance plan preceded its health insurance system by six years. Here again, public agencies have followed the lead of private employers, but this benefit, like others, is also becoming more common day by day in government employment.

The federal program permits employees to buy life insurance at extraordinarily low rates, with some accident benefits included, in amounts based on the size of their salaries. The government pays half the premium, the remainder being covered by payroll deduction. Employees may carry the insurance, without premiums, into retirement.

CREDIT UNIONS

Another feature of a broad welfare program is the credit union. To the low-salaried employee the problem of low-cost small loans is a very real one. Financial crises frequently arise in which it is necessary to borrow small sums, and if the employee is to be protected from the loan shark, a credit union of some sort is called for. The provision of this service can be justified not only on broad social grounds but equally from the standpoint of its effect upon morale. Financial worry is an important depressant which, if severe or long continued, may seriously affect efficiency.

The movement in the United States has had a steady growth since various states passed laws providing for establishment of credit unions and the Federal Credit Union Act was adopted in 1934. Now there are many thousands of credit unions in the country, over half of which are organized under the National Credit Union Administration (NCUA).[4] A substantial number of charters are issued to federal, state, and local employee groups.

The credit union is basically a cooperative enterprise, the capital being supplied by the members, who buy shares in small denominations. Loans are made only to subscribers at a very low rate per month, and dividends paid to shareholders cannot exceed a modest percent a year. The rapid spread of the credit union movement bears witness to its economic advantages.

OTHER COOPERATIVE POSSIBILITIES

There is scarcely any limit to the possible development of cooperative activities among employees, and new services can be added constantly under the guidance of alert administrators. The advantages of cooperative buying, housing, and the like, have scarcely been tapped in this country, although such activities are common throughout Europe, and particularly in the civil services. It needs to be recognized as a basic principle that anything which improves the way of life of the staff may also improve its work. The scope for group action by civil servants is broad, requiring in most instances only guidance from the personnel agency.

Personnel administrators in private industry discovered some time ago not only that organized social and recreational activities were valuable from the standpoint of employee health and welfare but also that they contributed greatly to the development of group solidarity. The latter advantage is especially likely to develop out of a social and recreation program in the public service, where there is often a more stable personnel than in industry. Moreover, a rather extensive program can be operated at little or no cost and often within already existing facilities.

*   *   *

IT IS QUITE evident that civil servants, like any other employees, deserve being regarded by their employer not only as workers performing essential services but as human beings worthy of care and cultivation. Of all those entities in our civilization that hire the services of people, the state can least readily justify disregard for the welfare of its employees.

---

[4] Having originally been a component of other agencies, NCUA was made an independent agency in 1970.

CHAPTER 15

Work Hours and Leave

PERSONNEL ADMINISTRATION IS of necessity concerned with the time employees spend at work and their privileges of absence from work. There was a day when such matters were established by individual offices or divisions of public jurisdictions with little central policy control, but this condition is almost nonexistent nowadays. Hours of work and leave privileges are much more often than not governed by law or by central administrative regulation or both.

Certainly this centralization of policy and direction is in the interest of uniformity and equity, administrative control, and opportunity for check-up on abuses and irregularities. Naturally, such policy and direction are subjects for the attention of the central personnel establishment in any jurisdiction.

WORKING HOURS

DURATION

In the public services generally the hours of work are comparable to those in private employment. Although during times of national crisis, such as the World War II period, longer workweeks may prevail, most public jurisdictions now operate in the range of thirty-five to forty-four hours as the standard week, the most common being forty. Of course, many public functions must be performed around the clock and therefore require several shifts of employees over the period of a week. Typical are police and fire departments, municipal water plants and other utilities, public hospitals, certain defense establishments, various postal operations, air traffic control, weather analysis, customs and immigration work, and the like. Most work shifts, whether for office-type operations or for twenty-four-hour-a-day activities, are designed to provide a five-day week for the employee.

Factual studies of the effect of different lengths of workdays and workweeks on performance, especially in nonindustrial types of work, are all too scarce. Research conducted primarily in business firms reveals a wide diversity of findings and conclusions. Indeed, it is most unlikely that there is a thing such as an optimum workday or workweek. The nature of the work, physical demands, mental strain, tension, surroundings, time of day —to say nothing of variable psychological factors—all contribute to different results. Such broad social considerations as the use of leisure time also enter into the picture. By and large, not much more light can be shed on the subject without more investment in research.[1]

Another factor that affects the will to work any given number of hours in a week arises from workers' expectations. As the social product has increased, workers' expectations of sharing its gains have heightened with respect not only to material goods but also to leisure. The employee expects his job to leave him time and energy to enjoy his family, participate in the life of his community, engage in recreation or hobbies, and, as a citizen, keep himself informed on civic and national issues. This sometimes leads to advocacy of still shorter workweeks.

The prospect, however, of anything like the four-day workweek becoming common appears remote for some years to come. The productivity of our economy, industrial automation, the international situation, the population explosion, and the willingness of workers to take an increased share of their income in the form of leisure are all examples of factors that will determine in one way or another the speed with which a shorter workweek may come about. From the viewpoint of productivity per hour in any line of endeavor there must certainly be a point below which there is no advantage to further reduction of working hours. Also, we must not overlook man's natural need to be constructively occupied. To assume that a reasonable goal of the good society is the ultimate elimination or near-elimination of disciplined human effort is not only to misread history, it is to misjudge the wellsprings of human satisfaction.[2]

Whatever the final policies settled upon, it stands to reason that the same quantity of working hours should apply to all employees working under comparable conditions in any given jurisdiction. This does not necessarily mean precisely the same total periods for all employees, but the

---

[1] The U.S. Department of Labor, especially through its Bureau of Labor Statistics, is a source of some useful information in this field.

[2] What little objective research that has been conducted shows is that there is no economic or social gain to be expected from further overall reduction in workhours. See Clyde E. Dankert, Floyd C. Mann, and Herbert R. Northrup, eds., *Hours of Work*, New York, Harper & Row, 1965, especially Chapter 9 by David G. Brown, "Hours and Output."

For a report on workweek developments, see Carmen D. Saso, *The Four-Day Workweek*, Chicago, International Personnel Management Association, 1972.

burden of proof should be on any deviation from a norm. It is unthinkable that such determinations can be left to individual units or administrators. Here we have one of the most obvious examples of the need for common personnel policy across the board.

SPECIAL ASPECTS

OVERTIME   Three additional points deserve mention. One is the matter of overtime. Although careful planning and organization of work can usually keep the necessity for overtime work within reasonable bounds, it can rarely be eliminated entirely. Periodic emergencies in public services are not often susceptible to prediction and are no respecters of the clock. In an earlier chapter we reviewed the importance of overtime compensation. Such premium payments serve the dual purpose of easing the inconvenience imposed on employees who work overtime and of acting as a fiscal restraint on the management which authorizes it.

One of the dangers of too much overtime, even where employees welcome it for the extra pay, is the wearing effect it may have on the health and ultimate productivity of the employees. A problem of no small proportions is the all-too-universal pressure on many public executives that requires them to devote many long, fatiguing hours—almost invariably uncompensated— beyond a normal workweek. Yet few personnel measures are designed to alleviate this situation. The executive is the "forgotten man" in public personnel administration so far as legislators and the general public are concerned. There is little hope for improvement in the inequities involved and in the damage to the health of these persons (and indirectly to the public welfare) until the general education of the public in the importance of public services, the dignity of public employment, and the character of executive leadership required is vastly extended.

REST PERIODS   The second supplementary point with respect to working hours has to do with rest periods. The provision of work breaks, particularly in factory production, was common in industry long before it became common in public agencies. For a long time there were legal objections to periods of cessation from work, the usual one being that there was "no authority for it." But as much by the pressure of group practice as by affirmative authorization, the rest pause has become almost universal. The "coffee break" or "coke break" is as much an institution in the public service as in the business world. Indeed, the problem now is not whether to allow it but how to control it, how to keep it from being abused by the few who are not highly motivated and who stretch ten-minute breaks into half-hour absences. The solution usually comes back to the quality of supervision, the selection and placement of employees, and the firm insistence on reasonable standards of performance and production.

The foregoing comments should not be taken to mean that rest periods are unjustified. The weight of evidence, particularly when work is monotonous or demands intense concentration, supports such breaks because they usually result in improved production and morale, and absenteeism is decreased by reduction of fatigue. Moreover, some breaks will be taken by workers whether authorized or not.

FLEXIBILITY On the third additional point concerning work hours, flexible schedules, public jurisdictions do not reflect anything like the enlightenment they show in handling overtime and rest periods. Many well-qualified people are denied opportunity for employment in their specialties because the only times open to them are the standard daytime, Monday-through-Friday schedules. Most jurisdictions still fail to make adequate use of women, handicapped persons, and other able prospects because they refuse to create irregular or part-time schedules. Married women, especially those with small children, often constitute an unexplored gold mine of talent because they so often must confine their time commitments to partial days or other nonstandard work arrangements. There is seldom good reason for government offices to fail to organize their tasks to take advantage of this resource. Precious few governments have done so in any significant way, but those that have usually report considerable success with such flexibility.

ANNUAL AND SICK LEAVE

The one employment perquisite in which government—particularly the federal service—has for many years had a more liberal policy than have private organizations is the area of leave with full pay. The only explanation for this appears to have a Washington orientation. When travel was slow and many federal functions were performed at headquarters, it seemed reasonable to allow the hundreds and later thousands of persons who had moved to Washington for government jobs an opportunity for a generous amount of time "back home." State and municipal leave practice (except in public school and college teaching) seldom equaled that of the national government, and still does not do so.

In the meantime the policies of private employers have brought general practice much closer to that in the public service.[3] In fact, there is considerable question whether the advantage is still as clearly with government employment as some would have us believe. In private corporations the equivalent of as much as a week or more over a year may be consumed by excused absences, not chargeable to formal vacation or sick leave, for such things as personal shopping, attendance at funerals, visits to the doctor, and tardy arrival, whereas the more formal systems in the public service usually require that every period absent, even those as brief as 15 minutes or a

---

[3] Maximum vacations of four or five weeks or more for long-service employees are now the predominant feature in labor agreements. (See periodic studies of the Bureau of Labor Statistics.)

half-hour, be charged to sick or annual leave. Hence a portion of government leave is almost invariably used up by an accumulation of minor absences.

ANNUAL LEAVE

Annual vacations have been accepted as desirable not only from the standpoint of increasing efficiency by allowing for physical and mental recuperation but for general social reasons as well. The purpose of a vacation is twofold: it provides both rest and a change in pace and type of activity. Such a change, whatever its nature, is usually of itself the most significant element in rejuvenation and in a preventive approach to good health.

Two to four weeks' annual leave is the range in which most state and municipal provisions fall. Apart from such special groups as the Foreign Service, which have still more generous features, the federal service has a graduated systems, with 13 workdays off per year for employees with less than 3 years of service, 20 days for those with 3 to 15 years, and 26 for those with 15 or more years. No paid leave may be taken during the first 90 days of employment, and not more than 30 days of leave may be accumulated for carry-over at the end of any year for use in succeeding years. This latter proviso tends to ensure that a reasonable amount of leave is taken each year and not postponed to a degree that could jeopardize both the employee's welfare and the continuity of his services.

Such a system based on length of service is typical of plans in business concerns. At one time, before 1932, annual leave in the federal government was a flat 30 days, going back to a statute in 1898. This was curtailed by executive action during the depression and superseded in 1936 by a flat 26-day system, which was in effect until the graduated system was adopted. All absences, except those for illness and for certain specified purposes such as jury duty or military training for reservists, are charged to annual leave.

It goes without saying that if vacation leave is to serve its purpose supervisory officials must plan their work to permit employees to take it when needed. Control must be exercised so that too many are not away at the same time, but within the bounds of reason this can be done with a mimimum of inconvenience to individual employees. Although the earning of leave is usually a right, it is up to management to control *when* leave is taken. Some employees need positive encouragement to take leave. The typical agency asks its supervisors to insist that employees take a minimum vacation period each year (usually two weeks or more) for rest and recreation, recognizing that such a policy is to the long-range advantage of both the worker and the employer. One other purpose served by a generous vacation policy is that it affords an opportunity for temporary assignment of subordinates to more responsible positions of their supervisors or colleagues while the latter are on leave, thus providing part of their development and a chance for evaluation of potential for possible advancement.

Any well-conceived leave system requires a carefully worked out method and set of forms for reporting, recording, and accruing leave. The procedures and regulations must ensure equity, uniformity, and accuracy, but must not be burdensome or unduly complicated.

SICK LEAVE

Since ill health is among the normal expectancies of adult life, definite provisions for sick leave are essential to intelligent employment management. Failure to provide for such leave with pay leads employees who are "under the weather" to report for work, thereby endangering their health and possibly, through contagion, that of their fellow workers. Employees coming to work while ill ordinarily constitute a greater problem than does abuse of sick leave.

Almost all states and cities have adopted uniform sick leave plans: 12 to 15 days a year are the usual allowances provided in the states. When not used, sick leave may be accumulated against future exigencies usually up to 90 days, but a few provide 60, some 150, and many have no limitation. The federal service allows 13 days with no limit on accumulation.

That there is danger of abuse unless sick leave provisions are carefully and conscientiously supervised cannot be doubted. Employees who are generally well selected, well motivated, and well disciplined are not likely, however, to claim sick leave for unauthorized absences when they are not ill. As in other matters of personal integrity, a great deal depends upon the moral climate of the agency and the character of the supervision. For one thing, employees can be made to appreciate that sick leave is a form of insurance to be safeguarded when really needed, not a free-time privilege to be exploited to the hilt. As a matter of fact, no formal studies brought to this author's attention have shown that public employees do abuse sick leave to any appreciable extent. There will always be a few who try it, but these can usually be dealt with individually.

To summarize, great progress has been made toward standardizing conditions of work in the public service as far as annual leave and sick leave are concerned. Leave policies in the public service in general compare favorably with those in private industry but require safeguarding through careful supervision.

ATTENDANCE

The problem of employee attendance arises from the highly developed use of machinery and the division of labor. The whole process of production has become a cooperative venture. Economic losses from tardiness and absenteeism do not end with the lost time of individuals who are tardy or absent but are increased many times by the more or less extensive repercussions on the work of others, involving delays in work processes, idle machines, and possibly lowered morale. As an organization is elaborated, such losses become ever more extensive.

Although the extreme regimentation of line production has not affected the public services to such an extent as private industry, these developments have not been without effect in this sphere. With the increase in specialization, teamwork becomes an increasingly important characteristic of efficient management. Teamwork requires good attendance.

CAUSES OF ABSENCE

Although the causes of irregular attendance are as varied as the ills and frailties to which man is heir, some of the more significant ones may be recognized. These can be grouped conveniently into three classes: (1) conditions arising in the personal life of the employee, (2) general conditions external to the service, and (3) conditions within the service itself.

Among the factors in the personal life of the employee which bear most directly upon attendance are sickness and disability, family complications, worry, fatigue, and the pressure of personal business. Some of these may originate in the work life of the employee, while others may be entirely due to personal situations. Some are avoidable through enlightened personnel procedure; some are not.

Among the general conditions external to the service which influence the regularity of attendance may be listed inadequate transportation facilities and unsatisfactory housing conditions. Another factor of no little significance is the prevailing attitude toward the public service. If the public assumes and expects inefficiency, if it regards public employment as a sinecure rather than as an opportunity for service, if, as in some jurisdictions, the prestige of the public service is low, then the problem of securing regular attendance is aggravated. Such attitudes undermine morale in a subtle and pernicious way, but a sound personnel program goes far toward retarding and counteracting them.

Many conditions within the service itself may contribute to attendance irregularities. Only by careful study of particular situations can the personnel administrator determine which factors are of significance. Thus, tardiness and absenteeism may arise out of the relations between the employee and an influential politician. Such backing may make him feel free to let his convenience dictate his working hours and to ignore the department rules and regulations. Then again, the relations between supervisor and employee may be so unsatisfactory that the latter is quite lacking in a sense of loyalty toward his job. Failure to appreciate the cooperative character of the enterprise or the absence of a feeling of personal identification with it, both caused by the neglect of proper induction, training, and the like, may be an important contributing factor. Unsatisfactory working conditions, such as inadequate or inequitable compensation schemes, excessive hours, monotony, and poor ventilation, are almost certain to give rise to poor attendance records. Indeed, the solution to the attendance problem is more likely than not to be found in the conditions of service.

CONTROLLING ATTENDANCE

The problem of controlling attendance has three general aspects: (1) the formulation and publicizing of rules and regulations governing attendance, (2) the installation of records and the measurement and evaluation of attendance irregularities as a basis for further control, and (3) the adoption and administration of a program aiming at reduction of poor attendance. Attention to each of these aspects is essential to control. The third concerns assistance to operating officials in providing a physical and psychological setting in which the employees' zest for the work of the organization is fostered and causes of absence are reduced. The factors that are significant for an employee's morale—his attitudes toward the specific features of his job, toward management, toward his immediate supervisors, toward his fellow employees, and toward outside influences—also militate for or against tardiness and absenteeism. If the conditions that determine these attitudes build a feeling that each employee is an important part of the organization and that his work contributes significantly to the goals of the organization, problems of absenteeism and tardiness tend to disappear.

Where there are excessive absenteeism and tardiness, a frontal attack on these specific evidences of low morale may be less effective than a broad program for improvement in the selection and training of supervisors, increased participation of employees in work design, the development of employee counseling and group activities, the prompt adjustment of grievances, and surveys of employee attitudes. The major safeguards against abuse of leave and attendance standards are the same as for any other facet of improving personnel administration—establishment of those conditions that exert a positive influence on work motivation.[4]

[4] See the discussion in Chapter 11.

PART V

Conduct

It is not the critic who counts; not the man who points out how the strong man stumbled, or where the doer of deeds could have done better. The credit belongs to the man who is actually in the arena; whose face is marred by dust and sweat and blood; who strives valiantly; who errs and comes short again and again; who knows the great enthusiasms, the great devotions and spends himself in a worthy cause, who at the best knows in the end the triumphs of high achievement; and who at the worst, if he fails, at least fails while daring greatly; so that his place shall never be with those cold and timid souls who know neither defeat nor victory.

Theodore Roosevelt

Surely this is the ultimate ethical postulate in a democracy: not that man is good, but that he is capable of good; not that he is wise, but that he is capable of valuing wisdom; not that he is free from corruption, but that he is desperately sick of it; not that he has fashioned the good society, but that he has caught an unforgettable glimpse of it.

Stephen K. Bailey, "The Ethical Problems of an
Elected Political Executive," in Harlan Cleveland and
Harold D. Lasswell, eds., *Ethics and Bigness,*
New York, Harper & Row, 1962, p. 36.

Those holding public office, as servants of the public, are not owners of authority but agents of public purpose.

Code of Ethics for Employees of Arlington
County, Virginia, adopted October 7, 1961.

There is no kind of dishonesty into which otherwise good people more easily and frequently fall than that of defrauding the government.

Benjamin Franklin

Those who expect to reap the blessings of freedom must, like men, undergo the fatigue of supporting it.

Thomas Paine

CHAPTER 16

Public Service Ethics in a Democracy

GOVERNMENT OFFICIALS AND employees are not only committed to loyal and effective performance but are obligated to carry out a *public* objective—which in any nation controlled by the people can mean only such purposes as are arrived at democratically. Ethics are truly a part of competence, and they are a part of democracy.[1] Those persons who look upon public employment as an opportunity for self-aggrandizement and for exercise of authority to favor themselves or their friends obstruct the interest of the commonweal both as to efficiency and as to service to all the people.

In comparing the ethical problems of government employees and those in private enterprise, writers commonly refer to the public service as if it were an occupation—on a par, for example, with law, medicine, business management, engineering, or chemistry. As a matter of fact, of course, it is a composite of *all* occupations, not one for which a separate discipline, a distinctive technical preparation, and a special code of conduct exist. It is a composite of occupations many of which themselves embrace definite ethical standards, in whatever context they may operate. Practically every occupation known to man is represented in the American public service.

Within public employment the group on which the greatest attention centers as to moral behavior is that comprising the professions, the managerial specialties, and the executive classes in general—occupations in which

---

[1] "In any civilized way of looking at public service, ethics are part of competence; if the public is not getting ethical service from its stewards, it is not getting effective service" (Frank J. McGilly, "Private Conscience and Public Service—Reflections on Codes of Ethics," *Horizons for Modern Governments*, Associated Institutes of Government of Pennsylvania Universities, February 1963, p. 18).

some degree of judgment or discretion is exercised in the execution of public policy. For many routine occupations it would be difficult to distinguish between the standards to be expected of those engaged in private employment and of those working in government. The same obligations of care and integrity prevail for clerical, skilled, and technical personnel in the public service as exist for these groups in the business world. The bookkeeper is under the same moral compulsions in one place as in the other. The laboratory technician's processing of blood samples in a hospital must be viewed in the same ethical light regardless of whether the institution is publicly or privately owned. But when we think of the bureau chief, the sanitation engineer, the tax assessor, the park ranger, the police officer, the personnel examiner, the public school teacher, we see categories of workers on whom special ethical obligations rest that have little counterpart in private enterprise. For it is in the hands of such persons that discretion lies in the application of the publicly (democratically) adopted laws and rules—however minor they may be—which constitute governance. Thus, while this is not the place for a disquisition on morality in general, it is worthwhile to give some attention to its special characteristics in the public service.[2]

To be sure, the most influential public servants, when it comes to ethical performance, are the officials at the top. They set the tone for an entire enterprise, and all that is said in this chapter applies most pointedly, though by no means exclusively, to them. In this connection, the agonizing period in American political experience of the early 1970s, commonly referred to as the Watergate-related scandals, posed some special issues. Here we had a concentration of concerns in several areas: abuse of presidential power; invasion of private rights; distortion of the meaning of organizational loyalty; and arrogant behavior of White House staff. Yet, even here, all of the errors can be summed up in a failure to appreciate the democratic base of public service ethics.[3]

---

[2] For a number of thoughtful discussions see the various papers in the following editions of the *Annals of the American Academy of Political and Social Science: Ethical Standards in American Public Life*, March 1952; *Bureaucracy and Democratic Government*, March 1954; *Ethical Standards and Professional Conduct*, January 1955; and *Achieving Excellence in Public Service*, August 1963.

Also, for a penetrating treatise of profound insight and relevance to today's problems, see Wayne A. R. Leys, *Ethics for Policy Decisions*, Englewood Cliffs, N.J., Prentice-Hall, 1952. This superb volume, organized around the teachings of the great philosophers of history, relates ethical principles to issues of the day. Also, see the useful exposition in George A. Graham, "Ethical Guidelines for Public Administrators: Observations on the Rules of the Game," *Public Administration Review*, January–February, 1974, pp. 90–92.

[3] An impressive report on these and other points appears in *Watergate: Its Implications for Responsible Government*, A Report prepared by a Panel of the National Academy of Public Administration at the request of the Senate Select Committee on Presidential Campaign Activities, Washington, D.C., March 1974.

RIGHT AND WRONG IN PUBLIC SERVICE

Over the centuries philosophers have debated the relative merits of ways of looking at and measuring moral behavior. Various sets of virtues and human goals have been advanced as the best ways to understand and to implement achievement of what is "good." Ethical pluralists, in more modern times, have argued that single laws of ethics cannot define the means to good ends or explain man's obligations. A variety of tests, they say, must be employed to ascertain when choices and decisions serve morally justifiable purposes. Elaboration of no one virtue—such as honesty, justice, selflessness, or courage—will provide the satisfactory measure. Good behavior emerges from applying them all. Certainly, the pluralistic approach has the appeal of common sense and would seem most applicable to performance in the public service.

But applying any tests to the goodness of behavior of public officials poses some very complex and anguishing problems that transcend those common to other human interrelationships. Some of the major issues deserve a brief review here.

THE DEMOCRATIC BASE

Problems of ethical conduct arise for the public official by virtue of the power and influence he commands and the commitment he undertakes of loyal and disinterested service to the public. In a democracy, authority is derived from the consent of the governed. Public administration therefore must serve the public in a manner that strengthens the integrity and processes of a democratic society. This fundamental principle has at least three implications for performance in a government position, especially as we move up the hierarchy to those of the greatest responsibility. It means (1) that all the people must be served, equally and impartially; (2) that this must be achieved with full respect for and reliance on representative institutions; and (3) that internal administration in public agencies must be consistent with these modes of behavior.

THE PUBLIC INTEREST   One of the most difficult concepts to define is the "public interest." But without getting lost in the fine points as to whether there is a single or whether there are multiple "publics" to be served, we can safely assert that the civil servant and politician should, above all, think in terms of the total welfare, the overall good, the long-range effect, and eschew the temptation to please just the individual or group pressing its case before him. The late Paul H. Appleby put it well: "In nearly all administrative decisions the sense of virtuous performance is to be pursued by attempting to inject some increased allowance for the more public interest and some increased concern for those citizens not immediately present or heard."[4]

[4] *Morality and Administration in Democratic Government*, Baton Rouge, Louisiana State University, 1952, p. 176.
Of special interest at this point is the statement by Wayne R. Leys in a passage

This simple counsel comes about as close to a universal definition of how to pursue the public interest as can be found. There is sometimes evident the administrative demagogue who, in his anxiety to appear friendly and cooperative with anyone seeking his favors, leaves the impression that the pleader's will is to be earnestly followed while failing to explain the countervailing interests that must also be taken into account.

On the safe side of outright dishonesty lies the wide range of political morality in terms of courage, independence of judgment and decision, and intellectual integrity. There are worse things than mere graft, and one of them is the reduction of politics to an empty process of wheeling and dealing, in which the personal fortunes of the contestants loom larger than the social issues which they evade, straddle and obfuscate in the hope of offending no one.[5]

The problems of overt corruption get all the attention, but the most subtle issue in public service ethics is how to find and attain genuine service to the broadest possible interest.

The objective is neither clear nor easy. It is not too difficult to regulate the behavior of officials on outright or potential conflicts of personal interest with public welfare, especially where a dollars-and-cents measure is involved. "The harder and infinitely more important issue of administrative morality today," says Frederick C. Mosher, "attends the reaching of decisions on questions of public policy which involve competitions in loyalty and perspective between broad goals of the polity (the phantom public interest) and the narrower goals of a group, bureau, clientele, or union."[6] As another writer expresses the point:

In public service much of the ethical uncertainty flows from a tormenting contradiction. The public servant is committed to serve the public, but it is never the abstract that asks for a favor, bids for a contract, or hopes for a job; it is always a concrete person. And action that would appear to be resplendent in the light of the public interest may lose its luster when it reflects upon the interests—perhaps the perfectly legitimate interests—of some person.[7]

---

on "good judgment":

"Ethics, as a discipline of questions, should unparalyze the mind at the moment of action. It suggests the unremembered or unperceived angles that may need investigation. If there is a logic of practical judgment, it is a logic of questions. It does not supply factual information, but it is a reminder of the kind of facts that may need investigating. Like Sam Goldwyn, ethics says: "For your information, let me ask you a question!" [Leys, *op. cit.*, p. 11.]

[5] Telford Taylor, "The Ethics of Public Office," *The Saturday Evening Post*, April 19, 1960, p. 46.

[6] *Democracy and the Public Service*, New York, Oxford University Press, 1968, p. 210.

[7] Frank J. McGilly, *loc. cit.*

Perhaps, as Harlan Cleveland suggests, the government executive cannot best measure the rightness of his prospective action by asking himself: "Will I be criticized?" For the answer to that question is always: "Yes." "He might better start by asking himself some such question as this: 'If I am publicly criticized, will I still feel that this is what I should have done, and the way I should have decided to do it?' "[8]

THE WILL OF THE PEOPLE   The responsibilities of government employees to the public, to the law, and to their current political leadership are tied together by the common bond of democratic consent—which leads us to the second implication that may be perceived in trying to understand the democratic base for public service ideals. One of the most difficult principles for the average civil servant to appreciate and to honor is his complete dependence on the will of the people. Having once achieved his post, he is quite understandably inclined to resent any intrusions upon his time and his authority that appear to sway him from pursuing his mission as he understands it. He has trouble seeing how any legislator or any citizen could possibly have an interest in what he does. He forgets that in exercising those discretions that are left to him he is obligated in his deliberations to listen to, to consider carefully, and to weigh the viewpoints of others as to the meaning, intent, and spirit of the law he administers. Even when he has grounds to believe that a decision being urged upon him is the self-serving traffic of some narrow, petty interest, he cannot ignore it. In effect, we are now looking at the obverse side of the coin from the one where we stressed the need to avoid being "taken in" by every personal or corporate pleading.

One of the tests of the public employee's dedication is his earnestness in recognizing the importance of letting "the people decide for themselves what policies and objectives the public service shall have."[9] He must have an abiding faith in democratic processes, in making certain that it is not just his personal view but that of the people as expressed in law and declared policy to which he gives effect. Where he has the latitude to make choices, he must continually apply the rule: is this action consistent with all the objectives and requirements that impinge on it? Democratic government can succeed only as its agents display a healthy respect for and intelligent understanding of the democratic environment.[10]

[8] Harlan Cleveland and Harold D. Lasswell, eds., *Ethics and Bigness: Scientific Academic, Religious, Political, and Military*, New York, Harper & Row, 1962, p. xlv.

[9] Gordon R. Clapp, "A Credo for the Public Servant," *Public Personnel Review*, January 1951, p. 14.

[10] Attention is called to the related discussion in the section on "Career Continuity and Political Leadership," in Chapter 2.

David M. Levitan expresses the idea this way: "We are forced to the conclusion that in the last analysis much of our success in the quest for a responsible bureaucracy will depend upon our ability to foster among the citizenry as a whole, and therefore among the bureaucracy, a respect and devotion to representative institutions" ("Administrative Responsibility," *Political Science Quarterly* [Academy of Political Science, Columbia University], December 1946, p. 598).

EFFECT OF INTERNAL POLICIES   Finally, in this dissection of democracy's meaning for ethical performance, we must consider the character of a public agency's internal administration. A cardinal tenet of our democratic faith is respect for human personality, for individual dignity and worth. If, as we have emphasized many times, the success—and coincidentally the moral behavior—of an administrative undertaking depends ultimately upon the capacity, the integrity, and the motivation of its workers, then it would be the better part of wisdom to view the manner of running the enterprise as a major contributing factor in achieving a moral climate.

We have seen that an organization is effective in almost direct proportion to the degree to which its employees have pride in its work, identify personally with its goals, and sense a genuine, open opportunity to participate to their fullest capacity in attaining its mission. Ethical necessities in their broadest sense require that administrators commit themselves to "a philosophy of personal and group living which allows everyone to live, work, and contribute to the general good."[11] To put it bluntly, it is unlikely that employees can have a consciousness of and be motivated toward a democratic role in relation to the public if there is little democratic practice and recognition of the dignity of man in internal administration. In other words, ethics begin at home.

THE LIMITS OF SPECIALIZATION

Both the specialization of the individual and of the institution give rise to some risks in the moral level attained by a governmental organization. Since specialization has its advantages and since it is idle to think of dispensing with it in any true sense, it behooves us to understand it and to live with it. But we must beware of its limitations. The public servant must not only assure that his technical judgments are enriched by value principles and his decisions infused with concern for human needs and goals, he must first of all try to see his whole field in perspective. In pursuit of the general welfare, "there must be care not to confuse one's professional viewpoint, functional preoccupation, or personal prejudices with the public interest."[12] Indeed, reconciliation of our necessary dependence on experts in government with the realities of public needs and with the inexorable pressure of change poses a central problem of statesmanship and is therefore at the heart of the civil servant's moral imperatives.

No one has elucidated the limitations of the specialist more brilliantly than Harold J. Laski earlier in this century. A political system which fails to keep the expert under control, he said,

> will lack insight into the movement and temper of the public mind. It will push its private nostrums in disregard of public wants. . . . It will mistake

[11] Hurst R. Anderson "Ethical Values in Administration," *Personnel Administration*, January 1954, p. 8.
[12] Appleby, *loc. cit.*

its technical results for social wisdom, and it will fail to see the limits within which it measures are capable of effective application. For the expert, by definition, lacks contact with the plain man.

At another point, he observed: "The expert, in fact, simply by reason of his immersion in a routine, tends to lack flexibility of mind once he approaches the margins of his special theme. . . ." And again: "*Expertise*, it may be argued, sacrifices the insight of common sense to intensity of experience. It breeds an inability to accept new views from the very depth of its preoccupation with its own conclusions. It too often fails to see round its subject."[13]

The public servant who does not see round his subject may, albeit unwittingly, violate the moral laws of balance, completeness, and sensitivity to the public will. Well-meaning concentration on narrow objectives with single-track techniques, by both bureaucrats and outside pressure groups, is undoubtedly the source of more unethical behavior than is outright corruption. It is a more undetectable and therefore more insidious evil. It can be practiced by otherwise good men with the noblest of intentions. Its remedy can never be reached by arbitrary restraints or punishment; it can only be treated by a wise personnel policy that makes the fullest use of all the methods for broadening the perspectives of specialized staff—continuous training exposures, periodic attendance at professional meetings, and diversification of experience through new assignments, rotation, and teamwork.

LOYALTY TO LEADERSHIP

Decisions in public agencies are rarely the product of a single individual. Arriving at a conclusion on some policy issue or on application of a policy to a case is almost invariably a shared process. Ideas and solutions are researched, debated, checked, and weighed sometimes to the point of exasperation for the interested citizen on the outside.

INSTITUTIONAL DECISION-MAKING   From the standpoint of making sure that an action truly serves the public interest and is consistent with law, a carefully followed procedure is both understandable and praiseworthy in the light of the very principles that have been enunciated here. But multiple reviews and checks also have their drawbacks. For one thing, they take time. For another, they inhibit maximum delegation of authority down the line— a cardinal principle of good management. Finally, they diffuse responsibility so widely that it becomes difficult to determine who did what. In spite of the usual newspaperman's conception of how bureaucratic decisions are made (springing miraculously from the head of the top administrator who thereupon calls in his lackeys to carry it out), the fact is that they are necessarily institutional products. They are the fruit of many minds, the emanation of numerous inquiries and discussions.

---

[13] "The Limitations of the Expert," *Harper's Magazine*, December 1930, pp. 106, 104, and 102.

Although there may be some comfort in all this sharing for the lone expert or executive from whose office the action appears to issue forth, there are some very perplexing problems posed for the conscientious performer and for the style of management the organization tries to maintain. How far can individual initiative be permitted and fostered within the hierarchy and still insure a proper role for institutional (or collective) responsibility? Where does zeal for the right end and insubordination begin? When does loyalty to a profession become disloyalty to the hierarchy?

THE MATTER OF CONSCIENCE   Such questions clearly occur when the individual employee finds himself in disagreement with his supervisor. Where the morality of a prospective action is involved, he must first of all decide for himself whether it is an isolated instance or whether it is part of a total pattern of behavior. He must also think in terms of the larger good. Is the supervisor's different view justifiable in that light, even though he may continue to think of his own view as preferable in a more limited context? Is it possible that others will find as much rationality in the supervisor's judgment as in his own? In short, can he be certain that he is right and his supervisor is wrong?[14]

These are some of the agonizing questions that torment many a conscientious public servant. Generally, however, the issues are of a nature on which reasonable men can properly differ. Only when the employee has serious evidence of willfull violation of the law, blatant corruption, or equally obnoxious misdeeds is he in a position to take his case outside the organization. Differences in point of view or interpretation are part of the normal grist of the bureaucratic mill. But the other issues do arise, and the potentiality of facing up to them should be part of every intelligent civil servant's fund of mental and emotional preparation. The accumulation of case histories illustrating ethical and other administrative issues in the public service, available through a number of university research programs, provides useful material for such preparation.

CONFLICTS OF INTEREST

By now it must be clear that there are many subtleties and ramifications to the matter of ethics in public employment, but the one area that gets the most publicity and is always highlighted by members of the legal profession is that of "conflicts of interest." Although it is rarely the most important or the most intricate of the various fields of potentiality for good or bad behavior, it is important and complicated enough and certainly deserves some substantial attention at this point.

MEANING   By a conflict of interest is meant any situation in which an individual's private best interest (usually economic) might run counter to serv-

---

[14] Reference may be made again to Chapter 2, section on "Career Continuity and Political Leadership." Of special relevance to the Watergate period and its paranoid interpretation of institutional loyalty is O. Glenn Stahl, "Loyalty, Dissent, and Organizational Health," *The Bureaucrat*, July 1974, pp. 162–171.

ing the public interest or appear to do so. The problem permeates all branches of government—the legislator who steers through or at least votes for a bill that benefits an enterprise in which he has some monetary investment, the judge who hears a case involving a person with whom he has business dealings or a corporation in which he holds stock, and the public executive who has decision-making authority affecting the fortunes of persons or businesses with which he has economic connections. The latter confrontation of interests is particularly noted in the consideration and decision-making of regulatory commissions, purchasing and contracting officers, tax assessors, inspectors of various kinds, and the like.

In passing, notice may be taken that judges almost always recuse themselves from trying lawsuits involving parties in which they have an interest, and administrative officials are usually hedged about with numerous checks, constraints, and audits that make it rare for them to get away with overtly self-serving decisions. Not so with legislators. Infinitely the greatest virgin territory for ethical reform in the United States is in the halls of Congress, state legislatures, and city and county councils. However, since the behavior of legislators is not directly within the purview of a book on personnel management in administrative agencies of government and since many other sources deal most adequately with the subject, what is said here about conflicts of interest is essentially in the context of public administration.

NATURE OF RESTRICTIONS   Restrictions on what public officials may or may not do in the economic realm have been on the statute books for many years. Most of the proscribed actions are laced with penalties imposing fines or imprisonment for violations. At the federal level there are detailed provisions of law occupying many pages in the U.S. Code, with numerous annotations and cases,[15] that apply generally to the entire service, and still further prohibitions on the specific conduct of employees of a number of individual agencies, especially the regulatory commissions. Some states and cities are still without any clear-cut legal foundation for this troublesome aspect of public administration, but many do have written codes of conduct and ethics against which performance may be measured.

In the federal service a comprehensive executive order was issued in 1965 prescribing standards of conduct, forbidding most gift-taking, requiring reports of personal financial interests by all presidential appointees and designated career employees, establishing regulatory and directive authority in the Civil Service Commission, and directing agency heads to supplement the standards with controls befitting their special functions.[16] Although embracing certain other areas of conduct, the order's principal orientation was to prevent conflicts of interest. As stated in the order, the intent of the standards prescribed is to avoid any employee action which "might result in, or create the appearance of (1) using public office for private gain; (2)

---

[15] 18 *U.S. Code* 11, "Bribery, Graft, and Conflicts of Interest."
[16] Executive Order 11222, May 8, 1965, "Prescribing Standards of Ethical Conduct for Government Officers and Employees."

giving preferential treatment to any organization or person; (3) impeding government efficiency or economy; (4) losing complete independence or impartiality of action; (5) making a government decision outside official channels; or (6) affecting adversely the confidence of the public in the integrity of the government."[17] The Commission's regulations on the subject constitute the nearest thing to a central body of standards, and these are supplemented by the detailed regulations of each department.

Obviously, all this effort to anticipate every potential avenue of wrongdoing creates a monstrous task of detection and enforcement. A particularly difficult problem is in enforcing the restrictions on subsequent employment, by industries doing business with the government, of military officers and civilians from the Department of Defense, the General Services Administration, and other large government buyers of services and goods.

APPEARANCE VERSUS SUBSTANCE Granting the necessity for spelling out the goals of ethical behavior and some of the principal misdeeds that should be forbidden, one cannot help but note the preoccupation with appearances more than substance. Much space in the federal order and regulations is devoted to proscribing the acceptance of gifts. The purpose of the reporting of financial interests is to ascertain whether any official has economic investments in any field that might be affected by his official responsibilities. Both in pursuance of this order and in the concerns expressed in senatorial committee hearings when nominations for presidential appointment are before them, there is a disposition to insist on disclosure of the individual's holdings and, where there may be a potentiality of conflict, on divestment of such holdings. The assumption appears to be that once a man sells his stock in a corporation, for example, or abstains from accepting any free meals, he no longer has an interest in that corporation or will no longer be tempted to favor it. And there is the further assumption that an executive is utterly unable to rise above the temptation to use his power to augment the fortunes of a corporation in which he is a stockholder or from which he accepts a small gift, including the subassumption that he knows or thinks about the precise impact a decision of his might have on such an enterprise.

While they may be necessary under certain circumstances, it is naive to assume that forbidding gifts or that disclosure and divestiture of stocks solves all problems. They focus attention on the prospect of temptation, instead of on the crime.[18] They create the impression that all is well once these steps are taken. And they ignore the plain fact that men of integrity

[17] Section 201 (c).

[18] In a moment of bemusement over the executive order in 1965, the author came up with this limerick:

A bureaucrat worked like a soldier
To keep his career from foreclosure,
  But a spurious conflict
  Made him a convict,
Because he failed on disclosure.

are quite capable of acting judiciously and fairly without regard to their own economic interests, and equally that men bent upon self-serving will find a way to achieve their ends regardless of such window-dressing as gift proscription or disclosure and divestiture.

As in the case of other aspects of ethical performance, the most satisfactory approach to reducing the evils that might come from conflicts of interest lies in the methods for initial selection of personnel, in character investigation where that is indicated, in sound internal management, in training, and in all the other requisites of good administration.

THE COMMUNITY ENVIRONMENT

THE DOUBLE STANDARD

As often as the facts have been pointed out, there is still a failure on the part of the general public to appreciate that a public service can hardly be expected to rise much above the level of its environment, that it derives most of its temptations for wrongdoing from that environment, and that, on top of all this, a double standard is applied to public officials as contrasted with men in private life. Informed and fair-minded persons will certainly concede that we expect higher standards of conduct from our public servants than we do from businessmen. Unfortunately, there seems to be little opportunity outside of government for practice in the rigorous objectivity and impartiality demanded of public servants. In practically all but a few businesses and professions, the principals can buy and sell where they wish, can play favorites without fear of punishment, can disclose or conceal information on their operations largely as they please, can accept gifts without question of impropriety, and need seldom worry about conflicts of interest. Yet, when similar activities are discovered in any branch of the public service, we are shocked. "Our admiration goes out to the man who makes good in business even though his methods may be ruthless and he may keep within the letter rather than the spirit of the law. The same admiration does not go to the man who makes a full-time job of politics in an effort to win power and wealth."[19]

It was a subcommittee of the U.S. Senate that was among the first to cite the effects of the double standard:

> We . . . believe that the ethical standards of public officials are probably higher than those prevailing in business and other walks of life. On this point . . . there was persuasive testimony from men of experience in both Government and business and from observers of both. Public officials appar-

[19] E. Pendleton Herring, *The Politics of Democracy; American Parties in Action*, New York, Norton, 1965. The double standard was also pointed out by Herbert Emmerich, "A Scandal in Utopia," *Public Administration Review*, Winter 1952; and by Senator Paul H. Douglas, *Ethics in Government*, Cambridge, Mass., Harvard University Press, 1952. Likewise, see the thought-provoking discussion by Walter Lippmann, *The Public Philosophy*, Boston, Little, Brown, 1955.

ently are more conscious of the problem of moral standards. The resentment which public officials sometimes show when subjected to public criticism may be explained in part by their awareness of the fact that some of their critics would be even more vulnerable to criticism if the same standards were applied.[20]

OVERLOOKING THE GREATER EVILS

Not only is the standard between public and private life different, but there is a tendency in times of scandal to focus more on minor bribery than on really extensive fleecing of the public. A Department of Interior official is credited with observing:

> The American people wouldn't bat an eye if a real estate syndicate stole one of the Dakotas, but no matter how high up in government you are, they'll hound you out of office if you take a deep-freeze or a vicuna coat. That's something they can understand. An oil lease, a grazing permit, a mining license, who cares? If you lean toward larceny, swipe a multimillion dollar government patent or a million acres of government land, but don't ever take a washer-dryer combination. That's fatal.[21]

Further perspective on the real depredations against the public weal is supplied by the following:

> The law's reach is necessarily limited, and much of the most dangerous and destructive corruption of our times is entirely legal. The law itself may be used to reap enormous rewards at public expense, as through subsidies or manipulation of the tax structure. Silver was once the favored metal of the wild Western radicals; now oil is the magic mineral of the "nouveau riche" Southwestern magnates. In comparison with special-interest legislation of such dimensions, the little fees and favors of the five per centers are trivial enough. As the old English rhyme has it:
>
> > The law locks up both man and woman
> > Who steals the goose from off the common,
> > Yet turns the greater felon loose
> > Who steals the common from the goose.[22]

SOCIETY'S RESPONSIBILITY

In the last analysis society as a whole must bear the responsibility for ethical conduct in public affairs. Those who complain of corruption but

[20] U.S. Congress, Senate Committee on Labor and Public Welfare, Subcommittee on Ethical Standards, *Ethical Standards in Government*, 82nd Cong., 1st sess., 1951, p. 12.

[21] Reported in John D. Weaver, *The Great Experiment*, Boston, Little, Brown, 1965, p. 167.

[22] Telford Taylor, *op. cit.*, p. 94.

busy themselves with seeking special benefits not available to the general public are the more serious corruptors. Said one great senator, now deceased: "Until the citizen's own moral code prevents him from debasing himself by procuring corruption of public servants, the problem of corruption and morality in public life will remain very real and earnest."[23] And as the man who served as staff director of the Task Force on Personnel of the second Hoover Commission put it:

> The business executive who thinks only in terms of his corporation, the labor leader who thinks only in terms of his union, the leader of organized agriculture who thinks only in terms of his farm organization are all a menace to the basic integrity of the nation. . . . In a free society the responsibilities of the statesman fall on everyone, and upon each person in accordance with his power and ability.[24]

If the facts were known, we would unquestionably find more people dedicated to the public interest as a whole within the public service than outside it. Many persons are attracted to government in the first place by a genuine zeal for identification with a larger good than some narrow economic, social, or sectional interest. Perhaps this explains why corruption is as rare as it is in government employment. The good society will not come from the pressure of special interests. Whenever the medical doctor looks upon his own prosperity as synonymous with the status of the public health, whenever an association of manufacturers opposes legislation for the general welfare, whenever the labor leader mistakes the sanctity of his union structure for the protection of all citizens, whenever a veterans' organization exploits patriotism for class legislation, whenever the voter views his congressman merely as a channel to get favors and special consideration, we fall short of our goal of the highest possible public ethics. The onus is not just on those in public employment, it is on every citizen.

THE REMEDIES

Aside from the larger remedy of a change in public avarice, enforcement of good behavior in government service may be built upon a variety of methods. Some have already been mentioned; others may be derived from statements that follow.

CODES AND PUNISHMENT

Of course, the most common way of dealing with the subject is to punish misbehavior. Most jurisdictions provide that the grosser forms of

---

[23] Senator Estes Kefauver, in *Annals of the American Academy, op. cit.*, March 1952, p. 7.
[24] George A. Graham, *Morality in American Politics*, New York, Random House, 1952, p. 305.

corruption, such as the giving and acceptance of bribes, the use of intoxicants to excess, and clear-cut violations of law, are punishable at the minimum by dismissal from office and sometimes by fines or imprisonment, or both. In addition, it has been the practice in many places to adopt positive codes of ethical conduct, which set forth the ideals that public employees undertake to uphold. Some people are inclined to ridicule codes of ethics as pious hopes, unrelated to reality, but they do have two virtues: (1) they emphasize the positive, not just the negative, and thereby avoid the error of trying to conceive of and block all the wrongdoing that might come to pass; and (2) they provide a criterion, a measure against which unanticipated behavior may be weighed. The trend has been to have a common code for both elected and appointed officials.[25]

INTRINSIC CONTROLS

There are other, more informal controls that induce moral behavior but are commonly overlooked. Some of these are internalized forces from within the individual, such as conscience and reason. Others spring from a number of human associations, ranging from religious affiliations to social or neighborhood inducements. Such associations, in addition to any direct restraint they may supply, also help develop the personal motivations of conscience and reason. Perhaps the most influential controls of the association type are those implicit in membership in a professional or other occupational society. The exposure to avowed ideals of a profession and the pride that flows from identification with a service motive operate as strong forces for individual high standards. Not only should they not be overlooked in the public service, every effort should be made to rein them in—to work out the reconciliations that will make clear the unity between occupational standards of conduct and serving the public interest.

NEGATIVE EFFECTS

Two conditions almost certain to weaken public ethics are ones that are usually intended to have the opposite effect: (1) overemphasis on arbitrary restrictions, such as the conflict-of-interest type of controls already cited; and (2) a ceaseless drumfire of negative and scantily supported criticism of public officials.

Calling attention to the chronic problem of attracting high-quality people to the highest government posts and the hazards to careers that merciless exposure to public scrutiny imposes, a distinguished law school dean admonishes: ". . . any additional hurdle thrown before the government in its effort to attract men of ability to public office is costly and even dangerous.

---

[25] See, for example, the model code developed by the International City Management Association, which contains an explanation for each suggested provision. It is a very well worked out standard that any municipality could be proud of adopting (ICMA, *A Suggested Code of Ethics for Municipal Officials and Employees*, Chicago [now located in Washington, D.C.], 1962).

But we are setting up just such a hurdle with every new restraint on public officials imposed in the name of preventing conflicts of interest."[26] Reliance on unreasonably restrictive controls could ensure a supply of nonentities or unventuresome souls who would never add luster or imagination to public programs and could deny government the dynamic, creative persons who, confident in their distaste for venality, will have no truck with an employer who suspects them of wrongdoing even before they get started.

All of which leads us into our next point, the negative impact of low expectations. The theme might well be taken from the couplet: "Men might be better if we better deemed of them./ The worst way to improve the world is to condemn it."[27] Or, to borrow phraseology more directly on our subject: "The best way to make a man trustworthy is to trust him. And the best way to attract men of dignity to public office is to treat them as men of dignity."[28] The government employee's best impulses can hardly be strengthened by abuse and undiscriminating attacks heaped upon him by demagogues, the press, or members of the general public. Fortunately, this kind of field day at the expense of public servants has considerably abated in recent years, but whenever there does happen to be some wrongdoing uncovered, the temptation to generalize and to tighten up restraints on everyone indiscriminately becomes almost irresistible.

A MATTER OF PERSPECTIVE

It should not be necessary to belabor the point that the proportion of people devoted to the public interest is without doubt higher within the public service than in any other sector of our society. Whatever failings government men have, they are more likely to stem from circumstances such as overspecialization and reluctance to expose their work and their thinking publicly than from any lack of regard for high standards of ethics per se. In this light, they deserve the most tolerant kind of understanding and treatment commensurate with the burdensome demands of their offices. The following thoughts are pertinent:

> If administration officials are to appreciate the high role of the citizen and to accord him the dignity becoming free men, they must themselves experience the blessings of free men. Harassed employees—themselves deprived of the privileges and immunities of citizenship—will be ill prepared to accord to others that which is denied to them. A dual interpretation—one applicable to government employees and another to others—of the due process and

---

[26] Bayless Manning (then Dean of the Stanford Law School), "The Purity Potlatch: An Essay on Conflicts of Interest, American Government, and Moral Escalation," *Federal Bar Journal*, Summer 1964, p. 249.

[27] Attributed to Philip James Bailey, by Herbert Emmerich, "Ethics in Public Administration," *Democracy in Federal Administration*, Jump-McKillop Memorial Lectures; Washington, D.C., U.S. Department of Agriculture Graduate School, 1955, p. 23.

[28] Manning, *op. cit.*, p. 254.

other liberty guaranteeing clauses of the Constitution is repugnant to the philosophy of the Constitution. Nor is there room in America for two classes of citizens—those who work for the government, and those who do not.[29]

*   *   *

THAT WE ARE achieving a relatively high standard of public moral conduct in the United States within a system of tenure and competence—and without the cruder efforts at democratization that characterized the Jacksonian era—is to the credit of most political leadership, of the quality of our civil servants, and of the public consciousness of a great many of our responsible citizens. A continuing strengthening of the moral base for public administration is not likely to be inspired by further tightening of conflict-of-interest laws, an extension of penalties, or resort to sensational legislative investigations. Steady and durable progress can be found most dependably in preentry education and in-service training clarifying the imperatives of the modern state, in enlightened, democratic internal administration, in greater communication of the accomplishments of public service to the general public, in emphasis on positive codes of ethics, and in continuing recognition —by citizen organizations, universities, and foundations—of the distinguished achievements of government agencies and of government servants.[30]

The theory here espoused may be disputed by some, but it is very simple and clear: a proud public servant is a good public servant. Our efforts should be directed toward building and maintaining that pride.

[29] Levitan, *op. cit.*, p. 587.

[30] A helpful general discussion of ethics for modern man appears in the admirable little volume Henry B. Veatch, *Rational Man: A Modern Interpretation of Aristotelian Ethics*, Bloomington, Indiana University Press, 1962.

CHAPTER 17

Employee Conduct in the Community

THE PROFOUND AND special obligations which rest upon public servants as the instruments of government *of* the people and *for* the people have long been close to the heart of political and administrative developments in every democracy. This nation has also been concerned with the healthy participation of public workers in government *by* the people, especially since these workers constitute a significant portion of the population. Whatever one's views of the merits of the expanded role of government, he must face the fact that there is little indication that it will diminish. The significance of the outlook and behavior of public employees, both on duty and off, is substantial because of their strategic position and because of the extent to which they represent the government in the everyday life of their fellow countrymen.

It is beyond the scope of this book to deal with all the social issues in this situation. However, it is necessary to discuss the subject within a broader frame of reference than that provided by attempts to balance the civic rights of persons who are also public servants against the need for official impartiality, to balance the private life of the official against the public interest in the quality of his character, and to balance the authority of political bodies against the bars set up to block the spoilsmen. Here we must balance the broad interests of a free and open society against the necessity for the very survival of that society, to reconcile government protection and order with freedom itself—particularly as it involves the public employee.

LOYALTY AND SECURITY

THE PROBLEM

IMPORTANCE OF MEANS   The basic characteristic of totalitarianism which distinguishes it most strikingly from democracy is its complete subordination of the individual and his rights to the interests of the state. In contrast, the governments of the United States, Canada, and the western European and other democracies are founded on the precept that the dignity and worth of the individual are supreme. Personal liberty, civil rights, and government by the consent of the governed are rooted in this fundamental philosophy. Likewise, the principles of the leading religions in these democracies are based on this same respect for the person, for the individuality of man, and on the belief that each individual has a self-determining will of his own.

To be sure, in all governments, totalitarian or democratic, laws and rules are set which govern the individual's conduct in his relation to others and to society as a whole. But the methods by which these controls are arrived at and the protection which a citizen enjoys against arbitrary action affecting his person and his possessions comprise the major area of distinction between totalitarian and democratic government. In democracies *means* are as important as *ends*; in other governmental systems they are not.

SUBVERSION   In a democracy this business of means—evidenced in the supremacy of the individual and the institutionalization of consent—becomes a special problem when the life of the state itself is threatened from without or by subversion from within. Subversion is a process of infiltration into a society of treasonable intentions and acts under the guise of other aims. One who subverts seeks to overthrow a whole system of government, not just certain leaders or policies, but pretends to work within the framework of the system. Under our Constitution this process constitutes treason when it may be construed as "levying war against" the United States or in "adhering to their enemies, giving them aid and comfort."[1] The transmission of secret information or assistance to an enemy state would thus presumably be treasonable.[2]

Although by no means new to history, subversion has become a particular problem of the twentieth century, because its potentiality is strengthened by modern communication and transportation, by the very complexity of civilization, by the size and impersonality of governments, and by the critical importance of key facilities such as military bases and weapons, industrial concentrations, and natural resources. The periodic upsurges of fascism and the alarming spread of communism have already destroyed several democratic systems and continue to threaten others. At the same time, a democracy by

---

[1] Constitution of the United States, Article III, sec. 3.
[2] "A finding of disloyalty is akin to a finding of treason" (*Bailey* v. *Richardson*, 182 F 2nd 46 [March 1947], p. 66).

its own precepts is under compulsion to deal with subversion in a manner that does not do violence to civil rights and to democratic processes, lest the very treasure it seeks to protect be lost. It is often difficult to distinguish ordinary political dissenters from subversive individuals who mask their treasonable aims with just such harmless cloaks. This is the situation that has periodically plagued the United States.

Unfortunately European history abounds with instances in which an established government punished political dissenters at least as vigorously as felons. Autocracies in the past and totalitarian governments today have survived in part on the outright suppression of all opposition. Democracies, in order to remain democracies, must confine any suppression to actual enemies of the state, to those who seek to destroy the democratic system itself. Safeguards against the extension of such restriction in the United States are found in our traditions and laws guaranteeing freedom of speech and assembly, confrontation of witnesses, habeas corpus and jury trial, the presumption of innocence, and the outlawing of bills of attainder, ex post facto laws, and self-incrimination.

STATUS OF PUBLIC EMPLOYEES   Of particular difficulty in this regard is the matter of controlling those who work for the state—the employees of government. The United States has been alert to this problem especially during and since World War II. Throughout the throes of wrestling with subversion in the federal government or the threat of it, Congress and the executive branch have had to be conscious that under our traditions of liberty we have in the past based punishment for treason on *acts*, not *beliefs*. Our laws have not sought to mold social behavior but to penalize overt antisocial action. When this tradition is brought to bear on government employment, it runs up against another truism, namely, that no citizen has a *right* to hold a government job. Yet dismissal or disbarment from a government job on any grounds short of treasonable acts, while consistent with an employer's privilege to determine who will work for him, can so brand the denied individual that his opportunity for livelihood and normal social behavior is jeopardized. This raises the question of whether he has not suffered the equivalent of criminal punishment without the benefit of constitutional safeguards.[3]

Here lies the heart of the issue: to what extent should the government as an employer apply the Bill of Rights to the acceptance or retention of accused persons in its employ? Must it protect its informants in loyalty investigations or should it allow employees or applicants to learn who their

[3] A detailed discussion appears in David H. Rosenbloom, *Federal Service and the Constitution: The Development of the Public Employment Relationship*, Ithaca, N.Y., Cornell University Press, 1971. For a summation of parts of this book and a discussion of the relationship of civic and political rights to a "representative bureaucracy," see Rosenbloom's article "Forms of Bureaucratic Representation in the Federal Service," *Midwest Review of Public Administration*, July 1974, pp. 159–177.

accusers are and to cross-examine those accusers? Is the employee innocent until proved guilty, or must any doubt be resolved in favor of the government as employer? Who has the burden of proof? Are congressional investigating committees the proper vehicles for uncovering and adjudicating charges against employees? Is the risk of subversion such that an exhaustive inquiry into every aspect of the life of every worker and every applicant selected for work is essential for safe public employment? Is the case of a fired public employee essentially different from indictment and conviction of a private citizen or alien on "security" grounds?[4]

FEDERAL ACTIONS

At this point it may be well to look at the facts of recent history on this issue. The constitutional loyalty of public employees has been of concern primarily in the federal government, although a number of states have passed laws requiring loyalty oaths or other checks on their employees. It should be understood that ever since its establishment the U.S. Civil Service Commission has been checking applicants and new appointees for "suitability," based on searches of police records, character references, and the like. To a certain extent, particularly in times of war, these investigations have taken into account evidence casting doubt on the loyalty of the individual to the American form of government.

Under the 1939 act restricting political activities of federal employees and under various appropriation measures during and following World War II, removal has been required of any person who advocated or belonged to any organization which advocated overthrow of the government of the United States by force or violence.[5] In addition, in the interest of national security department heads have authority to remove any employee without regard to normal civil service removal procedures, but the scope of application is limited (by Supreme Court ruling) to positions directly concerned with the national security.[6]

HISTORICAL HIGHLIGHTS   The first comprehensive federal loyalty program, inaugurated in 1947 by executive order, required investigations (inquiries among anonymous as well as identified informants) by the Federal Bureau of Investigation regarding all existing and prospective federal employees.[7] The results of these inquiries constituted the basis for review and action by de-

---

[4] These and related issues are discussed in most of the works on loyalty-security cited in the bibliography for this chapter at the end of the book. Note particularly the writings of Bontecou, Biddle, Barth, Brown, Ginsburg, and Hyman, all of whom deplore the excesses of the post–World War II "witch hunt" for communists in the government.

[5] 53 Stat. 1148, August 2, 1939. See also footnote 21.

[6] A 1950 law, P.L. 733 (81st Cong., 2nd sess.), was construed by the Supreme Court to permit extraordinary dismissal procedures only in "sensitive" positions, that is, activities directly affecting the national security (Cole v. Young, June 11, 1956).

[7] Executive Order 9835, March 21, 1947. For a history of the loyalty program up to 1953 see Internal Security Manual, Sen. Doc. No. 47, 83rd Cong., 1st sess., 1953.

partment heads concerning any individuals who appeared to be members of suspected subversive organizations. Bolstered by an elaborate appeals set-up, the procedure actually uncovered comparatively few suspects.[8] In the meantime a special authority that had been developing in Defense and other sensitive agencies became known, separately, as a "security program." In effect, it was "designed to eliminate unintentionally as well as intentionally dangerous employees—the indiscreet as well as the disloyal."[9]

In 1953, both loyalty and security factors were combined into one system of standards and adjudication.[10] Under this system, investigations are now conducted principally by the Civil Service Commission; heads of departments and agencies are still responsible for all individual determinations; and a few major agencies conduct their own investigations.[11] The Attorney General makes interpretations and sets standards. The Commission conducts purely factual, unevaluative investigations, referring to the Federal Bureau of Investigation all cases involving allegations of actual disloyalty. Although this 1953 program is still in effect, it is limited, as noted previously, to activities and positions directly concerned with the national security.

SOME RESULTS   The first criticism of the combined program, aimed at its lack of appellate procedures and its use of the term *security risk* to embrace every misdeed from chronic alcoholism to outright disloyalty, was somewhat ameliorated by this limited application. It is significant, nevertheless, that the American Assembly in its report of October, 1954, a Senate Civil Service Subcommittee in 1955, and the joint legislative-executive Commission on Government Security in its 1957 report all urged greater safeguards for accused employees, including less decentralization to individual departments and some system of central appeal rights.[12] So far, only hearings by security hearing boards in individual agencies are available to the accused.

---

[8] After millions of forms were processed and thousands of full field investigations were conducted, the overwhelming proportion of suspects had been cleared and only 557 persons had been dismissed by April 1953, when new procedures went into effect (U.S. Civil Service Commission, *1953 Annual Report*, Washington, D.C., p. 27; and U.S. Civil Service Commission Loyalty Review Board, "Report on the Loyalty Program," June 30, 1953 [mimeo]).

[9] Alan Barth, *The Loyalty of Free Men*, New York, Viking, 1951.

[10] Executive Order 10450, "Security Requirements for Government Employment," April 27, 1953.

[11] Among the federal agencies having their own investigative and security systems are the Department of State, the Central Intelligence Agency, certain Defense activities, and the Nuclear Regulatory Commission. One interesting point is that the last-named agency, whose work is surely as vital to the national security as any agency's, is the only one that permits a rejected *applicant* as well as employees to have a hearing before an administratively established committee.

[12] American Assembly, Sixth, *The Federal Government Service: Its Character, Prestige, and Problems*, final ed., New York, Columbia University, Graduate School of Business, 1954, p. 184; U.S. Congress, Subcommittee of the Senate Committee on Post Office and Civil Service, *Administration of the Federal Employees' Security Program*, Report No. 2750, 84th Cong., 2nd sess., Washington, 1956; and Commission on Government Security, "Federal Civilian Loyalty Program," in *Report of the Commission on Government Security*, Washington, D.C., 1957, pp. 3–107.

The security system actually embraces many standards for dismissal or disbarment which are indistinguishable from those that have guided such action in the U.S. civil service for many years, as well as in all other progressive jurisdictions. Thus, drunkenness, criminal records, or other immoral behavior have long been factors in keeping or taking a person out of the civil service on grounds of not meeting suitability requirements. Although several thousand employees were removed under the 1953 order, the great majority of these actions would have occurred under normal civil service suitability procedures if no security order had been on the books. Even more recent developments have further reduced the impact by restricting the situations under which police records or sexual deviation can have an adverse effect on employment. In fact, current social policy encourages giving rehabilitated ex-offenders a chance at jobs that are not sensitive to the nature of their past offense and for which they are fully qualified.

It is also important to note that the intent of the 1953 order was to simplify and consolidate the previous systems, to place everything under the concept of security, and to remove the stigma of disloyalty on employees who were removed for simple defects in character. After the program had been in operation, it became clear that the stigma of security risk was associated with disloyalty as much as if the latter term were used, when as a matter of fact suspicions of disloyalty occurred in only a small minority of security cases. Some critics allege that, so far as specific discovery of communists is concerned, there have been extremely few or none found in the government since 1949.

In 1968 the Civil Service Commission, following extended study by an interagency committee, issued uniform minimum criteria to be used by all agencies that conducted field investigations of applicants and employees for appointment to critical-sensitive positions in the competitive civil service. These standards, the first issued on a governmentwide basis, included criteria for the selection, training, and supervision of investigators and strong safeguards against unwarranted invasions of privacy, including restrictions on the use of the polygraph or lie-detector. This action was in part a response to increasing concern expressed in the Congress and elsewhere that many persons were being subjected to unjustified questioning as to their sex life and other highly personal matters that appeared remote from any relevance to the job being filled, were being subjected to questionable dependence on the unverified determinations of machines, and were handicapped by the special procedures of some agencies that varied from other practice. Among other things, the standards limit use of the polygraph to intelligence activities and prohibit questioning about sex unless the case contains allegations indicating sexual misbehavior with job-related effects.

STATE AND LOCAL MEASURES

So far as the loyalty-security issue is concerned, the actions of most state and local governments have not been in the forefront like those of the federal government. Checks on applicants have tended to rely on investigation of police records and prescription of loyalty oaths as bases for questioning their employability. Since at these governmental levels there has not been as much in the way of functions relating to the national security as there has been at the federal level, public anxiety over the problem has not been as marked.

Nevertheless, there have been some very real concerns from a civil-liberties viewpoint, particularly about loyalty-oath requirements. This has been noted especially in the imposition of oaths requiring prospective public school teachers to declare their beliefs regarding the nation, the constitution, political party affiliation, and the like. In some states, following protest by independent-minded applicants, courts have declared such oaths unconstitutional, usually on the grounds of violation of the citizen's right to equal protection of the laws—that is, the unfairness of singling out teachers or any other candidates for public positions by use of special oaths that were not required of all citizens or, in some cases, not even of elected or legislative officials. In other instances, laws requiring dismissal of teachers who allegedly uttered treasonable statements were outlawed by courts on the grounds of their vagueness and susceptibility to varied interpretations by unscrupulous or overavid accusers. Preoccupation with the general problem has not been as heated, however, as it has been with the national government, and there appears to be an acceptance for the most part of judicial decrees on the issue.

THE BRITISH AND CANADIAN APPROACHES

Although based on the same premises of the necessity for protection of the state and proscription of the activities of its suspected enemies, the British and Canadian approach has been substantially different from that in the U.S. federal government. These nations are not as concerned about trying to keep communists out of every unit of government but rather out of positions that might have access to state secrets. Further, they reason that the most dangerous enemy agents would not be so foolish as to associate themselves with any organization that would inspire suspicion, such as the Communist party. Therefore, these governments rely more heavily on counterespionage and less on exploring with whom or what groups an individual appears to associate. Where communists or others are denied employment or dismissed, the action is usually a very quiet affair without publicity. So far, there seems to be little evidence that the United Kingdom or Canada have had any less success in countering subversion in their countries that we have in the United States.

EVALUATION

The federal government's efforts to ensure the loyalty and security of its work force may have overlooked the effectiveness of counterespionage and the utility of psychiatric-psychological examination in critical spots as ways of discovering or preventing disloyal acts. None of the handful of convictions widely publicized in the late 1940s and early 1950s were the result of findings under the loyalty-security programs; nor would the names of those few individuals found guilty of giving secret documents to foreign agents likely have shown up on any subversive membership lists. The fact is that they were uncovered by good detective work, following up leads on serious cases.

ALTERNATE METHODS   Perhaps some of these unfortunate betrayals could have been forestalled by careful testing and psychiatric examination of all assignees to jobs involving access to state secrets. Some highly successful experience in gauging the emotional maturity of individuals and predicting their character, fitness, and integrity under stress was gained by the Office of Strategic Services in selecting candidates for overseas intelligence positions during World War II.[13] An exhaustive program of testing and creation of stress situations, covering periods of days and weeks, typified this plan. Although the information is not available, it can be hoped that the current Central Intelligence Agency and the National Security Agency today are benefiting from and making use of this experience in selecting personnel for their supersensitive activities. One cannot help wondering whether scientific testing would not be a more rational approach to ferreting out subversive persons or security risks than overreliance on decisions by laymen based on interviews of neighbors, colleagues, and anonymous informants.

In fairness, it must be acknowledged that the program of checking on all employees at least to some degree, with the rule of thumb of suspicious membership determining the degree of further inquiry, probably has had a deterrent effect on subversive entrants into the service. Some voluntary resignations also may have reflected fear of discovery.

The high cost of psychological methods, however, is not a critical factor, because they could not be more expensive than the process of full field investigations on all names showing up on certain lists. Memberships or lists of names often represent innocent contributors to seemingly worthy causes; others have been compiled by ignorant and irresponsible demagogues or their hirelings, who do not understand the difference between liberals and totalitarians or who seek only to discredit as many "bureaucrats" as they possibly can. Even more important is that many thousands of innocent employees and applicants have been subjected to full field investigations[14] and, in hundreds of cases, to suspension and formal hearings, events which could not be kept completely confidential. The results of these steps, which more often than not reveal no cause for alarm, are not as widely known as their frequency. Clearance in such cases has a hard time sticking. Cases are re-

---

[13] See U.S. Office of Strategic Services, Assessment Staff, *Assessment of Men: Selection of Personnel for OSS*, New York, Holt, Rinehart and Winston, 1948, a detailed report by a group of eminent scientists and scholars under Dr. Harry Murray, Harvard Medical School.

[14] The general public, now more familiar with the fact that many government workers are investigated routinely, is probably getting away from the earlier impression that there "must be something wrong" with a person about whom investigators make inquiries.

opened every time the branded individual moves to another agency. For many innocent and cleared persons the aura of suspicion lingers on or crops up periodically in the minds of overcautious appointing officers.

It should also be acknowledged that many highly placed individuals in the federal service have bent every effort to assure fairness in adjudication of cases that raise doubts about a person's past or current associations. Present practice requires department heads to review adverse action cases personally and to weigh carefully the probable dependability of the sources of derogatory information. A loyalty-security program dependent on final responsibility reposed in department heads nevertheless runs the risk that there will be some unevenness in justice.

The completely disciplined, systematically organized, and well-trained instruments of totalitarian imperialism and those who have deliberately chosen to follow parallel courses have nothing in common with the warm-hearted, individualistic, and independent rebels who have often enriched American development at the price of their own careers and popularity. Nor can the adherents of groups dedicated to the destruction of the government or of the constitutional rights of others by violent means be dealt with by the same means which have been used to prevent the abuse of power by supporters of either of the two great political parties, both of which, regardless of their differences or faults, are agreed on the broad outlines of our political and economic structure. How, then, shall we proceed to combat extraordinary threats within the framework of our traditional freedoms and limited government?

ACTS VERSUS APPEARANCE   The object of a loyalty program should be *loyalty*, not *orthodoxy*. "If there is any fixed star in our constitutional constellation, it is that no official, high or petty, can prescribe what shall be orthodox in politics, nationalism, religion, or other matters of opinion, or force citizens to confess by word or act their faith therein."[15]

A loyalty program should be concerned with the substance of disloyalty, not the shadow; with the fact, not with appearance. It should therefore always take into consideration the fact that subversive movements are often able to enlist through various subterfuges the support of completely patriotic Americans. Moreover, there must be an awareness that the technique of "boring from within" has been used successfully to take over from the inside organizations which originally had no subversive characteristics. Under such circumstances, guilt by association is not only an un-American criterion to apply; it is misleading. Membership in an organization should be no more than one piece of evidence which may or may not be helpful in arriving at a conclusion in a particular case.

On the other hand, certain organizations have so clearly identified them-

---

[15] Opinion of the Supreme Court in the Barnette case, *West Virginia State Board of Education* v. *Barnette*, 319 U.S. 624, 1943.

selves with the advocacy of violence, with the destruction of constitutional government, and with subservience to foreign powers that it would seem that any civil servant who now joins them manifests a degree of irresponsibility, to say the least, which would justify the most searching inquiry. A policy which does not discourage employees or applicants from joining or supporting loyal organizations, liberal or conservative, should rule out the sort of witch-hunting which would reduce American men and women to the soulless, unthinking cogs who are the very type of bureaucrats desired by dictatorial governments and who are the worst possible citizen of a free country.

The question is frequently raised as to why this difficult and involved attempt must be made at all to reach a balance between guilt by association and recognition of organized disloyalty. Why not follow the centuries-old traditions of the common law and the American constitutional provisions governing treason and exclude from the service only those who have been proved guilty of an overt act criminal in character? The answer lies in the nature of twentieth-century totalitarian and other extremist movements. Their plans contemplate a variety of tactics over a period of years, and the leaderships assign to selected disciples and followers roles which require abstinence from overt acts until the crucial moment comes. At that time such men must throw aside the camouflage of being servants of the duly constituted government and must attack whatever sector of democracy has been assigned to them. A government which kept such sworn enemies on its payroll until the hour of danger would be inviting the fate which befell several democracies in the past.

The definition and designation of organizations as subversive have implications which transcend the field of personnel administration and are not discussed here. Much of the criticism leveled at the actions of the federal government has been aimed at the use of such labels by the executive branch, based upon the very general wording of the political activities acts, various appropriation and defense measures, and the constitutional clauses relating to the executive powers of the President. Even those critics who believe in the need for categorical indictments include a number who urge that such determinations should be made through a judicial rather than a legislative or an administrative process.

THE STIGMA   Both the standards set forth and certain decisions made by federal authorities have been further criticized because people are discharged under the stigma of disloyalty without their status having been proved beyond question. The legality of a policy of dismissal based on reasonable doubt of loyalty, as distinguished from clear conviction, is founded on the right of government to set the requirements for hiring its aides, and it has apparently been upheld by the courts.[16] Nevertheless, the dangers to morale and to

---

[16] See *Friedman* v. *Schwellenbach*, 159 F 2d 22, cert. denied 330 U.S. 838.

individual freedom which misuse of such a policy, however legal, can produce are too obvious to require comment.

Additional fire has been directed at the fact that such findings of doubt can be arrived at by an administrative process which, although it provides for appeals and hearings, does not establish standards of evidence equal to those observed by other administrative tribunals, not to mention courts, and denies to the accused sufficient opportunity to challenge such evidence or any opportunity to confront his accusers and to cross-examine witnesses against him. If it is incumbent upon employees to avoid even the appearance of disloyalty, it is likewise incumbent upon the government to avoid even the appearance of star-chamber proceedings. Determinations of disloyalty should be based on the statements of unidentified informants and undisclosed evidence *only* when the national security would be directly and vitally compromised by open proceedings or by the retention of the accused in the service.

We have centered our attention on the issues arising out of a presumption of disloyalty based on association with subversive organizations, because it is organized disloyalty which is the most effective in modern society. Obviously, individuals may be disloyal who belong to no group or who are members of the most respected and trustworthy organizations. Acting as individuals, however, without central direction, they can accomplish little without resort to the type of overt act which can be dealt with under normal disciplinary rules and procedures.

SOME ADMONITIONS   By way of conclusion, two further points, though seemingly at opposite ends of the spectrum, deserve special mention: (1) the danger of character assassination by irresponsible and sometimes anonymous accusers; and (2) the danger of making heroes out of persons who are caught disclosing government secrets.

As for point one, we must say this: when measures to protect the national security are so operated that informants or other employees "bearing false witness" against employees are as sharply dealt with as a security suspect himself, then some of the major objections to a security system will be removed and we will have restored some measure of the traditional American ideal of assuming innocence until guilt is proved. As the American Assembly concluded, "Basic human values are at stake when an employee is charged with disloyalty. Security charges in today's climate of public opinion cast a stigma on the employee which may quite literally ruin him and his family."[17] This is a grave responsibility. Our system must make certain that a removal is clearly identified when it is for subversive action or threats as distinguished from when it is for reasons not vital to security in other employment. Even more important, the decision must be right and just.

[17] Sixth American Assembly, *op. cit.*, p. 184.

On point two, we must also make certain that excesses in ferreting out unwarranted disclosures or other misdeeds by government workers do not result in relaxation of standards of behavior toward which such excesses were directed. During the period of preoccupation with the paranoias and abuses of the Watergate-related affairs and the need for better public oversight, newsmen and others were prone to applaud anyone who furtively released government documents regardless of their sworn obligation to protect them. Nor should government employees who violate their oaths escape punishment just because higher officials, in an excess of suspicion, use illegal methods to gather further evidence against them.[18]

CIVIC AND POLITICAL STATUS

Even in periods of stability, when the fate of the nation is not thought to be in the balance, civil servants in every country have been subject to restrictions and obligations with regard to their behavior in the community, as well as on the job, beyond the general responsibilities of citizenship. Governments of every political complexion have realized that private as well as public misconduct of officials, and to a lesser extent of subordinate workers, could reflect on the prestige of the regime. Dictatorial and aristocratic governments have proceeded to a maximum of regulation of their minions around the clock, while in democracies emphasis has been on finding the balance between infringement of personal liberties and maintenance of public confidence in the integrity and impartiality of the service.

PERSONAL STANDING

The standards of personal behavior for civil servants as members of the community are usually expressed in very general prohibitions, such as those of "conduct unbecoming an officer," "disgraceful or notoriously immoral conduct," and "vicious habits." Almost universally, a civil servant is liable to discharge upon being convicted of a crime or serious misdemeanor even when there is no violation of official duties. Specific prohibitions or restraints in the way of private conduct in the community cover a great variety of subjects from one jurisdiction to another. The general attitude toward activities outside the scope of formal administrative control is illustrated by this federal statement of policy, referring to the 1965 executive order on ethics: "This policy is based on recognition that the maintenance of unusually high standards of honesty, integrity, impartiality, and conduct by Government em-

---

[18] It was a travesty of justice that Daniel Ellsberg, a key employee in the Department of Defense, should have been acquitted in 1973 of illegally releasing government documents (the "Pentagon Papers") just because certain White House officials themselves engaged in an illegal act by ordering a break-in to the offices of Ellsberg's psychiatrist. True justice would have punished perpetrators of both offenses as entirely separate matters. Any questions as to the appropriateness of the security classification of Ellsberg's revelations or of their seriousness are beside the point. The simple fact was that he breeched his trust just as much as did the men in the White House.

ployees . . . through informed judgment is essential to assure proper performance of the Government's business and the maintenance of confidence and respect of the citizens in their Government."[19]

CIVIL SERVANTS AND POLITICS

When it comes to latitude or restraints on public employees in the way of self-expression off the job or political activity, the roots of practice in the United States may be traced to the spoils system and the efforts to eradicate it. The most vigorous defenders of spoils in the form of job patronage were political party henchmen both on and off the public payroll. Much of the inefficiency of bureaucracy was ascribed to the time and energy devoted by employees to partisan activities and to the selection, promotion, and retention of the incompetent at the behest of party wardheelers and bosses. Hence, improving the civil service became identified with removing individual civil servants from politics.

Little wonder, then, that federal, state, and local merit system laws were replete with restrictions on what civil servants could *not* do in the political arena. Somewhat less attention was given to what could not be done *to* civil servants and to what their status as citizens should be. This is still the dominant theme in many jurisdictions that have not matured too far beyond the first two or three decades of this century. Generally, however, the history since that time of anxiety over purity as distinct from performance has been one of gradual liberalization of restrictions that at first characterized the civil service reform movement.

To be sure, public employees have hardly ever been disenfranchised. Almost invariably they have had the opportunity to express their sentiments at the voting booth quite like other citizens. Generally, too, they have been able to express their convictions on public issues in private (especially when off duty), even though their freedom to propagandize or argue their case through public media has usually been circumscribed. It may be noted, as will be found in connection with unionism, that federal employees were protected in their right to petition Congress, individually or collectively, as early as 1912 by the Lloyd-La Follette Act. At least they have been able to communicate with their elected representatives as freely as other members of the community. Nevertheless, taking to the hustings to publicize their stand on political issues of the times or otherwise to use their offices to influence public opinion has been restricted, sometimes drastically.

Gradually, new dimensions have been added to the picture by way of restraints on what politicians or others can do *to* civil servants—rules against

---

[19] *Federal Personnel Manual*, 735-3 (U.S. Civil Service Commission). The basic policy is in Executive Order 11222 of 1965.

Expectation of higher standards in public employment and problems of uniqueness in every instance were the main reactions found in a survey among 41 municipal executives as to off-the-job behavior issues (W. D. Heisel and Richard M. Gladstone, "Off-the-Job Conduct as a Disciplinary Problem," *Public Personnel Review*, January 1968, pp. 23–28).

intimidation, against party treasury assessment, against enforced political service at elections or otherwise, and against pressure from party leaders to exert pressure on other citizens.

Concurrent with these developments, the widespread cynicism or disdain as to political party activity in general complicated matters. As long as "politics" was a dirty word in American public life, as long as the intelligentsia or the business classes did not stoop to participate in party affairs, it was not thought that restriction on civil servants' participation was a serious deprivation. But this is precisely the area wherein a dramatic change has been taking place across the country. The great issues of our times have stimulated citizens from many walks of life to "get involved," to look to standard political processes as the means through which to deal more effectively with problems of housing, transportation, education, racial discrimination, poverty, disarmament, environmental pollution, and all the other crises that plague our urban society. As a major and relentlessly growing sector of that society, public servants cannot be ignored in this process, in this awakening to the critical needs of our civilization and to the possibility that determined collective effort might conceivably alleviate them.

Coincidentally, we shall explore later the development of public employee unionism and the tendency for these groups to take upon themselves lines of political activity that are denied to employees as individuals, such as actively supporting or opposing candidates for elective office, supplying huge sums for campaign expenditures of favorite candidates, lobbying for or against legislation, and conducting political advertising campaigns on various issues. Here arises the question whether public workers can achieve by indirection what they are prohibited from doing directly.

Before examining some of these seemingly insoluble problems in greater depth, it is well that we review just what the typical limitations on government employee political behavior have been.[20]

SPECIFIC RESTRICTIONS

The principal limitations on political activity of American career public servants fall into three groups: (1) those dealing with political candidature; (2) those prohibiting campaign activity; and (3) those prohibiting the solicitation of party contributions and the holding of office in party organizations. Provisions on these points have been covered in federal law since 1939, under what is still popularly known as the Hatch Act, although prior to that the Civil Service Commission had covered the same ground in its rules which are promulgated by the President.[21] In 1940, limitations on political activity

---

[20] For a definitive history of the legal status of government workers as to their political rights, see Rosenbloom, *op. cit.*

[21] All of the Hatch Act provisions (named after Senator Carl Hatch, who had sponsored the idea of putting them into statutory form) have been codified since 1966 in 5 *U.S. Code* 1501–1508 and 7324–7327. The original Hatch Act of 1939 was largely a statutory extension of the then existing Civil Service Rule on the subject.

were extended by law to state and local government employees whose principal employment was in connection with federally financed functions. Although there was some intent by this measure to improve the character of state and local merit systems, some of which were of a fledgling status at the time, the primary purpose of the 1940 amendments was to secure more efficient and impartial administration of federal funds.[22] In addition, of course, most of the state and local jurisdictions have political activity restrictions of their own, usually as part of their legislation on merit systems.

CANDIDATURE   Practically all jurisdictions forbid civil servants from running for partisan political office unless they resign their career jobs. The laws in this respect tend to be considerably more stringent than those in other countries, reflecting no doubt the bitter experience in the United States with the excesses of the spoils system. The usual reasons given for this denial are persuasive. It is felt that the civil servant who strives for elective office divests himself of the cloak of impartiality in the eyes of the public, that he would find it difficult to behave impartially if or when he should return to the service, and that there are extraordinarily delicate and awkward issues to face in determining a person's exact status upon any such reinstatement either after defeat for the elective post or at the expiration of his term of office. Such problems seem to have been surmounted in many other nations, however, where it is common practice to permit career men and women to go on leave without pay during any period of campaigning for public election.

Exception to the policy does occur in this country when it comes to serving in part-time nonpartisan posts, such as on local school boards. The chief example of this latitude lies in the federal provision permitting candidacy in local elections where *all* the candidates are nonpartisan, that is, not representing a major political party, and in localities where federal workers constitute a majority of the electorate, permitting nonpartisan candidacy even though party candidates are also running for the office in question. This policy obviously makes a difference among federal employees in their freedom to run for election depending on the accident of the degree of concentration of their fellow workers in a particular local jurisdiction. Of course, in all cases the office sought can be held only if its duties can be performed without interference with the civil servant's full-time responsibilities with the federal government.

CAMPAIGNING   Only a step removed from candidature, although not as visible to the general public, is the act of campaigning or helping in the campaign of candidates for office. Generally, career people are prevented from

---

[22] *U.S. Code, ibid.* This was known as the second Hatch Act. As pointed out later in this chapter, these restraints on state and local employees working in federally aided programs were substantially relaxed in 1974.

taking any active part in political party management or campaigning, including making speeches, organizing or conducting political rallies, and publishing or distributing campaign literature. In the federal service these restraints do not go as far as preventing employees from *attending* political meetings, without any leadership role, or actively supporting referenda on bond issues and the like. Also, the exceptions mentioned for candidacy in certain local elections apply to campaigning as well. On the other hand, some state and local jurisdictions still have some extreme restrictions that even prevent, for example, employee attendance at political meetings simply as an observer. For the most part, however, the prevailing policy parallels that in the federal service—partly, no doubt, because the federal law itself applies to large portions of the state and local governments.

SOLICITING   Finally, we come to the area of monetary contributions to political parties or campaigns, representing the least open and visible level of political involvement. In many jurisdictions civil servants are not only protected from the necessity of contributing to such political purposes but are themselves enjoined from soliciting contributions for these purposes. Some go as far as prohibiting voluntary contributions on the part of public employees. Federal practice and that of many other jurisdictions, however, permits voluntary contributions but protects government workers from exploitation on this score. The desirability of protecting employees from coercion to make political contributions is unassailable, but they should not be denied a privilege close to that of voting itself merely because they might be coerced. Punishment should be directed instead at those who impose the coercion, whether they are within or outside the government.

It should be noted that, in some states and localities, unions or other employee organizations are barred from political activities, on the theory that individuals should not do by association what they are prohibited from doing individually. In practice, however, this has proved to be a most difficult area to control. Unions have in fact seldom felt seriously inhibited in exerting political pressure in favor of or against candidates for office, especially behind the scenes. Nationwide unions are certainly not handicapped when restrictions on their "politicking" are confined to limited localities.

CIVIL SERVANTS AS CITIZENS

As public employees have increased markedly in relative proportion of the working population, concern has increased over the number and degree of constraints imposed on them in their capacity as citizens. A new ferment has been generated in one place after another demanding that shackles on civil servants as voters, as public speakers, as political activists be removed. Traditionally, it is possible that they have been too timid in their own self-assertion, fearing that even private expression of viewpoints on issues of the day might run them afoul of the law. However, a new sense of strength and independence has awakened many employees to an awareness of their responsibilities as well-educated, well-informed citizens and to resentment at confinement of their self-expression. Curiously, the resentment is sometimes directed against imaginary restraints that have not in fact existed as legal prohibitions.

EXPRESSION OF VIEWS   Although the *private* expression of views on public issues is not barred, the problem is defining when *public* expression is not compatible with official responsibilities and when it may jeopardize the pursuance of a legitimately arrived-at policy. In other words, where does protection of the employee's freedom of speech reach the point where the supposed agents of government are undercutting the responsibilities they swore to uphold? To add a further complication, can postal employees be allowed to protest a matter of foreign policy while those engaged in foreign affairs are forbidden to do so? Conversely, might foreign affairs employees argue publicly for or against a Postal Service policy that postal employees are obligated to enforce? Such questions are hypothetical, but they are quite illustrative of numerous real-life issues that have arisen.[23]

A good rule of thumb would appear to be this: *a public employee ought to have the right to state his views in public, especially when the issue under debate does not relate to his own duties; but when such expression might compromise the integrity or impartiality of action on his job, then he should face up to the alternatives that any honest and courageous person would expect to follow, namely, to restrain his expression or to resign.* As one noted chairman of the U.S. Civil Service Commission once stated:

> Again we come to the need for balance. The Federal employee is a full citizen and entitled to express his views—publicly if this is his choice; however,

[23] The controversy over the Vietnam War and over poverty-alleviation measures created many such occasions where the obligations of employees had to be neatly balanced with their rights as citizens. Drawing the line becomes especially difficult in the field of foreign affairs, as in the case of two police officers at the Panama Canal who sued the government for curtailment of free speech when they were dismissed for repudiating publicly the Canal Zone administrator's policy of hiring qualified Panamanians for police and guard jobs, thus contributing to strained relations between the United States and Panama and jeopardizing Latin American relations in general. They received scant consolation in a U.S. Circuit Court of Appeals decision (*Meehan* v. *Macy*, D.C. Cir., 392 F 2d 822 (1968), modified on reconsideration, August 23, 1968 [C.A.D.C. No. 29, 812]).

The Canal Zone situation provides a good illustration of how the selfish interests of a small group of government workers cannot be allowed to subvert American foreign policy and jeopardize our international position. Many employees in the Zone are of a second or third generation of ex-patriates who enjoy extraordinarily generous allowances, who have done little to relate to the citizens of the host country, who disdain learning Spanish, and who want to keep Canal jobs in the family of nineteenth-century-type colonialists still evident among the employees in the Zone.

Nevertheless, some disputes are not so simply disposed of on the grounds that the public interest must always override private benefit. On some issues, where there is a generally divided opinion among the populace as a whole, it becomes a question of how far civil servants may stand up and be counted when their stand runs counter to their employer's decided policy.

he cannot proceed blindly down this path in perfect immunity. He is responsible for his actions, like any citizen. He does indeed have special obligations connected with his own role in his agency's programs, when these come into question. And he must keep his private activities strictly apart from his use of official time or Government property. Last, but not least, he needs to be aware of any special regulations which may bear on his participation.[24]

GROUP ACTION   Aside from what employees may do as individuals, there is the question of what they may do in concert with others. When it comes to public parades or demonstrations of protest, the above rule of thumb would still seem to be applicable, but active association in leadership roles of standing political parties poses some special problems of its own. The traditional purist position ducks the issue by the blanket prohibitions of the type cited earlier. But it is hardly enough to console the civil servant with the advice that there are citizens' associations, parent-teacher groups, bond drives, and other nonpartisan local activities in which he may participate freely. The great issues of the day are ones on which the major parties take a stand and on which leaders chosen by these parties are judged. To deprive public employees entirely of any part in such processes is not only to deny full democatic citizenship to a very large sector of our society but to appear to put the stamp of community approval on the posture that politics is so inherently corrupting and government workers so inherently lacking in integrity that most such men and women are unable to be active party members *and* impartial public servants.

ADDRESSING THE EQUITIES   Indeed, there is a persuasive argument that, if government employees can be deprived of political participation because they might get involved in a corrupting or at least an unfair influence on public policy, then on the same grounds we logically could prohibit farmers, veterans, businessmen, doctors, union leaders, and many others from engaging in political activity, since they clearly have a large and direct interest in expenditures, regulations, subsidies, and a host of other practical determinations by government.[25] As one student of the subject observed:

A democracy is always open to the abuse of its instruments or the extraction of special privileges by interest groups which gain ascendancy among the conflicting social and economic forces operative within the community. The political neutralization of a specific group based upon the possibility of such undesirable consequences would seem to constitute a repudiation of institu-

[24] John W. Macy, Jr., in an address before the D.C. Chapter of the Federal Bar Association in Washington, May 22, 1968.

[25] See the thesis taken by Supreme Court Justice Hugo Black in *United Public Workers of America (CIO)* v. *Mitchell*, 330 U.S. 109, and by Dalmas H. Nelson in "Public Employees and the Right to Engage in Political Activity," *Vanderbilt Law Review*, December 1955.

tional arrangements which have become an integral part of the apparatus of a modern democratic state.[26]

If some groups in society, equally identified with governmental affairs through subsidies or by virtue of being regulated enterprises, are free to exert political pressure and operate through established parties, then why not civil servants? The injustice is further compounded by the facts that proscription of political activity is punishment for *potential* offenses and that all public employees are being restrained because of the acts of some.[27]

Thinking through the maze of considerations in this eternal dilemma of how to balance citizen rights with employee obligations would be facilitated if we distinguished between neutrality as a person and impartiality as an employee. Ideally, it ought to be possible for a high-principled person to be *impartial* without necessarily being *neutral* about the law or the policy he is administering. He may be as aware or perhaps more aware than outsiders of the shortcomings of a given policy, in which case it is his duty to acknowledge them while at the same time continuing to apply the existing policy impartially and without prejudice.

UNION ROLES   The remaining issue has to do with the role of employee unions in political activity. Whatever limitations may have been imposed on union engagement in political campaigns, reality suggests that they have not been very effective. Behind-the-scenes maneuvering and financial support are as difficult to trace in this case as they are in the political machinations of giant corporations or individual magnates. It could be said that the plight of the civil servant in political expression has been offset to some degree by the reality of power in his organizing for the welfare of his group and by the resulting collective negotiations of such organizations with management and their lobbying directly with legislative bodies. It must be acknowledged, however, that with rare exceptions the political business to which unions have turned has been that of seeking more favorable conditions of work and remuneration for their membership, not the substantive issues of government policy.

[26] Morton Robert Godine, *The Labor Problem in the Public Service: A Study in Political Pluralism*, Cambridge, Mass., Harvard University Press, 1951, pp. 186–187.

[27] Arch Dotson, "The Emerging Doctrine of Privilege in Public Employment," *Public Administration Review*, Spring 1955, especially p. 84. Dotson says that denial of basic constitutional safeguards such as free speech, peaceable assembly, and petition to public workers is part of the erroneous conception of public office as a privilege and the specious theory "that since there is no right *to*, there can be no right *in* public employment." This position, he observes, means that government employees would have no protection against arbitrary dismissal, no participation in determining the conditions of their retention in the service, and no way of participating in the debate of issues that profoundly concern them. They would be restricted to "silent voting."

David H. Rosenbloom, bringing this issue more up to date, observes that the doctrine of privilege has clearly lost ground to a doctrine that lays greater stress on protection of public employees' constitutional rights (*op. cit.*).

SIGNS OF CHANGE

Thinking along the lines presented in this discussion has been the force behind a series of developments that serve as harbingers of change in the whole realm of political activity of public servants. In addition to those already cited, a number of students of the issues involved have concluded that there should be an overall liberalization of political activity restrictions.[28]

COMMISSION ON POLITICAL ACTIVITY   Under a 1966 act of Congress, the federal government set up a Commission on Political Activity of Government Personnel, which in its report of 1967 proposed notable moves in the direction of liberalization, although only a few such changes had actually taken place at this writing. The basic thrust of the recommendations was to expand the permissive area of political activity for federal employees, and even more so that of state and local employees working on federally financed programs, while strengthening the sanctions against coercion and misuse of official position. Asserting that "the best protection that the government can provide for its personnel is to prohibit those activities that tend to corrode a career system based on merit," the commission declared that "these limits should be clearly and specifically expressed" and "beyond those limits political participation should be permitted as fully as for all other citizens."[29] The major changes proposed were these:

1. That public employees be allowed to express their opinions freely in public on any political subject or candidate.
2. That federal employees be permitted to hold or campaign for any local office, regardless of location or the partisan nature of the electoral process, that does not interfere or conflict with the conduct of their federal duties.
3. That they be allowed to serve as delegates to political conventions so long as such service does not interfere with their federal responsibilities.
4. That prohibited activity be confined to partisan fund-raising, actions while on duty, campaigning for or holding other than local offices, serving as watcher or recorder at polling places, and serving as a principal officer of a political party.
5. That states with systems for controlling political activities, with the approval of the U.S. Civil Service Commission, be given responsibility for enforcement within their own jurisdictions, including application to federally financed functions.

---

[28] See, for example, the convenient summary of the problem at all governmental levels and of possible solutions in Donald Hayman and O. Glenn Stahl, *Political Activity Restrictions: An Analysis with Recommendations*, Personnel Report No. 636, Chicago, International Personnel Management Association, 1963.

[29] The Commission on Political Activity of Government Personnel, *A Commission Report: Findings and Recommendations* (Vol. I), Washington, D.C., 1967, p. 3.

6. That penalties for violations be made more flexible than the present requirement of either dismissal or a minimum suspension of thirty days of the offending employee.

7. That more funds be appropriated for administration of the law.[30]

STATE AND LOCAL EMPLOYEES   Even before the report of the federal commission a number of states had lifted political restrictions to a degree at least as significant as those proposed. A number actually have no limitations at all and are affected only by the federal requirements imposed on grant-assisted programs. Changes in some states in recent years have paralleled the thesis advanced by the federal study commission, namely, that restrictions should be relaxed on after-work-hour politicking but that provisions should be stringent against coercion of employees into giving money or service to aid a political candidate. Some of these liberalizing actions have been instigated or abetted by court decisions made in response to suits by public workers protesting curtailment of their constitutional rights.[31]

The only nationwide liberalization of political activity restrictions has affected state and local employees engaged in programs under federal financing. A surprise clause accomplished this in the Federal Election Campaign Act Amendments of 1974, a measure designed primarily to tighten controls on campaign spending for election to federal congressional seats. The new law continues prohibitions for state and local workers against (1) use of official authority to influence or interfere with election results, (2) coercion of employees to make political contributions, and (3) being a candidate for elective office in a partisan election. But it extends state and local permissable activities by: (1) clearly authorizing free expression of opinions on political subjects and candidates; (2) allowing solicitation and collection of party contributions, without coercion; (3) permitting active participation in party organizations short of holding a party office; and (4) permitting active campaigning on behalf of partisan candidates.[32]

It should be understood, of course, that where state law establishes more strict prohibitions on the political activity of state and local employees, these prohibitions remain in effect. The federal action does, nevertheless, remove a number of constraints in those states that already had fewer or no limitations on their employees who were not connected with federally financed programs.

[30] A minority of the members of the commission disagreed with opening local partisan offices to federal employees, and the commission divided evenly on whether they should be permitted to hold offices in local party organizations (*ibid.*, pp. 5–6). Summaries of the recommendations and of provisions of a proposed draft bill to give them effect appear on pp. 3–6 and 39–43.

[31] Legislative and judicial developments are usually reported in the biennial volume of the Council of State Governments, the *Book of the States.*

[32] These provisions appear in section 401 of the Act and became effective on January 1, 1975.

THE FUTURE   The trend toward liberalization seems clear, although a tidal wave of change has not yet occurred. Nor does there appear to be much likelihood of the more radical proposals—letting down all the bars—being enacted. Certainly protections against coercion and the more incompatible activities are likely to continue.

In any case, it is doubtful that a standard pattern can be prescribed for all jurisdictions at all times. The political stability of the governmental unit involved and the maturity of its career public service would have to be taken into account. Where the tradition of a merit system is not well fixed in the public mind or in the habits of political leaders, any move away from standard restraints on political activity may have to be postponed or slowed down to the capacity of the community to absorb change without damage either to public employees or to the quality and impartiality of their performance of official duties.[33]

*   *   *

IN THESE FATEFUL days, it is dangerous for any significant group of citizens to stand aloof from the functioning of the party system through which our democracy works. It has therefore been the contention of this writer that, while we keep partisan politics out of the civil service, we must work toward the day when citizens who are also civil servants can return to at least limited political responsibilities after duty hours.

This restored freedom should not include latitude to support totalitarian movements designed to destroy the Republic or to suppress constitutional liberties. It should, however, encompass the traditional right of any American to defend the status quo or to advocate far-reaching changes and unorthodox ideas as long as he does not contend for unconstitutional means to achieve the ends. Pursuant to these principles, loyalty-security programs and political activity limitations should ensure that national security and impartial public service are safeguarded without causing civil servants to lose that confidence in the fairness of their government, that faith in justice, that courage of conviction, and that independence of spirit which set apart the servants of a free people from the servile tools of dictatorships.

---

[33] See the proposals in Hayman and Stahl, *op. cit.*, pp. 16–19.

CHAPTER 18

Discipline, Removal, and Appeals

FROM SOME PASSAGES in this book one might infer that government employees can do no wrong. We have tried to stress the positive side of the managerial process and searched for ways to expect and secure the best from each worker. In all fairness, however, we must concede that uncorrectable bad performance and intolerable misconduct do in actuality occur. Except where remedial measures are practicable and effective, the net result is some negative action, some kind of punishment. No organization is so perfect, no executive so ingenious, no personnel system so infallible that measures of correction and punishment can be completely avoided. The purpose of this chapter is to lay down a few points of definition, give a brief assessment of practices, and outline a few principles and precautions.

DISCIPLINARY ACTIONS AND EXECUTIVE RESPONSIBILITY

PRINCIPAL FORMS OF CORRECTION

Penalties for violation of rules, for misperformance, or for nonperformance vary widely in severity. The more usual forms of disciplinary action are warning or reprimand, reassignment, suspension without pay, demotion, and dismissal.

REPRIMAND   The least severe punishment, warning or reprimand, often proves sufficient to correct a situation. Proper handling, with due regard for a person's self-esteem—that is, directing the charge against the specific behavior, not the whole man—can send an employee back to his work with a new perspective and a new feeling of loyalty toward the service. The personal contact occasioned by an informal oral reprimand presents an opportunity for constructive counsel that the good supervisor does not overlook.

REASSIGNMENT   Although not always evident as disciplinary punishment, reassignment to other duties may well be induced by bad performance. Since reassignment is more likely to be used as a developmental technique, it is well that when it is used for disciplinary purposes its intent be made clear to the individual involved. Banishment to less desirable duties or a less desirable location is sometimes resorted to in the case of police officers, field workers of various kinds, or others who can be moved about without disruption to the services concerned. It is a dubious practice at best, for even though it may be effective on occasion, it hardly seems to be a constructive way to make placements. Assignments should be based on fitness, not unsuitability.

SUSPENSION   One of the most common forms of punishment is suspension without pay. In many jurisdictions this is the most extreme penalty that can be imposed by an operating official without the possibility of reversal by a higher authority. Since an indefinite suspension might be tantamount to dismissal, it is customary to limit the period for which an employee may be suspended. Commonly, thirty days is the maximum, although longer periods are by no means unknown.[1]

Use of suspension is likewise of doubtful practicality, if the objective is to improve performance. Loss of salary for even a couple of weeks can be a serious financial blow to a civil servant's family, in effect amounting to a fine. How such a measure might rectify any wrongdoing is seldom clear. If a lengthy suspension is intended as a means of easing an offender out of the service, outright dismissal would be more forthright and honest. The main utility for suspensions is in cases where some unfortunate incident of misconduct on the job requires temporary removal of the employee from the work environment or where doubt about guilt in some instance necessitates a period of investigation. In such cases, the quicker the issue is resolved the better.

DEMOTION   A more severe penalty than suspension, although sometimes more rational in terms of making the best use of employee skills, is demotion to a position of lower rank or grade. Carrying a more continuing stigma, demotion must be used with caution. As in the case of lateral reassignment, it can be justified only when the new assignment gives promise of making more effective utilization of the individual's capacity and aptitude than the previous one. If it is intended simply as punishment for some breach of duty,

---

[1] In the federal service, suspensions over thirty days are appealable to the Civil Service Commission on the merits of the issues involved. Others are subject to this review only as to whether proper procedures have been used.

either reprimand or dismissal would be more appropriate, depending on the seriousness of the offense.

DISMISSAL   Dismissal or removal from the service is the most extreme disciplinary action but, second to reprimands, probably the most common. Many times it is the most humane action if the reasons are serious, for it permits the employee to make a completely new start elsewhere, which should not be a remote possibility in a near-full-employment economy. It is, nevertheless, a drastic action and an awkward and often embarrassing one to consummate. In some instances, as in the case of certain criminal or security offenses, the dismissed person may be barred from future reemployment anywhere within the governmental entity that "fired" him, either for some specified period or permanently. Dismissal or removal is the one penalty that requires more extended comment later.[2]

OUTMODED PUNISHMENTS

A few other forms of discipline, besides those mentioned, have been used from time to time, but most of them have been discarded as outmoded or ineffective. One has been the practice of placing demerits against an employee's record, which has usually had the effect of retarding his chances for promotion. In situations where the individual has corrected his performance or behavior, such a continuing black mark on his record would seem to be decidedly unfair. Another device has been the imposition of cash fines deducted from pay, a practice that has all but disappeared in civil services except in a few police departments. As in the case of suspension, a money penalty injures the employee's family as much as the employee, to say nothing of the fact that such a punitive measure seems utterly incompatible with the dignity of government employment.

FREQUENCY OF DISMISSALS

Contrary to the lingering popular assumption that government employees under merit systems cannot be "fired" or "sacked," the fact is that many thousands lose their jobs in this fashion every year. In spite of the unavailability of directly comparable statistics, there is every reason to believe that the annual rate of removal ranging from a little less than one to about one and a half percent in public jurisdictions in the United States as a whole is exceeded, if at all, only in certain categories of private employment, such as a few areas of manufacturing.[3] When we bear in mind the generally more

[2] When no disciplinary element is involved, involuntary separations in some services are called *discharges* or simply *separations*, for example, removals due to retrenchment. In the federal service, the latter are called *reductions in force*.

[3] Periodic statistical reports of the U.S. Civil Service Commission on federal dismissals and of the U.S. Bureau of Labor Statistics on dismissals in some fields of industry, plus occasional periodical articles on such actions in state and local governments, may be consulted for comparisons in any current year, but most of the figures are not collected for exactly parallel circumstances.

exacting methods of initial hiring in the public service, expectancy for a high rate of removal should actually not be as great as it is in private business. If, indeed, incompetency is condoned anywhere, it is no more a feature of civil services than it is of other sectors of our society.

The fact is that the failure to make more "surgical operations" on bad performance and conduct is attributable to pretty much the same causes in both industry and government: (1) the tendency of employee unions to make a fortress out of the removal procedure, making it so complex and painful to management that it is avoided more than it is used; and (2) the natural reluctance of executives to take such drastic action.

If anything, the latter reason is the more dominant one. Firing is a distasteful business in any organization. Seldom is the justification so clear to the employee himself that he accepts it with good grace. With conspicuous exceptions, even seasoned executives shrink from dismissal and try every device possible to avoid it. There is certainly no monopoly on this reluctance in the public service. "Kicking a man upstairs," "palming off" a poor employee on another division, and overlooking the faults of a long-time worker are just as common in industry as in government. There is a natural unwillingness to hurt people severely for what may be easily rationalized as minor human failings, as well as a reluctance to accept the consequences of drastic action whether it be facing a protesting union official or legislator or the procedural requirements of a personnel system. Under the circumstances, the sizable volume of removals that do take place in American government is probably as substantial as can be expected.

EXECUTIVE HANDICAPS

There is, however, still a further dimension to the subject in the public service. The battle against the spoils system of job patronage and against corruption in government became merged with hostility toward politics and politicians generally. Since key public executives are elected or selected by political means, it has been easy to confuse civil service reform with restrictions on executive power. To an increasing extent, of course, it is being realized that a mature citizenry should rely less on negative restraints and more on positive means of selecting a capable executive in the first place, giving him the necessary control over the agencies through which the people's will is to be carried out, and holding him accountable (and his subordinates through him) for the administration of the popular mandate. Even today, however, foreign students of American public administration continue to be astonished at the heavy weighting of the division of powers against the executive when it comes to matters of internal administration.

In this one area of authority to determine when an employee is failing to measure up to what the job demands and to be able effectively to do something about it, the American public executive is unduly handicapped. Superficially, no one can quarrel with the standard requirements that executives give a period of advance notice in anticipation of a dismissal or other severe disciplinary action, a statement of reasons for the proposed action to the employee (usually in writing), and an opportunity to the employee to make a reply before the ax falls. Nor can the interested citizen complain about the criterion for removal in the federal service, paralleled in many other jurisdictions, namely: "only for such cause as will promote the efficiency of the service."[4] But the legalisms and abracadabra that have been added thereunto, and particularly the highly protectionist language of the Veteran Preference Act of 1944, as interpreted by the Civil Service Commission and the courts, has made removal an extraordinarily technical and time-consuming process.

For example, the necessary thirty-day notice and the requirement that reasons given for dismissal must be stated "specifically and in detail" have given lawyers and courts a field day in narrowing down the discretion of federal executives to extremely precise terms.[5] As a result, the merits of a case are all but lost in the wrangling over procedural fine points, instigated by veteran organizations, unions, and attorneys who make a specialty of taking up the cases of fired workers. The courts have not ordinarily substituted their judgment for that of administrative authorities on the substantive issues, that is, the validity, desirability, or necessity of taking the action, but the detailed procedural requirements have provided them an opportunity to indulge in a whole new field of law, often to the discouragement of conscientious administrators who are trying to maintain reasonable standards of performance.

If dismissals for the good of the service are to stand up, there is no question but that they must measure up to certain standards. The right of the accused employee to know what he is charged with and to have an opportunity to state his view of the situation is unassailable. Also, disciplinary control, if it is to be effective, must be prompt, firm, and consistent. Further, there can be no room for favoritism or revenge. And, finally, in most cases disciplinary authority should be vested in the responsible executive administering the public program concerned. The ultimate remedy for the employee who feels that he is being treated unjustly is resort to an appeal, the subject taken up shortly. Nevertheless we must guard against adulteration of the disciplinary process itself by preoccupation with the technicalities of the indictment instead of the overall fairness and justice of the action.

POWER TO INITIATE ACTION

One more principle requires mention. In almost all jurisdictions, responsibility for initiation of disciplinary measures rests with the department head, often with the power to delegate it to lower officials. This is as it should be. However, some places require review of such actions by the personnel agency, a practice reflecting an excess of caution against the possibility of prejudicial

[4] Originally in the Lloyd-La Follette Act of 1912, now codified in 5 *U.S. Code* 7501.
[5] *U.S. Code* 7512.

action by overzealous, politically appointed department heads. Rather than tying the hands in this way of all principal executives in maintaining discipline, it would seem more sensible to provide for removal of the offending manager if such reprehensible action is ever demonstrated.

There is one kind of situation where another party, preferably a multi-member body, may wisely be called into play in initiation of an adverse procedure against an employee. This is in those instances where the supervising official is not in a good position to have observed the behavior or performance of the employee, such as in the work of police officers, school teachers, or hospital attendants. In these cases, where the employee necessarily works alone without immediate supervision and is concerned with delicate human relationships rather than a reviewable product or service, it serves a useful purpose to have a committee or board inquire into the facts when the official is first confronted with an accusation against an employee. Police departments often refer to such bodies as "trial boards." In effect, such a process equips the official with substantiating evidence (if the body so finds) as a basis for judgment, since he is unlikely to have any direct knowledge of the circumstances from personal observation. Even here, it should be noted, the power to proceed in the case should be and normally is vested in the administrator, not the board acting alone.

APPEALS

In an earlier chapter we have discussed the need for grievance procedures in every well-managed organization.[6] A grievance or complaint by an employee growing out of some disciplinary measure initiated by management is what is referred to here as an "appeal."[7]

GENERAL PRACTICE

Most jurisdictions provide employees who wish to avail themselves of it an opportunity to have an appeal, including a hearing, against a serious disciplinary action, particularly a removal. Where a service is politics-ridden, the legal right to notice and hearing may offer the employee only the shadow of protection against arbitrary action. But in a well-run merit system appeal rights are generally meaningful and do act as a brake on hasty, ill-conceived decisions.

Appeals are customarily heard by a multiple body—often of three persons—which is established by statute or which is appointed ad hoc by the

[6] Chapter 11, "Liberating the Will to Work."

[7] This is the more common term used in the public service, connoting a special safeguard to protect civil servants from abuse. The prevailing term used in private industry, *grievance*, embraces both objections to adverse actions taken by management against individuals and complaints of any kind against working conditions, management policy, or alleged sins of omission as well as commission by management.

head of the department. Frequently, one member is elected by employees or, in the case of ad hoc boards or committees, is selected by the appellant. An ad hoc hearing panel may select its own chairman by joint agreement of the management representative and the employee representative. Occasionally, representation of the general public is required on appeal boards.

Whatever their constitution, these appellate bodies usually follow informal procedures rather than the processes of a court of law, and their decisions are ordinarily advisory rather than binding on the department head. Where they are set up to make final determinations, they take on the characteristics of an administrative court. True appeal boards are distinguished from the aforementioned "trial boards" in that the former are invoked only at the behest of the employee *after* disciplinary action, whereas the latter constitute the instrument by which the initial action itself may be decided on.

FEDERAL SYSTEM

Following periods when individual agencies of the federal government were encouraged and later required to operate appeals systems within their own bailiwicks, with further appeals to a Civil Service Commission body under certain circumstances, the federal service finally established a one-level appellate system under which: (1) agency appeal systems were eliminated; (2) a final agency determination on a dismissal or other adverse action must, before the action takes place, be made by a higher authority than the official who signed the proposed measure; (3) an employee affected by such action may appeal it to a professional appeals officer on the staff of the Commission, such officers being located at the Commission's ten regional office centers; (4) the appeals officer directs whatever investigation is needed, holds hearings, and makes the final appellate decision for the Commission; and (5) an Appeals Review Board in the Commission may review such determinations only in the limited instances where there is a showing that new material evidence is available, a misinterpretation of law, regulation, or policy has taken place, or the case is precedent-setting for new policy.[8] Only a minority of persons removed actually avail themselves of this process; that is, most people against whom a removal or similar drastic action is directed may protest it while it is in process but in the last analysis accept it without formal appeal.

Whether the federal system does violence to the principle of executive responsibility for discipline remains to be seen. The head of an agency or his agent does have an opportunity to reconsider an adverse action against an employeee before the action goes into effect, but the central personnel

[8] This system is provided for in Executive Order 11787, June 11, 1974. The order revoked authorization for the previous agency appeals systems. It applies to the competitive civil service and not to the various satellite personnel systems in the federal service. More detailed descriptions of the new appellate plan and its origins appear in articles in the *Civil Service Journal*, April–June 1973 and July–September 1974.

agency has the power to overrule the agency's decision. The latter step can, of course, be viewed as a final determination on behalf of the chief executive, the President, if we accept that the Commission is, at least in some respects, his agent. The new plan was designed to eliminate the complexities of multiple tiers of appeal, and it certainly achieves at least that objective.

Reflecting the particular sensitiveness of the federal government to the problems of women, blacks, and Spanish-speaking citizens, a separate system of review and appeal is provided in the federal service for "equal opportunity" issues, that is, instances alleging discrimination in employment, advancement, or training because of race, color, religion, sex, or national origin. Special procedures of informal adjustment, investigation, and hearing are set up within each department under civil service regulations to apply to such cases, but complainants may carry their grievances as far as the Appeals Review Board in the Civil Service Commission.[9]

The larger the jurisdiction the more desirable it is to have an appeals system that permits and even encourages settlement of issues as close to the point of origin as possible while still providing for review of actions by higher administrative authority than that which initiated them. Another point is that any third-party adjudication outside the department involved should definitely be by a governmental authority. The desire of some unions to call in private arbitrators to settle disputes over the status of individuals in the service should be resisted as firmly as using them to settle policy issues. Executive responsibility for personnel performance would only be further eroded by such a process.

SAFEGUARDS VERSUS PROTECTIONISM

We have already observed that problems of discipline, removal, and checks on management action are not peculiar to the public service. Union contracts with private employers vie with state civil service laws and the federal Veteran Preference Act in their provisions circumscribing management's disciplinary authority. The minimum formality in union contracts is that discipline and dismissal must be "for cause." No fair-minded individual would deny the face validity of such a safeguard; every person is entitled to fair and reasonable treatment. The question is one of reasonableness from the standpoint of the public or consumer interest.

PROCEDURAL FORMALITIES

Formal and detailed statement of the "for cause" principle opens the door to a chain of interpretations and thereby results in a significant shift in the employer-employee relationship. As one student of the subject observed:

[9] See Civil Service Regulations, Part 713, under authority of Executive Order 11478, "Equal Employment Opportunity in the Federal Government," August 8, 1969.

The prime effect of the phrase "for cause" has been procedural. It puts the burden of proof on the employer for any corrective action prejudicial to the employee. In nonlegal language, this means simply that the employer must prove that discipline is justified instead of the employee having to prove that it was arbitrary, inconsistent, or unfair. The difference is important; it puts the employer or his representatives on trial, with the employee presumed innocent until shown to be guilty. . . . In the nature of things, the rule of "burden of proof" is not stated in the agreement between the company and the union, but it has become the fundamental rule of fair play to millions of employees working under union contracts in the United States.[10]

Similar conclusions can be drawn from experience with appeals requirements in public jurisdictions where there is a tendency to get enmeshed in excessive procedural formalities. This is in spite of the obvious truth that the purpose of procedure is to assure reasonable justice, not to provide an arena for adversaries to see who can best manipulate the requirements or outmaneuver each other. Some of the more recent merit system laws in state and local governments show little sign of avoiding the traps of overproceduralization. A few have gone so far as to make discipline almost impossible.[11]

NEED FOR BALANCE

The issue is not whether employees should have fair treatment. Nor is it whether management should have a free hand. The more serious issue is what the effects will be on our social fabric and productivity. Trends in both private and public employment clearly demonstrate (1) a desirable awareness of the need for protection of workers in all employment against arbitrary or capricious discipline, but also (2) a danger that a protective philosophy is gaining such ascendancy that reward or condonement of incompetence and mediocrity is the result in many cases.

A very delicate balance in values is at stake. Our civil rights heritage and sense of justice lead us to extend to the work place the ideals we espouse in relationships between citizen and state or among citizens. Hence, we naturally think of parallel protections in the arena of employment. Innocent until proved guilty, sufficiency of evidence, due notice and hearing, and similar hallowed concepts have come to be applied by workers who are protesting a dismissal, a demotion, or other action adverse to their employment. This has its risks as well as its virtues. There is ample evidence that a

[10] Orme W. Phelps, *Discipline and Discharge in the Unionized Firm*, Berkeley, University of California Press, 1959, p. 33.

[11] The 1960 personnel law of the state of Washington was described by a professor of Washington State University as evidencing "overemphasis on seniority, overspecificity, and oversolicitude for employees subjected to administrative discipline" (Paul L. Beckett, "Operation Self-Help: Washington State's New Merit System Law," *Public Personnel Review*, January 1963, p. 58).

civilization is on the decline when it loses discipline and "goes soft."[12] Many sincere and responsible people are concerned that we are too lenient with those who do shoddy work or no work at all. Such payroll leeches too often succeed in securing extraordinary protections and even the same rewards as those who produce and produce well. It is much like the schoolchild who feels put upon when forced to meet high standards or when punished for laziness or misbehavior. Too often it is the teacher who gets the "third degree" by the overprotective parent. A productive civilization cannot survive in this kind of atmosphere.

It is difficult at best to square responsibility with equity. The main source of trouble is in mistaking procedural refinement for equity. A major frustration to responsible officials in some public services as well as in private employment is the labyrinth of procedure that must often be followed not only to the letter but to various implied meanings of the letter, and the insistence of some courts that things such as length of notice or the manner in which a statement of reasons or charges is drawn up are more important than ridding the service of an undesirable employee. Some judges have mistaken such statements of reasons for indictments. The employee is not being charged with a crime; he may simply be ineffective or unable to do the job. If the employer fails to be as specific as an indictment requires in every respect, is this a proper basis for preventing the action obviously needed? The employee is not being sentenced to jail; he may simply not deserve as good a job as he has been holding. Or perhaps he could do better on a different job. Must the procedural compulsions be the same for the supervisor as for a jury?

Procedural errors have allegedly resulted in restoring to duty a police officer whose mental condition was sufficiently questionable that his carrying a revolver constituted a danger to the public he was supposed to protect, a postal clerk who defied authority and spent most of his energy on nonproductive activity, an attorney who produced little and spent most of his time preparing diatribes against his superiors about their infringement of his rights, and others too numerous to mention but just as alarming. It is not easy in such cases for executives to catologue exact events as to time and place or the precise significance of the sins of omission as well as commission. Yet they are often tripped up for not doing just such things, even when there is no denial of inadequate performance or improper conduct by the employee. Sometimes the fault lies in the law itself, but more often it is in the interpretation, by either administrative or judicial authorities.

We must guard against such an excessive concern for worker protection that laxity and mediocrity come to be equated with integrity and superiority. A society founded on individual enterprise cannot long survive a dead-leveling influence that gives a person a property right in employment with

---

[12] The most formidable support is found in Arnold Toynbee's famous 10-volume *A Study of History*. See abridgment by D. C. Somervell, New York, Oxford University Press, 1947, 2 vols., *passim*.

little or no obligation on his part to merit the rewards that go with it. Dedicated and competent employees get no incentive from conditions which condone and even protect poor performance or conduct. We cannot risk losing that incentive. The race should still go to the swift, the battle to the strong.

*   *   *

THERE WILL BE occasion in even the best administrative worlds when one must resort to punitive measures. In the enforcement of discipline, the executive should enjoy sufficient authority to enable him to maintain a competent work force. His discretion should be limited only by a few basic legal provisions and policies which are safeguards against arbitrary procedure and punishment without just cause being duly shown. Although it is desirable to provide for administrative review of the actions of supervisors, the final decision of an appointing authority should be subject to reversal on appeal only where there has been a violation of fundamental principles and rights.

PART VI

Employee Organization and Collective Relations with Management

It has been the experience of government employees everywhere that the amelioration of their material status must have organized self-pressure as its initial impetus.

Walter R. Sharp, *The French Civil Service:*
Bureaucracy in Transition, New York,
Macmillan 1931, p. 493.

Unionism springs from the basic aspirations of those employees who become convinced that they can gain more through membership in a union than by "going it alone." . . . Instead of regarding unionization solely as an evidence of ingratitude on the part of employees or a failure by management, wise managers take the initiative in attempting to develop constructive relationships with the new organization representing their employees.

Paul Pigors and Charles A. Myers, *Personnel*
Administration: A Point of View and a Method,
7th ed., New York, McGraw-Hill, 1973, p. 161.

We believe that in the cities, counties, and states there are other claimants with needs at least as pressing as those of the public employees. . . .

The trouble is that if unions are able to withhold labor—to strike—as well as to employ the usual methods of political pressure, they may possess a disproportionate share of effective power in the process of decision. . . .

Make no mistake about it, government is *not* "just another industry."

Harry H. Wellington and Ralph K. Winter, Jr.,
The Unions and the Cities, Washington, D.C.,
The Brookings Institution, 1971, pp. 25 and 202.

Whatever else may be said about public management at the bargaining table, one point stands out: Public administrators have a right to manage. Indeed they have an obligation to manage because they are protectors of the public interest and custodians of the public welfare. But they must also understand the shift in the climate of management-employee relations; it is away from one-sided paternalistic management and toward two-party cooperative management. . . .

Management's success at the bargaining table will depend in large measure on its ability to think ahead and to prepare for tomorrow.

Kenneth O. Warner and Mary L. Hennessy,
Public Management at the Bargaining Table, Chicago,
International Personnel Management Association,
1967, pp. 331 and 310.

CHAPTER 19

Development
and Impact
of Unionization

Just as at the turn of the century the prime concern in public administration was the contest of the merit system with an outmoded method of staffing government bureaucracy, just as a few decades later there was a concern for a broader view of the personnel function and a new concept of government careers, so in the last third of the century we see increasing concern with the substance and form of employee welfare and a new militancy in seeking accommodation to employee interests from the general public as employer. Not that the current stage in evolution is anything really new or without its roots deep in the past. Public servants in the United States began to develop some consciousness of common needs and interests even before the merit system idea flourished and certainly before the phrase "personnel administration" was used in organized enterprise.

However, unionization in public jurisdictions did not get seriously under way until the 1880s, since the haphazard status of public employment before that time was hardly conducive to the development of solidarity among civil servants and since, as in most nations, the example and impetus of the general labor movement was required to get government employee organization really off the ground. It is due to this followership, perhaps as much as any other one cause, that the parallels with private industrial-union history in circumstances, problems, and resolutions tend to be taken for granted. As we shall see in the course of our examination, such parallels are greatly overdrawn.

CURRENT STATUS

Employee organization in the public service must be understood not only as an extension of the age-old confrontation between private employers and exploited labor but also as a typical issue of the body politic—one in which the contest is between the special interests of a minority and the dominant interests of the majority. What has become critical in recent times is the rapid growth in relative size and strength of the minority—public employees—in the face of increasing resistance by the majority—the general voting and taxpaying public—to mounting governmental expenditures. The issue is not altogether different than it was in the 1880s; it is just immensely bigger.

The American habit over the years of disparaging public employment, of looking upon investment and operational expense paid from public revenues as some kind of inherent evil—all during the time when the people have demanded new and enlarged public services—is now bearing, as it did in times past, some unpleasant and unexpected fruit. Militancy and strikes in the most unexpected places are commanding public attention as never before.

Police officers, public school teachers, and postal employees were among the first in the latter part of the nineteenth century to organize for prosecution of their own welfare. The movement spread gradually over many reaches of the municipal, state, and federal services. But never has unionization spread as rapidly in so short a time as it has from the late 1950s onwards. Curiously, this is occurring at the very time that union membership in the private economy has been declining both relatively and absolutely as a portion of the total work force of gainfully employed persons. Naturally, this new focus of labor strength brings with it new militancy and new conflict; yet, it also brings new significance and opportunity.

It is almost impossible to keep up with the full extent of public employee organization nationwide. The great majority of municipal employees are represented by unions, with the larger cities having the more extensive organization and with police and fire personnel leading the field in proportions organized. A large percentage of state employees also belongs to either individual state associations or to one of the national unions of government workers. Likewise, union organization in the federal service has grown markedly, especially since presidential encouragement in 1962.

Public employees more than ever before are demanding to be heard. As a major share of the nation's working population, their interests and concerns are entitled to a sympathetic hearing. But so are the interests and concerns of the public as a whole. Before attempting to analyze some of the practices in existence and the policy issues that arise, it is well that we take a look at the history and some of the elements of unionism in the American civil service.[1]

---

[1] Some of the more important recent works (listed here chronologically) on the general subject of public employee organization and representation are: Kenneth O.

DEVELOPMENT OF CIVIL SERVICE UNIONISM

Almost all the public employee organizations in existence prior to 1880 were benevolent societies, established for welfare and protective purposes, found principally among the municipal police forces. A possible exception was the National Teachers' Association, first organized in 1857. During the remainder of the nineteenth century, numerous organizations of both a professional[2] and a union type sprang up. As might be expected, groups along trade-union lines appeared first among the skilled and semiskilled workers in various government industries, such as at military installations. The unionization of government printers, machinists, carpenters, and other craftsmen lagged but little behind the general labor movement. In the main, whether as the result of this proximity or not, such workers are employed at about the same wage scales and for about the same hours as prevail among their fellow tradesmen in the same locality.

FEDERAL SERVICE UNIONISM

POSTAL   The first strictly public service unions emerged in the Postal Service, primarily as a protest against the all but intolerable working conditions at the time but also because of its size and far-flung staff, its industrial character as compared with many other services, and the relative standardi-

---

Warner and Mary L. Hennessy, *Public Management at the Bargaining Table*, Chicago, International Personnel Management Association, 1967; Lloyd Ulman, ed., *Challenges to Collective Bargaining*, Papers Prepared for the Thirtieth American Assembly, Columbia University, Englewood Cliffs, N.J., Prentice-Hall, 1967; Felix A. Nigro, *Management-Employee Relations in the Public Service*, Chicago, International Personnel Management Association, 1969; W. Donald Heisel, *State-Local Employee Labor Relations*, Lexington, Ky., The Council of State Governments, 1970; Michael H. Moskow, J. Joseph Loewenberg, and Edward Clifford Koziara, *Collective Bargaining in Public Employment*, New York, Random House, 1970; Harold S. Roberts, ed., *Labor-Management Relations in the Public Service*, Honolulu, University of Hawaii Press, 1970; O. Glenn Stahl, *The Public Personnel Function—Two Issues*, Detroit, Citizens Research Council of Michigan, 1971; Harry H. Wellington and Ralph K. Winter, Jr., *The Unions and the Cities*, Washington, D.C., The Brookings Institution, 1971; David T. Stanley, *Managing Local Government Under Union Pressure*, Washington, D.C., The Brookings Institution, 1972; J. Joseph Loewenberg and Michael H. Moskow, *Collective Bargaining in Government; Readings and Cases*, Englewood Cliffs, N.J., Prentice-Hall, 1972; Sam Zagoria, ed., *Public Workers and Public Unions*, Papers Prepared for the Fortieth American Assembly, Columbia University, Englewood Cliffs, N.J., Prentice-Hall, 1972; and Jack Stieber, *Public Employee Unionism: Structure, Growth, Policy*, Washington, D.C., The Brookings Institution, 1973.

The International Personnel Management Association maintains a service in the form of periodically issued pamphlets, cases, and fact sheets, identified as the *Public Employee Relations Library* (PERL). The Bureau of National Affairs in Washington, D.C., publishes a weekly news sheet containing information on rulings, agreements, and decisions affecting management-union relations in governmental employment. Another loose-leaf service is that of Prentice-Hall, Englewood Cliffs, N.J., appearing in its two-volume work *Public Personnel Administration; Labor-Management Relations*, 1974.

[2] For example, the International Association of Fire Chiefs (1873), the International Association of Chiefs of Police (1893), and the Association of American Food and Drug Officials (1897). Many of these professional organizations play a prominent role in the improvement of standards and practices of administration, but they are not the direct concern of this chapter.

zation of its operations.[3] The 1880s and 1890s saw, in rapid succession, the formation of unions for letter carriers, post office clerks, rural carriers, and railway mail clerks. Most of them started independently, and in some instances mergers took place when rival organizations appeared. In the early 1900s groups representing various postal supervisor and postmaster categories began to develop, but since they actually represent particular tiers of management they can hardly be considered typical of true unionism. The dominant post office unions today are the American Postal Workers Union (embracing former unions of postal clerks), the National Association of Letter Carriers, and the National Federation of Rural Letter Carriers, the first two being affiliates of the American Federation of Labor–Congress of Industrial Organizations (AFL-CIO).[4] A few smaller unions also continue in the giant Postal Service. Collectively the postal unions wield extraordinary influence in the Congress and in the operation of the Postal Service.

OTHER FEDERAL   The unionization of federal employees outside the Postal Service and the established trades lagged far behind and is a phenomenon of the periods since World War I and the depression of the 1930s. Leaving out of consideration some developments that left few permanent marks, the resulting organizations of general coverage are the American Federation of Government Employees (AFGE is affiliated with AFL-CIO) the National Federation of Federal Employees (NFFE is not affiliated), and the National Association of Government Employees (NAGE is not affiliated). The last-named body also embraces some local-government employee unions.

In addition, several limited coverage groups exist, such as the National Treasury Employees Union, the National Customs Service Association, and several in the Immigration and Naturalization Service. Employees in the Navy yards, the arsenals, other defense establishments, the Government Printing Office, the Bureau of Engraving and Printing, and similar industrial-type establishments are heavily organized, usually in the well-established AFL-CIO trade unions. AFGE, NFFE, and NAGE, as general-purpose organizations, are the only ones that offer broad-coverage representation for white-collar workers, and the AFGE has greatly outstripped its competitors in membership in recent years. A number of professional associations, of course, include among their other purposes the advancement of the welfare of their practitioners.

THE TVA EXAMPLE   The pioneer of a modern and sophisticated approach to public service labor relations was the Tennessee Valley Authority, beginning in the 1930s. Although some formal consultative arrangements had

---

[3] Accounts of the early unionization of the Postal and other services are to be found in Sterling D. Spero, *The Labor Movement in a Government Industry: A Study of Employee Organization in the Postal Service*, New York, Macmillan, 1927, and his *Government as Employer*, New York, Remsen, 1948.

[4] The combined parent organizations that affiliate together most of the major trade unions in the United States.

been started and discontinued in the Postal Service earlier, TVA is credited with inaugurating the most thorough collective negotiations paralleling collective bargaining in the private sector that have existed in the American public service. Later, many municipalities and some of the public power operations in the Department of the Interior, such as the Bonneville Power Administration, implemented comparable policies in dealing with employee unions.

The essence of the TVA plan embraced an affirmative encouragement of employees to belong to a bona-fide union, a willingness to submit major issues of pay and working conditions to full joint exploration and discussion with union representatives, and a genuine effort to find bases for agreement between management and labor on all such issues. TVA was among the first public enterprises to enter into written agreements with unions that approximated in character and effect the binding labor contracts in the private sector. TVA had two conditions that facilitated its enlightened policy: (1) the major portion of its work force was made up of blue-collar workers who were accustomed to unionism and who formed the nucleus with which the policy was first developed; and (2) it had much wider statutory latitude in matters of pay and working conditions than did other federal establishments. TVA's success in achieving constructive labor peace was a trailblazing one, particularly its insistence that it would deal with employee unions only if they federated themselves to work with management as a unit. This specific policy helped reduce the disadvantages of negotiating with numerous separate craft unions as isolated entities. TVA now has one annual negotiation session and an annual agreement on pay and related matters with a consolidated group of blue-collar unions and one with a similar unified body of white-collar organizations.

CURRENT POLICY   Meanwhile, as in the case of the Department of the Interior, the Postal Service, and a number of military installations, the relations between management and organized labor were being worked out department by department, or establishment by establishment. It was not until 1962 that a full-scale federal-wide policy was promulgated by the President making consultation with employee organizations an affirmative aim of government management and setting forth the conditions for such arrangements.[5] This was substantially revised and strengthened in 1969.[6] The major elements of the federal policy include: (1) declaration of employee participation in personnel-policy development as a positive good; (2) affirmation of

[5] Executive Order 10988, "Employee-Management Cooperation in the Federal Service," January 17, 1962. It is interesting that, because of its independently developed and going program, TVA was exempted from this order.

[6] Executive Order 11491, "Labor-Management Relations in the Federal Service," October 29, 1969. Note the more unequivocal title of the order, indicating more ready acceptance of traditional terminology used in the private sector. Further amendments in 1975 permitted negotiation agreements to override lower-level agency regulations (but not those issued from agency headquarters) and facilitated consolidation of bargaining units (Executive Order 11838, February 6, 1975; effective May 7, 1975).

employee rights to join or not join labor organizations; (3) a Federal Labor Relations Council to administer the policy, decide major policy issues, and handle appeals on matters such as units of representation, union eligibility, and negotiability of subjects; (4) a Federal Service Impasses Panel to settle impasses on substantive issues in negotiations; (5) consultative arrangements applicable only to unions that have exclusive representation of the majority of employees in a given unit; (6) provision for written agreements; (7) elimination of agency mission, budget, organization, number of employees, technology of work, and internal security from negotiability; (8) prohibition of strikes, work stoppages, slowdowns, or picketing; (9) prescription of standards of conduct for labor organizations and fair labor practices for agencies; and (10) engagement of an Assistant Secretary of Labor to determine union eligibility, elections, and appropriate units for representation, and the Civil Service Commission to guide and assist agencies through technical advice, training, and inspection of operations.

The foregoing policy is designed primarily to apply to matters that are within the jurisdiction of individual federal departments and agencies so far as personnel policy is concerned, thus including grievance systems, work shifts, vacation schedules, safety practices, services to employees, working conditions, certain supervisory practices, promotion systems, reduction-in-force procedures, and the like, but governmentwide policy in any of these areas cannot, of course, be abrogated. Unions also have an intimate participative role in the determination of local blue-collar pay rates in each geographical area where federal employees are located, under the Coordinated Federal Wage System.

Including the long well-unionized Postal Service and the crafts and trades largely located in the Department of Defense, nearly two-thirds of the federal service is covered by units in which one union or another has the privilege of exclusive recognition of the unit's employees. There are written agreements on various working conditions between management and unions covering the great majority of employees in these units.[7]

In brief, the general federal practice is about the equivalent of that initiated by TVA in the 1930s. There is no new source for governmental authority or action; laws and regulations on personnel management are intact. But there is an orderly and workable means whereby the views of organized employees groups can be fully taken into account in development of personnel policy and procedure.

STATE AND MUNICIPAL UNIONISM

The organization of state and local employees got under way much more slowly than that of federal workers, owing no doubt to the greater hold of the spoils system on the states and cities and to a wider dispersion of

---

[7] For detailed data, see various U.S. Civil Service Commission bulletins, particularly the booklet *Union Recognition in the Federal Government—November 1974*, Washington, D.C., 1975.

personnel. The established craft groups were early allied with the appropriate local craft unions, and benevolent societies existed in great numbers in 1890 among the teachers, the police, and the firemen. Outside the recognized crafts, however, organization along union lines has taken place largely since 1910. By the 1970s the proportion of state and local government employees in unions was greater than in private industry, even excluding public school teachers, who are the most highly organized.[8]

OCCUPATIONAL FOCUS   The earliest *national* unions of state and local employees were of the craft variety. The first of these appeared among the teachers, who have generally exhibited greater solidarity than many other groups. The American Federation of Teachers is the main education group that espouses the trade-union point of view. The more professional organization of teachers, the National Education Association, while heretofore showing less inclination to behave like a union, has assumed a more militant stand in recent years. Another occupational union of national scope is the International Association of Fire Fighters, which is affiliated with the AFL-CIO. Police officers remain organized mainly in strictly local units, although statewide affiliations exist in many cases and there are several national federations of police unions, only two of which—the International Conference of Police Associations and the Fraternal Order of Police—account for large memberships.

AFSCME   The main national union of *general* coverage is the AFL-CIO-affiliated American Federation of State, County, and Municipal Employees (AFSCME). Interestingly, it is this powerful group of unmistakably trade-union-minded employees with which the aforementioned National Education Association has joined forces, along with the National Treasury Employees Union and the American Nurses' Association. The result is the largest union (in membership) in the world.[9]

AFSCME is probably the fastest-growing union in the country and also one of the most militant. This organization even asserts the right to strike and frequently practices it. Its insistence on complete bargaining rights for public employees and sponsoring of federal legislation to secure them in all states are indicative of its assertiveness in the realm of determining the conditions of employment in state and local government throughout the United States.

[8] For periodic reports on unionization, see the following: for cities, *The Municipal Year Book*, Washington, D.C., International City Management Association; for states, *The Book of the States*, Lexington, Ky., The Council of State Governments (published biennially). The basic source is the *Census of Governments*, Washington, D.C., Bureau of the Census, published every five years.

[9] This merger, under the name of Coalition of American Public Employees (CAPE), is more of a loose federation than a cohesive union. Nevertheless, it represents a most significant amalgamation of union power (*The Washington Post*, January 23, 1973, and April 30, 1975).

STATE ASSOCIATIONS   In contrast to AFSCME, the older statewide "associations" of employees in a number of states have represented a somewhat less militant stand. These organizations, originally with more focus on welfare and recreational aims, have come together under a national umbrella known as the Assembly of Governmental Employees. Generally, the state associations have been less insistent on full bargaining procedures and have eschewed use of the strike weapon.[10]

OTHER STATE-LOCAL ORGANIZATIONS   Aside from the national organizations and the older state associations, the variety of employee groups at state and locals levels almost defies analysis. Powerful organizations of general jurisdiction exist in a number of the larger communities. Also, innumerable local organizations of a craft or vertical type are to be found in cities and counties. Thus, the multiple unionism that is conspicuous in the federal service also characterizes employee organization in state and local governments—a factor which handicaps worker solidarity and collective negotiation. In spite of this, the organization of public workers in terms of sheer volume has proceeded unabated.

RECOGNITION AND AFFILIATION

RECOGNITION   Antiquated as the issue may seem now, the first problem concerning public employee union membership had to do with whether civil servants could belong to such bodies at all. In the first decade of this century two presidents in succession—Theodore Roosevelt and William Howard Taft—issued orders forbidding federal workers from associating together to solicit pay increases or other benefits from Congress and confining their congressional contacts to channels through their respective department heads.

In the face of this crippling of the growing postal unions and at a time of grave demoralization of the railway mail service, Congress retaliated with legislation in 1912 that clearly specified the right of postal workers (and, by later interpretation, all federal employees) to organize and to petition Congress on matters affecting their employment conditions and compensation.[11] Gradually, the right of association was recognized by practically all public jurisdictions in the country, with President Franklin Roosevelt giving positive support to the cause in 1937 by acknowledging that employee organizations "have a logical place in governmental affairs."[12] Meanwhile, the affirmative program of TVA and the stance of various civic organizations on the issue clearly supported the right of civil servants to organize and to be represented on matters pertaining to their own welfare.

[10] The best study of these state associations is found in U.S. Department of Labor, *State Civil Service Employee Associations*, Washington, D.C., 1973.
[11] The Lloyd-La Follette Act of 1912, 5 *U.S. Code* 7501.
[12] In his letter to Luther C. Steward, then president of the NFFE, August 16, 1937.

AFFILIATION   A later issue had to do with the question of affiliation of government unions with the general trade-union movement. Although affiliation was implicitly upheld in the federal legislation of 1912 and although most other jurisdictions have not denied the practice, there are still some vestiges of resistance to it on the grounds that it is incompatible with the stance of public employees in serving all the people. However, the prevailing thinking is to emphasize the need for difference in tactics and action by government unions without denying their freedom of association with trade unions in private employment. Affiliation of public unions with the private labor movement has also long been accepted by the governments of the United Kingdom and western Europe.

THE CHECK-OFF   One of the most important innovations in government labor relations policy that has contributed immensely to union growth has been adoption of the industrial practice of deduction of union dues from employee pay checks wherever the employee authorizes it. This voluntary policy of the employer to act as a collection agent for the union, known as the "check-off," obviously makes for stability of membership and indirectly aids management by assuring it of the representativeness and continuity of the employee organizations with which it deals. The practice is now generally used in the federal service and receives increasing acceptance in state and local employment.

OTHER EFFECTS   In response to the later militancy of state and local unions, official action at the state level has shown an increase in provision for collective consultation and negotiation arrangements. Also, a few have legislated provision for compulsory arbitration of disputes but usually where the arbitrators are themselves public officials and therefore duly endowed with legal authority. At the same time, state after state has enacted firmer laws against public service strikes, although several permit them under limited circumstances. These developments go to the heart of the deeper issues in management-employee relations about which we shall have more to say later.

WELLSPRINGS FOR UNIONIZATION

Without doubt, the principal force leading to public employee unionization has been the need sensed by these employees for a showing of solidarity in support of better working conditions and of improved rewards for work performed. A great many government jurisdictions in this country may never have awakened to the lack of regard for and mistreatment of civil servants if there had not been an attention-getting process like that generated by unions. The longstanding public apathy toward the bureaucracy and its members clearly accelerated employee organization. If such organization had to be justified purely on rational grounds, it could certainly be defended as a necessary antidote to public neglect.

Yet, this is hardly the whole story. Reasons and motivations for unionization are in reality more complex. This should be evident, if on no other bases, from the fact that unions continue to expand in the public service even after the conditions of employment have been vastly improved and modern personnel management is widely practiced. To be sure, some of this phenomenon may be interpreted as an effort to preserve gains already enjoyed, but perhaps the following circumstances or factors also go far to explain why unions hold and increase their membership:

1. *The union makes it possible for employees to express their point of view to the legislative branch and to management as a whole.* We must acknowledge that there are many matters in the fundamental employment relationship—pay, for example—which are commonly beyond the scope of authority of the executive side of government and certainly outside the jurisdiction of individual managers. Even if the legislative branch is not involved, many personnel policy matters cannot be settled within the typical employee-supervisor relationship. A personnel issue that cuts across the board in a public agency or in a whole governmental jurisdiction calls for collective representation of employees. One of the most effective ways of securing such representation on a valid basis has been through voluntary association of employees into organized groups, whether they be labeled unions or otherwise.

2. A corollary to this collective purpose of unionism on overall policy matters is *the convenience to management that a union provides when management honestly wants to secure the real opinions of employees as a group,* rather than to rely wholly on the faulty distillation of opinion that slowly filters through the supervisory line.

3. *A union is something belonging to the employee.* What it seeks and what it does is a part of him. It provides a feeling of identification with the securing of certain personnel objectives that is not present when the solution to personnel policies—even when they are highly acceptable—is handed to workers by management. Employees want to do something for themselves, no matter how enlightened an organization's personnel administration is.

4. *A voluntary employee organization provides an outlet for natural social aspirations of employees which the work in office or shop may not make possible.* This is particularly the case for workers at routine, repetitive tasks. Whether it be garbage collection or operating a duplicating machine, guarding a museum or reading water meters, making out tax bills or typing reports, the work may be such that all of one's job satisfaction cannot be derived from performance of the duties themselves, as may be more likely in professional and executive positions. Union membership gives

the employee a chance at a kind of association and even avenues of recognition and advancement not present on the job. If job satisfaction can be increased in this way, it is to management's advantage to permit and encourage voluntary unionism even though management may also be doing all it can to make the work satisfying and attractive.

The foregoing considerations make for more reconciliation than may appear on the surface between management's responsibility for the welfare and motivation of employees and the acceptance of unionism as a continuing feature of our society. The growth and continuation of union organizations does not make good personnel management any less important; nor does enlightened personnel practice eliminate a useful role for unions. Some advice from the industrial world is relevant here:

> Managers who have tried to do everything for their employees are often bewildered, hurt, or angered when these employees want to do something for *themselves* through membership in a labor organization. These employers gain little by regarding unionization as an insult or as an evidence of failure on their part. . . . The real challenge is for these managements to deal constructively with this new organization which their employees have chosen to represent them.[13]

INFLUENCE OF UNIONIZATION

Study of the constitutions of some of the older staff-association-type organizations would suggest that they are comparatively conservative bodies. Improving working conditions and employee welfare ranked as only one among such purposes as promoting solidarity and comradeship, protecting and extending the merit system, and improving the quality of public administration. These high-flown objectives were ostensibly sought through social and recreational activities, service and benevolent functions, educational and propagandistic undertakings, and representation of employees before administrative officers and legislatures. Promoting efficiency in government service and protecting the merit system still find expression in many association constitutions.

The more definitely union-type organizations, like AFSCME, take a typical trade-union stance, declaring their "God-given" right to organize and confining their aims to employee welfare and unity. Their concentration, to be sure, has been on matters of pay and general working conditions. At times, however, especially in the case of school teachers and police, such unions have sought to influence public policy on the substantive issues of administration—such as educational method, budgets, crime-fighting, and the like.

[13] Paul Pigors and Charles A. Myers, *Personnel Administration: A Point of View and a Method*, 7th ed., New York, McGraw-Hill, 1973, p. 153.

FOSTERING REFORMS

Often it was union backing that helped put across personnel measures that management itself should have been soliciting on behalf of good administration. Enlightened management in general and improvement of the lot of public employees in particular have not always received wholehearted and unrelenting initiative from the managerial side. Perhaps this has been due in part to the popular distrust and antipathy toward government workers that so long clouded American public administration. Bringing pressure to bear on legislative bodies to enact progressive personnel statutes too often became the task of the employees themselves. Occasionally they had the support of enlightened civic groups like the National Civil Service League, one of its local counterparts, or a League of Women Voters, but even more potent was employee union affiliation with the general labor movement, an element especially useful in rallying legislative and public support for needed personnel laws.

Examples of legislation at the federal level for which unions can take considerable credit are the first Classification Act, the Retirement Act, and the many liberalizations of these laws in subsequent years. Particularly in state and local legislative halls the presence of union representatives has served as a check on inroads upon the merit system and has facilitated establishment of machinery for employee-management consultation. Unions have historically been at the fore in the fights to sustain and extend the merit system and in numerous instances have been responsible for introduction of position-classification plans, salary standardization, and similar reforms.

NEGOTIATION AND BARGAINING PROCEDURES

The most notable impact of union organization and pressure during recent years has been in establishment by law or practice of formal methods for structuring the relations between management and employee organizations. The example of the private sector has been exploited to the fullest, whether justifiably so or not. With varying results, and perhaps with debatable effects in many jurisdictions, procedures closely resembling those of collective bargaining in private industry have been widely adopted. The merits and risks of these processes will be discussed later, but quite apart from any value judgments that might be made about them, the fact is that formal representation, negotiation, bargaining, and contractual agreements have become the order of the day in settling numerous personnel policies for great segments of municipal, state, and federal government.

SOME SHORTCOMINGS

Aside from any reservations that may be discernible later about collective bargaining or any of several other issues in management-union relations in the public sector, note must be taken here of certain evident deficiences of unionization—in terms of the long-range public interest. In at least the following three respects public union behavior has borrowed too heavily from that of industrial unions: (1) the tendency to insist that all workers on identical or roughly similar tasks must receive the same pay, regardless of the productivity resulting from the effort, initiative, or attitude the individual worker brings to his job; (2) the assumption that the desirable work standard is the minimum acceptable rather than maximum or optimum accomplishment; and (3) the continuous pressure that, above all else, the seniority principle must prevail.[14] In serving such ends, unions can hardly be said to foster the public interest.

In addition, government unions have tended to overemphasize the security aspects of employment and to be overzealous in the defense of their members, no matter what the circumstances. They have too often failed to support reasonable measures to ensure discipline, tending to take the tack that whatever management does by way of restraint or punishment administered to an employee must ipso facto be wrong. They are inclined to favor rigidity in administrative procedures and to resist the exercise of administrative discretion. In all these respects, unions render a disservice to their cause, for the conditions of protectionism and inflexibility to which their attitudes give rise are damaging to the prestige of public employment. None of these postures contributes in the long run to the best interests of well-motivated, hard-working civil servants.

THE FUNDAMENTAL QUESTION—HOW DIFFERENT IS GOVERNMENT?

Before we undertake a closer analysis of practices and problems in formal collective relations and an evaluation of the major unsettled issues on the whole subject, a more basic question must be faced. That there are economic, social, and psychological justifications for union organization in the public service is not to be gainsaid. Without giving the matter much thought, many persons—union leaders, managers, legislators—articulate these justifications solely in terms of parallelism with private employment and thereby jump to the conclusion that all implementing policies and processes in government should parallel those in the private sphere.

A few moments study and reflection almost certainly elicit recognition that there are some inescapable differences between government as employer and industry as employer. The more refined questions are: how important are these differences? and to what extent must they influence the assump-

---

[14] Industry has been taken to task for having come to accept, for the most part, such concepts: Herbert L. Marx, Jr., "Union Philosophy: The Basic Fallacies," *Personnel*, September–October, 1959, p. 31.

Because government unions purport to represent employees and to support good government, it does not follow that their activities are always in the public interest. Frederick C. Mosher points out: "The most cogent argument against some public unions today concerns not political democracy and popular sovereignty, but their pressure toward conformism and mediocrity" (*Democracy and the Public Service*, New York, Oxford University Press, 1968, p. 200).

tions and practices involved in relations between public managers and public unions?

GOVERNMENT—REPRESENTATIVE OF ALL THE PEOPLE

Those who oversimplify the nature and problems of organized labor relations in the public service tend to overlook the fact that *government is not just another industry.* It is not just slightly different; it operates in a markedly different milieu.

In the private sector, the owners and managers on the one hand and the organization of their workers on the other are essentially equal powers before the law. They jockey for advantage or accommodation in an ostensibly free contest, inhibited only by the pressures of economic competition and by the ground rules set up by government as expressed in law and regulation. Neither side has any peculiar role or obligation to represent or even to seek the general *public* interest. Whatever they can agree to, without destroying their enterprise in the give and take of the marketplace, they are free to pursue.

Government—even a single local government—is not merely one of two parties before the law. It is the instrument of democracy. What its legislators decree becomes the law, and what its officials are under oath to administer is a fair and impartial enforcement of that law as it applies *to all parties.*

The most important single democratic control by the people is the control of government expenditures. Specific processes are set up by constitution and statute as to how much money is to be spent and for what purposes it is to be spent. Administrative agencies submit budgets; chief executives review, modify, and promulgate these budgets into consolidated fiscal programs; and legislative bodies accept, modify, or reject these programs and enact tax measures to supply the necessary revenue. Since salaries of public employees constitute overwhelmingly large proportions of these budgets—especially in state and local governments—this subject of pay, the main ingredient of industrial labor relations, is subject to a vastly different set of influences in government. In short, it is part of the total political process. And so is every other policy, expenditure, or practice that affects the government worker's employment relationship and working conditions. Such subjects are not simply the concern of employee unions and a few public managers. Through legislators and executive officials, they are the concern of the *whole people.*

Thus, the interests of government employees is *one of many competing interests* that must be ultimately resolved in the political arena, not just a contest between the organization representing those employees and a particular government executive or body of executives. As two discerning writers put the matter, in reference to the typical city mayor: "What he gives to the union must be taken from some other interest group or from taxpayers. His is the job of coordinating these competing claims while remaining politically viable."[15] These statements express in capsule form the most fundamental distinction that must be kept in mind between labor relations in private business and management-employee relations in the public sector. In essence, *anything in the public arena is a political issue*, and no special procedure or philosophy borrowed from the private sector can alter that reality.

Furthermore, government—and its employees—is the very body that sets the rules for the private arena. Beginning with the ballot and activated through duly established agencies administering laws and programs legislated by elected representatives of the people, it is the agent of the whole people. This means that the public as a whole must have the ultimate power in setting and operating the rules for labor relations within the public service. As we shall see later, this fact has the most profound effect on the *meaning and content* of negotiation, bargaining, and agreement (or dispute) between public employee unions and public officials.[16]

THE MANDATE OF THE LAW

A second distinction between the public and private sectors is an extension of the political-issue reality just discussed. Most of the conditions of employment in the public service, including pay, have been mandated by law. Unless or until those laws are changed, the executive arm of a government cannot enter into a bilateral agreement with its employees that abrogates or even modifies those laws. This is why public unions frequently pay more attention to legislative bodies than to executive managers in public jurisdictions. This fact alone makes for a major difference from the atmosphere and machinery of labor relations in the business world.

To be sure, these very laws can and do delegate authority to and obligate government executives to recognize unions of their employees, to deal with them in prescribed ways, and to make agreements in specified areas of policy. Examples of such prescription will be forthcoming in the next chapter. The important point here is simply that, in government, one party to the usual labor relations process itself sets the rules. It is not just an "equal" with employee organization.

DIFFUSION OF AUTHORITY

As a corollary to the foregoing points, there is the simple fact that decision-making authority in government is far more diffused than it is in private

---

[15] Wellington and Winter, *op. cit.*, p. 21. These authors are among the few who have cogently pointed out the distinguishing political characteristics of unionism in the public service. Most union leaders and many politicians seeking votes are in the habit of drawing thoughtless and false parallels with industrial labor relations.

[16] The distinction even affects some employees' so-called right to organize. For example, state-employed labor mediators and federal employees of the National Labor Relations Board or Federal Mediation Service must play an impartial role in dealing with labor disputes in the private sector over which they have jurisdiction. How can they maintain even the appearance of impartiality if they are allowed to be members of unions that are affiliated with national organizations embracing groups that are on one side of disputes they must help settle?

industry. The great bulk of public employees work for *one branch* of government, the executive or administrative branch. Even within that branch, power is not only circumscribed by principle, criterion, or precedent set out in law, but it is shared and checked and rechecked at many points. There is cogent reason for such diffusion, although there are many instances where it has unquestionably gone too far. It has, nevertheless, been quite deliberate —to prevent the overconcentration of power in public officials. Oversimplified talk about collective bargaining in the public service seems to ignore this reality. Any suggestion that union representatives should share or be *equal* partners with public officials collectively in determining any kind of public policy, even personnel policy, would imply that they should have power beyond that of the officials themselves who are supposed to be so thoroughly checked by this very diffusion of decision-making authority.

Especially relevant to the concerns of public employee unions is the problem of identifying whom to deal with. Just who constitutes management? Who has the power to make commitments? Is it the head of a particular establishment? Is it at no less a point than the chief executive of the state or municipality or other jurisdiction involved?

The answer varies, of course, with each situation and usually with each subject of concern. As already noted, pay may be set by law, so that even the chief executive can only recommend, not act finally, in that area. In contrast, the working environment, supervision, performance evaluation, training programs, and the like, may well be within the province of the department or institutional administrator. Under some circumstances, even facets of pay scales, schedules for special groups of occupations, or procedures for implementation of pay standards are under the control of chief executives or their agents, and they have the power to make agreements with unions in those areas. But they almost never can make commitments that involve major expenditures of funds beyond those already appropriated.

Obviously the government union may have to negotiate with both executive management and the legislative body on some matters, while on others it may settle its concerns or even "bargain" with the head of an agency or his representative. No such diffusion exists in the ordinary private enterprise. One clearly identifiable set of managers represents the owners or stockholders on every conceivable personnel issue that comes up.

Although the diffusion of authority in the public service, mostly designed to ensure democratic control, poses problems for organizing a practicable relationship between management and unions, it also has its advantages from the union point of view. When union leaders and the employees they represent are unable to achieve their ends in concert with administrative officials, they may and usually do turn to the political process to attain their goals. This may entail bringing pressure on the appropriate legislative body, making or withholding contributions to political campaigns or causes, or otherwise seeking to influence elections or public policy development. Often they work both the bargaining-with-management approach and the political process at the same time. Nothing betrays the positive uniqueness of government employee labor relations more clearly than this simple fact of public union behavior.

SIGNIFICANCE OF DIFFERENCES

The purpose of this analysis is not to belabor the issue of sovereignty. Sovereign or not, government is the creature and agent of the total citizenry; and the only institution that can supersede it is some higher level of government. To hold otherwise would give democracy no meaning. Nor is this presentation meant to despair of a meaningful kind of policy and procedure to govern labor relations in government employment. Rather, the objective here is to rid our minds of the simplistic notions so often expressed that processes or even principles of labor relations in the private sector are transferable to public employment.

The net effect of what has been said adds up to the following significant conclusions on the character of relationships between government management and organized government employees:

1. One party to the relationship—the employer, including all branches of government—must and does set the rules, for it is the instrument of the whole people. It is not just an ordinary employer.
2. Many aspects of personnel policy are and will continue to be established by law. The union role in this respect is simply one of a competing interest in the political arena. Wellington and Winter state the point as clearly as it can be said: ". . . the principal issue in public employee unionism is the distribution of political power among those groups pressing claims on government."[17]
3. The subjects available for negotiation and settlement between administrative management and unions will almost invariably be more limited than is the case in the private sector.
4. As a result of the foregoing conditions, the processes of negotiation and bargaining will be substantially different from those in private business.
5. Likewise, the settlement of disputes will follow quite different patterns from those prevailing in private employment.

The implications of these conclusions will become clearer as we explore more fully the experiences and problems of collective negotiation and bargaining in the public service.

---

[17] *Op. cit.*, p. 202. The need for broader representation of interests is also well presented in Sara Silbiger, "The Missing Public — Collective Bargaining in Public Employment," *Public Personnel Management*, September-October, 1975.

CHAPTER 20

Collective
Negotiation
and Bargaining

WITHOUT DOUBT THE most dramatic impact on public personnel administration in the United States during the 1960s and 1970s, particularly in local governments, has been brought about by the growing bilateralism in determining personnel policy. Government leadership, including legislative bodies, has come to recognize the necessity for systematic sharing of its personnel decision-making with representatives of organized public employees. This development has been consonant with burgeoning urbanization, increasing demands for public services, and the attendant upsurge in numbers of municipal employees.

In the preceding chapter reference was made at various points to collective negotiation and collective bargaining. These are the processes of management-union communication and joint determination that give rise to the term *bilateralism*. They refer to a series of procedures under which certain issues affecting employee welfare, compensation, advancement, or working conditions are determined, not by unilateral action of management, but by agreement with employees collectively.

The phrase "collective bargaining" was borrowed from labor relations parlance in the private sector without much regard for the essential differences in circumstances in government employment. Technically, it cannot mean in the public service exactly what it means in industry, but it has been appropriated so widely and even is used in state statutes, so that it becomes pointless to avoid using the term in government entirely. If bargaining is defined as a process in which two *equal* parties with *equal* power seek to come to some mutual understanding on a proposition, then what we have in govern-

338

ment is actually something different. This is for the simple reason, already discussed at length in the preceding chapter, that government leadership as one party—often including legislative, executive, and judicial branches—necessarily possesses the superior ultimate power. What is called bargaining in the public service is not in reality a contest between equals.

This situation has led some authorities to prefer the term *negotiation*.[1] Considering the final powers inevitably and understandably reserved by the government involved and the usual narrower range of issues dealt with in public labor relations, this would be the preferable terminology. Nevertheless, no single writer can buck an overwhelming trend in the use of language. Hence, we shall use the words *negotiation* and *bargaining* in referring to the preliminary and more sophisticated stages, respectively, in formalized management-union relations in government employment—fully recognizing that we are not talking about the fuller, more traditional meaning of the words as they were developed in the private sector.

THE NEED FOR BILATERALISM

That there is a need for representation on the part of employees and for consultation and shared decision-making on the part of management may properly be inferred from all that has been said not only in this part of the book but in the various references to a participative type of administration that is espoused time and again in these pages. Certainly representatives of employees as a group are likely to secure a more respectful hearing from management and to speak with more assurance and authority than would employees speaking individually. Management, in turn, has much to gain from seeking employee viewpoints collectively.

1. Quite apart from the quality of daily supervision and other attributes of the motivational environment, management frequently needs to test employee interest and gauge employee opinion on service-wide policy matters that are beyond the jurisdiction of individual executives or work units.
2. Soliciting employee views on prospective personnel policy avoids pitfalls that may not always be perceived by management acting alone, preoccupied as it is with the bird's-eye view.
3. Consultation with employees usually creates better understanding and acceptance of change. Ideas or reforms that might have been resisted if sprung on employees at a full-blown stage may actually enlist their support when employee representatives are brought in on the ground floor of initial planning.

---

[1] E.g., Felix A. Nigro, *Management-Employee Relations in the Public Service*, Chicago, International Personnel Management Association, 1969, p. 20 and *passim*. Another book refers to importation of full private-sector bargaining into the public service as "mindless" (Harry H. Wellington and Ralph K. Winter, Jr., *The Unions and the Cities*, Washington, D.C., The Brookings Institution, 1971, p. 202).

4. Management frequently benefits by the positive ideas and proposals initiated by employee groups.
5. Mutual discussion promotes rapport and understanding that builds a useful continuing relationship and reduces the potentiality of conflict.

Of course, such consultation may be secured in a variety of ways. Where no employee organization of any kind exists, it behooves public management to contrive some way to get the collective viewpoints of the employees as a body. This may be done through an established system of councils to which employees are asked to elect representatives from among their number. If a staff association or union peculiar to the particular establishment exists, such as a firefighters' association or a customs officers' union, this would be the logical organ through which to ascertain the staff views. Similarly, if employees are organized in a union of general jurisdiction and affiliated with outside groups, management would likewise find it advantageous to deal with that entity. Ordinarily, the better and more simply organized employees are, the easier it is for management to know how to proceed and with whom to negotiate.

It follows that responsible unionism can be a positive asset, not only in attaining sound personnel policies and good working conditions for employees but in assuring management that the policies and conditions finally established are understood and acceptable to employees. It is a standard tenet of administration that the most effective and durable actions are those in which there has been the widest participation in their development. Responsible unionism entails assurance that all or most employees in an organization are being honestly and accurately represented in their desires and concerns, that employees will live up to their end of any bargain arrived at, that union leaders will discipline their members to comply with agreements, and that these leaders, as well as management, can be depended on to keep their word and to cooperate in effectuating agreed-upon policy. These are the ideal results that may properly be expected to flow from judicious and sensible collective bargaining.

GROWTH OF NEGOTIATION AND BARGAINING PRACTICES

Whether these ideals are being achieved will be a subject for continuing evaluation by managerial and union participants, by scholars, and by the American public in general. But one thing is not in doubt: the formalization of management-union relations into one variety or another of collective negotiation or bargaining is rapidly gaining headway throughout the American public service.

All but a few states now have laws on their statute books authorizing some degree of formalized relationship between management and unions, ranging from acknowledgement of the right of union membership and representation, to procedures for consultation ("meet and confer"), to collective bargaining in the fullest sense in which it can be applied in the public service.[2]

Almost all major cities, whether controlled by state statute or not, are engaged in some degree of the process of bargaining, especially with school teachers, police officers, and various crafts and trades. Various agencies of the federal government engage in bargaining arrangements, especially the TVA, which initiated the practice, and the Postal Service, which has "collective-bargaining agreements" specifically authorized in its enabling legislation. In brief, the existence of formal systems for negotiation and bargaining is one of the hallmarks of the current era in public personnel administration.[3]

DEVELOPMENTS IN STATE AND LOCAL GOVERNMENTS

STATES   Almost all state laws governing management-union relations were passed in the 1960s and 1970s. They do not supersede basic merit system laws but obviously affect their administration. Most of the laws set forth the conditions and steps to be followed in negotiation and consultation, and many provide explicitly for bargaining procedures and written agreements between management and unions. Usually they define the negotiable subjects and exclude matters covered by law and civil service regulation, thus preserving current provisions for merit system employment. "The intention of this legislation clearly is to guarantee the employees as large a scope for collective negotiations as is possible in government, with adequate protection at the same time for the management and the public against irresponsible employee actions."[4] The laws generally apply to local government employees and unions as well as to state agencies. Some are applicable only to specific categories, such as public school teachers.

The typical state law provides for various contingencies in the event that agreement cannot be reached between management and unions (an "impasse" in labor relations parlance) or when grievances occur over the manner in which

[2] See W. Donald Heisel, *New Questions and Answers on Public Employee Negotiation*, Chicago, International Personnel Management Association, 1973. This is a useful manual stressing practical approaches for conferring, negotiating, and bargaining with organized employees.

[3] Both Canada and the United Kingdom, with whom we share much of our cultural and legal background, have moved ahead with even greater speed and sophistication in developing labor-management relations in the public service. Canada has long had most of the elements of collective bargaining as known in the private sector in its dealings with unions in the provinces and municipalities, and has extended much of what has been learned in the process to its federal government. The United Kingdom has, since World War I, channeled its consultation with "staff associations" through a hierarchy of Whitley Councils (named after the founder, J. H. Whitley), consisting of individual councils in each department, supplemented by district and office "works committees," and a National Whitley Council on overall policy. These councils, each with equal representation from the "official side" and the "staff side," come to agreement on matters within their respective spheres of competence, which understandings become operative unless Parliament acts otherwise, thus preserving legislative authority. Similar councils have evolved in British local governments.

[4] Nigro, *op. cit.*, p. 20.

agreements are being implemented. Most provide for mediation and some ultimate adjudication of the issue. Those that provide for arbitration by a third party almost invariably require confirmation or permit veto by either the chief executive or the legislature or both. Such a procedure is understandable in view of "the inescapable fact that government is government," as one official expressed the point.[5]

A few states have acknowledged possible use of the ultimate sanction of organized employees—the strike. But in such instances either certain employees—such as those engaged in health and safety activities, like hospitals, fire protection, or police work—are excluded from the strike possibility, or various procedures are devised to override a strike and outlaw it whenever it jeopardizes public safety. The overwhelming majority of states, even where they have adopted modern collective bargaining laws, continue to prohibit public employees from resorting to a strike or any kind of work stoppage.

MUNICIPALITIES   The labor relations practices of most cities, at least in broad outline, are governed by state law. In those instances where state controls are minimal or nonexistent, municipal governments have had to work out their salvation in this field independently. It was in this arena that unions such as the AFSCME and the American Federation of Teachers made their greatest conquests during the 1960s and early 1970s. Many a mayor and city council, or local school board, acceded to full collective bargaining processes or to pay raises and other gains that might never have been established if they had not felt the threat of isolation from state or federal intervention and the prospect or reality of a debilitating work stoppage.

Furthermore, the internal politics of the situation has made the municipality the most vulnerable to union power, in some instances to the loss of other interest groups with at least equal claims. A united front by a city employer in a labor dispute is almost impossible. For example, under any threat of a strike by teachers, police, or other critically needed workers, a large part of a mayor's political constituency will, in many cases, press for a quick elimination of the threat (or end to the strike if it has already occurred) with little concern for the cost of settlement.[6]

Little wonder that the focus of concern about the impact of collective bargaining has been on the cities. This is where the controversial action has primarily occurred. It is where nationally directed unions have displayed their most strident militancy and exerted their greatest power and where public officials were the least prepared and sophisticated to protect the interests of the general public. Few major cities have escaped the discomfort

---

[5] Robert D. Helsby, Chairman, New York State Public Employment Relations Board, in a statement presented at the 1972 National Conference on Public Information in New York City.

[6] This is the observation of Wellington and Winter, as a result of their intensive study of the behavior of American municipalities in labor relations (*op. cit.*, p. 25 and *passim*).

and even dangers to the public welfare occasioned by serious labor disputes. This is not to say that what the unions gained was always too much or that the gains were not deserved, but only to say that, in principle and practice, many a jurisdiction was unprepared, and effective procedures had not been established. Now that most states have legislated in this field and as municipal officials have become better prepared psychologically and technically to cope with labor issues, there is prospect of more balanced handling of such matters in the general public interest.[7]

DEVELOPMENTS IN THE FEDERAL SERVICE

Various branches of the federal service have had long experience with unionization and at least the "meet-and-confer" type of negotiations. Only a few, however, can be said to practice genuine collective bargaining, even in the limited sense used in public employment. Most notable among these are the Postal Service and TVA.

TVA   While TVA was a trail-blazer in the field as early as the 1930s, its relationships with unions are entirely the product of administrative discretion and many years of management-union agreement. The outstanding features of the TVA experience are its comparative freedom from statutory personnel controls so typical of the average public agency and its insistence on dealing with unions only through collective vehicles instead of with each union separately.[8]

POSTAL SERVICE   Unions in the Postal Service had a long history of potency in the political sense, primarily with committees of the Congress concerned with postal and civil service affairs. For many years they set the pace for pay scales and other benefits applying to the total federal service. It remained for the Postal Reorganization Act of 1970, however, to establish the full complement of bargaining procedures for postal workers. Consistent with the Act's basic thrust to operate the Postal Service like a private corporation and to reduce congressional involvement in postal affairs, the Act provides for practically all the trappings of unionization, exclusive recognition, bargaining, and arbitration that obtain in private enterprise.

---

[7] Intensive training in management obligations and techniques in bargaining and in handling work stoppages have been conducted by organizations such as the National League of Cities, the International City Management Association, and the International Personnel Management Association.

A great many books, too numerous to list here, on unionism and collective bargaining in public education and police administration have appeared in recent years. The most important are listed, with annotations, in the bibliography for this chapter at the end of the book. Mention many be made here of a briefer treatment that gives a good overview of the situation in police departments: Harvey A. Juris and Peter Feuille, "Employee Organizations," appearing as Chapter 11 in *Police Personnel Administration*, O. Glenn Stahl and Richard A. Staufenberger, eds., Washington, D.C., Police Foundation, 1974.

[8] See the discussion in somewhat greater detail in Chapter 19.

The main difference between bargaining in the Postal Service and that in the typical industrial setting lies in the scope of subject-matter open to negotiation. Although the major personnel components, including basic pay levels, are available for the bargaining table, a number of personnel laws of general application throughout the federal service continue to apply to the Postal Service, such as retirement, injury compensation, and veteran preference.

Labor disputes in the Postal Service, following the usual course of fact-finding and mediation efforts, may ultimately be settled by final and binding arbitration. In this respect, not even the usual power reserved to chief executives or legislatures can overturn an arbitration award. Except for the authority of the President of the United States to appoint, with Senate approval, nine members of the eleven-member Board of Governors, the American people at large have lost any direct control or influence over the operations of the U.S. Postal Service. In other words, postal employees, through their unions, have a far more effective voice in postal affairs than does the presumed beneficiary of postal services, the general public. Only by change in the basic legislation itself can the public interest be asserted, and even such change could not abrogate any contract that had previously been entered into by the Postal Service.

DEFENSE   Especially in connection with the many thousands of trades and labor employees in arsenals, munitions plants, laboratories, military bases, and repair facilities, there is also a long history of management-union relations in the nation's largest public agency, the Department of Defense. For many years units of this department, after consultation with appropriate unions, set the hourly pay rates for blue-collar trades and labor jobs in hundreds of locations throughout the nation and the world. Although these rates are now established under a governmentwide coordinated system, Defense is still the largest and most influential user of the process. The procedure that is followed, while allowing for a very strong union input through governmentwide bodies on which unions have rotational membership, cannot be considered an actual process of bargaining.

In Defense alone the volume of bargaining units and written agreements executed numbers in the thousands. As in other departments of the federal government, subjects covered in bargaining embrace promotion procedures, grievance adjudication, safety conditions, overtime and vacation scheduling, various areas of union representation and responsibility, and a host of working-condition items.

GENERAL POLICY   The main elements of federal labor relations policy, applying to Defense as well as other agencies, have already been summarized in the preceding chapter. Founded solely on executive order, the policy prescribes the conditions under which individual departments, agencies, or sub-units of these may negotiate collectively with unions and enter into binding agreements. The major deviations from industrial bargaining practice are:

(1) final settlement of disputes not resolvable at the bargaining table is reserved to a Federal Service Impasses Panel made up of seven persons appointed
by the President; and (2) matters such as agency mission, budgets, organizational arrangements, the technology of work processes, determination of
numbers of employees needed for any given function, and matters of internal
security are removed at the outset from any negotiability with unions.

Bilateralism, in spite of some limitations and a contention by unions that
a statutory base for the system is necessary, is clearly a way of life in the
federal service, as it is in most major cities and many states. One piece of
evidence that the current federal policy works reasonably well is the fact that
comparatively few instances of bargaining have required third-party
involvement.[9]

THE ELEMENTS OF BARGAINING

Collective bargaining, though scarcely a half-century old in the private sector,
has built up a formidable technology that makes it a field of study in itself.
Insofar as industrial issues have been adjudicated by the National Labor
Relations Board and by the courts, a great volume of case law has developed
—a condition that keeps a major segment of the legal profession fully
occupied, whether they work for employers or unions or mediation and
arbitration organizations.[10] The steps in the process, the nomenclature, the
classification of problems and issues, the successes and failures, the legal
decisions, the perennial counsel from scholars and practitioners on approaches
that work and pitfalls to avoid—all combine to make it the most complicated,
the most elusive, and consequently the most written-about aspect of the
personnel function. Add to this the unique and special problems of application in the public service, and the subject becomes a very technical one
indeed. Therefore, in a book of this dimension, we can only deal with the
highlights, try to clarify a few definitions, and point up some of the pros and
cons relating to the most important problems that emerge.

UNIT DETERMINATION

The basic structural step necessary to a practicable bargaining environment
is determination of the "unit"—either organizational or occupational—
within which and regarding which bargaining is to take place. The usual
definition is that a unit is any group of employees who have a "community
of interest" either by virtue of having a common occupation or being engaged
in the same activity or program of work. The unit is not necessarily co-

---

[9] As of 1974, less than 16 percent of bargaining situations had to be moved to third-
party settlement, and most of these involved only mediation (Robert E. Hampton
[Chairman, U.S. Civil Service Commission], "A Report on Bilateralism in the Federal
Service," *Civil Service Journal*, July–September 1974, p. 7).

[10] With considerable justification, some shrewd observer has dubbed the advent of
collective bargaining and all its trappings "the lawyers' full employment plan."

terminous with an organizational segment (department, division, branch, etc.) identifiable in a public agency. Seldom is it an entire jurisdiction, a state service or a municipal service. In the federal government it is rarely an entire agency.

Determining the bargaining unit in industry is comparatively easy. Usually a plant or operation is a homogeneous entity, employing a body of workers with obviously equal or similar concerns. The layers of supervision are readily distinguishable. Ordinarily only groups such as engineering or maintenance personnel pose questions of separate treatment.

In public jurisdictions, the interorganizational relationships, the range of occupational skills, frequent geographical dispersion, across-the-board application of basic benefits like pay, retirement, and leave, and the existence of a variety of interrelated services rather than physical products—all contribute to far greater complexity in deciding on an appropriate unit in which a single union can represent employees. Extreme specialization in unionism adds further to the complications. Organization by craft and trade often prevents a reasonable solution and sometimes results in ridiculously small units composed of only three or four employees, simply because they refuse to be identified with any other group.

A variety of methods for resolving issues of unit determination are resorted to. In some places arbitration is used; others allow a specified neutral official to settle the matter; and in some instances the issue is determined in courts of law. The program in the federal service calls for final decisions in disputes over unit determination to be made by a designated Assistant Secretary of Labor. This is an example of a condition already emphasized in the preceding chapter—the fact that in the last analysis some branch of officialdom must act as arbiter in making bargaining work.

In the long run, the only sensible solution to unit determination is to insist on dealing with general-purpose or so-called industrial-type unions or on requiring occupational-type unions in a given agency to create a common mechanism for bargaining purposes, as TVA has successfully done for many years. The objectives of constructive management-union relations are not served when management is put to the continuing expense and trauma of negotiating separately with multifarious craft-type unions when common working conditions apply to them all. It makes good sense from the employee point of view as well as management's for general-purpose unionization to be promoted as the most direct, simple, and effective form of employee representation.

EXCLUSIVE RECOGNITION

Contrary to the theory of labor relations that employees are yearning for representation and know exactly what they want, both industry and government are rife with instances of more than one union competing for membership among the same group of employees. Sometimes even when only one union is involved, it may be striving merely to convince most employees in an establishment that they should be represented at all. Thus, determining the unit for representation does not end the problem of finding who should represent employees. The rational solution in collective bargaining practice is to recognize only a union that can muster the support of a majority of employees in a given unit. Such a union becomes the exclusive representative, and management is not expected to (or is required not to) deal with any other organization purporting to speak for the same unit of employees. This principle is known as "exclusive recognition."[11]

Obviously, if there is competition or if there is any doubt about a union actually having a majority of the employees in a given unit as its members, the question can be resolved only by an election. In such a ballot employees are asked whether they want one or another union to represent them or whether they prefer to have no union at all. If no one union gets a majority, then whatever bargaining procedures are specified in a jurisdiction simply cannot be put into effect in the particular unit involved. Usually, substantial intervals of a year or more are required before another election may be held. Elections are ordinarily conducted or monitored by an outside third party or by a state labor department or the U.S. Department of Labor.

MANAGEMENT REPRESENTATION

The general question of "Who is management?" in the government milieu has been explored in the general discussion on diffusion of authority in the preceding chapter. The main point to be made here is that when it comes to the explicit process of bargaining, management must be represented by that official, or his agent, who is responsible for the policies and operations of the unit concerned. This leaves aside (for this purpose only) the matter of involvement of higher management, the legislative body, and others. Clearly, then, the assumption here is that what is negotiable and bargainable for a given unit is only that collection of policies and practices over which the designated manager has definite responsibility.

Ordinarily the head of the establishment cannot personally sit through all the negotiating sessions, which may carry on for days, weeks, or even months at a time. Although there are numerous exceptions, the tendency is for the personnel agency or office to carry on the discussions on behalf of management. This is a thoroughly logical practice, providing competence of the character needed is present in the personnel establishment.

If there is any question about such competence, it should be just as much a matter of concern with regard to other aspects of the personnel function as it is in relation to conducting negotiations with unions. In other words, if this

---

[11] ". . . exclusive recognition by labor organizations is the only meaningful form of employee representation and should be the only sanctioned form" (Marvin J. Levine, "Dealing with Inadequacies in Collective Bargaining in the Federal Government," *Public Personnel Review*, July 1969, p. 168). Since this article was written, the federal government adopted exclusive recognition as its basic policy for representation. Similarly, this principle is applied almost universally in state and municipal bargaining units.

office is ably equipped to handle the total personnel operation, it is competent to perform this role as well. The expertise on all policies affecting employees is presumably located here, and the personnel office is in the best position to coordinate and unify the management position on issues that arise. Acknowledgedly, it will have to consult the head of the agency or the budget and fiscal officers frequently, but such checking would be essential for any negotiator selected.[12] It is reasonable for a jurisdiction to set up special machinery for adjudicating unit determination, conducting elections, and resolving impasses in negotiations, but there is no good reason for a well-staffed and competent personnel organization to be bypassed when it comes to representing management at the bargaining table.

SUBJECTS FOR BARGAINING

Much has already been said about the restriction on bargaining created by so many features of public personnel systems being embedded in law and regulation. From the viewpoint of the general public, this is as it should be. When ultimate decisions are made on fundamental matters such as merit principles and practices, or on any action that might involve substantial expenditures of funds, there are many groups in the body politic besides a union of government employees and a small coterie of administrative officials who have a legitimate interest in the result and just cause for participating in arriving at the decisions. Examples are the clientele of government services that may be slighted if certain public employees get all they want, legislators who were elected to represent the general interests of their constituencies, citizen or professional associations that are concerned with the volume or quality of public services, organizations of taxpayers, voters' leagues, and the like. Hence, before limitations on subject-matter for bargaining are looked upon as unwarranted constraints, as many union officials do seem to view them, the recipients of public services, taxpayers, and all average citizens—most of who are employed in private enterprise (some of them no doubt unionized)—should think twice before succumbing to the mindless doctrine that because all facets of personnel policy are available for bargaining in the business sector the same should prevail in government employment.

The subjects that *are* normally open to negotiation and bargaining in the public service are not insubstantial. Promotion policy, vacation and overtime scheduling, safety practices, performance evaluation, training opportunities, grievance procedures, and working conditions are often core issues even in private employment. They, along with numerous others, make up the bulk of subjects taken up in government service bargaining.

And it should be borne in mind that when it comes to matters such as basic levels of salaries, wages, and fringe benefits, which often are not open to bargaining, government employee unions have more effective access to the

[12] A good case for using the personnel office for this purpose is made by Kenneth O. Warner and Mary L. Hennessy, *Public Management at the Bargaining Table*, Chicago, International Personnel Management Association, 1967, pp. 291–305.

political process where these levels are decided than any other interest group, because they have inside information, have long and established relationships with legislators, and usually through their own memberships speak for an influential block of voters.

An equally serious issue arises when unions seek to bargain on substantive public policy as distinguished from personnel policy. The problem is well summarized in the following:

> Welfare workers want to negotiate the level of benefits available to their clients. School teachers want to negotiate textbook selection, class size, curriculum, even the amount of the budget for underprivileged schools. Police organizations want to negotiate the number of men assigned to patrol cars.
>
> Most of these proposals have a bearing on "conditions of employment." The police officer working in a patrol car by himself can reasonably argue that he is not as safe as if he had a partner. The teacher can claim that the textbook she uses is her tool, in much the same sense that a crane operator is concerned about the type or condition of his crane.
>
> On the other hand, these matters bear heavily on agency policy. When decisions on such policy matters become matters of bilateral decision-making, with only the two parties involved, public participation in policy formation is reduced. It is one thing to determine salaries bilaterally; it is a different thing to determine educational curriculum in that manner.[13]

Unions everywhere, once their periods of initial organization are over, seem invariably to seek enlargement of the area of bargaining. In the public service both executive management and legislators must be ever mindful of ensuring that subjects that are of equal concern to other groups or to just the general public are not preempted for the two-sided closed-door bargaining of unionized government employees and specific program managers. Major expenditures and basic program policy are the proper domain of the various elements of the political process, not of collective bargaining. At the same time, it is pointless and shortsighted to place unreasonable restrictions on what is bargainable when a matter is of legitimate relevance to the welfare of employees. A sound guide for the powers that should be reserved to management is found in the policy of the federal government, cited in the description of general federal policy presented earlier in this chapter.[14]

One additional point deserves emphasis. As more and more salary authority becomes vested in executive branches of government, so that basic pay becomes more susceptible to the bargaining process than to the older political

---

[13] W. Donald Heisel, *State-Local Employee Labor Relations*, Lexington, Ky., The Council of State Governments, 1970, p. 18.

[14] These reserved powers of management are spelled out in Section 12 of Executive Order 11491, October 29, 1969 (effective January 1, 1970). They were not altered by the amendments of 1975 (Executive Order 11838, February 6, 1975; effective May 7, 1975).

arena, provision must be made for reflecting the results in budget planning and appropriation of the necessary funds. If bargaining can be so timed that executive management and unions can come to terms in time to have the results reflected in the budget for the next period and to allow for whatever legislative action is necessary for appropriation, any time lag can be reduced to a minimum and the power of the people through the legislative process is not frustrated. Another alternative is for the legislative body to authorize a certain percentage of flexibility in salary appropriations so that executive management can act promptly, upon culmination of an agreement with unions on basic pay levels, at least up to the point of any limitation imposed on the authorization.

INJECTING THE PUBLIC INTEREST

This is the logical place to consider some methods for ensuring attention to the public interest in government bargaining, over and beyond the foregoing matter of allowing for adequate operation of the expenditure authorization process. It is not always possible to anticipate just which bargaining sessions may extend beyond the "bread-and-butter" issues of conditions of employment that are within the legitimate province of administrators to bargain on. The essential need is to provide an opportunity for other groups besides the employees to have their say and for management to learn what these views are before it commits itself to any agreement with the employee union. This consideration may apply even to issues that are normally viewed as personnel policy but that may be of substantial concern nevertheless to the general public. Sometimes such issues have a way of being inextricably mixed up with what on the surface appear to be the conventional employment matters.

One series of steps that might help assure representation of the general public interest would be the following:

1. The appropriate agency, such as a local school board, could appoint a community-wide group, broadly representative, to discuss and try to develop a consensus on any issues that are anticipated in forthcoming bargaining sessions with unions.
2. This discussion and exploration could be conducted openly, with participation by any interested organizations or individuals and with full access by the news media.
3. Any possible consensus arrived at by the community-wide group, say, for example, on aspects of educational policy potentially affected by prospective demands of a teachers' union, could be reported to the school board before it crystallizes its own position on these subjects. It could then take this into account in its negotiations with the union.
4. If the timing is such that bargaining has had to proceed apace, provision could be made for management to reopen negotiations, perhaps even

including a public hearing, if the public reaction to the preliminary negotiations is adverse.

5. A variant might be to consider all negotiations and agreements tentative, to allow for a waiting period during which public hearings would permit airing of the views of all groups, and to require management to reopen negotiations with the union for final settlement only after it has the benefit of this public reaction.[15]

Still another approach in local services like public schools would be for the state legislature in effect to take over as bargaining agent, by centralizing salary and other major determinations statewide. This would ensure parity among school districts on bargainable issues and no doubt greater parity among occupations, for example, teachers versus general government employees. It would, however, deprive localities of much of their autonomy in financing and even in many other policy areas.[16]

Any contention by public employee unions that measures such as those described deprive them of equal rights with unions in the private sector must be rejected on the simple grounds that the public interest in any government action must always be paramount. If such procedures as those outlined are infeasible in practice, then others that are better must be found. A policy of drift and thoughtlessness that leaves major segments of public policy to be determined solely under a process in which any body of government employees exerts more than its rightful power is not in the interest of democracy or of all government employees as citizens.

WRITTEN AGREEMENTS

Some years back the typical product of public management consultation with an employee organization was an oral understanding or at most an exchange of letters articulating the results. Under collective negotiations and bargaining the common conclusion is now reflected in a written agreement. Taking a leaf from the tradition that built up in the private sector since passage of the National Labor Relations Act in the 1930s, such an agreement is supposed to constitute a "contract" between management and labor, enforceable in courts of law. Whether this is truly the case in the public sector is not quite so clear, since such agreements may sometimes be challenged by taxpayers or others on the grounds that they abrogated the rights of some other group or of the general public welfare. In this respect, as in so many others, the peculiar situation in government employment must be taken into account.

[15] These ideas are adapted from comparable ones suggested in Warner and Hennessy, op. cit., p. 318.

[16] This suggestion is explored in Charles R. Perry and Wesley A. Wildman, *The Impact of Negotiations in Public Education: The Evidence from the Schools*, Worthington, Ohio, Charles A. Jones Publishing Co., 1970. This book describes results of a study of actual experience in twenty-four school districts over a five-year period.

As noted previously, TVA was a pioneer in development of the written agreement. Now such agreements are commonplace in the Postal Service, many other federal departments (especially Defense), and in most large cities. Naturally their contents are confined to the subjects to which bargaining is limited. Nor can they ordinarily encroach on or supersede laws or regulations relating to a given personnel system.

In many branches of private industry the scope of such agreements in effect constitutes a total personnel system. Not so in the public service. Nevertheless, although they were once feared as unwarranted encroachments on governmental authority, agreements are now for the most part widely accepted simply as recordations of understandings that are properly within the province of the parties to carry out. Viewed in this perspective, they have often been a vehicle for the easing of tension between management and union and have helped ensure a solid basis for each party to see that the other side lives up to its commitments.

IMPASSES AND GRIEVANCES

An impasse in bargaining is just what the term usually implies. It is a breakdown in negotiations when neither side is willing to "give" on some point and when a stalemate is reached. Many of the state laws and the federal program provide expressly for the procedures to be followed when such a deadlock occurs. These are dealt with in some detail in the next chapter.[17]

Of a lesser order than an impasse in *arriving* at agreement are instances in which it is alleged that one party or the other has *violated* it in practice. As previously noted, when such a complaint is initiated by a union or employee, it is known as a *grievance*. Unfortunately there is still confusion over use of this term, for in government the traditional meaning of grievance was a private complaint by an employee that he had been unjustifiably "done in" by his superiors, found some working condition intolerable, or was unwarrantably disciplined by his superiors—not a contention that some agreement with management had been violated.[18] On the other hand, the traditional usage in private employment has been that a grievance is a complaint against a violation of a contractual agreement. For the time being at least, we shall have to live with a spectrum of meanings for this term.

Adjudication of grievances in the agreement-violation sense is usually provided for in the agreement itself. Unless otherwise established to the satisfaction of employees, the agreement may also provide for settlement of grievances of the more personal type when contract violations are not directly involved. Nevertheless, the more common invocation of a grievance in circumstances in which there are written agreements is one involving agreement interpretation or application. A common mode of resolution of such disputes is through arbitration by an outside third party. This party may be

---

[17] See the discussion on dispute settlement in Chapter 21.
[18] See the discussion on adjustment of grievances in Chapter 11.

an official located elsewhere in the governmental hierarchy or, more frequently, a professional arbitrator. Elaborate procedures are often set up to govern such settlements.[19]

UNFAIR PRACTICES

Another standard item of labor relations parlance is the concept of "unfair practices." Borrowed from the private sector, this phrase has now become commonplace in the public arena. Either through state law (or executive order in the federal service) or by virtue of provision in labor agreements themselves, a series of actions by both management and union are proscribed. Commission of these labor "crimes" may automatically be the basis of complaint by and ultimate adjudication on behalf of either party.

Typical of practices prohibited to the employer are: (1) interfering with employee rights guaranteed by statute, order, or other source; (2) initiating, dominating, or interfering in any way with creation of an organization of employees; (3) giving financial support to an employee union; (4) discouraging union membership; (5) disciplining an employee for filing a grievance; (6) refusing to recognize a qualified union; (7) refusing to negotiate or bargain with a union in good faith; and (8) violating a bargaining agreement.

Usual actions in which unions are forbidden to engage are: (1) seeking to induce the employer to coerce an employee for opposing union leadership; (2) coercing an employee into joining the union; (3) refusing to represent a member in exercising his rights under an agreement; (4) refusing to negotiate or bargain with management in good faith; (5) discriminating against an employee on matters of union membership because of race, color, creed, sex, age, or national origin; (6) calling or engaging in a strike, work stoppage, or slowdown of work where such actions are forbidden by law; and (7) violating a bargaining agreement.[20]

By and large, no objective person could challenge the reasonableness of prohibitions such as those enumerated. One of the beneficial results of collective bargaining is the introduction of a discipline in management-union relations that flows from such standards of conduct for both sides.

SOME IMPLICATIONS OF BARGAINING

Greater reliance on bilateralism in determining personnel policy, no matter how much of it must be reserved to law and the political process, carries in its train several important effects. Some of these, because they have the stature

---

[19] See the detailed report by Arnold Zack, *Understanding Grievance Arbitration in the Public Sector*, Washington, D.C., U.S. Department of Labor, 1974. Thirty-seven pages in double-column fine print are devoted to the various facets of this subject.

[20] In drafting this summation of typical unfair practices on the part of both management and union, we drew upon Executive Order 11491 in the federal situation (section 19) and, for state and local government examples, relied upon W. Donald Heisel, *op. cit.*, p. 17.

of major issues, are analyzed at some length in the next chapter. Here we shall look especially at a few points that grow out of the bargaining process itself.

ADVERSARY PROCEEDINGS AND POWER

A few scholars and administrators have deplored what they consider to be a reduction of human relationships in the public service to a process of adversary proceedings. Others feel that the same procedures guarantee a constructive kind of joint determination on matters in which both management and employees have a warranted stake. If we consider the variety of conditions and circumstances that can exist in this field, no doubt both are right. At least, few would contend that collective bargaining is a perfect answer in achieving wise and fair public administration.

Thoughtful persons may, however, be justified in expressing concern about the impact of adversary contests on the *quality* of decision-making. A subtle but nonetheless significant effect of settling complex issues through the bargaining process is that professional or objective analysis of problems tends to get subverted. Too often the "leverage" that one side or another possesses is a more potent determinant of the result than the merits of the case. Two authorities who studied actual results of teacher bargaining in twenty-four school districts over a five-year period have observed:

> Reliance on power as the arbiter of conflict tends to place a premium on disingenuousness. It also tends to reduce flexibility and opportunities for problem-solving in favor of commitments to formal rules or positions and debate over right and wrong. In short, clinical approaches to problems may be supplanted by adversary approaches to issues.[21]

NEED FOR MORE MANAGEMENT INITIATIVE

A number of students of the effects of bargaining in the public service, including those wholly sympathetic with the process, have called attention to the tendency of government administrators to overlook the utility of using the procedure to extract concessions from union negotiators. Too often they have missed opportunities to bargain hard and have merely used a defensive strategy in responding to union demands. They have not understood the quid pro quo character inherent in bargaining.

Several gains for the public interest can be sought when employees are seeking some improvement in their own lot via a salary increase, better fringe benefits, or otherwise. Most important among these potentialities for management are getting commitments to better performance and higher productivity. As one scholar who surveyed experiences in nineteen urban governments put it: "In some units they could bargain for increased productivity, improved work quality, or work rules conducive to efficiency. Such

---

[21] Perry and Wildman, *op. cit.*, p. 222.

management aggressiveness of course requires skilled work by the union relations staff and high resolution on the part of executives."[22]

Winning explicit collaboration from organized employees to enforce performance standards, to devise productivity improvements, and generally to be supportive instead of resistant in matters of better service to the public can be a net asset worth fighting for. In addition, management could bargain for other concessions such as eliminating or reducing seniority policies that induce mediocrity and getting union cooperation in enforcing discipline. Some of the shortcomings of unionization referred to in the preceding chapter could be substantially alleviated if more public administrators took an aggressive stand on actions along these lines.

NEED FOR MANAGEMENT TRAINING

As already implied, for management to take such an approach calls for better preparation. We have seen how municipal officials especially have frequently been caught off guard by confrontation with experienced and skillful negotiators on the labor side who have national organizations to back them up and who may draw upon the cumulative wisdom of compatriots in the industrial field. To keep up with them, public officials must carefully study their own roles, confer with their counterparts in other jurisdictions, and take advantage of every educational facility and program available to prepare themselves in the economic, legal, and psychological aspects of negotiation and bargaining.[23]

Two authors who have studied bargaining problems with police unions contend: "Responsible public officials appear to be completely unqualified to appropriately arbitrate police labor disputes. Thus, they must equip themselves with the necessary background knowledge and develop practical plans for any eventuality in this area."[24]

Some critics have gone further and compared untrained managers with unlicensed professionals who visit untold damage upon their clients by their inadequacy.[25] Whether the situation among public administrators is still that

[22] David T. Stanley, *Managing Local Government Under Union Pressure*, Washington, D.C., The Brookings Institution, 1972, pp. 150–151.

[23] See the counsel of Kenneth O. Warner, "Cities at the Bargaining Table," *Nation's Cities*, September 1966, p. 11.

[24] Allen Z. Gammage and Stanley L. Sachs, *Police Unions*, Springfield, Ill., Charles C Thomas, 1972, p. 122.

[25] People need licenses to drive a taxicab, practice medicine, install plumbing or crop corns. Yet I have watched labor-management negotiators, who ought not to be allowed to cross the street without a seeing-eye dog, inflict hardship on millions of their fellow-citizens through sheer incompetence at the bargaining table—and there is not one thing anyone in the community can do to arrest them for reckless use of a dangerous economic weapon. No remotest relationship exists between the capacity or social responsibility of the bargainers and the degree of damage their status enables them to visit on the economy. [A. H. Raskin, "Collective Bargaining and the Public Interest," in *Challenges to Collective Bargaining*, Papers prepared for the Thirtieth American Assembly, Columbia University, Lloyd Ulman, ed., Englewood Cliffs, N.J., Prentice-Hall, 1967, p. 155. Mr. Raskin is a noted labor relations authority.]

lacking is doubtful. After all, most of them are quite accustomed to bargaining with and among other groups in society, and some of these skills are transferrable. The problem arises from the lack of acquaintance with the particular milieu of collective bargaining and the failure to press for some "give" as well as "take" from the union side.

*   *   *

TO BE SURE, government unions have made great strides and the lot of public employees has been much improved. On the other hand, the general public interest must be maintained, and managers have much to learn to make themselves fully effective in its protection. That there are continuing problems is unquestioned. The most critical of these will be explored in the next chapter. But, as David Stanley reminds us, "there seems to be little prospect that the transaction will become overbalanced against management, given the continued functioning of the American political system and the exercise by management officials of a reasonable mix of resolution, ability to listen, decisiveness, labor relations knowledge, and good will."[26]

[26] *Op. cit.*, pp. 151–152.

CHAPTER 21

Continuing Issues in Union Relations

AT SEVERAL POINTS in the preceding two chapters controversial questions had to be raised because they were so intimately bound up with the process or development under immediate examination. Occasionally reference was made to still other issues, but no attempt was made to go into them in any detail. In this chapter we have reserved discussion of these, the most important and difficult problems facing management-union relations in the public service. None of the problems is neatly divisible from the subjects already covered, but for the sake of clarity and brevity the effort is made here to give these issues their due without overlapping what has already been said and without attempting to relate them back fully to any or all principles or processes previously explored.

MEMBERSHIP ISSUES

UNION SECURITY

The tradition in the private sector has been that the powerful unions have managed to achieve a status vis-à-vis employers that, to one degree or another, guarantees their membership—and hence is referred to as "union security." The rationalization from the standpoint of unions is obvious; the rationalization from the standpoint of employers is that it stabilizes their relationships by ensuring the continuity of the organizations with which they must deal.

Primarily three different forms of union security have evolved: the "closed shop," under which the union supplies all candidates for employment; the "union shop," under which all employees hired by the employer must, after some period of time, join the union; and the "agency shop," under which all employees must eventually submit to the check-off from their salaries for union dues whether they join the union or not. None of these relationships has any proper place in the public service.

Closed Shop   To this author's knowledge, there is no employment through a closed shop anywhere in the American public service. If there ever should be, it would constitute a complete denial of the government's right to choose its workers and would negate the whole concept of a merit-based system with equal opportunity for all qualified applicants. Fortunately, there have been very few advocates of such a drastic and inappropriate borrowing from private practice, where it applies incidentally to only a tiny proportion of total employment. But occasionally the argument is made by extremist labor advocates who apparently have no qualms about allowing a private group—especially if it is theirs—to control entry to the public service and thereby control the service itself without accountability to the public. Anything more undemocratic (indeed, it would be nothing less than oligarchy) can hardly be imagined. It would reinstitute a form of spoils system, this time through union instead of political party machinery.

Union Shop and Agency Shop   The union shop is only a shade or two less drastic. Not only does such a policy—forcing hired employees to join a union—seriously abridge their personal rights, but it discourages entry into public employment by many persons who find such a requirement offensive. Public employees have enough special obligations and restriction as it is, without imposing such a duty in the name of promoting labor-management relations. Only a hair's breadth away in seriousness is the agency shop, wherein one of the major obligations of union membership, paying dues, is imposed without necessarily having the employee's consent.

The argument made in support of the union shop or agency shop is that employees who benefit from union representation should be forced to support the cause. Such reasoning presumes that in any instance the union is performing a sound and constructive service on behalf of the employees without undermining the public interest and that all employees perceive its actual role in such favorable terms. The answer is that a union, like any other social or economic organization, should *earn* its reputation and its strength. A flat guarantee of membership or at least of income makes union leadership complacent and flabby. An energetic union need have no worry about membership, even if it never achieves 100-percent support.

A few localities have, to the loss of their citizenry, succumbed to permitting the union shop or agency shop in some parts of their services.[1]

---

[1] From a sampling of nineteen jurisdictions, it was found that four (among them Philadelphia) had permitted the union shop and three (Boston, Dayton, and Detroit) the agency shop. Unfortunately, the device seems to be spreading, even though its main virtue is to simplify life for union leaders. For a report on the survey, see David T.

Not only is such a practice questionable from the viewpoint of the general public, there is no evidence that employees are any better off in jobs where these union-security measures prevail than they are where unions have to "sell" their worthwhileness to employees on a continuing basis. It is the considered view of objective analysts that membership guarantees serve no useful public purpose, that they do not serve sound management-union collaboration, and that in the long run they do not even promote the best interests of employees.[2]

THE SUPERVISORY DEMARCATION

The industrial labor movement traditionally abhorred the idea of mixing any ranks of supervision into unionization with rank-and-file workers. Supervisors at any level were identified with management, and that was that.

The situation in government has been quite different. The earliest public employee organizations clustered around functions or broad occupational groups, including one or more supervisory levels. Even the general-purpose or so-called industrial-type unions that followed later drew no special line for supervision when it came to accepting members. Indeed, the pattern in many state associations and in federal agencies at least up the 1940s was that middle management and sometimes higher officials were found on the membership rolls. They had not viewed the organizations as vehicles for confrontation with anybody in the administrative hierarchy, but rather as means for collective representation of career-service interests before legislators and elected officials.

The advent of affiliation with the general labor movement, the growth of governmental employment, the failure of many jurisdictions to treat their employees as anything more than second-class citizens—all combined to place great strains on the easy-going, open membership policies of so many of these public employee unions. Leaders and members of such groups resisted the idea of freezing out people because they happened to occupy positions of substantial importance or to carry some measure of supervisory responsibility. Old-time union organizers from industry, who began to infiltrate the public sector, were appalled at this lack of sensitivity to what they considered a cardinal tenet of classic unionism: all supervisors take their orders from, act on behalf of, behave like, and therefore *are* management.

Naturally, this difference in attitude has led to compromises. Many government unions, including those affiliated with the AFL-CIO, do admit first-level, subforeman, or straw-boss types of supervisors into their member-

---

Stanley, "What Are Unions Doing to Merit Systems?" *Public Personnel Review*, April 1970, pp. 108–113.

Agency shop contracts are also permitted in a few state services, among them Michigan, Rhode Island, and Hawaiii (International Personnel Management Association, *Personnel News*, September 1973, p. 62).

[2] Note the strong recommendation against such measures by the Advisory Council on Intergovernmental Personnel Policy, cited near the conclusion of this chapter.

ships. Others provide for organization of lower-level supervisors into separate union chapters with separate representational units. The Postal Service has for many years had supervisory unions. Although obviously not carrying the weight of numbers that are in the rank-and-file unions, they exert considerable influence, know how to bargain hard, and frequently take stands on issues contrary to those being pressed by their nonsupervisory colleagues.

The ultimate relationship of supervisors to government unions is still in the process of evolution. Lack of resolution of the issue continues to be one of the reasons for reluctance of the older state associations and several federal unions to affiliate with the general labor movement.

THE PLACE OF THE PROFESSIONALS

Of almost equal stature and even greater complexity has been the question of where to fit in professional employees. As in the case of supervisors, they often had been members of the older state associations or federal unions that confined their efforts for the most part to legislative lobbying. With the new militancy and labor movement orientation of groups such as the AFSCME and AFGE, most professionals—engineers, lawyers, doctors, scientists— shy away from membership or at least from leadership roles. They often want the benefits of the bargaining power they see other employees acquiring and frequently seek separate identification in separate units of recognition. But, when it comes to general-purpose unionization, they tend to resist identification with those in less prestigious occupations.

It is difficult for most professional workers to disentangle themselves from the objectives and concerns of management. One such body of professionals has explained:

> The professional is typically either a part of management or closely associated with management. Either he exercises delegated authority or he influences policy through the strength of his ideas. Right down to the most junior level, the professional is generating the advancement of knowledge, improvements in services, and sound bases for decisions at higher levels of authority.[3]

The dilemma they face is understandable. They do not want to be overlooked or left out in the cold in the decision-making processes affecting their welfare, but they clearly have interests, perspectives, needs, and problems quite different from people in the other occupations.

Curiously, in those instances where one field of professionalism dominates in a public agency and is the principal avenue through which the agency's services are delivered, a totally different situation prevails. We are thinking

[3] From the "Statement on Federal Professional Employees and Their Relationships" by Ewan Clague, President, The Federal Professional Association, July 22, 1974, presented to the House Committee on Post Office and Civil Service in connection with the latter's consideration of bills to establish a statutory base for government labor relations policy.

here of groups such as teachers in public schools, hospital nurses and related specialists, and social case workers. In these situations the central functions of the entity are critically in the hands of this one professional group. And where the members have been highly organized, they have shown at least as much aggressiveness and militancy in advancing their interests as any of the old-time trade unions, even indulging in use of the strike weapon in defiance of law.[4]

As in the case of drawing the line for supervisors, the future role of professional groups in management-employee relations is still in a developmental stage. By and large, neither the influence nor the welfare of professional employees seems to be suffering any diminution.

IMPACT ON THE MERIT SYSTEM

An issue engaging increasing attention is the effect that collective agreements between units of management and units of employees in various jurisdictions are having or might have on a merit-based system of employment. It would be well at this point to recall the definition of a merit system as stated in Chapter 3. Note that it comprehends much more than a technical mode of initial entry into the service: it embraces the means by which the requirements of jobs are determined and made known; it involves a genuineness of equal opportunity; it entails advancement in the service on the basis of competence and performance; it is the principal component of the career concept; in short, it is infused in all personnel policies that influence competence and continuity in public administration. Whatever impact recent developments in management-union relations may have on such a vital area in democratic government, it certainly is not to be taken lightly.

As yet, there is no firm conclusion on what the impact has been. Most unions and associations of public employees still give lip service at least to the merit idea, and some are found supporting it effectively in legislative halls and in practice. Others are less interested or nibble away at both principle and technique without attacking the idea head on. The old-line state associations and police and fire unions generally support not only the principle but often insist on particular techniques such as written tests which, in other quarters, are under challenge. Surveys that have been conducted

[4] Speaking of public employee unions, Frederick C. Mosher observes:

Somewhat surprisingly, amongst the most aggressive are certain categories of professionals, especially those principally employed by and therefore principally dependent upon public employers: school teachers, social workers, nurses and other hospital specialists. It is worth noting that the concessions now being demanded by the labor movement with respect to unilateralism and individualism are essentially parallel to those demanded by the organized professions and their career services. . . . [*Democracy and the Public Service*, New York, Oxford University Press, 1968, p. 199.]

Mosher's thesis in this book is that government professionals exercise considerable power through various channels, especially the influence of their expertise.

suggest that there has not been a paramount interest or activity in this area on the part of most government unions.[5]

A distinction must be made between vital principles and questionable methods in carrying them out. Some personnel agencies mistake their particular techniques for principles; some unions mistake the methods used in a specific localized case as the full-blown merit ideal. Thus, we can have a spirited defense of a technique as if it were the very embodiment of the merit principle, and an equally spirited attack on principle as if some particular technique completely represented it. Neither, of course, is a rational reaction. The fact is that if some unjustifiable or faulty method in selection is deemed by some union to be present in a system, few would say that the union has no right to seek to have the flaw remedied. But it need not attack the merit system per se (or "civil service," to use the usual mistaken jargon), nor does management need to view the issue as such an attack. Whenever issues of methodology can be isolated and treated for what they are, all parties will be better off and the merit concept is likely to be preserved.

On the other hand, efforts of some government unions do have the insidious effect of undermining not only technique but principle as well. Examples are these: (1) installation of closed-shop, union-shop, or agency-shop schemes; (2) establishment of seniority as the governing factor in selection for promotion or in reemployment following lay-off; (3) preference for employees of a given bargaining unit in promotion to positions within or outside the unit; and (4) allowing labor agreements in particular units or agencies to supersede governmentwide merit regulations. Apparently not too many jurisdictions have succumbed to these ill-conceived attacks on the public interest. The anathema that the first three examples pose for good government is fully discussed elsewhere.[6] The fourth example is the worst of all, because it is a gateway to slow strangulation of any governmentwide personnel policy without the benefit of participation of the duly constituted agencies and officials who have the perspective and the responsibility for such policy. At the very minimum, any proposed action that affects governmentwide policy in a jurisdiction, particularly merit considerations, should be dealt with at the governmentwide level and should not be made the hostage of specialized interests or spineless management in some subordinate unit.[7]

In spite of instances to the contrary, most observers do not find that public

[5] Of relevance here are such works as David T. Stanley, *Managing Local Government Under Union Pressure*, Washington, D.C., The Brookings Institution, 1972, especially pp. 32–45; and W. Donald Heisel, *State-Local Employee Labor Relations*, Lexington, Ky., The Council of State Governments, 1970, especially pp. 23–26.

[6] The first one is covered earlier in this chapter; the second and third are analyzed in Chapter 10, "Selection: From Inside the Service."

[7] Connecticut is one state that has the alarming provision that any agreement between a municipal employer and a union regarding police and fire personnel must prevail over statutes, charters, or regulations, whether enacted by legislative bodies or personnel boards or commissions (Heisel, *op. cit.*, pp. 24–25). In this case, since the provision is a matter of state law, it is the state legislature that has sold out not only its own responsibilities but those of municipalities and the people as well.

merit systems have been seriously compromised by the pressures of collective agreement. Indeed, one team goes so far as to say: ". . . there is now sufficient evidence to justify optimism that collective bargaining and merit systems can be made compatible."[8] Although partisans of the public interest may devoutly hope this to be the case, it is well that they fortify their convictions and their arguments against the blandishments of those who reason that what is good for industry is good for government. Our concluding statement on this subject can best be capsuled in the following:

> Selection of personnel for entry or advancement in the service should not be bargainable—that is, the basic criteria for selection and the actual selections themselves. For entry to the service this proscription should be near absolute. In promotion processes, however, methods for ascertaining qualifications, identifying talent, or establishing competition may well be subject to negotiation, but not such questions as to whether seniority should replace merit as a criterion for promotion or whether a particular position demands the possession of certain skills or knowledge. Any surrender by management of such factors in the selection process to bargaining is an abandonment of managerial responsibility. Suggestions may, of course, be received—but not bargaining.
>
> No group of public workers should be in a position of controlling—even to the extent of having a fifty–fifty weight of influence—its own reproduction or perpetuation. Whenever this occurs, democracy ceases. Entry, advancement, and utilization in the service must remain instruments under full, unadulterated public control.[9]

One may contend, of course, that high-quality and competent people have found their way into various areas of employment without the benefit of a merit system. But that side-steps the problem; the problem is one of the prevailing tendency and the importance to the public interest of attracting, selecting, and holding as much quality as possible in public services. The price paid for a nonmerit system is not the total absence of competence but the overwhelming presence of mediocrity.

IMPASSES AND DISPUTE SETTLEMENT

Several kinds or levels of dispute can arise in the course of normal relationships between management and organizations representing employees. One type may occur from the complaint of an individual worker which the union takes up on his behalf or as illustrative of a policy problem. Another may arise out of difference in interpretation of a published rule or of a written

---

[8] Felix A. Nigro and Lloyd G. Nigro, *Modern Public Administration*, 3rd ed., New York, Harper & Row, 1973, p. 273. Less assurance is expressed by Heisel, *op. cit.*

[9] O. Glenn Stahl, *The Personnel Function—Two Issues*, Detroit, Citizens Research Council of Michigan, 1971, p. 22.

labor agreement or of some other previously established policy. The usual adjudication process for settling such disagreements or misunderstandings is through the grievance procedure.

Still another, and usually more aggravated dispute, may arise in the course of negotiations on some major policy front, such as pay. In this case, the employee group is seeking some kind of change, and management is holding out for an alternative. Ordinarily more is at stake in this last type of issue. Such inability to reach agreement, by compromise or other mutual adjustment of positions, is, as previously noted, referred to as an "impasse." It is primarily this kind of dispute that creates tension and may lead to a strike.

MODES OF SETTLEMENT

Over the years several methods of settlement have evolved that always entail participation of some third party but differ in the degree to which that participation prevails. These resolution procedures are generally known as: mediation, fact-finding, voluntary arbitration, and compulsory arbitration. The last two methods involve decisions that are binding on both parties.

MEDIATION   Mediation is a noncoercive process in which an agreed-upon neutral party maintains the flow of communication, offers tentative solutions, presses each party to modify its position so that the two can come to terms, or otherwise seeks to bring about agreement. It is the most commonly used process and, in the public sector, has been quite successful in many jurisdictions.

FACT-FINDING   If mediation fails or is not used, the next stage is usually a fact-finding procedure in which a neutral party holds a hearing, makes such other inquiry as he sees fit, thoroughly analyzes the situation, and finally makes a recommendation as to what he deems the terms and conditions in dispute should be. Although in this procedure there is no commitment to accept such a recommendation, the power of the process lies in the possibility that the public will accept the fact-finder's neutrality and support his decision, thereby putting pressure on the disputing parties to accept it.

VOLUNTARY ARBITRATION   The term *arbitration* in labor disputes has come to mean a binding decision. In the case of voluntary arbitration both parties agree in advance to abide by the determination of the arbitrator. This, in effect, is fact-finding with advance agreement to accept the result.

COMPULSORY ARBITRATION   The meaning of "compulsory" in conjunction with arbitration is that, either by law or some other enforceable dictum, the parties to a dispute *must* submit it to binding arbitration at some stage in the proceedings. In some instances this stage is arrived at when one party requests such action; in others the final arbitration procedure is triggered by a predefined set of circumstances having been reached, such as expiration of some period of time or failure of other methods of settlement. Compulsory arbitration is essentially no different from adjudication of a civil dispute in a court of law, except that in arbitration interpretation of law plays less of a role, economic and value judgments are more significant, and the arbitrator is usually a specialist in labor settlements rather than an officially appointed or elected judge. In some jurisdictions, however, arbitrators are provided by state labor departments or other official sources. In those cases where ultimate resolution of a disagreement requires some legislative action, the legislature or local governing council in effect acts as arbitrator by means of its final passage of a controlling measure.[10]

POWER OF NEUTRAL PARTIES   Industrial disagreements are typically referred to private arbitrators who are in the business of settling such cases. Obviously, to rely on outside individuals or panels of arbitrators to make final decisions in disputes between government jurisdictions and civil service unions would appear to usurp the authority of legally established executive or legislative bodies to make final determinations of policy.[11] Hence, two alternative solutions have been suggested. One is known as "advisory arbitration," which takes the finality out of the decision, leaving its acceptance up to the two parties, thus preserving the government's prerogative to disavow it if it chooses.[12] The other is to use public officials as the arbitrators. Providing the officials chosen are impartial, judicious, and competent, as well as authoritative, this latter procedure would appear to be the more desirable. Even where legislative bodies in effect exercise the final determination as to public labor agreements, we have to all intents and purposes arbitration by a higher government power. In the federal service the Assistant Secretary of Labor

[10] Experience in government jurisdictions demonstrates that mediation is the most commonly used procedure and results in settlement in the majority of cases in which it is used. A survey of use and results of all the modes of settlement in 160 jurisdictions is reported in *Impasse Techniques Survey*, prepared by the Prentice-Hall Editorial Staff and the International Personnel Management Association, Englewood Cliffs, N.J., Prentice-Hall, 1973. This pamphlet also presents case histories, experiences with strikes, and discussion of effectiveness of various procedures.

A detailed manual on the subject is Arnold Zack, *Understanding Fact Finding and Arbitration in the Public Sector*, Washington, D.C., U.S. Department of Labor, 1974. Also see Thomas P. Gilroy and Anthony V. Sincropi, *Dispute Settlement in the Public Sector: The State-of-the-Art*, Washington, D.C., U.S. Department of Labor, 1972.

[11] Nigro observes, however, that government already delegates its powers to private arbitrators in settling disputes under construction and purchasing contracts. Felix A. Nigro, *Management-Employee Relations in the Public Service*, Chicago, International Personnel Management Association, 1969, pp. 27–28. He does not, however, urge the use of private arbitrators in public service labor disputes.

[12] Sterling Spero maintains that the question of whether arbitration awards are binding or not misses the point. It is their mere issuance and the influence which they generate that is important. "The general acceptance of advisory opinions indicates that the significance of arbitration lies not in the compulsory character of the awards but in their mutual acceptance" (*Government as Employer*, New York, Remsen, 1948, p. 421).

and the Federal Service Impasses Panel act as arbitrators on the issues assigned to their respective areas of responsibility.

IMPACT OF ARBITRATION ON BARGAINING   One of the longstanding objections to arbitration has been the contention that its potentiality as a last resort in the minds of bargainers inhibits serious and fruitful collective bargaining. This is based less on proven experience than conjecture. The argument goes that the parties are tempted to stick rigidly by their original positions, lest they be caught with having given up too much in advance in the event the case ultimately goes to arbitration.

Just as good an argument can be made that compulsory arbitration provides a motive for arriving at agreement. Many civil suits in our law courts are settled out of court because the threat of a final adjudication beyond the control of either party and which neither can predict leads them to come to terms. The same potential of ultimate third-party judgment in a collective bargaining impasse should be an inducement, not a handicap, to agreement.[13] The fact is that we settle every other kind of dispute among individuals or groups, economic differences and all others, by judicial processes similar to mandatory arbitration. Such actions do not always eliminate controversy or reduce tensions, but at least there is an orderly, legal way to resolve the differences based ostensibly on justice, not on power. The suspicion is reasonable that the unarticulated reason behind much of the objection to arbitration, whether from the labor or management side, rests on the fear that one side or another will not be able to invoke sufficient economic or political power to affect the result of an arbitration award, as it might through a stalemate, strike, or appeal to public concern.

SOME ALTERNATIVES TO STANDARD ARBITRATION

Nevertheless, if we accept that at least in some circumstances the prospect of traditional arbitration may jeopardize bargaining, then several remedies are worth considering. The most common one is to require the arbitrator to select the final offer of either the union or management. This is supposed to have the effect of inducing each side to come as close to a moderate posi-

---

[13] One authority states: "I am not impressed with the argument that, if you had compulsory arbitration anywhere in the picture, the raw material of employer-union exchange would dry up to such an extent that even the most inventive of government peacemakers would have nothing out of which to fabricate useful ideas." He states further:

> much as I believe in the preferability of private decision-making, I find it hard to be impressed by the creativity of the bargaining process. When I try to tick off the settlements of recent years that have shown any distinctive qualities of originality in meeting the problems of automation or of membership discontent over the obliterating effect of submergence in a mold of big industry and big unionism, I find I run out of outstanding examples before I run out of fingers to count them on. [A. H. Raskin, "Collective Bargaining and the Public Interest," *Challenges to Collective Bargaining*, Papers Prepared for the Thirtieth American Assembly, Columbia University, Englewood Cliffs, N.J., Prentice-Hall, 1967, pp. 160 and 159.]

tion as possible, so that its final offer is not deemed too extreme and untenable. The idea certainly has a plausible rationale. How well it works in practice has not been adequately tested.

Another alternative is to provide automatically for a fixed period, say, thirty days, between the arbitrator's award and its effective date. During this period the two parties could bargain further, and if they still do not come to agreement within the deadline, the original decision of the arbitrator would go into effect. Again, too little experience with the procedure hampers appraisal.

Aside from the mechanics of making arbitration decisions effective, still other devices have been suggested as means for settling disputes in public sector bargaining. Some would simply assert the obligation of elected officials or legislators to make final determinations, which is the procedure consistent with governmental authority in a democracy. Others would submit major unsettled disputes to voter referenda. This too comports with democratic tenets, but it is obviously clumsy and expensive. Many issues of equal or greater import are regularly left to the duly constituted authorities. Still other concerned persons have suggested creation of a series of specialized, non-partisan labor courts to adjudicate disputes in the public sector. This latter proposal has much to commend it, especially two points: (1) it squares with the judicial structure we use to settle all other kinds of disputes in our society; and (2) it leaves the ultimate power in agencies of government where it belongs.

RESORT TO THE STRIKE

The most controversial and emotion-laden issue in public service labor relations centers on organized refusal of employees to work—the strike. Although occasional brief references to strikes have been made earlier in these three chapters on unions and collective relations with management, we have deliberately reserved full discussion of the subject until this point in our study. The issue is too important in itself to be dealt with as merely incidental to other matters.

The literature on this issue is almost invariably laced with arguments about the "right" of public employees to strike. What this means is not some inherent or constitutional right but a right that can be conferred (or withheld) by statutory law. This is as true of the private sector situation as it is of the governmental arena.[14] Hence, the present discussion will focus on the realities of the issue: the increase in strikes in the public service, the arguments over

---

[14] Federal courts have been quite clear in pointing out that neither the U.S. Constitution nor the common law confer a "right" to withhold labor in concert with fellow workers. Availability of the strike weapon in the economic sphere comes only from express provision in state laws and in the National Labor Relations Act (Benjamin Werne, "Public Employees and the Right to Strike," *Personnel Letter No. 255*, Chicago, International Personnel Management Association, September 1973, p. 7).

their tolerability, the status of their statutory acceptance or outlawing, and methods of coping with them.

THE SPREAD OF STRIKE ACTION

No amount of debate or theorizing seems to curtail the tendency of some civil service unions to try the strike weapon against public jurisdictions. Strikes had occurred spasmodically in earlier years, but there was a definite upsurge in the 1960s and this continued, though slightly abated, in the 1970s.[15] School teachers, police and fire protection personnel, and blue-collar tradesmen predominated in the earlier walkouts. Teachers still seem to be in the vanguard, possibly reflecting something missing in the quality of administration or in public oversight of our public schools. In addition, groups such as nurses, social workers, sanitation employees, and, in a few instances, postal employees have swelled the ranks of striking civil servants.

Three points of fact are worth noting: (1) the greater proclivity of professional workers to strike in recent years, outstripping the tendency among the more traditional unionized occupations; (2) the relatively small portion of the public service that has actually been affected by strikes; and (3) some signs that the frequency, volume, and duration of government strikes are declining. It is possible that, in the heady atmosphere of new and expanding union organization among government employees, union leaders have been more precipitous in counseling strike action and in testing the reaction to it than they will be in the future.

THE CONTINUING DEBATE

The position taken by some union heads and writers on the subject is that strikes are to be avoided if at all possible but that conditions in some jurisdictions are so intolerable and elected officials so intransigent that to deny the right to strike is to maintain civil servants in a status of serfdom. A few unions have rescinded the no-strike pledges that were once common in public union constitutions. The assumption is made, of course, that a strike is the only way to bring the case to public attention, if indeed the public would recognize conditions as intolerable. Since there may be in-

---

[15] For the early history see David Ziskind, *One Thousand Strikes of Government Employees*, New York, Columbia University, 1940. The number in the title is misleading, because over half the cases included are from the ranks of temporary depression workers under the Works Progress Administration, not regular employees.

A summary of the situation in the 1960s appears in Sheila C. White, "Work Stoppages of Government Employees," *Monthly Labor Review*, December 1969.

Some of the most crippling municipal strikes that received nationwide attention were transit workers in 1966, and teachers and sanitation workers in 1968, all in New York City; Memphis sanitation workers in 1968; and the neighboring Montreal police in 1969 —the latter really demonstrating what a thin veneer civilization is when it comes to relying on self-restraint without the presence of law enforcement. Until 1970, only minor walkouts of very short duration occurred in the U.S. federal service, but postal workers and air traffic controllers in New York and elsewhere, in that year, became the first to violate the law with serious work stoppages.

stances where reluctant taxpayers are unwilling to face up to their responsibility to their public servants, the real issue is whether there are not less damaging alternatives than the strike that can produce results fair to both government workers and the general public.

Another common position taken in defense of allowing public employees to strike is that such a power or threat on the labor side is essential to meaningful collective bargaining. The specious parallel with experience in private industry is at the heart of this argument. Not only the considered appraisal of experts on the subject but the facts of extensive and fruitful bargaining where strikes are prohibited seriously weaken this contention.[16]

The tendency of some analysts is to assume that strikes in the public sector should be acceptable unless it can be proved that grave damage to the public welfare has resulted from giving some government workers the strike privilege. Aside from the fact that such damage could no doubt be proved if only all the data were assembled, no one needs to be entrapped into assuming this burden of proof. The fact is that the issue is far more complex than is implied by this approach.

There was a time when the relative infrequency and minor impact of government strikes suggested that statutory strike prohibition was less important than guaranteeing employees fair treatment. But the public's capacity to tolerate interruptions in vital public services like transportation, police and fire protection, trash and garbage collection, hospital care, and education has reached the saturation point. Some students of the subject have suggested that a distinction be made between "essential" government services and others, on the grounds that nonessential activities might as well be given the same freedom as the private sector, since many functions controlled by private corporations, such as utilities, are no less vital to the public than are many government operations. But determining just which work is essential has not been found easy, since all kinds of categories of personnel are interwoven into the complex government structure performing a vital service—some outside

---

[16] Note the comments of Jerome T. Barrett (Chief, Division of Public Employee Labor Relations, U.S. Department of Labor) in "Governmental Response to Public Unionism and the Recognition of Employee Rights," *Oregon Law Review*, Fall 1971, particularly p. 128.
Another expert observes:

> In the collective bargaining arena, we are witnessing something that students of labor-management relations have for a long time held (and may continue to hold) could not exist, namely "no strike bargaining." If the recent trend in state legislation continues, mediation, fact-finding and other methods of settling disputes will be used more extensively than ever before. To the extent that these approaches are successful, they may have some application to disputes in private industry. If they fail, it will provide additional ammunition to those who contend that collective bargaining without the right to strike is meaningless. [Jack Stieber, "Collective Bargaining in the Public Sector," in *Challenges to Collective Bargaining, op. cit.*, p. 88.]

In this same volume, A. H. Raskin, in the article previously cited, supports "non-crisis bargaining" even in the private sector.

the specific organization charged with the service who are necessary to its operation and some inside who are not as necessary. Besides, one might well ask: why not turn the issue around? Why not extend the no-strike rule to those private operations that are essential, instead of seeking to identify nonessential public functions for exemption? If there are such things as nonessential functions, what are they doing in the public sphere anyway?[17]

The most telling point made in the debate is the following by Wellington and Winter: "Distortion of the political process is the major, long-run social cost of strikes in public employment. The distortion results from unions' obtaining too much power, relative to other interest groups, in decisions affecting the level of taxes and the allocation of tax dollars."[18] In other words, we cannot escape the unique character of management-union relations as they exist in government employment. More and more authorities seem to be coming to the conclusion that the strike weapon is too drastic for the special conditions of government labor relations.[19]

STATUS OF THE LAW

Even in the face of increased resort to strikes by public employees, legislation prohibiting them has, for the most part, held fast. Federal law has been explicit since 1946, forbidding employment to and imposing criminal penalties on persons who strike, assert the right to strike, or belong to an organization that they know asserts the right to strike.[20] Almost all states continue to prohibit strikes to one degree or another, but two contradictory developments have taken place: (1) a number have strengthened their prohibitions by clarification and penalty imposition or by providing a clear alternative through collective bargaining and dispute settlement; while (2) a few have granted a limited or qualified right to strike to all or some of their public employees. In the latter instance, either specific categories are excluded from the new right (for example, police, firefighters, prison and mental hospital guards, etc.) or courts may enjoin a strike if there is a danger to the public welfare, health, or safety.[21]

[17] A fairly balanced treatment of the subject appears in Robert Booth Fowler, "Normative Aspects of Public Employee Strikes," *Public Personnel Management*, March–April 1974. But also see this author's rejoinder in a letter to the editor appearing in the July–August 1974 issue.

[18] Harry H. Wellington and Ralph K. Winter, Jr., *The Unions and the Cities*, Washington, D.C., The Brookings Institution, 1971, p. 167.

[19] See, for example, Merton C. Bernstein, "Alternatives to the Strike in Public Labor Relations," *Harvard Law Review*, December 1971, pp. 459–475.

[20] Originally contained in clauses attached to appropriation acts, subsequently enacted into substantive law in 1947, and further refined in 1955 (5 U.S. Code 7311). Efforts are currently under way by postal unions to get this prohibition lifted.

[21] A total of seven states had the new liberalized laws as of mid-1975. Only Alaska permits an ultimate right to strike, even if dispute-settlement efforts fail, without court interference. Pennsylvania has its law under reconsideration due to the controversy stirred up over the marked increase of strikes in the state. Vermont's law applies only to municipal workers, and the Montana law only to public health nurses. The other three states involved are Hawaii, Minnesota, and Oregon.
The best source summarizing the situation is Antone and Grace Aboud, *The Right*

In a new measure applying to most of its federal employees, Canada has established a comprehensive labor relations program that includes a qualified right to strike under certain circumstances.[22] The most notable exception to the program is the Royal Canadian Mounted Police. Prior to this, Canadian provinces and municipalities have had a long record of collective bargaining experience, along with some varied toleration of strikes. By implication, some European countries still permit at least some government employees to strike, but in most cases police and certain other functional categories are not among them, and the compulsory arbitration provided in some nations implies enforcement of decisions by governmental authority.

Most observers do not anticipate any sudden abandonment of antistrike legislation in the United States. If this to to be the case, then the American people must face up to the compelling necessity of treating civil servants as first-class citizens. Otherwise no amount of strike prohibition is going to work. Basically, public employees should properly expect:

1. An affirmative right to organize and be represented in collective negotiations with governmental authorities.
2. Pay and benefits comparable to those for equivalent employment in the general community.
3. A reasonable method for impartial settlement of grievances.
4. A reasonable method for resolution of disputes that cannot be settled by negotiation, with the final arbitrating authority vested in an impartial governmental body superior to or independent of the administrative entity involved in the dispute.

Most jurisdictions will probably continue to heed the words of the former governor of New York: ". . . it is proper for government employees to have the right to organize, to bargain collectively and to have grievance procedures," but "they should not have the right to paralyze public services as a club for obtaining their objectives."[23] Civil servants are entitled to the

---

to Strike in Public Employment, Ithaca, N.Y., Cornell University, 1974. Their conclusions are that each of the seven laws "presupposes significant differences in public and private employment"; that vague language on public welfare, health, and safety may lead to uneven enforcement; that no two laws are alike; and that in only one instance, Pennsylvania, has increased strike activity followed passage.

[22] The Public Service Staff Relations Act of 1973, under which a union bargaining agent may choose either of two dispute-settlement routes: (1) a conciliation process, including a qualified right to strike except for employees essential to public safety or security; or (2) a binding arbitration process, via which strikes are prohibited. Strikes are also illegal wherever the employees involved are not members of a certified bargaining unit, where conciliation steps have not been exhausted, or where the employees are covered by an agreement that has not yet expired (Aboud, *op. cit.*, p. 25).

[23] Nelson A. Rockefeller, in a message to the state legislature urging new antistrike legislation. Reported in *From the State Capitals*, Asbury Park, N.J., Bethune Jones, January 3, 1969, p. 2.

foregoing guarantees, and with their having them the public is entitled to absolute continuity of service.

COPING WITH STRIKES

PLANS   Facing up to realities has led many public administrators to lay contingency plans for carrying on government services in the event a walkout occurs among any segment of their work forces. Such plans may include: (1) an adequate system of communication with all supervisors and other key personnel; (2) provision for longer workdays to permit adequate services to be maintained by fewer employees; (3) clear identification of those functions or processes that are postponable, at least for limited periods, without loss to the public welfare; (4) specification of those operations that are so vital that temporary employees must be hired to help carry them on, and plans for quick appointment of such emergency personnel; (5) a system for adequate protection of public premises and property; (6) a system for adequate protection of supervisory or other personnel engaged in providing continuity of services to the public; (7) means for initiation of appropriate legal actions designed to get strikers back to work, such as seeking court injunctions, suits to impose penalties, or charges of unfair labor practice; (8) methods for keeping the general public informed of changes in services, schedules, etc.; and (9) methods for maintaining open channels to leaders of the striking union, so as to keep alive the possibility of a settlement.

The foregoing are by no means all the elements of a comprehensive plan for dealing with a situation that, at best, is difficult and, at worst, could pose a serious threat to the public safety. Some of the items in a plan may seem inconsistent, in that they must anticipate a range of possibilities not all of which will happen, or at least not at once. But that is precisely the reason for a plan. Every responsible public official, especially those in local governments, should be prepared to meet his obligations to the public in the event any part of his work force stops work.[24] Having a plan on the books permits thinking through in advance many complex and troublesome problems that otherwise would have to be coped with under the stress and time constraints of an emergency. Even where the plans have to be altered at the last minute because of some unanticipated event, energies can be concentrated on the change rather than expended on a whole array of issues.

PENALTIES   Administration of penalties against striking employees and unions has been uneven. In many municipalities the final relief that came from ending a strike has left little disposition in officialdom to bring criminal indictments against the strikers even though such were provided by law. In

---

[24] The best guides for this purpose are two publications of the International Personnel Management Association: Carmen D. Saso, *Coping with Public Employee Strikes; A Guide for Public Officials*, Chicago, 1970; and Lee T. Paterson and John Liebert, *Management Strike Handbook*, Chicago, 1974. The latter booklet is issuance no. 47 in IPMA's *Public Employee Relations Library* (PERL).

the federal service, postal workers who participated in the work stoppages of 1970 went scot free, while air traffic controllers involved in slowdowns the same year in a number of instances were fined or lost their jobs. The lack of justice in enforcing antistrike laws has contributed to skepticism about the feasibility of such prohibitions.

The trend, nevertheless, seems to be in the direction of enforcement of penalties. They have been imposed in a number of critical cases, with unions forced to pay fines on behalf of their members and with jail sentences meted out against both organizers and strikers.[25] Although in a major crisis the ultimate police power of the state could always be invoked, the existence and enforcement of realistic sanctions against union leaders and union treasuries should not be written off as impractical. Only in extreme cases would it appear feasible to consider outright dismissal of the offending employees themselves.

STRIKE SUBSTITUTES   Although not widely supported, some very intriguing proposals have been made that would fall in a category one might label as "eating one's cake and having it too." One of these is the "nonstoppage strike." This idea calls for both the employer and the union involved in a stalemate to pay specified amounts of money into a special fund daily or weekly throughout a period of continued dispute, while the employees continue at their jobs. In effect, the procedure imposes an ever-expanding fine on both parties for not coming to agreement. Determination by a special committee of respected community figures is suggested as the device for ultimately deciding on what to do with the fund, such as subsidizing some community service, creating a recreational facility, or contributing to local charities. It is contended that a nonstoppage strike would avoid interruption of public services (although the agency's contributions to the special fund would have to come from tax revenues), would cost both the striking employees and the public agency less than a work stoppage, and would eliminate any problem of penalties. Present likelihood of acceptance of such a procedure, as against third-party settlement such as arbitration, seems remote.

Another idea advanced is that of the "graduated strike." Under this proposal the striking union would reduce services gradually until some minimum floor of service is reached that would still not jeopardize the public welfare or safety. Thus, it would involve a proportionate loss of pay by

[25] In New York City, AFSCME had to stake 6300 of its bridge and tunnel operators to about a million dollars in fines in 1972, and the head of a Teamsters Union affiliate was indicted, with the threat of a prison term. In New Jersey about the same time, striking school teachers were jailed. Such action, along with pressure from outraged taxpayers, has led one authority to suggest that "there are growing signs of a rethinking of the strike issue by both public unions and public workers" (Sam Zagoria [Director, Labor-Management Relations Service, of the National League of Cities, the U.S. Conference of Mayors, and the National Association of Counties], "Administration of Labor-Management Relations in Local Government," paper delivered at the national conference of the American Society for Public Administration, New York City, March 23, 1972).

the strikers (for the time not worked) and an equal proportionate loss of service to the public. It would ensure that, in any case, a minimum number of employees or all employees for a minimum period of time would report for duty. The net effect would be to draw a boundary line on how much of a strike could be accepted as legal.[26]

For still another modification of the traditional strike model, we have to turn to the private sector. The reference here is to the unprecedented experiment worked out between ten major steel companies and the United Steelworkers of America (AFL-CIO). Committing themselves only for the duration of the experiment (but with the obvious prospect for extension), the parties agreed upon a special negotiating arrangement that includes: protection of existing benefits for employees; certain guaranteed preliminary benefits; free negotiation on all other economic or benefit issues; voluntary arbitration of any unresolved issues; and, most important, elimination of a nationwide strike or lockout. One might characterize this as a "minimum guarantee" plan. If employees can be assured of some minimum achievement that they consider vital, then they are willing to forego use of the economic power of a strike and to leave remaining issues up to bargaining or arbitration. Whether any aspect of this plan is transferable to the public sector would require some careful watching and some careful evaluation in the light of government's special responsibilities.[27]

So far, no alternative for public employment has been tried or put forward that offers any more utility or is any freer of shortcomings than mandatory arbitration. Where it is necessary to avoid interruption in public service and where some appropriate branch in the government structure has the ultimate power to make, accept, or veto any independent third-party decision, it would seem to be the most viable procedure to ensure justice to both civil servant and citizen-consumer-taxpayer.[28]

[26] Both the nonstoppage strike and the graduated strike are best explained in Bernstein, *loc cit.* This proponent objects to compulsory arbitration on the ground that it preempts the authority of public officials from deciding on policy issues. His defense of the strike substitutes is this:

> A blanket ban on strikes does not work. Illegal strikes are bad for labor relations and even worse for the rule of law. However, conventional strikes, if legalized, would be ill adapted to the complex procedures of public labor relations. Yet the public must accord its employees reasonable procedures that produce responsible bargaining. Under my proposals, bargaining could perform its salutary function, but without the disruption caused by the conventional strike and in ways adapted to the peculiarities of the public's needs and the government's intricate procedures for allocating resources. [p. 475.] (Copyright 1971 by the Harvard Law Review Association.)

[27] This procedure, known as the Experimental Negotiating Agreement, covered the three-year period from 1971 through 1974. It is explained, along with other ideas, in an eighteen-article symposium on "Exploring Alternatives to the Strike," *Monthly Labor Review*, September 1973. The discussions embrace both the private and public sectors. Few of the writers are willing to circumscribe the strike weapon to any significant degree, even in the public sphere.

[28] A caveat worth emphasizing here is one by A. H. Raskin: "The citizens must be prepared to pay the price of economic justice for their state and municipal employees and not expect them to subsidize the agencies for which they work by taking less" (*loc. cit.*, p. 166).

IMPLICATIONS FOR THE PRIVATE SECTOR

Before leaving the strike issue, we cannot escape giving attention to those factors that overlap between the public and private sectors of our economy. Many services constituting the lifeblood of the community—and provided by government in practically every other country—are operated by privately owned enterprise in the United States. Typical are the utilities in transportation, communication, electric power, heating gas, and the like. Although regulated by government as to rates of charge and their financial return, their employees are under no constraints regarding work stoppages. Yet, the essentiality of the services performed is as critical as for many of those rendered by government. Almost as necessary to the viability of a technological society are industries engaged in the manufacturing and distribution of food products, petroleum products, steel, textiles, automobiles, and many kinds of technical equipment.

The simple fact is that a large proportion of private-sector strikes are more damaging to the public than to the parties in dispute. As some would say, major strikes nowadays are called not against employers but against average citizens and consumers. Instances where the contending parties suffer little or no loss while the rest of society bears the brunt of the stoppage are legion. Even in a strike of newspaper printers—a case with seemingly mild public impact—the strikers are able to get temporary employment promptly and the employer saves money from their unpaid wages, but other businesses, retailers, and employees suffer serious economic dislocation.

When the demands of organized employees are not against exploitation, as they once were, but for the purpose of reaching still higher levels of affluence (as in the case of highly paid airline pilots), their pay claims are not made upon the employer but upon the society which uses their services. It is the customer, not the employer or the stockholder in the company, who must eventually pay the bill. A noted economist has observed: "That the compensation a man receives rests on his union leader's capacity to hold a community to ransom, exacting a price for his power instead of using reasoned evaluation, should be questioned." And again: "Business organizations, through price changes, and workmen, through a labor union, can make and collect demands whose payment will exploit the consuming public exactly as old-line employers exploited their labor."[29]

[29] Adolf A. Berle, *Power*, New York, Harcourt Brace Jovanovich, 1969, pp. 246 and 237 respectively. Berle, in addition to questioning the strike's legitimacy in private employment, makes a devastating attack on its consequences in the public service, such as in the New York City transit strike of 1966, which, he observed, in order to settle the pay of 34,000 civil servants,

> disoriented several million citizens, caused losses of irrevocable millions of dollars, and also imposed an immeasurable amount of discomfort and personal suffering. For the able-bodied, walking several miles to and from work was time-wasting rather than hardship. For the sick who could not reach doctors or hospitals and the tiny shops for which the loss of two weeks' business was a crushing blow, the effects were disastrous. [P. 243.]

Berle also suggests outlawing strikes where the issue is "how affluent the workers ought

We arrived at the concept of the right to strike, as an adjunct of a free society, mainly because it is a logical consequence of our insistence on minimizing control over free enterprise. If employers are to be free to exploit, then workers must be free to withhold their services. The strike is a labor counterweight to capital's economic power. It should follow that, as management is actually less and less free to exploit, by virtue of laws affecting hours, wages, and conditions of work, then the reason for an unlimited right to strike becomes less and less cogent.

Acceptance of the inevitability of the strike is coming more and more into question. Initial understandings as to limitations on the strike weapon seem more sensible than resort to court injunctions when a crisis faces the public. Whatever its durability in the most immediate future, the arrangement with the steelworkers previously described is a straw in the wind for the long run. One specialist sees a danger to unions themselves in persistent resort to the strike where it endangers the community: "The current threat to union status comes not from crooks, racists or interunion raiders; it comes from the public's irritation over crippling strikes and settlements that aggravate the upsweep in living costs."[30] Of equal relevance is the expansion of automation, which permits some industries (for example, telephone utilities) to provide a substantial measure of service even with unionized workers off the job. This is making many unions think twice about the wisdom and utility of the strike method for inducing management acceptance of their goals.

Perhaps we do not need to accept strikes in any sector of society, much less the public sector, if some criteria of economic justice can be established and machinery set up for mandatory settlement of disagreements. In any event, with all these trenchant questions being raised from responsible quarters about strikes in private employment, now hardly seems to be the time to abandon the longstanding policy against strikes in the public service. As another noted labor economist states the point: "A strike prohibition in public employment should be effective if ways and means other than the strike are available to insure a fair and equitable disposition of employee claims."[31]

THE QUESTION OF NATIONAL LEGISLATION

One of the most debated issues of the 1970s is centered on union pressures for national legislation that would put a statutory base under and extend the federal labor relations policy for federal workers and would require all states

---

to be" and the strike "presses on the community rather than the employer," but not where pay and conditions of workers are below a set "reasonable level" (p. 241).

[30] Raskin, *loc. cit.*, p. 162. A *New York Times* editor at the time, Raskin is an award-winning expert in labor relations.

[31] George W. Taylor, "Strikes in Public Employment," *Good Government*, Spring 1968, p. 13.

to adopt and implement a policy for state and local employees that conforms to detailed federal standards. A number of members of the Congress who are generally sympathetic to labor causes look favorably on such a law. They are faced, however, with surprisingly stiff opposition from the management side across the country.

At the federal level, the finger is pointed at the Postal Service as already having a specific collective bargaining plan embedded in statute. It is difficult to contest the argument that other federal employees are entitled to similar assurances by law. All recent presidential administrations and the U.S. Civil Service Commission have consistently opposed such a measure on the grounds that, as it has evolved, the current collective bargaining system is working well and that freezing provisions in statute would handicap future adaptations of the kind that have been cooperatively made with unions in the past. The very large components of professional employees in the federal service (who are minimally represented in the Postal Service) are also quite skeptical of what a statutory system might do to their own interests. They fear, and probably correctly, that there would be less flexibility to permit adaptation to their special circumstances and needs but that if they are left out entirely, they would become the forgotten workers.

With respect to state and local governments the concern is even more manifest and the opposition more determined. The contention here is that most states already have labor relations legislation on the books, that most of them are working well, and that their diversity is simply a manifestation of the proper workings of the federal decentralized system. The argument certainly has considerable potency that to deprive states of local control of fundamental relationships with their organized employees would be an unconstitutional interference with the powers ostensibly left to the states and would hamstring healthy local experimentation and assumption of responsibility by imposing standardized systems and methods.

A formidable array of public interest organizations has asserted strong opposition to such bills, among them, the National League of Cities, the National Association of Counties, the International City Management Association, the National Public Employer Labor Relations Association, and the International Personnel Management Association. The aggregation of old-line state employee associations, the Assembly of Governmental Employees, does not go along with AFSCME and other unions that seek federal standardization. It proposes instead a measure that would simply encourage states that have not done so to enact their own forms of collective bargaining laws. Likewise, as we shall see later, the Advisory Council on Intergovernmental Personnel Policy urges that the matter be left to the individual states.

Considering the fact that public employees generally are very well off in comparison with workers in the business world, the need for a drastic step such as federal intervention in this field is hardly impressive. The movement for such legislation looks suspiciously like a bald attempt of nationwide labor leaders to consolidate union power.

VIEWS ON THE ISSUES

This chapter would be incomplete without a more systematic examination of the considered views of professional and other groups that are informed on the problems of labor relations in the public service and have systematically deliberated on them in concert with others. The occasional references to these judgments in the preceding pages are inadequate to get an overall picture of their tenor.

UNION STANDS

We will not catalogue here quotations of employee-union viewpoints on the various issues. There is even greater diversity of attitudes on the staff side than there is on the managerial side. There is no one source to turn to for voicing the prevailing opinions. Nevertheless, we have noted at various points what most union leaders have stood for or have sought to establish. Suffice it to say that most public unions have come around to supporting the idea of collective bargaining, most of them pay obeisance to at least the *principle* of merit in public employment, many demand an equal voice with management in setting pay and other conditions of employment, a few assert a right to bargain on substantive matters of public policy (particularly those in public education), a number assert an inherent right to strike, many object to compulsory arbitration, and those of nationwide coverage for the most part favor federal standardizing legislation on collective bargaining. Apart from these generalizations, little more could be said to summarize the typical government union point of view.

AMERICAN ASSEMBLY

The American Assembly is an enterprise conducting sessions on broad public policy, held about two times a year, under the leadership of a staff affiliated with Columbia University. For whatever subject is selected, from fifty to a hundred known leaders and interested persons are invited to spend about three days studying preconference papers and participating in discussions relating to the general subject. Usually a brief statement is prepared at the conclusion of the meeting designed to portray points on which there appears to be general agreement, but no one is asked to sign it, and it is not assumed that every participant subscribes to every recommendation.

Two such Assemblies have been held in recent years on labor relations in government, one in 1966 and another in 1971.[32] Union leaders, public officials from all levels of government, and scholars made up most of the participants. In the final report of the 1971 session, we find support for federal legislation

---

[32] The publications containing the preconference papers for each session have been referred to from time to time in this chapter. The two meetings were the Thirtieth and Fortieth Assemblies.

to provide collective bargaining for federal workers but not to standardize practice in the states. Instead, the Assembly urged each state to pass its own law, modeled after the Assembly's recommendations. A majority of this Assembly sanctioned "a limited right to strike after public unions have exhausted obligatory procedures." It considered this preferable to compulsory arbitration but also concluded that "strikes which imperil the public health or safety should be restrained or limited by court injunction." In relation to merit-based civil services, the report had this to say:

> The extension of collective bargaining in the public sector is clearly modifying the civil service system. The Assembly believes that while the trend is both inevitable and desirable, the principle of merit as it relates to the recruitment and hiring of public employees should not be eliminated.
>
> The Assembly further believes that comparability between public and private sector wages and fringe benefits is a desirable principle and more likely to be achieved through collective bargaining than through traditional civil service procedures.[33]

NATIONAL LEAGUE OF CITIES

In a comprehensive statement on all aspects of municipal government policy adopted by the National League of Cities (NLC) in 1972, considerable attention was given to personnel administration in general and to labor relations in particular. A few of the highlights of this declaration relating to unions were these:

1. The League observed that unionization and bargaining require "that public employers be fully prepared and skilled in public employer-employee relations and in methods of resolving disputes without disrupting services essential to the health, safety and welfare of the community."
2. It urged cities to enact labor relations laws or seek state legislation to to assure "reasonable, equitable and effective methods of governing relationships" between management and unions.
3. It was very insistent that strikes be prohibited, accompanied by "adequate enforcement," but it also avowed that "binding arbitration of terms of a contract should be prohibited."
4. It asserted that, as a matter of principle, "the establishment of hours of work, scales of salaries and wages and any other working condition of municipal employees must be determined by and left to the discretion of municipal government management."

---

[33] *Collective Bargaining in American Government,* Report of the Fortieth American Assembly, October 28–31, 1971, Arden House, Harriman, N.Y. (obtainable from Graduate School of Business, Columbia University), pp. 5, 6, and 8.

5. Finally, it strongly opposed federal legislation affecting municipal employee conditions of work.[34]

The positions taken by the NLC, among the stances of public sector organizations, are probably the most pointedly opposite to the aspirations of most unions. The policy statement, for example, does not even countenance the prospect of bargaining; it speaks only of allowing unions to "meet and confer" or to "negotiate in good faith." It does, however, support the idea of "exclusive recognition."

ADVISORY COUNCIL ON INTERGOVERNMENTAL PERSONNEL POLICY

Authorized by the Intergovernmental Personnel Act, the Advisory Council on Intergovernmental Personnel Policy was appointed by the President of the United States for the purpose of advising the federal government on a range of issues embraced by its title and explicitly on needs for policy changes or new legislation. The Council submitted two reports, including its basic recommendation for extension of merit principles to states under all federal grant programs.[35] The Council consisted of fourteen leaders in public life, including one state governor, one head of a state civil service agency, four city or county administrators, two federal officials, one consultant, two professors of government, one federal judge, and two representatives of national unions of state and local employees.

In its second and last report, submitted in 1974, the Council included a lengthy section on "Labor Management Relations." Its recommendations in this area are so pertinent to our study that they are quoted here in full:

1. Public sector employee management relations should be conducted within the framework of State law—not Federal law. The statute or statutes should be applicable to State employees, local government employees, and employees of other public and quasi-public agencies.
2. Employee Management Relations statutes should establish or designate a special impartial and independent board to administer the law.
3. Employe management relations statutes should require employer recognition of employee organizations which meet basic criteria; the different acceptable types, or levels of recognition should be specified in the law along with the associated criteria.
4. States should require reporting and disclosure of financial transactions and administrative practices, bonding requirements, and standards for

[34] *National Municipal Policy*, Adopted at the Forty-ninth Congress of Cities, November 26–30, 1972, Indianapolis, Ind. Washington, D.C., National League of Cities, 1973, section 4.300.

The NLC is the national spokesman for nearly 15,000 municipal governments located in all parts of the United States. Included is the vast majority of cities of over 30,000 population.

[35] See the discussion on intergovernmental personnel problems in Chapters 2 and 3.

trusteeships and election of officers modeled after the Labor Management Reporting and Disclosure Act of 1959.

5. Public employee organizations should be assured rights to become involved in the political process equal to, but no greater than, those of other public groups.

6. States, in framing their statutes, should take into account that different approaches to employee management relations are required in the public sector from those in use in the private sector. These necessary differences in approaches grow out of the very basic and very real differences between the two sectors. State statutes should contain provisions, among others, to assure the rights of all citizens and groups to be heard in the public policy making process and to establish the IPA merit principles as the basis on which comprehensive systems of public personnel management, including effective employee management relations programs, are built.

7. Employee management relations statutes should clearly and specifically establish the framework for collective negotiations.

8. State and local governments should establish as a high priority appropriate education and training both for those who will represent the public in labor negotiations and for the supervisors and managers who must implement agreements on a day to day basis. The Federal Government should increase substantially the information and technical assistance services it presently provides to States and local governments.

9. The legislature must be considered a part of management for employee management relations purposes. The results of public sector collective bargaining must always be made public. Agreements should not be implemented unless they are ratified by the appropriate governing body(ies), (executive and/or legislative).

10. Public management should be constrained from negotiating in certain areas. The negotiating table should be used as a problem-solving device on conditions of employment, not as a means of establishing public policy (i.e., the jurisdiction's mission, standards of service to the public, etc.).

11. The closed shop, the union shop, and the agency shop are unacceptable forms of union security for the public service. An agreement providing for the establishment of service fees for non-organization members in an exclusive bargaining unit, however, would not be contrary to merit principles so long as the fee schedule is approved by a vote of a majority of the unit; is for non-members on an individual basis only for those services which the individual requests and are actually provided; and does not exceed either members' dues or the actual cost incurred. Employee organizations should not be legally obligated to represent non-members on the individuals' complaints or grievances without appropriate compensation.

12. Strikes by public employees should be prohibited by law. Machinery

should be established to resolve impasses. Workable, usable, acceptable, and flexible strike penalties should be available.

13. The State statute should provide for a standard, commonly accepted means of determining unit size and assuring that bargaining units are comprehensive and cohesive.

14. The specific form for grievance handling where there is an exclusive bargaining unit should be negotiated, not legislated.

15. There should be available a wide range of alternatives for resolving negotiations impasses. Arbitration is an alternative of last resort.

16. Unfair labor practices for both employers and employee organizations should be delineated and prohibited.[36]

Although the two union members of the Council took exception to a few of these proposals, there was a remarkable amount of unanimity among the other members. The statement, taken as a whole, is undoubtedly the best prescription for action that has been issued by an official body. If the Council's recommendations became the basis for future policy in all jurisdictions, the reasonable distinctions from the private sector would be upheld, public employees would have an appropriate degree of influence apart from the political process, and the general public interest would be maintained.

*   *   *

THE SIGNIFICANCE OF our subject in the past three chapters is captured effectively in the following:

> In both public and private sectors, organized employees use power to affect the distribution of resources and the management of men and materials. In the private sector they do this primarily *as employees*. In the public sector they exert influence *as employees, as pressure groups, and as voting citizens*. "Management" officials in government, who are responsible directly or indirectly to the voters, are in this sense in a weaker position than are corporation managers in dealing with the demands of organized employees. This three-dimensional structure of public employee power greatly complicates the employment transaction in government and elevates it to a major problem in public administration, public law, and public finance.[37]

Thus, as we ponder the ethical standard that public officials have an obligation as well as a right to manage, the equity principle that public employees are entitled to nothing less than simple justice, the democratic postulate that both officials and employees owe responsibility, independence, integrity, and impartiality to the people, the efficiency criterion of effective and continuous

---

[36] The Advisory Council on Intergovernmental Personnel Policy, *More Effective Public Service*, The Supplementary Report to the President and the Congress, July 1974, pp. 14–37 (available through the U.S. Civil Service Commission).

[37] Stanley, *op. cit.*, p. 20.

performance—we can appreciate the enormous complexity that surrounds the modes and consequences of employee organization and representation in the public service. Participative management imposes great obligations on government managers, on politicians, on organized employees, and on the public. So much attention has been focused on rights that the obligations tend to be overlooked.

PART VII

Separation

Adversity has the effect of eliciting talents which in prosperous circumstances would have lain dormant.

Horace

Cowards die many times before their deaths; the valiant never taste of death but once.

Shakespeare

Though we seem grieved at the shortness of life in general, we are wishing every period of it at an end. The minor longs to be at age, then to be a man of business; then to make up an estate, then to arrive at honors, then to retire.

Addison

There is more to life than increasing its speed.

Gandhi

CHAPTER 22

Tenure, Turnover, and Staff Reductions

THE DESIRE TO be sure, to be protected, to find equanimity, to fulfill one's desires—in short, to be secure—is not the peculiar malaise of those who work for public authorities and draw their income from tax revenues. It is a basic human instinct to organize one's life so as to reduce to a minimum the conflicts, the stresses, the risks, the uncertainties that create threats or do harm to our mental, spiritual, or physical welfare. Indeed, we continually strive to organize ourselves so that life contributes *positively* to these needs. The only difference between the civil servant and the businessman in this respect is his standard of values—the goals he sets for himself and therefore the methods necessary to achieve them. Both seek security in one form or another.

In fact, striving for security is universal; for the quest is found in all stages and walks of life. Is it not being sought by the primitive hunter stalking game and storing provisions? By the entrepreneur inaugurating and consolidating a new enterprise? By employee unions seeking an annual wage or stability of employment? By big business promoting diversity of markets and adequate volume to assure continuity? By a nation legislating in behalf of the aged, war veterans, and the physically handicapped, or negotiating for international understanding and mutual aid, or training a military force? By the politician "mending his fences"? By the worker probing the work plans and intentions of his boss?

SECURITY OF TENURE

Security of tenure in the public service must be viewed in the context of this universal quest for security. Narrowing the application of the term to employment, we see that the problem of security in the public service differs from that in private industry only in the need to deal with the peculiar threats to security in government organizations—principally the danger of making employment contingent upon factors other than the performance of the worker. Meeting this danger was precisely the aim of the security of tenure espoused by the early civil service reformers and carried out in the tradition of merit system laws. And it has very substantial counterparts both in private employment and in the general economic system: provisions in union contracts and agreements, informal understandings between workers and owners in small organizations, price supports on agricultural products, subsidies to certain transport and other industries, guaranteed rates of return on investment to privately owned public utilities, various tax exemptions or allowances to protect certain industries, protective tariffs, and reciprocal international trade agreements.

MERIT-BASED TENURE

In essence, what is meant by employment tenure may be inferred from what has already been said about removal procedure. Where dismissal from a position may be based only on causes relating to the individual's performance and conduct, where it is for the good of the service and not to serve some ulterior or partisan interest, and where special procedures are laid down to ensure that terminations are governed by such principles, it may be said that job tenure prevails.

Note that it does *not* mean an absolute right of an employee to retain a position, nor an inability of management to separate an employee regardless of his behavior or the needs of the service, a view which some uninformed persons persist in holding about government employment. Separations under any merit system may take place when either the employee's action or inaction or the public agency's work requirements indicate that a termination is necessary. The only protective element in tenure—at least as it was initially intended—lies in procedure, that is, the assurance that the employee has an opportunity to contest any separation action so as to offset any possibility of prejudicial, arbitrary, or capricious decision by management. Where tenure goes beyond this elementary principle it does violence to the very foundation of the merit system idea—the concept that genuine merit on the part of the employee and genuine need for his services on the part of management should control employment, and that nothing else should interfere.

GENERAL TENURE LAWS

Until passage of the Veteran Preference Act of 1944 the emphasis in the federal civil service was laid more heavily on the entry process than on separation. The only references in statute until then had been the protection in the original Civil Service Act of 1883 against removal for refusal to contribute funds or service to political parties and the limitations of the Lloyd-La Follette Act of 1912 requiring that removals "promote the efficiency of the service" and that reasons be given in writing.[1] As already brought out, even with the additional prescriptions of the 1944 legislation and the appellate processes now applicable, a surprising number of separations of personnel do take place. The danger lies in the attitudes of those who still behave as if every separation is at least suspect and who wish to put management on ceaseless trial.

The basis for removal under state merit systems is usually as broad as it is in the federal civil service. Commonly, state laws limit dismissal to situations where there is "just cause," but occasionally more specific criteria, such as incompetency or misconduct, are specified. In several states, standard provisions extend to counties and cities within their respective jurisdictions. Hearings are allowed in almost all of these removal procedures.

Any difficulty in separating inefficient employees from merit system jurisdictions is not primarily attributable to the basic statutes concerning tenure. It is difficult to conceive how most of the laws could have been worded more broadly or have left more discretion to administrative authorities and still have provided some reasonable assurance that dismissals would serve the cause of merit alone. Reluctance of administrators to act and excessive pressures by court decisions and regulatory processes are the more probable reasons for a feeling of frustration in some quarters that getting rid of poor workers is more trouble than putting up with their shortcomings.

TENURE OF PUBLIC SCHOOL TEACHERS

The one area of public service in which tenure has asserted itself most strongly and in which the statutes are very explicit and restrictive is in school teaching. Over the long road to recognition of their occupation as a profession and as protection against favoritism and patronage, organized teachers have succeeded in promoting detailed tenure laws in the overwhelming majority of states. Under most of these tightly drawn statutes a school board must consider the competence of teachers very carefully during a probationary period, usually three years in length, and must grant tenure status where justified by performance. The degree to which this probationary scrutiny is conscientiously handled by school administrators is the degree to which reasonable restrictions on the dismissal process make sense. But loose entry during probation makes a tight tenure law a burden by protecting the incompetent along with the competent.[2]

The greater reliance on statutory provisions for teacher tenure, as contrasted with the rest of the public service, leads not only to somewhat less administrative latitude but also to more involvement of the courts. In addition to the steps of due notice and hearing common to all civil service

[1] See the discussion in Chapter 18. The respective statutory citations are 5 *U.S. Code* 7321 and 7501.

[2] Facts on teacher tenure laws are conveniently summarized by the Research Division of the National Education Association, Washington, D.C., in *School Law Summaries— Tenure and Contracts*, (loose-leaf), revised every December.

dismissal procedures, the process for teachers often expressly provides a role for the courts or at least encourages use of the judiciary as the forum of last resort. In some state laws the judicial branch is called into the process to make an initial settlement, unless the teacher wins his or her case at the school board level.[3]

This writer is well aware of the hazards of leaving final dismissal authority in the hands of local school boards and of the fact that the caliber of board members in some jurisdictions leaves much to be desired. But he is equally firm in the opinion that appeal to a higher level in the state school system should provide adequate recourse for an aggrieved teacher. Involvement of courts of law is out of place, except in the most extreme circumstances, in the making of such essentially administrative decisions as those affecting personnel. The only exception might be where charges against the teacher challenge his loyalty to the nation. The principle of tenure must never be distorted to mask a maudlin overprotection of mediocrity—which is what can occur when the legalisms of the court room replace administrative judgment and flexibility.

TURNOVER

Employees leave their jobs for a variety of reasons. Regardless of the degree of job security or tenure provided, this loss and replacement of workers—known as turnover—occurs in all large organizations. For convenience we may categorize departures from the job as (1) employer-initiated cases, such as instances of transfer, lay-off, or removal; (2) employee-initiated cases, chiefly those of voluntary resignation or optional retirement; and (3) uncontrollable events, such as instances of death or mandatory retirement. The rate of separation due to death or retirement may be a measure of the quality of staffing planning or the age of the organization. Turnover from these causes may be expected to be slight in relatively new agencies. For the sake of clarity, it must be acknowledged that most references to turnover contemplate only that variety of terminations culminating from resignations or voluntary "quits."

THE SIGNIFICANCE OF DEGREE

It has been commonplace in the industrial world for many years to view the heaviest incidence of turnover of workers—that is, voluntary separations

---

[3] In California, for example, if a teacher demands a hearing upon receiving a dismissal notice, the school board, unless it rescinds its action, must file a complaint in superior court, asking it to make inquiry and determine if grounds for dismissal are supportable. Court-appointed referees first hold hearings and report back to the court, after which a regular trial is held by the court itself, whereupon it decides whether the board may dismiss the teacher. Thus, any contested case calls the judiciary into the action. This is perhaps the most extreme instance of abridgement of executive power in American school administration.

The Commission on Professional Rights and Responsibilities of the National Education Association in its pamphlet, *Fair Dismissal Standards*, February 1969, clearly contemplates appeal to the courts as an essential part of fair procedure.

—as an unmitigated evil. And understandably so. The replacement and retraining of workers is an expensive process, and when such operations are unnecessary, they are certainly wasteful. To a considerable degree, perhaps for the masses of employees, the same principle applies to the public service.

MOBILITY   We must bear in mind, however, as we proceed with the ensuing discussion, that the objective of reasonable mobility of certain professional and managerial employees among public jurisdictions suggests that the traditional abhorrence of turnover, at least as far as these classes of workers are concerned, may be misplaced. In a democracy it may be desirable to ensure a certain amount of movement in the upper reaches of our public enterprises, without doing violence to merit and tenure principles, in order to ensure representativeness, freshness of viewpoint, and breadth of experience on the part of key workers. Hence, many of the comments about turnover, while applicable to the mass of employees in government activities, must be modified when we speak of categories for which a certain amount of mobility is an asset.

Another consideration applies generally. Even where mobility per se is no advantage, it must be acknowledged that the rate of movement out of an organization ultimately determines the opportunities for promotion within it. Thus, the annual rate of deaths, retirements, removals, and resignations is one factor that throws light upon the attractiveness of the organization to new recruits.

Nevertheless, a high incidence of resignations or other voluntary separations would seem to be the most significant index of the relative acceptability of employment conditions in the particular organization as compared with such conditions generally. It is for this category of turnover that a high rate is peculiarly a danger signal. Thus, the task of government management is to avoid the Scylla of a stagnant service while steering clear of the Charybdis of inordinate instability. This is not an easy task. It implies constant effort to improve methods of recruitment, selection, and placement, so that workers are well adjusted at the outset; it necessitates careful consideration of the policies in regard to compensation, promotion, transfer, and removal, and attention to working conditions in general. But the initial steps in dealing with the turnover problem are to record the facts and analyze the factors leading to separations, whether of a voluntary or an involuntary sort.

MEASURES   Turnover involves not only movements out of employment (separations) but movements into the service (accessions). The employee brought in as a replacement may be recruited from the outside or transferred from some other branch or department. There is no universally accepted formula for the measurement of turnover, and various studies have indicated wide divergences in the methods employed by personnel managers. Some have used the rate of accession, some the voluntary separation or quitting rate, others the rate of replacement. The last leaves out of account those employees whose services have terminated but who have not been replaced.

Theoretically, the replacement rate is the most accurate general measure of turnover, but the separation rate is the most widely employed measure and will suffice for most purposes in the public service. This rate is arrived at by dividing the total number of separations in a given time period (week, month, or year) by the average number of workers employed by the given agency or service for the period. It is customary to reduce this to a percentage.

The question arises as to the place of transfers in turnover calculation. Obviously, from the standpoint of the calculation of departmental rates, transfers out must be considered as separations. On the other hand, transfers within the department do not enter into that department's turnover, although they would enter into the turnover rates of the bureaus within the department. Finally, in computing the rate for the service as a whole, transfers are not considered.

ANALYZING SEPARATION RATES   The total separation rate is useful as a general average but suffers because of its composite character; that is, it is valuable in the same way as a fever chart. Just as when a patient's temperature rises above or falls below a certain norm, need for a diagnosis is indicated, so the turnover rate should be continuously checked and resolved into its several constituents: death rate, retirement rate, voluntary quitting rate, lay-off and removal rates, and so forth. When this has been done, the personnel manager is in possession of a serviceable tool for analysis of the employment situation in relation to economic and other pertinent conditions.

In general, the separation rate supplies a gauge of the general attractiveness of the service as a whole, in comparison with other employment opportunities. It is also an aid in analyzing differences between various units within a given service and between various grades and classes of employees. Further, it throws light on the relations among employees of differing age and length of service, at different locations, at different levels, and in different occupations.

There is no single desirable rate of turnover for all establishments, except that it should be sufficiently large to prevent stagnation and sufficiently small to reflect healthy working conditions. Within these broad limits, wide variations are likely, depending on the nature of the occupations, the kind of employees, their maturity, and other factors. For example, it is usual to find a much higher rate of turnover among younger workers, those with less total service, and those in lower grades. At one time it was assumed that turnover would always be higher among women employees, but in more recent years there are signs that the rates for men and women are approximating an equal level, when comparison is made on like work.[4]

In spite of the dearth of turnover data on public jurisdictions in general, such information as exists suggests that turnover in government employment is at least as low as in most private employment and actually lower than

---

[4] U.S. Department of Labor, *Facts About Women's Absenteeism and Labor Turnover*, Washington, D.C., August 1969, p. 2.

that in manufacturing industry.[5] This may be partially explained by the fact that a smaller proportion of public workers falls in the blue-collar labor groups, where movement from job to job generally tends to be higher. The one point that is most certain is the evident need for more reporting of data by state and local governments and for more analysis of the incidence of turnover by occupation, level, and cause. As in so many other aspects of personnel administration, here is an area where research could profitably serve the appraisal and development of policy.

Costs   The cost of hiring and training a new employee in private business has been calculated to run anywhere from a few hundred to several thousand dollars, depending on the industry and the occupation. Replacements in the civil service are probably even more expensive. Not only are the methods of recruitment and selection more complex but in many cases the work requires experience not obtainable outside, so that training and development expenses are often higher. Yet, few attempts have been made to estimate the cost of turnover in the public service. There is no reason why the overhead costs of the selection process could not be calculated, as well as the continuing operating costs such as lowering of output due to the presence of inexperienced workers, waste of materials, the time of trainers, and the general impairment of morale which is likely to accompany high turnover.[6]

CONTROL OF TURNOVER

From the standpoint of management, the problem of controlling turnover may be divided into two parts: first, determining the causes of the various types of separation; second, adjusting and developing the personnel program in the light of these causes.

Exit Interviews   The causes of labor turnover are numerous and complex, and many influences may be involved to which statistics can give only a lead. One of the most fruitful methods for uncovering the real factors involved in turnover is the exit interview—an interrogation of each employee who has signified his intention to quit, in order to ascertain his reasons and probe his feelings in general. This device has been widely employed by industrial personnel agencies and public organizations, and there is fairly general agreement among those who have used it concerning its value.

The functions of the exit interview may be listed as follows:

1. To learn all pertinent facts about each employee and his reasons for seeking employment elsewhere.

[5] This is the category of industry regularly reported in the *Monthly Labor Review*, published by the U.S. Department of Labor. For public service data, see U.S. Civil Service Commission, *Federal Employment Statistics Bulletin* (monthly), and information from annual reports of various state and local jurisdictions.

[6] For a general discussion of turnover measurement and costs in the industrial field, see Frederick J. Gaudet, *Labor Turnover: Calculation and Cost*, Research Study No. 39, New York, American Management Association, 1960.

2. To give information, whenever advisable, regarding opportunities in the organization and how the employee may best take advantage of them.
3. To serve the employee, taking into consideration his own best interests and the interests of the organization, and consequently to create a favorable attitude toward the organization.

The first function, that of discovering the real reasons for quitting, is not always easily accomplished because of the reluctance of many workers to reveal the true state of affairs. It is the most important of the three functions listed, because it may throw light on employment conditions that affect others and should be remedied. A standard classification of reasons for leaving can be used to make certain that comparable data can be compiled from the reports of various officers making exit interviews. The second function, pointing out alternative opportunities and making adjustments where they seem both desirable and possible, is essentially a last-minute placement effort, a part of the process of fitting workers to the right jobs. To be effective, of course, it requires a flexible transfer policy. Finally, the third function aims at building up one of the most valuable assets of any organization—good will.

It goes without saying that the exit interview is the proper responsibility of the personnel organization, either at the department level or in smaller jurisdictions at the offices of the central personnel agency. The techniques of the exit interview are not unlike those used in interviews for selection, except that more care may be required to elicit responses from individuals who have signified their intent to depart the organization than is necessary in talking with those who are seeking to join it.

CORRECTIVE MEASURES   The second phase of controlling turnover consists in making whatever adjustments in personnel policies or working conditions that have been suggested by the analysis of reasons for employee departures. Just as specific reasons for separation may vary widely, so the particular adjustments must vary from organization to organization and from time to time. Where employee dissatisfaction exists, it may in general be explained by either (1) failure to fit the person to the job or the job to the person, implying unsatisfactory selection and placement procedures, or (2) undesirable conditions relating to the work environment or rewards. To diagnose the causes and to design the appropriate remedial measures are clearly responsibilities of a high order of importance in any first-rate personnel program.

REDUCTIONS IN STAFF

One of the factors affecting the stability of any employment is the degree of fluctuation in the activity itself. Although much employment in the public service is more stable than that in many competitive industries, complete stabilization is impossible, even if desirable. Government, like industry, is frequently confronted with the unhappy task of curtailing its payrolls. In industry and in many local public services these retrenchments are commonly termed *lay-offs*. In the federal civil service they are known as *reductions in force*. The occasions for retrenchment are far less frequent in the ever-expanding state and local governments.

POLICY GUIDES

The necessity for a reduction in staff arises not only when a certain piece of work has been completed or when a contraction in governmental activity occurs at some point, but also when a cut in appropriations calls for a general reduction in the work force, with or without a reduction in the functions performed. In the first instance, the curtailment affects a particular agency or a particular type of employment; in the second, the effect is general, applying throughout the whole service. The two situations call for different treatment.

As a general principle, it should be the purpose of every employer to provide continuity of employment so long as the employee's services are satisfactory. Although not always feasible, it should at least be the guiding concept. Accordingly, if a staff reduction is found necessary in some agency or among a group of employees, every effort should be made to place those threatened with lay-off into other positions by means of the transfer process. The spectacle of one agency dismissing efficient employees while another is recruiting new ones for similar positions betokens poor management and a lack of appreciation of the workers' welfare. Judicious use of transfer machinery can do much to reduce this form of unnecessary and undesirable turnover.

When conditions demand a general reduction in force, affecting a number of departments and establishments, the situation becomes different. The problem then is one of selecting which employees are to be laid off or dismissed. Two factors are generally employed as criteria for such purpose: length of service and performance. The former is more commonly adopted. Thus, in many jurisdictions in the United States, it is provided that, in case of a reduction of force, employees be laid off in inverse order to the order in which they were hired. Similar procedures have been widely followed in industry.

Such a procedure has the advantage of fulfilling the responsibility of the employer to an employee who has a long record of service. It also has the advantage of simplicity in administration and can be applied without fear or favor. But since the primary aims of personnel administration are to bring into and retain in the service the best-qualified persons, it is open to objection. Seniority is not much better as a basis for retention in the service than it is for promotion. In both instances, due consideration should be given to the performance of the employees.

This fact has been recognized in the more progressive jurisdictions in this country. For example, some provide that the least efficient permanent employee as shown by the most recent efficiency ratings be laid off first, and so on in order of efficiency. This rule makes no provision for the weighing of factors other than those measured by the performance rating scheme. It may work out well, but it presupposes more discriminating records than are maintained in most jurisdictions.

As the result of union pressure, performance-related lay-off policies are being replaced in some jurisdictions by strict adherence to seniority. Such total abandonment of merit is obviously not the answer in the interest of a better public service.

FEDERAL EXPERIENCE

The problem of lay-offs in state and local jurisdictions is rarely as critical as it is in the U.S. civil service. In addition to the major contractions which took place in the federal service following World War II and again following the Korean emergency, there have been continuing changes in program and organization which have led to reductions in particular agencies. On top of this, the critical review of budgets and appropriations each year, creating the threat of retrenchment almost annually, is responsible for a highly charged atmosphere each spring and summer, particularly in the headquarters of agencies in Washington, D.C. More often than not, the threat of appropriation cuts is more serious than the final outcome. The morale-shattering effect of this annual effort to impress upon the bureaucracy that it is "swollen" and must retrench is rarely considered by politicians bent upon making a showing to their constituents back home, who are eager to see the bureaucracy reduced in the mistaken belief that it would make a significant difference in their taxes.[7] The advantage of budgeting and appropriating on a three-year or five-year basis, at least for most activities, is not often assessed from the viewpoint of sound personnel management.

Lay-offs in manufacturing industry are at a higher rate than those in the federal civil service, only because the former has a higher proportion of blue-collar workers. These craftsmen and laborers bear the brunt of industrial production shifts and technological changes. There is a similar disparity in separations due to lay-offs between manufacturing industry and white-collar enterprises, such as insurance companies. Even within the government, there are as sharp contrasts between different agencies or different activities within an agency as there are between certain kinds of government activity and certain kinds of business.

ORDER OF LAY-OFF   In the federal service the attempt has been made to combine various criteria for order of lay-off, including length of service and

---

[7] A surprisingly small percentage of federal expenditures (around 15 to 16 percent) goes to pay salaries of civilian employees. The bulk of federal taxation pays for munitions, maintenance of the armed services, interest on the public debt, veterans' benefits, and state grants-in-aid for welfare, highways, etc.—in other words, mostly for past and future wars, for materials and equipment, and for income maintenance.

performance, as established by the rules of the Civil Service Commission and by certain statutes. The present provisions may be summarized as follows:

1. Whenever an agency must reduce personnel, it must first determine which job categories can be eliminated with least damage to program.
2. Then it must consider all employees in the same commuting area who occupy such positions in which interchange of personnel is feasible. The highest retention preference is given to employees holding career appointments and the lowest to those holding appointments definitely limited to one year or less. An intermediate group is composed of career employees who are serving probationary periods and "career-conditional" employees —those who have not completed the three years of service required for career appointments.
3. Within each of these three groups there are two subgroups, veterans having higher retention preference than nonveterans. (Veterans who have been restored less than one year previously, under statutory provisions for restoration of permanent employees after military service, have the highest separation in one group of positions must, under certain conditions, be assigned to other positions.
4. Within each of the subgroups, retention preference is based on length of service, with credit added for outstanding performance. An exception to the regular order of selection may be made only when the employee to be retained is engaged in necessary duties which cannot be taken over without undue interruption to the activity by any employee with higher standing on the retention register. Permanent employees reached for separation in one group of positions must, under certain conditions, be assigned to other positions.
5. Any employee who believes that the regulations have not been correctly applied in his case may appeal to the Civil Service Commission. Any corrective action recommended by the Commission is mandatory upon the agency.

CHANGES PROPOSED   The first Hoover Commission recommended that the statutory base and regulations governing reductions in force be changed so that there would be more realistic ranking of employees from the standpoint of their overall usefulness to the agency in question and that such ranking be approached from the point of view of "which employees should be retained" rather than which should be eliminated.[8] The recommendation raises serious procedural difficulties when the competitive area includes positions under a number of supervisors. The second Hoover Commission suggested a sharp curtailment of veteran preference in connection with staff reductions. In 1955 this body urged a reduction in veteran advantage in retention by placing

[8] Commission on Organization of the Executive Branch of the Government, *Personnel Management: A Report to the Congress*, Washington, D.C., January 1949, pp. 34–35.

nonveterans with fifteen or more years of service in the same category as all veterans except those who are disabled. It did not go so far as its task force, however, which recommended elimination of veteran preference as a retention factor during lay-offs, even though continuing the counting of military service toward seniority.[9] This would be in line with the concept of preference as a readjustment aid in initial employment rather than as a continuing reward.[10] Once a person is in the service, considerations of merit and seniority would be the guiding controls for retention of the veteran as well as of the nonveteran.

REASSIGNMENT, REEMPLOYMENT, AND EARLY RETIREMENT

It is desirable that efficient employees separated from the service because of reduction in staff be given opportunity for reassignment where possible or for reemployment if an expansion in staff occurs within a reasonable time. Only by conferring upon this group a preferred status for a short time can the government's responsibility for continuity of employment be expressed. In both reassignments or reemployments, however, enthusiasm to "take care" of those with lay-off notices should not blind administrators to the necessity of maintaining the principle of merit.

LIBERAL TRANSFERS   In reassignments, the widest possible opportunity for displaced workers to be considered for other jobs should be fully exploited. Certainly, temporary or other transitional employees should not be kept on the rolls while career people are being separated. The system must be lubricated to assist in exploring every possible placement consistent with the laid-off employee's qualifications. But care must be taken to make certain that those placed are genuinely qualified for the work to which they are transferred. In the federal civil service, where many such reassignments must be made every year to avoid separations, a generous procedure facilitating placement of displaced employees is in operation, but in all such cases the individual must meet fully the qualification requirements of the position into which he is moved.

REEMPLOYMENT   It becomes necessary, also, to surround any subsequent reemployment procedure with restrictions to assure that it contributes to the good of the service. This is a particularly difficult task. If separations on account of reduction in force are based primarily upon the criterion of efficiency, as they should be, those laid off may be in fact "the halt and the lame" of the service. The question then arises whether they should have what amounts to a lien on employment or should be required to enter into open competition for any future vacancies.

[9] Commission on Organization of the Executive Branch of the Government, *Personnel and Civil Service*, Washington, D.C., February 1955, p. 73, and *Task Force Report on Personnel and Civil Service*, Washington, D.C., February 1955, p. 104.

[10] See the discussion in Chapter 9 relating to veteran preference.

This illustrates again the dependence of one aspect of the personnel program upon others. Assuming, first, recruitment and selection systems which bring the best available talent into the service and, second, a vigorous exercise of the removal power to rid the service of any misfits who do secure appointment, the advantages of according a limited preferred status to laid-off employees are clear. Many factors enter into this point of view, among them the beneficial effect upon the morale of those still in the service. The responsibility of the government toward employees separated through no fault of their own has been quite generally recognized.

A sensible procedure would seem to be one that gives top priority to laid-off employees for any vacancies that occur in a given geographic area and occupational category, provided their work records have been entirely satisfactory. In addition, it has been suggested that laid-off workers be kept on the payroll for several months or until they are assigned to new jobs, with the idea that they constitute a kind of reserve in which the employing organization has a considerable investment and toward which it has a distinct obligation.[11] Although this is an accepted procedure in the military service, it may be some time before it is regarded as feasible in civil services by those who guard the interest of the taxpayer—even though in the long run such a policy may be in that very interest.

EARLY OPTIONAL RETIREMENT   Where the retirement system is sufficiently flexible to permit it, the prospect of lay-off can be an occasion to trigger an early retirement. In the federal civil service, for example, it is possible for an employee who receives a reduction-in-force notice to elect to take a "discontinued service annuity" under the retirement plan, provided he has met age and service requirements that are considerably more relaxed than those necessary for ordinary optional retirement. Employees threatened with involuntary separation due to staff reductions who are at least fifty years of age and have twenty years of service, or those who have twenty-five years of service, regardless of age, may avail themselves of this opportunity if such retirement would lessen the overall number of separations in the particular unit or category in which they are competing for retention. This is a model provision which other jurisdictions would do well to emulate. It is generous to the persons who choose the retirement route, and it eases the impact on younger employees who do not have such an alternative.

UNEMPLOYMENT INSURANCE

The guarantee of some minimal income to workers for limited periods following a lay-off has been a cornerstone of American social security since 1936. Administered through separate state systems, this plan of unemployment insurance has been available to state and local governments from the

---

[11] The 1949 Hoover Commission made such a proposal (*Personnel Management,* p. 37).

beginning. Although federal financial assistance to the state systems on the basis of a tax offset plan does not apply to state or local government employees, most states (and the District of Columbia) provide this insurance coverage to their public employees—usually including local as well as state workers. Unemployment insurance was not made applicable to federal workers until 1955. Considering the frequency of reductions in force in the national establishment, it is strange that nearly two decades elapsed before extension of this elementary justice came to pass.

In the meantime federal employees relied on payments for their accumulated annual leave as cushions in the event of lay-off. Apart from the arbitrary limitations on such accumulations, these leave payments represent amounts already earned by the workers to which they would be entitled in one form or another regardless of whether they were laid off and should not be viewed as a proper substitution for unemployment insurance.

Although the general plan is complex in administration, owing to the operation through fifty somewhat varying state systems, federal agencies have worked out a standard procedure for compliance with individual state laws. When a laid-off employee applies to a state employment agency in the area where his last federal establishment is located, his former employer certifies (on standard forms, used with all the states) as to his earnings and the reasons for separation. Until the state agency can find him another job reasonably appropriate to his skills or until the maximum period of insurance is reached, the state pays him weekly compensation bearing some relation to his previous earnings, within the particular minimum and maximum rates paid to other unemployed workers in that state.

*　　　*　　　*

ASSUMING VIGOROUS EXERCISE of the power of rejection during the probationary period and courageous use of the removal power at any time to weed out the unfit, then the public employer is obligated to be aware of what is happening by way of turnover, to engage in constant revamping of policy and working conditions to assure retention of the best in the service, to stimulate a healthy degree of mobility, and to demonstrate a genuine concern for the utilization and welfare of any employees threatened with separation through no fault of their own. Nothing less is worthy of enlightened personnel administration.

CHAPTER 23

Retirement and Disability

ONE OF THE areas of personnel administration which was slow to evolve was systematic and humane attention to the matter of separation of employees by reason of age, disability, or death. Until a comparatively few decades ago this critical aspect of the husbanding of the human resources of organization was handled in manners ranging from the haphazard to the unjust. Neglect and failure in this area was at least as true of industrial personnel management as it was in the public sphere. In turn, evolution of the modern concept of retirement systems has run the gamut from expediency and charity to the idea of the employee's right to a *deferred salary* upon completion of a career.

ORIGINS AND PURPOSES

THE BRITISH EXAMPLE

Great Britain was far ahead of the United States in establishing funds and schemes to compensate for *superannuation*.[1] With roots going back to a pension plan for the British Customs Service as early as 1712, the first comprehensive law created a generous arrangement for all civil servants in England in 1810, with important revisions in 1857 and others later. Privilege and corruption in the civil service near the end of the eighteenth century had led to the drive for paying pensions entirely out of public funds. The main features of the 1857 revision—a noncontributory plan (fully financed

---

[1] A term contrived to convey a point in one's career where usefulness on the job demonstrably begins to decline because of advanced age.

by the employer), a scale of pensions based on annual increments, and recognition of the age of sixty years as the normal time of retirement—are still in force.[2]

AMERICAN DEVELOPMENTS

By comparison, developments in this country were slow and halting. The federal government has had a retirement system for its civil employees since 1920, which became a true annuity plan based on actuarial principles in 1930 and was greatly revamped and liberalized in 1956 and subsequently.[3] States and municipalities followed suit during the decades following, so that today all states have some kind of contributory system for retirement annuities.[4] A determining factor in promoting public service retirement systems was the passage of the Social Security Act of 1936 which had compelled private employers and workers, with few exceptions, to contribute to reserve funds to be used for a nationwide annuity plan. Public jurisdictions had little choice but to provide at least equivalent arrangements. An amendment in 1950 gave further impetus to government retirement plans by extending coverage of the general social security law to public workers not yet under retirement systems and gave annuitant survivors greater protection than that allowed in many of the state and local plans then existing. Most important, it provided continuity of minimal protection for workers who shifted from one job to another in public employment or between public and private employment, without weakening in any way existing public retirement systems or affecting their independence.

The history of public retirement legislation in the United States has been one of multiple plans covering particular jurisdictions, departments, or employment categories, beginning with those for which there was strong employee organization pressure, special public appeal, or concern about hazardous duty. The first groups covered therefore were, not surprisingly, police, firemen, and school teachers. More recently, there has been a steady trend toward statewide retirement systems covering municipal and other local employees, thus resulting in a gradual decrease in purely local plans.

As the national social security underpinning was extended to public services, retirement systems were usually revised to provide supplementary

---

[2] Marios Raphael, *Pensions and Public Servants; A Study of the Origins of the British System*, Paris, Mouton, 1964, *passim*. Interestingly, separation before age sixty could occur with medical certification (the antecedent of disability retirement); sixty was the age after which retirement could take place without such certification. Another book on British pension systems, covering both government and nationalized industries, is Gerald Rhodes, *Public Sector Pensions*, London, Royal Institute of Public Administration, 1965.

[3] The current provisions are in 5 *U.S. Code* 8301–8348.

[4] Payroll deductions range from three to six percent; almost all plans have disability benefits, and almost all have some provision for "vesting" of contributions so that employees may be certain to recover their contributions in some form, if not in annuities. Council of State Governments, *Fringe Benefits in State Government Employment*, Chicago, May 1968, Table 10.

protection in such a way that the total protection under the two systems was greater than could be provided under either alone. Also, it is an accepted fact that statewide systems are virtually essential for small localities, on the grounds that a broad base is necessary to spread the risk and to permit advantageous investment of funds, as well as for reasons of efficient administration and audit. Even more important, a common system throughout a state makes for greater possible mobility of employees among governmental units within that jurisdiction.

PURPOSES

From the standpoint of the government as employer, the primary object of an adequate retirement system is, to put it in the simplest terms, improvement of the staff. It facilitates the graceful and humane elimination of the superannuated and those who otherwise become incapacitated. The fact that a worker could be kept at his desk or bench until he died, as was typical of American civil services for all too long a time, meant not only poor performance but less opportunity for promotion of others. It is fully recognized now that a retirement plan contributes to employee advancement opportunity and therefore to incentive, and also to planning for recruitment and replacement. Although at one time objectives were expressed primarily in humanitarian terms, the more realistic look suggests that reasons of administrative efficiency are sufficient unto themselves to justify a proper retirement program. Where no retirement system existed, the actual result—in performance of the superannuated—tended to be *pensions at full pay.* Such a condition appeals neither to the conscientious administrator nor to the intelligent taxpayer.

The advantages of retirement annuities to employees are obvious. It assures them against a penniless old age or against pauperism due to disability. It serves as a needed supplement to income received during their working careers that has seldom been of dimensions permitting accumulation of substantial savings.

In effect, then, a retirement annuity upon leaving the service for reasons of age or disability (or for discontinuance of the job) is genuinely a form of *deferred compensation.* The benefit is not a gratuity but a straight business proposition serving the interests of the service and the employee in equal measure.

Simultaneous with the development of retirement systems in public employment, comparable pension arrangements were blossoming in private industry under the same twin stimuli of hard-headed practicality and the impetus of national social security. Today most large employers sponsor retirement plans that supplement basic social security, and the details are frequently the subject of union-management agrements. The history of such systems has, like those in government service, evolved from considerations of business expediency to those of social responsibility based on the concept of the deferred wage. The tendency in these plans has been to make the financing of pension funds entirely the employer's responsibility, but with many permitting augmentation by employees, whereas those in the public service have almost without exception been jointly supported (or "contributory"). Where private employees do regularly contribute a share of the upkeep, the percentage of payroll deduction is usually substantially less than that in most public jurisdictions. On the other hand, the public plans are, more often than not, the more rewarding in ultimate benefits.[5]

CHARACTERISTICS OF SYSTEMS

By way of definition, the term *retirement system* is used here to embrace both a *method of financing* of deferred compensation and any of several *conditions of payment*. The latter include:

1. annuity upon separation from the service *by virtue of age*, acquired under one or another of the following conditions:
   a. *optional retirement*, after a specified minimum age and minimum service,
   b. *mandatory retirement*, upon attainment of a specified *maximum* age and minimum service, *or*
   c. *flexible retirement*, under sundry combinations of circumstances;
2. annuity upon separation due to physical or mental *disability*, following some minimum period of service;
3. annuity upon separation due to *retrenchment* of staff; *and*
4. annuity to *survivors or dependents* upon *death* of an employee in the service or during retirement.

[5] Typical of the literature in the business arena are: Dan M. McGill, *Fundamentals of Private Pensions*, 2nd ed., Homewood, Ill., Richard D. Irwin, 1964; and Joseph J. Melone and Everett T. Allen, Jr., *Pension Planning; Pensions, Profit Sharing, and Other Deferred Compensation Plans*, Homewood, Ill., Dow Jones-Irwin, 1966. Both of these books are comprehensive texts on the concepts and technical elements of industrial retirement and related systems of deferred compensation. A volume that demonstrates the prevailing inferiority of American industrial plans (in coverage, benefits, and vesting) is Merton C. Bernstein, *The Future of Private Pensions*, London, Free Press, 1964.

Two of the recent works on retirement systems in the United States are: (1) Gordon F. Streib and Clement J. Schneider, S.J., *Retirement in American Society: Impact and Process*, Ithaca, N.Y., Cornell University Press, 1971, which reports the results of research (among several thousand retirees) on the characteristics and activities of retirees and on the effects of having a major sector of the population in a state of retirement; and (2) James H. Schulz, Guy Carrin, Hans Krupp, Manfred Peschke, Elliott Sclar, and J. Van Steenberge, *Providing Adequate Retirement Income: Pension Reform in the United States and Abroad*, Hanover, N.H., The University Press of New England, 1974, which focuses mainly on national social security systems and compares U.S. developments with those in foreign countries, principally Canada, Belgium, Germany, and Sweden.

Retirement systems in the private sector are now subject to vesting and fiduciary standards prescribed by the federal government, under the *Employee Retirement Income Security Act of 1974*. This Act also initiated a study to determine whether state and local government retirement plans should be regulated in similar fashion. A report was to be made by December 31, 1976.

The supporting mechanisms and the various considerations that enter into all of these alternatives deserve further examination.

FUNDING AND ANNUITY SYSTEMS

CASH AND ACTUARIAL FORMS

The financing for retirement systems may be classed generally as either of the "cash disbursement" variety or of the "actuarial reserve" type. As the name implies, the cash disbursement method entails appropriation of sufficient funds each year out of current revenues to pay the annuities due that year. An actuarial reserve, or "funded," plan is one in which there is current provision for meeting future liabilities. In other words, a portion of the retirement annuities payable to each employee in the future, calculated on an actuarial basis, is presumed to be accrued during each year of the employee's active service, thus building up a reserve fund which may be invested and earn interest. The mathematical calculations involved include projection of anticipated earnings on the reserve plus the periodic contributions, so as to keep the amount sufficient to meet benefit obligations as they mature.

In spite of the simplicity of the annual cash appropriation and disbursement approach, based as it is on annual estimates of how much must be paid out in annuities, it is a shortsighted and irresponsible method of meeting future obligations. Its attractiveness in the youthful days of a retirement system, when income from contributions is high and payments out are low, conceals the financial burden which is being postponed to future generations when the number of annuitants to be paid will mount. The danger, of course, is that political pressure to curtail, or at least to resist liberalization of, the retirement benefits will mount with equal insistence.

ADVANTAGES OF ACTUARIAL RESERVE

Sound fiscal planning clearly supports the actuarial reserve or some equivalent method over such a piecemeal approach, for these reasons: (1) it results in approximate leveling of annual cost, with a fairly uniform ratio between the amount of the annual payroll and the contributions to the retirement fund; (2) it is in accord with the concept of retirement expenditures as a continuing charge for depreciation of the work force; (3) the annual cost is reduced by the interest earned on investment of the funds accumulated; (4) the very existence of the reserve provides reasonable assurance that benefits will definitely be paid; and (5) the higher cost in the early years, as compared with the initially lower but constantly rising cost of the cash plan, acts as a brake on unwise or overliberal improvement of benefits, since the precise cost can be more readily discerned currently as well as in the future. Consequently, there is little argument over the desirability of the actuarial funded method.

It is not surprising that most public retirement systems are now funded under an actuarial reserve plan, but a few persist with the unsound cash payment method. Curiously, the largest system of all, that for the federal civil service (covering close to three million persons) survived for fifty years before it was placed on a fully financed, cost-guaranteed basis. Because of substantial contributions by both employees and the government and because of the constant growth in size of the work force, thus keeping contributions ahead of annuity claims, it managed to develop enough of a fund to meet all obligations, but projections clearly showed that the fund would be depleted in the 1970s. In 1969, following periodic efforts by successive presidents and civil service commissioners to get some relief in the situation, the Congress passed legislation that provides, in addition to adequate contribution formulae, for permanent indefinite appropriations and payment of interest to the fund equal to what would be earned on a true actuarial reserve.[6] In this way, future liabilities are guaranteed to be met. This approach, while the equivalent to an actuarial system and entirely practical for an institution as supreme and powerful as the federal government, would hardly be practical for the average public jurisdiction. Hence, reliance on standard actuarial funding is the only viable financial approach for the typical public retirement system.

CONTRIBUTORY AND NONCONTRIBUTORY SYSTEMS

Accepting the philosophy of the annuity as deferred compensation and the principle of the mutuality of interest between the employer and the employee, it seems reasonable that the cost of retirement benefits should be shared by the two. In effect, this is what happens anyway. Even under the so-called noncontributory systems, although the employing organization presumably bears the entire burden, it may be in part borne by the employees through lower salaries. It is much more desirable to recognize this fact by the adoption of a joint contributory system. As a matter of fact, the arguments for either the contributory or the noncontributory system are more largely psychological than economic. As far as the cost of the retirement benefits is concerned, it makes little difference which of the two principles is adopted, although there does appear to be a greater tendency for contributory systems to be operated upon an actuarial reserve basis.

Among other advantages, it is sometimes easier to establish and maintain a system under the contributory principle, because the apparent burden is divided, and further, this may check extravagant demands on the part of employees, since it is clear that a part of the cost would be borne by themselves. Moreover, in accord with the theory that the faculties of the employee

---

[6] PL 91–93, October 29, 1969. The Secretary of the Treasury is required by this law to credit to the fund annually interest based on the amount of "unfunded liability" computed for that year. It also provides for more or less automatic financing of any new liberalizations in benefit provisions. The payroll deduction for employee contributions is set at 7 percent.

are being used up by the organization in which he is employed as well as by his own personal pursuits, a joint responsibility rests upon the employer and the employee for building up the resources that would sustain the employee during the time when these faculties will have declined.

Generally speaking, the joint contributory principle appears to have found greater favor in the United States than the noncontributory. The federal system and almost all state and municipal systems are contributory. Although noncontributory systems continue in the military service and seem to maintain a substantial popularity among private business concerns, there has been a noticeable trend among the latter toward contributory plans.

At this point it may be noted that, whatever the contribution formulae, a first-rate retirement system will seek constantly to adjust its features to the needs of the service. Factors of size, age distribution, turnover, mobility, and the like, must be continuously analyzed by persons with actuarial training to make certain that the system will be responsive to future requirements. Since so many of the calculations and projections necessary are based on the law of averages, a system encompassing and serving large numbers is more reliable in this respect than one for a small group. Indeed, from almost any standpoint, the larger the coverage of a retirement plan the more dependable and flexible it is likely to be. The independence and separatism of so many of our public plans is certainly not consistent with the best that can be anticipated in public personnel administration.

BENEFITS

RETIREMENT FOR AGE   Provision of a retirement annuity for persons who have reached some combination of age and service is the primary justification for a retirement system and likewise the most common manifestation of one in practice. Originally, the emphasis was on compulsory separation at an advanced age in order to protect the service from the declining efficiency of the superannuated. But, as annuity income has become more common and relied upon, pressures have developed to liberalize systems so that a greater variety of options become available—with the result that, quite the opposite from the situation before such systems were commonplace, more and more employees (at least those in jurisdictions that have generous systems) seek provision for and avail themselves of retirement privileges as soon as they can.

The typical system makes it possible for varying combinations of age and service to qualify for an annuity. Age spans tend to range from 55 to 70, and service length from 25 years on up. Generally, more service would be required of the younger retiree than of the older, and the benefits in the form of annuities are usually actuarially reduced as lesser age-service combinations apply. Anything short of separation at a mandatory maximum age limit is referred to as "optional" retirement, while separation at the maximum age is termed "mandatory" or "compulsory" retirement. The maximum age for pensions under private business schemes, frequently around 62 to 65, tend to be lower than those in the public plans, which run more in the 65 to 70 range.[7]

The public service practice of rather high mandatory age requirements is more consistent than industrial practice with society's need to keep people in productive employment as long as they are capable and to make the latter years of workers healthier and more meaningful. As life expectancy increases, the support of an increasing proportion of nonproducing older citizens would also heavily burden the relatively smaller group of younger people. Hence, rather high-age compulsory retirement provisions make sense, if indeed there needs to be an absolute maximum at all. Both the increasing proportion of persons in the older age groups in the population and the advancing life expectancy in general have led many students of the subject to question whether there should be absolute mandatory features to retirement systems and to suggest more flexible arrangements instead. Partly as a result of these searching inquiries and concomitant proposals, the trend toward more flexible systems has been marked, both in industry and government.

Flexibility takes any of several forms: provision for rehiring annuitants after retirement where their services are especially needed and their capacities unquestioned; development of alternative assignments, sometimes part-time, permitting a more gradual detachment or "tapering off" from the organization; or abandonment of the maximum age proviso entirely, leaving compulsory retirement up to ad hoc determinations by panels of colleagues and experts in the organization which act on the basis of a more reasoned appraisal of the individual's continued usefulness than that afforded by the arbitrary indicator of chronological age.[8] The purpose of eliminating the truly superannuated may be better served by depending on examination of individual health and aptitudes, the nature of the work, and the possibility of "tapering off" assignments than by sudden separation based only on an arbitrary criterion.

At the same time, and based equally on the fact of individual differences and the imperatives of different work situations, the opportunity for early optional retirement makes sense. In some cases, the type of work, such as unusually hazardous or physically strenuous jobs, might call for express provision for earlier retirement options than those available to the general em-

---

[7] The minimal combinations of service and age under the federal civil service system are as follows:

Age	Service	
55	30	*(Optional)*
62	15	*(Optional)*
70	15	*(Mandatory)*

[8] Along with the high age for mandatory retirement (70), the federal system has long permitted reemployment of annuitants where there is special need for their services. Fears that such a policy might lead to keeping too many of the superannuated on duty have been totally unfounded, especially since only a small percentage of retirees wait until the maximum age to terminate their careers.

ployee population.[9] In others, such as in professional work, it may be salutary to encourage employees to avoid going stale on the job by taking advantage of early retirement options and engaging in some self-renewing alternative activity, a possibility especially available to many professionals. It may also be argued that, if the option of early retirement is open to the employee, it ought also to be open to management. Thus, when minimal conditions of age and service have been met, a dignified separation with annuity, instead of ordinary dismissal, can be made of persons who are unable to measure up to demanding jobs. This is an especially reasonable and humane procedure for termination from tension-packed executive posts and where outright removal would seem unduly harsh after an individual has in general served an honorable and useful career. In such cases, a decision by a panel of superiors and peers could avoid the suspicion of prejudicial or arbitrary action.

In sum, there is everything to be said for a flexible approach to retirement from all points of view. Unfortunately, the tendency has been for employee organizations to press for more liberal and flexible opportunities for their members to retire but at the same time to resist efforts to allow management to exercise the same options, even when the latter would have applied only to higher-level professional and managerial personnel.[10]

RETIREMENT FOR DISABILITY   No retirement system is complete without a plan for premature retirement of workers who become so handicapped as the result of illness or accident that they are unable to perform their duties. Most public systems provide annuities for this purpose regardless of whether the disability occurred in line of duty (commonly referred to as "service-connected") or as the result of something that happened off the job. A minimum period of service is almost invariably required before disability benefits may be paid under a plan. The amount of the annuity ordinarily depends on the salary and amount of service the individual has had. Where employees are covered under a workman's injury compensation law, the retirement system may simply pay the difference between the injury compensation and the benefits due under the disability clause.

It goes without saying that an employee physically unable to perform the duties of his current job should first be given an opportunity to perform other work for which he is qualified and physically suited, if that should be his preference and if such reassignment can be made without displacing someone else. In such cases, as well as in making the disability determinations

[9] For example, police and fire protection. The federal system has long permitted persons engaged in investigation, apprehension, or detention of suspected or convicted criminals to retire when they reach the combination of age 50 and 20 years of service.

[10] Discussions of "flexible," "selective," or "gradual" retirement are replete in the literature, concentrating principally on the industrial setting. Attention is particularly called to Geneva Mathiasen, ed., *Flexible Retirement*, New York, Putnam, 1957; and Richard A. Beaumont and James W. Tower, *Executive Retirement and Effective Management*, Industrial Relations Monograph No. 20, New York, Industrial Relations Counselors, 1961.

in the first place, it is obvious that the services of one or more physicians are required. Also, it should be clear that any retiree who recovers from his disability sufficiently to warrant reemployment should be required to give up his annuity and offered the chance to return to work. If part-time remunerative employment is possible, his annuity could be reduced accordingly. For those workers who become disabled before meeting minimum service requirements, the state injury compensation law ordinarily provides the only income protection.

RETIREMENT DUE TO RETRENCHMENT   We have already taken note how reductions in staff can be ameliorated by use of the retirement system. Typically, as in the federal service (which is the only one where reductions of any consequence normally take place), a lesser combination of age and service factors than that ordinarily required permits drawing an annuity whenever an individual is laid off. This procedure can supply an extremely valuable cushioning effect in the trying times of retrenchment.

DEATH   Under a sound retirement system the minimum benefit to survivors upon death of an employee would be the amount of the employee's contributions to the retirement fund plus accumulated interest. If the organization also has a group life insurance program, the foregoing is all that need be expected of the retirement system. However, in any instance where death is in line of duty, a greater obligation falls upon the system to provide a more generous benefit. A fair plan is to base such an extra insurance feature in some fashion on the amount of the employee's salary.

WITHDRAWAL FROM SERVICE AND VESTING   Obviously provision must also be made for appropriate disposition of the employee's accumulated contributions in case he leaves the service before he is eligible for retirement. Such disposition may take any of the following forms: return of the contributions with interest in lump sum to the employee upon his departure; payment of an annuity deferred until an optional retirement age is reached; or allowing the employee to choose either the immediate refund or the deferred annuity. Ordinarily some minimal period of service is necessary to authorize the deferred annuity alternative.

Making it possible to draw such a deferred annuity applies the principle of "vesting," that is, a kind of investment permitting some level of annuity in later years even when total service in the system is less than qualifying for full annuity. Vesting not only contributes to the purpose for which the system was designed (to provide an income for old age), but it eliminates the bane of many of the early retirement systems, namely, the binding of workers to one employer because of severe penalties attached to leaving.

ANNUITY COMPUTATION   There is probably no aspect of retirement plans in which more variation takes place than in the manner by which annuities are calculated. The most that can be said by way of universal application is confined to some very general precepts.

First of all, the size of the annuity is related to the salary level of the employee, on the theory that the more he is paid the more he can afford to set aside for retirement and the more he will need to approximate the standard of living to which he has become accustomed. The salary level is usually arrived at by averaging the pay for some portion of the period of service, such as the most recent or the highest-paying several years.[11] Some stipulated fraction is then usually applied to this salary average, and the total is thereupon multiplied by the number of years of service to arrive at the annual benefit or annuity. Under most retirement systems, the worker in the medium salary brackets and with substantial total service can count on an annuity approximating half his pay, increasing to as high as 75 or 80 percent with extraordinarily long service.

One unfortunate feature of many retirement annuities is that the recipient finds his income "frozen" in times of price inflation, so that what he had earned as a lifetime benefit gradually erodes in the wake of constantly increasing living costs. Since 1962, this problem has been solved in the federal retirement systems (general civil service, foreign service, and military) by a periodic percentage adjustment in annuities that is automatically triggered by specified increases in the cost-of-living index.[12] This plan, based on a generally fair though complex formula, has worked well. However, the extraordinary inflation of the early 1970s and the resulting dramatic increases in federal annuities have stimulated criticism from some sectors in American society that are not so fortunate and are unwilling to see such generous treatment for what they consider a "favored" group.

SURVIVOR PROTECTION   Although it was not characteristic of the first retirement systems, most now provide that the retiree, by electing a somewhat smaller annuity, may ensure a continuation of a portion of his annuity for his spouse or other dependents who survive him. Amounts of the retiree's annuity and of that of his survivor are computed on an actuarial basis, taking into account the probabilities of life expectancy. Needless to say, with the greater sophistication among the general population on matters of insurance, this matter of survivor protection has come to be one of the most important features of the whole idea of retirement income. It is the rare (and probably not very discerning) individual who fails to choose the annuity option that ensures an income for his survivor.

---

[11] In the federal system the average salary for the three highest paid years is used as the base. Other systems use an average of anywhere from two to five years, and some take whatever is the most recent actual salary.

[12] An alternative method for adjusting annuities would be to use general wage and salary changes as the guide rather than the cost-of-living index. This would permit reflection of changes in standard of living as well as in purchasing power. So far, it has not been tried.

ADMINISTRATION

The central personnel agency is the logical location for administration of a jurisdiction's retirement system. Costs of administration are customarily borne by the government involved. Because of public concern over the potentialities of misuse of reserve funds, it is not uncommon and not unwise for a policy board of some kind to oversee the operation of the system. Where a joint contributory plan is in effect, representation on such a board of employee groups covered under the plan is desirable. Their money, along with that of the government, is being managed, and they should be expected to share the responsibility for its safe and effective use, especially when it comes to investment and the relationship between earnings and benefits. The board of trustees or overseers should, however, confine its role to that of determining general policy. As to the actuarial and other technical work required in sound administration of the system, the career staff designated for the purpose should have the requisite authority for daily transactions and methodology.

Except perhaps when a new system is being installed for the first time, membership in a retirement system should be compulsory for all full-time, continuing workers as a condition of their employment. This policy is necessary to ensure a broad-based system covering an adequately representative range of people as to vocation, age, and life expectancy, to provide management the guarantee that the superannuated can be separated without deprivation of income, and to make certain that employees participate in assurance of their own protection for their advancing years. Temporary, limited-term, or part-time employees are more appropriately made subject to the compulsory national social security system alone, without augmentation by the staff retirement system.

PREPARATION FOR RETIREMENT

More and more employers, public and private, are concerning themselves with the obligation to help prepare employees who want and need the help to make the transition from a work environment to retirement. Especially for those who have not given the matter much thought or whose intellectual or educational preparation is not as adaptable, sudden adjustment to retirement can be a traumatic experience. On the other hand, many who have abundant emotional and mental resources to adapt to a new life are quite prepared for the experience. In either case, nevertheless, some adjustment is likely necessary to a new level of income. All will be concerned with their continuing health. Some will need advice as to avocational pursuits, travel, or other use of leisure time.

It is with such subjects that anticipatory planning before retirement deals. For those whose retirement is in sight, conference groups, movies, and reading matter can provide useful information and ideas. Progressive public agencies regularly make such programs available to prospective retirees. As in so many aspects of personnel administration, however, relationships with employees in retirement preparation or counseling must be highly flexible to permit individualized treatment. Higher-level and better-educated employees, feeling more self-sufficient than others, may even resent too much advice—which they may consider paternalistic or at least superfluous. On the other hand, they may welcome some of the information that would not otherwise be readily accessible to them. Proffering of assistance by the organization should make clear that attendance or participation in preretirement programs is entirely voluntary. Perhaps as more flexible retirement policies are developed, the emphasis in preretirement counseling will be on winning acceptance or instilling understanding of a "tapering off" or some other gradual transition instead of preparation for complete severance of connection from the work place.[13]

RETIREMENT AND MOBILITY

Retirement systems are now so widely accepted that it is commonly overlooked that one of the sales arguments used in their original adoption was the attraction they would have to employees to remain with any employer who had a plan. In other words, it was frankly anticipated that the prospect of pensions and the loss of eligibility upon resignation would deter employees from casual job-jumping and thus reduce costly turnover. There is no doubt that this has been one of the effects of individual systems localized with single employers.

NEED FOR MOBILITY

More recently, the American public service has been faced with an opposite problem—how to facilitate, not obstruct, the movement of at least certain professional and managerial personnel among public jurisdictions and in some instances even between the public service and private fields of endeavor. The interrelationships among federal, state, county, and municipal functions in almost every area of governmental policy—education, housing, welfare, health, agriculture, road construction, employment, taxation, and various others—point up the need for more diversified experience of public servants at all levels.

This means increasing opportunities for employees to work for more than one jurisdiction during their careers, for an individual to be able to move freely from one government to another where his services are needed without

---

[13] The following publication contains results of a survey of practice and experience with preretirement preparation in federal government agencies: American Association of Retired Persons, *Preparation for Retirement; A New Guide to Program Development*, prepared under the direction of William L. Mitchell, Washington, D.C., 1968.

Following this study and a supplementary one among annuitants conducted by the U.S. Civil Service Commission, preretirement activities among federal departments have been broadened and extended.

Countless books and pamphlets appear in American libraries advising retirees on ways to find usefulness and happiness during their retirement years.

sacrifice of his "investment" in the fringe benefits, and particularly the retirement system, of his original jurisdiction. A specialist in one state can develop a new perspective and acquire a new fund of ideas if he has a few years experience in one or more other states. A federal official who spends some time working at the local level is likely to sharpen his understanding of problems at the "grass roots" for which, in his federal job, he is expected to prescribe certain policies or standards. Conversely, the local expert who serves a period in a federal agency will undoubtedly come away with a better appreciation of the national import of his subject. Municipal employees will be able to utilize their skills more fully, and municipalities better able to capitalize on them, when employment arrangements encourage advancement from smaller jurisdictions to greater responsibilities and opportunities in larger cities.[14]

IMPACT OF RETIREMENT POLICY

To be sure, many conditions can influence persons to reject such opportunities for mobility. Pay scales, selection procedures, residence requirements, housing availability, educational considerations for children, and other factors may well block an employee's motivation to transfer. But the holding power of a retirement system can also be a major deterrent, especially in those instances where the individual has already built up considerable credit in one system and this is neither transferrable nor available to him as a deferred annuity (that is, not vested) if he should leave. Aside from those states that have statewide systems applying to all public workers in all jurisdictions within the state, which are still in a small minority, there are many hundreds of local retirement systems of very small size scattered throughout the United States. Many of these still do not have any provision for vesting or other deferrable annuity.[15] Although the great majority of state and local government employees are now covered under the national social security system, which constitutes a kind of common floor among the public systems of which it is a part, the added benefits provided by a local staff retirement plan may be controlling in determining an employee's economic motivation to remain with or move from his location.

SOLUTIONS

The ideal solution would appear to be a nationwide retirement system applicable to all government employees—federal, state, and local. Even if it were open to only state and local civil servants, it would solve many problems. Such a proposal was indeed made by a responsible body that studied the manpower needs of American municipalities.[16] To bring about

---

[14] See the earlier discussions on mobility in Chapters 2, 4, and 13.

[15] Working in several jurisdictions that have a deferred annuity arrangement would enable an individual, upon reaching retirement age, to make up his retirement income by piecing together the deferred annuities from each place of employment.

[16] The Municipal Manpower Commission, *Governmental Manpower for Tomorrow's Cities*, New York, McGraw-Hill, 1962, p. 116.

a nationwide plan encounters strong resistance from the custodians of the many local systems who jealously guard their little fiefdoms, but, more important, entails enormous problems of coordination and legal adoption in our highly pluralistic system of government. It is interesting, however, that one pioneering example of retirement coordination exists in American higher education, spanning both public and private institutions. This is the well-known Teacher's Insurance Annuity Association of America (TIAA), with which almost all universities and colleges in the nation are affiliated. Under this plan faculty members are able to move about from institution to institution while building up continuous credit in a common retirement investment.

Given the multiplicity of general civil service retirement systems throughout the country, apart from the field of higher education, it must be acknowledged that achieving a measure of coordination among public jurisdictions is enormously complex. Yet something in the way of interrelationship among systems is bound to be worked out. The increasing interdependence among various units and levels of government intensifies the need for greater mobility of technical personnel. Reciprocity of annuity credits or extension of the principle of vesting, permitting deferrable annuities, are among the possible alternatives short of a nationwide retirement system.

The Advisory Commission on Intergovernmental Relations, rejecting the idea of a unified national system on grounds of impracticality, proposed a twin approach of consolidation of plans within each state, plus provision for vesting in each plan, with no more than five years of service required of the employee to get the benefit of vesting in any one system.[17] Parallel recommendations are made by other students of the problem, including one who suggests that the federal government supplement the costs of state and local retirement vesting so that inadequate vested benefits earned by a mobile employee could be raised to the level paid by the system from which he retires.[18]

An encouraging sign is the fact that a number of states have moved in the direction of statewide retirement systems or have expressly provided for retention of retirement coverage when an employee goes to work for another governmental unit. Still others continue coverage for state employees who work for a university or undertake advanced study to increase their qualifications.[19] Likewise, as noted in an earlier discussion of mobility, the Intergovernmental Personnel Act underwrites mobility by guaranteeing against losses due to shifts to different retirement coverage in the case of government-sponsored temporary moves between the federal government and state and local governments.[20] Undoubtedly, the wave of the future is in the direction

---

[17] Advisory Commission on Intergovernmental Relations, *Transferability of Public Employee Retirement Credits Among Units of Government*, Washington, D.C., March 1963.

[18] Harold Rubin, *Pensions and Employee Mobility in the Public Service*, New York, The Twentieth Century Fund, 1965, p. 85.

[19] See Tables 10 and 15 in Council of State Governments, *Fringe Benefits in State Government Employment*, Chicago, May 1968.

[20] See especially Chapter 4.

of more compatible arrangements among public retirement systems to facilitate much needed mobility of professional and managerial personnel.

*   *   *

BY WAY OF summation, the characteristics of modern public retirement systems as to broad elements of funding and benefits are no longer matters of controversy. The future policy in this area will most likely continue to emphasize the following:

1. Flexible provisions, both to respond to the needs of an aging population and to permit deviation, especially for key positions, from a slavish dependence on chronological age as the only determinant of super-annuation.
2. Consolidation of retirement systems within states and cities, promoting wider coverage, greater economy, and more equitable benefits.
3. Invention of devices of reciprocity and interchange to encourage greater movement of public workers in the professions and managerial fields among different jurisdictions without hazard to their accumulation of retirement credits.
4. Adjustment of annuities periodically, on the basis of changes in wage or cost-of-living indexes, so that the retiree's income always approximates its original value and reflects improvements in standards of living.

PART VIII

Personnel
Organization

Chaos is a name for any order that produces confusion in our minds.

George Santayana, *Dominations and Powers:*
Reflections on Liberty, Society, and Government,
New York, Scribner's, 1951, p. 33.

Personnel administration is the utilization of the best scientific
knowledge of all kinds to the end that an organization as a whole
and the individuals composing it shall find that corporate purpose
and individual purposes are being reconciled to the fullest possible
extent, while the working together of these purposes realizes also a
genuine social benefit.

Ordway Tead, *The Art of Administration,*
New York, McGraw-Hill, 1951, p. 145.

CHAPTER 24

The Central
Personnel Agency

UNDER THE IMPETUS of the early civil service reform movement, central personnel agencies in the form of bipartisan commissions were created with the primary aim of freeing the public servant from allegiance to and dependence upon the politician. The end determined the means. Hence, the first civil service commissions were merely examining agencies, designed to make certain that persons *entered* the service only through merit, regardless of what happened to them thereafter. The commissions were "politics eliminators" and little more. The system of control which developed was intended to prevent specific abuses, without particular reference to other aspects of the employment situation. Most significantly, in order to ensure elimination of political influence, the typical commission was organized independent of and largely external to the administrative hierarchy.

LIMITED SUCCESS OF THE COMMISSION FORM

There is no question but that the selection of personnel through open competition, under the auspices of a special agency established for the purpose, has been the major contribution toward checking the evils associated with the job-patronage spoils system. During the near century since enactment of the national Civil Service Act, federal, state, and municipal jurisdictions have made significant progress in the direction of establishing a public service loyal to the state as a whole and ready to serve whatever party may come to power. To be sure, this progress has been far from uniform. In certain jurisdictions it has been negligible, and in others the commmission has been little more than an irritating obstacle to be hurdled. Despite this unevenness, however, the generalization is valid that a notable advance has been made.

419

Yet, it is not at all evident that the civil service commission is the sine qua non of the merit system. Indeed, many factors other than the commission system have contributed to the gradual liberation of the civil servant from political spoilsmen. Chief among these is the ever more technical nature of both the instruments and the objects of public administration, which, in many spheres of government enterprise, has made the old spoils system intolerable. Another contributing factor is to be found in the increasing costs of government, which have aroused the public to demand the elimination of waste and inefficiency. Such a demand has influenced administrators to give more heed to personnel matters.

Nor does the evidence show that the bipartisan civil service commission has always been successful in the elimination of politics with respect to personnel—that is, any more successful than any other agency functioning under a merit system law might have been. Like other government agencies, it is run by human beings and is subject to manipulation to serve the ends considered desirable by those in control. Here, as in other instances, the American people have placed undue confidence in the saving power of machinery, apparently little realizing that the manner of administration is of more importance than the system prescribed in the law. Indeed, there have been some commissions which constituted a focal center of political influences and to which only those giving the political countersign had entry.

REASONS FOR SHORTCOMINGS

A number of conditions and developments contributed to the limited success of the commission form of organization. These were founded principally on the bipartisan and amateur character of commission membership and on the relative isolation of commissions from the executive machinery of government.

COMMISSION STRUCTURE   The standard civil service law provided for three commissioners, not more than two of who could be members of the same political party, each serving overlapping terms. The latter feature was to prevent "packing" the commission by any one executive having the appointing power. *Bi*partisanship was expected to insure *non*partisanship. The inherent contradictions in such a set-up apparently escaped notice in the early days of the reform wave. Some commissions, as has been noted, were themselves too politically minded to resist the depredations of spoilsmen. A variety of schemes were contrived in many a jurisdiction to circumvent the merit law—ranging from clever manipulation of examination weights or ratings to outright favoritism. Even in the appointment of commissioners, the common pattern was cynically observed to be one of naming "a lady, a lame duck, and a friendly Indian."[1]

[1] As students of the American political scene will no doubt recognize, a "lame duck" is a politician who has lost an election but who still has part of a term of office to serve or who seeks further shelter in political appointment. A "friendly Indian," using terminology of the early American frontier, conveys the idea of an innocuous member of

MEDIOCRITY Naturally, it was not uncommon for civil service commissioners to be rank amateurs at their tasks. In addition to professional politicians, categories such as farmers, housewives, lawyers, and journalists typified the range of occupations from which commissioners were drawn. Even when they were professional and well-motivated people, they frequently were ill informed and had naive notions of how to go about their jobs. Unfortunately, what were supposed to be citadels of training, competence, and independence, too often came to be (and some still are) the dumping ground for mediocre personalities who could not be trusted with what were considered to be the more significant political assignments. It was lack of respect for the personnel function that led so many chief executives, at least in the early days of civil service commissions, to downgrade its effectiveness by naming to its leadership individuals considerably below the caliber originally envisaged by the reformers.

Both the element of mediocrity and the structuring of commissions contributed to their separatism from the mainstream of public administration. In theory they were supposed to have considerable independence from executive influence to ensure their guardianship of merit processes. Yet, instead of providing that assurance, they too often either knuckled under to partisan domination or developed a style and impression about the personnel function that made it an obstacle to progress in attaining competency and responsiveness in the public service.

LEGISLATIVE INTERFERENCE Such conditions were not always conducive to the best of relations with legislative bodies, although here too, collusion in political maneuvering or in neglect of progressive management practices were by no means unknown. Legislators have been all too ready, with or without the connivance of inept commissioners, to disrupt sound merit system procedures by exempting too many jobs from the career service, by giving sweeping preference to veterans, by placing undue restrictions on removals, by interfering in individual matters of promotion or disciplinary action, or by otherwise jeopardizing the pursuit of competence as the only valid measure for entry or retention in the service.

POOR FINANCIAL SUPPORT Of greatest negative impact has been the parsimonious behavior of legislative bodies when it came to appropriations for the personnel agency. Many a commission has been hamstrung through

---

the opposition party. The appointment of a "lady" was simply an effort to demonstrate due regard for representation of the interests of women.

In spite of the implications of this allegation, the fact was that the majority of appointments to commissionerships could not be so neatly categorized. For example, in many places, instead of the minority party commissioner being a weak personality, he often stood out as the strongest member, assuming leadership in personnel program improvement that had been neglected by the majority members. This was true over a long span of years during the 1930s and 1940s in the federal Civil Service Commission. To this extent, *bi*partisanship produced a healthy antidote to mediocrity even where it did not necessarily ensure *non*partisanship.

lack of adequate funds. This was the main cause for collapse of several merit systems in years past. Even today a niggardly money policy seriously curtails the effectiveness of all too many commissions. Nothing could provide better assurance of a placid and unimaginative central personnel organ than the understaffing and lack of equipment induced by a policy of penury. It means a lower quality staff, a staff overwhelmed by the daily drudgery of the bare essentials of examination processes, the absence of necessary steps such as positive recruitment and test validation, slow responsiveness to operating needs of the service, inability to maintain close working relationships with operating officials, poor job-classification maintenance, and usually the complete neglect of in-service personnel activities such as training, monitoring good promotion and transfer practices, dynamic pay administration, employee consultation, and the like. It was the reaction to such conditions which led to citizen demand in some jurisdictions that the personnel agency be guaranteed a fixed percentage of the government budget each year.[2]

POSITIVE ACHIEVEMENT

A mere listing of the foregoing shortcomings of many civil service commissions would seem to condemn them as an instrument of modern public administration. This is not the intent of this analysis. Nor is it by any means reflective of the character or performance of a major proportion of these bodies. It is to the credit of many dedicated civil service commissioners that, in spite of great obstacles thrown in their way, a worthwhile job has been done. Many public executives will testify to the positive contributions to the staffing of governmental programs that wisely led and professionally oriented personnel agencies have spearheaded. Commissions, especially in the larger and more affluent jurisdictions, have been instrumental in winning acceptance of modern methods of personnel administration that would never have come about without their leadership.

PROPOSALS FOR CHANGE

Reaction to the commission form has nevertheless been a mixed one. Partly because of poor or unimaginative performance, but more often because of lack of funds or remoteness from day-to-day operating problems of the particular jurisdiction, the so-called independent commission has been the target of much complaint as the traditional form of organization for direction of public personnel administration.

ATTEMPTS TO STRENGTHEN EXECUTIVE DIRECTION

Criticism reached a peak when the Municipal Manpower Commission recommended abolition of the independent civil service commission or its

[2] The State of Michigan is an example, with such a proviso in the state constitution. For a discussion of legislative involvement in personnel administration in general, see Joseph P. Harris, *Congressional Control of Administration*, Garden City, N. Y., Doubleday Anchor, 1965; chapter on personnel administration.

limitation to an advisory role and urged the vesting of clear-cut authority for directing the personnel function in the chief executive.[3] Although this study staunchly supported the appointment and advancement of public personnel exclusively on merit principles,[4] it aroused a great deal of resentment on the part of those conscientious personnel administrators who had come to feel that the independent commission form of organization had been successful and that it was the only guarantee against spoils politics—as indeed it was in many a locality. Despite resistance and sincere doubts about its efficacy, the Municipal Manpower Commission's recommendation has been implemented in many cities, at least to the extent of making the chief personnel officer accountable to the chief executive.[5]

Concurrently, at the federal level, various proposals have been advanced to emphasize the executive character of the personnel function. Unfortunately, instead of suggesting a change in the headship of the U.S. Civil Service Commission from a three-member body to a single administrator (as was initially put forward as early as 1937),[6] these proposals mainly call for creation of additional mechanisms to carry on executive personnel activities but would leave the Civil Service Commission in existence with a truncated and somewhat anomalous role.[7]

---

[3] Municipal Manpower Commission, *Governmental Manpower for Tomorrow's Cities*, New York, McGraw-Hill, 1962, pp. 106–108.

[4] *Ibid.*, p. 109.

[5] In a 1972 survey, the great majority of city personnel directors were found to report to the chief administrator (*Profile of the Public Personnel Officer*, Englewood Cliffs, N.J., Prentice-Hall, 1973). The survey, conducted jointly by the International Personnel Management Association and the Prentice-Hall Editorial Staff, covered over two hundred municipalities of a wide range of sizes.

[6] Floyd W. Reeves and Paul T. David, *Personnel Administration in the Federal Service* (President's Committee on Administrative Management), Washington, D.C., 1937, p. 4.

[7] The so-called Clark Bill (S. 1638, 86th Cong., April 1959, and June 1960; and S. 1402, 87th Cong., 1st sess., March 1961) proposed establishment of a separate personnel office in the White House but would have bifurcated the personnel function between it and the Commission.

Likewise, a subgroup of the Committee for Economic Development, in its proposal for an "Office of Executive Personnel," would have divided personnel administration into layers, the top to be handled by its recommended new office and the remainder by the Commission (*Improving Management in the Federal Government*, A Statement on National Policy by the Research and Policy Committee, Prepared by the Committee for Improvement of Management in Government, New York, Committee for Economic Development, 1964).

In its recommendation for a thorough reappraisal of the federal personnel system, made in 1974, the panel of the National Academy of Public Administration (NAPA) urged that serious consideration be given to establishment of a separate agency to maintain merit standards, prevent political influence in the career system, and adjudicate appeals and complaints of employees. Although it did not make a specific recommendation of its own, the NAPA panel was apparently thinking of leaving the "managerial" aspects of personnel administration in separate hands (*Watergate: Its Implications for Responsible Government*, A Report Prepared by a Panel of the National Academy of Public Administration at the Request of the Senate Select Committee on Presidential Campaign Activities, Washington, D.C., March 1974, p. 114.)

At this writing, none of the proposals to divide the personnel function in the federal service seems destined for adoption. The only one that might possibly carry some weight

The fact is that the federal Commission is already an instrumentality of the chief executive. Not only does the President appoint the commissioners but he is required to approve and issue the Civil Service Rules, in the form of executive orders. Especially since 1950 or so, the Commission has had close ties with the presidency and has to all intents and purposes been the personnel arm of the chief executive, but without jeopardy to its direct responsibility for administration of a lengthy catalogue of laws and policies relating to employment, classification, training, and all the other facets of a modern personnel program. Its behavior as an executive personnel agency was made clearer when, in pursuance of a recommendation of the first Hoover Commission in 1949, its chairman was given responsibility for administrative direction of its work, with the other two commissioners serving only to pass on issues of policy and to act on appeals that reach that level.[8] Hence the need for de-emphasizing "independence" and for stressing executive responsibility is largely academic in the federal service. The only remaining issue is whether the central personnel agency might be better operated completely under a single headship than by a three-man body.[9]

Returning to the state and local government scene, one must acknowledge that the separation of central direction of the personnel function from the chief executive has remained more pointed there. Nevertheless, reconciliation between the personnel agency as watchdog and as executor of a personnel program has been achieved in many a progressive jurisdiction. Since this subject continues to be debated among students and practitioners of public administration, it remains the central issue of public personnel organization.

---

is the idea of creating a special adjudicatory body to handle employee appeals, and to serve as a kind of ombudsman and public watchdog or auditor calling attention to misfeasance and malfeasance in connection with the personnel system, thus leaving the Civil Service Commission or a successor agency to concentrate on development and administration of personnel policy on behalf of the President and the executive branch generally. As a matter of fact, the Commission's leadership and initiative in this role have not only, for the most part, met the standards of merit and quality needed but also served the operating requirements of the federal government. Its dynamic performance is attested by the range of achievements related in the Commission's lively and informative annual reports of recent years. For this reason, as well as others, the pressure for organizational change is not likely to be very insistent.

[8] Accomplished by the President's Reorganization Plan No. 5 of 1949, which was approved by the Congress.

[9] This is not to say that the Commission is without its problems, both within the service and vis-à-vis the general public. As Donald R. Harvey observes:

> To the merit system zealot, it is the only hope for good government—even though its performance is sometimes disappointing, since it does not always appear ready to commit the final act of heroism in defense of principle. To the jobseeker, it is a high blank wall or an open door, depending upon his success at finding the job he wants. To the politician desiring a position for an influential constituent, it is a group of bothersome bureaucrats. To the busy federal executive, it is a required nuisance, welcome when protecting him from the importunities of the unwanted jobseeker but a handicap when preventing an action he wishes to take. To the federal career employee, it is an institution that should be doing a lot more about many things. [*The Civil Service Commission*, New York, Praeger, 1970, pp. 30–31.]

THE CONTINUING DEBATE

Due to sad experience in some communities and states with efforts by chief executives and legislators alike to sabotage the merit system, it is understandable why some authorities argue that a commission—independent of real control by political leaders—is an absolute necessity to ensure forthright administration of the personnel law. The question, however, is whether complete and genuine independence can in actuality be maintained and, further, whether any substantial subversion of executive accountability is not too large a price to pay to protect the public from the occasional unprincipled scoundrel.

It is inescapable in a democratic system that legislators are elected to make all laws, personnel laws included, and that mayors, governors, and presidents are elected to enforce them. As a long-time exponent of the merit system once stated: "Why such grave concern about independence of the personnel agency any more than other vital agencies of government for which the chief executive must be responsible to the electorate?"[10] Still another way of looking at the realities is this: if a chief executive wants good administration, why should we not expect him to support the efforts of his personnel agency? Conversely, if the agency does not have such sympathetic and actively demonstrated support, then how can it hope to carry out its functions effectively, regardless of its touted independence?

There is little doubt but that the device of independent civil service commissions was essential in the first instance to implant acceptance of the merit principle and the habit of competition in an atmosphere of hostility and skepticism. Although the dangers of using public jobs for political currency are always still with us, the practice has been so thoroughly discredited as a normal method of staffing, and a quality public service based on relative merit has been so completely accepted, that protection against the spoilsman simply pales into insignificance alongside the overwhelming need to maintain a dynamic personnel system on all fronts that attracts, utilizes, and motivates the best talent available for governmental purposes.

A classic rationale for the independent commission was once formulated by a British expert in an exhortation to a colonial official:

> Governments through the Empire have set up Public Service Commissions which exercise almost independent powers and the reasons for their independence are twofold. First, a Public Service Commission is an extremely expensive body. If a householder engages a cook at a high salary to cook his

[10] H. Eliot Kaplan, as reported in Thomas Page, ed., *The Public Personnel Agency and the Chief Executive: A Symposium*, Personnel Report No. 601, Chicago, International Personnel Management Association, 1960, p. 29. Mr. Kaplan also asked, as to the contention in favor of the independence of personnel agencies: "Independence of what, and of whom? And while we're at it, what price should we be willing to pay for alleged independence?"

meals, it is a mistake equally detrimental to his purse and his digestion to cook them himself or to interfere in the culinary operations of his servant. He lays down his gastronomic policy and leaves it at that. Secondly, a Public Service Commission acquires a fund of knowledge and experience of service matters which neither the Government nor any one else possesses. The Commisson may be wrong in its decisions but there is no one else of whom it may be said that they are more likely to be right.[11]

As with so much of the reasoning demonstrated by classically trained minds, this exposition is, to paraphrase Mencken, "neat, plausible, and wrong." Assignment of responsibility does not mean abandonment of scrutiny. Expertise should never be left unaccountable. Surely the independence of a civil service agency should never rest on such superficial, specious grounds.

PROS AND CONS FOR CHANGE

The arguments for and against executive control of the personnel function may be most conveniently summarized by stating the case in terms of the most extreme positions: abolition or retention of the commission-form of organization.

FOR ABOLITION OF COMMISSIONS   The proponents of a personnel structure in which the traditional bipartisan commission disappears and in which personnel administration becomes simply one of the auxiliary management functions of the chief executive generally argue their case along the following lines:

1. Chief executives must have control of personnel policy and processes in order to be held accountable for the results of their operations, for the very reason that the quality and motivation of employees are vital to the success of any enterprise. If these managers have control, their incentive will be to appoint and energize good people.
2. These executives can be held as accountable to the electorate in this area of their responsibilities as they can in any program field. There is no more reason to question their integrity or judgment in personnel matters than in the technical subjects in which they have been trained.
3. Providing chief executives with real control over personnel processes, even though they are obligated to abide by principles of merit in appointment and advancement of workers, permits attuning personnel policy and operations to the daily needs of agency management and to the inexorable influences of technological and social change.

[11] Sir Ross Barker, in his Memorandum submitted to the Indian Statutory Commission, *Extracts from Official Oral Evidence*, vol. XV, London, His Majesty's Stationery Office, 1930, paragraph 14. The term *Public Service Commission* is still used in many of the former British colonies as the name of the central recruiting agency. Also, its "independence" is being questioned more vigorously than before in these new states now that they are free of colonial domination.

4. Civil service commissions, by their establishment and operation on the sidelines of public program administration, are out of touch with daily administrative needs and with the dynamics of administrative change.
5. Commissions tend to become overprotective of employee interests that are not consistent with government agency effectiveness. Not feeling an obligation to achieve program goals, as is the case with those immediately responsible to the chief executive, they are overimpressed with employee complaints and are less disposed than program managers to discipline laxity or inefficiency.
6. Chief executives for the most part are just as interested in maintaining the quality of their career staffs as are civil service commissions, but they have too little say in the methods by which merit is to be determined. Civil service commissions have no corner on integrity or on interpretation of what constitutes merit.
7. The most serious ill effects of spoils politics and patronage are passé in most communities. The negative function of commissions in keeping political favorites as against qualified applicants from acquiring government jobs is outmoded. The modern-day task is to attract and motivate well-qualified persons to respond to great challenges, to work enthusiastically at public causes, and effectively to implement democratically conceived government programs.
8. The chief executive in each jurisdiction should therefore have a single personnel administrator responsible to him who is charged with all aspects of the personnel function, including recruitment and selection, just as he has responsible administrators in each of the other areas of his concern and accountability to the public. There should be no question, of course, but that the chief executive should be obligated to make his personnel decisions in accordance with principles of merit and that his subordinate program chiefs should likewise be so guided.

Obviously, this line of reasoning accords with the precepts of management in private enterprise. Persuasive as it is, the question remains whether operating large government agencies in the public interest can be equated entirely with running a business concern. It is reasonable to expect that the arguments on the other side of the issue are equally cogent.

AGAINST ABOLITION OF COMMISSIONS Those who defend the need for multimembered, bipartisan civil service commissions or boards, with some degree of independence of executive control, rest their case primarily on points of practical experience:

1. In the best-run public personnel systems there is no breakdown of communication, no hiatus with line management. The soundly administered personnel programs by independent central personnel agencies are arrived at with a large measure of operating executive participation and with the

objectives of government program ends distinctly in mind. Hence, many of the complaints about civil service commissions do not by any means fit all or even most cases.

2. The organization of jobs, the setting of work standards and qualification requirements, the development of recruiting and examining methodology, and the making of selections to government positions are already strongly in the hands of operating executives. Final approval of personnel policies in some jurisdictions that have civil service commissions still rests with the chief executive. In brief, up-to-date and dynamically administered commissions enlist a great deal of involvement of program administrators, including the chief executive, in making the judgments that profoundly affect entrance into and progress in the service. In these cases the "independence" of the commission from direct and immediate responsibility to the chief executive does not actually insulate it from the concerns of program operations, does not result in its being on the sidelines or outskirts of daily program objectives.

3. Chief executives usually are empowered to appoint members of civil service commissions. The practical effects of terms and turnover are such that by and large they appoint a controlling proportion of commission members. Is their power to make these appointments any less significant than the power sought to appoint single personnel administrators?

4. Following on this point, as well as on the habits of practical operations, many modern commissions are really part of the executive family. The best example is that of the federal government, although it is recognized that this condition obtains less frequently in state and local government.

5. Almost all commissions have single executive secretaries or directors who are the executive heads of the personnel agencies subject only to commission policy direction and who have considerable operating responsibility. The operational role of these directors tends to identify them in spirit and concerns with other line operators in their jurisdictions. Their understanding and communication with operators is a natural and real part of their daily decision-making.

6. Flowing from the foregoing conditions, it cannot be assumed that governors, mayors, city managers, or county executives make poor appointments to civil service commissions where these bodies exist but not to single personnel directorships where these offices exist separate from commissions.

7. The temptations of political party organizations to exploit the potentiality of public jobs for serving partisan purposes is by no means nonexistent; spoils politics, in other words, is not dead. Petty-minded politicians interested only in officeholding, with no commitment to issues or purpose, are always standing in the wings ready to take advantage of any opening to use government jobs as political capital and government employees as pawns in maneuvering for party benefit. This realistic condition suggests several subpoints:

a. Many government executives welcome the existence of a commission of some independent status as a protection and refuge against patronage predators.

b. Too much latitude for executives in the personnel field breeds irresponsibility more than it builds responsibility, because they sense less accountability for their actions in the sensitive personnel area when there is no multiheaded body looking over their shoulders.

c. The inexorable reliance on specialists in government program fields—accountants, lawyers, doctors, welfare workers, police, educators, etc.—means that not all persons reaching managerial ranks are sophisticated in either the realities of political pressures or the arts of personnel management. They are often the unwitting victims of manipulators who exploit their naiveté for party or personal ends.

d. If it is generally acknowledged that civil service commissions were necessary in the beginning of merit system establishment in order to ensure the maintenance of merit in the face of hostility and skepticism, then it would follow that in all new installations of merit procedures, where there has been no tradition to rely on, a commission form of organization would likewise be a necessity.

This last point suggests the possible utility of basing personnel organization on the degree of maturity of a jurisdiction in living with merit-based processes. Moreover, the fact must be taken into account that merit systems have worked effectively under both forms of central personnel organization and that failures likewise have been found under both. Perhaps the greatest reliance can be placed on the conclusion that, above all, an unwavering, doctrinaire position on the issue of personnel organization should be avoided.[12]

THE INGREDIENTS OF ACCOMMODATION

As with so many issues of administrative form, the best decisions will be founded on careful analysis of functions and on accommodation to the particular needs of a public jurisdiction. If personnel organization is, at least in part, a function of the maturity of a merit system, then this factor will have to be taken into account. The newer the system, that is, the less tradition of acceptance present, the more likely the need to maximize protective features and to minimize executive control.

It is perhaps equally true that, under the most favorable conditions, a watchdog role must be assigned somewhere on a continuous basis for insurance purposes. For purposes of this objective, a distinction must be made

[12] The foregoing pro and con arguments are drawn from the author's paper, *The Public Personnel Function—Two Issues*, Detroit, Citizens Research Council of Michigan, May 1971.

Where a commission or board on personnel affairs exists, whatever its scope or role, a useful manual on its operation is the following: Winston W. Crouch, *Guide for Modern Personnel Commissions*, Chicago, International Personnel Management Association, 1973.

For the federal service, a former Commission Executive Director urges retention of the commission form of organization. (See monograph cited at end of Chapter 3.)

between "doing" and "auditing." An auditor must have detachment and independence, and for this purpose there is need in public personnel administration for some authority to review what is going on, to report on it, to try to achieve correction of what it deems to be flaws, and, when all else fails, to expose its findings to public view and the potentiality of legislative or judicial correction.

On the other hand, such functions as on-going recruitment, examination, selection, position classification, training, and all that go with them, are "doing" functions—that is, they are essentially executive in character. It is idle to pretend that they can operate properly without close association with and indeed without the participation of the agencies that are performing government services and exercising its controls. These functions are performed through manpower, manpower for which these operating agencies must answer in serving the public. Whatever assistance a central personnel agency provides in setting common standards, monitoring recruitment, supervising selection, and initiating all manner of personnel policy, this can be only part of the process, a process that is inescapably executive and shared with every administrative instrument of government that employs the services of human beings.

It seems inevitable, as time goes on, that modern government will move more and more in the direction of greater executive responsibility in administration of personnel policy. At the same time, a mechanism is required to ensure accountability in performance of this function that has such a proneness to corruption. Attention may be directed, then, toward current and future design of the central personnel organization for the typical public jurisdiction.

THE EXECUTIVE PERSONNEL AGENCY

In actuality, personnel agencies have moved in the direction of closer membership in the family of executive agencies of government. The facts at the federal level have already been cited. In the states, although the civil service commission as an institution still predominates, both the newer and several reorganized systems have a director of personnel who has a direct relationship with the governor. In a few cases he serves at the pleasure of the governor, although this is not typical.[13] Under these plans, policy and appellate responsibility is usually placed in a personnel board or commission, of which the personnel director may be either chairman or executive officer. A similar evolution toward the executive-type organization has taken place in the cities and counties, particularly where the city-manager plan exists. Thus,

[13] In Minnesota, for example, the Commissioner of Personnel serves for the term of the Governor, while the Personnel Board is advisory and appellate in function only (*Personnel News*, Chicago, International Personnel Management Association, September 1973).

more and more units of government have established single personnel administrators, backed up by a citizen policy board. In the development of this
form of organization there appears to be no evidence of serious erosion of the
merit concept, and in most places it seems to have been strengthened.

A MODEL PLAN

One model of personnel organization is offered here that seeks to preserve both merit principles and executive responsibility:

1. A single personnel administrator:
   a. would report directly to the chief executive,
   b. would be appointed by the chief executive from the most highly quali-
      fied persons who could be referred by a panel of unimpeachable public
      and private leaders, on the basis of specified standards of ability, train-
      ing, and experience,
   c. would be removable only on the grounds of poor performance or con-
      duct, with the same procedural safeguards applicable to other civil
      servants, and
   d. would have responsibility for development and administration of a full
      range of personnel policies and programs.
2. Major policy decisions, in the form of rules or regulations, would require
   the approval of the chief executive.
3. A part-time, staggered-term, nonpartisan (without regard to party affiliation) personnel advisory board:
   a. would be appointed by the chief executive from specified prestige
      sources (such as university presidents, distinguished professors, cor-
      poration presidents, civic association heads, prominent professional
      men, publicists, etc.,) and
   b. would perform the following functions:
      —advise the personnel administrator and the chief executive on all
        major policy issues under consideration, and
      —whenever it saw fit, report independently and publicly its views on
        such policy proposals and decisions.

Under this plan a range of lay views would be afforded, and the public
would be informed of what is going on with little danger of concealment.
Policy development would be the task of a professional staff. But, most important, all this would take place without impairing the executive's power
to act or his assumption of responsibility for his acts. The chances of skulduggery by a corrupt, devious, or ineffectual executive would be remote.
He could hardly risk the almost positive assurance of exposure through
adverse publicity. Yet his capacity to give leadership to the personnel function
if he chose to do so and his power of direction over the personnel affairs of
subordinate units would be fortified.

It is not suggested that employee appeals be handled by the advisory board. This function could best be centered in a separate body within the service.

It should be noted that this model differs markedly from proposals that tend to divide the personnel function by subject matter or by level of civil servants affected.[14] Commissions or other multiheaded bodies, under such plans, would be left with some administrative functions or with responsibility for certain layers of the civil service, as well as with appellate duties and bits and pieces of policy initiative. The model plan keeps the personnel function as a unified area, with one central agency responsible to the chief executive for that function. The web of interrelationships that always characterizes personnel policy issues and day-to-day personnel management would be under unified direction. Only the quasi-judicial role of processing appeals might be set apart, perhaps vested in some administrative tribunal. And the duty of the multimembered board suggested would be strictly advisory, to serve as a source of ideas and reactions and as a safety valve for exposure when necessary. It would not be in the decision-making line, and even major policies would not require its approval.

SCOPE OF FUNCTIONS

Whatever form central personnel agencies might take, there can be no question about the vast expansion of their functions during recent decades. In sharp contrast to the original examining agencies of the late nineteenth and early twentieth centuries, the modern personnel organization is a principal entity of government wherever it operates and carries on a myriad array of activities associated with the human resources of government.

FEDERAL   The U.S. Civil Service Commission has evolved from a negative-oriented monitor of entry tests to the largest and most highly developed personnel establishment in modern government, with many initiatives entrusted to its ingenuity and a vast range of responsibilities entrusted to its care. In addition to administration of a number of regional and subsidiary offices servicing federal installations scattered throughout the nation and abroad, it superintends numerous decentralized boards of examiners that are manned by experts from the operating departments; it plans and directs an extensive recruitment network; it develops and establishes the polices and

---

[14] Although it is not explicit in the statutory language, Reorganization Plan No. 2 of 1970, establishing an Office of Management and Budget in place of the Bureau of the Budget, was transmitted by the President to the Congress with an explanatory statement that included reference to personnel matters. It said that the new office would "be charged with advising the President on the development of new programs to recruit, train, motivate, deploy, and evaluate the men and women who make up the top ranks of the civil service," but that it would "not deal with individuals," relying on "the talented professionals of the Civil Service Commission and the Departments and agencies themselves to administer these programs." Only time can tell what this might possibly mean for the unified direction of personnel administration.

standards governing the entry, classification, advancement, and separation of the civilian work force; it administers a broad program of investigation of candidates for employment; it conducts and supervises a wide variety of training activities; it adjudicates appeals and acts on thousands of complaints and inquiries; it inspects the personnel management of federal departments; and it operates directly the retirement and insurance plans for federal employees. Its principal role in many of these functions is that of policy-making and standard-setting, with much of the daily personnel work being decentralized to the departments, subject to inspection as to its adequacy by the Commission.

STATE AND LOCAL   Similarly, the roles of state and municipal personnel agencies have expanded greatly over the years. It is heartening to see that so many have been able to develop and support well-rounded personnel programs. Some, especially those in the burgeoning metropolitan areas, have performed almost herculean tasks of recruitment, classification, and training in the face of insistent and sometimes overwhelming demands. Many of our public personnel agencies deserve no small part of the credit for the relative success of one jurisdiction after another in measuring up to the mounting needs for public services of all kinds. Schools, hospitals, sanitation, streets, police and fire protection, and all the other requisites of modern urban existence are insatiable consumers of manpower—much of it highly technical, scarce, and difficult to retain. For the most part, public personnel agencies have demonstrated the drive, the adaptability, and the innovativeness to facilitate the acquisition, preparation, and retention of this manpower. This has been done in many a location in spite of the heritage of outworn personnel laws and cumbersome organizational frameworks.

THE SUBSTANCE   Whether it is a civil service commission of the traditional mold or a streamlined executive personnel office, the modern central personnel agency must be prepared to:

1. Determine the coverage of merit procedures;
2. Develop sources of personnel supply, keep qualification requirements realistic, cooperate with educational institutions and occupational associations, and otherwise undertake the recruiting efforts necessary to attract able candidates to the service;
3. Examine applicants, develop lists of eligible candidates, and direct related operations in the operating departments;
4. Administer the use of eligible lists and the system of probation and reinstatement;
5. Establish standards for the duties classification of positions, and where necessary, classify individual positions;
6. Administer pay schedules, and make or recommend adjustments based on factual analysis of competitive conditions;

7. Establish policies and procedures for movement of personnel by transfer and promotion, for attendance and leave, for conduct and discipline, for separation, and for appeals and grievances;

8. Develop guides and stimulate the best practice in supervision, in working conditions, in organization of tasks for motivational utility, in health and safety, and in performance evaluation;

9. Conduct in-service training that cannot be provided feasibly within individual departments and training in fields common to several departments;

10. Operate employee retirement, life insurance, and health insurance systems (unless these are provided from a higher jurisdiction);

11. Conduct basic and applied research in personnel measurement, in behavioral aspects of management, and in appraisal of the impact of personnel policies on productivity and morale;

12. Maintain a constructive practice of public reporting and public relations;

13. Consult or bargain with employee unions on personnel policy issues;

14. Take action on, or recommend to the chief executive or the legislative body, changes and improvements in personnel policy and practice; and

15. Carry out all of these duties with full appreciation of and attention to the imperatives of the day—social issues, equal opportunity, pending legislative interests or measures, and the inexorable requirements of the operating agencies of government.

Wherever practical, the personnel agency must collaborate with other jurisdictions in pursuing these functions. Likewise, in larger jurisdictions, its consultation with operating departments will be faciliated by relying on advisory groups of their personnel officers—commonly referred to as personnel councils. A number of states, a few major cities, and the federal government utilize such councils as a means for policy consultation with the personnel specialists who are close to the firing line. They have generally contributed to good communication, to better understanding of policy and of problems, and to orderly implementation of change.[15]

PUBLIC RELATIONS

Central personnel organizations have several "publics" to serve. Internally there are the operating executives and the rank-and-file employees. Elsewhere in the government there are the legislators and other elected political leaders. Outside, but looking in with special interest, there are potential candidates for jobs and various organizations with a particular concern about the public personnel system—civil service leagues, unions, taxpayers' groups, veterans' organizations, universities, et cetera. Finally, there is the channel through

---

[15] A still relevant study on this subject is Theodore H. Lang, *Public Personnel Councils*, Personnel Report No. 583, Chicago, International Personnel Management Association, 1958.

which the unidentified general public is reached—newspapers, radio and television, and periodicals, collectively known as the "media."

THE POSITIVE ROLE   The personnel agency may be conscious of a somewhat different role before each of these categories. The common denominator in its relations with all of them is its special responsibility for maintaining a favorable image of government employment and therefore of government services and of the general climate in its particular jurisdiction. Almost all successes in administration of public personnel affairs ultimately hinge on the attitudes of people, both within and outside the service, toward the public service as a place of employment. Hence, a progressive personnel agency will be very much concerned with the accuracy and intensity of those attitudes.

This is a far cry from the original conception of the personnel agency as a mere arbiter or policeman in sorting out candidates who were presumed to be clamoring for public jobs. As we have stressed in an earlier chapter, government is a competitor for talent in the general economy. It must therefore make certain that both its performance and knowledge of its performance are of as high quality as it can generate. It must be mindful of the views held by different sectors of the public, of any prejudices or misconceptions prevailing, of justifiable criticisms made, and of ways to correct the causes for unfavorable notions about its character or quality. It does not follow that a public agency must be a weak reed bending to the whims of every pressure group. But prudence requires that it be aware of potential sources of difficulty, that innovations in policy be carefully explained, that the ground be prepared for desirable change in practice or service, and that public relations "boners" be prevented. Obviously all government agencies share in these obligations, but the personnel agency is in the best position to sum them up, to supply the capstone of general image about the total service that is so important to high quality, responsive public administration.

OBJECTIVES   The substance of sound public relations is well expressed in the following advice from a professional handbook:

1. *Public relations is positive, not negative.* You tell the people what you are going to do and how you are going to do it before they hear a distorted "grapevine" version. You tell them how it worked, even what mistakes you made. And you don't forget to tell them how you corrected your mistakes.
2. *Public relations is everybody's business.* Your public relations can't be solely the responsibility of a public relations man. The acts and attitudes of each and every public employee make or break public relations. The employees who come into daily contact with the public are in a sense the "public relations ambassadors" of the agency. But everybody is on the team. A misfiled letter or a needless set of forms can be just as much a public relations hazard as an ill-tempered answer to a citizen's question. You've got to make public relations everybody's business.

3. *Public relations is a continuous activity.* You can turn your publicity on and off, but the public is still going to draw some conclusions about you. Better keep them informed. And here is one public relations rule you must never violate: Employees must be told before a new policy or program is announced to the public.

4. *Public relations is in everything you do.* Many people think public relations is a news release, an annual report, a speech, an employee newsletter. It is. But it is more than that. It is your tone of voice when you answer the telephone; it is the way you write letters and the way you type them; it is the way you housekeep your office; it is the way you announce examinations; it is how you notify delinquent taxpayers; it is the dependability with which you pick up garbage; it is the neatness of a cop's uniform. Public relations is the effect everything you do has upon your public.[16]

METHODS   A positive program, based on the idea that public relations are constantly in the making, will embrace: (1) systematic opinion sampling and analysis, to ascertain the attitudes and viewpoints of the various publics; (2) planning specific informational releases and media outlets to disseminate facts and human-interest data about the civil service involved; and (3) permeation of the staff, through training programs and otherwise, with an appreciation of the public relations implications of all that they undertake. Unless some other establishment is set up to superintend all of these activities, the personnel agency might well take the lead. It should be particularly well equipped to give direction to those efforts relating to employee performance, such as:

1. Seeing that letters written to members of the public are simple, clear, and friendly;
2. Seeing that regulations and instructions are so drafted that they are sensible and understandable;
3. Making employees conscious of their telephone manners, so that they will be cordial and responsive;
4. Informing employees of the major programs of the organization or jurisdiction and of the policies and problems pertaining to them, so that employees can serve as sympathetic interpreters to the public;
5. Encouraging key personnel to accept speaking invitations from local organizations and providing speech training and other services to facilitate this policy;
6. Campaigning for good physical appearances, so that offices exhibit cleanliness and order, and so that equipment such as automobiles and trucks are kept washed, attractively painted, and clearly identified; and

[16] Eleanor S. Ruhl, *Public Relations for Government Employees: An Action Program,* Personnel Report No. 524, Chicago, International Personnel Management Association, 1952, pp. 15–16.

7. Alerting employees to problems or issues that are causing or might cause unfavorable reactions, and equipping them to deal with them constructively.

In addition, all units of the governmental entity can be encouraged to keep friendly contacts open with citizen groups that are concerned with their operations. The best public relations are always anticipatory. Public agencies should solicit the views of interested groups from time to time, getting their consultation and if practicable their participation in the development of policy. The creation of citizen advisory committees is one technique that is useful. Such involvement is likely to make both the citizen groups and the public agency more responsive to the total public interest. Here again, the personnel establishment can be of service, through its training and employee relations experts for example, in organizing and operating liaison relationships with representatives of the general public.

Many central personnel agencies have had notable success in one or more programs such as those outlined. Few, however, can boast of leadership in a comprehensive approach, embracing all these goals and methods across the board. An element most commonly lacking is the systematic and persistent probing of public opinion. For this purpose, a research staff is essential, just as in the case of internal attitude surveys.

The utility of good public relations is without question. The degree of success in developing the in-house attitudes and in using the techniques that contribute to good relations may well determine the image that the average citizen has of his government, its functions, and its employees. In turn, such impressions exert a stimulating or depressing effect on recruitment and retention in the service. Even if there were not other good reasons for the effort, specialized attention to public relations by the personnel agency can be justified entirely on its contribution to effective recruitment and to the maintenance of sound, publicly supported pay and working conditions for the public service.

PROGRAM EVALUATION

Just as positive public relations can contribute to an informed and interested citizenry, and therefore to the vitality and permanency of democracy, a further logical step in stewardship for carrying out the public business is found in evaluating public programs. Such appraisal is also, of course, valuable for purposes of internal analysis and self-improvement.

When it comes to public personnel administration, this poses no easy task. Without help, the average citizen is patently ill equipped to pass critical judgment on most of the policies and procedures of personnel organizations. He is unlikely to have a knowledge of what constitutes the best practice in the field, and he has no clear norms by which to judge. The operations of the fire prevention department or the public health agency are not only more visible but most susceptible to quantitative and qualitative evaluation. This situation makes all the more compelling the development of criteria for and modes of reporting and appraisal of the personnel function.

DATA NEEDS   Although only portions of personnel work are reducible to quantitative terms, one of the areas in which improvement is called for is in statistical reporting and analysis. The dearth of research-type activities in personnel agencies has made it difficult to evolve the doctrine and technique that are so much needed. Reasons for the neglect have ranged from inadequate budgets to lack of imaginative leadership. Now, with the widespread use of automated computer technology, there is less excuse for inadequate data and for lack of standardization.[17]

Even in the federal service it has been only in recent years that a real effort has been made to standardize and extend data-gathering on personnel employment and movement so that comparisons could be made among individual departments. Theretofore, selective information on promotion trends, on turnover, on the effects of training, on the characteristics and talents of various groups in the employee population, on the impact of separation policies, and the like, was for a long time either not comparable or completely lacking.[18]

Of course, the ideal would be a standardized system of reporting that would permit comparisons among municipalities, states, and counties. Disparate enterprises such as libraries and hospitals have achieved relatively standard methods of statistical reporting. There is no congenital reason why personnel agencies could not do the same.

DEPARTMENT EVALUATIONS   Another device for augmenting the general deficiency in personnel program evaluation is that of having a continuous

---

[17] A quick appreciation of both the operational and research possibilities made practicable by computerization may be derived from the following:

> How many employees can speak German, have had experience in production control, and would be willing to move overseas? If we changed from the present incentive wage system to a measured daywork, what would happen to labor costs? How many employees have not had a wage increase in the last eighteen months, and how does this fact correlate with their performance appraisals? These questions might present difficult problems for some personnel departments, but if the department used a computerized system, the answers could be furnished easily and quickly. [J. D. Dunn and Elvis C. Stephens, *Management of Personnel; Manpower Management and Organizational Behavior*, New York, McGraw-Hill Book Co., 1972, p. 504.]

[18] The following piece describes the central reservoir of personnel information in the U.S. Civil Service Commission, drawing upon 1,500 data points and including a general statistical data bank, a detailed skills inventory on the qualifications of 80,000 middle-management employees, and standardized data elements that all federal agencies use so that information can be pulled together for special report or research purposes: Victor J. Cavagrotti, "Solving Personnel Problems by the Thousands," in *A Record of the Proceedings of the Second Conference of Human Resources Systems Users*, New York, Information Science Incorporated, 1972, pp. 105–116.

and well-staffed function in the central personnel agency to make periodic appraisals of the personnel operations in each of the departments of the jurisdiction. Aside from the rather extensive activity of this kind in the federal service, relatively few civil service commissions or agencies systematically undertake regular personnel evaluation among their constituent departments. Certainly many conditions would lend themselves to study and reporting—turnover, the effectiveness of promotion processes, employee attitudes, supervisory attitudes, complaints and appeals, the extent and quality of in-service training, the prestige the organization enjoys among candidates for employment, and so on.

Still other methods may well be devolped that will strengthen the processes of personnel program appraisal. But great strides in administrative improvement would be made if the techniques of statistical reporting and of general evaluation by central personnel agencies of departmental operations were given the attention that they deserve.

THE MULTIPLICITY OF JURISDICTIONS

The central personnel agency is among those governmental institutions that are severely handicapped by the bewildering hodgepodge of separate and often overlapping jurisdictions characterizing American local government. The expansion of suburbia has exacerbated the situation, so that it is not uncommon in metropolitan areas to have anywhere from several to a dozen or more individual jurisdictions within a radius of ten to twenty miles. The values of having as many elements of government as close to home as possible are not to be gainsaid, but the irrational, confusing, and inefficient maze of subdivisions with their separate bureaucracies, to say nothing of the outright overlapping of powers among counties, townships, and cities, has reached a point of becoming intolerable. In essence, structures that suited a largely rural society are straitjacketing the urban sprawl that is no respector of political boundaries.

IMPACT ON PERSONNEL OPERATIONS

Obviously, the problems of personnel recruitment, of maintaining comparable working conditions and salaries, and of providing challenging work and career opportunities are compounded by the close proximity of numerous governments, each competing with the others on almost every administrative front. Jurisdictions that are tiny, that evolved piecemeal, that are often duplicative, certainly do not lend themselves to the development of the kind of public personnel program envisaged in this book. Furthermore, whenever a local government does make the effort to undertake imaginative recruitment, sophisticated in-service training, or constructive labor relations, to name only a few earmarks of high quality personnel management, it pays a disproportionate price—one much more costly per unit of return than would be the case if several jurisdictions had a combined program.

REMEDIES

Without further belaboring the issue, we turn to examination of some of the possible remedies. The ideal is to dispense with the bureaucratic labyrinth by consolidation or integration of the jurisdictions themselves, abolishing overlapping functions and broadening their base. Examples are supplied by the various forms of unification that have taken place in Miami and Dade County, in Jacksonville, in Indianapolis, and in several other metropolitan areas. Another model is found in Toronto, where a two-level system has emerged, federating thirteen originally independent municipalities into a metropolitan government but leaving some functions to five boroughs incorporated within the federation. The top level operates such functions as property assessment, expressways, and regional parks; the lower levels handle such purely local matters as street lighting and community centers; and there are shared powers between the two levels over roads, water supply, sewage disposal, and traffic control. Unification of any of these varieties greatly simplifies the tasks of personnel administration. In view of the discussion in the preceding section, it might also be noted that the public relations of a personnel agency are immeasurably facilitated by such consolidating moves.

Short of elimination of the multiplicity of jurisdictions themselves, a number of steps can be taken by the personnel units in a metropolitan area to ameliorate their problems and serve mutual purposes. They can contract with each other to conduct common examinations for similar job categories; they can consolidate many training activities and thereby attract more skillful leadership and more competent lecturers; they can set up inter-jurisdictional pay commissions to gather data and report on prevailing rates in the total area; they can try to standardize their job classification systems, so as to facilitate the setting of comparable pay scales; they can adopt liberal transfer policies, honoring each other's recruitment processes by permitting movement among jurisdictions without reexamination; they can, in short, use creative imagination to work out joint activities of many kinds and to approximate as nearly as possible the conditions of a unified metropolitan public service.

A boost to such cooperative endeavors came from the Intergovernmental Personnel Act in several ways: (1) it authorizes cooperative recruiting and examining between the federal service and state and local governments; (2) it permits, upon request of a state or local government, certification of candidates for employment from federal examination lists; (3) it authorizes interstate compacts for cooperative efforts and mutual assistance in state and local personnel administration or training; and (4) through its grant programs, it encourages joint endeavors among state or local jurisdictions in any aspect of public personnel administration.[19] Each of these authorities has resulted in a

[19] See particularly sections 204, 207, and 202 of the Intergovernmental Personnel Act of 1970 (approved January 5, 1971), Public Law 91-648.

number of practical achievements in the way of interjurisdictional collaboration, with benefits and economies to all concerned.

Needless to say, not all collaborative arrangements to offset our incomprehensible jumble of governmental jurisdictions need depend on legislation. Initiative by enterprising personnel administrators themselves could go a long way toward circumventing the obstacles that stand in the way of providing a modern personnel program at all levels of government.

CHAPTER 25

The Operating Personnel Office

THE EARLY STRUGGLES to gain acceptance of the merit principle in the American public service naturally led to preoccupation with the establishment and strengthening of central personnel agencies. But, important as they are, they have by no means been the only professional personnel influence in the picture. As governments have grown larger, as individual departments have expanded into major bureaucracies of their own—not only in the federal service, but in the more populous states and cities too—attention has become increasingly centered on the personnel function in an operating agency, whether it be a giant municipal hospital and health facility, a state department of taxation, highways, or welfare, or one of the mammoth federal agencies. It is at this point that the bulk of the daily personnel transactions take place, the point where policy meets up with practice, where the contending forces to get work accomplished bring out all the tests of the efficacy of personnel theory and require hour-by-hour adaptation of broad rule to specific event.

PERSONNEL ROLE AND RELATIONSHIPS

It is the thesis of this chapter that personnel management is simply an aspect of general administration and therefore a responsibility of all who have any kind of leadership authority. It is interwoven into all levels of a hierarchy and into all facets of supervision and direction. Far from being the sole concern of a special office carrying the name "personnel," the function permeates the everyday acts of each supervisor or unit chief, as well as those of the top executive. It is part of the policy and part of the machinery of administration, part of the system by which they get their work done.

And it is a very distinctive and difficult part. From surveys that have been conducted, it is not unusual for personnel administration to be ranked by executives as first among their most troublesome problems. Its uniqueness is quite clear:

> Unlike such specialties as electrical engineering or finance, management involves *human beings*. The engineer, for instance, need never give a thought to the impact his maintenance program will have on the "personality" of his equipment. The accountant busies himself with tractable, obedient figures. But the manager must keep himself constantly alert to the impact of his personnel administration on the employee as an individual and as a citizen. And he must understand the subtle relationships that prevail between corporate efficiency and employee satisfaction.[1]

Thus, as the function of maintaining effective human resources and human relations in an organization, personnel management is largely a *manner* of administration.

As distinguished from the considerations discussed elsewhere throughout this volume, the problem of concern here is how to equip operating management to carry out its personnel responsibilities in the best fashion. Specifically, we must explore what specialized staff assistance is needed, what the proper role of that staff should be, and what form its organization and methods should take. In the larger organizations this has meant the establishment of a special office or division composed of professionally trained persons giving their full time to leadership in personnel administration.

THE NETWORK OF AUTHORITY

SERVICE AND CONTROL Whether such an operating personnel office exists purely as a service or as a control immediately comes to mind.[2] The concentration of personnel activities in an office attached to the top executive of an agency renders a service to that executive. But there are at least three ways in which it also provides either a strong influence or a control: (1) it will of necessity be the unit best prepared to interpret to the manager what is intended by the directives and rules emanating from the chief executive and the central personnel establishment of the overall jurisdiction; (2) it usually is expected to formulate and propose to the agency executive the internal policies and procedures on personnel matters required within the agency; and (3) it is

---

[1] Leonard R. Sayles and George Strauss, *Human Behavior in Organizations*, Englewood Cliffs, N.J., Prentice-Hall, 1966, p. 473. At another point the authors observe: "As the administrator makes choices between organizational efficiency and the satisfaction of individual needs, he is acting as a mediator in this inevitable, and, we believe, socially useful, divergence of interests" (p. 489).

[2] The issues surrounding the concepts "line and staff" were discussed at some length in Chapter 2.

ordinarily used by the executive to apply these policies and to see that they are enforced throughout the organization. It may even be given delegated powers in some areas, such as in position classification or in setting up promotion panels, to act in his name. In short, it is one of the channels through which he manages the organization.

Thus, what is a service at one point in the hierarchy may be a control at another. This perspective on personnel "services" is not always acquired by middle and minor supervisors, who sometimes insist that the personnel unit is there to serve *them*, giving them exactly what *they* want regardless of whether it is in line with directives of the agency's top manager. Like all other specialists in the elements of management, such as budget examiners, fiscal controllers, organization and methods analysts, and space and equipment technicians, the personnel officer is employed by the executive expressly for the purpose of taking the load off the latter's shoulders in guiding, information, helping, and, if necessary, restraining subordinate levels in the line in matters involving the particular specialty. This in turn imposes a great responsibility upon the staff specialist to so exert his influence and, where he must, so exercise his controls that they will be readily understood and accepted by the line operators. This duty calls for a maximum of tact, skill, and persuasiveness, especially when applied to the personnel field. For, we reiterate, good personnel administration can be realized only as its objectives and techniques are woven into the whole fabric of the organization and as every supervisor is aware of and concerned with his responsibilities in this regard. Rather than there being an issue here between "service" and "control," the problem comes down to one of joint endeavor and teamwork between line supervisor and staff specialist, which calls for suitable personality and adequate training on the part of both.

USING THE PERSONNEL STAFF   Mention should also be made of the ways in which a top executive can use his personnel staff. Some suggestion of these ways is implicit in the discussion in the preceding paragraphs. Beyond that, attention should be called particularly to the need for the chief personnel officer to participate in all top staff meetings and in general program planning. Without this inside status he can hardly contribute his maximum; this is one of the principal ways in which he can keep alive an awareness of the human aspects of the machine through which the organization gets its work done. It is much better that his counsel be brought to bear in the formative stages of a new program, a new public policy, or a revised organization than to have it after decisions are reached and commitments made. If the personnel specialist is worth having at all, he is worth having when his knowledge and insight can count, not when it is too late. This is far more important than merely having the personnel officer report directly to the executive head of the agency, on which some writers have laid too much stress. It is the degree to which he and his staff are used on important problems and their status as "insiders" that are significant.

Related to this point is recognition by the executive of what a personnel office is for. To make the most of it, he must see it as an instrument for influencing the morale and efficiency of the work force. When there are problems of developing staff enthusiasm, when need for greater understanding and cooperation is evident, when insularity or animosity within the organization is to be dealt with, when the most effective utilization of principal staff members is in question, when, in short, anything involving the attitudes, behavior, and usefulness of the agency's officers and employees is up for attention, the personnel office should be represented in the deliberations. If it is worth its salt, it will make a contribution. If it is viewed as a mere recruiting and placement unit for lower-level personnel and a source of information on rules and regulations, it will be just that and little more.

Yet, even in its routine functions, the constructive place of the personnel office should not be overlooked. Especially in the public service, which is circumscribed more closely by law and regulation than is industry, the personnel organization can be immensely useful in suggesting how certain objectives might best be achieved within the scope of personnel policy. Even civil service laws are not always as rigid as popularly supposed; and under these laws administrators can usually do whatever good management requires, so long as they recognize that what needs to be done may only be done in certain ways. As one sage public administrator (not a personnel man) once counseled the political head of any public enterprise: "If he will put to career administrators in the department a statement of his *general* objective and ask them to tell him how to reach it, they will find a way. The incoming administrator is likely to make the mistake of attempting to issue orders based on some one particular way of attaining an objective, and the way may be, and frequently is, utterly illegal."[3] This wisdom is especially applicable to the field of personnel administration.

MODES OF OPERATION

If we look at the role of the personnel office from the standpoint of technique of operation, taking into account its daily relations with managers and employees, the following features would be the most evident:

1. The first and most basic means through which a personnel office operates is the *development of policy*. It must see both the need for policy and the possible solutions to problems, so that it can take the initiative in management-employee cooperation in policy formulation.
2. Closely related is the *development of written instructions*. The primary problems in this connection are writing the instructions in simple, usable styles, organizing or indexing them for easy reference, keeping them up to date, and seeing that they reach and are used by all officials who need them. The ideal plan, of course, is a classified loose-leaf manual system.

[3] Paul H. Appleby, *Big Democracy*, New York, Knopf, 1945, p. 45. After more than three decades, this little volume is still one of the most insightful and informative pieces on public administration ever written.

The most formidable example of such a system is the U.S. Civil Service Commission's *Federal Personnel Manual,* which is the core upon which any federal department must build its supplementary policies and instructions. It is continuously updated.

3. A personnel office also operates through the *establishment and interpretation of various personnel standards.* These may relate to position classification, qualification requirements, testing criteria, performance minima, safety measures, and the like. Such standards are usually not the exclusive product of a personnel office; they are more often a joint product, with the various operating specialists in the agency supplying the technical information and scrutiny on those matters that affect occupations under their direction. The function of the personnel division here is to see that the standards *are* developed, to supervise their development, to reconcile differences in viewpoint, to coordinate related standards with each other, and to see that they are used.

4. Another channel of personnel staff operation is *training of the operating line.* It is the duty of a personnel unit to use every technique possible, ranging from group meetings to individual consultation and "shot-in-the-arm" circulars, in order to keep supervisors aware and fully informed of their personnel responsibilities. Here is the crux of the personnel job, for only as line management is permeated with an understanding and acceptance of good personnel policies and methods can an organization expect to achieve good personnel administration. This had led some authorities to refer to the personnel man's role as one of "working himself out of a job." But unless we can envisage the day when all operating supervisors are paragons of personnel skill and virtue, attainment of such an objective is an unlikely prospect.

5. The personnel division also serves as a *catalytic agent for bringing top management and employee representatives together to solve mutual problems.* This end is achieved in developing employee representation plans themselves, in soliciting employee participation in policy development, and in keeping management reminded of the profit to be gained from gleaning employee ideas and viewpoints.

6. In a more formal relationship, the personnel staff is the logical one to *speak for management in negotiations and bargaining with unions.* Personnel officials must counsel with key managers on both the substance and tactics involved in such consultation procedures. They are the natural source for relevant facts to be called into play. And, in extended negotiations, they may often have to be the principal figures who sit through lengthy sessions and serve as spokesmen for management's concerns.[4]

7. Frequently a personnel office engages in *certain direct services.* Thus, it may maintain a clearing house of information for employees on recreation resources, housing, outside educational opportunities, social agencies, and

---

[4] This role of the personnel office is discussed at greater length in Chapter 20.

the like. It may operate an emergency loan fund. It may supply the service of writing job descriptions for busy supervisors on the basis of oral information given by the latter. Where there are large numbers of persons to be hired in very routine occupations and the individual discretion of operating officials is not vital, the personnel unit may even make final selection of appointees. All such direct services must necessarily vary in type and volume, depending upon the needs and conditions of the particular organization.

8. Finally, personnel divisions must work to some extent by the *exercise of certain controls*. These controls are largely in the fields of selection and position classification. Final determination of the class into which a position falls cannot be left, without some review, to every supervisor; the very essence of the process calls for the utmost in uniformity. This does not mean, however, that the judgment of supervisors and experts in specific occupations has no part to play in job evaluation. More often than not such judgments are the ones that prevail, but there must be a neutral point somewhere to avoid inequities and to restrain the myopic views of some specialists. These controls are ideally exercised with the assistance of review committees made up of operating officials, to advise on the evaluation of highly technical and of borderline positions.

The other area in which controls are commonly exercised by personnel offices is that of selection of personnel. In this field, some staff unit must of necessity see that all reasonable sources of candidates for the given situation are used, that minimum qualification requirements are adhered to, that irrelevant factors such as race and sex are not determining, and that all laws relating to oaths of office, citizenship, age, and the like, are complied with. Certainly the personnel office is the logical unit to perform these tasks.

ORGANIZATION DYNAMICS

Operating personnel units, as distinguished from central personnel agencies, will generally be found to be organized around either of two concepts: (1) a corps of specialists for each branch of personnel subject matter, whose skills, counsel, or work products are coordinated by the top personnel officer; or (2) a crew of so-called personnel generalists, who individually work with particular segments of the organization but deal with all the subspecialties of the personnel function. At one time there was lively debate over the relative virtues of these two approaches, but the resolution has not been to prescribe one as the universal better answer over the other. The conclusion seems to be that some situations call for the one form of organization, some for the other, and some for elements of both.

FUNCTIONAL SPECIALISTS   The earlier form, and still widely employed, especially in very large departments, is organization around the several functional specializations: classification and pay administration (pay is sometimes separate); employment, placement, and promotion (occasionally there are separate units concerned with testing); training; and employee relations (usually including miscellaneous services to employees). There are, of course, a variety of combinations of these common categories. Also, some offices have additional units responsible for functions such as investigations, procedures and instructions, or public relations.

The drawbacks of the specialist approach tend to be these: (1) Supervisors are forced to identify which personnel specialty their problems or needs come under and to deal with each specialty separately. (2) Supervisors fail to get continuing, overall advice on an integrated basis. (3) The personnel office tends to see problems in fragments, frequently failing to bring these together so that their interrelationships are understood and can be dealt with. (4) This approach, unless accompanied by rotation in assignments, narrows sharply the development of the individual personnel technician.

PERSONNEL GENERALISTS   The generalist arrangement, developed mainly during and after World War II in the federal service but having spread quickly to many states and municipalities, involves the organization of the personnel office along the lines of the main functional subdivisions of the parent organization. General personnel representatives in each unit handle all personnel matters for a given segment of the agency (usually one representative for each entity of about three to five hundred employees). Functional specialists are not necessarily eliminated in such plans, but where they exist they are called into play only to take care of unusual or knotty problems. Of course, the generalist approach has always been used in small operating offices or bureaus where the volume of work did not permit a personnel staff of sufficient size to warrant having separate functional specialists.

Some of the reservations about the generalist form of organization are: (1) Personnel representatives may develop only superficial familiarity with specialized personnel functions. (2) There is less opportunity for expert advice on any one specialty. (3) A personnel generalist may become so interested in and identified with the operating view as to particular cases that he loses his professional objectivity and becomes merely an advocate of what some supervisor wants. (4) Training and employee relations work, on the one hand, and classification and employment, on the other, call for somewhat different education, interests, and talents. (5) It is difficult to develop well-rounded generalists at junior and intermediate levels, since there is too little time for them to become adequately skilled in each of the techniques. (6) The generalist plan does not fit all situations—an example being a central staff personnel office in a large department which performs policy-making and reviewing functions but not operating personnel services.

COMBINATIONS   A number of steps may be taken to minimize the adverse effects of each plan and still enjoy their benefits. One would be, under the generalist system, to provide for rotation of the personnel representatives from time to time, both between specialist and generalist assignments and among different generalist assignments. Another is to be more exacting in the initial selection of general representatives and in their training by functional specialists. Also, specialization could be preserved primarily at the head-quarters level of a department, with generalists working out of bureau personnel offices. It seems clear that only the extremes are intolerable—where specialists are too narrow-gauged or where generalists are too poorly informed. With careful selection and adequate training, combinations of the two approaches would seem to fit most situations. As in so many aspects of public administration, adaptability and moderation are the elementary requirements.

Another consideration relating to personnel office relationships is the role of a general administrative officer, concerned with all management staff services, in a given program bureau, division, or operation. This official on the immediate staff of line administration of the particular unit may represent that unit on policy issues and may carry out instructions of a personnel office which is servicing several such units. If the personnel office handles its relationships with that unit largely through this admin-istrative officer, the latter is in effect performing like the generalist. An important difference is that in this case the generalist is on line manage-ment's staff rather than on the personnel office staff. Hence, it may be argued that a still more desirable adjunct of the generalist idea is to give the line operating official the maximum delegation of personnel responsi-bility by placing the generalist on his immediate staff. This obviously would leave the personnel office with little reason to have more than a group of functional specialists, since no one would propose both a line unit administrative officer and a personnel office generalist as intermediaries between individual supervisors and personnel technicians.

OTHER ORGANIZATIONAL CONSIDERATIONS   Space does not permit full discussion of other aspects of personnel office organization. There is, for ex-ample, the special problem of relationships on personnel matters between headquarters and field establishments. Related to this is the companion prob-lem of decentralization or delegation from one level in the hierarchy to sub-ordinate levels. Should the personnel offices at the bureau level be part of a central personnel set-up, or should they be part of the bureau line organiza-tion? How far should department-level personnel offices go in exercising line controls? These and similar questions must be left to continuing experience and research for answering.

Note has already been taken, in the discussion on central personnel agencies, of the utility of personnel officers' assemblages in the form of councils serving as advisory bodies to the central body. As the personnel function develops at the operating level, the meeting together of these officials to discuss common policies and problems becomes more and more necessary. A number of states and localities have found such councils useful not only to the central agency but also to each of the participating departments. The Interagency Advisory Group, previously the Federal Personnel Council, is the mechanism through which this objective is served in the federal civil service. Both the U.S. Civil Service Commission and the government departments regard it as a successful and almost irreplaceable enterprise in personnel management for the vast and complex federal bureaucracy.

Supplementing such official bodies, or substituting for them where they do not exist, are the several professional associations in the governmental administrative field. Organizations such as the American Society for Public Administration and the International Personnel Management Association have field chapters in various centers throughout the country, with a few even abroad. Their meetings and publications have exerted a stimulating and healthy influence on the administration of public affairs. In addition, research and professional inquiry have been fostered by the American Political Science Association, the American Academy of Political and Social Science, and the National Academy of Public Administration.

In line with the thinking that personnel organizations are the links between any work enterprise and the social environment of which it is a part, the operating personnel office is playing an increasingly significant role in the life of public agencies everywhere.

FUNCTIONS OF THE PERSONNEL OFFICE

The larger the department of government the more highly developed its personnel office is likely to be. Therefore, the fullest range of personnel functions is found in the more heavily populated states and cities and in the federal government. Smaller agencies, of less than one or two hundred employees, can seldom afford to have full-time personnel specialists on their staffs. But even in such cases, some official, if only as a part-time matter, should be responsible for seeing that needed personnel policies are developed and followed.

SCOPE OF FUNCTIONS

Without attempting to repeat the details of personnel programs as presented at length throughout this book, an effort is made here simply to sketch in outline form the typical duties carried on by a well-rounded personnel office in an operating agency of government:

1. *Policies and instructions:* developing these in all areas of personnel administration, for management approval, and promulgating them in usable form.
2. *Job analysis and evaluation:*
   a. Assisting supervisors in developing facts about new or changed positions.

b. Evaluating positions in accordance with class standards.

c. Developing or interpreting class standards.

d. Contributing to analysis of organization problems.

3. *Staffing:*

a. Ascertaining and organizing staffing needs for recruitment purposes.

b. Working with the central personnel agency in establishing qualification and testing standards; developing and administering tests in specialized areas peculiar to the agency, or organizing boards of examiners to do so; participating in developing sources of qualified candidates; requisitioning lists of eligibles.

c. Investigating work histories of persons outside the agency.

d. Maintaining a qualifications index on present employees; checking with other agencies for candidates when necessary; referring candidates as vacancies occur.

e. Assisting the selecting and appointing officials in evaluating candidates from inside the agency, from other agencies, or from examination registers.

f. Processing appointments, promotions, and other actions; checking for adherence to law and regulation.

g. Interviewing and corresponding with all applicants and employees interested in placement.

h. Evaluating placements through follow-up inquiry.

4. *Salary and wage administration:*

a. Where discretion is authorized, making wage and salary studies as the basis for setting pay scales; or interpreting and executing relevant provisions of law on compensation.

b. Convening and guiding negotiations with employee unions on pay matters.

c. Administering special pay provisions for satisfactory service, for outstanding performance, for geographic, cost-of-living, or hazard differentials, and for movement from job to job.

5. *Employee services and working conditions:*

a. Advising management on all administrative matters that affect human motivation and morale.

b. Counseling with employees and supervisors on human relations problems.

c. Sponsoring suggestion programs and other means of eliciting employee participation in work improvement.

d. Arranging for provision of adequate health services.

e. Maintaining a safety education program; facilitating provision of injury compensation.

f. Checking on adequacy of physical working conditions.

g. Establishing machinery for adjustment of grievances, and umpiring its use.

     h. Interpreting leave policy.

     i. Assisting in or providing recreation and other services.

6. *Performance standards and evaluation:*
   a. Assisting supervisors in making and recording objective appraisals of employee performance.
   b. Directing and assisting in setting up performance standards.
   c. Guiding the staff in focusing efforts on performance development and improvement.
   d. Stimulating use of various forms of employee recognition.

7. *Staff training and development:*
   a. Analyzing and pointing up training needs; conducting training methods research.
   b. Working with supervisors in perfecting on-the-job training techniques, in organizing group training, and in evaluating training.
   c. Planning and conducting such orientation, supervisory, clerical, and other training as can best be handled centrally in the agency.
   d. Maintaining liaison with outside educational institutions on preentry training curricula and on supplementary in-service training.
   e. Preparing training materials.
   f. Encouraging or developing "house organs."

8. *Separation:*
   a. Conducting exit interviews.
   b. Advising on and processing retirements.
   c. Conducting reductions in staff in accordance with policies and rules.
   d. Advising supervisors on disciplinary suspensions and removals.

9. *Employee rights and obligations:* keeping employees informed of various rights and obligations pertaining to their public employment status.

10. *Union bargaining and agreements:*
    a. Keeping up needed data relevant to union negotiations.
    b. Anticipating issues and advising top management on their resolution.
    c. Representing management as necessary at the conference table.
    d. Participating in drafting agreements with unions.
    e. Monitoring adherence to agreements on behalf of management.

11. *Records and reports:*
    a. Maintaining statistical records on employee population, turnover, and movement.
    b. Maintaining all files on employee work histories.
    c. Reporting to top management, supervisors, and employees on all developments that affect or potentially affect the human resources and morale of the agency.

12. *Personnel research:*
    a. Conducting attitude surveys.
    b. Studying and validating testing, interviewing, and rating devices.
    c. Analyzing exit interviews, turnover, absences, and tardiness.
    d. Improving forms and procedures.

13. *Public relations:*
   a. Presenting information on personnel operations of interest to the public.
   b. Conducting helpful, considerate correspondence in reply to all inquiries.

This is not a comprehensive tabulation. Nevertheless, a mere recitation of the list, when used in conjunction with the more substantial treatments of the various subjects in earlier chapters, is enough to give a broad idea of the part the personnel office must play in personnel administration. Many functions duplicate those in the central personnel agency but on a smaller scale.

Such a skeleton outline may not seem to take into account the time-consuming special fields of personnel concern that are incidental to one or another of the activities listed. For example, in many jurisdictions, personnel offices must give a great amount of attention to matters such as arranging for employee suitability or security investigations, receipt of clearances, and any related suspensions or removals; answering debt collection letters and credit inquiries; assuring adherence to laws and executive orders prohibiting discrimination in personnel actions on account of race, sex, religion, or color; enforcing veteran preference requirements in selection, reduction, or movement of personnel; answering letters and calls from members of the legislative body; and commenting on the wisdom and feasibility of proposed legislation on pay, recruitment, retirement, hours, leave, and the like. These are illustrative of facets of the personnel office job that are inherent in many of the activities previously listed.

To be sure, not all operating personnel offices in the public service are covering the whole range of functions outlined, and not all are meeting their highest purpose as staff advisers, but an increasing number are doing so.

RECORDS AND REPORTS

Because it is not given special attention elsewhere, a special word is necessary here regarding the record-keeping and reporting functions of the operating personnel office.

PERSONNEL RECORDS   Personnel records are, in the main, of the following broad types: (1) records on employees, (2) records on applicants, (3) records on positions, (4) policy and procedural directives, rules, and regulations, (5) payroll, leave, and retirement records, and (6) correspondence files. Several of these deserve special comment.

In the first place, *payroll, leave, and retirement records* may not be personnel records at all. Because of the processes involved, many organizations regard these primarily as fiscal records that can best be kept by persons skilled in bookkeeping and accounting. For this reason, payroll, leave, and retirement records are often maintained by finance offices rather than personnel offices, particularly in the federal service. This in no way diminishes the personnel office's responsibility for pay, leave, and retirement policy and interpretation from a substantive standpoint. A frequent practice in state and local agencies, however, is still to carry on these record-keeping functions within the personnel office or within the same office which handles requisitions for eligibles. In fact, in the early days of merit system control, the "checking of the payroll" by the central personnel agency was considered a sine qua non of such a system. It was by this control that recalcitrant division heads could be prevented from surreptitiously slipping a political appointee on the rolls.

The category of *records on employees* is the most complex. Ideally it should consist of (1) individual employee folders covering the total employment history and training of each employee; (2) confidential files on some employees, containing inquiries, complaints, or other data which are of such a nature that for them to remain in the regular folders, which are often referred to supervisors interested in candidates for jobs, might unjustifiably prejudice the employees' opportunities for employment success in the organization; (3) an index (by computerized methods or otherwise) of employee qualifications necessary for placement purposes and other indexes or cards needed for statistical reporting; (4) placement contact records to maintain continuity of relationships and make adjustment simpler in those instances in which interviews or inquiries are conducted between placement officers and employees; (5) health examination records and reports of special health conditions or treatments, which probably should be kept in the health room. A personnel operation is not likely to be very up to date unless it contains an orderly system of files for each of these purposes. It is impossible to say what proportion of public agencies measure up to these elementary criteria.

Records on applicants are primarily of three types: (1) those on applicants from other departments in the same jurisdiction who are eligible for transfer; (2) those on persons seeking reinstatement; and (3) registers or certificates of eligible candidates from outside. Some of the principles governing the content of such files are covered in the chapters on staffing. Suffice it to say here that, where applications of persons eligible for selection are kept, it is necessary to have an occupational and qualifications index similar to that used for current employees. Only in this way can the personnel office be assured that all such candidates will always be considered for any openings that they are qualified to fill.

Necessary *records on positions* consist, of course, of individual job descriptions, class specifications, organization charts, and other program or comparative information that will be of use in the evaluation of duties and responsibilities.

Notable examples of modern record-keeping are the following standard practices in the federal service: a decentralized leave-reporting form and system; a standard personnel folder on individual employment history that is transferred between departments when the employee transfers; a standard summary personnel card; and use of electronic equipment for qualifications indexes and for statistical reporting. Comparable systems are found in a number of other jurisdictions. Indeed, some have led the way.

PERSONNEL REPORTING Reporting is a less developed aspect of personnel management. Few will claim that they have found the ideal plan for reporting to top executives on personnel activity and trends in their organization. The statistical side of the problem is commonly taken care of by mechanical means, with basic data punched or coded on cards or tapes that are subsequently sorted and tabulated by computers, by hand-operated "keys," or by other devices. Thus, the facts on numbers and movement of personnel, pay rates, location, promotions, separations, and so on, can readily be compiled for periodical reports or for ad hoc requests.

Pointing up significant developments, analyzing workloads, demonstrating areas of need for personnel work, showing what factors and conditions are influencing motivation, and indicating trends in the organization that call for action are much more difficult to synthesize and report on. But they are nonetheless essential. The better a personnel office's regular reporting system, the better prepared it is to meet the special requests for reports that it continuously receives from the chief executive, the central personnel agency, the budget authorities, and the legislative body.[5]

THE PERSONNEL OFFICER

Regardless of how much we like to profess that ours is a government of laws and not men, the fact is that personality and capacity have a great deal to do with both politics and administration. Nowhere is this more true than in the case of the manager at the head of the personnel operation. The personnel officer must be many things to many people. He must set an example, and he must be an adviser. He must be an interpreter but also a controller. Above all, he must be a diagnostician. To fill such a bill successfully requires talents of the highest order. Certainly the key personnel job in any organization cannot be a refuge for the mediocre. It is not the assignment for the person who simply "likes" or "understands" people. It is a professional responsibility calling for thorough preparation and experience and personal qualifications of insight and tact that would do credit to an ambassador.

The personnel official cannot be a passive observer. If anyone must be an activist, he must be. He should be good enough that when creative efforts are needed to solve management problems the top executive of the agency will automatically want him involved. He should not be content merely with technical implementation at the point when a decision has been reached. He should participate in making that decision.

[5] A useful reference on this subject is Merrill J. Collett, *Streamlining Personnel Communications*, Chicago, International Personnel Management Association, 1969.

The current and next generation of personnel managers have to be more than specialists in the several facets of personnel technique. They must have the general perspective and understanding to sense the role of government in modern life and the particular relationship of their agency to that role. They must therefore have an appreciation for the great issues faced by society and for the contributions and responsibilities of all levels of government in their treatment. This means seeing beyond one's own jurisdiction; it means a readiness to participate in intergovernmental relationships.

On top of these underlying considerations, the personnel official must understand how motivation is derived from the work itself, how education is going to be a continuing part of work, how behavioral science can contribute to problem-solving and policy-making. He must perceive the sociological changes that are going on about us, the renewed emphasis on equality in its fullest sense, and the special problems of labor relations.

At the same time the personnel officer must be cognizant of the latest techniques employing quantitative methods and computers, of those involving engineering of jobs, and of those affecting modes of testing and measurement. With all of this, he is expected to be a person of extraordinary human qualities, one with general managerial skills, gifted in problem-solving, decision-making, writing, and speaking. Above all, he must be an innovator.[6]

It takes little perception to accept that an advanced education is a necessity for professional personnel work, especially for those who expect to carry on leadership functions in the field—as is the case with key personnel officers. No apprenticeship in clerical work—not even that associated with the personnel office—can possibly provide the preparation needed. Only with rare exceptions can the breadth of experience, the professional outlook, the knowledge of the job world in the modern social environment, of human values, and of motivational influences be acquired in any way other than that afforded by the intensity, the continuity, and the discipline of a full collegiate education, preferably at graduate level and of the broadest scope.

If the personnel function is to live up to all that is being expected of it, its leaders will have to be persons of extraordinary understanding, of outstanding ability, and of unassailable integrity.

---

[6] See O. Glenn Stahl, "Tomorrow's Generation of Personnel Managers," *Public Personnel Administration—Progress and Prospects*, Personnel Report No. 681, Chicago, International Personnel Management Association, 1968, pp. 41–46; plus the commentary by Edward C. Gallas, pp. 47–49.

PART IX

Developmental Areas

Government policy "can be judged to be right only by its fitness to further the aims of the government, these aims in turn can be judged only by the interests of the nation, and these interests only by the philosophy of the judge."

George Santayana, *Dominations and Powers: Reflections on Liberty, Society, and Government,* New York, Scribner's, 1951, p. 461.

We need men with ideas, but even more, we need ideas with men.

Anonymous

A "Gresham's Law" of administration: "Operations drive out thinking."

Anonymous

The ability of the nation to solve its most critical problems— education, law and order, environmental decay, urban blight—rests squarely upon the ability of the public services of the country to attract, retain, motivate, and utilize human talent.

John W. Macy, Jr., *Public Service: the Human Side of Government,* New York, Harper & Row, 1971, p. vii.

CHAPTER 26

Personnel Research

MANY PERSONNEL AND related administrative subjects are as speculative and imponderable as they are because of the dearth of facts and systematic analyses that permit an objectively drawn finding or conclusion. At various points throughout this book reference has been made to problems and issues that are ultimately resolvable only through the techniques of painstaking research. But the investment and hence the progress in research in personnel administration has been much less than the costlier habit of trial and error and "bumbling through."

STATUS OF BEHAVIORAL RESEARCH

A MATTER OF PRIORITIES

The problem is not the total absence of research in human affairs, but the comparative neglect of it; not the inability to cope with the complexities of the subject, but the failure to devote sufficient resources to it. In the last analysis it comes down to a matter of priorities. We have gone to extraordinary lengths to contrive ways to permit man to walk on the moon, but we still have not learned to govern ourselves on earth. We have spent billions to split the atom but hardly pennies to unite humanity. The identification of human talent, the kindling of human motivation, the improvement of human relationships in our institutions of productive effort are a major part of governing ourselves. They continue to elude our grasp more than does the physical universe, because we study them with far less dedication and in far less magnitude than we study our physical environment.

Just one example of the contrast in approach dramatically illustrates the effects. Realization of the dangers inherent in pollution of the air, the water, and the other ingredients of our natural heritage points up no lack in the physical data as to how to deal with the problems technically. The lack is on the social, political, and economic sides. There have been practically no studies on the value judgments, on the methods, on the organizational arrangements necessary to bring about a complete change in direction and emphasis.

We now know something of the conditions that make for productive, smooth-running enterprises, but careful and persistent research in the field is still a hit-or-miss, haphazard venture, the preoccupation of a comparative handful of managers and behavioral scientists. One student of the situation observes:

> The most significant thing that the industrial social scientists have done is simply to make good their claim that the complex events of business life are useful fields for research. Whether their work ultimately leads to anything worthwhile—for example, to greater human satisfactions in work, to greater productivity, to lessened waste and strife—will depend as much on the ingenuity of managers of all kinds as on that of the social scientists. For research has already indicated that the more burdensome problems of industrial life, such as apathy, restricted output, strikes, demoralized older workers, anomie, and all the rest, are not inevitable. It has even suggested that the feelings of self-fulfillment in work which have traditionally been experienced by very few people can be made available to many more and that the results of such an opportunity might well be an amazing surge of creativity and efficiency.[1]

SIGNS OF PROGRESS

Actually, the truly substantial advances in the art and science of personnel administration have been based on research. Such has been the case with the work of psychometrists in test research, that of pay experts in assembly and analysis of pay data, that of educators in the elementary principles of learning, and that of health specialists in showing the relationship of preventive health and safety measures to productivity and job satisfaction. The military services have never been slow to rely on heavy investment in research. Examples of successful use of research in civilian pursuit have been the studies of selection and motivation of volunteers in the Peace Corps; the exhaustive inquiries into the selection, care, and nurturing of astronauts by the National Aeronautics and Space Administration; and the longstanding studies by the Public Health Service on various categories of health personnel.

More recently, the funding of several projects in the public personnel field offers promise that the climate for research is finally beginning to change. The National Science Foundation has made grants to universities to study various

---

[1] Saul W. Gellerman, *Motivation and Productivity*, New York, American Management Association, 1963, p. 292.

aspects of productivity, industrial organization, and job satisfaction. The National Training and Development Service, with funds from the Department of Commerce, undertook a study of the quality of job satisfaction in state and local government. The U.S. Civil Service Commission has directed a small portion of its research resources into subjects such as productivity and performance evaluation. A few states have ventured into the uncharted areas of personnel research that involve state personnel.[2] Nevertheless, much remains to be done.

THE CONTINUING NEEDS

Agendas of needs for personnel research prepared some years ago are still apropos, because so little has been done in the meantime. A selective list of conclusions from two noteworthy reports is worth summarizing:

1. Of the nation's total research budget (governmental, industrial, university, foundation, etc.), only about 1 percent is devoted to the social or behavioral sciences.
2. Technical areas that have received very little attention have been: training methods and the learning process, job analysis, performance evaluation, pay and fringe benefits, and the special problems of personnel management in government.
3. Selection and testing have received more emphasis in research than any other area of personnel administration.
4. Important research needs appear in the following:
   a. How to engineer work for human effectiveness.

---

[2] Notable among the states that have personnel research units are California and Michigan. On the federal level, the Departments of Agriculture and Air Force stand out in this regard.

The following, addressed to private industry but equally applicable to government, suggests a source or two for research support:

> we must put some of our resources aside, and with blood, sweat, tears and cash dig into the basic problems of understanding, as well as pursuing the task of attempting to put out fires armed with an arsenal of ignorance. If instead of sending 500,000 people to management development programs each year, we sent only 250,000 and spent the rest on basic research, we would have a chance to get some place. If instead of spending $1000 per year per employee on fringe benefit placebos, we spent half of this on basic research—we might get something for our money. If we raised our sights from the non-thinking level—for example, the plethora of surveys of personnel practices and policies—we might begin to see what we are missing. [Herbert G. Heneman, Jr., "Manpower Management: New Wrapping on Old Merchandise," address at the 18th Annual Industrial Relations Conference, University of Minnesota, Industrial Relations Center, Minneapolis, April 13–14, 1960.]

A popular summary of the influence of early modern research in the social sciences appears in Stuart Chase, *The Proper Study of Mankind*, New York, Harper & Row, 1948. See also the stimulating first chapter in Dwight Waldo, *Perspectives on Administration,* Tuscaloosa, University of Alabama Press, 1956.

b. How to use the fruits of increased productivity.

c. How to identify and release creative talent.

d. The effect of the governmental setting (e.g., legislative bodies, statutory controls, city managerships, court actions, etc.) on public personnel administration.

e. The effect of political parties and patronage.

f. Organization for the personnel function in government.

g. Comparative analysis of career systems.

h. Intergovernmental mobility of professional and managerial personnel.

i. Significance and effects of veteran preference.

j. Professionalization of the personnel executive and specialist.

k. Nature and causes of public attitudes toward the public service.

5. Personnel administrators should become more research conscious.

6. All governments should perform or arrange for much more research in the personnel field.[3]

The foregoing list may be expanded to include a number of other needs:

1. To develop more sharply the genuine, as distinguished from the presumed, qualifications needed to perform various classes of work.

2. To find the optimum ways of reconciling career stability with the infusion of new blood.

3. To learn how to balance personal freedom with the necessities of bureaucratic impartiality and ethical behavior.

4. To devise fresh ways of developing employee skills in motivation and supervision.

5. To discover practical means of reporting and evaluating personnel policies and practices.

6. To ascertain the impact of computer technology on work, on people, and on work products.

7. To find out how to modify concepts and practices in labor relations to accord with democratic control of the bureaucracy and to avoid a self-governing civil service.

8. To explore the relation of personnel selection processes to the awareness and responsiveness of civil servants.

---

[3] This listing only partially reflects the impressive array of findings and ideas set forth in these two significant documents: Cecil E. Goode, *Personnel Research Frontiers: A Review of Personnel Research Activities and Facilities, with Special Reference to their Implications for Government*, Chicago, International Personnel Management Association, 1958; and Wallace S. Sayre and Frederick C. Mosher, *An Agenda for Research in Public Personnel Administration*, Washington, D.C., National Planning Association, 1959.

Briefer but nevertheless excellent discussions on research processes and needs appear in: Dale Yoder, *Personnel Management and Industrial Relations*, 6th ed., Englewood Cliffs, N.J., Prentice-Hall, 1970, pp. 718–750; and Nesta M. Gallas, "Research Needs," Chapter 12 in *Police Personnel Administration*, O. Glenn Stahl and Richard A. Staufenberger, eds., Washington, D.C., Police Foundation, 1974.

9. To determine the relation of political activity restrictions (or changes in them) to employee performance and behavior and to public agency performance.[4]

Essentially we are concerned with a most important area of social science research. The workaday life of man occupies more of his time and attention than any other element of his active life. Common sense alone would suggest that we know as much about it as possible. To do that, we need to employ the information and techniques of the anthropologist, the sociologist, the psychologist, the psychiatrist, the political scientist, the economist, the engineer, the statistician. In other words, we must discipline ourselves to rely not just on hunch and guess, but on systematic, orderly study and appraisal of controlled and observable experience.

Research is still conspicuous by its absence among public personnel agencies. Very few states have personnel research units worthy of the name. The U.S. Civil Service Commission devotes a modest expenditure to research, but it is overweighted with emphasis on the traditional test and measurement area. Few of the largest federal departments have special staffs for the purpose. In short, the function has not achieved anything like the stature that is required if modern government is to profit from what we already know about the utility of sound and continuing research in personnel administration.

THE RESEARCH ATTITUDE

The research approach is epitomized as much in a point of view as it is in a process. It is the willingness to venture a new hypothesis, to act on facts and not conjecture, to experiment, to learn and revise on the basis of organized study of experience. It is the attitude of the diagnostician, the inquiring mind, the entrepreneur, the innovator. It is the facing of facts by assembling them systematically, validating them rigorously, and interpreting them carefully. In essence, it is the scientific method.

Research is a combination of theorizing, experimenting, and discovering. Some research may proceed no further than the descriptive stage. Some may be analytical. That which ventures forth with new ideas and dares to try them out under rigidly controlled conditions is creative.

Some administrators make the mistake of assuming that, once research is conducted on a particular subject with some success, it is transferable to all related situations. Every organization needs to shape its own inquiries in the context of its own environment. The findings in one place can be immensely helpful, but more often than not they require repeated verification in the light of the circumstances of each organization. Unlike the natural sciences,

---

[4] The last two items were inspired by reading David H. Rosenbloom, "Public Personnel Administration and Politics: Toward a New Public Personnel Administration," *Midwest Review of Public Administration*, April 1973, pp. 98–110.

the results of social science research are not highly borrowable. The most that a study in one place can do is to suggest a line of approach. Only after a great many repeats under a wide variety of conditions can anything like some enduring conclusions be expounded.

Likewise, the techniques of research evolve. In this respect the natural and social sciences are one. Both subject matter and lines of approach change. Perhaps that is why research is never complete. Only the naive would suggest that once a set of answers is found the study may be discontinued. There is much enduring truth in this statement:

> In the 1920's, management thought of personnel research in terms of stop-watches and test blanks. In the 1930's, the Hawthorne investigators . . . proclaimed the importance of the interview. Uses as well as methods of personnel research—or fact finding for the guidance of administrative decisions on personnel—have changed in response to changing emphases in administration.[5]

And so will tomorrow's research call for new insights and new designs. The important thing is that there be a mechanism and a habit of research to permit a response.

Public agencies may draw upon many sources for research guidance and assistance, in addition to equipping their own offices to engage in it. Nearby universities are often ready and willing to collaborate. Joint studies with industrial concerns are sometimes productive. The case for the research attitude and for enterprising methods of implementing it is well stated in the following:

> Research . . . begins with an attitude—a lively and imaginative curiosity, coupled with a determination to ferret out and make explicit the assumptions on which one operates from day to day and then to test them in the cold, bright light of objectivity. Adequate internal funding and staffing are important for personnel research. At the same time, there are external sources of assistance which few personnel agencies have explored.. Personnel research cooperation among jurisdictions can be particularly rewarding. . . . If positive personnel administration is to be more than a a shibboleth, it must be responsibly based on a sound bedrock of research.[6]

*   *   *

THAT THERE HAVE been great advances in the physical and natural sciences cannot be denied. But they will come to naught—indeed they may annihilate

---

[5] Elinor G. Hayes, "New Uses for Personnel Research," *Personnel Administration,* October 1945, p. 5.

[6] Kenneth A. Millard, "Action Programs to Improve Research in Personnel Agencies," *Extending the Horizons of Public Personnel Administration,* Personnel Report No. 671, Chicago, International Personnel Management Association, 1967, p. 41.

us—unless there are equally great advances in the human sciences.[7] ·The advances in that field, as in the other, will be founded on unrelenting and rigorous research. The altar of physical science is laden with gold—and with grave dangers.

Man's life in the work place is no small part of the neglected field of human affairs. Until detached fact-finding and analysis win better support from executives, from personnel officials, and from those who hold the purse strings, personnel administration will fall short of its supreme goals of creating and maintaining a highly motivated work force serving the public interest. If personnel research and inquiry does rise to the occasion, it will have been a potent force in assuring that public administration meets its tremendous challenges.

[7] Many a thoughtful physical scientist has acknowledged this truth. They have particularly been concerned that spectacular achievements in the physical world may have been at the expense of projects that would have offered more prospect of advancing human welfare. One such was the Director of the Oak Ridge National Laboratory of the Nuclear Regulatory Commission, who mused that when history looks at the twentieth century, it may find our pyramids, our cathedrals, our palaces in the form of huge rockets, high-energy accelerators, and high-flux nuclear reactors—which may serve us no better than the Roman Colosseum staved off the barbarians or the Sphinx made Egypt a modern wealthy state.

> Those cultures which have devoted too much of their talent to monuments which had nothing to do with the real issues of human well-being have usually fallen upon bad days. . . . we must not allow ourselves, by short-sighted seeking after fragile monuments of Big Science, to be diverted from our real purpose, which is the enriching and broadening of human life. [Alvin M. Weinberg, "Impact of Large-Scale Science on the United States," *Science*, July 21, 1961, p. 164.]

CHAPTER 27

Public Personnel Policy Around the World

IN TODAY'S WORLD no nation stands alone. The concepts and issues of public personnel administration are no exception to this condition. Interest in what is taking place in this field outside one's own country develops as rapidly as information and communication permit. Although a reasonable feeling of self-sufficiency about their personnel practices may be sensed within most of the highly developed nations, many, through publications and at international meetings, display an increasing curiosity about what is going on elsewhere.

Guardians of the more established personnel systems are more self-critical and more receptive to exploring how their policies came to be what they are. The developing nations aspire to finding the presumed secrets and devices that will improve the effectiveness of their civil services. The gradual extension of international organization is forcing more interchange of ideas and reconciliation of views in order to make rational and operable the personnel mechanisms to which all nations must subscribe and contribute. In short, the development and the implementation of public personnel policy become more transnational and international as each year goes by.

Such considerations are merely part of the interdependence and oneness of humanity being recognized by thoughtful persons everywhere. As one distinguished international figure has expressed it: "Before long, humanity will face many grave difficulties that can only be solved on a global scale."[1] And, so, it becomes necessary that we take the existence of "one world" into account in the policy-making processes, in the public administration, and in

[1] Edwin O. Reischauer, *Toward the Twenty-first Century: Education for a Changing World*, New York, Alfred A. Knopf, 1973, p. 4.

the education of youth in every quarter of the earth, for, to quote further, "the world is sinking into a single vast unit which will survive as a whole—that is, as a global community—or not at all."[2]

In addition to such global realities, regard for how well the world's work gets done suggests the desirability of examining the major facts and problems in the personnel field that face all governments together. This cannot be accomplished in any exhaustive way within the confines of one chapter. However, we can look at the scope and depth of American involvement in human resource development around the world, outline briefly the principal aspects of the more fully developed public personnel systems, analyze in some measure the special personnel problems of developing countries, and scrutinize the distinctive issues facing personnel administration in international organizations.

RANGE OF AMERICAN INVOLVEMENT

In the decades since World War II the United States has vastly extended its worldwide interests and operations—both official and unofficial. Quite apart from any appraisal of its successes and failures on the world scene, the fact of American influence and presence—economically, culturally, militarily, politically—cannot be denied. A brief recitation of the many forms of this involvement that have an impact on the marshaling and development of human resources is in order.

AMERICAN BUSINESS ABROAD   Approximately 3000 U.S. commercial and industrial companies have operations in at least 114 countries.[3] They generally employ many more local nationals in each host country than they do Americans but the special problems of employment and pay policy in a non-U.S. environment have given rise to a whole new field of business administration.[4] In addition to these direct operations, various American consulting and research firms are actively engaged in services to foreign governments and

[2] *Ibid.*, p. 19. Reischauer further observes: ". . . a reorientation of education so as to give young people everywhere a sense of the shared interests and basic oneness of mankind and to prepare them for effective participation as members of a world community is, I believe, a clear necessity for human survival in the twenty-first century" (p. 195).

[3] Burton W. Teague, *Compensating Key Personnel Overseas*, New York, The Conference Board, 1972, p. 2.

[4] A substantial number of books have appeared in recent years on management of multinational corporations, embracing issues relating to Americans overseas, to employment of foreign nationals in U.S. businesses abroad, and to the problems of intercultural relations. Typical of such works is Barry M. Richman and Melvyn Copen, *International Management and Economic Development, with Particular Reference to India and Other Developing Countries*, New York, McGraw-Hill, 1972.

An even more international example is Joseph L. Massie and Jan Luytjes, eds., *Management in an International Context*, New York, Harper & Row, 1972, which contains a collection of essays on industrial managerial developments in and from fifteen nations.

businesses. The pervasiveness of American products and American managerial methods is quite obvious to anyone who has traveled the world.

DIPLOMATIC AND CONSULAR SERVICES   The growing number of national states in Africa and Asia has accounted for an equivalent increase in U.S. political outposts abroad. At the same time, the expansion of international communication and commerce has required a substantial increase in traditional representation and data-gathering services at U.S. foreign missions in all nations. Accordingly, the personnel system for the regular U.S. foreign service has taken on new importance. Little wonder that its relative isolation from the rest of the federal civil service and its greater tendency toward an elitist mentality have brought some of its features into question.[5]

SUPPLEMENTARY OFFICIAL PROGRAMS   By no means has the American official presence abroad been confined to the regular diplomatic and consular operations. Outranking these in volume, personnel, and expenditure have been the programs of the U.S. Information Agency (USIA), including the Voice of America broadcasts, and those of the two agencies focusing on the developing nations, the U.S. Agency for International Development (USAID) and the Peace Corps. Although the latter two organizations have been gradually reduced in size and scope, they have exerted a marked influence among the poorer countries, as shall be noted more explicitly later in this chapter. Naturally, they brought in their train a host of personnel issues not heretofore involved in U.S. foreign missions. The most distinctive aspect of these supplementary programs has been the introduction of the short-term expert—the provision of special services in technical aid to developing nations through direct hires of specialists and through contracts with university, professional, and consulting organizations.

At the same time, every federal agency in the U.S. Government has been getting involved in overseas activities to one degree or another. Although

---

[5] Perhaps the best overview of this subject is that in Chapter 17, "The American Public Servant Beyond the Borders," in John W. Macy, Jr., *Public Service: The Human Side of Government*, New York, Harper & Row, 1971. For a review of the structural history and of various studies regarding the foreign service, see Arthur G. Jones, *The Evolution of Personnel Systems for U.S. Foreign Affairs*, New York, Carnegie Endowment for International Peace, 1965. In summarizing, Jones reports that the bodies studying foreign affairs personnel have favored:

> retention of the career concept but would add more flexibility on intake; at least a partial merger of overseas and domestic personnel within the foreign affairs agencies; increased attention to specialization and executive needs; a more rational personnel structure and elimination of unwarranted status distinctions; improved management machinery, organization, and procedures; and greater use of the Foreign Service to meet overseas needs of domestic agencies when these activities have distinctly foreign affairs implications. [P. 135.]

Still another source is W. Wendell Blancké, *The Foreign Service of the United States*, New York, Praeger, 1969, which gives a description of the character of and life in the foreign service.

overshadowed by the giant Department of Defense and its many civilian support operations at military installations abroad, other agencies—the National Aeronautics and Space Agency, the Departments of Agriculture and Commerce, the Internal Revenue Service, the Federal Aviation Administration, to name only a few—also have contingents of civil servants working regularly in foreign countries.

The scope of federal involvement in international affairs certainly makes continuance of a separate foreign service personnel system highly questionable.

MILITARY MISSIONS   At least two kinds of American military establishments exist in various foreign nations: (1) provision of teams of military advisers, usually at the request of the host government; and (2) military bases, with sizable complements of personnel, usually established at the request of the United States for maintenance of strategic power centers in the interest of American military security. Those missions in the first category are few both in total number and in the number of U.S. military personnel located in any one country. The number of military people at any one installation in the second category may be quite large, but they are most often housed as well as employed in separate American compounds on the military bases themselves.

In neither case are the American personnel involved (except at the top), including U.S. civilian support workers, as intimately associated with the officialdom and citizenry of the host nation as are those American personnel working in the embassies, USAID, USIA, the Peace Corps, and other such civilian operations. It is part of the functions of many engaged in the latter activities to work intensively and on a daily basis with counterparts in the host government or among the host citizenry, a relationship likely to exist only on the part of a few senior officers on the military side. It is common for the American personnel of the civilian agencies to "live on the local economy," that is, in residential quarters intermixed with homes of local nationals and with supplies acquired on the local market; such practices are far less often found among U.S. military personnel.

The Defense Department's installations abroad, however, often employ many nationals of the host country and are thereby deeply involved in sensitive economic and labor relations issues on the local scene. In these matters they must operate under the general policy direction of the American ambassador in the particular country.

EDUCATIONAL PROGRAMS   One of the most striking and influential evidences of American international activity has been the employment of our vast educational resources in programs designed especially for foreign nationals. In addition to a substantial influx of regular foreign students on university campuses, numerous methods have evolved that encourage and sustain thousands of persons, particularly from the poor countries, to study in the various professions and managerial fields that have been most highly developed in the United States. Support of such programs has been both official, through longstanding government appropriations, and unofficial, ranging from private business endowment to establishment of many scholarships by philanthropic or religious organizations.

Most noted among the official programs have been the Fulbright[6] scholarships for visiting students and scholars and for sustaining American lecturers at foreign universities. Another variant has been the underwriting of educational and cultural visits to this country of foreign officials and experts, as a means of improving intellectual and cultural exchange. Furthermore, American money and educational institutions have been responsible for establishment and, to a considerable extent, operation of numerous educational ventures *within* foreign nations—especially institutes in developing nations created for technicians and civil servants whose skills need upgrading. More often than not, both for programs based within the United States and those carried on abroad, the personnel of American educational institutions have been utilized to staff these various enterprises.

Private Voluntary Services   Typical of the American pluralistic and unfettered approach to the world's needs is the array of private ventures in the realm of international betterment. The oldest example, of course, has been the missionary programs of the major religious groups in the United States. Well beyond the aim of religious conversion or proselytism these organizations were the first to contribute to improving education and health standards in the poorer parts of the world, although the volume and impact of such humanitarian efforts were modest by comparison with what followed under official auspices.

Especially noteworthy on the international scene have been the large American foundations—notably the Ford Foundation, the Rockefeller Foundation, and the Asia Foundation. These bodies, while retreating in their degree of financial commitment in recent years, have funded many educational, health, and agricultural activities and have often worked hand in hand with official U.S. and international agencies engaged in technical and economic assistance in developing countries. Likewise, the American business community has, among other ventures, contributed to the technical aid process by organizing and funding the International Executive Service Corps, an organization that supplies experts in manufacturing and other business practices to counterpart companies in nations trying to build up an industrial capability. Other worthy enterprises are the relief and health activities of CARE and the American Friends Service Committee.

Americans in International Agencies   Scarcely noticed in the mass media of communication but nonetheless potent in the American involvement

---

[6] Named after Senator William Fulbright, long-time chairman of the U.S. Senate Foreign Relations Committee, who sponsored the idea in the early days after World War II.

in the international arena is the employment of many U.S. citizens in the U.N. Secretariat and in the various other international and regional agencies of modern transnational civilization. Small as these organizations may be by comparison with our largest national governmental agencies, their significance for world well-being and therefore for public administration everywhere must not be underestimated. Only a few thousand Americans work in these international organizations, but the uniqueness of their service along with that of other international civil servants should not be overlooked. Perhaps the relevance of this statement will be clearer upon a reading of the last section of this chapter.

Superficial and incomplete as it is, the foregoing catalogue of ways in which the people of the United States, through both governmental and private institutions, are involved in worldwide affairs may further reveal the degree to which a book on public personnel administration must give attention to the development and administration of personnel policy around the world.

THE ESTABLISHED SYSTEMS

It is most unusual to find a public personnel system that has been established without reference to those in other nations. Just as the American system has its roots in the British ideas of competitive examination, so most of the industrialized states can trace their personnel structures and policies to the influence of neighbors or of more dominant powers. Likewise, the systems found in new nations that were former colonies of European-based empires are almost invariably prototypes, at least in general terms, of those in the central governments that had colonized them. International organizations, in turn, having been first set up in western Europe, have tended to adopt personnel arrangements that imitated in their principal features the national systems in that part of the world.

THE EUROPEAN MODELS

In the discussion of career systems we have already given considerable attention to some of the elements of major European personnel structures, particularly the British, as they are reflected in the issues regarding closed systems and rank-in-corps.[7] Among the circumstances that had an impact on the evolution of the European models were the social stratifications in each society and the gradual shift over the past two centuries from absolute monarchies to democratic governments or parliamentary monarchies. Undoubtedly the origins and morphosis of governmental and social forms have helped shape common denominators in these personnel systems such as the following: (1) the subdivision of the civil service into broad categories roughly paralleling the major classes in the society, as reflected in level of

---

[7] It would be well to review this analysis in Chapter 4. It is the foundation for much of what is said in the chapter at hand.

education achieved; (2) the barriers to movement among such categories, which tended to be relaxed somewhat as democratization progressed; (3) the elitist character of the upper strata of the service, and the prestige that accompanied this condition; (4) the strong protection of the service from political manipulation, and the almost absolute tenure assured; (5) the domination of seniority in governing advancement; (6) the unwritten codes of impeccable conduct on the part of career men; (7) the permissiveness as to the unionization of civil servants and as to union representation of their interests; and (8) anomalous as it may seem, the tendency to keep the monetary rewards of public service relatively low as compared with the private economy.

Not all these features apply in equal measure to each country, but, for the most part, they have all existed and still substantially exist in the civil services on the continent and in the British Isles.[8] Certainly they spell out some of the distinguishing characteristics of these public services as compared with that in the United States. We are speaking here principally of the British, French, German, Italian, and Spanish personnel systems, although those of the smaller nations—Austria, Belgium, the Netherlands, the Scandinavian group, and Switzerland—fit the prescription about as well. In short, they have been highly stratified civil services of great prestige and almost untouchable when it came to transformation or dislodgement. Yet they also displayed a kind of monastic dedication and expected self-denial that have shown signs of changing only since World War II.

The development of the bureaucracy in the Soviet Union appears to have taken quite different turns. Putting aside the role of the Communist party in recruitment, the competitive entry, job classification, performance evaluation, and promotion features of the USSR system seem to be much more like policy in the United States than are the comparable aspects of personnel administration in the western countries, with which the United States has had much stronger cultural ties. This is evident not only in the meager literature on the subject but from discussions and positions taken at international seminars and conferences in which civil service practice comes up for consideration, such as when application to developing nations or international organization is involved. From what can be ascertained, the civil services in the other eastern countries are patterned after the Soviet model but with foundations that are still not unlike those in western Europe. An example of Soviet practice paralleling that in the United States is in the treatment of the higher positions in its service, which are not set aside as the special preserve of an administrative corps but which are filled by persons specialized in each subject-matter field who are trained in supervision and management.

---

[8] Among other sources, a report of the International Institute of Administrative Sciences (IIAS) confirms these generalizations: Aryeh Attir, *Adaptation of Public Personnel Administration to Changes in Society*, based on a questionnaire survey and on the meeting at the Fourteenth IIAS Congress held in Dublin in September 1968; published by IIAS, Brussels, 1971.

OTHER SYSTEMS

The situation in the most highly industrialized nation in Asia, Japan, cannot be neatly bracketed with any other category. During the military occupation by the United States following World War II, it was almost in the position of a developing country accepting technical assistance in a wide range of its governmental activities. The influence of American technicians on its civil service policy during this period was obviously great. But Japan was vastly different from the peasant societies that make up the bulk of the developing world. It had already had extended administrative experience, having added to indigenous systems selective features of Confucian, Buddhist, British, French, and German thought and practice, as well as American ideas acquired before the war. It had, moreover, never been exploited by colonialism. Its amalgam of policy and its well-developed National Personnel Authority do not fit any precise pattern but have unquestionably been affected by the American exposure more than by any other outside influence.[9]

Aside from the common denominators among the European civil services just cited, the established personnel systems around the world vary widely in several respects. Most of them are based on the rank-in-corps concept. The notable exceptions, aside from the United States, are Canada, the Soviet Union, a few Latin American and Middle East nations, and to a certain extent Japan. Canada and the United States, having collaborated professionally over many years, have many common features in their personnel systems. Other members of the British Commonwealth, such as Australia, India, Pakistan, and New Zealand, have followed the British civil service pattern more faithfully. Even where categorization into cadres or corps is the foundation of a system, however, there are infinite variations as to form and detail. When it comes to *openness and fluidity of the system,* so far as movement of personnel is concerned, Canada and the United States are probably unexcelled.

Merit and competitive examination are cardinal principles almost everywhere, but with wide variations in approach and organization. The objective, short-answer test is nowhere as highly developed as it is in the United States.

---

[9] A convenient summary of European civil service system appears in Marshall E. Dimock and Gladys O. Dimock, *Public Administration,* 4th ed., New York, Holt, Rinehart and Winston, 1969, pp. 185–191. Other useful references are Brian Chapman, *The Profession of Government: The Public Services in Europe,* New York, Macmillan, 1959; Edward McCrensky, *Scientific Manpower in Europe; A Comparative Study of Scientific Manpower in the Public Service of Great Britain and Selected European Countries,* New York, Pergamon, 1958; Edward McCrensky, "Personnel Management—Soviet Style," *Personnel Administration,* September–October 1960, pp. 45–51; Eric Strauss, *The Ruling Servants: Bureaucracy in Russia, France—and Britain?,* New York, Praeger, 1961; Gwendolen M. Carter and John H. Herz, *Major Foreign Powers,* 4th ed., New York, Harcourt Brace Jovanovich, 1962; and Marshall E. Dimock, *The Japanese Technocracy —Management and Government in Japan,* New York and Tokyo, Walker/Weatherhill, 1968, Chapter 9.

Central personnel agencies of one kind or another usually have responsibility for supervision of the merit system, but in many countries they do not control the total personnel management function. Likewise, they vary in the degree of "independence" from executive leadership. In some cases, special units attached to the chief executive officer (president or prime minister) have certain policy initiative and directoral authority not shared by the central recruiting agency.

One of the civil service problems receiving major attention in the industrialized nations has been the matter of labor relations. As has been noted in the chapter on that subject, some have very highly developed programs, while others have not reached that stage. Few have proscribed strikes on the part of public employees to the same extent as has the United States (and they have had more strikes, too!). An international committee of the International Labor Organization has enunciated some guidelines in the field of union-management relations, but it has avoided taking flat positions on collective bargaining and strikes. It did suggest that, "appropriate to national conditions," the member states should promote the widest development of collective bargaining and consultation procedures relating to employment conditions, including promotion, training, safety, and health.[10] Not many governments in developed countries really fail to live up to this elementary precept.

THE AMERICAN MODEL

With all of its problems, mistakes, and challenges, the American system of public personnel administration does not have to take a back seat to any other of the established systems. Its openness to lateral entry from industry, universities, and other levels of government; its comparative lack of reverence for seniority in promotions (up to now at least); its stress on decentralization of authority to act; its vigorous pursuit of education and training in the service; its insistence on the combination of technical and administrative skills in its highest jobs; its involvement of operating management in the development of personnel policy; its provision of latitude for adaptation of general policy to the peculiar needs of specific units or programs; its relative professionalization of the personnel function; its elevation of public pay scales to levels comparable with the general market; its emphasis on the job and the work to be done rather than on personal status; its informality of communication lines; and, above all, its freedom from class distinctions (with few exceptions)—

[10] International Labor Organization, *Meeting of Experts on Conditions of Work and Service of Public Servants*, Geneva, 1963, pp. 25–32. The experts specifically urged that governments guarantee to their civil servants freedom of association and protection of the right to organize, and that they allow staff representatives to appear before decision-makers, to use government premises for meetings and for posting announcements, to collect dues during working hours, and to defend members of their unions before appropriate adjudicative bodies.

have been the distinguishing marks of civil service administration in the United States that are to its genuine credit. The American reputation for productivity and efficiency must be attributed to many conditions—the vast spread of education among its masses; an extraordinary elasticity in its economic system; freedom of expression; endowment of great natural resources; and an attitude and spirit of achievement. But the structure and operation of its personnel system, especially in government, are part of this milieu and deserve a reasonable share of the recognition.

Illustrative of the testimonials to the general quality of personnel practice in this country are two that come from other nations. We have already taken note of the impact of the Fulton Report in the United Kingdom, which clearly follows the American model in its criticism and proposed reform of the class structure of the British civil service.[11] Its endorsement of an open system, with more stress on fitting the capacities of civil servants to the needs of jobs, has attracted worldwide attention, because it challenged the foundations of a system that had been so widely imitated in the former British colonies. Its rejection of the cadre concept, by which a civil servant's career was determined at the point of entry, is near revolutionary in its implications for most of the personnel systems now in existence and a vindication of the basic philosophy of the American approach. The British have made considerable progress in implementing the basic thrust of the Fulton Report.

Referring primarily to American industry, a modern Frenchman produced a best-seller in Europe when he published his thesis that American technology surpasses that of European nations because of certain identifiable characteristics of American managerial practice. Among the policies to which he gave special credit were genuine delegation of authority to the point where action has to take place; confidence in people to carry out decentralized responsibility; and personnel procedures based on evaluation of performance, on respect for organization objectives, on achievement as the criterion for advancement, and on inadequate results as the grounds for dismissal.[12] These are, of course, features of public personnel systems in the United States as much as of industrial systems. His contention was that, from the standpoint of enterprise management, Europe would never catch up unless it abandoned some of its traditional practices that contravene these principles.

The problems and shortcomings of public personnel administration in this

---

[11] See the discussion on "Job-Oriented Careers and Rank-in-Corps" in Chapter 4.

[12] Jean-Jacques Servan-Schreiber, *The American Challenge*, New York, Atheneum, 1968.

Illustrative of American practice, reflected in both private and public sectors, is the greater emphasis on performance than on status and rank. Two observers of U.S. business overseas point out: "American subsidiaries in Europe, as a whole, have a reputation for basing promotions and pay increases more upon evaluated performance than upon seniority and experience, as native European companies have tended to do" (Herbert J. Chruden and Arthur W. Sherman, Jr., *Personnel Practices of American Companies in Europe*, New York, American Management Association, 1972, p. 10).

country, which are amply highlighted throughout the present volume, may not seem so formidable when compared with the deficiencies noted by critics of other national civil services. To whatever degree this comparative advantage is in fact true, however, it should never be allowed to become a cause for complacency. For the problems of prestige of public employment, the need to extend mobility of professional and managerial personnel, the necessity for working out better consultative arrangements between public management and unions, and the imperative need for expanded research are but a few of the issues that must be squarely faced and met before citizens, politicians, and public administrators in the United States can rest comfortably on their laurels.

THE DEVELOPING COUNTRIES

Concern for the technical and administrative capacity of governments in developing countries is a phenomenon of the post–World War II period. Some of this concern may be attributed to competition among the great powers to win the support and indebtedness of the transitional societies in the latters' quest for economic and social progress. Some may be attributed to the direct clamor of the developing nations themselves for assistance. Some may be accounted for by the responsibility of international organizations, especially the United Nations and its specialized agencies, for improvement of the standard of living in all quarters of the globe—a goal naturally fostered by the many member states that stand to gain from such a policy.

Much of the common thread running through all these explanations is enlightened self-interest on the part of the industrialized world—an awareness that the resources on this planet cannot be so marshaled to serve any society adequately unless all societies reach some minimal point of economic development and justice. This is not said in cynicism, but rather with profound respect for the statesmen who moved the developed nations to a realization of this fact of life, for it was a humanistic and altruistic stance that had never before in history characterized the relations among nations and one that bids fair to transform the whole quality of international affairs, to say nothing of its hoped-for direct effect on the world's standard of living.

The important consideration for our interest in personnel matters is that the more underdeveloped a transitional society happens to be, the more dependent it is on *public* policy and administration for at least the direction of change. As one student of the subject has expressed it:

> There are a few elites in developing countries today which espouse *laissez-faire*. All of them accept a substantial measure of governmental activity. These measures may range from the construction and operation of infrastructure facilities like schools, roads, and power plants; through measures of governmental financing, stimulation, and regulation of economic activities

performed in the private sector; to planning and guiding the main lines of development policy; and at the far pole, to state monopoly of all significant economic enterprises.[13]

Public personnel management finds itself in the very center of such a picture. Where bureaucracies may have been nonexistent or of minimal impact before, they now become vital and face rapid expansion.

THE EXTRAORDINARY PROBLEMS

Appreciation of the magnitude of the personnel challenges in the public service of a developing nation may be gained if we look first at the major tasks the nation faces:

1. Achieving security against external aggression and ensuring internal order.
2. Establishing and maintaining consensus on the legitimacy of the regime.
3. Integrating diverse ethnic, religious, communal, and regional elements into a national political community.
4. Organizing and distributing formal powers and functions among organs of central, regional, and local governments and between public authority and the private sector.
5. Displacement of vested traditional social and economic interests.
6. Development of modernizing skills and institutions.
7. Fostering of psychological and material security.
8. Mobilization of savings and of current financial resources.
9. Rational programming of investment.
10. Efficient management of facilities and services.
11. Activating participation in modernizing activities, especially in decision-making roles.
12. Achieving a secure position in the international community.[14]

All of the foregoing undertakings require government leadership of an order that would tax the most experienced statesmen, and achievement of most of them is critically dependent upon the quality of administration.

THE INTERPLAY OF POLITICS AND ADMINISTRATION

The tasks facing a transitional society being as formidable as they are, it is understandable that experts from outside the country debate the degree to which various factors bear on the success of development. The nature of the political system, the intensity of participation by large segments of the

[13] Milton J. Esman, "The Politics of Development Administration," in John D. Montgomery and William J. Siffin, eds., *Approaches to Development: Politics, Administration and Change*, New York, McGraw-Hill, 1966, p. 77.
[14] Excerpted from *ibid.*, pp. 61–63.

society, the manipulation of media and special interests, and other conditions certainly play important and sometimes critical roles. As our previously cited authority observes:

> Nation building and socio-economic progress are not only technical, but profoundly political, processes. To counter the resistance of bitter and often powerful opponents of development programs, to mobilize clientele to relate effectively with governmental activities, to overcome apathy or suspicion through discussion, demonstration, and persuasion—these are not arts in which most bureaucrats shine, especially in developing countries. . . . When under pressure, they usually opt for safety in order to protect their careers.[15]

While some would argue that the main ingredient of a success formula is the technical capacity of a small group of public officials and entrepreneurs, others would contend that this is secondary. But there seems to be general agreement that, whatever its relative weight in influencing progress, the better equipped and more capable public administration is, the better the prospect for growth and development in a society. Although there may be instances where accent on administrative improvement has had little impact because of political obstacles, it would be difficult to find a situation where investment in such melioration has been counterproductive. This is not to disparage the relative importance of the nonadministrative factors, for political organization and related efforts can be extremely useful both in shielding administration and in directing and energizing it. The point is that the combination is indispensable. Inspired leadership produces nothing without effective administration; however able and well-intentioned, it cannot push very far beyond its bureaucracy. But the expertise and continuity essential to development also desperately need political support and protection.

At the same time, the leadership both external to and within the bureaucracy must have a moral quality that rises above the immobility of a peasant society's past. The value content of a development program and of its operation can be one of its most enduring benefits. Respect for the human individual, for intellectual integrity, for simple everyday honesty, for fair and equitable dealing—these are the elemental virtues that must be as much a part of successful administration as technical knowledge and skill. Moralizing as this may sound, the fact is that in many emerging states experience with organized human effort on any substantial scale has been so relatively unknown that articulation or even awareness of ethical considerations has been as underdeveloped as technical proficiency. It should not be overlooked in any assistance rendered to a youthful government struggling with its enormous development tasks. Nor should western moral values be confused with eco-

---

[15] *Ibid.*, pp. 81–82. Unlike Esman, some students of comparative politics and administration have dealt with the subject in such abstruse and esoteric terms, of interest to only a select few, that their research and observations are of little help either to developing nations or to those providing technical assistance.

nomic individualism and our theories of private property. Decent regard for human welfare and human rights can be fostered regardless of the degree of socialization of the means of production.[16]

PERSONNEL SYSTEM ISSUES

Many of the compelling needs of public personnel systems in developing countries are more or less obvious. Almost invariably one finds shortages of skilled manpower, absence of manpower planning, inadequate examination methods, penurious pay scales, use of the service as a haven for lawyers and economists who have no other likelihood for employment, lack of statistical data for evaluation, underutilized or inadequate training, dearth of clear-cut policy directives, low incentive, poor attitudes toward achievement, outright corruption, and many other conditions that are natural concomitants of low standards of living in the society, limited educational opportunity, and slight economic resources. To say that these deficiencies are obvious is not to say that they are unimportant. The point is simply that they are fairly readily discerned and are often acknowledged by leaders within the developing country.[17]

Certain other characteristics of transitional civil services are somewhat more subtle and therefore more difficult to detect and to understand. A few typical conditions are worth brief exposition:

CULTURAL CONSTRAINTS   The effects of religion, race, tribe, or caste—all representative of deeply engrained cultural traits or influences—are the most sensitive and complex circumstances that usually must be faced. These are the most difficult for local politician and bureaucrat alike to deal with because of their understandable desire not to compromise their power or position by needless offense to any clientele group. Yet, although these "facts of life" can impose serious obstacles to progress in civil service reform, they are not always as inexorable as some people too close to the situation may feel. Sometimes more forthright and courageous dealing with the problem on the part of the officialdom would go far to minimize adverse effects of cultural habit or doctrine. For example, interference of tribal or caste predispositions with rational classification or training schemes may well be ameliorated by enlisting tactful but persistent statements by political leaders to explain the benefits of new ideas and, above all, to get people within and outside the civil service sufficiently accustomed to hearing about such notions over a period of time that they no longer seem strange or threatening to their welfare. Too often a "can't-be-done-because-of-our-

[16] See the two essays by John D. Montgomery: "A Royal Invitation: Variations on Three Classic Themes," in Montgomery and Siffin, eds., *op. cit.*, pp. 257–294; and "Sources of Bureaucratic Reform: A Typology of Purpose and Politics," in Ralph Braibanti, ed., *Political and Administrative Development*, Durham, N.C., Duke University Press, 1969, pp. 427–471.

[17] Summaries of the personnel systems in many developing countries appear in Harold F. Alderfer, *Public Administration in Newer Nations*, New York, Praeger, 1967, pp. 95–118.

heritage" philosophy perpetuates resistance to change by the very repetition and reinforcement of myths and fears that could be substantially dissipated if they were frankly questioned or even ignored as irrelevant.

FORMER COLONIAL STATUS   An overwhelming majority of the states we now identify as transitional or developing were once colonies of European powers. The impact of the colonial period on their civil services has usually been profound. With rare exceptions, the new government bureaucracies tend to ape those that had been established locally by the colonists. Even though the colonial period in no case reaches back very far in modern history, it is not uncommon for average citizens and even well-educated people in a developing country to mistake as part of their indigenous "culture" some legacy in personnel structure or practice that was actually conferred upon them by their former masters.

The tendency to defend the system as "native" is not necessarily deleterious, but it does not create a good climate for change when everyone (often including the apologists for the status quo) acknowledges the desirability of change. It should be recognized that the legacy of the colonizing powers has more often than not been a good and supportive one in smoothing the transition to self-government, by providing a model on which the new leadership could lean for administrative viability while consolidating its control. The British did a particularly good job of setting the example, training the personnel, and creating the mechanisms for competent and impartial performance that have generally made their former colonial civil services the most effective ones among the newer states. But the models established were largely those of the nineteenth and early twentieth centuries, and the new governments have seldom kept abreast of the changes and adaptations that were taking place in the meantime in the bureacracies of the "mother country." Recognition that a civil service that has ostensibly declared its independence is not continually beholden to its origins in the womb of the colonizing power would create receptivity to change or reform where it is clearly essential to economic, political, and social progress.

ENTRENCHED ELITES   Related to the foregoing point is the problem of vested interests in the bureaucracy of the developing country. Such entrenchment of special governing elites takes any of several forms. Sometimes it simply means a holding on to positions of influence and authority by older civil servants or by representatives of well-to-do families, neither of which groups is likely to be of a frame of mind receptive to policy or structural changes in the personnel system. In other instances, the key elements in the bureaucracy may represent a branch of the society that has been passed by in thinking and development by other sectors that have emerged in more recent times, such as a group of well-trained military officers or a newly energized body of industrialists and other entrepreneurs. As these developing subsocieties acquire some of the keys to power in the society at large, the civil service may face the prospect of upheaval and overturn unless it is capable of adaptation and reform from within.

The model of the "closed service," implanted particularly by the British and the French, has played into the hands of vested bureaucratic interests in many a transitional society. Entry only at junior levels, advancement primarily on the basis of seniority, emphasis on passive "neutralism" rather than programmatic zeal, and excessive reliance on security of tenure—the usual attributes of closed services or cadres—create conditions ideal for maintenance of the status quo and for resistance to change. Indigenous elites that have no intention of surrendering their privileges and powers in such a civil service are extremely hard to retrain or remotivate and, where extreme steps are essential to progress, to dislodge or replace.

LOW PRESTIGE OF SPECIALISTS   An especially aggravating situation that is repeated in so many of the newer nations, and is also attributable to the colonial model, is the relatively low incentive for professional and technical personnel—a most regrettable condition when one considers the overwhelming need in all developing societies for technological advancement. The plight of engineers, medical doctors, and scientists, to say nothing of supporting technical workers, derives in part from the vested interest problem just cited but more particularly from the kind of personnel structure that exalts the "administrator" (the so-called generalist) above all other occupational groups and reserves for him all or nearly all the key career posts. The result has been that the professional man, by virtue of practicing his vocation and not having entered the service via an administrative cadre, cannot aspire to hold any of the very top positions, because the latter have been traditionally the closed preserve of those who were trained in the liberal arts, the classics, or the humanities and whose careers were built around a series of assignments concerned with the methodology, the techniques, and the procedures of administrative clearance and coordination. It is this top rung of posts to which the professionals are denied access that provides direct and continuous policy counsel with the ministers, deputy ministers, and other political heads of state.

The age of technology and specialization clearly makes the exclusive hegemony of the "generalist" an anachronism. There are doctors in these countries who are quite capable of holding and eager to serve in the highest career posts in health ministries but who are barred because of their vocation and their "corps," not because of any defined personal deficiencies. Engineers in road building or hydroelectric construction, agriculturists in soil conservation or food production and storage, educators engaged in expanding school services, understandably resent domination by "administrative" men, often their juniors in age and service, who are rotated into their respective departments over their heads with no program knowledge or commitment. The idea that breadth, vision, balance, or any other requisite of high executive responsibility can be manufactured only under a liberal arts curriculum and through a limited avenue of experience, the notion that administration is always a thing apart from the program administered, are completely out of tune with the needs of modern government everywhere.

Of course, this was the very argument of the Fulton Committee in its analysis of the shortcomings of the British Administrative Class and its insistence that more opportunity be given to professional personnel in the British civil service. Fortunately, similar conclusions are coming to the fore among developing nations which had patterned their personnel practices after such a system. No modern civil service can afford long to stultify those occupational categories in its employ that constitute the backbone and hope for technological leadership and advancement in their development programs. The solution will, of necessity, be along the lines of training the specialists, both in formal educational courses and by planned progressive assignments, to gain the perspective and knowledge beyond their special fields that will enable them to compete successfully for the very highest career positions for which they are peculiarly qualified by subject-matter orientation and interest.

GOVERNMENT AS ALMONER   There seems to be an inescapable tendency among the poor nations to use government employment as a means of livelihood for sectors in society that might not otherwise have an avenue for gainful pursuits. The objects of such welfare-oriented use of government jobs may be college graduates as well as the unskilled or extremely destitute. In short, where there is no other way of providing sustenance, public jobs become a mode of welfare assistance, whether the jobs are really needed or not. In some societies, even well-educated people have difficulty securing employment because of inadequate industrialization or a dearth of sophisticated institutions that might utilize their skills. Under such circumstances, the public service seems to be the only way to keep them off the streets, from plotting revolution, or from otherwise prostituting their talents.

The very poor also become objects for minimal employment by government. In one of the largest developing nations it has been estimated that at least 50,000 messenger or menial-service jobs in the government's headquarters were really not needed but existed only to provide work for the chronically poor.

Such a condition is hardly conducive to a rational salary policy, and accordingly government salaries in these circumstances are usually depressed. The dilemma for such governments is this: if salaries are kept low, the public service cannot attract or hold the best people in competition with any growing industrial sector or any other outside alternative; but if salaries are made too favorable, the payroll grows beyond the government's means, especially when it may embrace many who do little or no work on jobs that exist only to provide an income. The usual result is to keep salaries abysmally low.

THE BRAIN DRAIN   Another condition that plagues developing societies is the loss of their best brainpower to more attractive opportunities outside the country. Exposure to the richer nations, where they may have acquired their training in the first place, often creates temptations for young people to accept employment in a more attractive and rewarding environment than that afforded by the overwhelming problems of their native country. Some of the poor societies have sought to impose sanctions to induce their trained manpower to return or remain at home. In some instances the industrialized countries have cooperated by facilitating their return or at least not permitting their stay in the richer country beyond a period of training.

The brain drain has occasioned much thoughtful analysis in international circles, to say nothing of much hand-wringing and pointless recrimination. Ultimate solutions are still not in sight, for the international competition for able, highly trained men and women is severe and unabating, and those who have looked objectively at the problem find that migration of talent is much more an *effect* than a cause of underdevelopment in the poor nations.[18] Among other steps that might help are those that would reform the more indefensible features of personnel systems, such as the low recognition given to technical manpower in many societies that have been conditioned to exalt the literary scholar or the administrative generalist. Correcting such misguided attitudes and improving the prospects, challenges, and rewards for technical specialists in the home environment might well slow down the drain of educated manpower from the country of origin to more promising opportunities elsewhere.

SOME REDEEMING FACTORS AND DEVELOPMENTS

A recitation of personnel problems in developing administrative systems creates an unfortunate atmosphere of hopelessness and may make the obstacles seem so formidable as to discourage efforts at improvement. This need not, of course, be the conclusion drawn.

In the first place, in many of the countries there are a number of redeeming conditions. As already implied, some of the very places that have been handicapped by heritage of outworn colonial systems of administration have also been blessed with some useful traditions of merit, dedication, and distinguished public service by indigenous civil servants. Noteworthy in this regard are the civil services of India and Pakistan, which are illustrative of the best products of British colonial tutelage. These are conditions to build upon, not to reject

---

[18] See the following study, which assembles reports and factual data from all continents: Committee on the International Migration of Talent, *The International Migration of High Level Manpower; Its Impact on the Development Process*, New York, Praeger, 1970. Supporting the point that the brain drain is not a prime cause of underdevelopment, this report states: "Among the more serious factors are dependence on one crop economies, static cultures based on status, shortage of capital, shortages of foreign exchange, political instability, and inflation" (p. 670). The loss of technical manpower is not likely to be markedly reduced until at least some of these more basic deficiencies are dealt with.

outright. If necessary changes in compartmentalization, closed cadres, and the like, can be undertaken without weakening the affirmative qualities of such bureaucracies, a happy and effective combination will have been achieved. There is no derogation of the quality and high standards of conduct with which the British impregnated the subcontinent of Asia; there is simply the necessity to accept that some of the forms and methods implanted are no longer in keeping with the exigencies of modern government.

Another hopeful sign is the readiness of a considerable portion of the political and bureaucratic leaderships in a number of countries to make a case, and if necessary fight, for change. India, Pakistan, Nepal, Thailand, the Philippines, and other nations are pressing forward on programs of personnel reform to one degree or another. The emphasis on more job-oriented personnel policies in the U.N. workshop of Asiatic nations held in Bangkok in 1968, the substantial changes in the same direction proposed by entirely indigenous official commissions in India and Pakistan, the receptivity in Nepal to introduction of job evaluation—are all recent examples, at least in one area of the world, where the prospects for elimination of some of the more flagrant deterrents to a well-motivated and productive (not just competent) public service seem reasonably good.[19] From the standpoint of population, these nations mentioned constitute a major part of the less than fully developed world. For sheer magnitude, therefore, any progress there is especially noteworthy.

TECHNICAL ASSISTANCE

The amount of technical and economic aid that has been poured into the less fortunate areas by the United Nations, by the World Bank, by the United States, by various European countries, by Canada, by Australia, by Japan, and by private groups such as the Ford Foundation, CARE, and the American Friends Service Committee—has been little short of prodigious during recent decades. No one has yet assembled the full dimensions of this collective and unilateral (and sometimes competing) effort, but isolated reports on parts of the activity and for limited periods confirm the undeniable magnitude of the total undertaking. Only in the mid-1970s did the volume of such activity

[19] Several of these instances are mentioned at greater length in Chapter 4 on "Career Systems." It may be noted here that, from the 1950s onwards, there has been almost uniform criticism of closed cadres and elitism in the civil services of Pakistan, India, and Nepal by a series of outside consultants. Under auspices of the Ford Foundation, Rowland Egger in 1953 and Bernard Gladieux in 1955 in Pakistan, Paul Appleby in 1953 in India, and myself in 1969 in Nepal all came to approximately similar conclusions. These viewpoints have also been seconded from time to time by public administration advisers supplied to these nations by the U.S. Agency for International Development (USAID) and by the United Nations. A commission in Pakistan was the first to come to the same conclusion for itself (1962), although the report was suppressed from public view for seven years.

In 1973 Pakistan abolished its antiquated, compartmentalized system and began building an open civil service under a single broad structure of pay levels.

begin to decline, although some of the change is represented by a shift of program direction and responsibility from individual donor nations (particularly the United States) to international agencies.

AID IN SUBSTANTIVE FIELDS   Initially the concentration of technical advice and assistance was on agriculture, health and sanitation, education, and engineering, and these fields together still compose the greater part of the effort from all these quarters. More recently the subject of birth control and family planning has been commanding greater prominence in technical assistance, as the world's population explosion has come to be understood as the major obstacle to improvement of living standards. Gradually, there has also been increased attention given to public administration problems. As experts in technical fields attempted to establish skills and understanding in developing societies, they encountered inadequate or a total vacuum of infrastructure upon which to build. There simply was insufficient knowledge of organization and methods, an absence of a tradition of collective effort, and a lack of administrative and social structure to provide the necessary underpinnings on which to construct technical improvements in agriculture, sanitation, and all the other areas of need.

ADMINISTRATIVE AID   Awareness that scientific and technical improvements were foundering on the shoals of managerial ineptitude (on the part of the technical advisers, as well as the recipients) and realization that government in the transitional societies would have to be the main vehicle for conveying and directing all social and economic advances led to more positive methods to bolster public administration from local to national levels in each country. The United Nations and USAID especially stepped up their projects to be of assistance in the ways and means of public administration. In addition to help on specific reorganizations, on introduction of new financial and procedural methods, on installation of new personnel policies, and on similar one-time projects, both these giants in the technical assistance field initiated or helped operate over seventy training institutions to provide continuing education to both prospective and current public servants in developing nations.[20] These institutions may well prove to have more lasting effect in building administrative capacity in these countries than any other technical assistance undertaking that has been devised.

The experience generated by the total technical assistance effort, and particularly that part of it directly concerned with public administration, has demonstrated that there are many pitfalls to be avoided and many obstacles still to be surmounted. It has been found, for example, that a narrow, technical method—especially of a physical variety—applying to one of the subject-matter fields such as agriculture was easier to introduce than an

[20] Approximately seven more were inaugurated by the Ford Foundation.

administrative change, because the latter impinged more directly and perceptibly on local traditions and habits. This seemed to be true even though the enduring effectiveness of the technical change itself was dependent ultimately on the administrative alteration. Consequently, much of the prime content of preparation for technical assistance, especially in administration, has been focused on matters such as cultural empathy, sensitivity to value systems in the host country, personality characteristics of advisers, and analysis of the transferability of techniques. The latter point includes such factors as isolating elements of a field that hold promise of universal application and finding methods for building transitional bridges or means for "phasing in" new ideas or procedures.[21]

The future of technical assistance, although it is tapering off in total volume and cost, will probably include more emphasis on combining administrative directly with technical aid. That is, a medical, educational, agricultural, or construction project would be offered to a host government only if administrative change to accommodate it is part of the package. The specialist rendering assistance would have to be trained or supplemented by persons who are trained in ways to create the climate, to suggest the organizational machinery or devices, and to develop the understandings within the developing society that will make the introduction of the new technology practicable on a continuing basis.[22]

[21] The possibility that there are some universal principles and features of administration cannot be overlooked. Basic findings of social science research and spreading industrialization led Rensis Likert to postulate that there are many common denominators in management regardless of culture and degree of development:

> The studies in India have found that the same general principles as those found in the U.S. are applicable there. For example: general supervision yields better productivity and overall performance than does close supervision; the more adequately supervisors communicate with subordinates and the greater freedom subordinates feel to approach their superiors, the greater is the productivity of the work groups; the more subordinates participate in planning a change in their work, the greater is the productivity of the work group after the change is made; the work groups in the higher producing units more often than those in the low-producing units display greater skills in group interaction processes, have greater group pride and loyalty, and more often use group decision-making to deal with work related problems. [From an address before the 13th International Management Congress, New York, 1963, entitled: "Toward a World-Wide Theory of Management." Released by the American Society for Public Administration, Washington, D.C., p. 4.]

[22] The following is a practical guide written for advisers, technicians, and teachers engaged in developing new or revised institutions in emerging or developing societies: Hiram S. Phillips, *Guide for Development: Institution-Building and Reform*, New York, Praeger, 1969. Phillips proposes, in reference to all direct hire, contract, and loan-financed specialists, that American "foreign-assistance agencies establish special programs for the training of all long-term personnel *prior to* assignment overseas." The training he has in mind would include: the technology relevant to the assignment; the development process; institution-building; and relevant aspects of the culture and history of the host country (p. 270).

Many books and pamphlets have appeared in the literature that deal with the subject of training specialists for service in developing countries.

PERSONNEL REFORM

No small part, and probably the most difficult aspect, of assisting governments in public administration is the area of personnel reform. The scope and the content of what must be dealt with and revised have already been suggested by the personnel issues that face developing nations. At this point it may be useful to set forth a few considerations of possible univeral application and, derived for these, outline what the main elements of a basic personnel or career service law and policy might ideally be like.

CROSS-CULTURAL PRINCIPLES   Some of the universals that could govern personnel reform almost anywhere are these:

1. *Personnel administration should be viewed as a part of general administration,* not a function isolated from the mainstream of public management. It is a matter of emphasis, an attitude, a way of looking at administration —a consciousness of the complexities of human relationships and of the importance of human resources in getting work done. Therefore, the personnel function should be integrated with the executive management of government.
2. *Personnel administration should be viewed as dynamic,* not static. It is under constant growth and change. Hence, career service foundations should be sufficiently flexible to accommodate to change.
3. *The selection, motivation, and retention of public employees should always be based primarily on quality and merit,* in the broadest sense of those terms. Merit should be understood to embrace interest in and zeal for the public programs to which employees are assigned.
4. *A personnel system should provide good conditions of employment—* satisfactory environment, adequate rewards, and enlightened supervision. Unless these conditions are secured, the higher motivations and absolute integrity are almost impossible to attain on any general scale.
5. *The character and direction of a career service should demonstrate recognition of the dignity of the individual and of respect for human personality.*
6. *The administrative climate*—the systems of authority, the confidence in people, the minimizing of status or class, the brand of executive direction— *should be sufficiently motivating and supportive that it stimulates the release of human energy and ideas in the interest of the objectives of the public service.*

These are obvious generalizations, but their meaning will be patently clear when specific policies and practices are measured against them.

No attempt will be made to identify the precise elements of the ideal public personnel system to fit all places and all times. Most personnel methods and techniques are not so standardized that they can be uncritically exported from one country to another. It is because such exportation was attempted, during the colonial period at least, that so many developing nations are in need of civil service reform today.

A MODEL LAW   Nevertheless, we can proceed somewhat beyond the level of fundamental and broad principle. We can list the most important elements of a personnel or career service law that may serve as a model for the transitional societies around the world, without committing ourselves to concrete structures and devices.[23] The main features of the statutory foundations for a viable personnel system to serve the needs of modern government would seem to be these:

1. *The law should have a clear and substantial statement of purpose,* setting forth a forward-looking, comprehensive set of ideals.
2. *The law should be clear but flexible,* with as much of its content as possible expressed in principle but leaving a large measure of discretion to executive and personnel authorities to adapt those principles to different parts of the service and to changing conditions.
3. *The law should stress authority and the nature and scope of functions rather than institutional forms.* Too many personnel laws now in existence expend all their force on the establishment of a personnel agency and structure and on the details of their operation.
4. *The law should be an instrument of public management, not merely a bill of rights and protections for public employees.* The main thrust should be effective operation of the administrative agencies of government and the establishment of a bureaucracy of high standards responsive to the will of the people. Although the law may include provisions that serve as guarantees to employees, these should be clearly subordinated to the overriding purpose to guarantee to the people of the nation that the personnel system is designed as a high-quality instrument to serve the interests of the state and through it the people.
5. *The law should establish personnel administration as one of the normal executive powers.* Along with the objectives and some of the methods of exercise of that power, it should provide for clear authority vested in a chief executive (the president or prime minister) but with equally clear encouragement to delegate specific responsibilities to department heads and personnel offices. This proposal is based on the notion that good personnel administration depends, in the last analysis, on well-motivated executive leadership, on vigilant citizen interest in supporting that leadership, and on making that leadership feel a sense of responsibility for sound personnel management.
6. *The law should establish a strong single administrator,* reporting to the chief executive, to be in charge of the personnel function, *and a part-*

---

[23] For the principal features of such a law the author drew heavily from his paper "A Career Service Law for Developing Countries," presented at the Inter-American Bar Association Conference in San Jose, Costa Rica, in April 1967.

time board or commission of three to five members to exercise a "watch-dog" role in the development and application of personnel policy. Provision may be made for selection of the personnel administrator on the basis of technical and personal qualifications and of the members of the overseeing body on the basis of previous public service and unimpeachable character and standing. The administrator would initiate policy, make recommendations to the chief executive, take actions delegated to him, and operate the personnel system. The board or commission would insure that personnel policies or actions would not be decided in secret, that there would be a flow of information on the status and problems of personnel administration kept open to the public, to legislators, and to the chief executive—but it would not be empowered to pass on issues before action on policy could take place.

7. *The law should specify the criteria for coverage of the career service.* It might also lay down the general number and type of posts that may be left to political discretion for appointment. One device could be to permit the chief executive to exempt positions from the career system only after soliciting the advice of the personnel board or commission.

8. *The law should include general provisions authorizing:*

—*recruitment based on merit,* without consideration of irrelevant factors, and utilizing techniques of competitive examination to be prescribed by the personnel administrator;

—*classification of positions* into types and levels consistent with the skills and knowledges necessary to perform the work;

—*establishment of pay scales* by the chief executive, upon advice of the personnel board or commission, and within broad fiscal limits set by the legislative body;

—*separation of employees from the service for poor performance or misconduct,* or when there is no longer need for their services due to reduction in workload;

—*paid leave,* including that due to illness and for vacation;

—*life and health insurance* for employees and their families;

—*a retirement plan* to ensure deferred income for employees after some minimum period of service;

—*advancement, transfer, and other movement within the service on the basis of merit and the needs of the service;*

—*an in-service training program* for orientation, skill improvement, and preparation for advancement;

—*a flexible system of performance evaluation and awards;*

—*health and safety care* on the job;

—*establishment of the hours and other conditions of duty.*

9. *The law should place legal restrictions on political party activity of employees only to the extent necessary* to avoid conflicts with the principle of impartiality of the civil servant, thus allowing a reasonable measure

of political freedom. Negative restrictions might be confined to prevention of assessment on employees of party contributions, prohibition of leadership roles by employees in party activities, and limitation of candidature for elective office to situations where the employee can take extended leave of absence for the purpose.

10. *The law should establish clear standards of ethical conduct* for public employees, preventing conflicts of interest, acceptance of gifts or bribes, and unauthorized use of official information for personal gain.
11. *The law should set forth very general provisions for employee grievances and appeals* against management actions.
12. *The law should provide for employee representation and consultation* when changes in personnel policy or benefits are under consideration, with the details of relationships to be established by the personnel administrator.
13. *The law should make ample provision for financial support of personnel operations*, possibly in the form of a minimum percentage of the total payroll, so as to ensure that the objectives are not sabotaged or weakened for want of necessary staff and facilities.

With provisions of the type outlined, a personnel or career service law would obviously leave many policy decisions and all procedural features to the daily administration of the system. The principles, however, would be unmistakable. And the character and aims of the personnel system would be sufficiently explicit that an alert and informed citizenry, operating through its representatives, could insist on faithful execution of the law and high standards of performance under it.

INTERNATIONAL ADMINISTRATION

SCOPE

Although by standards of national civil services, international administrative agencies may seem comparatively small in numbers of personnel employed, they are of importance far out of proportion to their size. In fact, they represent both the most ambitious and the most difficult administrative undertakings of mankind. To appreciate the boundless complexity of their operation, one would have to multiply several times almost every problem encountered in the organization and direction of human affairs on the national level, and then add several others.

Some international agencies, such as the Universal Postal Union (UPU), date back to the nineteenth century, but most of them are the product of the period between the two world wars and, even more so, following World War II. They range in jurisdiction and type from the United Nations itself and its various affiliated specialized agencies, such as the Food and Agriculture Organization (FAO), the World Health Organization (WHO), the International Labor Organization (ILO), the U.N. Educational, Scientific, and

Cultural Organization (UNESCO), the International Civil Aviation Organization (ICAO), the International Telecommunications Union (ITU), and the UPU, to a variety of other entities of great import in the fields of commerce and finance, science, and international law and justice. The International Bank for Reconstruction and Development (World Bank) and the International Monetary Fund (IMF) are major vehicles of economic impact throughout the world as the result of their investments and loans. Still other bodies are engaged in exchange of meteorological and hydrographic information, in atomic energy development, in regulation of weights and measures, in studies of the production and distribution of major commodities, in collaboration among national police, and in arbitration of international disputes. Finally, there are the several regional organizations of vital importance to their respective spheres of the world, such as the Organization of American States (of which the Pan American Union is the central organ), the Organization for African Unity, the North Atlantic Treaty Organization (NATO), the Southeast Asia Treaty Organization (SEATO), and the three European bodies that are directed by a single European Commission: the European Economic Community (EEC, or the Common Market), the European Coal and Steel Community (ECSC), and the European Atomic Energy Community (Euratom).

Including the staffs of some of the subordinate regional bodies, the secretariats of the worldwide organizations number close to fifty thousand persons and are growing as each year goes by.[24] The employees of these secretariats, coming from all member nations which compose the particular organizations, are engaged in staff services to international deliberative bodies like the U.N. Assembly and Security Council and the legislative organs of the specialized agencies; in the regulation of technical operations, such as international air traffic, postal service, and radio and cable communication; in the conduct of research and dissemination of information of worldwide interest; in the investigation of the economic feasibility of loans (such as for the World Bank); in the planning and conduct of international meetings, conferences, and seminars; and, above all, in rendering technical assistance to developing nations along the lines described earlier.

The significance of these international organizations and, as we shall see, many of their perplexing problems derive from their being at one and the same time the creatures of nations and yet above and beyond the interest or power of any one nation. But their very existence represents one of the notable progressive steps in human history. Referring to the United Nations,

[24] The total staff of the U.N. Secretariat and its affiliated specialized agencies exceeds 33,500, over 35 percent of which is in the professional and managerial category (as distinguished from general service and clerical occupations). Over 5,000 of these professionals are engaged in limited-term assignments in developing countries. Including the World Bank and the International Monetary Fund, as well as other nonaffiliated organizations, the total international civil service surpasses the 49,000 mark. The number of U.S. citizens employed in this complex of international agencies is under 6,000. (Data are as of December 31, 1974; supplied by the Office of International Organization Affairs, U.S. Department of State.)

and its predecessor the League of Nations, a great Secretary-General of the United Nations once said:

> one of the essential points on which these experiments in international co-operation represent an advance beyond traditional "conference diplomacy" is the introduction on the international arena of joint permanent organs, employing a neutral civil service, and the use of such organs for executive purposes on behalf of all the members of the organizations.[25]

UNIQUE CONDITIONS OF INTERNATIONAL SERVICE

One might infer from what has already been said that a number of conditions of employment in international secretariats have few or no precedents in national public administration. Several of these warrant mention before we explore specific personnel policies and problems in the international jurisdiction.

LANGUAGE PROBLEMS   The first and most obvious condition that creates both confusion and unusual expense is the necessity for dealing with several languages. Even though the "small-language" countries defer to the more widely used tongues, every international agency, to meet the demands of its member states and to accommodate its multinational staff, adopts at least two or three official languages. This means that every document, every written communication must be translated one or more times. Since there must be someone in each subunit of the organization who can use or translate into one of these official languages, it means that the distribution of staff must always take this factor into account. It means that oral conferences are often impeded by inability of employees to understand each other fully or clearly, or that simultaneous interpretation must be provided. It means, in short, that as many as possible of the staff members must be bilingual or multilingual.[26] Only the fact that English is the most widely known single language among the international set (some would say that it has become the closest thing to an international language) has made day-to-day communication as feasible as it is.

VARIATIONS IN ADMINISTRATIVE TRADITIONS   A second barrier to understanding and teamwork is the wide variation in concepts of organization and

---

[25] Dag Hammarskjold, *The International Civil Servant in Law and in Fact*, A Lecture Delivered to Congregation on May 30, 1961, Oxford, Clarendon Press, 1961, p. 3.

[26] Even more difficult is finding words in another language that connote exactly what a term conveys in the language of the person initiating the statement. One of the classic illustrations of misunderstanding is the case where an inept translator converted the French *Je demande* into "I demand," because of the misleading similarity in the words, when the accurate translation would have been "I request" or "I ask for." The implications of such a slip are obvious. Problems have arisen even among the nationals of English-speaking countries when different connotations are placed on such words as "administrative" and "executive." Americans tend to use the terms almost interchangeably; certainly no lower order of affairs is intended to be conveyed by "executive," as is the case where British traditions prevail.

administration among the various nations. Although, as communication and publication progresses, there is prospect for gradual alleviation of the most striking differences and misunderstandings, reconciliation among these viewpoints is still almost a daily necessity in international agencies. Some of these conceptual differences have already been referred to in the discussion relating to the established national personnel systems and to those in the developing countries; others will be evident from the several personnel issues presented later in this chapter.

WORLDWIDE RECRUITING   The first two difficulties arise from the fact of multinational staff; the third complication is caused by the very need to ensure that this multinational composition be maintained. The international organization must deal with a worldwide recruiting ground. As we shall see later, this creates the problem of equating employment terms and conditions to meet each country's distinctive situation and automatically makes many selection processes inappropriate or impracticable.

INTERNATIONALISM   A fourth problem stems from the international civil servant's relationship to his home country, that is, a question of his loyalties and his capacity for neutrality on political issues. The ideal requires that he place loyalty to his employing agency above loyalty to his own country. He is expected to have a broad international outlook and detach himself from national prejudices and narrow national interests. Most of the time this ideal can be lived up to by abstaining from receiving or acting on instruction from his home government. But sometimes secretariats are required to carry out what at least some states would brand as political duties. The deliberative organs of the United Nations, for example, do on occasion impose on the Secretary-General (and therefore the staff) the necessity for political decision-making, as in the case of peace-keeping activities, which may not be in accord with the views of some member states. Thus, the staff may in some instances be forced to depart from neutrality in the literal sense, but it should still act without taking instruction from any member state. In this role, it is acting as a true international agent, loyal to the higher ideal, as distinguished from an intergovernmental broker.[27] Consequently, the occasions for agonizing ethical evaluation on the part of key staff members are surely more numerous than in public services at the national level.

RELATIONS WITH HOST COUNTRY   A fifth set of issues derives from the peculiar relationship of an international agency, and hence its employees, to the host country in which its headquarters are housed. For one thing, there is the matter of relying on the host government for protection of

[27] To switch the role to an intergovernmental one would run the risk of a "Munich of international cooperation." "To abandon or to compromise with principles on which such cooperation is built may be no less dangerous than to compromise with principles regarding the rights of a nation. In both cases the price to be paid may be peace" (Hammarskjold, *op. cit.*, p. 28).

premises and persons, an awkward situation if there should be a dispute between that government and the international organization. Fortunately, this issue has seldom reached the point of a showdown in any real instance, but the possibility is there. Next is the question of privileges and immunities for staff members, as in the enforcement of certain laws, such as traffic control. Among other considerations, to what extent should employees who happen to be citizens of the host country (who may even have lived in the host city for all or most of their lives) enjoy an exceptional status that none of their fellow citizens may attain? Finally, there is the matter of taxation and pay. Generally, international employees (by agreement among the states or with the host government) are not subject to taxes on their incomes received from the international employer. But such a privilege necessitates adjustments in basic compensation, so as not to bring it completely out of line with pay standards in the local community. The pay scale also requires some degree of rationalization between local prevailing pay and the standards in the several home countries of employees who come from nations outside.

THE INTERNATIONAL CIVIL SERVICE COMMISSION

Following repeated efforts to create an enduring mechanism for common personnel policy among the U.N.-related international organizations, the U.N. General Assembly finally established an International Civil Service Commission (ICSC) in late 1974. Up to that time coordination had to depend more completely on advisory bodies and on independent action by each organization. Instrumental in achieving some common policies in the past on pay, leave, retirement, and other benefits had been the International Civil Service Advisory Board (ICSAB), the Administrative Committee on Coordination (ACC), and the latter's subordinate agent, the Consultative Committee on Administrative Questions (CCAQ).

For the first time, an interorganizational device exists that has some direct policy powers of its own. Most knowledgeable persons close to the international scene had long ago urged stronger central machinery and a firmer foundation for a truly international civil service. Creation of the new ICSC offers greater hope of progress in that direction.

The ICSC is a fifteen-member body (each member is from a different nation) which is enjoined by its enabling statute to carry out understandings reached between the United Nations and the specialized organizations that aim at "the development of a single unified international civil service through the application of common personnel standards, methods and arrangements."[28] Although some of the Commission's functions are still advisory, it has authority to act directly in establishing: (1) job-classification standards for all staff categories in fields common to several of the international organi-

---

[28] *Statute of the International Civil Service Commission*, Article 9; U.N. General Assembly, Twenty-ninth Session, Agenda item 82, January 17, 1975. Only two of the Commission members serve full-time, and meetings of the full body are required at least once a year. A moderate-sized staff is provided.

zations; (2) the classification of duty stations for the purpose of applying pay adjustments to different posts; (3) rates of allowances and benefits, other than pensions and certain special allowances for professional staff on which General Assembly action is required; and (4) the methods by which conditions of service are determined in accordance with Assembly-set principles. The Commission's recommendatory powers embrace the following subjects on which it makes proposals to the General Assembly: (1) scales of salaries and post adjustments for professional and higher staff and for locally recruited service staff; (2) allowances and benefits reserved for General Assembly action; (3) broad principles for determining conditions of service; and (4) staff assessment. The Commission must further recommend action to the specialized organizations on: (1) development of common staff regulations; (2) development of consistent job-classification plans; (3) standards of recruitment; (4) development of recruitment sources; (5) setting up competitive examinations or other selection processes; and (6) evaluation, training, and career development.[29]

That the effectiveness of international organizations depends in no small measure on the quality of their career staffs is a truism that hardly needs elaboration. Making the situation all the more compelling are the special handicaps under which such agencies must recruit, reward, and motivate their staffs. Predicting the continuing expansion of international bodies and calling for a "more fully developed international civil service," a prominent individual who had held high posts in the U.S. government and in the United Nations observed:

> the rapidly growing family of member states must be persuaded that their own collective self-interest lies in supporting the development of a high-quality international civil service as a flexible and creative force that will apply ever higher levels of skill to the resolution of problems among nations in the crowded and shrinking neighborhood of mankind.[30]

Establishment of the ICSC is at least a first step in achieving these lofty goals.

PROGRESS IN SPECIFIC POLICY AREAS

A more detailed examination of several of the major aspects of personnel administration in the international arena is now in order.

STAFFING   Aside from clerical and custodial employees, who are usually recruited primarily from local residents at whatever site the agency (headquarters or branch) is located, almost all international organizations are

---

[29] *Ibid.*, Articles 10–15.

[30] John W. Macy, Jr., *op. cit.*, p. 283. Also, see the discussion of the factors and problems involved in international administration in the last chapter of Felix A. Nigro and Lloyd G. Nigro, *Modern Public Administration*, 3rd ed., New York, Harper & Row, 1973.

expected to maintain some reasonable balance of representation from the various states that compose their memberships. As a result, the common practice is to establish some kind of quota for staff from each member nation. In the U.N. Secretariat and the U.N.-affiliated agencies the quota is based on the proportionate amount contributed by the member to the budget of the organization. The compulsion for equitable geographic distribution of staff is not applied, however, to project personnel when the work is being financed out of voluntary contributions instead of the regular budget.

The range of logistical problems posed for a worldwide recruitment system is staggering, even apart from the matter of geographical balance. For example, common standards of education among different countries, to permit fair comparison between candidates, do not exist; the contact points through which candidates may be sought in each country are many and varied; arriving at a standard method for recording educational and experience backgrounds on application blanks is complicated by the great variety of circumstances to be allowed for; the use of written tests is impracticable (except for clerical jobs, in the language of the host country); interviews or other face-to-face contacts are rare; most of the recruitment must be concentrated at intermediate and senior levels, especially for the personnel needed in technical assistance; many professions or other occupations being recruited for do not exist in the less-developed nations; and the negotiations with prospective appointees drag out over extensive periods of time because of lack of familiarity of many candidates with the terms of employment and the living conditions in the expected location, because of the need to check references at long distance, and, of course, because of reliance on postal service that may require a several-week interval between each round of correspondence.

Most of the major nations have set up central coordinating committees to receive requests for personnel from the U.N. Secretariat and the specialized agencies and to act as recruiting agents for them in generating candidacies within their boundaries. Unfortunately, the United States (the chief supporter of the United Nations financially) has never gotten around to establishing such a body, although a very modest effort in this direction is carried on within the State Department. The result is that the United States is consistently under its quota for technical staff. However, a law passed in 1958 and liberalized in 1969 does facilitate both loans and transfers of U.S. federal government personnel to international organizations for up to five years, without loss of status as to retirement or other benefit eligibility, and permits salary augmentation to equalize pay levels.[31] The President in 1964 and again in 1970 did ask all federal departments to encourage and assist

[31] The Federal Employees International Organization Service Act, 5 *U.S. Code* 3343, 3581–3584. Extensions up to three years beyond the five may be made in certain loans or transfers. The purpose of salary equalization is to avoid the disincentive of an international salary that is lower than the one being received by the federal employee involved.

able employees from their ranks to accept assignments with international agencies.[32]

It is evident that there are limits to the application of merit principles in international secretariats. In addition to all the factors cited, the most powerful member nations demand and normally obtain the more important posts. Hence, an international civil servant making a career of the work can seldom expect to attain a position of the highest responsibility because of the overriding necessity for political representation on the organization's staff and "because of the national identity which for personal stability he usually feels he must preserve but which at the same time for professional reasons he must minimize or ignore."[33]

Whether international organizations can maintain an objective international civil service, in the face of pressures for national patronage, is from time to time brought into question. In addition to the longstanding tactic of member nations' seeking national "representation" in *key* posts, it has been alleged that in recent years the pressure to appoint specific persons to represent their native lands has extended to the middle and lower levels of the international bureaucracy. A report made by a respected research institute in 1975 was especially critical of practice in the U.N. Secretariat in this regard.[34] To whatever extent such charges are true the international civil service falls short of our highest hopes. Certainly, if any criterion other than personal merit and *supra*national loyalty is followed, we cannot expect that some of these organizations can be entrusted with technical and administrative responsibility for international action in areas such as food supply, population planning, environmental control, global economics, and exploitation of ocean resources. Fortunately, some U.N. divisions and some of the specialized organizations have reputations for resisting the planting of "deadwood" and "political watchdogs" in their offices, but others seem to be viewed as "dumping grounds" for just such cast-offs from member nations.

In spite of all these obstacles and complications, the caliber of personnel assembled by the United Nations and other organizations has been better than commonly supposed. Particularly in technical assistance, the United Nations has been able for the most part to provide competent experts who were well suited to their assignments.[35] Furthermore, there appears to be

[32] Memorandum to the Heads of Executive Departments and Agencies, August 17, 1964; and Executive Order 11552, August 24, 1970.

[33] Robert S. Jordan, "International Civil Servants," *The George Washington University Magazine*, Spring 1965, pp. 14–15.

[34] Report by the Ralph Bunche Institute on the United Nations, cited in *The Washington Post*, January 11, 1975.

[35] After an exhaustive study, one scholar concluded that "the vast majority of U.N. technical assistance experts have satisfactorily performed their assignments" and that "although technical assistance missions have had a share of failure, most of the setbacks resulted neither from technical incompetence nor from improper personality of experts, but rather from the combinations of forces and factors over which experts were powerless to act" (Yonah Alexander, *International Technical Assistance Experts; A Case Study of the U.N. Experience*, New York, Praeger, 1966, p. 174).

no evidence that the proportion of a nation's representation in any international secretariat has affected the impact of that nation on the organization's policy. Contrary to allegations by some partisans, the United Nations and other secretariats are largely involved in nonpolitical work. Also, it should be noted that for some years the United Nations has sponsored the imaginative plan of providing to developing countries that ask for the arrangement, transnational experts who work, not as advisers, but as integral members of the key staff of the host government. These have been designated as "Operational, Executive and Administrative Personnel" (OPEX).

By and large, international organizations have not done badly, considering all that they have been up against. However, the U.N. Secretariat and its related agencies have some distance to go to live up to the injunction of the well-known section 3 of Article 101 of the U.N. Charter:

> The paramount consideration in the employment of the staff and in the determination of the conditions of service shall be the necessity of securing the highest standards of efficienty, competence, and integrity. Due regard shall be paid to the importance of recruiting the staff on as wide a geographical basis as possible.

CLASSIFICATION AND PAY   The international agencies have vacillated between systems of rank-in-corps and rank-in-job in their basic position and salary structures.[36] In its initial years the U.N. Secretariat tried the American position-classification plan but, because of lack of familiarity with it and inadequate means to administer it, later shifted to the corps scheme. More recently, the United Nations appears to be reintroducing the ideas of job evaluation and classification. At the very minimum this may be inferred from the functions assigned to the ICSC, with its several references to common job-classification plans and standards. It is also noteworthy that the U.N. handbook, designed as doctrine for the national civil services of developing countries, certainly gives the edge of support to the idea of duties classification, even though the advantages of both job-oriented and rank-oriented systems are enunciated.[37]

With a background of earlier recommendations for common professional job and recruitment standards made by the previous ICSAB, the new ICSC is clearly enjoined to promote more effective administration of the basic job-oriented system. Leaders among the agencies in the job-classification approach

---

[36] It may be helpful to review the meaning of these terms by referring to the discussion in Chapter 4, "Career Systems."

[37] United Nations, *A Handbook of Public Administration*, Department of Economic and Social Affairs, New York, 1961. It concludes that posts of similar duties and responsibilities should have a similar grade or rank; that the grade should attach to the post, and not to the individual; that each post should be analyzed for proper allocation; that the qualifications needed for each class and grade should be determined; that the number of grades or ranks should be "reasonably few"; that the salary plan should be based on classes of positions and grades; and that promotion should be only on demonstrated capacity to assume higher duties and responsibilities (pp. 39–40). Not much room for rank-in-corps features is left in such a prescription.

have been the World Health Organization and the International Civil Aviation Organization.

As for salary plans and schedules, even before establishment of the ICSC a common general system applied to all the U.N.-affiliated agencies. Still other organizations, such as the World Bank and the International Monetary Fund (IMF), have cooperated in some measure with these guidelines. Prior to the 1960s pay practices among the international entities were about as varied as their functions. At least the base salary scales and pattern of allowances for the professional categories are now the same or comparable among all the agencies, although the World Bank and the IMF have the highest rates. General service employees (clerical, custodial, etc.) are usually paid in local currency in accordance with the best prevailing conditions in the locality.

Special allowances include an adjustment differential for each post to equalize the purchasing power of salaries, with those in Geneva serving as a base. In addition, there are allowances for dependency, for installation, for language proficiency, and for the education of children. Even though the system would appear to be quite generous, there has been difficulty in keeping base salaries abreast with the almost universal inflationary pressures around the world. Several major adjustments have been made from to time, and more are undoubtedly due to come.[38]

We have already alluded to the matter of income tax liability of international employees. As a general rule, they are exempt from national income taxes. Instead, the group of agencies which follow the common salary system operates a staff assessment plan, which in effect is a levy in lieu of taxes. Where the host country levies an income tax on the employee, the agency reimburses him for the amount paid. Gross salaries, including the amount assessed, can therefore be used for salary comparison purposes without the tax exemption feature distorting the relationship.

Both leave and retirement provisions under the common system have reached a point of reasonable liberality. Leave amounts to six weeks a year, plus home leave every two years for those working away from their native country. The U.N. Joint Staff Pensions Fund is based on contributions by employees of 7 percent of salary and 14 percent by the employer. Contributory life and health insurance and generous sick leave round out the system.

LOYALTY Of a more intangible nature, but nonetheless complex and confounding, is the issue of the international civil servant's loyalties. On this subject, the celebrated Article 100 of the U.N. Charter has this to say:

1. In the performance of their duties the Secretary-General and the staff shall not seek or receive instructions from any government or from any other authority external to the Organization. They shall refrain from any action

---

[38] In setting up the ICSC the General Assembly asked the new body to review "as a matter of priority" the entire U.N. salary system and to report to the thirtieth session of the Assembly in 1976.

which might reflect on their position as international officials responsible only to the Organization.

2. Each member of the United Nations undertakes to respect the exclusively international character of the responsibilities of the Secretary-General and the staff and not to seek to influence them in the discharge of their responsibilities.

The ideal could not have been stated more directly and eloquently.

In line with this policy, permanent staff members are prohibited from holding any other employment, public or private, from receiving any honors, favors, or gifts, and from running for political office. By now the tradition has been well established that the international public servant's loyalty must transcend mere faithfulness to his own country. Some may contend that this asks a citizen to render primary fealty to a jurisdiction other than his native land. The more sensible view is that international loyalty is not a negation of national loyalty but an extension of it to a higher plane. The international employee is serving the highest interest of his own country by serving the international organization.

A special problem was created when, at the height of the hysteria over disloyalty and subversion in the early 1950s, the United States ordered a loyalty check on all Americans who were employed by or under consideration for appointment to the U.N. Secretariat or other international agencies.[39] These bodies, after some initial hesitation, accepted an arrangement whereby they would receive the security reports on all U.S. citizens but without any commitment that the information would affect the organization's action as to employment. Decisions on retention or employment of persons challenged by the United States are made by the head of the international organization, with ultimate appeal allowed to the international appellate body, the Administrative Tribunal. Since the U.S. investigative reports contain information as to an individual's character and related aspects of his background, the international agency oftentimes finds the inquiry useful in appraising whether it wishes to hire the person. Only a handful of instances were ever uncovered, however, in which the U.S. Government suspected individuals of being linked with efforts actually to sabotage American interests.[40]

The action of the United States raised some very difficult questions. At first, there was the mere problem of delays in completing investigations and transmitting clearances to the international organizations, all of which only served to inhibit the employment of Americans on their staffs—a condition hardly in the interest of U.S. policy. Eventually, however, this problem was

---

[39] Following Senate hearings and a federal grand jury inquiry, the President ordered the checks and clearances in Executive Orders 10422 and 10459 (1953).

[40] The International Organizations Employees Loyalty Board, the instrument in the U.S. government for handling these cases, determines whether the employee or candidate is "cleared." Even if there is no loyalty question, the board may summarize character information for such disposition as the international employer wishes to make of it.

largely surmounted. Nevertheless, other awkward questions still have to be faced: Does the U.S. action violate the independence of the international body? Is it unconscionable influence by a member state? Is it evidence that an international civil servant, if suspect in his own country, is taking instruction from another? How far must the concerns of the host nation be honored? Conversely, can an international agency successfully be composed of men who have disowned or been disclaimed by their own governments? On the other hand, does not the U.S. practice add fuel to the tendency of other countries to expect their nationals in the international secretariats to "represent" their homelands? Final answers have not been arrived at, but keeping such questions alive should help keep the general issue in perspective and avoid excesses in one direction or another.[41]

TRAINING   Probably the most deficient area of international personnel administration is that of training. Various groups, both multinational and American, have from time to time issued reports on the subject and generally have urged more attention to the need for staff preparation and development, but performance has not measured up to conceptualization.

Several major universities in the United States have sponsored substantial programs in the preentry area for international administration. A few such ventures also exist in western Europe. But little of this effort has been stimulated or coordinated by the international agencies themselves.

As for in-service training, the most highly developed programs are operated in such specialized agencies as the World Bank, WHO, and the Pan American Union. The U.N. Secretariat has long carried on training for its staff in languages and, to some extent, in clerical procedures, but it has not ventured far into the fields of professional or administrative training. Some use of regular educational institutions in the United States and elsewhere has been made to supplement knowledge and skills of certain staff members, but the volume of such activity is still low in proportion to the productive possibilities that could be utilized. Undoubtedly, as the international organizations mature, we shall see more emphasis on this all-important aspect of the management of human resources.

EMPLOYEE REPRESENTATION AND GRIEVANCES   For the U.N. group of agencies there is an established procedure for consultation with representatives of the staff on personnel rules and regulations. Although not approaching the stage of bargaining, a Joint Advisory Committee, composed of both management and staff representatives, carries on a dialogue relating to staff

---

[41] Some of this analysis of the issues was developed in Alagappa Alagappan, *Personnel Administration in the United Nations: Some Aspects of Article 101 of the Charter,* Doctoral Dissertation, New York University, 1967, p. 196.

A viewpoint that rejects the U.S. procedure as serving no good purpose and as infringing on the independent operation of the international civil service is expressed in Edwin H. Fedder, "United States Loyalty Procedures and the Recruitment of International Personnel," *The Western Political Quarterly,* December 1962, pp. 705–712.

conditions and is expressly called upon to consider personnel policy changes. The pattern seems somewhat like the Whitley Council device in the United Kingdom, but without the element of compulsion to arrive at agreement. In this connection, it is interesting that the ICSAB once recommended that, for resolving disputes in this area of staff relations, recourse to "outside parties" should be avoided.[42] This position is, no doubt, dictated by a desire to prevent the development of any institution outside the established international framework that might jeopardize the independence of the regular international agencies.

Individual employee grievances or appeals among the U.N. agencies are processed first through a Joint Appeals Board of the United Nations, following which a further appeal my be taken to the Administrative Tribunal which was established by the U.N. General Assembly in 1949. This is, in effect, a kind of employee court of last resort. It is composed of seven members, each of a different nationality, any three of who may sit on a case. Its jurisdiction is limited to issues arising out of application of personnel regulations and to instances of alleged nonobservance of contracts with staff members. It is not empowered to redress injustices fully, but it can award monetary compensation for damages. The need for such a tribunal is evident from the fact that, while wide discretionary power must be vested in the leadership of an international agency, there must be some avenue to assure that the interests of the rank-and-file are not unjustly encroached upon.[43]

GENERAL STATUS OF INTERNATIONAL PERSONNEL MANAGEMENT Much remains to be done before the many perplexities facing international organizations can be reduced to the level of normal administrative problems. More work on common standards is essential, more planning and systemizing of the recruitment effort is called for, and, above all, there is need for a much more intensive investment in in-service training of all types.

A fair appraisal would suggest, however, that international personnel administration has come a long way—especially considering the barriers to effectiveness that it continually faces. At the price of mutual concessions among nations and the international secretariats and of some difficult adjustments, the international civil service, as one authority puts it, "has taken firm root in the international soil." No more fitting capstone can be found than the observation of this distinguished French scholar:

> Experience has abundantly shown that the international civil service is a unique instrument for ensuring the continuous and effective cooperation between modern States in every sphere, whether they have common or divergent interests. There can be no doubt that mankind would be threatened with chaos

---

[42] *Report of the Seventeenth Session of the Board*, United Nations, 1969, p. 15.
[43] Byung Chul Koh, *The United Nations Administrative Tribunal: Legal Guardian of the International Civil Servant*, Doctoral Dissertation, Cornell University, 1963, *passim.*

if it ceased to exist. Its economic, social and cultural achievements have been striking. . . .

The fact that the administration is effectively international—and not only intergovernmental or multinational—is part of the historic process of the drawing together of mankind. . . . It is impossible to imagine the world of the future without such a factor; necessary in the past, it will be doubly so in the future.[44]

*   *   *

THE DIFFICULTIES AND challenges of public personnel administration in the industrialized world are perplexing enough. Those in developing societies and international organizations are doubly so. Individually and collectively, all nations will have to invest their unstinting resources and the best of their brainpower to develop the personnel function to the point where it fully meets the needs of public services everywhere.

[44] Georges Langrod, *The International Civil Service; Its Origins, Its Nature, Its Evolution*, Dobbs Ferry, N.Y., Oceana, 1963, p. 324.

CHAPTER 28

Prospects

THE FOREMOST TASK of administration is the management of staff, for high-caliber and strongly motivated personnel constitute the most valuable asset of any large-scale organization. The enthusiasm, good will, and cooperativeness bred by sound conceptions about and direction of this vital resource are the bases for human satisfactions, for the constant improvement of operations, and for long-range effectiveness. With payrolls comprising the largest single item in the operating budgets of most public jurisdictions, personnel administration should be in the forefront of public policy. As public administration continues to become larger and more complex, the policies and relationships that make up the personnel function will surely command more and more of the attention of top executives of all governments.

It is not the purpose of this chapter to recount all the achievements, the needs, the shortcomings, the challenges, and the forecasts that have been enumerated throughout this book. Rather, the intention is to single out a few ideas that represent a synthesis of more specific ones cited earlier and to add some that did not fit neatly into the exposition of material as presented. If repetition of some points appears, it is because of their critical importance and the fact that they are of an order that does not permit exclusion.

The chapter is written in the belief that public personnel administration is in less need of improved technology than it is of a broader philosophy. Accordingly, it needs more philosophers in proportion to technologists. And it needs more searching inquiries in the realm of ideas and less concentration on methods.

THE MILIEU

We explored at some length in Chapter 2 the normal and continuing environmental influences on the public personnel function. Now we should take note of some of the unusual, and to some degree the unique, characteristics of our times that have implications for the management of people.

Not all we see is consistent. There appears to be a renewed regard for human rights and individuality, but the population explosion makes it all the more difficult to bring them to reality. Youth is ostensibly looking for ways to serve higher causes, but portions of their vintage alienate support for such objectives. There is an exciting new awareness of the importance of our natural environment, but callous disregard of personal responsibility by individual and corporation alike continues unabated. There are signs that the American public is maturing in its recognition of the role of government in modern society, but resistance to necessary taxation is as strong as ever. Peace and disarmament have won new adherents, but crime, dope addiction, and violence are at an all-time high. The hysteria over loyalty to the state has died down, but few advocate a brand of internationalism that would modify national sovereignty. There is much talk about the general welfare, but the special interest groups are still the most powerful ones in our society. Employees are in need of collective representation, but the traditional unions have become about the most conservative and change-resistant forces in the nation. Our national legislature, the Congress, has generated great quantities of laws on a bewildering array of subjects, but it is severely hobbled by a committee and seniority system that is utterly unsuited to the demands of the age. Public administrators and professional individuals are for the most part serving the public interest valiantly, but some among them show even greater zeal for improvement of their own lot. Meanwhile, somehow the governing of mankind goes on.

If there could be a harnessing of all the good and altruistic motivation that seems to be evidenced in this milieu, if our institutions—educational, economic, governmental—could be designed to capitalize on the good in people, if there could be some genuine implementation of that glorious gauntlet thrown down by President Kennedy: "Ask what you can do for your country," perhaps the contrasts and offsetting influences to the hopeful trends in modern life would be less potent.

THE PLACE OF THE PERSONNEL FUNCTION

In this kind of context, it is rather difficult to get excited over methods of examination and devices for performance evaluation, over pay scales and retirement systems, over collective negotiations and agreements. This is why the personnel function should be much more than a collection of data and doctrine on such subjects. This is why we must have a philosophy of personnel administration, and why this must be a philosophy not just of so-called specialists in that field but of every manager and worker, every professional person and craftsman, in public enterprise. It bears repeating once more: personnel administration, especially in the public service, is not so much a collection of techniques as it is a way of life. It is, above all else, an understanding of, a willingness to spend time at, and an investment of meticulous care in the marshaling and husbanding of the human resources of productive organization.

With the challenges of our day in mind and with this conception of the personnel task, what are the truly outstanding needs and the most significant developments that should be fostered in public personnel administration? Without demeaning in the slightest the many other enthusiastic recommendations made in this book and elsewhere, what is the minimum agenda for the personnel goals and policies of tomorrow? The answers ventured here are organized under nine rubrics.

AN AGENDA FOR PERSONNEL ADMINISTRATION

1. PUTTING MEANING IN MERIT

The continuing growth and strengthening of the merit idea in public employment seems for the most part to be assured. The real issue is what constitutes merit.

What needs to be underscored, among other considerations, is the intangible but nonetheless important factor of interest in and zeal for the public program to which a public servant is assigned. Without minimizing the vital necessity of technical preparation and knowledge and the ample methods for ascertaining their presence among candidates (both within and outside the service), the element that has been too little stressed, sometimes almost ignored, is the degree to which an individual is genuinely concerned about the field of work for which he is ostensibly prepared, the degree to which he is "committed." We must find the ways to assemble the facts and to permit the judgments that will assure that, for those positions or careers in which it counts, adequate weight is given to this factor. In the public service, one person with enthusiasm is worth ten who look upon their jobs merely as a source of income.

At the same time, merit must encompass more opportunities for women, older persons, and youth by use of part-time and more flexible working schedules and by more imaginative organization of tasks. Likewise, through improved education, more comprehensive in-service training, and better selection methods, the merit ideal must demonstrate that it can embrace greater employment and advancement opportunities for qualified minority members while still maintaining a quality work force. The purpose must be to eliminate non-work-related barriers, not to create non-work-related preference. In the long run, only the highest standards of competence and productivity on the part of public workers will guarantee to all elements in society the caliber of public administration that a high-level civilization requires.

2. MAKING THE MOST OF TALENT

The two conditions that contribute most surely to the best utilization of talent are the openness of the service and its facilitation of mobility. A static service is a stagnant service. Nothing more energizing has been found than the occasional infusion of new blood in an organization and the stimulation of a new assignment for an employee.

As the cruder evils of a blighted personnel management have been vanquished in most places, more attention must now be given to a greater linking of public services at all levels of government. Monolithic careers in a single jurisdiction or in a single field are giving way to interchange and movement. Indeed, this mobility is extending to industry, to education, and to the international scene. Where selection processes, retirement systems, or other elements of personnel policy inhibit such movement, modifications should be made to encourage it.

Obviously, for mobility to mean anything, the concept of "closed" careers and cadres must go by the board. The essential characteristics of such personnel systems are nonadaptive and simply do not square with the dynamic, ever-changing imperatives of modern government.

3. MAKING EDUCATION CONTINUOUS

Training while in the service is the one enlightened policy that has won the most acceptance and implementation in the personnel area. But it is still viewed, in somewhat disconnected fashion, as a series of opportunistic "courses" for workers rather than a way of work. The wave of the future is that in-service training and supplementary education will be a planned and regular part of the work career. It must be so, if public administration is to keep abreast of the inexorable fact of change. Just as is already the case in the military services and among certain scientific pursuits, we must prepare ourselves to recognize that the average professional and managerial employee of the future will spend a major share of his career, perhaps as much as a quarter or more of his occupied time, in formal training. The day of looking upon this as an absence from or an exception to the normal work situation is past. In today's environment, training is one of the natural and inevitable phases of work itself. Administrators, legislators, and citizens must accept it as such in a modern public service.

4. KEEPING THE ENVIRONMENT ETHICAL

The ethical behavior of public servants is higher than that in most sectors of the American society, but it can never rise much above the standards of its environment. Many things can be done in government departments to ensure high motives, unflinching integrity, and uncompromising serving of the public interest as against private interests. But the surest device, if we can imagine the millennium in this respect, would be for the general public and specific publics to refrain from seeking aggrandizement of their own welfare at the expense of others. The bulk of disservice to the broad public interest comes from the undue pressures and resulting influence of self-seeking citizens and organizations brought to bear on public legislators and administrators. If this tendency in a democracy could in some way be reduced, the rest of the ethical problem in government would be easy.

5. BASING MANAGEMENT ON CONFIDENCE

The role of everyday management in personnel affairs is not so much in the across-the-board policy areas of personnel systems, pay and benefits, and employee consultation but in the manner of organization of work and in the assignment and utilization of people. It is here that the wellsprings of motivation and drive can be most fully tapped. It is here that we can recognize and build on human differences and capitalize on human individuality. It is here that managers can challenge and give vent to man's desire to achieve and to create.

These principles suggest a style of administration that extends responsibility as far as the law allows, that dares to give subordinates authority—yes, even give them the opportunity to make mistakes! It means delegation based on faith and confidence in the natural motivation of workers to do their best.

As responsibility is shared down the line, so must many personnel decisions (as well as others) be shared laterally. The inhibitions of vertical authority—too much holding of authority at the top—must be reduced to the minimum necessary to satisfy the law and public demand. This does not mean that the substitute is a martinet somewhere down the line. When it comes to such matters as selection for promotion, providing opportunities for training, predictions of potential performance, and other personnel decisions of some moment, single supervisors should not be in the position of "playing God," of affecting the lives and fortunes of others on the basis of their own limited perspectives. To avoid the even worse alternative of reliance on automatic systems, such as seniority, the major personnel decisions should be shared decisions. That is, there should be participation of several responsible persons in their making. The classical judgment of the supervisor should, wherever practicable, become one of a committee or panel of persons who in some degree are familiar with the situation and with the personalities involved in the decision.

The concept of shared decision-making may well apply to other facets of the managerial process, as well as to personnel decisions. In effect, we are saying that the management of tomorrow, while shaking off unreasonable restraints and inhibitions of "vertical" direction, should be prepared to share its most critical judgments in a "horizontal" fashion.

6. EARNING THE CONFIDENCE

The relationships between management and the worker are a two-way street. Employees should earn the faith in them that management should start with. Both in their individual capacity and collectively employees have obligations, as well as rights. So much emphasis has been placed on the latter that some people enter a work situation with a chip on their shoulders, having had their concerns directed more to themselves than to the mission to be accomplished.

It is every public employee's obligation, first of all, to fulfill the requirements of his job. It was not created to provide him an income (at least, we must presume this to be the case!); it was designed to render a service to the public. It is the obligation of the employee who accepts the conditions of employment in the job to give it the full measure of his capacity and, if necessary, to move with the job. One of the most trying circumstances faced by a harassed administrator is that of an employee who considers it an imposition to be assigned to another location when the needs of the service and his own career development clearly call for such a transfer (and when, more often than not, the possibility of such moves was part of the understanding in his initial employment).

Likewise, employee organizations have some obligations, not merely privileges. Granted that advances in personnel policy and practice have not diminished the feeling of need for employee unionization, granted that the representational function of unions is useful to a farsighted management as well as to employees, there is much room for reform on the union side before management-employee relations in the collective sense can achieve all that is hoped for. The tendency of unions to resist recognition of human differences, to fight efforts to discipline poor workers, to display little regard for quality performance, to press for seniority as the main criterion for advancement and retention—does nothing to facilitate their wholehearted acceptance as partners in setting the tone of public enterprise. Also, until there is greater unification or coordination among unions and until there is a more progressive and responsible brand of leadership in many of them, the full possibilities of constructive consultation and negotiation will not be realized.

Militancy, work stoppages, defense of mediocre workers, and appeal only to the most selfish interests of their members does not build the kind of trust that is needed to develop a participative relationship with management in determining the terms of employment. The voice of employees is one that must be heard; its clarity and effectiveness must not be compromised by transmission through leadership that is still living in the days of the industrial revolution and that sees all management as some kind of cross between Scrooge and Simon Legree. Insistence on outmoded work methods and work relationships (such as the union shop or agency shop), a holding to traditional arrangements that are particularly characteristic of unions of the craft variety, will only serve to weaken ultimate union influence. The innate conservatism of the American union and its resistance to technological, social, and organizational change is the most serious deterrent to worthwhile union-management relations in the public service.

7. MEETING THE WORLDWIDE CHALLENGE

Organization for public services everywhere has become so big and so essential, and yet so difficult to fathom and to control, that governments of all degrees of development and sophistication are crying out for answers to the perplexing questions of public management. Studies and recommendations for administrative reform are the order of the day in all but the most complacent of societies. Transmitting ideas and methodology from culture to culture has been a trying but necessary experience. If we consider the obstacles, remarkable progress has been made in improvement of personnel administration in the industrialized nations, in organizing for and initiating modern practices in developing countries, and in reconciling varying philosophies to operate an international civil service.

There is bound to be more, not less, of this concern and this activity. It behooves the thoughtful leaders in the public personnel field around the world to continue to seek out and articulate the principles and methods of potential universal application and to persist with equal vigor to develop the adaptations and modifications of ideal or tested methods to meet the needs of particular jurisdictions in as full measure as possible.

8. TAKING THE SCIENTIFIC APPROACH

The term *scientific* is used here to connote the research method, not the prescription of some single "right answer" to managerial problems. If public personnel administration is to continue to progress, it must be based more completely on objective research than it has been in the past. Too much policy is still determined by trial and error, by intuition, and by the compulsion to weather a crisis.

General issues on attitudes toward public employment, on personnel organization, on political privileges of civil servants, on ethical standards, on collective negotiation procedures, or other such basic subjects can best be studied by professional scholars outside the service and in private or public agencies of national scope. But each governmental jurisdiction, to provide a foundation for its own policies suitable to its own needs, has many issues that are researchable only within its own premises. Local matters of leadership, motivation, pay, evaluation, incentives, training, employee complaints, and many others can be dealt with intelligently only when there are regular and systematic procedures for research as the standard basis for considering them. The accumulation of local and comparative information on any issue is essential to rational decision. Changes in policy are still undertaken without precise knowledge of the effects of the previous policy or the experience that others have had with the new one.

Hence, every jurisdiction of reasonable size should have a research unit and staff, and should be prepared to augment it from time to time as occasions require. Such a staff is certainly at least as necessary in administration of personnel affairs as it is in the engineering aspects of the average manufacturing concern, where it is taken for granted. Trial and error, informed guessing, and exchange of professional opinion, while useful at times, are not reliable or complete enough to serve as a continuing basis for the solid progress in personnel administration that every public service must seek if it is to be responsive to the unrelenting demands that are being made upon it.

9. SELLING THE PUBLIC SERVICE

Deserving and developing public respect for government service is all the more insistent now that most people have come to recognize that big government is here to stay. Public management in general and public personnel operations in particular can never rise much above what the public expects of them. When they are viewed contemptuously, it makes all the more difficult the attraction of high-caliber persons to the public service. Prestige is both an effect and a cause of performance.

Gradually, we have moved away from the more extreme invectives and diatribes that it was once fashionable to hurl at public agencies and public employees. In the face of the senseless disparagement by ignorant and sometimes malicious people that has taken place at various episodes in our history, it has been little short of a miracle that our public jurisdictions have been able over the years to attract and to hold such a large share of able, devoted civil servants.

Formerly, the source of the problem was in considerable measure the businessman's exaltation of money-making and the tendency of the more thoughtless among them, by way of self-justification, to strike out at alternative modes of making a living, such as those of college professors and bureaucrats. Now the tables are turned. The stock market, manufacturing, and commercial selling are not the attraction to young people that they once were. There is a yearning for reformation, an impatience with injustice, poverty, war, and ecological mass suicide. There is a desire to identify with aims and causes beyond self-interest.

It is not clear how genuine these notions are on the part of all who voice them. Nor has the role of government in this renaissance of humanistic protestations been well articulated. Some who profess their interest in correcting society's wrongs seem anarchistic in their attitudes, rejecting governmental institutions along with the rest of what is contemptuously called the "establishment."

Aside from the extremists of both left and right, there are those of the great majority of the younger generation who seem to have a healthy respect for man's progress to date but who are unhesitatingly opposed to the self-serving institutions in this country and elsewhere that inhibit more than they serve human welfare. The idealism, innovativeness, and enthusiasm of this great mass of the more youthful sector of our population would seem to be wholly reconcilable with the kinds of activities that are, for the most part, carried on in government. Indeed, the striking improvement in recent years in the ability of government at all levels to attract able people in the younger age group would suggest that its missions (with the probable exception of waging war!) form the touchstone of attraction to those who want to see something done about the world's problems.

Where mankind is facing up to its needs, there you find government. It is in the nature of things in this highly interdependent world that every human issue of any consequence must be dealt with collectively, and therefore at some point by government. The challenge to enhancing and maintaining the prestige of government in the future is to harness in its behalf the public surges of altruism and motivation for service. The challenge to youth and to all others seeking ways to better the lot of mankind is to recognize that government is a going concern already engaged in just such human endeavors.

Whether it is international service, construction of great public works, or alleviating poverty, or whether it is simply engaging in ways and means to make the economic or social system, or the government itself, to work better, public employment offers an opportunity to work at causes with which high-minded people can proudly associate. The interest of so many in today's generation is not unlike the enthusiasm of those in the 1930s who became part of the great initial expansion of government to serve the needs of the age.

Satisfaction and fascination, if they do not derive from the objectives of a public program, may come from the excitement of sheer magnitude or complexity. Many another generation whose members sought outlets for a service motive experienced that satisfaction and fascination. Certainly the probabilities of government's serving noble causes well are greater when it is bolstered with talent and dedication from within than when it is sniped at from without. Thus, the need to maintain the prestige of the public service is as great as it ever was.

*   *   *

ONE OF THE activities that gives promise of keeping government an effective as well as a potent force in modern society is administration of public personnel policy in a manner that will maintain and improve the quality and motivation of all civil servants. The personnel function itself calls continually for new talent and fresh approaches. The public business is the foremost enterprise of the nation. No more fruitful or inspiring cause can be generated than that of developing the policies and conditions to enlist in the public service the enthusiastic participation of men and women with capacities and concerns commensurate with its vast responsibilities.

Bibliography

I. BIBLIOGRAPHICAL SOURCES

Various single-volume bibliographies on public administration or related subjects have been issued from time to time, but all of these are now too old or too limited to be of much value.

A. U.S. Civil Service Commission Library

The only continuous bibliographical service on public personnel administration is that provided by the U.S. Civil Service Commission Library. Beginning with *A Bibliography of Public Personnel Administration Literature,* published in Washington, D.C., in 1956, and followed by a series of supplements extending to 1958, it is now maintained by periodic issuances of special bibliographies on specific aspects of personnel administration, covering almost every subfield, such as employment, labor relations, training, personnel organization, and so on. Each of these is identified in the "Personnel Bibliography Series" and by a series number, and all current ones are dated since 1960. In 1963 (Series Number 9) there was a *Bibliography of Bibliographies in Personnel Administration.* Any scholar attempting to make a thorough study of an issue in or phase of the personnel function would find the Personnel Bibliography Series invaluable.

B. Basis for this Selective Bibliography

The literature in the field of administration is so voluminous that any bibliography must be selective. These considerations influenced this one:

1. The main emphasis is necessarily on the public service.
2. Only the major works on industrial and business personnel management are included.
3. No attempt is made to list all the major publications in the English language, such as those from England, Australia, Canada, Ireland, India, Pakistan, and New Zealand.
4. Periodical articles are cited only if they (a) are of extraordinary significance or (b) offer a primary source of information on a subject that is not adequately treated in book-length publications.
5. Some items are included that may not seem to be directly on the subject but do enrich understanding of personnel management from a theoretical, political, or pragmatic standpoint.
6. Publications before 1960 are listed only if they are of an outstanding or enduring character, or have not been superseded on the same subject.

The annotations are designed to give the scholar or practitioner some idea of content and, where practicable, this writer's appraisal of the work.

II. GENERAL BOOKS

A. Emphasis on Private Business

While perusing the many volumes on industrial personnel maagement, one is struck not by their diversity and distinctiveness but by the almost inevitable similarity among them. The proliferation of texts demonstrates widespread use in schools of business administration and a great sensitivity to the personnel function. Yet, few of them show even slight concern with that function in the public sector, and most reveal a total lack of awareness of the literature in the burgeoning and profoundly significant field of public personnel management. Except where otherwise noted, practically none of the books listed in this section, in spite of their quality for industry, gives more than a nod to the governmental area.

Nevertheless, they are useful in gaining an understanding of the personnel function in general, and several works in this listing are classics in the field.

Barnard, Chester I., *The Functions of the Executive*, Cambridge, Mass., Harvard University Press, 1939.
> A masterful "first" in the literature, giving particular attention to the "informal" organization, leadership functions and qualities, and the physical, biological, and social foundations of organization.

Blum, Milton J., and James C. Naylor, *Industrial Psychology: Its Theoretical and Social Foundations*, New York, Harper & Row, 1968.
> Relates in great detail the products of psychological research and theory to motivation, performance, leadership, and the whole range of concerns as to industrial personnel administration.

Calhoon, Richard P., *Personnel Management and Supervision*, New York, Harper & Row, 1967.
A condensation and updating of an earlier book that covers modern industrial personnel management.

Chase, Stuart, *The Proper Study of Mankind*, New York, Harper & Row, 1948.
A brilliant, popularly written synthesis of progress made by social science research in solving human relationship problems, including those in the work place.

Chase, Stuart, *Roads to Agreement*, New York, Harper & Row, 1951.
A practical description of successful methods used in reducing conflicts.

Chruden, Herbert J., and Arthur W. Sherman, Jr., *Personnel Management*, 4th ed., Burlingame, Calif., Southwestern Publishing, 1972.
A well-organized text, with cases and bibliography, including some attention to government.

Crichton, Anne, *Personnel Management in Context*, London, B.T. Batsford, 1968.
Concentrates on British private enterprise, with a sociological approach; but also gives substantial attention to the civil service.

Cunning, Maurice W., *The Theory and Practice of Personnel Management*, 2nd ed., London, Heinemann, 1972.
Focuses on British industry but shows much greater interest in the public sector than is found in American business management books.

Dunn, J. D., and Elvis C. Stephens, *Management of Personnel; Manpower Management and Organizational Behavior*, New York, McGraw-Hill, 1972.
A good coverage of the subject, emphasizing employee productivity and satisfaction, and with unusual chapters on computerization and on personnel problems in overseas operations.

Etzioni, Amitai, ed., *Readings on Modern Organizations*, Englewood Cliffs, N.J., Prentice-Hall, 1969.
A collection of significant essays of the twentieth century that relate to management.

Famularo, Joseph J., ed., *Handbook of Modern Personnel Administration*, New York, McGraw-Hill, 1972.
Eighty-one chapters on the personnel function written by various authors with perspectives on American business.

Fleishman. Edwin A., and Alan R. Bass, eds., *Studies in Personnel and Industrial Psychology*, 3rd ed., Homewood, Ill., Dorsey, 1974.
Articles on industrial personnel problems that lend themselves to psychological measurement or analysis.

Flippo, Edwin B., *Principles of Personnel Management*, 3rd ed., New York, McGraw-Hill, 1971.
A general textbook for college use, with selected cases.

Follett, Mary Parker, *Dynamic Administration: Collected Papers*, New York, Harper & Row, 1942.
> Lectures by one of the pioneer thinkers in management, revealing a profound insight into leadership and human relationships. Focused on business practice but with much wider application for the orderly control of human affairs—governmental and international.

French, Wendell L., *The Personnel Management Process: Human Resources Administration*, 3rd ed. Boston, Houghton Mifflin, 1974.
> A general text organized around a "process-systems" approach to industrial personnel administration.

Gilmer, B. von Haller (with collaboration by eight other authors), *Industrial Psychology*, 3rd ed., New York, McGraw-Hill, 1971.
> A study of how modern psychology fits into the industrial complex.

Ginzberg, Eli, *The Development of Human Resources*, New York, McGraw-Hill, 1966.
> Selected chapters from earlier books by the author, setting forth a thorough case for more deliberate and purposeful planning and utilization of manpower resources.

Glueck, William F., *Personnel: A Diagnostic Approach*, Dallas, Business Publications, 1974.
> A thorough text, logically organized, with considerable emphasis on career development.

Haire, Mason, *Psychology in Management*, 2nd ed., New York, McGraw-Hill, 1964.
> A good summary of theory and findings in applied psychology as they relate to industry.

Huneryager, S. G., and I. L. Heckman, eds., *Human Relations in Management*, 2nd ed., New Rochelle, N.Y., Southwestern Publishing, 1967.
> Readings covering the usual range of subjects on human behavior, supplemented by introductions at various points by the editors.

Jucius, Michael J., *Personnel Management*, 7th ed., Homewood, Ill., Richard D. Irwin, 1971.
> A general work, taking cognizance of the contributions of the behavioral sciences, the impact of technology on personnel management, and current issues.

Kindall, Alva F., *Personnel Administration: Principles and Cases*, 3rd ed., Homewood, Ill., Richard D. Irwin, 1969.
> A collection of real cases, experienced in business and government, illustrating the problems of personnel management.

Knowles, William H., *Personnel Management: A Human Relations Approach*, New York, American Book, 1955.
> Unlike most texts, this book leaves the technical and procedural aspects of personnel management to others and instead stresses the impact of ideology,

ethics, and the social sciences on the personnel function. Shows how personnel work is essentially interdisciplinary.

Knudson, Harry R., Jr., ed., *Human Elements of Administration; Cases, Readings, Simulation Exercises*, New York, Holt, Rinehart and Winston, 1963.
A teaching tool with essays by leaders in personnel management theory, supplemented by real-life cases and exercises.

Ling, Cyril C., *The Management of Personnel Relations: History and Origins*, Homewood, Ill., Richard D. Irwin, 1965.
A factual record of the development of the personnel function in American industry.

Lyons, T. P., *The Personnel Function in a Changing Environment*, London, Pitman, 1971.
A brief, practical, no-nonsense treatment of personnel management needs in British industry.

Maier, Norman R. F., *Psychology in Industrial Organizations*, 4th ed., Boston, Houghton Mifflin, 1973.
Covers the range of psychological measurements and insights into industrial manpower management.

Margerison, Charles J., and David Ashton, eds., *Planning for Human Resources*, London, Longman, 1974.
Selected papers on some major aspects of personnel policy in British industry.

Matteson, Michael T., Roger N. Blakeney, and Donald R. Domm, eds., *Contemporary Personnel Management*, San Francisco, Canfield, 1972.
An assembly of readings, with substantial orientation to behavioral studies and theories.

Mayo, Elton, *The Social Problems of an Industrial Civilization*, Boston, Harvard School of Business Administration, 1945.
A landmark study, stressing man's persistence in association and in seeking cooperative activity. Points up need for research in and systematic methods of easing individuals from one group of associates into another. Mayo was the guiding spirit behind the renowned Hawthorne studies.

McClelland, David C., *The Achieving Society*, New York, Van Nostrand Reinhold, 1961.
The first significant study of the effect of man's achievement on economic growth, covering the history of achieving societies, the sources of achievement motivation, and its relationship to other factors in entrepreneurial behavior and economic development. Of special importance to developing countries.

McGregor, Douglas, *The Human Side of Enterprise*, New York, McGraw-Hill, 1960.
One of the outstanding works; a penetrating and challenging analysis of human motivation. Renews faith in man's will to achieve.

Megginson, Leon C., *Personnel: A Behavioral Approach to Administration*, rev. ed., Homewood, Ill., Richard D. Irwin, 1972.
A comprehensive text, emphasizing modern trends, manpower development, and performance improvement in industry and, to a limited extent, in government.

Milton, Charles R., *Ethics and Expediency in Personnel Management: A Critical History of Personnel Philosophy*, Columbia, S.C., University of South Carolina Press, 1970.
A synthesis of the historical impact of various philosophies on the personnel function in industry, especially the significance of a humanistic approach; also proposes an ideal model for a modern personnel philosophy.

Miner, John B., *Personnel and Industrial Relations: A Managerial Approach*, New York, Macmillan, 1969.
A first-rate basic text that introduces some new terminology and relates the personnel function thoroughly to its environment and to organization maintenance in industry.

Nash, Allan N., and John B. Miner, eds., *Personnel and Labor Relations: An Evolutionary Approach*, New York, Macmillan, 1973.
A collection of outstanding articles and papers in the personnel field, encompassing most of the work done in the twentieth century.

Odiorne, George S., *Personnel Administration by Objectives*, Homewood, Ill., Richard D. Irwin, 1971.
Stresses the role of the personnel department and management in general especially in relation to professional, managerial, and technical personnel.

Patten, Thomas H., Jr., *Manpower Planning and the Development of Human Resources*, Wiley-Interscience, 1971.
A comprehensive treatise on education and training for productive employment, including manpower planning within business firms and in society at large and embracing training at all levels, from apprentice to executive. Reflects a stimulating and farsighted view of "management of our most precious resource."

Pigors, Paul, and Charles A. Meyers, *Personnel Administration: A Point of View and a Method*, 7th ed., New York, McGraw-Hill, 1973.
A sound general text on industrial personnel matters, taking at least some note of the problems in and literature on personnel administration in government. Contains a unique organization of material and a lengthy section on cases.

Pigors, Paul, Charles A. Myers, and F. T. Malm, eds., *Management of Human Resources; Readings in Personnel Administration*, 3rd ed., New York, McGraw-Hill, 1973.
A comprehensive collection of readings, containing leading articles by authorities from government, industry, and academia.

Roethlisberger, F. J., and W. J. Dickson, *Management and the Worker*, Cambridge, Mass., Harvard University Press, 1939.
The precedent-shattering work describing the results and theories evolving

from the Hawthorne studies of the Western Electric Company, covering a twelve-year period.

Schultz, Duane, *Psychology and Industry Today*, New York, Macmillan, 1973.
A standard treatment of industrial psychology.

Smith, Henry Clay, and John H. Wakeley, *Psychology of Industrial Behavior*, 3rd ed., New York, McGraw-Hill, 1972.
A goal-oriented text relating psychology to industrial organization and performance.

Sokolik, Stanley L., *The Personnel Process: Line and Staff Dimensions in Managing People at Work*, Scranton, Pa., International Textbook Co., 1970.
A thorough work on the industrial personnel scene, stressing the division of work between operators and personnel people.

Strauss, George, and Leonard R. Sayles, *Personnel: The Human Problems of Management*, 3rd ed., Englewood Cliffs, N.J., Prentice-Hall, 1972.
A comprehensive text on business practice, with a unique and useful organization of material and containing illustrative problems.

Tead, Ordway, *The Art of Leadership*, New York, McGraw-Hill, 1935.
A vanguard book, thought-provoking, analytical, and basically supported by research findings of others in subsequent years.

Tead, Ordway, *The Art of Administration*, New York, McGraw-Hill, 1951.
Advances the thesis of allowing the widest freedom for personal initiative to capitalize on the natural human inclination to produce high-quality work.

Tiffin, Joseph, and Ernest J. McCormick, *Industrial Psychology*, 6th ed., Englewood Cliffs, N.J., Prentice-Hall, 1974.
The only general text on industrial personnel administration that stresses both behavioral science and job analysis as techniques for understanding and applying modern psychological knowledge.

Whyte, William H., Jr., *The Organization Man*, New York, Harper & Row, 1956.
A provocative report, in journalistic style, challenging commonly held notions about group work and subordination of the individual, derived from American business practice.

Worthy, James C., *Big Business and Free Men*, New York, Harper & Row, 1959.
A theory of the place of enterprise in our society but including ideas on internal organization and management; intended primarily for business audience, though having wider application.

Yoder, Dale, *Personnel Management and Industrial Relations*, 6th ed., Englewood Cliffs, N.J., Prentice-Hall, 1970.
One of the major books on industrial personnel management, emphasizing manpower planning and development, executive competence, management audits, and research.

B. Emphasis on Public Service

Advisory Committee on Merit System Standards, *Progress in Intergovernmental Personnel Relations*, Washington, D.C., U.S. Civil Service Commission, 1968.
Having studied social and administrative issues facing state governments, this body proposed various ways by which merit systems could be made both stronger and more flexible.

Advisory Council on Intergovernmental Personnel Policy, *More Effective Public Service*, First Report, January 1973; Supplementary Report, July 1974, Washington, D.C., U.S. Civil Service Commission.
Two outstanding reports of a council authorized under the Intergovernmental Personnel Act. Includes significant recommendations regarding merit system improvement and extension in state and local governments and concerning labor relations and equal employment opportunity.

American Assembly, Sixth, *The Federal Government Service*, 2nd ed., Wallace S. Sayre, ed., Englewood Cliffs, N.J., Prentice-Hall, 1965.
An updating by the same authors of papers originally prepared for the Sixth American Assembly held in 1954, discussing the history and problems of the bureaucracy. The five scholarly analyses explore relations with parties, Presidents, and the Congress, as well as the significance of personnel systems. Packed with thoughtful insight and critiques.

Appleby, Paul H., *Big Democracy*, New York, Knopf, 1945.
A book rich with wisdom and quotable observations on the nature of the public interest and the administrative process, with much of import to personnel administration.

Berkley, George E., *The Craft of Public Administration*, Rockleigh, N.J., Allyn and Bacon, 1975.
A practical guidebook aimed at public administrators, particularly at the local level.

Brown, Fred R., ed., *Management: Concepts and Practice*, Washington, D.C., Industrial College of the Armed Forces, 1967.
A handy resumé of modern practices written by various experts, laying heavy emphasis on quantitative, behavioral, and environmental considerations.

Carpenter, William Seal, *The Unfinished Business of Civil Service Reform*, Princeton, N.J., Princeton University Press, 1952.
A brief appraisal of the achievements of civil service reform, urging greater control of administration by the executive as the main "unfinished business."

Case, Harry L., *Personnel Policy in a Public Agency: The TVA Experience*, New York, Harper & Row, 1955.
The authoritative and stimulating story of TVA personnel administration.

Charlesworth, James C., ed., *Bureaucracy and Democratic Government*, Philadelphia, American Academy of Political and Social Science, March 1954.
An excellent series of papers on identification of and cures for so-called bureaucratic tendencies in the American public service.

Commission of Inquiry on Public Service Personnel, *Better Government Personnel,* New York, 1935.

This is the official report of the commission which set goals for American civil service administration for many years following its issuance. It was a milestone in developing appreciation of public personnel problems, being the first to emphasize policies to provide career opportunities, both within a jurisdiction and among all levels of government.

Twelve monographs prepared by outstanding authorities of the time present specific factual and conceptual treatments of this subject, including analyses of four European personnel systems.

Commission on Organization of the Executive Branch of the Government:

(1) *Personnel Management: A Report to the Congress,* Washington, D.C., February 1949.

A summary of major shortcomings in federal personnel administration, with general recommendations for improvement.

(2) *Federal Personnel,* Task Force Report, Washington, D.C., January 1949.

A more detailed study of the points covered in the foregoing report of the commission.

Commission on Organization of the Executive Branch of the Government:

(1) *Personnel and Civil Service,* Washington, D.C., February 1955.

The best of the 1955 crop of Hoover Commission reports, with some important proposals regarding federal civil service based on its Task Force recommendations.

(2) *Task Force Report on Personnel and Civil Service,* Washington, D.C., February 1955.

One of the great documents on the federal civil service, containing challenging recommendations that emphasize managerial competence (the "senior civil service" proposal) and strengthening of the merit system.

Crouch, Winston W., *Guide for Modern Personnel Commissions,* Chicago, International Personnel Management Association, 1973.

The only book of its kind, designed to inform lay commissioners or board members about the nature of their responsibilities.

Crouch, Winston W., ed., *Local Government Personnel Administration,* 7th ed., Washington, D.C., International City Management Association, 1976.

An authoritative handbook for city managers and mayors on personnel practices in cities.

Davis, James W., Jr., *An Introduction to Public Administration; Politics, Policy, and Bureaucracy,* New York, The Free Press, 1974.

An unusual but instructive slant on the administrative process, emphasizing bureaucratic behavior, clienteles, and power.

Dimock, Marshall E., *Administrative Vitality,* New York, Harper & Row, 1959.

A first-class treatise on the innovative role expected of the executive.

Dimock, Marshall E., and Gladys D. Dimock, *Public Administration,* 4th ed., New York, Holt, Rinehart and Winston, 1969.

An outstanding textbook, giving substantial space to and demonstrating keen understanding of the personnel function. Material is organized in a unique and useful manner.

Feldman, Herman, *A Personnel Program for the Federal Civil Service*, House Doc. No. 773, 71st Cong., 3rd sess., Washington, D.C., 1931.
One of the old "classics" in the field, now useful as history.

Gibson, Oliver, and Herold C. Hunt, *The School Personnel Administrator*, Boston, Houghton Mifflin, 1965.
A solid work on public school personnel administration, demonstrating much more awareness of the general literature and concepts of public administration and managerial doctrine than is common among public school executives.

Golembiewski, Robert T., and Michael Cohen, eds., *People in Public Service: A Reader in Public Personnel Administration*, Itasca, Ill., F. E. Peacock, 1970.
For a course on the personnel function, a useful supplement of papers, organized in an interesting fashion and tied together by instructive commentary by the editors.

Golembiewski, Robert T., Frank Gibson, and Geoffrey Y. Cornog, eds., *Public Administration; Readings in Institutions, Processes, Behavior*, 2nd ed., Chicago, Rand McNally, 1972.
An unconventional collection of articles and book chapters, with stimulating viewpoints on a wide range of issues.

Golembiewski, Robert T., and Michael White, eds., *Cases in Public Management*, New York, Rand McNally, 1973.
A brief collection of cases for graduate study.

Hills, William G., Voyle C. Scurlock, Harold D. Viaille, and James A. West, eds., *Conducting the Public Business: the Framework and Functions of Public Administration*, Norman, Okla., University of Oklahoma Press, 1973.
An important assembly of modern readings on major aspects of public administration.

Hyneman, Charles S., *Bureaucracy in a Democracy*, New York, Harper, 1950.
A classic treatment of the problems of leadership and control of the bureaucracy, as relevant today as it was at mid-century.

International Personnel Management Association, *Guidelines for Drafting a Public Personnel Administration Law*, Chicago, 1973.
A first-rate effort to present the principles and systems that should be established in statute, discussing alternative approaches and forms at various points rather than seeking to set forth a single "model."

International Personnel Management Association, *Policies and Practices in Public Personnel Administration*, Chicago.
A series of books on major aspects of the field, published from time to time; cited individually in appropriate places in this bibliography. Includes: Baruch (*Position Classification in the Public Service*); Byers (*Employee Training and Development in the Public Service*); Donovan (*Recruitment and Selection in the Public Service*); Lopez, (*Evaluating Employee Performance*); Nigro, (*Management-Employee Relations in the Public Service*); Stahl (*The Per-*

sonnel Job of Government Managers); and Warner and Donovan, (*Practical Guidelines to Public Pay Administration*). These are among the most complete and authoritative works on these respective subjects.

Kaplan, H. Eliot, *The Law of Civil Service*, New York, Matthew Bender, 1958.
A compilation and synthesis of issues on merit system laws that had been adjudicated up to that time in the courts; many points still relevant.

Kramer, Fred A., ed., *Perspectives on Public Bureaucracy: A Reader on Organization*, Amherst, Mass., University of Massachusetts, 1973.
A highly selective group of ten articles, including ones on motivation and decision-making.

Leighton, Alexander, *The Governing of Men*, Princeton, N.J., Princeton University Press, 1945.
The first winner of the Society for the Advancement of Management Human Relations Award. Based on experience in governing the relocation camps for Japanese during World War II, the second part of the book sets forth findings and principles on human motivation and cooperation that were pace-setting at the time.

Lippmann, Walter, *The Public Philosophy*, Boston, Little, Brown, 1955.
The essays of a great journalist, demonstrating that collective action is necessary for conservation of resources, for restraint on unbridled individual license, for free speech, and for preservation of democracy itself.

Macmahon, Arthur W., and John D. Millett, *Federal Administrators*, New York, Columbia University, 1939.
The first study of its kind, giving a realistic profile of the origins, qualifications, and education of executive personnel at the time.

Macy, John W., Jr., *Public Service: The Human Side of Government*, New York, Harper & Row, 1971.
The seasoned perspective of a former high-level federal official on the problems and successes of public personnel management, providing keen insight into federal practices and wise counsel for the future.

Mayers, Lewis, *The Federal Service: A Study of the System of Personnel Administration of the United States Government*, New York, Appleton-Century-Crofts, 1922.
One of the first systematic studies of personnel policies and therefore a "classic" for historical purposes.

Meriam, Lewis, *Public Personnel Problems from the Standpoint of the Operating Officer*, Washington, D.C., The Brookings Institution, 1938.
The first treatment of the subject that recognized the managerial approach.

Messick, Charles P., *An Adventure in Public Personnel Administration*, Newark, Del., University of Delaware, 1973.
The principal addresses and reminiscences of one of the great early leaders in the field. Remarkable for its grasp of current issues. Published in Messick's ninety-second year.

Millett, John D., *Government and Public Administration*, New York, McGraw-Hill, 1959.
Explores the ways and means of subjecting public service management to responsible political direction.

Mosher, Frederick C., *Democracy and the Public Service*, New York, Oxford University Press, 1968.
A penetrating analysis of the meaning for democratic government of developments in modern civil services, including forms of career systems and the impact of influences such as unionization and professionalization.

Municipal Manpower Commission, *Governmental Manpower for Tomorrow's Cities*, New York, McGraw-Hill, 1962.
A detached appraisal of the manpower predicament in American cities plus some trenchant proposals for dealing with it.

National Academy of Public Administration, Panel of, *Watergate: Its Implications for Responsible Government*, Washington, D.C., 1974.
Prepared by a panel of the Academy at the request of the Senate Select Committee on Presidential Campaign Activities, this discerning report offers prescriptions for governmental reform across the board, including keen analyses and proposals regarding ethics and public service issues.

Nigro, Felix A., and Lloyd G. Nigro, *Modern Public Administration*, 3rd ed., New York, Harper & Row, 1973.
A first-rate scholarly text dealing with contemporary issues as well as with basic principles.

Novogrod, R. Joseph, Gladys O. Dimock, and Marshall E. Dimock, *Casebook in Public Administration*, New York, Holt, Rinehart and Winston, 1969.
Eighteen detailed case studies on a whole range of policy issues facing public managers.

Pfiffner, John M., and Robert V. Presthus, *Public Administration*, 5th ed., New York, Ronald Press, 1967.
A very good text, with emphasis on the impact of modern organizational and behavioral theory on management of public services.

President's Commission on National Goals, *Goals for Americans*, Report of the Commission and Accompanying Papers, Englewood Cliffs, N.J., Prentice-Hall, 1960.
Administered by the American Assembly of Columbia University, this commission outlines a magnificent set of objectives for American society, including several regarding government processes and administration. The supporting papers, including one on "The Public Service" by Wallace S. Sayre, constitute an appraisal and an agenda worthy of a liberal education.

Public Personnel Administration; Policies and Practices for Personnel, Englewood Cliffs, N.J., Prentice-Hall, 1973.
A publisher-prepared loose-leaf manual of principles and practices, including sample policies and forms used in specific jurisdictions. Supplemented with bi-

weekly bulletins announcing developments among American governments at all levels.

Reeves, Floyd W., and Paul T. David, *Personnel Administration in the Federal Service,* Washington, D.C., President's Committee on Administrative Management, 1937.
One of the studies prepared for the President's committee, advocating comprehensive reforms in federal personnel administration, including the proposal for heading the central personnel agency with a single administrator.

Rosenbloom, David H., *Federal Service and the Constitution: the Development of the Public Employment Relationship,* Ithaca, N.Y., Cornell University Press, 1971.
A detailed, legalistic analysis of the historical development of the rights and obligations of public employees, including the areas of spoils, reform, loyalty, political freedom, and equal opportunity. A useful reference work.

Sharmansky, Ira, *Public Administration: Policy-Making in Government Agencies,* 2nd ed. Chicago, Markham, 1972.
A textbook that stresses the political milieu in which public administration takes place and the large role that administrators play in policy-making.

Sherman, Harvey, *It All Depends: A Pragmatic Approach to Organization,* Tuscaloosa, University of Alabama Press, 1966.
An excellent summary, valuable to student and practitioner alike, of the principles, problems, and pitfalls of organization theory and practice.

Siegel, Gilbert B., ed., *Human Resource Management in Public Organizations: A Systems Approach,* Los Angeles, University Publishers, 1973.
An impressive collection of papers and articles on public personnel problems.

Simon, Herbert A., *Administrative Behavior,* 2nd ed., New York, Macmillan, 1957.
An innovative analysis of the sociological aspects of administration: structure, communication, motivation, ethics, and informal organization, establishing a kind of *realpolitik* of administrative decision-making.

Spero, Sterling D., *Government as Employer,* New York, Remsen Press, 1948.
The first comprehensive treatment of unionism in the public service.

Stahl, O. Glenn, *The Personnel Job of Government Managers,* Chicago, International Personnel Management Association, 1971.
A brief primer for chiefs of line operations in the public service; the only book of its kind available. Provides background thinking and practical advice on personnel problems for government executives of all levels.

Stahl, O. Glenn, and Richard A. Staufenberger, eds., *Police Personnel Administration,* Washington, D.C., Police Foundation, 1974.
Recognizing the critical human factor in modern police forces, this book assembles a series of papers written by police and personnel officials that are designed to aid police administrators in improving the quality, motivation, and utilization of police officers.

Sweeney, Stephen B., and James C. Charlesworth, eds., *Achieving Excellence in Public Service*, Philadelphia, American Academy of Political and Social Science, August 1963.
A symposium of informative papers by administrators and educators on the weaknesses, strengths, and prospects of American public servants for meeting the needs of the times.

Thompson, Victor A., *Modern Organization*, New York, Knopf, 1961.
Presents a theory as to the innate conflict between traditional systems of authority and modern specialization, urging coordination through mutual interdependence among specializations.

Tolchin, Martin and Susan, *To the Victor—Political Patronage from the Clubhouse to the White House*, New York, Random House, 1971.
A popularized story of examples of use by political leaders of government jobs, purchases, subsidies, contracts, and decisions in order to maintain party and general citizen support. Job patronage is found to be a declining aspect of the ability to grant or withhold favors.

U.S. Civil Service Commission, *Biography of an Ideal*, 2nd ed., Washington, D.C., 1974.
An official history of achievements in improving public personnel management, including new informative sections on "The Past Fifteen Years, 1958–1973" (covering the federal picture) and "State and Local Personnel Administration."

Uveges, Joseph A., Jr., ed., *The Dimensions of Public Administration*, 2nd ed., Boston, Holbrook Press, 1975.
Readings on aspects of administration that constitute current issues and are of special concern to public executives.

Van Riper, Paul P., *History of the United States Civil Service*, New York, Harper & Row, 1958.
A political scientist's insightful history of events and trends, comprising the most important single-volume history of federal personnel administration.

Waldo, Dwight, *Perspectives on Administration*, Tuscaloosa, University of Alabama Press, 1956.
Outstanding lectures on the social science bases for public administration.

Warner, W. Lloyd, "The Careers of American Business and Government Executives: A Comparative Analysis," in George B. Strother, ed., *Social Science Approaches to Business Behavior*, Homewood, Ill., Richard D. Irwin and the Dorsey Press, 1962.
The informative results of a major research project confirming, among other points, the superior educational backgrounds of federal executives as compared with business counterparts.

Warner, W. Lloyd, Paul P. Van Riper, Norman H. Martin, and Orvis F. Collins, *The American Federal Executive*, A Study of the Social and Personal Characteristics of the Civilian and Military Leaders of the United States Federal Government, New Haven, Conn., Yale University Press, 1963.

The detailed report of the latest survey of the backgrounds, education, and qualifications of all categories of federal leadership, including political appointees.

Weaver, John D., *The Great Experiment, An Intimate View of the Everyday Workings of the Federal Government*, Boston, Little, Brown, 1965.
An extraordinarily informative and readable story of the daily grist and achievements of federal agencies and bureaucrats.

White, Leonard D., *The Federalists*, 1948; *The Jeffersonians*, 1951; *The Jacksonians*, 1954; and *The Republican Era*, 1958, New York, Macmillan.
Collectively, these four volumes comprise the most complete and penetrating administrative history of the federal government in existence.

White, Leonard D., *Government Career Service*, Chicago, University of Chicago Press, 1935.
The first full-scale discussion of the problems involved in creation of a true career civil service.

III. PROFESSIONAL PERIODICALS

Not all the journals listed specialize in governmental affairs, but only those business-oriented periodicals that give steady attention to this field are included. A few publications from England, because of their general importance and quality, are also listed. The division between general administration and personnel administration is for convenience of classification; subjects covered in the respective types of journals are never so discrete as to permit absolute categorization.

No annotation is feasible because of wide variations in coverage and quality over the years. Four items about each publication are presented: the organization sponsoring the journal; the city in which the organization or other publishing entity is headquartered; the year in which the journal or its predecessor, if any, first appeared; and the frequency of issuance.

A. General Administration

Administration and Society, Beverly Hills, Calif., 1969–. Quarterly journal published by Sage Publications. (Formerly *Journal of Comparative Administration*.)

Advanced Management, New York, 1936–. Quarterly journal of the Society for the Advancement of Management.

American City, The, Pittsfield, Mass., 1909–. Monthly publication of the Buttenheim Publishing Corporation.

American Political Science Review, Washington, D.C., 1906–. Quarterly journal of the American Political Science Association.

Annals of the American Academy of Political and Social Science, Philadelphia, 1891–. Bimonthly publication, each on a separate theme, of the academy.

Book of the States, The, Lexington, Ky., 1935–. Biennial encyclopedia on American state government, published by the Council of State Governments.

Bureaucrat, The, Beverly Hills, Calif., 1972–. Published quarterly by Sage Publications; founded by the National Capital Area Chapter of the American Society for Public Administration.

Government Executive, Washington, D.C., 1969–. Published monthly by Executive Publications, Inc.

International Review of Administrative Sciences, Brussels, 1928–. Quarterly journal (published in English, French, and Spanish) of the International Institute of Administrative Sciences.

Management Review, New York, 1926–. Monthly journal of the American Management Association.

Midwest Review of Public Administration, Parkville, Missouri, 1967–. Quarterly journal published by the Central States Conference on Public Administration.

Municipal Review, London, 1930–. Monthly organ of the Association of Municipal Corporations in the United Kingdom.

Municipal Year Book, Washington, D.C., 1934–. Annual encyclopedia on city government, published by the International City Management Association.

National Civic Review, New York, 1911–. Published eleven times a year by the National Municipal League.

Nation's Cities, Washington, D.C., 1963–. Monthly journal of the National League of Cities.

Public Administration, London, 1923–. Quarterly organ of the Royal Institute of Public Administration.

Public Administration Review, Washington, D.C., 1940–. Quarterly journal of the American Society for Public Administration.

Public Management, Washington, D.C., 1919–. Monthly organ of the International City Management Association.

Sage Public Administration Abstracts, Beverly Hills, Calif., 1974–. Quarterly publication of several hundred abstracts of periodical articles; published by Sage Publications.

State Government, Chicago, 1926–. Monthly journal of the Council of State Governments.

B. Personnel Administration

Civil Service Journal, Washington, D.C., 1960–. Official quarterly organ of the U.S. Civil Service Commission.

Good Government, Washington, D.C., 1881–. Quarterly publication of the National Civil Service League.

Human Relations, London and Ann Arbor, 1948–. Quarterly journal of the Tavistock Institute of Human Relations in London and the Institute for Social Research at the University of Michigan.

Human Resource Management, Ann Arbor, Mich., 1961–. Quarterly journal of the Graduate School of Business Administration, University of Michigan. (Formerly *Management of Personnel Quarterly.*)

International Prospect, Journal of World Service, Canterbury, England, 1969–. Privately published bimonthly, as an international manpower information medium.

Journal of Applied Psychology, Washington, D.C., 1917–. Bimonthly journal of the American Psychological Association.

Monthly Labor Review, Washington, D.C., 1915–. Official monthly publication of the Bureau of Labor Statistics of the U.S. Department of Labor.

Personnel, New York, 1915–. Quarterly journal of the American Management Association.

Personnel Administrator, The, Berea, Ohio, 1948–. Published eight times a year by the American Society for Personnel Administration (an association of industrial personnel executives).

Personnel and Guidance Journal, Washington, D.C., 1922–. Published ten months a year by the American Personnel and Guidance Association.

Personnel Journal, Baltimore, 1922–. Privately published eleven times a year.

Personnel Management, London, 1945–. Monthly journal of the Institute of Personnel Management in the United Kingdom.

Personnel Management Abstracts, Ann Arbor, 1927–. Quarterly publication of the Graduate School of Business Administration, University of Michigan.

Personnel Psychology, Washington, D.C., 1948–. Privately published quarterly.

Psychological Abstracts, Washington, D.C., 1927–. Monthly publication of the American Psychological Association.

Psychometrika, Princeton, N.J., 1936–. Quarterly journal of the Psychometric Society.

Public Personnel Management, Chicago, 1972–. Bimonthly journal of the International Personnel Management Association. (A consolidation of the former *Personnel Administration,* 1938–1972, and the former *Public Personnel Review,* 1940–1972.) This is the principal journal in the public personnel field, but it also includes articles on industrial experience.

Supervision, Burlington, Iowa, 1939–. Published monthly by the National Research Bureau.

Vocational Guidance Quarterly, Washington, D.C., 1952–. Quarterly journal of the National Vocational Guidance Association.

Worklife, Washington, D.C., 1969–. Official monthly publication of the Employment and Training Administration of the U.S. Department of Labor.

IV. LEADING REFERENCES BY CHAPTERS

Not all items alluded to in footnotes are listed here by chapter. Only the most important sources that relate to the subject of the chapter are included. Reference should also be made to the section in this bibliography on "General Books" for additional materials on the respective subjects. Individual parts of the books cited in that section, or occasionally the entire work, may be relevant to a particular topic. In two or three instances, items cited under one chapter are also relevant to another, but they are not repeated. The additional subject coverage will be evident from the annotation.

Chapter 1. THE SERVICES OF CIVILIZATION

Bailey, Stephen K., "The Excitement of the Public Service," *Civil Service Journal,* July–September 1963.
  An exciting article about an exciting subject.

Galbraith, John Kenneth, *The Affluent Society*, Cambridge, Mass., Riverside Press, 1958.
  An economic analysis of the anomaly of public poverty in the midst of private opulence.

Nelson, Charles A., *Developing Responsible Public Leaders*, A Report on Interviews with 52 Leading Americans, Dobbs Ferry, N.Y., Oceana Publications, 1963.
  Demonstrates that American leaders support a public-oriented philosophy as needed, to offset the popular stereotype and disposition toward purely private values.

Storing, Herbert J., "Political Parties and the Bureaucracy," in Robert A. Goldwin, ed., *Political Parties, U.S.A.,* Chicago, Rand McNally, 1964.
  An excellent perspective on the role of the career service.

U.S. Civil Service Commission, *Civil Service Inventors*, reprinted from *Civil Service Journal*, July–September 1962 and October–December 1962, Washington, D.C., 1962.
  Examples of the initiatives and contributions of civil servants to science and business, ranging from radar and heart pumps to industrial packaging and pain-killing drugs.

Wilson, Woodrow, "The Study of Administration," *Political Science Quarterly,* reprinted in December 1941 (originally published in 1887).
  One of the great "classics" of all time in public administration.

Chapter 2. THE PERSONNEL FUNCTION IN SOCIETY

Ginzberg, Eli, *Manpower Agenda for America*, New York, McGraw-Hill, 1968.
  A well-reasoned plea for manpower planning and recognition of the importance of the public sector.

Kilpatrick, Franklin P., Milton C. Cummings, Jr., and M. Kent Jennings, *The Image of the Federal Service*, Washington, D.C., The Brookings Institution, 1964.
The most comprehensive of several studies on the prestige of public employment, indicating the complexity of the subject and some of the inherent contradictions.

Kuhn, Delia and Ferdinand, eds., *Adventures in Public Service*, New York, Vanguard Press, 1963.
An interesting insight into honorable civil service careers through description of the lives of eight Rockefeller Award winners.

Mann, Dean E., with Jameson W. Doig, *The Assistant Secretaries: Problems and Processes of Appointment*, Washington, D.C., The Brookings Institution, 1965.
The only systematic study of the sources and quality of appointments to assistant-secretaryships.

Stahl, O. Glenn, "The Network of Authority," *Public Administration Review,* Winter 1958, and "More on the Network of Authority," Winter 1960.
Critiques on the concept of "line" and "staff."

White, Leonard D., *Further Contributions to the Prestige Value of Public Employment*, Chicago, University of Chicago Press, 1932.
The final report of the first studies on public attitudes toward government employment.

Chapter 3. DEVELOPMENT OF THE MERIT SYSTEM

In addition to the following items, reference should be made to listings under "General Books" by Crouch; International Personnel Management Association, *Guidelines*; Macy; Messick; Mosher; Rosenbloom; U.S. Civil Service Commission; Van Riper; and White.

Berkson, I. B., *Ethics, Politics, and Education*, Eugene, University of Oregon Books, 1968.
A rational treatment of the importance of recognizing human differences.

Curtis, George William, *Orations and Addresses*, ed. by C. E. Norton, New York, Harper & Row, 1894, three vols.
The public papers of one of the great leaders in the civil service reform movement.

Fish, Carl Russell, *The Civil Service and the Patronage*, Cambridge, Mass., Harvard University Press, 1904.
The first great history of the reform period.

Gardner, John W., *Excellence; Can We Be Equal and Excellent Too?* New York, Harper & Row, 1961.
A masterful discussion of the necessity for a democratic society to recognize ability and achievement.

Graves, W. Brooke, *Federalism and Public Employment,* Washington, D.C., Federal Professional Association, 1965.
    An eloquent and well-supported plea for more intergovernmental cooperation and uniformity in public personnel administration, federal, state, and local.

Hoogenboom, Ari, *Outlawing the Spoils—A History of the Civil Service Reform Movement, 1865–1883,* Urbana, University of Illinois Press, 1961.
    The most intensive history of the pre–Civil Service Act period, with some interesting interpretations.

Sorauf, Frank R., "The Silent Revolution in Patronage," *Public Administration Review,* Winter 1960.
    The best piece showing how unnecessary patronage is to party success.

U.S. Civil Service Commission, *Directory of State Merit Systems,* Washington, approximately biennially.
    A useful listing of offices and coverage of state merit systems.

Chapter 4. CAREER SYSTEMS

Fulton Committee, *The Civil Service,* vol. 1, Report of the Committee, London, Her Majesty's Stationery Office, 1968.
    The dramatic critique of the class structure in the British civil service.

Leich, Harold H., "Rank in Man or Job? Both!" *Public Administration Review,* Spring 1960.
    A spirited demonstration of how the best of two concepts can be merged.

Stahl, O. Glenn, "Of Jobs and Men," *Public Administration Review,* July/ August 1969; first published in the *Indian Journal of Public Administration,* April–June 1968.
    A critique of the effects of closed, functional rank-in-corps systems.

Stanley, David T., *The Higher Civil Service; An Evaluation of Federal Personnel Practices,* Washington, D.C., The Brookings Institution, 1964.
    Analysis of facts and viewpoints, and presentation of some perceptive alternatives, as to how career patterns and other aspects of personnel administration can be dealt with at executive levels in the federal service.

U.N. Economic Commission for Asia and the Far East, *Workshop on National Personnel Systems,* Bangkok, November 1968.
    A report urging more job-oriented features in public personnel systems of developing countries.

Chapter 5. CLASSIFICATION OF POSITIONS

Baruch, Ismar (chairman of drafting committee), *Position Classification in the Public Service,* Chicago, International Personnel Management Association, 1941, reprinted in 1965. (Now in process of extensive revision).
    The standard work on the subject, of sufficient merit that it was reprinted a quarter of a century after it was originally published. Largely the work of Baruch.

Ingraham, Albert P., and Carl F. Lutz, "Managing Positions—the Key to Effective Organization, Compensation, and Productivity," *Human Resource Management*, Summer 1974, pp. 12–21.
  The best up-to-date case for the manifold benefits of job analysis and evaluation.

Lutz, Carl F., and James P. Morgan, "Jobs and Rank," Chapter 2 in *Police Personnel Administration*, O. Glenn Stahl and Richard A. Staufenberger, eds., Washington, D.C., Police Foundation, 1974.
  A very good succinct treatment of the issues.

Report of the Job Evaluation and Pay Review Task Force to the United States Civil Service Commission, printed for the Committee on Post Office and Service, U.S. House of Representatives, January 12, 1972 (92nd Congress, 2nd Session; Committee Print No. 16).
  A lengthy volume proposing changes in the federal classification system, only a few of which were deemed worthy of adoption by the USCSC.

Stahl, O. Glenn, "The System Takes the Rap," *Civil Service Journal*, October–December 1961.
  Clarification to offset some of the misconceptions about job evaluation.

Chapter 6. COMPENSATION

Comptroller General of the United States, *Critical Need for a Better System for Adjusting Top Executive, Legislative, and Judicial Salaries*, Report to the Congress, February 25, 1975.
  An excellent analysis of a still neglected area of federal personnel administration.

Council of State Governments, *State Institutional Employee Maintenance*, Lexington, Ky., March 1967.
  Encyclopedic information on how the various states handle allowances for quarters, meals, etc.

Personnel Classification Board, *Closing Report of Wage and Personnel Survey*, Washington, D.C., 1931.
  The first notable survey of pay and other conditions of employment in the public and private sectors.

U.S. Civil Service Commission, *Pay Structure of the Federal Civil Service*, Washington, D.C., published annually.
  A standard reference tool on federal pay provisions for all categories of personnel.

Warner, Kenneth O., and J. J. Donovan, eds., *Practical Guidelines to Public Pay Administration*, Chicago, International Personnel Management Association, vol. I, 1963; vol. II, 1965.
  The best compendium of papers on different aspects of compensation policy and practice.

Chapter 7. MANPOWER PLANNING AND ATTRACTION

Lester, Richard A., *Manpower Planning in a Free Society*, Princeton, N.J., Princeton University Press, 1966.

A lucid primer on the need for more information, planning, and leadership in the development and mobility of persons for gainful employment.

Levitan, Sar A., Garth L. Mangum, and Ray Marshall, *Human Resources and Labor Markets*, New York, Harper & Row, 1972.

For the most part a good detailed overview of national manpower policy and practice, emphasizing remedial issues but with inadequate attention to government as employer, especially the fastest-growing segment of the economy—local public services.

National Manpower Council, *Government and Manpower*, New York, Columbia University Press, 1964.

The most complete exploration of issues relating to government's impact on the manpower market, both as an employer and as an economic determinant.

U.S. Civil Service Commission, *Equal Employment Opportunity in State and Local Governments—A Guide for Affirmative Action*, Washington, D.C., 1972.

A practical working outline of steps essential to true equal opportunity, embracing job structuring, recruitment, selection, training, and other areas.

Wolfle, Dale, *The Uses of Talent*, Princeton, Princeton University Press, 1971.

A good analysis of the need for balance between (1) manpower and educational planning and (2) allowing free play for educational and occupational opportunity.

Chapter 8. METHODS OF EXAMINATION

American Psychological Association, *Standards for Educational and Psychological Tests*, Washington, D.C., 1974.

A professional and authoritative resource on the quality of tests and their proper use.

Anastasi, Anne, *Psychological Testing*, 3rd ed., New York, Macmillan, 1968.

A standard work on principles, with examples of major types of tests in use.

Buros, Oscar Krisen, ed., *The Seventh Mental Measurements Yearbook*, Highland Park, N.J., The Gryphon Press, 1972.

A compendium of critical reviews, by many specialists, of hundreds of published test instruments on a wide range of subjects, including intelligence, aptitude, personality, and numerous vocational fields. Use of this volume enables test users to avoid tests that are of doubtful validity or are otherwise worthless.

Campbell, J. T., L. A. Crooks, M. G. Mahoney, and D. A. Rock, *An Invalidation of Sources of Bias in the Prediction of Job Performance: A Six-Year Study*, Final Project Report, Princeton, N.J., Educational Testing Service, 1973. (Also reported more briefly in *A Management Summary*, July 27, 1972.)

This study, in which ETS and the U.S. Civil Service Commission collaborated, focused on several occupations in the federal service and confirmed that well-constructed tests are just as predictive of performance for minority groups as they are for others.

Cronbach, Lee J., *Essentials of Psychological Testing*, 3rd ed., New York, Harper & Row, 1970.
A standard text surveying the total scene of mental assessment.

Donovan, J. J., ed., *Recruitment and Selection in the Public Service*, Chicago, International Personnel Management Association, 1968.
The most complete and up-to-date book on public personnel selection, consisting of essays by authorities throughout the country, mainly on the various aspects of testing but including several chapters on the planning and recruitments areas.

Gehlmann, Frederick L., L. W. Ferguson, and John F. Scott, *Personality Tests— Uses and Limitations*, Personnel Report No. 561, Chicago, International Personnel Management Association, 1956.
Sound warnings about efforts at personality measurement.

Getzels, Jacob W., and Philip W. Jackson, *Creativity and Intelligence*, New York, Wiley, 1962.
Based on research conducted by University of Chicago faculty members among students, this report concludes that traditional intelligence tests fail to identify creativity in individuals, a much needed talent in our civilization. The subjects of the research tended to be concentrated within the upper ranges of intellect, but there was no correlation between "smartness" and "originality."

Ghiselli, Edwin E., *The Validity of Occupational Aptitude Tests*, New York, Wiley, 1966.
An authoritative reference on all aspects of aptitude testing.

Guion, Robert M., *Personnel Testing*, New York, McGraw-Hill, 1965.
Research bases for testing and administrative requisites for use in selection and placement.

Lawshe, C. H., and Michael J. Balma, *Principles of Personnel Testing*, New York, McGraw-Hill, 1966.
A text and handbook providing a complete survey of the testing function.

Lopez, Felix M., Jr., *Personnel Interviewing: Theory and Practice*, 2nd ed., New York, McGraw-Hill, 1975.
Broad guidance on use of the interview as a management tool.

Mandell, Milton M., *The Selection Process: Choosing the Right Man for the Job*, New York, American Management Association, 1964.
A readable treatment, directed primarily to private employment, drawing upon research bases and presenting practical examples of recruiting, testing, and interviewing processes.

Super, Donald E., and John O. Crites, *Appraising Vocational Fitness by Means of Psychological Tests*, rev. ed., New York, Harper & Row, 1962.
One of the outstanding works on measurement, designed for vocational guidance and choice.

Taylor, Vernon R., *Test Validity in Public Personnel Selection*, Public Employment Practices Bulletin No. 2, Chicago, International Personnel Management Association, 1971.
A first-rate summary of the main points on the subject.

U.S. Office of Strategic Services, Assessment Staff, *Assessment of Men: Selection of Personnel for OSS*, New York, Holt, Rinehart and Winston, 1948.
The fascinating story of gauging the capacities of prospective intelligence agents for service during World War II.

Wright, Grace H., ed., *Public Sector Employment Selection: A Manual for the Personnel Generalist*, Chicago, International Personnel Management Association, 1974.
A full-scale how-to-do-it manual, containing a comprehensive bibliography and the best analysis of validation and legal issues relating to equal employment opportunity.

Chapter 9. SELECTION: FROM OUTSIDE THE SERVICE

Berwitz, Clement J., *The Job Analysis Approach to Affirmative Action*, New York, Wiley, 1975.
An exposition of principles, as well as a technical manual, built on the contention that affirmative action to ensure opportunity for women and minorities is nothing more than good personnel management and that a basic key to sound practice is reliance on the methods of job analysis and of relating persons' skills to job needs.

President's Commission on Veterans' Pensions, *Veterans' Benefits in the United States: A Report to the President*, Washington, D.C., April 1956.
Amidst proposals on all aspects of veteran legislation, this report recommends curtailment of the perpetual eligibility feature of veteran preference in federal employment.

Stahl, O. Glenn, *A Fair Look at Fair Employment*, Chicago, International Personnel Management Association, 1971.
A record showing how well-run merit systems provide the most equal employment opportunity.

U.S. Civil Service Commission, *History of Veteran Preference in Federal Employment, 1865–1955*, Washington, D.C., 1955.
The best summary of the facts; no evaluative discussion.

U.S. Commission on Civil Rights, *For All the People—By All the People: A Report on Equal Opportunity in State and Local Government Employment*, Washington, D.C., 1969.
A comprehensive and fair survey of the practices of state and local jurisdictions with respect to employment and advancement of black and other minority groups. It does not attack the merit concept but demonstrates that it is not always lived up to.

Chapter 10. SELECTION: FROM INSIDE THE SERVICE

Corson, John J., and R. Shale Paul, *Men Near the Top; Filling Key Posts in the Federal Service*, Supplementary Paper No. 20 issued by the Committee for Economic Development, Baltimore, The Johns Hopkins Press, 1966.
    The product of an intensive survey of program managers, managerial-support personnel, and professional employees in the highest civil service grades, showing what they do and how they arrived where they are, and suggesting how competence may be developed and siphoned into such posts in the future.

Lynch, Edith M., *The Executive Suite—Feminine Style*, New York, Amacon (American Management Association), 1973.
    A lively and informative exposition of the breakdown in myths and prejudices about women in executive jobs.

Stahl, O. Glenn, "Perspective on Promotion Policy," *Public Personnel Review*, July 1954.
    Presents the major issues relating to movement and advancement of personnel within the federal service.

Chapter 11. LIBERATING THE WILL TO WORK

The lengthy list of references for this chapter reflects the popularity of the subject among modern academicians. Motivation, human relationships, and leadership have been perceived to be central to the ever-present problems of productivity and smooth-running organizations. There has been much writing on these subjects for several decades. Centering on intergroup and interpersonal relations in business organizations, the number of books published since 1960 has been phenomenal. Only representative volumes are therefore listed here.

Also, it should be noted that several works cited under the heading "General Books" are especially relevant to the subject of this chapter, such as those by Barnard, McClelland, McGregor, Roethlisberger, Tead, and Worthy. They were of such an outstanding character that they deserved more general notice than listing under a single chapter.

Annotations are made in this chapter only where something unique about the book deserves attention; otherwise, citations are listed without annotation.

American Assembly, Forty-third, *The Worker and the Job: Coping with Change*, Jerome M. Rosow, ed., Englewood Cliffs, N.J., Prentice-Hall, 1974.
    Seven papers on sociological and attitudinal changes that are affecting work and satisfaction from work. Prepared for the Assembly, "The Changing World of Work," held in November 1973.

Argyris, Chris, *Integrating the Individual and the Organization*, New York, Wiley, 1964.

Bellows, Roger, Thomas Q. Gilson, and George S. Odiorne, *Executive Skills: Their Dynamics and Development*, Englewood Cliffs, N.J., Prentice-Hall, 1962.

Berelson, Bernard, and Gary A. Steiner, *Human Behavior: An Inventory of Scientific Findings*, New York, Harcourt Brace Jovanovich, 1964.

Bernstein, Marver H., *The Job of the Federal Executive*, Washington, D.C., The Brookings Institution, 1958.
A report on the deliberations of a group of distinguished political and career executives regarding their leadership roles.

Bittel, Leslie R., *What Every Supervisor Should Know*, 3rd ed., New York, McGraw-Hill, 1974.

Blake, Robert R., and Jane S. Mouton, *The Managerial Grid—Key Organizations for Achieving Production Through People*, Houston, Gulf Publishing, 1964.

Chase, Stuart, *Men at Work*, New York, Harcourt Brace Jovanovich, 1945. A A classic in its time, based on early behavioral research.

Cleveland, Harlan, *The Future Executive*, New York, Harper & Row, 1972.
A stimulating perspective on the role and challenges of the public executive.

Coffey, Robert E., Anthony G. Athos, and Peter A. Raynolds, *Behavior in Organizations: A Multidimensional View*, 2nd ed., Englewood Cliffs, N.J., Prentice-Hall, 1975.

Cooper, William W., Harold J. Leavitt, and Maynard W. Shelly II, eds., *New Perspectives in Organization Research*, New York, Wiley, 1964.

Davis, Keith, *Human Behavior at Work*, 4th ed., New York, McGraw-Hill, 1972.

Davis, Keith, ed., *Organizational Behavior: A Book of Readings*, New York, McGraw-Hill, 1974.

Downs, Anthony, *Inside Bureaucracy*, Boston, Little Brown, 1967.
A synthesis of theories on organization structure, relationships, and decision-making, relying heavily on absolutes and large doses of cynicism but containing much good counsel. Outdoes all other behavioral-oriented works by the sheer volume of its detailed pontifications on almost every conceivable facet of organization life.

Dubin, Robert, ed., *Human Relations in Administration*, 4th ed., Englewood Cliffs, N.J., Prentice-Hall, 1974.
A collection of over one hundred outstanding essays on organization, administrative action, and personnel administration, with introductory comments by the editor.

Ford, Robert N. *Motivation Through the Work Itself*, New York, American Management Association, 1969.
The most impressive assembly of facts and ideas, based on experiments in various plants of the American Telephone and Telegraph Company, on the importance of work as a motivator. Illustrates how jobs can be enriched to make them more meaningful for their incumbents.

Gellerman, Saul W., *Management by Motivation*, New York, American Management Association, 1968.
A first-rate interpretation of the impact of social science research on human motivation and behavior in a work environment.

Glover, John Desmond, Ralph M. Hower, and Renato Tagiuri, eds., *The Administrator: Cases on Human Aspects of Management*, 5th ed., Homewood, Ill., Richard D. Irwin, 1973.
An extensive assembly of classic essays on life, each illustrated by several cases involving application to the administrative process.

Golembiewski, Robert T., *The Small Group*, Chicago, University of Chicago Press, 1962.
An evaluation of concepts and methodology in research on small groups.

Golembiewski, Robert T., ed., *Perspectives on Public Management; Cases and Learning Designs*, Itasca, Ill., F. E. Peacock, 1968.

Greiner, Larry E., "What Managers Think of Participative Leadership," *Harvard Business Review*, March–April 1973, pp. 111–117.
A balanced appraisal of a complex philosophy of management.

Guest, Robert H., *Organizational Change: The Effect of Successful Leadership*, Homewood, Ill., Dorsey Press, 1962.
The story of how a new manager of an automobile assembly plant changed it from the poorest of six sister plants to the best, in terms of productivity, cost, and quality.

Herzberg, Frederick, *Work and the Nature of Man*, Cleveland, World Publishing, 1966.

Herzberg, Frederick, Bernard Mausner, and Barbara Bloch Snyderman, *The Motivation to Work*, New York, Wiley, 1959.
Originates a theory of job satisfaction, based upon Maslow's "hierarchy of needs" theory, to the effect that "hygiene factors" (conditions of pay, fringe benefits, etc.) can detract from worker satisfaction or leave it unaffected, but that real improvement can come only from restructuring jobs and emphasizing personal growth in the organization.

Hinrichs, John R., *High-Talent Personnel; Managing a Critical Resource*, New York, American Management Association, 1966.

Ivens, Michael, and Frank Broadway, eds., *Case Studies in Human Relations, Productivity and Organization*, London, Business Publications, 1966.
Cases from British business experience on human problems in personnel administration.

Jacobs, T. O., *Leadership and Exchange in Formal Organizations*, Alexandria, Va., Human Resources Research Organization (under contract with Office of Naval Research), 1970.

Katz, Daniel, and Robert L. Kahn, *The Social Psychology of Organizations*, New York, Wiley, 1966.

Lawrence, Paul R., and John A. Seiler, eds., *Organizational Behavior and Administration; Cases, Concepts, and Research Findings,* rev. ed., Homewood, Ill., Richard D. Irwin and the Dorsey Press, 1965.
A voluminous compilation of cases and interpretative articles by an array of distinguished scholars.

Leavitt, Harold J., *Managerial Psychology,* 2nd ed., Chicago, University of Chicago Press, 1964.
A highly readable, "common-sense" book, giving a balanced, sensible appraisal of what is going on in the managerial sciences.

Leavitt, Harold, and Louis R. Pondy, eds., *Readings in Managerial Psychology,* Chicago, University of Chicago Press, 1964.

Levinson, Harry, *Emotional Health in the World of Work,* New York, Harper & Row, 1964.
One of the few books devoted to industrial health problems.

Likert, Rensis, *New Patterns of Management,* New York, McGraw-Hill, 1961.
A synthesis of the significant findings made by the Institute for Social Research at the University of Michigan over a fourteen-year period, advancing a novel integration of theories of management and motivation.

Likert, Rensis, *The Human Organization; Its Management and Value,* New York, Mc-Graw-Hill, 1967.
Reports additional research results from the Institute for Social Research that support a science-based approach to management.

Mailick, Sidney, and Edward H. Van Ness, eds., *Concepts and Issues in Administrative Behavior,* Englewood Cliffs, N.J., Prentice-Hall, 1962.
A series of first-rate papers and lectures dealing with decision-making, values, communication, and human relationships in administrative organizations.

Marrow, Alfred J., David G. Bowers, and Stanley E. Seashore, *Management by Participation,* New York, Harper & Row, 1967.
The story of improvement of a failing organization through introduction of new management policies based on behavioral science research.

Maslow, A. H., *Motivation and Personality,* New York, Harper & Row, 1954.
A collection of the brilliant essays by this innovator in behavioral science, including his classic "A Theory of Human Motivation," first published in 1943, in which he advances the concept that human needs rank in a "hierarchy of relative prepotency," so that when basic needs for food, drink, etc., are satisfied, then more complex needs for belongingness, esteem, self-realization, and esthetics come into play.

McCormick, Ernest J., *Human Factors Engineering,* 2nd ed., New York, McGraw-Hill, 1964.
More than other books, stresses the psychological aspects of man-machine systems in production environments.

Neff, Walter S., *Work and Human Behavior,* New York, Atherton Press, 1968.
A study of the meaning of and attitudes toward work through the ages.

Parker, S. R., R. K. Brown, J. Child, and M. A. Smith, *The Sociology of Industry*, London, George Allen and Unwin, 1967.

Petrullo, Luigi, and Bernard Bass, eds., *Leadership and Interpersonal Behavior*, New York, Holt, Rinehart and Winston, 1961.
A collection of excellent papers by a distinguished group of scholars presented at a symposium sponsored by the Office of Naval Research.

Pfiffner, John M., and Marshall Fels, *The Supervision of Personnel: Human Relations in the Management of Men*, 3rd ed., Englewood Cliffs, N.J., Prentice-Hall, 1964.

Presthus, Robert V., The *Organizational Society; An Analysis and a Theory*, New York, Knopf, 1962.

Reeves, Elton T., *The Dynamics of Group Behavior*, New York, American Management Association, 1970.

Roethlisberger, F. J., *Man-in-Organization: Essays of F. J. Roethlisberger*, Cambridge, Mass., The Belknap Press of Harvard University, 1968.
Papers by one of the great behavioral scientists written over a span of forty years.

Sanford, Aubrey C., *Human Relations; Theory and Practice*, Columbus, Charles E. Merrill, 1973.

Shaw, Marvin E., *Group Dynamics: The Psychology of Small Group Behavior*, New York, McGraw-Hill, 1971.

Steiner, Ivan D., *Group Process and Productivity*, New York, Academic Press, 1972.

Trowbridge, Lowell S., *Human Relations*, Waterford, Conn., National Foreman's Institute, 1968.
Probably the briefest, most lucid, and most readable of the several books written in popular style but covering the full range of the findings and truths emanating from behavioral research, punctuated with clarifying anecdotes.

Van Dersal, William R., *The Successful Supervisor in Government and Business*, 3rd ed., New York, Harper & Row, 1974.
A first-rate succinct review of managerial effectiveness and training.

Walker, Nigel, *Morale in the Civil Service; A Study of the Desk Worker*, Chicago, Aldine Publishing, 1962.

Whyte, William Foote, *Organizational Behavior: Theory and Application*, Homewood, Ill., Irwin-Dorsey Press, 1969.

Chapter 12. EVALUATION AND INCENTIVES

Barrett, Richard S., *Performance Rating*, Chicago, Science Research Associates, 1966.
A technical manual on rating scales and administration.

Foundation for Research on Human Behavior, *Performance Appraisals; Effects on Employees and their Performance*, Ann Arbor, 1963.
> Reports by several research men on the effects of the evaluation process on performance and how it might contribute positively to achievement.

Gardner, John W., *Excellence: Can We Be Equal and Excellent Too?* New York, Harper & Row, 1961.
> Fundamental wisdom on society's need to hold high standards and to be unafraid of evaluating people. An enduring work.

Katz, Elihu, and Brenda Danet, eds., *Bureaucracy and the Public: A Reader in Official-Client Relationships*, New York, Basic Books, 1973.
> A unique collection of articles on the behavior of public servants.

Kellogg, Marion S., *What to Do About Performance Appraisal*, New York, American Management Association, 1965.
> A handbook stressing especially the "coaching appraisal" and appraisal of potential.

Lopez, Felix M., Jr., *Evaluating Employee Performance*, Chicago, International Personnel Management Association, 1968.
> The most thorough and authoritative work on the subject. Broadly based both from the standpoint of conceptual thinking and research, it deals adequately with technique and is problem oriented, but yet looks to essential purpose and contains much practical doctrine.

McGregor, Douglas, "An Uneasy Look at Performance Appraisal," *Harvard Business Review*, May–June 1957.
> One of the great provocative pieces, challenging several traditional concepts.

Meyer, Herbert H., Emanuel Kay, and John R. P. French, Jr., "Split Roles in Performance Appraisal," *Harvard Business Review*, January–February 1965.
> A report of significant research discrediting all-purpose ratings.

Odiorne, George S., *Management by Objectives: A System of Managerial Leadership*, New York, Pitman Publishing, 1965.
> Enunciation of a management philosophy under which achievement and recognition rest on evaluation of managers in terms of the results that they and their subordinates produce.

Chapter 13. STAFF DEVELOPMENT AND TRAINING

Byers, Kenneth T., ed., *Employee Training and Development in the Public Service*, Chicago, International Personnel Management Association, 1970.
> A symposium of doctrine on the subject by authoritative practitioners and scholars. The most up-to-date treatment in the literature.

Gardner, John W., *Self-Renewal; The Individual and the Innovative Society*, New York, Harper & Row, 1964.
> An excellent bit of Gardnerian philosophy about the compelling need to gear up for change in a relentlessly changing society.

Golembiewski, Robert T., and Arthur Blumberg, eds., *Sensitivity Training and the Laboratory Approach: Readings About Concepts and Applications*, Itasca, Ill., F. E. Peacock, 1970.
> The best source of articles on this popular but controversial technique for learning about oneself.

Heisel, W. D., E. R. Padgett, and C. A. Harrell, *Line-Staff Relationships in Employee Training*, Washington, D.C., International City Management Association, 1967.
> The results and conclusions drawn from a survey of training organization, policies, and levels of activity in a number of municipalities and other local jurisdictions.

Investment for Tomorrow, A Report of the Presidential Task Force on Career Advancement, Washington, D.C., U.S. Civil Service Commission, 1967.
> An imaginative analysis and set of recommendations for training in the federal civil service.

Kellogg, Marion S., *Closing the Performance Gap: Results-Centered Employee Development*, New York, American Management Association, 1967.
> A handbook of counsel for managers and foremen on creating a climate for staff training, including self-development.

Lambie, Morris B., *Training for the Public Service*, Chicago, Public Administration Service, 1935.
> A reliable review of the early history of preentry training.

Laski, Harold J., "The Limitations of the Expert," *Harper's Magazine*, December 1930.
> One of the great "classics" in modern political-administrative literature, demonstrating the shortcomings of overspecialized educations and, implicitly, the need for broadening of specialists in public administration.

Lynton, Rolf P., and Udai Pareek, *Training for Development*, Homewood, Ill., Richard D. Irwin, 1967.
> A detailed manual on training planning, methodology, and strategy, supplemented with illustrative readings by other authors following each chapter. Compares training approaches and results in developing and developed countries, using India and the United States as examples.

Odiorne, George S., *Training by Objectives: An Economic Approach to Management Training*, New York, Macmillan, 1970.
> A presentation of learning theory and of a systems approach in training managers.

Stahl, O. Glenn, "Public Service Training in Universities," *American Political Science Review*, October 1937.
> One of the first proposals that universities should concentrate training in public administration on in-service programs and on supplementation of technical school curricula.

Stahl, O. Glenn, *Training Career Public Servants for the City of New York*, New York, New York University, 1936.
> The first intensive study of preentry and postentry training in a major jurisdiction, showing the relationship to local educational institutions and to job opportunities.

Stewart, Ward, and John C. Honey, *University-Sponsored Executive Development Programs in the Public Service*, Washington, D.C., U.S. Office of Education, 1966.
> A survey of university-operated advanced courses for middle- and upper-level executives and professionals in the public service.

Sweeney, Stephen B., ed., *Education for Administrative Careers in Government*, Philadelphia, University of Pennsylvania Press, 1958.
> The product of a conference on the subject, this series of papers presents an excellent overview of preentry and executive training issues by some of the leading academic minds of the period.

Tickner, Fred, *Training in Modern Society*, Albany, Graduate School of Public Affairs, State University of New York, 1966.
> A skillfully drawn review and critique of training practices in government and industry in both the western societies and developing countries.

Tracey, William R., *Evaluating Training and Developing Systems*, New York, American Management Association, 1968.
> A handbook on quality of preparation for and methodology of evaluation of formal training courses. Neglects evaluation of results, however.

United Nations, Public Administration Branch, *Handbook of Training in the Public Service*, New York, 1966.
> An authoritative volume describing preentry and in-service training for public service in the nations of the world, including analysis of training organization, content, methods, and problems.

Chapter 14. HEALTH, SAFETY, AND WELFARE

Council of State Governments, *Fringe Benefits in State Government Employment*, Chicago, May 1968.
> A compilation of state practices, including health and welfare provisions, as well as leave and retirement plans.

Jacobson, Walter O., *Compliance with the Occupational Safety and Health Act*, Personnel Report No. 741, Chicago, International Personnel Management Association, 1974.
> A manual for administrators on the national standards for health and safety.

Chapter 15. WORK HOURS AND LEAVE

Dankert, Clyde E., Floyd C. Mann, and Herbert R. Northrup, eds., *Hours of Work*, New York, Harper & Row, 1965.
> A practical symposium of articles, mostly based on objective research, that

suggests, among other things, that there is no economic or social gain to be expected from further overall reduction in work hours.

Saso, Carmen D., *The Four-Day Workweek*, Chicago, International Personnel Management Association, 1972.
One of the few reports on developments in this area.

Chapter 16. PUBLIC SERVICE ETHICS IN A DEMOCRACY

In addition to the items listed here, reference should also be made to a number of materials in the section on "General Books", especially the report on Watergate by the Panel of the National Academy of Public Administration.

Appleby, Paul H., *Morality and Administration in Democratic Government*, Baton Rouge, Louisiana State University, 1952.
Some solid wisdom on the subject of ethical performance.

Association of the Bar of the City of New York, *Conflict of Interest and Federal Service; Report of the Special Committee on Federal Conflict of Interest Laws*, Cambridge, Mass., Harvard University Press, 1960.
A significant proposal for statutory improvement.

Bailey, Stephen K., "Ethics and the Public Service," *Public Administration Review*, December 1964.
A first-rate delineation of the moral qualities of the ethical public servant, expressed as: optimism, courage, and fairness tempered by charity.

Callender, Clarence N., and James C. Charlesworth, eds., *Ethical Standards in American Public Life*, Philadelphia, American Academy of Political and Social Science, March 1952.
Papers on ethical problems in various public arenas, including the government service. The principles are still relevant.

Cleveland, Harlan, and Harold D. Lasswell, eds., *Ethics and Bigness: Scientific, Academic, Religious, Political, and Military*, New York, Harper & Row, 1962.
An impressive assembly of essays and commentaries, with heavy emphasis on government problems, by a distinguished group of authors who have had significant political, philosophical, religious, and academic experience.

"Ethics and Morality in Government," a symposium in *The Bureaucrat*, April 1975.
A series of articles inspired by the aftermath of the Watergate-related experiences.

Geis, Gilbert, ed., *White-Collar Criminal; The Offender in Business and the Professions*, New York, Atherton Press, 1968.
An interesting collection of essays, old and new, concerning the depredations on society, and possible remedies, caused by unprincipled people of the "upper world"—in government, business, and the professions.

Graham, George A., *Morality in American Politics*, New York, Random House, 1952.
One of the insightful discussions of the subject.

Graham, George A., "Ethical Guidelines for Public Administrators: Observations on the Rules of the Game," *Public Administration Review*, January–February 1974, pp. 90–92.
A sound statement of the main considerations affecting administrative action.

Landis, Benson Y., ed., *Ethical Standards and Professional Conduct*, Philadelphia, American Academy of Political and Social Science, January 1955.
Papers on ethical issues in various professions, including the public service.

Leys, Wayne A. R., *Ethics for Policy Decisions*, Englewood Cliffs, N.J., Prentice-Hall, 1952.
A brilliant treatment of the relation of the classical philosophical "systems" to modern ethical problems, including some in public administration.

Nader, Ralph, Peter J. Petkas, and Kate Blackwall, eds., *Whistle Blowing: The Report of the Conference on Professional Responsibility*, New York, Grossman, 1972.
A documentation of various public complaints by government or corporate employees as to their organizations' misdeeds against the public interest and a presentation of various methods to ensure employee rights and obligations in such "whistle blowing."

Stahl, O. Glenn, "Loyalty, Dissent, and Organizational Health," *The Bureaucrat*, July 1974, pp. 162–171.
This piece draws the line between constructive loyalty and blind conformity.

Taylor, Telford, "The Ethics of Public Office," *Saturday Evening Post*, April 16, 1960.
One of the outstanding articles that puts the issues in perspective.

U.S. Congress, Senate Committee on Labor and Public Welfare, Subcommittee on Ethical Standards (Senator Paul Douglas, Chairman), *Ethical Standards in Government*, 82nd Con., 1st sess., Washington, D.C., 1951.
The best official report on the subject.

Veatch, Henry B., *Rational Man: A Modern Interpretation of Aristotelian Ethics*, Bloomington, Ind., Indiana University Press, 1962.
An incisive discourse on ethics for modern man.

Walton, Clarence C., *Ethos and the Executive; Values in Managerial Decision-Making*, Englewood Cliffs, N.J., Prentice-Hall, 1969.
While focusing primarily on the world of private business, this volume is one of the most profound on managerial ethics and conveys many overtones applicable to the public administrator.

Chapter 17. EMPLOYEE CONDUCT IN THE COMMUNITY

Barth, Alan, *The Loyalty of Free Men*, New York, Viking, 1951.
A powerful critique of government security measures as limitations on civil liberties.

Brown, Ralph S., *Loyalty and Security*, New Haven, Conn., Yale University Press, 1958.
  The most detailed treatment of the subject, recommending restraints on the security program.

Commission on Political Activity of Government Personnel, *A Commission Report: Findings and Recommendations*, vol. I, Washington, 1967.
  A forward-looking appraisal, urging major liberalization of federal political activity restrictions.

Dotson, Arch, "The Emerging Doctrine of Privilege in Public Employment," *Public Administration Review*, Spring 1955.
  A challenge to traditional concepts of restraint on the private actions of civil servants.

Hayman, Donald, and O. Glenn Stahl, *Political Activity Restrictions: An Analysis with Recommendations*, Personnel Report No. 636, Chicago, International Personnel Management Association, 1963.
  An appraisal of the situation in state and local governments, presenting a formula for differentiated solutions depending on merit system conditions.

Nelson, Dalmas H., "Public Employees and the Right to Engage in Political Activity," *Vanderbilt Law Review*, December 1955.

Nelson, Dalmas H., "Political Expression Under the Hatch Act and the Problem of Statutory Ambiguity," *Midwest Journal of Political Science*, February 1958.

Nelson, Dalmas H., and Paul J. Hoffman, "Federal Employees and Voting in Federal Elections," *The Western Political Quarterly*, September 1969.
  These three articles expose some of the mythology about civil servants' actual or potential political behavior and raise challenging questions about the premises underlying the "no-political-activities" policy.

Chapter 18. DISCIPLINE, REMOVAL, AND APPEALS

Phelps, Orme W., *Discipline and Discharge in the Unionized Firm*, Berkeley, University of California Press, 1959.
  About the only general work on the subject and confined to the industrial setting, but well done.

Other reading on this subject is available in individual chapters in the general works on personnel administration and in periodical articles.

Chapter 19. DEVELOPMENT AND IMPACT OF UNIONIZATION

Heisel, W. Donald, *State-Local Employee Labor Relations*, Lexington, Ky., The Council of State Governments, 1970.
  A general guidebook for state and local government officials.

Federal Labor Relations Council, *Labor-Management Relations in the Federal Service*, Washington, D.C., U.S. Civil Service Commission, 1971.
Describes the status of federal labor relations.

Miernyck, William H., *The Economics of Labor and Collective Bargaining*, Boston, D. C. Heath, 1965.
A good reference for a history of the labor movement.

Nigro, Felix A., *Management-Employee Relations in the Public Service*, Chicago, International Personnel Management Association, 1969.
The most complete and authoritative volume on the subject. Presents the environmental and political considerations as well as the procedures and problems of collective negotiation and agreement.

Public Employee Relations Library, Chicago, International Personnel Management Association.
This refers to a loose-leaf compilation of papers, to which additions are made from time to time, on all aspects of labor relations in the public service. A very useful reference tool.

Public Personnel Administration: Labor-Management Relations, 2 vols., Englewood Cliffs, N.J., Prentice-Hall, 1974.
Detailed loose-leaf manuals on policies and practices, supplemented with biweekly bulletins on latest developments.

Roberts, Harold S., ed., *Labor-Management Relations in the Public Service*, Honolulu, University of Hawaii Press, 1970.
A compendium of federal and certain state statutes and regulations governing public sector labor relations, plus several articles commenting on issues.

Smith, Russell A., Harry T. Edwards, and R. Theodore Clark, Jr., *Labor Relations Law in the Public Sector: Cases and Materials*, Indianapolis, Bobbs-Merrill, 1974.
A comprehensive reference on all aspects of the legal framework of labor relations in government.

Spero, Sterling D., *The Labor Movement in a Government Industry: A Study of Employee Organization in the Postal Service*, New York, Macmillan, 1927.
The first account of the early history of unionism in the Postal Service.

Stieber, Jack, *Public Employee Unionism: Structure, Growth, Policy*, Washington, D.C., The Brookings Institution, 1973.
A sound, objective overview of the developments, issues, and prospects.

U.S. Department of Labor, *State Civil Service Employe Associations*, Washington, D.C., 1973.
A thorough report on the old-line state organizations.

Warner, Kenneth O., ed., *Management Relations with Organized Public Employees*, Chicago, International Personnel Management Association, 1963.
A series of articles presenting a cross-section of views from management, unions, and other sources, including factual accounts of experience in a number of jurisdictions.

Chapter 20. COLLECTIVE NEGOTIATION AND BARGAINING

Heisel, W. Donald, *New Questions and Answers on Public Employee Negotiation,* Chicago, International Personnel Management Association, 1973.
Stresses practical approaches for conferring, negotiating, and bargaining.

Kaye, Seymour P., and Arthur Marsh, eds., *International Manual on Collective Bargaining for Public Employees,* New York, Praeger, 1973.
Papers on practices in six western countries.

Koslow, Neil, James H. Breay, and Howard A. Kenley, "A Model Public Employees Collective Bargaining Act," *Harvard Journal on Legislation,* May 1969.
A constructive proposal for states.

Loewenberg, J. Joseph, and Michael H. Moskow, eds., *Collective Bargaining in Government; Readings and Cases,* Englewood Cliffs, N. J., Prentice-Hall, 1972.
A first-rate collection of articles on the subject.

Moskow, Michael H., J. Joseph Loewenberg, and Edward Clifford Koziara, *Collective Bargaining in Public Employment,* New York, Random House, 1970.
A balanced and informative treatment.

Perry, Charles R., and Wesley A. Wildman, *The Impact of Negotiations in Public Education: The Evidence from the Schools,* Worthington, Ohio, Charles A. Jones, 1970.
A discerning study of actual experience in twenty-four school districts over a five-year period.

President's Task Force on Employee-Management Relations in the Federal Service, *A Policy for Employee-Management Cooperation in the Federal Service,* Report of the Task Force, Washington, D.C., November 1961.
The foundation for the first federal-wide policy on relations with employee unions and other organizations.

Stahl, O. Glenn, *The Public Personnel Function—Two Issues,* Detroit, Citizens Research Council of Michigan, 1971.
Includes a discussion of collective bargaining in relation to a merit system.

Twentieth Century Fund, *Pickets at City Hall,* Report and Recommendations of the Twentieth Century Fund Task Force on Labor Disputes in Public Employment, New York, 1970.
A brief exposition of the elements of a sound labor relations policy that should minimize the risk of strikes among government workers.

Vosloo, William B., *Collective Bargaining in the United States Federal Civil Service,* Chicago, International Personnel Management Association, 1966.
The only intensive review of federal policy during the period between the 1962 and 1969 executive orders on the subject.

Warner, Kenneth O., and Mary L. Hennessy, *Public Management at the Bargaining Table,* Chicago, International Personnel Management Association, 1967.
An important review of practice and doctrine among public jurisdictions

in the United States and Canada, stressing advice and counsel to management on its role, responsibilities, and pitfalls. Includes illustrative appendices.

Besides the book by Perry and Wildman listed previously, a great many on unionism and collective bargaining in public education and police administration have appeared in the 1960s and 1970s. They are too numerous to list and annotate here, but a few examples are:

Blum, Albert A., ed., *Teacher Unions and Associations: A Comparative Study*, Urbana, Ill., University of Illinois Press, 1969.

Burpo, John H., *The Police Labor Movement: Problems and Perspectives*, Springfield, Ill., Charles C Thomas, 1971.

Cole, Stephen, *The Unionization of Teachers: A Case Study of the UFT*, New York, Praeger, 1969.

Gammage, Allen Z., and Stanley L. Sachs, *Police Unions*, Springfield, Ill., Charles C Thomas, 1972.

Juris, Hervey A., and Peter Feuille, *Police Unionism: Power and Impact in Public Sector Bargaining*, Lexington, Mass., D. C. Heath, 1973.

Miller, William C., and David N. Newbury, *Teacher Negotiations: A Guide for Bargaining Teams*, West Nyack, N.Y., Parker, 1970.

Shils, Edward B., and C. Taylor Whittier, *Teachers, Administrators, and Collective Bargaining*, New York, Thomas Y. Crowell, 1968.

Stinnett, T. M., Jack H. Kleinmann, and Martha L. Ware, *Professional Negotiation in Public Education*, New York, Macmillan, 1966.

Wollett, Donald H., and Robert H. Chanin, *The Law and Practice of Teacher Negotiations,* Washington, Bureau of National Affairs, 1973.

Chapter 21. CONTINUING ISSUES IN UNION RELATIONS

Aboud, Antone and Grace, *The Right to Strike in Public Employment*, Ithaca, N.Y., Cornell University, 1974.
A brief summary of actual experiences in strike situations.

Advisory Commission on Intergovernmental Relations, *Labor-Management Policies for State and Local Government*, Washington, D.C., 1969.
A thorough analysis of practices and problems in state and local jurisdictions, plus a series of significant recommendations, including one on the flat prohibition of strikes.

Anderson, Arvid and Hugh D. Jascourt, eds., *Trends in Public Sector Labor Relations*, Chicago, International Personnel Management Association, 1975.
A collection of articles and legal decisions bearing on the future of developments in this field. Covers material generated during 1972 and 1973.

Berle, Adolf A., *Power*, New York, Harcourt Brace Jovanovich, 1969.
Contains a stimulating discussion of union power and its consequences.

"Collective Bargaining for Public Employees and the Prevention of Strikes in the Public Sector," *Michigan Law Review*, December 1969.
> A comprehensive report on the situation from the standpoint of law and law enforcement. Warns against oversimplified parallels with private-sector bargaining. Concludes that neither outright prohibition of strikes nor wholesale promotion of collective bargaining is a satisfactory solution.

Liston, Robert A., *The Limits of Defiance: Strikes, Rights, and Government,* New York, Franklin Watts, 1971.
> A sensible, balanced appraisal.

Motta, Malcolm S., *Arbitration of Labor-Management Disputes,* New York, Amacom (American Management Association), 1974.
> An authoritative volume on arbitration settlements in both private and public sectors. Includes discussion, case analyses, and copies of pertinent statutes.

Saso, Carmen D., *Coping with Public Employee Strikes,* Chicago, International Personnel Management Association, 1970.
> A practical "battle plan" for public officials to prepare for all contingencies and to provide continuity of services in the event of any work disruption.

Stanley, David T., *Managing Local Government Under Union Pressure,* Washington, D.C., The Brookings Institution, 1972.
> A thoughtful exploration of the issues, based on first-hand information from nineteen jurisdictions.

Taylor, George W., "Strikes in Public Employment," *Good Government,* Spring 1968.
> A useful analysis of realities and alternatives.

Ulman, Lloyd, ed., *Challenges to Collective Bargaining,* Papers prepared for the Thirtieth American Assembly, Columbia University, Englewood Cliffs, N.J., Prentice-Hall, 1967.
> Includes two especially fine pieces: (1) A. H. Raskin, "Collective Bargaining and the Public Interest," which recognizes the limitations of bargaining in the private economy; and (2) Jack Stieber, "Collective Bargaining in the Public Sector," which gives a fair evaluation of the issues facing governmental units.

Walsh, Robert E., ed., *Sorry . . . No Government Today: Unions vs. City Hall,* Boston, Beacon, 1969.
> An anthology of articles on issues of unionization, collective bargaining, and strikes in the public sector.

Wellington, Harry H., and Ralph K. Winter, Jr., *The Unions and the Cities,* Washington, D.C., The Brookings Institution, 1971.
> A groundbreaking discourse, daring to challenge the bland assumption that what suits the private sector is also workable in government. Forthrightly points out how too much union bargaining power disrupts the democratic process.

Zagoria, Sam, ed., *Public Workers and Public Unions,* Papers prepared for the Fortieth American Assembly, Columbia University, Englewood Cliffs, N.J., Prentice-Hall, 1972.
> Eleven insightful papers on all the major issues.

Chapter 22. TENURE, TURNOVER, AND STAFF REDUCTIONS

Gaudet, Frederick J., *Labor Turnover: Calculation and Cost*, Research Study No. 39, New York, American Management Association, 1960.
>   An industry-oriented study focusing on statistical methodology.

Stahl, O. Glenn, "Security of Tenure—Career or Sinecure?" *Bureaucracy and Democratic Government*, Philadelphia, American Academy of Political and Social Science, March 1954.
>   Some perspective on the significance of tenure policies in the public service.

U.S. Civil Service Commission, *Federal Employment Statistics Bulletin*, Washington, D.C., monthly.
>   The official periodic report on the location and turnover of federal manpower.

U.S. Department of Labor, *Facts About Women's Absenteeism and Labor Turnover*, Washington, D.C., August 1969.
>   As with other studies, demonstrates more attendance disparity between different occupational and age groups than between sexes.

Chapter 23. RETIREMENT AND DISABILITY

In addition to books such as the following on systems and issues relating to retirement from remunerative employment, there are countless books and pamphlets in American libraries directed to the retiree, advising him on ways of keeping useful and happy during retirement years.

Advisory Commission on Intergovernmental Relations, *Transferability of Public Employee Retirement Credits Among Units of Government*, Washington, D.C., March 1963.
>   A thorough exploration of the issues, concluding that a unified national retirement system is impractical but urging consolidation of public plans within each state and universal vesting of contributions after no more than five years of service.

American Association of Retired Persons, *Preparation for Retirement, A New Guide to Program Development*, Government Edition, prepared under the direction of William L. Mitchell, Washington, D.C., 1968.
>   A study of practice and experience with preretirement preparation in federal government agencies.

Baker, Helen, *Retirement Procedures Under Compulsory and Flexible Retirement Policies*, Research Report Series No. 86, Princeton, N.J., Princeton University, Industrial Relations Section, 1952.
>   One of the first comparative analyses of compulsory and "flexible" retirement plans.

Beaumont, Richard A., and James W. Tower, *Executive Retirement and Effective Management*, Industrial Relations Monograph No. 20, New York, Industrial Relations Counselors, 1961.
>   An informative survey of prevailing practices concerning retirement of executives in private industry.

Mathiasen, Geneva, ed., *Flexible Retirement*, New York, Putnam, 1957.
A product of several technical committees of the National Committee on the Aging, this volume summarizes experiences and viewpoints concerning some of the problems of making retirement policies more adaptable to the realities and needs of an aging population and of industrial management.

Raphael, Marios, *Pensions and Public Servants; A Study of the Origins of the British System*, Paris, Mouton, 1964.
Because of the much earlier start of the British in this field, this work is important historically.

Rhodes, Gerald, *Public Sector Pensions*, London, Royal Institute of Public Administration, 1965.
Another work on British systems, covering both government proper and nationalized industries.

Rubin, Harold, *Pensions and Employee Mobility in the Public Service*, New York, The Twentieth Century Fund, 1965.
A good evaluation of the situation, with some constructive recommendations.

Schulz, James H., Guy Carrin, Hans Krupp, Manfred Peschke, Elliott Sclar, and J. Van Steenberge, *Providing Adequate Retirement Income: Pension Reform in the United States and Abroad*, Hanover, N.H., The University Press of New England, 1974.
Compares U.S. experience with foreign, mainly that in Canada, Belgium, Germany, and Sweden—all of which were ahead of the United States in providing general security for the aging. Main emphasis is on national social security systems.

Streib, Gordon F., and Clement J. Schneider, S.J., *Retirement in American Society: Impact and Process*, Ithaca, N.Y., Cornell University Press, 1971.
Reports results of a research undertaking among several thousand subjects, relating to the character and activities of retirees and the effects of having a major segment of the U.S. population in a retirement status outside the realm of productive work.

Chapter 24. THE CENTRAL PERSONNEL AGENCY

Reference should also be made to several works appearing under "General Books," for example, the report on Watergate by the NAPA panel; and Crouch, *Guide for Modern Personnel Commissions*.

Cavagrotti, Victor J., "Solving Personnel Problems by the Thousands," *A Record of the Proceedings of the Second Conference of Human Resource Systems Users*, New York, Information Science Incorporated, 1972, pp. 105–116.
Describes the central reservoir of personnel information in the U.S. Civil Service Commission, drawing upon 1,500 data points and including a general statistical data bank, a detailed skills inventory on 80,000 middle-management employees, and standardized data elements that all agencies use so that information can be pulled together readily for research or special report purposes.

Cohen, Michael, "The Personnel Policy-Making System," in Robert T. Golembiewski and Michael Cohen, eds., *People in Public Service*, Itasca, Ill., F. E. Peacock, 1970.
A good discussion of the process in the federal government, including the role of the U.S. Civil Service Commission.

Committee for Improvement of Management in Government, Research and Policy Committee, *Improving Executive Management in the Federal Government*, New York, Committee for Economic Development, 1964.
A proposal to divide the personnel function by assigning that relating to executive manpower to a new office in the White House and the remainder to the Civil Service Commission.

Greenlaw, Paul S., and Robert D. Smith, eds., *Personnel Management: A Man-Science Approach*, Scranton, Pa., International Textbook, 1970.
A collection of essays on uses of computer and other modern techniques in analyzing personnel problems.

Harris, Joseph P., *Congressional Control of Administration*, Garden City, N.Y., Doubleday Anchor, 1965.
The chapter on congressional involvement in personnel administration is the only published discussion of the subject and very illuminating.

Harvey, Donald R., *The Civil Service Commission*, New York, Praeger, 1970.
The definitive and authoritative (to say nothing of entertaining) analysis of the inner workings and problems of the federal government's central personnel agency, as an ex-insider reveals the influences on, the issues facing, and the achievements of the Commission, especially in recent years.

Lang, Theodore H., *Public Personnel Councils*, Personnel Report No. 583, Chicago, International Personnel Management Association, 1958.
A full report on the official deliberative bodies of personnel officers in federal, state, and municipal governments.

Page, Tom, ed., *The Public Personnel Agency and the Chief Executive: A Symposium*, Personnel Report No. 601, Chicago, International Personnel Management Association, 1960.
Includes an excellent overall discussion by Frederick C. Mosher, with commentary by six other authorities on issues relating to executive control over merit systems.

Ruhl, Eleanor S., *Public Relations for Government Employees: An Action Program*, Personnel Report No. 524, Chicago, International Personnel Management Association, 1952.
Still the outstanding publication on the subject, presenting model performance for all public jurisdictions.

Stahl, O. Glenn, *The Public Personnel Function—Two Issues*, Detroit, Citizens Research Council of Michigan, 1971.
Includes a discussion of the relative merits of an independent personnel commission versus an executive personnel agency.

Chapter 25. THE OPERATING PERSONNEL OFFICE

Collett, Merrill J., *Streamlining Personnel Communications*, Chicago, International Personnel Management Association, 1969.
The application of good communication and writing practice to personnel forms, records, correspondence, and instructions.

Stahl, O. Glenn, "Tomorrow's Generation of Personnel Managers," *Public Personnel Administration—Progress and Prospects*, Personnel Report No. 681, Chicago, International Personnel Management Association, 1968; commentary on this paper by Edward C. Gallas.
A prescription of the extraordinary knowledge and personal qualities that will be required of leaders in public personnel administration for the future.

Chapter 26. PERSONNEL RESEARCH

Gallas, Nesta M., "Research Needs," Chapter 12 in *Police Personnel Administration*, O. Glenn Stahl and Richard A. Staufenberger, eds., Washington, D.C., Police Foundation, 1974.
A perceptive analysis, with particular reference to police but with much general relevance.

Goode, Cecil E., *Personnel Research Frontiers: A Review of Personnel Research Activities and Facilities, with Special Reference to Their Implications for Government*, Chicago, International Personnel Management Association, 1958.
A thorough survey of activities, facilities, and needs in all areas of personnel administration research.

Millard, Kenneth A., "Action Programs to Improve Research in Personnel Agencies," *Extending the Horizons of Public Personnel Administration*, Personnel Report No. 671, Chicago, International Personnel Management Association, 1967.
A good outline of the requisites for a research program.

Sayre, Wallace S., and Frederick C. Mosher, *An Agenda for Research in Public Personnel Administration*, Washington, D.C., National Planning Association, 1959.
An imaginative list of subjects and issues susceptible of research, including many on the political and social effects on the personnel function.

Chapter 27. PUBLIC PERSONNEL POLICY AROUND THE WORLD

For other materials pertaining to the overseas and international scene, as they affect personnel matters, see relevant chapters in items listed under "General Books," including: Macy; McClelland; and any of several works on industrial personnel management, such as that by Dunn and Stephens, that have chapters in this area. In addition, a substantial number of books have appeared in recent years especially devoted to the management of multinational corporations, with particular reference to employment of foreign nationals in U.S. businesses abroad, using Americans overseas, and the problems of intercultural relations. Typical of such books is:

Richman, Barry M., and Melvyn Copen, *International Management and Economic Development, with Particular Reference to India and Other Developing Countries*, New York, McGraw-Hill, 1972.

Another example, with still more international flavor:

Massie, Joseph L., and Jan Luytjes, eds., *Management in an International Context*, New York, Harper & Row, 1972.
   A collation of essays on industrial managerial developments in and from fifteen nations.

Individual items for Chapter 27 continue as follows:

Akehurst, M. B., *The Law Governing Employment in International Organizations*, Cambridge (UK), University Press, 1967.
   The most comprehensive study of the legal principles underlying personnel relationships in international organizations.

Alagappan, Alagappa, *Personnel Administration in the United Nations: Some Aspects of Article 101 of the Charter*, Doctoral dissertation (microfilmed), New York, New York University, 1967.
   A first-rate study of the concepts and issues facing the U.N. Secretariat as to personnel matters.

Alderfer, Harold F., *Public Administration in Newer Nations*, New York, Praeger, 1967.
   A compendium of practices that includes a sketch of the personnel systems in many developing countries.

Alexander, Yonah, *International Technical Assistance Experts; A Case Study of the U.N. Experience*, New York, Praeger, 1966.
   An exhaustive study of the performance of U.N. technical assistance personnel, drawing generally favorable conclusions.

Attir, Aryeh, *Adaptation of Public Personnel Administration to Changes in Society*, Brussels, International Institute of Administrative Sciences, 1971.
   A report on practices in many nations, based primarily on a questionnaire survey but also on discussions at the Fourteenth Congress of the IIAS held in Dublin in September 1968.

Bailey, Sydney D., *The Secretariat of the United Nations*, U.N. Study No. 11, New York, Carnegie Endowment for International Peace, 1962.
   One of the best succinct treatments of the organizational and personnel problems of the U.N. Secretariat.

Blancké, W. Wendell, *The Foreign Service of the United States*, New York, Praeger, 1969.
   A standard description of the character of and life in the American diplomatic and consular corps.

Braibanti, Ralph, ed., *Political and Administrative Development*, Durham, N.C., Duke University Press, 1969.
A collection of weighty theoretical essays on the administrative development of emerging societies.

Chapman, Brian, *The Profession of Government: The Public Service in Europe*, New York, Macmillan, 1959.
A general study of bureaucracy, authority, and democratic control in western European countries, including reference to the structure and policies relating to personnel affairs.

Committee on the International Migration of Talent, *The International Migration of High-Level Manpower: Its Impact on the Development Process*, New York, Praeger, 1970.
The most extensive study of the subject, with reports and factual data from all continents.

Coombes, David, *Towards a European Civil Service*, London, Chatham House, 1968.
The political, legal, and career aspects and prospects of the secretariats of the European Economic Community, the European Coal and Steel Community, and the European Atomic Energy Community.

Dimock, Marshall E., *The Japanese Technocracy: Management and Government in Japan*, New York and Tokyo, Walker/Weatherhill, 1968.
A useful commentary on how the Japanese culture influences productivity and the governmental system, with a chapter on the civil bureaucracy.

Elder, Robert E., *Overseas Representation and Services for Federal Domestic Agencies*, New York, Carnegie Endowment for International Peace, 1965.
A review of how federal departments manage their overseas personnel in relation to the regular foreign affairs agencies.

Godwin, Francis W., Richard N. Goodwin, and William F. Haddad, *The Hidden Force*, A Report of the International Conference on Middle Level Manpower, San Juan, 1962, New York, Harper & Row, 1963.
A report demonstrating the importance of technicians, artisans, and other middle-level manpower in developing countries.

Gollin, Albert E., *Education for National Development; Effects of U.S. Technical Training Programs*, New York, Praeger, 1969.
A thorough survey and evaluation of American efforts to accelerate development through training.

Hammarskjold, Dag, *The International Civil Servant in Law and in Fact*, A Lecture Delivered to Congregation on May 30, 1961, Oxford, Clarendon Press, 1961.
One of the great statements on the independence and professionalization of the international civil service.

Jessup, Philip C., "The International Civil Servant and His Loyalties," *Journal of International Affairs*, vol. IX, no. 2, 1955.
Discusses conflicts in loyalties but attests to the existence of a loyal, efficient corps of international public servants.

Jones, Arthur G., *The Evolution of Personnel Systems for U.S. Foreign Affairs,* New York, Carnegie Endowment for International Peace, 1965.

A convenient review of the structural history of the American foreign service and of the several studies and reorganizations relating to it.

Knudson, Harry R., Jr., and David P. Gustafson, eds., *Management of Human Resources: Concepts for Developing Nations,* Palo Alto, Calif., Addison-Wesley, 1967.

A collection of essays intended to assist in managerial education in developing countries.

Langrod, Georges, *The International Civil Service; Its Origins, Its Nature, Its Evolution,* Dobbs Ferry, N.Y., Oceana Publications, 1963.

A carefully documented but humane and informative book tracing the history and operations of international secretariats from the Universal Postal Union through the United Nations.

Loveday, Alexander, *Reflections on International Administration,* Oxford, Clarendon Press, 1956.

Devotes six chapters to the special features of international service relating to qualities of personnel needed, to problems in recruiting specialized staff, and to morale.

Maddison, Angus, *Foreign Skills and Technical Assistance in Economic Development,* Paris, Development Centre of the Organization for Economic Cooperation and Development (OECD), 1965.

An excellent review, including much otherwise unpublished data, on the realities of technical assistance and the preparation needed by both donor and receiving countries to facilitate it.

Mailick, Sidney, ed., "Towards an International Civil Service: A Symposium," *Public Administration Review,* May/June 1970.

A series of nine articles identifying all the issues facing international bureaucracies and some of the prospective solutions.

McCrensky, Edward, "Personnel Management—Soviet Style," *Personnel Administration,* September–October 1960.

A good summation of the main characteristics of personnel practice in the USSR as compared with that in the United States.

McCrensky, Edward, *Scientific Manpower in Europe; A Comparative Study of Scientific Manpower in the Public Service of Great Britain and Selected European Countries,* New York, Pergamon Press, 1958.

A thorough study of the problems relating to specialized areas of manpower in some of the older civil services.

McNulty, Nancy G., *Training Managers: The International Guide,* New York, Harper & Row, 1969.

The only "encyclopedia" of institutions and courses carried on in many countries relating to all aspects of management, with the emphasis on the industrial sectors. Includes programs for government personnel when combined with industrial programs.

Montgomery, John D., and William J. Siffin, eds., *Approaches to Development: Politics, Administration and Change*, New York, McGraw-Hill, 1966.
    A book of nine papers examining public administration as an instrument of economic and social growth in developing countries, emphasizing the socio-political setting as well as other factors that influence progress.

Phillips, Hiram S., *Guide for Development Institution-Building and Reform*, New York, Praeger, 1969.
    A practical guide written for advisers, technicians, and teachers engaged in developing new or revised institutions in emerging or developing societies.

Reischauer, Edwin O., *Toward the Twenty-first Century: Education for a Changing World*, New York, Knopf, 1973.
    A thoughtful view of global realities and needs by a distinguished world figure.

Reymond, Henri, "The International Civil Service: Its Challenges and Problems," *Extending the Horizons of Public Personnel Administration*, Personnel Report No. 671, Chicago, International Personnel Management Association, 1967.
    A useful, concise statement of principles, practices, and problems on the international personnel front.

Schaffer, Bernard, ed., *Administrative Training and Development: A Comparative Study of East Africa, Zambia, Pakistan, and India*, New York, Praeger, 1974.
    Interesting analyses of how administrative training institutions have developed in nations that have the common denominators of poverty and underdevelopment.

Sharp, Walter R., *Field Administration in the United Nations System; The Conduct of International Economic and Social Programs*, New York, Praeger, 1961.
    An excellent study of the United Nations and its autonomous agencies, providing generous insight into personnel problems.

Stahl, O. Glenn, *A Strong Civil Service for Nepal; A Charter for Merit, Incentive, Control, and Simplicity*, Kathmandu, The Ford Foundation, June 1969.
    An example of a technical advisory report to the government of a developing country.

Strauss, Eric, *The Ruling Servants: Bureaucracy in Russia, France—and Britain?* New York, 1961.
    A study of the power of the permanent civil services in the continental countries, questioning whether similar tendencies are not evident in the United Kingdom.

Teague, Burton W., *Compensating Key Personnel Overseas*, New York, The Conference Board, 1972.
    A comprehensive survey of business practices applying to U.S. expatriates, local nationals, and third-country nationals. Interestingly, less than half the firms studied operate job evaluation programs in their overseas activities, but the trend to do so is upward.

Torre, Mottram, ed., *The Selection of Personnel for International Service*, New York, The World Federation for Mental Health, 1963.

An important series of papers embracing the cultural and psychological considerations underlying work among nationals of many countries and outlining what is known about the best indicators for selection of workers in international assignments.

Trail, Thomas F., *Education of Development Technicians: A Guide to Training Programs*, New York, Praeger, 1968.

An evaluation of programs by government, business, university, and voluntary organizations.

United Nations, Public Administration Branch, *Handbook of Civil Service Laws and Practices*, New York, 1966.

A detailed description of the personnel systems in developing nations, grouped by their basic patterns—those influenced predominately by British practice, by French practice, or by other sources.

United Nations, Public Administration Branch, *A Handbook of Public Administration*, New York, 1961.

A carefully drawn manual designed to provide administrative doctrine for the guidance of developing countries, including substantial material on personnel policy and operations.

United Nations, Public Administration Division, *Recruitment and Selection in the Public Service of Developing Countries*, New York, 1969.

A discussion of alternatives in the various aspects of the staffing process.

United Nations, Public Administration Division, *Report of the Interregional Seminar on the Development of Senior Administrators in the Public Service of Developing Countries*, Geneva, August 1968, vol. I: Report and Technical Papers, New York, 1969.

The product of a distinguished group of leaders in public service training programs, with recommendations for ways in which advanced training for senior civil servants could be undertaken in developing countries.

U.S. Office of Management and Budget, *A Study of Overseas Personnel Allowances, Differentials, and Benefits Granted to Federal U.S. Citizen Civilian Employees in Foreign Areas*, Washington, D.C., 1973.

Raises serious questions about the generosity of special payments for living quarters, education of children, cost-of-living, and other benefit categories.

Name Index

561

Subject Index